Drugs of Abuse

 Marshall Cavendish
Reference
New York

Copyright © 2012 Marshall Cavendish Corporation

Published by Marshall Cavendish Reference

An imprint of Marshall Cavendish Corporation

Website: www.marshallcavendish.us

This publication represents the opinions and views of the authors based on personal experience, knowledge, and research. The information in this book serves as a general guide only. The author and publisher have used their best efforts in preparing this book and disclaim liability rising directly and indirectly from the use and application of this book.

Other Marshall Cavendish Offices:

Marshall Cavendish International (Asia) Private Limited, 1 New Industrial Road, Singapore 536196 • Marshall Cavendish International (Thailand) Co Ltd. 253 Asoke, 12th Flr, Sukhumvit 21 Road, Klongtoey Nua, Wattana, Bangkok 10110, Thailand • Marshall Cavendish (Malaysia) Sdn Bhd, Times Subang, Lot 46, Subang Hi-Tech Industrial Park, Batu Tiga, 40000 Shah Alam, Selangor Darul Ehsan, Malaysia

Marshall Cavendish is a trademark of Times Publishing Limited

All websites were available and accurate when this book was sent to press.

Library of Congress Cataloging-in-Publication Data

Drugs of abuse / consultants, Michael J. Kuhar, Howard Liddle.
    p. cm.
Includes indexes.
ISBN 978-0-7614-7944-4 (alk. paper)
1. Drug abuse. I. Kuhar, Michael J. II. Liddle, Howard
RC563.D7718 2012
362.29--dc22
                                                2011004717

Printed in Malaysia

15 14 13 12 11   1 2 3 4 5

Consultants

Michael J. Kuhar, PhD, Charles Howard Candler Professor of Pharmacology, Emory University, Atlanta, Georgia

Howard Liddle, EdD, Director, Center for Treatment and Research on Adolescent Drug Abuse, University of Miami Medical School, Miami, Florida

Marshall Cavendish
Publisher: Paul Bernabeo
Production Manager: Michael Esposito
Indexer: Cynthia Crippen, AEIOU, Inc.

PHOTOGRAPHIC CREDITS

Ardea: François Gohier 201; **Art Explosion:** 135; **Brookhaven National Laboratory:** 70, 71, 190; **Corbis:** Annie Griffiths Belt 101, Bettmann 171, 245, Bob Kirst 265, Daniel Lané 163, Dave G. Houser 55, Ed Kashi 208, Gary Houlder 9, 17, 137, Historical Picture Archive 86, James Laynse 180, James Marshall 61, Jeff Albertson 192, Joseph Sohm/ChromoSohm Inc. 275, Karen Tweedy-Holmes 47, Michael Freeman 234, Morton Beebe 203, Najlah Feanny 289, Norbert Schaefer 21, Owen Franken 197, Patrick Ward 41, Pete Saloutos 157, Rick Doyle 146, Ricardo Azoury 91, Richard T. Nowitz 93, RNT Productions 218, Scott Houston 125, 259, Ted Streshinsky 189, The Cover Story 148, 151, Tom Stewart 255, Tony Arruza 266, Warren Morgan 50, W. Wayne Lockwood, MD 263; **Corbis Royalty Free:** 78, 79 243; Corbis Saba: Gustavo Gilabert 165; **Corbis Sygma:** John Van Hasselt 113, 116, Julien Hekimian 32, Pascal Le Segretain 117, Richard Ellia 112, Ricki Rosen 219; **Drug Enforcement Administration:** 99, 282; **Dynamic Graphics:** John Foxx & Images 4 Communication 133; **Imagingbody.com:** 159; **Mary Evans Picture Library:** 64; **Oxford Scientific Films:** John Netherton, 35; **PhotoDisc:** Doug Menuez 80, Keith Brofsky 269, Steve Mason 76; **Photos.com:** 38, 74, 222, 225; **Rex Features:** Alix/Phanie 216, Eric Vidal 195, Garo/Phanie 206, Image Source 257, Kim Ludbrook 84, Nils Jorgensen 182, 226, Ojala 284, Richard Young 89, Sakki 187, Sipa Press 178; **Science & Society Picture Library:** Science Museum 176; **Still Pictures:** Jean Jean 295; **Topham Picturepoint:** James Marshall/The Image Works 167, Parris Press 44, UPPA 153; **USDA:** Ken Hammond 290, Peter Manzelli 294.

Contents

Foreword

What does the word *drug* mean? The ancient Greeks' word for *drug* was "pharmakon," and it had three different but related meanings: remedy, poison, and magical charm. These three meanings apply to most substances called drugs. A specific drug can be a remedy, used to treat a symptom or disease; a poison, misused in some way to cause harmful effects; and a magical charm, when it is used in the belief that it is a "wonder drug" that will cure any illness and solve life's problems. The scientific definition of a drug is any substance, other than food, that by its chemical or physical nature alters the structure or function of a living organism, resulting in physiological or behavioral changes or both.

Various Definitions

The meaning of the word *drug*, however, often varies with the context in which it is used. For instance, the scientific definition of drug can include substances that are agricultural and industrial chemicals but are not intended for use by humans, because if humans were exposed to these substances, extremely harmful effects would occur. Substances used to treat symptoms and diseases in humans or to prevent health problems are considered drugs by almost everyone. There are drugs that require a prescription from a doctor before a patient can get the drugs from a pharmacist; these include antibiotics and tranquilizers. There are other drugs that people can get without a prescription from a pharmacy or supermarket, such as antacids, some allergy medications, and cough and cold remedies. The distinction between prescription and nonprescription drugs is based on laws and regulations passed as recently as the 1950s. Laws are one way of classifying different drugs. The Controlled Substance Act of 1970 created categories of drugs based on their abuse potential and value as medicines. Another way of classifying individual drugs is based on their psychoactive effects, for example, by classifying them as narcotics, stimulants, sedatives or depressants, and hallucinogens.

There are other substances that people use to treat health problems, such as herbal remedies, homeopathic medicines, and vitamins. Many people, especially most health professionals, consider these substances to be drugs, but the U.S. Food and Drug Administration does not legally define these substances as drugs; they are defined as nutritional supplements or foods. Most consumers do not think of their multivitamin pill or herbal tea as a drug, but the substances in the pill or tea can produce changes in the human body. In fact, the scientific definition of drug excludes, among other things, salt, sugar, and fruits and vegetables that contain vitamins. But all of these substances can produce changes in the human body. So the meaning of the word *drug* can vary, depending upon how it is used by particular people and the situations in which it is used. In this book, the focus is on drugs that may be abused and lead to harm, whether they are legal or illegal.

Recreational Drugs

There are drugs, such as caffeine, alcohol, and tobacco, that people use for reasons that are not medical. Is caffeine a drug? Most people who drink coffee each day do not consider caffeine, coffee's main ingredient, to be a drug. When heavy coffee drinkers do not get their daily dose of caffeine, however, they can experience unpleasant effects, which many scientists believe are withdrawal symptoms. A few decades ago, most people did not consider smoking tobacco to be the use of a drug (nicotine). But increasing public awareness of the many dangerous effects from smoking, including its ability to produce addiction, has led to the widespread realization that tobacco use is drug use.

Many drinkers of alcoholic beverages, especially most young people, do not think that they are using a drug. Yet alcohol produces many effects in the human body, can cause a great deal of harm, and represents the single, most important drug problem in society today. Many other drugs, including heroin and Ecstasy, are illegal to use for any reason. There is almost no confusion about considering these substances as drugs, but alcohol continues to occupy a unique position.

Sources of Drugs

Many drugs are substances that occur naturally in plants or other living things, and people can use the natural materials or extract the active ingredients from them. Examples include opium, cocaine, and mescaline, as well as the active ingredients in marijuana, tobacco, coffee, and many herbal remedies. Other drugs are made by humans using chemical processes to synthesize and manufacture compounds that act in the body and brain. Examples include most prescription medications, such as antidepressants, steroids, tranquilizers, sleeping pills, and painkillers. People also make alcohol.

In addition, the human body makes its own chemicals that act like drugs to help the body function. Examples of these are hormones (messenger chemicals), vitamins, and neurotransmitters (nerve and brain chemicals), such as serotonin, dopamine, and endorphins.

In *Drugs of Abuse,* each article on a particular drug includes a "Key Facts" panel, which details the drug's street names, form, dangers, and legal classification in the United States, the United Kingdom, and according to the International Narcotics Control Board (INCB). The 124 articles in this book are supplemented by other articles on the use of drugs in general, their effects on individuals, and the medical and social responses to drug abuse that can be found in the companion, single-volume work *Substance Abuse, Addiction, and Treatment.* Additional information is also available in the three-volume set *Drugs and Society* and the online *Drugs and Society* database at www.marshallcavendishdigital.com.

Michael Montagne, PhD, Massachusetts College of Pharmacy and Health Sciences, Boston, Massachusetts

Consultants and Contributors

Consultants

Michael J. Kuhar, PhD, Charles Howard Candler Professor of Pharmacology, Emory University, Atlanta, Georgia

Howard Liddle, EdD, Director, Center for Treatment and Research on Adolescent Drug Abuse, University of Miami Medical School, Miami, Florida

---

David E. Arnot, PhD, Institute of Cell, Animal, and Population Biology, University of Edinburgh, Edinburgh, UK

Kirk J. Brower, MD, Dept. of Psychiatry, University of Michigan Addiction Research Center, Ann Arbor, Michigan

Martin Clowes, BSc, Nottingham, UK

Cynthia A. Conklin, PhD, Western Psychiatric Institute and Clinic, University of Pittsburgh Medical Center, Pittsburgh, Pennsylvania

Ross Coomber, PhD, Dept. of Sociology, University of Plymouth, Plymouth, UK

William DeJong, PhD, Dept. of Social and Behavioral Sciences, Boston University, Boston, Massachusetts

Colleen Anne Dell, PhD, Dept. of Sociology and Anthropology, Carleton University, Ottawa, Canada

Jason Derry, BS, Dept. of Pharmacology, University of Alberta, Edmonton, Canada

Susan M. J. Dunn, PhD, Dept. of Pharmacology, University of Alberta, Edmonton, Canada

Erin J. Farley, MA, Center for Drug and Alcohol Studies, University of Delaware, Newark, Delaware

Graeme Fitzpatrick, BSc, University of Nottingham, Nottingham, UK

Dwayne W. Godwin, PhD, Dept. of Neurobiology and Anatomy, Wake Forest University Baptist Medical Center, Winston-Salem, North Carolina

L. John Greenfield, Jr., MD, PhD, Medical Director, Neurology Clinic, Medical College of Ohio, Toledo, Ohio

Wendy A. Horan, BSc, Croydon, Surrey, UK

Roger W. Horton, Professor, Pharmacology and Clinical Pharmacology, St. George's Hospital Medical School, London, UK

Richard G. Hunter, PhD, Neurosciences Division, Emory University, Yerkes Primate Research Center, Atlanta, Georgia

Jason Jaworski, PhD, Neurosciences Division, Emory University, Yerkes Research Center, Atlanta, Georgia

Judith L. Johnson, PhD, School of Psychology and Counseling, Regent University, Virginia Beach, Virginia

Ankur Kapur, BS, Dept. of Pharmacology, University of Alberta, Edmonton, Canada

Thomas H. Kelly, PhD, Dept. of Behavioral Science, College of Medicine, University of Kentucky, Lexington, Kentucky

Nathan Lepora, PhD, London, UK

Francesco Leri, PhD, Dept. of Psychology, University of Guelph, Guelph, Ontario, Canada

Ian L. Martin, Professor of Pharmacology, School of Life and Health Sciences, Aston University, Birmingham, UK

Duane McBride, PhD, Director, Institute for the Prevention of Addiction, Andrews University, Berrien Springs, Michigan

John McMahon, PhD, Centre for Alcohol and Drug Studies, University of Paisley, Paisley, UK

Darlene A. Mitrano, BS, Dept. of Molecular and Systems Pharmacology, Emory University, Atlanta, Georgia

Meryl Nadel, PhD, Social Work Department, Iona College, New Rochelle, New York

J. Glen Newell, PhD, Dept. of Pharmacology, University of Alberta, Edmonton, Canada

David E. Nichols, PhD, Dept. of Medicinal Chemistry and Molecular Pharmacology, Purdue University, West Lafayette, Indiana

Daniel J. O'Connell, PhD, Center for Drug and Alcohol Studies, University of Delaware, Newark, Delaware

Kenneth Perkins, PhD, Western Psychiatric Institute and Clinic, University of Pittsburgh, Pittsburgh, Pennsylvania

Kelly B. Philpot, PhD, Neurosciences Division, Emory University, Yerkes Primate Research Center, Atlanta, Georgia

Joseph P. Reoux, MD, Dept. of Psychiatry and Behavioral Sciences, University of Washington, Seattle, Washington

Henry Russell, MA, London, UK

Harry Shapiro, DrugScope, London, UK

Matthew D. Spigelman, BA, Dept. of Anthropology, University of Wisconsin, Milwaukee, Wisconsin

Lis Stedman, BA, Chelmsford, Essex, UK

John A. Tauras, PhD, Dept. of Economics, University of Illinois at Chicago, Chicago, Illinois

Yvonne Terry-McElrath, MSA, Institute for Social Research, University of Michigan, Ann Arbor, Michigan

Patricia L. Torchia, LCPC, CADC, Prairie Psychotherapy Associates, Springfield, Illinois

Aleksandra Vicentic, PhD, Neuroscience Division, Emory University, Yerkes Primate Research Center, Atlanta, Georgia

Chris Woodford, MSc, Burton-on-Trent, Staffordshire, UK

Joycelyn S. Woods, MA, President, National Alliance of Methadone Advocates, New York, New York

Acetaldehyde

Acetaldehyde is a poisonous substance that forms in the human body through the biotransformation of alcohol. Acetaldehyde can cause adverse reactions to alcohol consumption and a range of chronic health problems.

Acetaldehyde is an organic compound (formula CH_3CHO) that forms by the action of oxidizing agents on ethyl alcohol (ethanol, CH_3CH_2OH). The oxidation corresponds to the loss of two hydrogen atoms from each alcohol molecule.

In the human body, acetaldehyde is the first product in the sequence of reactions that eliminate alcohol from the bloodstream. The enzyme that promotes this reaction is alcohol dehydrogenase (ADH), which exists to deal with the small amounts of alcohol that are produced naturally by the human metabolism— around 1 ounce (30 g) per day—or that are ingested, for example, in fermenting food. When alcoholic drinks are consumed, these enzyme molecules in the liver are soon working at their maximum, converting around 0.3 ounces (8 g) of alcohol into acetaldehyde each hour for an average adult. In the normal course of events, another type of enzyme—aldehyde dehydrogenase (ALDH), also in the liver—rapidly converts acetaldehyde into acetic acid (CH_3COOH), which is quite harmless and can be excreted in urine.

Problems occur when the bloodstream concentration of acetaldehyde rises. This can happen because the ADH system is abnormally active, producing more acetaldehyde than the ALDH system can handle. Alternatively, the ALDH system can be the root of the problem, either because it is genetically deficient or because it has been knocked out by a substance that prevents the ALDH enzymes from working properly. In either case, the concentration of acetaldehyde increases with every alcoholic drink consumed.

Toxic effects

Acetaldehyde produces a broad spectrum of toxic effects, ranging from those that occur immediately after alcohol consumption (acute effects) to those that occur as a result of repeated episodes of acetaldehyde accumulation (chronic effects).

Acute effects. The immediate symptoms of an acetaldehyde buildup include reddening of the face and earlobes (flushing), nausea, dizziness, and a throbbing headache. These symptoms arise because acetaldehyde is a vasodilator—an agent that makes blood vessels expand and thus increases the flow of blood. The overall sensation is unpleasant enough to deter most people from drinking, which is the basis of disulfiram therapy for alcoholics. Alcohol-related flushing and associated effects occur in people who have unusually active ADH (and therefore convert alcohol into acetaldehyde rapidly) and people who have ALDH deficiency (and therefore dispose of acetaldehyde slowly).

Chronic effects. Acetaldehyde is highly reactive, and its reactions with amines and other nucleophiles (molecules attracted to a positive charge) feature in its chemistry. Acetaldehyde can react with proteins, DNA, and other molecules of the human organism that contain either nitrogen bases or other nucleophilic groups. When it does, it changes the structures and functions of these molecules. Reactions of acetaldehyde with proteins cause hardening of the arteries, wrinkles, and loss of skin elasticity; reactions with DNA cause abnormal cell functions.

Other damage occurs because acetaldehyde readily forms free radicals by oxidation in the body. Free radicals are fiercely reactive molecular fragments characterized by an unpaired electron. They react with a multitude of substances in the body, causing effects that range from cell damage and generalized aging to cancer. Acetaldehyde may also cause abnormal fetal development. Mothers who drink alcohol while pregnant run the risk of giving birth to a child with fetal alcohol syndrome. This syndrome is recognizable by physical and mental symptoms, such as learning disabilities, growth retardation, and facial abnormalities such as a small head size.

Racial variations

As already explained, the amount of acetaldehyde that builds up in the body and the length of time taken to eliminate acetaldehyde depend on the efficiency of the ADH and ALDH enzyme systems. Genes govern the formation of ADH and ALDH, and different forms of those genes, called alleles, code (specify the protein structure) for enzymes that differ in how quickly they transform alcohol into acetaldehyde, and acetaldehyde into acetate. Some alleles occur predominantly in people of specific racial heritages, and affect their drinking habits.

One such allele is ADH2*3, which occurs in some people of African or Native American heritage. ADH2*3 codes for a variant of ADH that is more efficient than others, so when a person whose ADH is of this type consumes alcohol, the enzyme produces acetaldehyde faster than would happen in other people. A mild flushing reaction results and is usually sufficient to discourage excessive drinking. The reaction is less severe than that which happens with disulfiram, since the ALDH enzyme still works but struggles to cope with the rapid production of acetaldehyde. Studies have shown that African American families who possess ADH2*3 are less likely to have alcoholic family members than the population as a whole. Pregnant women in this group are less likely to give birth to alcohol-damaged children, partly because they are less likely to be alcoholics who would drink during pregnancy. Similarly, there is evidence to suggest that some Jewish people may be protected from alcoholism by the presence of the allele ADH2*2, which in one study was found to be common in Jewish men with a low alcohol intake.

Another genetic variation that affects acetaldehyde metabolism occurs in peoples of East Asian descent; in this case, the affected enzyme is ALDH. In Japan, around 2 percent of the population are completely lacking in ALDH, and thus have no tolerance for alcohol, reacting to alcohol as if taking disulfiram. Almost half the population of Japan have a milder form of the genetic mutation, which reduces their ALDH system to one-third its normal capacity, and these people have a reduced tolerance to alcohol. Around 85 percent of the same groups of people also have a variant of ADH that is particularly active, so those who have hyperactive ADH and deficient ALDH produce acetaldehyde more rapidly but dispose of it more slowly than other people.

Despite the unpleasant consequences, some people with ALDH deficiency persist in drinking—often as a result of social pressure to drink with work colleagues or friends. The consequences of ignoring the flushing reaction can be serious, since the high concentrations of acetaldehyde signaled by the

Racial variations in alcohol metabolism may cause a different reaction in each of these girls.

flushing increase the risk of certain types of cancers. Almost 10 percent of alcoholics in Japan become so despite having an ALDH deficiency.

Acetaldehyde and alcoholism

The relationship between acetaldehyde and alcoholism is complex. While the physical symptoms of acetaldehyde accumulation are a clear disincentive to abuse alcohol in those who are sensitive to alcohol flushing, the action of acetaldehyde in the brain is less clear-cut. Acetaldehyde competes with certain neurotransmitters and reduces their inhibitory effect, making the brain more excitable. It can also react with neurotransmitters to form substances called isoquinolines. Some researchers suggest that isoquinolines, which are produced in higher quantities in people with ALDH deficiency, can interact with opioid receptors in the brain, and that this interaction could be a route to alcoholism.

M. CLOWES

SEE ALSO:
Alcohol • Disulfiram

Acetorphine and Etorphine

Acetorphine and etorphine are two of the strongest synthetic opioid analgesics manufactured. Useful for sedating wildlife, their effects can be deadly if taken by humans who are not aware of the danger of these compounds.

Acetorphine and etorphine are extremely potent narcotic analgesics that are commonly used by veterinarians to immobilize large wild animals. Both of these compounds are synthetic derivatives of opium alkaloids obtained from the poppy seed. Acetorphine, also known as 3-acetate etorphine or acetyletorphine, is the acetylated form of etorphine. Acetorphine is less toxic than etorphine and it is not used as often. It is rarely abused by humans; street names for etorphine include M99 and "elephant juice."

Etorphine was discovered by Kenneth Bentley's research team at McFarlan-Smith and Company in Edinburgh, Scotland, in the early 1960s. Etorphine was synthesized in an attempt to produce new non-steroidal anti-inflammatory drugs. However, as the legend goes, someone stirred the mid-morning cups of tea in the lab with a glass rod that, unknowingly, had been contaminated with etorphine. The group was tranquilized into an almost deadly state.

In 1966 the World Health Organization (WHO) recommended that both acetorphine and etorphine be added to Schedule I and IV of the Single Convention on Narcotic Drugs because of the liability of abuse and the lack of need for the drugs in human medical care. However, provisional statements were made to allow the veterinary use of the two drugs.

Etorphine is around 1,000 times more potent than morphine. Very small amounts can quickly lead to respiratory paralysis and death in humans. Etorphine is so toxic that it is usually dyed red for ease of recognition and is almost impossible to find in the United States outside of veterinary practice. Other opiates like codeine, morphine, and heroin are more popular for human abuse. In 1998 the *Wall Street Journal* reported that the British American Tobacco Company had once debated adding etorphine to its cigarettes to create an addictive craving for tobacco.

Etorphine produces its major effects on the central nervous system and bowel by acting as an agonist on the main opioid receptors. Its side effects are similar

KEY FACTS

Classification
Schedules I and IV (USA), Schedule I (Canada), Class A (UK), Schedules I and IV (INCB). Opioid.

Street names
M99, elephant juice, elephant trank

Short-term effects
Sedation, analgesia, decreased respiration, and irregular heartbeat

Long-term effects
Dependence, constipation, convulsions

Dangers
These drugs are hardly ever used by humans because they are 1,000 times more potent than morphine. Extremely dangerous, even in minute quantities.

to those of other opioid compounds and include a rapid heartbeat (tachycardia) and increased blood pressure, which can lead to capillary hemorrhage. However, the extremely potent nature of etorphine can easily lead to overdose and death caused by respiratory depression.

A 4-milligram dose of etorphine will immobilize an adult African elephant, and 1 milligram will knock out an adult rhino. The less toxic acetorphine is preferred to immobilize giraffes, which are harder to revive. The reversal agents naltrexone or diprenorphine are used to reverse the analgesic effects of etorphine.

K. PHILPOT

SEE ALSO:
Controlled Substances • Morphine • Narcotic Drugs • Opiates and Opioids

Acetylcholine

A chemical produced naturally in the body, acetylcholine carries signals in the brain and throughout the nervous system. Acetylcholine also controls the movement of muscles; blocking its transmission can lead to paralysis.

Acetylcholine is a simple molecule, yet as a neurotransmitter (chemical that transmits messages between one nerve and another in the brain) it plays an extremely important part in the communication of signals through many different parts of the nervous systems of humans and other species. The significance of acetylcholine as a neurotransmitter was discovered in 1921 by the German-born pharmacologist Otto Loewi, and the discovery set the criteria for classifying other chemicals produced within the body as neurotransmitters.

Nerve cells that transmit signals using acetylcholine are called cholinergic neurons. These cells produce acetylcholine from choline that is normally in the bloodstream as a result of digestion. If the diet lacks direct sources of choline for some reason, the body can also make it from the amino acid serine.

Once formed, acetylcholine collects in minute sacs called synaptic vesicles. After release from the synaptic vesicles, acetylcholine molecules cross the synapse and bind to receptors in the receiving end of the next neuron. There is little time for them to stay there, however, since the enzyme acetylcholinesterase rapidly breaks down acetylcholine into acetic acid and choline—usually within milliseconds—and the receptors become ready to receive another wave of acetylcholine molecules. Meanwhile, the choline molecules formed by the degradation of acetylcholine can be transported back into the transmitting neuron as raw material for making more acetylcholine.

Receptor types

There are many types of cholinergic receptors, but each belongs to one of two groups: muscarinic receptors and nicotinic receptors. These descriptions originate from the names of the naturally occurring compounds originally used to distinguish them. Nicotine is an alkaloid from the tobacco plant;

The acetylcholine system spreads extensively throughout the brain and into the peripheral nervous system in the body, where it primes the nerves to fire impulses. The projections from the brain stem are responsible for maintaining wakefulness and arousal; others are thought to be involved in memory and learning.

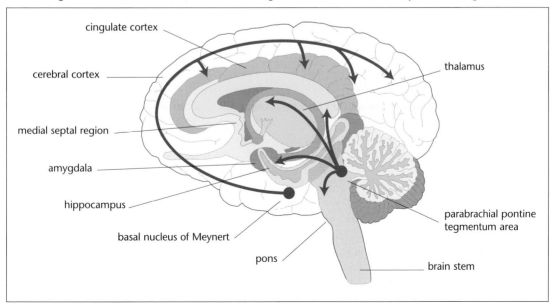

alkaloids are basic nitrogen compounds that occur in plants. Muscarine is an alkaloid present in the fly agaric mushroom *Amanita muscaria*. Muscarinic receptors have a stronger affinity for muscarine than for acetylcholine, and a weak affinity for nicotine. The reverse is true for nicotinic receptors.

Aside from their differing affinities for specific compounds, muscarinic and nicotinic acetylcholine receptors differ in structure and in the way they influence the cells on whose membranes they reside.

Muscarinic receptors. A muscarinic receptor is a protein that projects through the cell membrane. When acetylcholine attaches to the outside of the cell, the whole protein rearranges itself. This reconfiguration changes the properties of the section of protein that faces into the cell and triggers chemical reactions within the cell. There are at least five subtypes of muscarinic receptors, and each triggers a characteristic response within the associated cells.

Nicotinic receptors. Nicotinic receptors are adjacent to channels in cell walls that open and allow calcium ions (Ca^{2+}) to flow into a cell when acetylcholine attaches to its receptor. When this happens in a neuron, it becomes more likely to fire off a nerve impulse. In effect, a nicotinic receptor acts as a relay that passes impulses from one neuron to the next.

Peripheral nervous system

Acetylcholine plays a crucial role in all aspects of the peripheral nervous system, which carries signals from the brain to other parts of the body. In fact, all signals from the brain pass first through cholinergic nerves that release acetylcholine onto nicotinic receptors.

Voluntary and subconscious control of the skeletal muscles relies on the somatic nervous system, where cholinergic nerves from the brain signal directly to the nicotinic receptors on muscle cells to control contractions. On the other hand, fight-or-flight signals that prepare the body for action pass through the sympathetic autonomic nervous system. These signals result in the action of epinephrine or norepinephrine on appropriate receptors in target cells. The same target cells receive opposing "rest-and-recover" signals through the cholinergic nerves of the parasympathetic autonomic nervous system. In this case, the acetylcholine receptor is muscarinic.

Atropine is an extract from the deadly nightshade plant that blocks the action of acetylcholine at muscarinic receptors. Atropine eyedrops—traditionally known as belladonna—cause pupil dilation and were once a popular cosmetic product. Atropine now finds a use in medicines that alleviate stomach spasms and as an antidote for organophosphate poisoning.

The participation of acetylcholine throughout the peripheral nervous system explains why substances that disrupt cholinergic neurotransmission can have dramatic and often devastating effects on the human body. Organophosphate pesticides and related nerve gases, such as Sarin, disrupt normal functions by combining with acetylcholinesterase to form stable compounds that are unable to degrade acetylcholine. The concentration of the neurotransmitter then increases, causing all muscles to go into spasm, including those of the heart and lungs; the outcome is often fatal. The poison curare also induces paralysis, but this happens because its active ingredient tubocurarine blocks nicotinic acetylcholine receptors. Derived from a South American vine, tubocurarine is now used in controlled amounts to relax muscles for surgery.

Central nervous system

There are both muscarinic and nicotinic receptors in the brain, and their function appears to be to modulate the actions of other neurotransmitters. Nicotine from tobacco products increases neurotransmission, which explains why smokers feel more focused and alert almost immediately after lighting up. The effects are short-lived, however, and the nicotinic receptors gradually become desensitized. Hence, a long-term smoker requires regular fixes of nicotine to maintain normal levels of alertness and concentration. Nicotine is highly addictive, at least in part because it increases the concentration of dopamine in the brain. Dopamine is tied to the reward mechanism that makes people seek to satisfy cravings for food and sex, for example, so its involvement with nicotine gives smokers their cravings for cigarettes.

M. CLOWES

SEE ALSO:

Belladonna Alkaloids • Central Nervous System • Dopamine • Drug Receptors • Epinephrine • Nicotine • Norepinephrine

Adverse Reactions

Most drugs in clinical use produce effects that have been predicted during their development. These adverse reactions, or side effects, are suffered by users of legal and illicit drugs and, in some cases, can be severe enough to cause death.

An adverse drug reaction (ADR) is defined as an undesirable effect of a drug occurring during clinical use. The term relates to standard doses administered by appropriate routes and thus excludes deliberate or accidental overdosage.

ADRs are very common in medical practice. ADRs adversely affect a patient's quality of life and increase the cost of health care. About 10 percent of hospital inpatients experience an ADR and, although the data are less reliable, as many as 40 percent of patients outside hospital experience an ADR. Although most ADRs are not life threatening, 0.1 percent of medical inpatients die as a result of an ADR.

The simplest classification of ADRs is into type A (augmented) and type B (bizarre). Type A reactions are predictable from the known pharmacology of the drug. They are usually dose related and involve a significant proportion of patients. Type A reactions are usually mild, but they may be serious or sometimes fatal. They can often be managed by adjusting the dose. Mild type-A ADRs are often referred to as side effects. For example, propranolol is a drug widely used to treat high blood pressure and a number of other heart disorders. The drug acts by blocking beta-adrenoceptors in the heart and blood vessels. However, it also blocks beta-adrenoceptors in the lungs, and this can lead to a tightening of the chest and difficulty breathing (bronchospasm), particularly in individuals with asthma or bronchitis. Thus bronchospasm is a type-A ADR of propranolol.

By contrast, type-B reactions are unexpected from the known pharmacology of the drug. Generally they are unrelated to dosage, and although only a very small proportion of patients may be involved, they often cause serious illness and death.

Type-B ADRs usually require that the drug be taken out of use. A classic example is the case of thalidomide. This drug was marketed as a safe sleep-inducing agent. However, many thousands of women who took the drug early in pregnancy gave birth to babies with severe limb abnormalities. Another example is practolol, a drug developed to overcome the bronchospasm experienced by some patients receiving propranolol (*see above*). Practolol has a selective action on the type of beta-adrenoceptors found in the heart (beta$_1$-adrenoceptors) compared with those found in the lungs (beta$_2$-adrenoceptors), whereas propranolol affects both types equally. Practolol was seen as a significant clinical advance. However, about four years into its use, a bizzare syndrome involving the skin, eyes, and abdominal cavity was identified in a small proportion of patients receiving the drug. Some patients became blind, others needed surgery, and a few died. Sales of the drug were stopped. This syndrome was a type-B ADR of practolol.

The vast majority of ADRs are type A, and their factors and mechanisms involved are better understood than those for type B. There are three groups of factors: patient, prescribing, and drug factors.

Patient factors

ADRs are more common in the very old and the very young. Elderly people often have multiple illnesses and therefore take several different medicines together; both factors may contribute to their higher incidence of ADRs. Changes in the body with aging may also make the elderly more likely to develop ADRs. Enzymes in the liver that break down drugs are less active in the elderly, so older people have high blood levels of drugs circulating for longer periods of time. For example, benzodiazepines can accumulate in the bloodstream of the elderly and cause symptoms that can be mistaken for dementia or Alzheimer's disease. Similar effects may occur in the very young because the enzymes have not yet fully developed. Women are generally at greater risk of ADRs than men, although the reasons for this are not clear.

Patients who have liver and kidney disease are also more likely to develop ADRs. Liver enzymes break down many drugs, and these enzymes are often reduced in liver disease. Some drugs are not broken down by enzymes but are removed from the blood by the kidneys. Kidney disease may slow this process so that the patient is exposed to more of the drug for a longer time.

There are a large number of liver enzymes that break down drugs. They belong to a group called the cytochrome P450 super family. There are four main subfamilies, called CYP1-4, that are responsible for the breakdown of about 90 percent of the commonly used drugs in humans. Individual enzymes are identified by further numbers. For example, one of the most extensively studied enzymes is called CYP2D6. This enzyme is inactive in about 6 percent of Caucasians. These individuals are at risk of ADRs when given a range of drugs that are metabolized by CYP2D6. One example is codeine, which is converted by the enzyme to morphine, which produces painkilling effects. People who are unaware that they do not have the enzyme may take higher doses of codeine in an attempt to relieve their pain. Instead, they experience the side effects of codeine, which include nausea and vomiting, dizziness, constipation, and sedation. By contrast, people who have the enzyme and are coprescribed codeine with an antidepressant such as Prozac or Paxil may find that they feel no pain relief because the anti-depressant inhibits the enzyme's action.

Genetic differences also contribute to ADRs. A striking example is suxamethonium, a drug that relaxes muscle tissue, which is widely used in surgical procedures. It is a particularly useful drug because it is very short acting, and thus the patient recovers from its effects within a few minutes. Normally, the drug is very rapidly broken down by an enzyme within the blood called pseudocholinesterase. Some people have an abnormal enzyme that breaks down suxamethonium very slowly, so that its effects last for hours rather than minutes. Because one group of muscles affected by suxamethonium are those used in breathing, a long-lasting effect can be problematic.

Prescribing and drug factors

A surprisingly common factor in ADRs is that the dose of drug administered or the duration of administration is incorrect or that an inappropriate combination of drugs has been prescribed.

The single most common cause of ADRs is an interaction between two drugs, often prescribed for different illnesses, but sometimes for the same illness.

For example, digoxin and diuretics (water-reducing medications) are two drugs used to treat heart failure. However, certain diuretics cause a loss of potassium from the body, which increases the adverse effects of digoxin. Digoxin works by binding to a potassium-sensitive enzyme, and binding is stronger when the potassium concentration is reduced. Inadvertent combining of drugs that have the same type of effect, such as benzodiazepines with barbiturates, opioids, or alcohol, which all depress the central nervous system, can exacerbate their individual effects, leading to respiratory failure and death. The number of actual and potential drug interactions is vast and occupies a substantial part of all drug formularies.

Immunological mechanisms contribute to some type-B ADRs. Drug allergy is the most common form. A classic example is penicillin. Penicillin is not normally immunogenic but when bound to plasma proteins can result in the formation of antibodies that bind to a type of cell known as a mast cell. A subsequent exposure to penicillin, maybe months or even years later, results in an interaction that causes the mast cells to release their contents (large amounts of histamine and other substances), which often results in anaphylactic shock—a fall in blood pressure, breathing difficulties, and intense itching—which can be fatal. The patient has to be careful to avoid any future use of penicillins.

Minimizing ADRs

When a drug reaches the market, little is actually known about its safety. As few as 1,500 people may have been exposed to the drug, and only the most common ADRs will have been detected. Type-B ADRs are unlikely to have been identified. Ongoing surveillance is therefore essential to identify less common ADRs. Spontaneous reporting systems are the cornerstone of drug safety surveillance. In most European countries, a wide range of health care professionals are allowed to report. In the United States, patients can also report ADRs through the MedWatch system. Even though ADRs create risk to the patient, the risk-to-benefit ratio is justified because of the threatening illness.

R. W. HORTON

SEE ALSO:
Pharmacokinetics • Potentiation

Agonists and Antagonists

An agonist is a chemical substance that provokes a cell response. An antagonist is a substance that counteracts the effect of an agonist. Their actions can either enable chemical messages to be passed between cells or prevent them.

The related concepts of agonism and antagonism are fundamental to an understanding of how the body works, how drugs and certain other substances can modify the normal working of the body, and how one substance can be used to boost or counteract the impact of another on the body.

In order to understand agonism, it helps to think first about how the cells of the human body work together as a unified organism. The actions, symptoms, and reflexes that are typical of life—muscle contractions, allergic reactions, or changes in blood pressure, for example—can be traced back to cells changing from their normal states. A muscle contracts because its cells change shape, so the muscle as a whole changes shape and exerts a force. Such changes are not random, however: they occur in response to specific stimuli, and these stimuli can act on cells of a given type in one location or they can act systemically (on the body as a whole).

The stimuli that cause cells to undergo changes are chemicals that bind to sites on the external surfaces of cells. These sites are called receptor sites, and they exist in proteins embedded in the lipid bilayers that make up cell membranes. Once the chemical stimulus is docked at the receptor site, it causes a change in the way the protein chains coil together. This change also affects the parts of the protein chains that face into the cell, and it is the first of a sequence of events that cause the cell to change chemically, physically, or electrically. These stimuli are examples of agonists—substances that provoke cell responses.

Agonists that act locally include neurotransmitters, such as acetylcholine and dopamine. These substances are released from nerve cells in response to nerve impulses. The release sites are close to the cells where they act, which have corresponding receptors. Processes such as biotransformation and reuptake (reabsorption) mop up the neurotransmitter before it can reach more remote cells that might also have an appropriate receptor.

Agonists that act systemically include hormones, which are produced by glands, such as the gonads. Hormones circulate around the body, triggering responses at cells in diverse locations provided they have suitable receptors. Nonhormonal chemical messengers include histamine, a substance that is stored in cells around the body and is released in response to tissue damage and invading organisms.

Drug agonism and antagonism

Although the receptors on cells are perfectly matched to the natural agonists that usually bind there, they can sometimes be tricked into binding with substances taken into the body, such as drugs. For a

Agonists and antagonists often compete for the same receptor sites, producing a different effect on the cell.

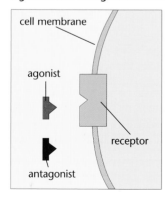

cell membrane

agonist

receptor

antagonist

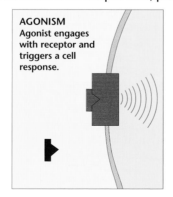

AGONISM
Agonist engages with receptor and triggers a cell response.

COMPETITIVE ANTAGONISM
Antagonist engages at the receptor without triggering a cell response.

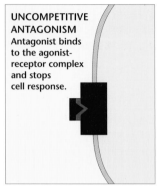

UNCOMPETITIVE ANTAGONISM
Antagonist binds to the agonist-receptor complex and stops cell response.

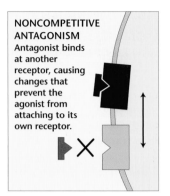

NONCOMPETITIVE ANTAGONISM
Antagonist binds at another receptor, causing changes that prevent the agonist from attaching to its own receptor.

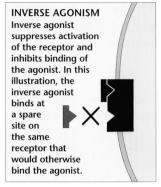

INVERSE AGONISM
Inverse agonist suppresses activation of the receptor and inhibits binding of the agonist. In this illustration, the inverse agonist binds at a spare site on the same receptor that would otherwise bind the agonist.

The action of antagonists and inverse agonists can prevent cell response by interfering with the receptor.

drug–receptor interaction to occur, there has to be a strong resemblance between part of the drug's molecular structure and the part of the natural agonist that binds at that receptor. If the drug can bind, its classification depends on the cell response it provokes. In broad terms, if the drug provokes the same response as the natural agonist, it is an agonist of that receptor; if the drug binds at that site but produces no response, it is known as a competitive antagonist.

Forms of agonism

A pharmaceutical agonist is a substance that binds to a receptor and mimics the effect of the endogenous (natural) substance that usually binds there. Provided the dose is sufficient, a full agonist produces a cell response equal to that caused by the endogenous substance. A partial agonist produces a weaker response regardless of dose, and it can even act as an antagonist by blocking a more effective agonist from receptor sites. A partial agonist moderates the activity induced by the main agonist, since the partial agonist maintains some stimulation of the receptor when no main agonist is present, but it prevents overstimulation when the agonist is present in full force. This buffering effect is useful in treating drug dependency.

Antagonists and inverse agonists

A substance that counteracts an agonist by occupying its receptor but provoking no cell response is a competitive antagonist. The term *competitive* refers to the fact that both agonist and antagonist vie for the same sites, and the overall cell response depends on the relative strengths of the interactions and the relative concentrations of the agonist and antagonist.

An example of a competitive antagonist in therapeutic use is naloxone, an opioid antagonist. Naloxone reverses opioid poisoning, such as a heroin overdose, by binding to the opioid receptors. Since it produces no cell response, the narcotic effects of other opioids are defeated and the risk of death is significantly reduced.

Uncompetitive antagonists are so called because they act by attaching to the receptor with the agonist in place rather than by competing for the same sites; the uncompetitive antagonist traps the agonist in its receptor and deactivates the receptor. Noncompetitive antagonists bind at receptors other than those where the agonist binds; they cause changes in the cell that make the agonist receptor inactive. Related to noncompetitive antagonists are the inverse agonists, which also bind to their own distinct receptors; they have the effect of switching off any receptors that become stimulated despite the absence of their agonist. Hence, an inverse agonist suppresses any baseline cell response in addiction to counteracting the agonist.

The most drastic form of antagonism occurs with irreversible antagonists, which form bonds that permanently inactivate the receptor. Their blocking effect lasts until the body can generate new cells with functioning receptors.

M. CLOWES

SEE ALSO:

Central Nervous System • Drug Receptors • Endorphins

Alcohol

Alcohol is the most widely used perception-altering substance and the most widely used psychoactive substance after caffeine. Moderate use of alcohol reduces inhibitions and has some health benefits, but its abuse can be harmful.

Alcohol is unique among psychoactive substances for the ambiguous reaction it provokes. It is consumed by both wine connoisseurs and down-and-outs—groups at opposite ends of the social spectrum. Even the restrictions on alcohol consumption can be ambiguous: U.S. law permits children and adolescents to drink alcohol if supervised by their parents or as part of a religious ceremony; under other circumstances, usually set by state law, the minimum drinking age is 21. Furthermore, some schools enforce alcohol-free policies that even forbid school groups from eating in establishments where other customers might be drinking alcohol.

Use and abuse

The apparent double standard society applies to alcohol stems from the difference between moderate use of alcohol and its abuse. In moderation, alcohol relaxes people and helps them interact in groups: a happy-hour beer brings work colleagues together, and a glass or two of wine can ease awkwardness among distant relatives at a family gathering. A few drinks too many, however, and the dangers of alcohol start to appear: an ill-judged comment can cause embarrassment in the workplace or offense between loved ones. Even more serious, party revelers who choose to drive home risk their own lives and the lives of others if they have consumed alcohol.

A single incident of excessive drinking can result in a hangover, and sometimes a missed day of work. When heavy drinking becomes a regular event, the risk of more serious consequences becomes significant. Damage to the liver, brain, and other parts of the body proceeds stealthily at first but can lead to life-threatening conditions such as cirrhosis of the liver. Behavioral changes such as diminished responsibility and irrational mood changes put personal relation-ships under stress and can lead to physical or emotional abuse of others; divorce and alienation from friends can result. A diminishing ability to function productively can result in unemployment. Without work or a social support network of sober friends, a habitual heavy drinker can easily become a vagrant.

Inappropriate use of alcohol is not confined to older drinkers. In 2010 the National Survey on Drug Use and Health (NSDUH) produced a report including data from 2009 concerning the drinking habits of U.S. citizens between the ages of 12 and 20. Across the age range, 18 percent reported having drunk five or more standard drinks on at least one occasion in the previous month. Medical studies show this type of consumption—sometimes called binge drinking—to be more damaging than if the same alcohol intake were spread evenly over several

A woman whose drinking matches that of a man of equal body mass runs a higher risk of health problems due to alcohol. Because women have smaller blood volumes, their blood alcohol concentration becomes higher from the same intake.

days. The developing brains of adolescents are more vulnerable to impairment by alcohol than are the fully formed brains of adults. Other studies suggest that up to 7 percent of U.S. adolescents are alcohol dependent.

Origins of alcohol production

If alcohol were a newly invented drug, it would almost certainly be subject to severe legal restrictions due to its potential to cause harm. One of the reasons that it escapes censure in most communities is that humans have consumed alcohol for so long. As far as historians can tell, the brewing of alcoholic drinks is as old as human civilization.

Alcohol forms from the fermentation of sugars in fruits, grains, and vegetables as part of a natural process that requires no human help. It is not known when humans discovered the intoxicating nature of the resulting brews or who first produced them intentionally.

Archaeologists believe Neolithic tribes made wines from fermented berries as long ago as 6400 BCE and the Chinese were brewing rice-based alcoholic drinks well before 5000 BCE. It is likely that even these early drinks were predated by mead, a brew fermented from honey mixed with water. Sumerian cuneiform tablets and Egyptian hieroglyphs dating from around 4000 BCE show that those peoples

BEER BREWING

The brewing of beer is essentially a two-stage process: the first stage converts the starches in grains into sugars, and the second stage converts those sugars into alcohol and carbon dioxide. The most usual grain for making beer is barley, although corn, wheat, and rice are alternative starting points. Indeed, Columbus found Native Americans brewing corn beer in the late fifteenth century, German *Weissbier* is a wheat beer, and Japanese sake is a potent rice beer.

The brewing process starts with malted grain, that is, grain that has been encouraged to germinate by soaking in warm water followed by several days' storage under warm and moist conditions. As the grain germinates, it forms enzymes that will break down starches in the brewing process. When the maltster determines that germination has progressed sufficiently, the process is halted by drying the grains in a kiln. Gentle heating simply stops germination and preserves the enzyme. Higher temperatures roast the malt, making it suitable for producing dark and strongly flavored beers. Roasting kills off some of the enzymes, and dark malts must be mixed with lighter malts to produce a mixture with enough enzyme for brewing purposes.

The brewer first crushes a suitable malt mixture, then mixes it with water at 120 to 130°F (49–54°C)

for 30 to 60 minutes. This softens the malt and helps extract its contents. The protein and fiber contents of the malt settle out and leave a clear liquid, the wort, that contains starch and enzymes.

Slow heating gradually raises the temperature of the mixture to around 140°F (60°C) to start the enzyme-catalyzed conversion of starch into sugars. This conversion, called mashing, is normally complete after about one hour, and the mixture is then strained to free the wort from the spent malt.

The wort is then boiled with hops for up to two hours. Hops are catkin-like flowers of the *Humulus lupulus* vine; they add a characteristic bitterness to the final beer and also act as a natural preservative. Further hops are added near the end of the boil to replace aromas that have boiled out of the first batch of hops. The brewer then siphons off the wort and allows it to cool to near room teperature.

Addition of yeast then starts fermentation, which is the enzyme-catalyzed conversion of sugars into alcohol and carbon dioxide. The fermentation temperature is usually just above 50°F (10°C) but can be as high as 100°F (38°C). The brew ceases to bubble with carbon dioxide when fermentation is complete. A small amount of sugar is added just prior to bottling or barreling; its purpose is to fuel a spurt of fermentation in the container, and the carbon dioxide that results gives the beer its fizz.

U.S. ANNUAL ALCOHOL CONSUMPTION				
	Beer	Wine	Spirits	Total
2006	1.19	0.37	0.71	2.27
2005	1.18	0.35	0.70	2.23
2004	1.20	0.35	0.68	2.23

The data show average consumption per person in gallons of ethanol per year.

Source: NIAAA Web site, August 2010.

produced beers from grains such as barley, the basis of most modern beers. Egyptian records from around 2500 BCE describe making wine from grapes.

Compared with the brewing of beers and wines, the production of spirits is a relatively modern invention. It requires the technique of distillation, which Chinese alchemists developed around 900 BCE for purifying the crude products of their chemical manipulations. It is possible that the first spirits were distilled from rice-based drinks shortly thereafter. In Europe, brandy and whiskey were certainly being distilled by the twelfth century.

Alcoholic drinks

Historically, the types of alcoholic drinks consumed in any given area depended on the crops that grew there. Wines are traditional in southern Europe, for example, where the soil and climate favor the growth of grape vines. Today, global trading has established many local products as international favorites.

Beer. Beer is by far the most popular alcoholic beverage in the United States (*see* table above), and its popularity is increasing as liquor drinkers move to lower-alcohol drinks. Most U.S. beer is brewed by mashing barley and fermenting the resulting wort (*see* box on page 18). The potency of such a beer is typically 4 to 5 percent ABV (alcohol by volume), although low-alcohol and superstrength beers are also available. Lager beer predominates in most of the Western world, and its name refers to the lengthy refrigerated storage period that conditions the beer before sale (*Lager* is German for "store").

Lager beer uses light malt, a moderate amount of hops, and yeast that settles out of the fermenting

wort. In contrast, ales have a shorter conditioning time, use varying types of malts and amounts of hops, and yeast that forms a froth on top of the wort. The color of an ale depends on the blend of malt that forms its basis. Stouts are heavily hopped and contain dark-roast and sometimes unmalted barley that gives a characteristic dark-brown color.

Wines. Wines are alcoholic drinks prepared by the fermentation of fruit juices. The necessary sugars for making alcohol are already present in the fruit, so simple juice extraction replaces the mashing stage of beer brewing. Almost all commercial wines are grape based; home winemakers use a variety of fruits.

All grape juice is pale straw in color, regardless of the color of the grape. The color of red wine arises by soaking the skins of red grapes in the juice during fermentation, which also allows tannin and other substances from the skins to soak into the juice. For white wines, the juice flows out of the juicing press but the skins remain inside, making white wine lighter than red in both color and flavor. For rosé wine, the skins of red grapes remain in contact with the juice long enough to impart a delicate pink color.

The primary fermentation of the juice, or must, uses the yeast that forms the bloom on grapes plus additional brewer's yeast. The optional addition of sugar before fermentation increases the final alcohol content. Fermentation proceeds at around 77°F (25°C) for 10 to 14 days and results in an alcohol content of about 12 to 14 percent ABV. A second fermentation takes place after a few months. It reduces acidity to produce a more palatable wine.

Fortified wines reach 18 to 20 percent ABV through the addition of spirits. Hard cider is made

ALCOHOLS, CONGENERS, AND DISTILLATION

Chemists use the term *alcohol* to describe any compound that has a hydroxy (–OH) group attached to a hydrocarbon ring or chain. The main alcohol in alcoholic beverages is ethanol (ethyl alcohol, formula CH_3CH_2OH).

Other alcohols, such as methanol (methyl alcohol, CH_3OH) and propan-2-ol (isopropanol, $CH_3CHOHCH_3$), can also produce a drunken state if consumed, but they are more toxic than ethanol. In particular, methanol can cause blindness. Nevertheless, some alcoholics resort to drinking household products that contain these alcohols if an ethanol-based drink is unavailable.

Ethanol and carbon dioxide are the principal products of fermentation, but they are accompanied by small amounts of various other compounds called congeners. These compounds include methanol and four- and five-carbon alcohols; aldehydes, esters, and fatty acids; and

miscellaneous compounds such as tannin. Some of these substances form during fermentation; others are present before fermentation starts.

Congeners impart the characteristic colors, flavors, and aromas of different alcoholic drinks, but many congeners are toxic and cause hangovers. As a general rule, dark beverages with heavy aromas and flavors contain more congeners and are more likely to give hangovers than are lighter-colored, more neutral-tasting drinks.

Distillation is a technique that separates substances according to their boiling points. The producers of spirits use distillation to concentrate the ethanol content of a fermented brew and to separate ethanol from congeners. High-quality vodkas undergo three stages of distillation and are practically free from congeners. Whiskies contain some congeners to give flavor and aroma, but other less palatable congeners are rejected.

from apples in a method similar to winemaking, but its alcohol content is closer to that of a beer.

Spirits. In theory, any alcoholic brew can produce a spirit by distillation. The contents contribute more or less to the flavor and color of the final liquor depending on how cleanly the distillation separates alcohol from other substances in the brew. The addition of water to the distillation product usually results in an alcohol content of 40 to 50 percent ABV (80–100 degrees proof). Some liquors are sold over proof, that is, at ABVs greater than 50 percent ABV.

Whiskey is essentially distilled beer. For Scotch and Irish varieties, the malted barley is dried over a smokey peat fire, and the smoke imparts a flavor to the grain before mashing. Rye whiskey starts with rye grain or a mixture of rye grain and barley malt; bourbon starts with at least 51 percent corn in a blend with rye and malted barley.

Gin is also a grain spirit, but with fewer original congeners (compounds formed during manufacture) than in whiskey. In its manufacture, the spirit from an initial distillation is mixed with juniper berries and other flavoring agents. A second distillation then

carries some of the flavors of these agents with the alcohol. Addition of water then results in a colorless liquor with a distinctive flavor and aroma.

Vodka manufacturers use one or more sources of starch as a starting material, including cereals such as wheat and root vegetables such as potatoes and beets. The exact blend is of little importance, since multiple distillations of the fermented brew yield almost pure alcohol with water. Charcoal filtration removes any remaining impurities, so the taste of pure vodka is that of a pure mixture of alcohol and water.

Many other spirits are obtained by distilling fermented brews, so brandy comes from wine, rum from fermented cane sugar, tequila from the fermented sap of the agave plant, and schnapps from the fermented pulps of fruits and berries. The distinctive flavors of these liquors depend on the congeners that distill over with ethanol.

Liqueurs. A liqueur is a spirit such as brandy or schnapps that has been steeped with flavoring agents and usually sweetened. Flavoring agents include spices, herbs, and fruits, such as black currant. Liqueurs are typically 25 to 40 percent ABV.

Red wine contains antioxidant polyphenols that protect against cardiovascular disease in later life. The recommended daily intake is about one glass.

Alcoholic soft drinks. Alcoholic soft drinks are a modern twist on liqueurs, although much weaker at around 5 percent ABV. They are typically mixtures of a neutral alcohol, such as vodka, with a carbonated fruit drink, such as lemonade. The fruit and sugar content mask the flavor of alcohol, so they appeal to people who dislike the taste of traditional alcoholic drinks. The manufacturers of these drinks have met harsh criticism for designing their packaging and marketing to appeal to underage drinkers. Critics view alcoholic soft drinks as gateway products whose purpose is to expand the alcohol market by developing drinking habits in people who would otherwise abstain.

STANDARD DRINK

The concept of the standard drink is intended to simplify comparisons of the effects of drinks of different potencies. It is the amount of an alcoholic beverage that contains the equivalent of 17.2 ml of pure ethanol.

The standard drink is roughly equivalent to 12 ounces (a can) of 5 percent ABV beer, 5 ounces (a glass) of 11 percent ABV wine, and 1.5 ounces (a shot) of 40 percent ABV liquor. The exact volume (in ml) of a beverage that constitutes a standard drink can be calculated by dividing 17.2 by the ABV as a fraction.

Alcohol in the body

Like all other psychoactives, ethanol must reach the brain to take effect. The first stage is diffusion from the digestive system into the bloodstream. Little alcohol passes through the stomach lining, but it passes rapidly into the bloodstream from the small intestine. Food in the stomach delays its arrival there, and drinking on an empty stomach hastens the absorption of alcohol. Blood alcohol concentration (BAC) peaks around one hour after drinking stops. For a given intake and body mass, women reach higher BACs than men because more of their body mass is fat, which absorbs little alcohol.

The body eliminates around 90 percent of alcohol by biotransformation of ethanol into acetaldehyde and then acetic acid in the liver. Around 10 percent of alcohol is excreted unchanged in urine, and traces leave the body in breath and sweat. A person of 150 pounds (68 kg) eliminates around one standard drink per hour, but chronic drinkers eliminate alcohol more rapidly.

Alcohol in the brain

Alcohol passes freely across the blood-brain barrier and interacts with neurotransmitter systems to produce the symptoms of drunkenness. The principal effect is to depress activity of the central nervous system (CNS) in two ways. First, it attaches to GABA (gamma-aminobutyric acid) receptors and strengthens their interaction with GABA itself. This is similar to the effect of benzodiazepines, so alcohol reduces anxiety by boosting the inhibitory system

BLOOD ALCOHOL AND BREATH TESTS

Since alcohol intoxicates by interacting with receptors in the brain, the extent of intoxication depends directly on the concentration of ethanol in the cerebrospinal fluid that permeates the brain. Direct measurement of that concentration requires a lumbar puncture—an uncomfortable and risky procedure whereby a needle is inserted into the spine to extract a sample of fluid. Fortunately, the concentration of alcohol in the brain correlates well with blood alcohol concentration (BAC), which can be measured by a simple blood test.

The effects of a given BAC depend on the individual, but BACs in the 0.03 to 0.10 percent range correspond to mild intoxication, with effects that include relaxation and reduced inhibition, impaired judgment and attentiveness, and poor coordination of movement. Such levels result from taking one to four standard drinks within an hour.

As BAC increases to 0.25 percent, coordination, balance, and reaction times worsen; vision becomes blurred; and memory is impaired. By 0.30 percent BAC, speech is slurred and confusion and dizziness set in; mood can become unusually aggressive, affectionate, or withdrawn. BACs of 0.40 to 0.50 percent cause stupor, unconsciousness, and even death from a variety of causes, such as cessation of heartbeat or breathing.

Alcohol intoxication is notorious for impairing the ability to drive, and it is now illegal in most states to drive with a BAC of 0.08 percent or more. Suspected drunk drivers are given a breath test, since breath alcohol concentration is proportional to BAC.

Early breath-test devices consisted of a tube packed with crystals and attached to a bag. The test subject would fill the bag with breath, thus ensuring that a standard volume of breath passed through the crystals. The crystals would then change color along a spectrum determined by the amount of alcohol in the breath sample.

Modern breath-testing devices use a fuel cell that produces an electrical current in proportion to the concentration of alcohol in a breath sample. The same devices are useful for testing whether a person is fit to operate potentially dangerous machinery in the workplace.

that suppresses neural activity. Second, alcohol blocks NMDA (N-methyl-D-aspartate) receptors of the excitatory glutamate system, which stimulates neural activity. These receptors also play a role in forming memories, which is why alcohol interferes with memory. The GABA and NDMA systems compensate for the presence of alcohol in chronic drinkers. The agitation and fits that accompany alcohol withdrawal result from this adaptation.

Alcohol also stimulates release of serotonin, which elevates mood and relaxes, and dopamine, which fuels the reward pathway. Since the reward pathway drives primal urges, the release of dopamine reinforces alcohol dependence.

Health effects

The short-term risks of alcohol abuse include injuries from accidents caused by poor judgment, coordination, or reactions or from violence related to reduced inhibitions. Interactions with other drugs can be dangerous or fatal, as can an extreme overdose of alcohol itself. Alcohol is diuretic and causes dehydration that contributes to the headache and lethargy associated with a hangover.

Doctors believe long-term moderate drinking—one or two standard drinks per day—can reduce the risk of heart disease and certain types of strokes by reducing anxiety and thinning the blood. The safe weekly limit is 7 to 13 drinks for women and 14 to 27 drinks for men. Above this intake, there is a dramatic increase in the risk of damage to the heart and liver, various types of cancer, and mental health problems such as depression and suicide.

M. CLOWES

SEE ALSO:

Acetaldehyde • Benzodiazepines • Ethanol

Amobarbital

Barbiturates comprise a family of addictive sedatives and hypnotics that have been largely replaced by the safer benzodiazepines. However, some barbiturates, such as amobarbital, are still used as prescription drugs for insomnia.

Amobarbital is a barbiturate. Barbiturates are central nervous system (CNS) depressants that bind to sites on the $GABA_A$ receptors that make the neuron less responsive to stimuli. Amobarbital acts as a sedative, hypnotic, and anticonvulsant. It is marketed under the trade names Amytal and Amylobarbitone and its street names include blue and blue angel.

Amobarbital is prescribed for insomnia (difficulty sleeping), as an adjunct to psychotherapy, as an anticonvulsant, or before surgery. It can be administered in three ways: intravenously, intramuscularly, or orally (capsules and tablets). The most common form of amobarbital is a bright blue capsule containing 60 milligrams of the drug.

Barbiturates are classified as ultrashort, short, intermediate, and long-acting. Amobarbital is an intermediate-acting barbiturate. This class is preferred by drug abusers, owing to its quick onset and relatively long-lasting effects. Amobarbital begins to work 15 to 40 minutes after it is taken orally, and the effects last up to 6 hours. Although amobarbital produces sedative and hypnotic effects, it does not produce euphoric or pleasurable feelings.

Owing to its high abuse potential, amobarbital is classified as a Schedule II controlled substance in the United States. A person can become dependent upon amobarbital without realizing it. Many people begin by taking the drug to induce sleep, and soon they cannot go to sleep without taking the medication. This type of dependence is termed *physical dependence*. Physical dependence can lead to serious withdrawal symptoms when drug use is ceased. Another serious side effect of amobarbital is its ability to produce tolerance. When tolerance occurs, a person has to keep increasing the dose of the drug in order to produce the same physiological effect. Therefore, one should not cease amobarbital use or increase the dosage without consulting a doctor first.

Common side effects related to amobarbital use include slurred speech, lack of coordination, impaired judgment, constipation, nausea, dizziness, drowsiness, and headache. Alcohol or other CNS depressants can increase the sedative effects of amobarbital and should not be consumed at the same time. Serious possible side effects include chest pain or tightness, muscle or joint pain, sore throat, fever, rash, severe depression, or confusion. Signs of overdose include slowed or fast breathing; cold, clammy skin; change in size of pupils; deep sleep; loss of consciousness; incomprehensibly slurred speech; and slow heartbeat. An overdose can also lead to respiratory failure and death. Withdrawal side effects include anxiety or restlessness, convulsions, feeling faint, nausea and vomiting, and trembling hands.

K. PHILPOT

KEY FACTS

Classification
Schedule II (USA), Schedule IV (Canada), Class B (UK), Schedule III (INCB). Sedative.

Street names
Blue, blue angels, -birds, -clouds, -devils, -dolls, -heavens

Short-term effects
Sedation, slurred speech, lack of coordination, nausea, dizziness, joint or muscle pain, confusion

Long-term effects
Physical dependence, tolerance, inability to sleep without the medication, need to increase dose

Signs of abuse
Incomprehensible speech, dilated pupils, impaired judgment, clammy skin, slow heartbeat

SEE ALSO:
Barbiturates • Benzodiazepines • Pentobarbital • Secobarbital • Sedatives and Hypnotics

Amphetamines

Amphetamines form a group of compounds that stimulate activity in parts of the central and peripheral nervous systems, producing feelings of alertness and euphoria. However, overuse can lead to addiction and psychosis.

The amphetamines are a class of compounds that share the basic chemical structure of the alpha-methylphenylethylamine (amphetamine) molecule. As the name suggests, they form a subgroup of the phenylethylamines (or phenethylamines), a class that includes drugs such as Ecstasy (MDMA). The phenylethylamines exhibit varying degrees of stimulant and hallucinogenic activity; this article concentrates on the stimulant activity of simple amphetamines, which is their predominant characteristic.

Physical peripheral effects
The physical effects of amphetamine mimic those produced by epinephrine (adrenaline), a chemically similar compound the adrenal glands release into the bloodstream at times of stress. The mechanism of action is quite different, however: epinephrine increases neural activity by stimulating adrenoceptors (receptors in neurons that respond to norepinephrine), whereas amphetamines act by prompting the release of norepinephrine from within neurons. Amphetamines have two further mechanisms for

boosting norepinephrine levels: they inhibit monoamine oxidase, the enzyme that inactivates some of the norepinephrine within neurons, and they block reuptake, the mechanism that carries norepinephrine from the synapse back into the neuron.

There are two classes of adrenoceptors, alpha and beta, and each class is subdivided into types 1 and 2. Stimulation of alpha$_1$ receptors is responsible for increased blood pressure, dilation of the pupils, and closure of the bladder sphincter, making urination difficult. Stimulation of the beta receptors increases heart rate, enhances contractility of the heart muscles, and causes the lung expansion that was the basis of early therapeutic uses of amphetamine to treat asthma.

Psychoactive effects
The effects of amphetamine that appeal to recreational users and can lead to dependency are those rooted in the central nervous system. There, the amphetamines stimulate release of neurotransmitters, such as dopamine and norepinephrine, into the synapses between neurons.

There is a similarity between the structures of amphetamines (left) and the neurotransmitters (right) whose activity they modulate as can be seen by substituting different atoms or groups at positions *X, Y,* and *Z.* Amphetamines do not act by binding to receptors, instead they prompt the release of neurotransmitters and then inhibit the reuptake of neurotransmitters into the transmitting neuron.

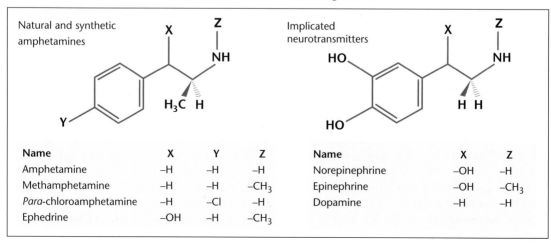

Name	X	Y	Z
Amphetamine	–H	–H	–H
Methamphetamine	–H	–H	–CH$_3$
Para-chloroamphetamine	–H	–Cl	–H
Ephedrine	–OH	–H	–CH$_3$

Name	X	Z
Norepinephrine	–OH	–H
Epinephrine	–OH	–CH$_3$
Dopamine	–H	–H

MECHANISMS OF AMPHETAMINE ACTION

Almost all drugs produce their effects by influencing a process natural to the human body. Amphetamines are no exception: they work by influencing the neurotransmission of nerve impulses by norepinephrine (noradrenaline) and dopamine.

Amphetamines displace neurotransmitters from the vesicles within the neurons that produce them. The result is an increase in the concentration of neurotransmitter in the synapses (junctions) between neurons and in the synapses between neurons and cells of the effectors they control,

such as muscles. High concentrations of neurotransmitters increase the level of neural activity by mimicking the pulses of high neurotransmitter concentration that occur when an action potential (nerve impulse) reaches the tip of a neuron.

Ephedrine is a natural amphetamine present in ephedra shrubs. It differs from typical synthetic amphetamines in that it acts directly on norepinephrine receptors, as well as prompting the release of norepinephrine from storage vesicles. Hence, it is considered a mixed-action norepinephrine receptor agonist.

The neural systems that respond to amphetamine are widespread throughout the brain, and their stimulation produces euphoria and alertness while suppressing appetite and fatigue. Neurons produce neurotransmitters at a finite rate, which imposes a limit on the effectiveness of amphetamine; it can only produce effects while there are reserves of neurotransmitter available for release. Hence, the tolerance to amphetamine increases with time. Furthermore, each episode of heavy amphetamine use is followed by a recovery period while stocks of neurotransmitter accumulate in the neurons. Neurotransmitter activity remains low during this time and is expressed in symptoms such as depression and fatigue. Behavioral tolerance to amphetamine's effects can also develop, as can cross-tolerance to other stimulant drugs.

Overstimulation of dopamine receptors caused by heavy amphetamine use resembles dopamine hyperstimulation in schizophrenics and is the cause of amphetamine psychosis. Tolerance to these effects develops at a slower rate than the tolerance to positive effects, which explains why long-term amphetamine users run a growing risk of psychosis as they take increasing amounts of amphetamine to achieve the intensity of the first hit.

Pharmacology

The amphetamines pass into the bloodstream most rapidly when smoked or injected, but snorting and ingestion (eating) also provide rapid onsets of

effects—typically within 15 to 30 minutes—that last 4 to 6 hours. The ease with which amphetamines pass through the blood-brain barrier to take effect on the central nervous system (CNS) depends on polarity: methamphetamine is less polar than amphetamine, so it enters the CNS more readily. The opposite is true for the neurotransmitters themselves, whose polar –OH groups would prevent them from traversing the blood-brain barrier, making them useless as CNS drugs.

The biotransformation reaction that deactivates amphetamine and begins its elimination from the body is oxidation to phenylpropanone by the action of liver enzymes. Although amphetamine binds to and inactivates monoamine oxidase (MAO), it does not become transformed in the process. This interaction can cause complications by adding to the effects of MAO-inhibiting (MAOI) antidepressants.

The effects of methamphetamine last longer than those of amphetamine because methamphetamine is not susceptible to the enzyme that deactivates amphetamine. Instead, another enzyme must first remove the methyl group to form amphetamine, which remains active until eliminated by the normal pathway.

M. CLOWES

SEE ALSO:

Amphetamine Sulfate • Dopamine • Epinephrine • Norepinephrine • Phenethylamines

Amphetamine Sulfate

Amphetamine is a stimulant drug that has therapeutic and recreational applications. It is most often produced in the form of its sulfate salt, a crystalline powder.

Amphetamine is the prototype of a group of psychoactive chemicals that also includes methamphetamine and various Ecstasy analogs. It is a stimulant and, at high doses, a mild hallucinogen; its hallucinogenic activity is mild in comparison to that of Ecstasy, however. The word *amphetamine* derives from alpha-methylphenylethylamine, an archaic name for the compound with the formula $C_6H_5CH_2CH(CH_3)NH_2$. This compound is a volatile liquid that darkens with age. The salt formed with sulfuric acid—amphetamine sulfate—is an off-white crystalline powder. Because it is more stable than the parent amine, it is a common form of street amphetamine.

Early uses

The first synthesis of amphetamine was achieved in 1887, but it took another 40 years for the pharmacological effects of amphetamine to attract interest. In the late 1920s, researchers discovered that amphetamine increases heart rate and blood pressure while causing constriction of blood vessels and dilation of the bronchial passages. The bronchodilatory effect helps counteract asthma attacks and relieve chest congestion, and it was this property that underlay the first pharmaceutical use of amphetamine—in the Benzedrine Inhaler, launched in 1932 by manufacturers Smith, Kline and French.

The Benzedrine Inhaler was a device that contained amphetamine-soaked wadding, and resourceful users soon learned to extract the amphetamine content by sawing open the inhaler and washing the wadding with water or alcoholic drinks. Drinking the resulting liquid caused a sustained buzz of alertness, euphoria, and self-confidence that made amphetamine a popular drug of abuse from then on. In the late 1950s, users seeking a more intense and rapid hit began to inject amphetamine from this source.

The 1930s also saw the psychostimulant effects of amphetamine put to clinical use for the first time when it was used to treat narcolepsy, a condition whose sufferers are prone to sudden and unpredictable bouts of deep sleep. The use of amphetamine to improve the attention span of hyperactive children started two years later, in 1937.

Amphetamine and warfare

By 1939, use and abuse of amphetamine was established enough for the drug to have acquired a track record of side effects including dependency and mental disturbances, including psychosis and profound depression. Nevertheless, the outbreak of World War II that same year would ensure the continued pharmaceutical production of amphetamine and methamphetamine, its longer-acting and

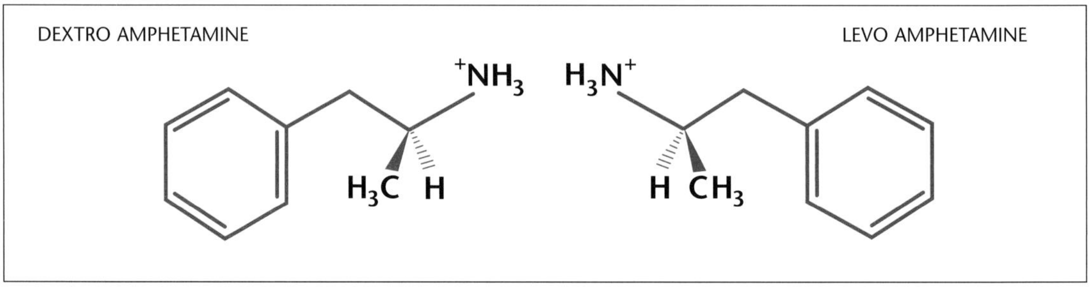

DEXTRO AMPHETAMINE

LEVO AMPHETAMINE

Amphetamine sulfate exists as two nonidentical mirror-image forms: dextro, shown at left, and levo. Chemical synthesis produces an equal mixture of the two forms, called a racemate. Pure dextro amphetamine, which is approximately twice as strong a stimulant as racemic amphetamine, is used in pep pills. Levo amphetamine has little stimulant activity but is an appetite suppressant used in the treatment of obesity.

KEY FACTS

Classification
Schedule II (USA, INCB), Schedule III (Canada) Class B (UK). Stimulant and antiobesity agent.

Street names
Amp, bennies, black bombers, pep pills, speed, uppers

Short-term effects
Mood elevation with increased alertness, self-confidence, and attention to detail. Dry mouth, sweating, tremor, insomnia, and reduced appetite. Increased heart rate and blood pressure, sometimes with palpitations. Higher doses can cause anxiety, paranoia, and psychosis.

Long-term effects
Lack of sleep and poor diet can cause fatigue, weight loss, malnutrition, ulcers, and psychological disturbances, such as depression and violent mood swings. Repeated heavy doses can cause brain damage that leads to slurred speech and confused thoughts.

Signs of abuse
Users can become talkative, persistent, and hyperactive. Depending on the amount taken and individual sensitivity, they may become paranoid, aggressive, or unusually self-confident. Habitual users can have spells of reclusion, prolonged irregular sleep, and depression between amphetamine-fueled "runs" of several days' activity without sleep.

led to illegal production in clandestine factories. The use of amphetamines as recreational stimulants (commonly known as speed) continued despite growing restrictions. This was particularly evident in 1960s, where a pill that could provide energy as required fitted well with the fast-paced "modern" lifestyle advocated by the popular-music culture of the time. The most popular amphetamine-based drugs were Dexedrine (pure dextro amphetamine sulfate, street name "dexies") and Drinamyl (a mixture of dextro amphetamine sulfate and a barbiturate). The mixture of a stimulant and a sleep-inducing barbiturate in Drinamyl might seem contradictory, but the mixture was intended to produce a nonsedating tranquilizer for clinical use; however, some users preferred it to pure amphetamine.

In 1970 the U.S. Controlled Substances Act (CSA) classified amphetamines in Schedule III; they were upgraded to their current Schedule II status a year later. With the increasing restrictions on amphetamine, many street users in the United States turned instead to cocaine and methamphetamine preparations, which are equally restricted and more potent. The amphetamine sulfate that was available was of poor quality and unreliable purity, often as low as 5 percent, and was cut with pseudoephedrine, caffeine, aspirin, or glucose. Such mixtures are in powder form and are intended for snorting or "bombing" (wrapping in paper balls, which are then swallowed). Insoluble impurities can clog veins if the user tries to dissolve and inject such powders, and there is a risk of adverse reactions to impurities however the drug is taken.

In recent years, a new source of amphetamine sulfate has become available in the form of Adderall. Prescribed for children and young adults with attention deficit disorder, it consists of a mixture of dextro and levo amphetamines with saccharin and aspartame. Although this drug has none of the risks associated with street speed, the amphetamine content makes it dangerous if the dose is exceeded or if it is taken by persons other than those for whom it is prescribed.

M. CLOWES

more potent relative. Production boomed as the drug was widely distributed to combatants who used it to stay alert on long tours of duty and to increase confidence under threat of enemy attack.

Civilian use
By the mid 1950s, amphetamine products were well established as over-the-counter pep pills and appetite suppressants. Then, from 1956, the classification of amphetamines as prescription drugs created a black market in prescribed amphetamines and ultimately

Anabolic Steroids

Anabolic steriods are hormones that promote muscle growth when used in conjunction with regular exercise. They are open to abuse by athletes and those wishing to create a more muscular body.

Anabolic-androgenic steroids (AASs) include the male sex hormone, testosterone, and its synthetic forms. Their name reflects the fact that they have both bodybuilding (anabolic) and masculinity-producing (androgenic) effects. AASs are sometimes called steroids for short, but AASs are only one kind of steroid. Another group of steroids, called corticosteroids, are commonly used to treat medical problems such as asthma, inflamed joints, and allergic skin reactions. Prednisone, cortisone, and hydrocortisone cream are examples of corticosteroids. Corticosteroids and AASs are both made from cholesterol in the body, and substances that resemble cholesterol in their chemical structure are called steroids. Corticosteroids and AASs, however, differ markedly in their effects: large doses of AASs can increase muscle size, whereas corticosteroids can cause muscle wasting. Street or slang names for AASs include roids and juice. The names of some commonly used AASs are listed in the table on page 31.

Chemical structure and pharmacology

Testosterone consists of 19 carbon atoms arranged in or around four rings (*see* diagram on p. 29). The carbon atoms are labeled from 1 to 19. Testosterone also contains atoms of oxygen and hydrogen. At the carbon-17 atom (C-17), there is a hydrogen (H) atom attached at the alpha position and an –OH (hydroxy) group attached at the beta position. Many synthetic forms are made by adding chains of carbon and hydrogen atoms (known as alkyl groups) with or without oxygen to the existing carbon atoms in testosterone. The chemical structure of a synthetic AAS determines its properties, such as toxicity, how long it lasts in the body, and whether it works as a pill, gel, or injection. The diagram also shows methyltestosterone, which is taken as a pill on a daily basis. A methyl (–CH_3) group has replaced the H atom at the C-17 alpha position, an example of a C-17 alpha-alkylated AAS. Another AAS shown is testosterone cypionate, a synthetic form that is taken by injection and lasts in the body for two to four

Weight lifters and body builders sometimes use anabolic steriods to promote muscle growth, but they run the risk of negative side effects such as liver problems and testicular shrinkage.

weeks. In general, pill forms of AASs are more toxic to the liver and have a greater effect on cholesterol levels than injectable forms. On the other hand, many of the injectable compounds are metabolized in the body to the female hormone estrogen, causing unwanted side effects, such as breast enlargement in men. Once in the body, AASs enter cells throughout the body, but especially muscle cells, sex organ cells, and brain cells. Once inside muscle cells, they bind specifically to proteins called androgen receptors. The AAS-protein complex then activates genes that cause muscle size to increase when combined with proper nutrition and exercise.

Legal and illegal use

Several AASs are available as prescription drugs to treat a small number of medical conditions. Most commonly, AASs are used to treat boys and men whose bodies are unable to produce testosterone in normal amounts, a condition known as male hypogonadism. Less commonly, they are used to treat hereditary angioedema (a rare skin condition), certain kinds of anemia (deficiency of red blood cells), and some breast cancers. AASs have also been used in patients with either acquired immune deficiency syndrome (AIDS) or serious burn injuries to stimulate appetite, weight gain, muscle mass, and improvements in mood. Prescribing AASs for these conditions and a few others is legal and within the scope of medical practice.

Outside the standard of acceptable medical practice, AASs are used to enhance athletic performance, physical appearance, and fighting ability. Because only rarely do doctors willingly engage in medical malpractice, a lucrative illicit market has developed to supply people who want to use AASs for these nonmedical reasons. Legally manufactured

AASs are sometimes diverted into the illicit market through illegal means. For example, AASs have been smuggled into the United States from countries where they are obtained over-the-counter without a prescription. AASs are typically sold in weight-lifting gyms by dealers who are weight lifters themselves. The result is that AASs are relatively easy to obtain.

Experts debate whether AASs actually do work to improve performance and appearance, because some scientific studies have failed to show an effect. Some experts argue that these studies were seriously limited by the ways in which they were carried out and what conclusions could be drawn from their results. Nevertheless, most researchers agree that AASs can enhance muscle size and strength in some individuals when combined with a proper exercise program and diet. However, AASs are highly unlikely to improve performance of aerobic or endurance activities.

Users of illicit AASs

Even though society has deemed nonmedical use of AASs as unacceptable or illegal, some people are willing to engage in illegal activity in order to obtain the perceived advantages of AAS use. They may be competitive bodybuilders, aspiring models, actors, or dancers, or merely individuals who want to improve their appearance. Some AAS users aim to enhance their physical power and aggressiveness in order to fight or intimidate others. They include bodyguards, bouncers, and gang members.

Many anabolic steroids are based on the structure of testosterone, a natural sex hormone. Manufacturers of illegal steroids use this structure to make new compounds that cannot be detected by drug-testing agencies.

Patterns of use

AASs are administered as pills, skin patches, and by injection. Injection occurs into large muscle groups (buttocks, thigh, or shoulder) or under the skin. Although AASs are not injected directly into veins, the risks of spreading diseases such as AIDS, hepatitis, and syphilis are the same as for intravenous drug users. Even without sharing needles, there are risks of infection: law-enforcement officials have confiscated nonsterile vials contaminated with bacteria that were ready to be sold.

Cycling refers to a pattern of use in which AASs are taken for 6 to 12 weeks, followed by 6 to 12 weeks off. Small doses are taken at the start of a cycle, increased to a maximum during mid-cycle, and then tapered at the end of a cycle. The reasons for cycling of AASs at periodic intervals are to minimize side effects, to avoid detection if subjected to drug testing, and to allow the body's own sex hormones to regain their natural balance. Stacking refers to a pattern of use in which multiple AAS drugs are used together. Users may take both pills and injections, for example. Different users have varying opinions about which "recipe" of combining and cycling particular AASs provides the most benefit. Everyone agrees, however, that higher than usual medical doses are required. Accordingly, illicit users usually take 10 to 100 times the amounts ordinarily prescribed for medical purposes, which increases their toxicity. The actual dose taken is difficult to know, however, because illicit AASs frequently contain preparations that are falsely labeled or are prepared for veterinary purposes or both. Drugs purchased illicitly do not always contain what is written on their labels, and an appropriate human dose of AASs designed for animals is not known.

Steroid users commonly take other prescription drugs, sometimes obtained illicitly, to offset the unpleasant side effects of AASs, to increase the body-building effects, and, in the case of competitive athletes, to avoid detection by drug testing. For example, tamoxifen and clomiphene are estrogen blockers that are taken to prevent breast enlargement, an obviously undesired side effect of high-dose AASs in men. Water pills (diuretics) are taken both to dilute the urine prior to drug testing and to eliminate fluid under the skin so that muscles look more defined. Human chorionic gonadotropin

KEY FACTS

Classification
Schedule III (USA), Schedule IV (Canada), Class C (UK). Not scheduled, INCB.

Street names
Arnolds, deca, depo-T, gym candy, juice, pumpers, roids, stackers, weight trainers

Short-term effects
Increased muscle size when taken with proper exercise and nutrition

Long-term effects
Possible side effects including increased aggression, liver disease, heart attack, stroke, sudden mood changes, and increased risk of suicide

Signs of abuse
In men: baldness or hair loss, reduced testicle size, and possible breast growth. Aggressive or violent behavior. In women: deepened voice, growth of facial and chest hair, and irregular menstrual periods.

(HCG) is a nonsteroidal hormone that when injected stimulates the testicles to produce additional testosterone and thus prevents them from shrinking. Human growth hormone is another nonsteroidal hormone that is injected to increase muscle and body size. Finally, nonmedical AAS users are not immune from, and may even have a greater risk of, using typical drugs of abuse such as alcohol, opioids, cocaine, and amphetamines.

Dietary supplements

Dietary supplements include vitamins, minerals, amino acids, protein supplements, creatine, caffeine, and testosterone precursors. Vitamins, minerals, amino acids, creatine, and protein supplements are not drugs of abuse and can be used in competitive sports. A testosterone precursor is a substance that is converted in the body to testosterone. The two most common precursors are dehydroepiandrosterone (DHEA) and androstenedione. Because these

ANABOLIC STEROIDS USED BY BODYBUILDERS

Generic name	Representative brand name
Injectable testosterone esters	
Testosterone cypionate	Depo-Testosterone Virilon IM
Testosterone enanthate	Delatestryl
Testosterone propionate	Testex, Oreton propionate
Other injectables	
Nandrolone decanoate	Deca-Durabolin
Nandrolone phenpropionate	Durabolin
Methenolone enanthate	Primobolan Depot
Veterinary injectables used by humans	
Trenbolone acetate	Finaject (Finajet) 30 Parabolan
Boldenone undecylenate	Equipoise
Stanozolol	Winstrol V
Pills (17-alkylated AASs)	
Ethylestrenol	Maxibolan
Fluoxymesterone	Halotestin
Methandrostenolone	Dianabol
Methenolone	Primobolan
Methyltestosterone	Android (10 & 25), Metandren, Oreton Methyl, Testred, Virilon
Oxandrolone	Anavar
Oxymetholone	Adroyd, Anadrol-50
Oxymesterone	Oranabol
Stanozolol	Winstrol

precursors such as DHEA. However, these substances are readily available in most countries without a prescription, regardless of age. In the United States, all dietary supplements have been unregulated since the passage of the Dietary Supplement and Health Education Act in 1994. An unfortunate consequence of no regulation is that the contents and labeling of these products are rarely checked. Thus, the actual dosage of supplements may vary from 0 percent to more than 100 percent of the labeled content. Moreover, products labeled as lacking testosterone precursors may still contain such substances.

Effects on bodily systems

Testosterone is normally produced in both males and females, with much higher amounts produced in males than females. The high amount produced in males prior to birth is responsible for the development of male sex organs. During puberty in boys, the physiological effects of testosterone cause adult male characteristics to appear, such as enlargement of the penis, hair growth on the face and pubic area, muscular development, and a deepened voice.

AASs have been associated with a variety of adverse events, including death. Deaths are expected when severely ill patients (with AIDS and anemia, for example) are medically treated with AASs, because such patients already have a higher risk for early death. Nevertheless, deaths among nonmedical steroid users have also been reported in the scientific literature from causes such as liver disease, cancer, heart attacks, strokes, and suicide. Therefore, anyone using AASs should have periodic health checks by a qualified health care professional.

Psychiatric effects. Most but not all studies in humans report that high doses of AASs increase aggressive thoughts and feelings. Some users may even think of this as a benefit, depending on their reasons for use. *Roid rage* is a slang expression used to describe extreme instances of aggressive behavior among AAS users. Reports of violent assaults and murder while taking AASs generate both alarm and widespread attention. Fortunately, the total number of such incidents is small. However, even when irritability does not lead to violent behavior, the feelings of aggression engendered by AASs can be distressing to users and people around them.

compounds have anabolic and androgenic effects after their conversion to testosterone, their actions and side effects are similar to, but generally less potent than, other AASs. The International Olympic Committee, all international sports federations, and some countries such as Australia ban testosterone

Using AASs is also associated with mood swings and psychosis. Steroid users commonly report feeling energetic, confident, and even euphoric during cycles of use. Their high energy level may make it difficult or undesirable to sleep. Appetite is typically increased and large amounts of food are eaten to support muscle growth and energy. When stopping use of an AAS, individuals may feel depressed, tired, or irritable. Appetite may decrease. Over longer periods of using AASs at high doses, moods may shift suddenly, so that the user feels energetic and euphoric for a while, then irritable and aggressive, and then depressed or anxious.

The term *psychosis* describes a mental state in which a person cannot distinguish between what is real and what is not. For example, a person may believe that other people intend harm when no real threat exists, or a person may believe that an impossible, life-threatening stunt can be performed with no problem. Such false beliefs are called delusions. The psychotic person may also experience hallucinations, such as hearing a voice that is not there. Most psychiatric effects of AASs tend to disappear soon after AASs are stopped, although a depressed mood may last for several months.

Effects on the liver. AASs can affect the liver in various ways, but the pill forms are generally more toxic to the liver than other AASs. Most commonly, AASs cause the liver to release extra amounts of enzymes into the bloodstream; this can be easily measured by a blood test. The liver enzymes usually return to normal levels when AASs are stopped. The liver also releases a substance called bilirubin, which, in high amounts, can cause the skin and eyes to turn yellow (a condition called jaundice). Although untreated jaundice can be dangerous and even fatal, jaundice usually disappears within several weeks of stopping AASs. Jaundice can also be a sign of other dangerous conditions of the liver, such as hepatitis, so a physician should always treat these symptoms. Another condition that occurs among patients treated with AASs is peliosis hepatitis, in which little sacs of blood form in the liver. Death can occur from bleeding if one of the sacs ruptures. Finally, liver

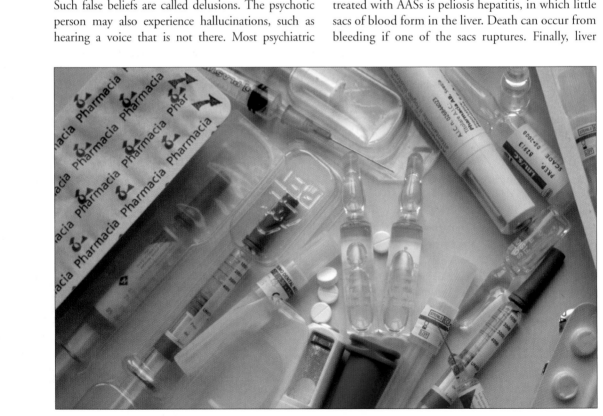

The increasingly sophisticated array of drugs available as pills, injections, and supplements to improve sports performance, combined with techniques to evade drug detection, makes testing for drugs increasingly difficult for sports authorities. New testing techniques must therefore constantly be developed.

DESIGNER STEROIDS

Athletes trying to outperform their fellow competitors sometimes use dietary supplements to give them an advantage. Lack of regulation over the labeling and content of supplements can mean that an athlete may not always be aware of what he or she is taking. A scandal broke in 2003 when antidoping officials were alerted to a new designer steroid that was being incorporated into food supplements. The substance, tetrahydrogestrinone or THG, was an analog of gestrinone, which is used to treat endometriosis (painful, heavy periods) in women. The new steroid had been deliberately manufactured to avoid detection. From a sample of THG passed to them secretly by a team coach, scientists were able to devise a test to reveal the presence of this steroid. Retrospective tests on urine samples from a number of leading athletes revealed the presence of THG. The drug has now been banned by all international sporting bodies.

tumors may occur in 1 to 3 percent of individuals (including athletes) using high doses of some pill forms of AASs for more than two years. Rare cases of liver tumors have also been reported with other types of AASs. Some of the tumors are cancerous, and although more than half of the tumors disappeared when AASs were stopped, others resulted in death.

Potential to affect the heart. Steroids, especially in pill form, can cause changes in cholesterol levels in the blood that are associated with an increased risk of heart attacks. When AASs are stopped, however, cholesterol levels return to normal. Another risk factor for heart attacks and strokes is high blood pressure. Studies have shown that AASs can cause small increases in blood pressure, which return to normal when AASs are stopped. Some but not all studies suggest that AAS users can develop a harmful enlargement of the heart. Further studies are needed to determine whether AAS users have a higher risk of heart attacks and strokes than nonusers.

Sexual side effects. AASs can alter the levels of several sex-related hormones in the body, resulting in many adverse effects. In males, the prostate gland can enlarge, making it difficult to urinate, the testes shrink, and sterility can occur. Steroids have been tried experimentally as male birth control pills, because they suppress sperm production when given in high amounts. The negative effects on the prostate, the testes, and sperm production reverse when AASs are stopped; however, at least one case of prostate cancer has been reported, which is not reversible. Males can also develop enlarged breast

tissue from taking AASs, an effect medically termed gynecomastia. Breast enlargement occurs because testosterone is chemically changed in the body to the female hormone estrogen, so excess testosterone causes males to have higher amounts of estrogen than normal. Painful lumps in the male breast may persist after stopping AASs, and they sometimes require surgical removal.

Females, however, may undergo shrinkage of their breasts as a response to higher amounts of male hormone than normal and the body shape becomes masculinized. Menstrual periods become irregular and sterility can occur as well. Deepened voice and an enlarged clitoris are effects in females that do not always reverse after stopping AASs. Women may also develop excessive hair growth in typically masculine patterns, such as on the chest and face. Finally, both males and females may experience increases or decreases in their desire for sex.

Other effects. In children of both sexes before the onset of puberty, AASs can initiate the characteristics of male puberty and cause the bones to stop growing prematurely. The latter effect can result in shorter adult heights than would otherwise occur. AASs can cause premature baldness in some individuals and can also cause acne, which is reversible with cessation of AASs. Other possible effects include small increases in the number of red blood cells, worsening of a condition called sleep apnea (in which afflicted persons stop breathing for short intervals during sleep), and worsening of muscle twitches (known as tics) in those who are predisposed.

Addictive potential

As with other drugs of abuse, dependence on AASs occurs when a user reports several of the following symptoms: inability to stop or cut down use, taking more drugs than intended, continuing use despite experiencing negative effects, tolerance, and withdrawal. Tolerance refers to needing more of a drug to get the same effect that was previously obtained with smaller doses, or having diminished effects with the same dose. As many as 12 to 18 percent of nonmedical AAS users report tolerance. Withdrawal refers to the uncomfortable effects users experience when they stop taking AASs. However, many of the undesirable effects reverse when AASs are stopped. Other undesirable side effects, however, can begin when the user stops taking the drug, such as depressed mood, fatigue, loss of appetite, difficulty sleeping, restlessness, decreased sex drive, headaches, muscle aches, and a desire for more AASs. The depression can become so severe that suicidal thoughts occur. The risk of suicide is thought to be highest during the withdrawal period.

Studies indicate that between 14 and 57 percent of nonmedical AAS users develop dependence, although dependence in women is rare. AASs, however, may differ from other drugs of abuse in several ways. First, neither physical nor psychological dependence on AASs has been reported to occur when AASs are prescribed for treating medical conditions. This differentiates the AASs from opioid painkillers and sedative-hypnotics. Second, dependence may develop primarily to the muscle-altering effects of AASs, rather than the mood-altering effects. Some researchers have questioned whether AASs produce dependence at all, because most definitions of dependence require that drugs be taken primarily for their mood-altering effects. Third, AAS users appear more preoccupied with their bodies and how they look than do users of other drugs of dependence.

Prevention and treatment

The two major strategies to prevent AAS use are drug testing and education. Drug testing is common in organized sports for elite athletes. It is employed to deter drug use and to ensure that no athletes have an unfair advantage over their competitors. Testing has caught many high-profile athletes, including the sprinter Ben Johnson. However, drug testing has also fueled the development of many techniques to conceal AAS use. Examples include stopping use prior to the testing season, ingesting substances to dilute the urine, and using AASs for which drug tests have not been developed. Drug-testing officials have responded with some measures to counter these tactics, such as year-round testing and testing for chemicals that may be added to urine to give a false reading. The result is an escalating competition between athletes and officials to conceal and detect AAS use, respectively.

Because of expense and unproven effectiveness, drug testing does not ordinarily occur in settings other than elite sports, yet approximately two-thirds of adolescent AAS users start at age 16 or younger. Therefore, educational prevention efforts must begin early and target those individuals at highest risk to use. Individual risk factors for use include being male, intensive weight lifting for sports or appearance, feeling smaller than peers, knowing people who use AASs, using other illicit drugs and dietary supplements, and engaging in other problem or risk-taking behaviors. Cultural risk factors include preoccupations with winning, physical appearance, and a "bigger is better" attitude. Research has shown that informing adolescents only about the negative effects of AASs is not effective. A program that provides a balanced review of known information about AASs, combined with techniques for optimizing weight training and nutrition, is believed to be most effective.

Treatment is indicated when users show adverse consequences of use. In addition to treating AAS-induced adverse effects, users should be assessed for symptoms of substance dependence. When persistent use despite adverse consequences or other symptoms of dependence are present, addiction-focused treatment may be necessary. If AASs are combined with other drugs of abuse, then traditional addiction treatment approaches may be used. In addition, treatment may need to focus on an over-reliance on physical attributes for self-esteem that is not usually observed with other substance-dependent individuals.

K. J. BROWER

SEE ALSO:
Analogs ● Hormonal Effects

Analogs

Analogs are chemical compounds that have similar chemical structures; analog drugs share some or all aspects of their pharmacological activity. These similarities of effect can be exploited to create legal versions of illicit drugs.

The fact that some related chemical compounds share similar profiles of biological activity is useful in developing medicinal or controlled drugs. Compounds that share this relationship are analogs of one another, but when one drug is more widely known or used than others in a group, the remaining members are classified as analogs of the principal drug.

The most common use of analogs is in the development of new drugs from existing ones. In some cases, the motive is commercial: a drug company might want to develop an analog of a drug that is under patent to another company, for example. These analogs are often called "me-too" drugs. They provide useful alternatives when selecting the treatment best suited to an individual, even if the average differences in effects are small. Clandestine producers of street drugs use the same approach to produce analog drugs that sidestep existing drug-control legislation; these analogs are the so-called designer drugs.

Reasons for developing analogs

Drug companies often seek to develop analogs with fewer or milder side effects than existing drugs. This can be achieved because the therapeutic effect and side effects occur when the drug binds to different receptor sites in the body. A superior analog might have a stronger affinity for the receptors responsible for the therapeutic effect, so it can be used in lower doses that produce fewer side effects than the original drug; alternatively, the analog might have a similar affinity for the therapeutic site but weaker affinities for sites linked to side effects, so it is milder at the standard dosage. An important example is the case of buprenorphine, an analog of heroin and morphine. Buprenorphine is a powerful painkiller—some 10 to 20 times as potent as morphine—so it is useful in the treatment of pain. Unlike morphine, buprenorphine has low addictive potential, and it is being introduced as a treatment for heroin withdrawal; buprenorphine prevents the onset of acute withdrawal symptoms but does not create a new addiction.

Some analogs improve the pharmacodynamics of an existing drug: that is, they reduce the time before the therapeutic effect takes hold. Rapid onset requires the drug to pass rapidly into the bloodstream if taken as a tablet or syrup (intravenous injection puts it there instantly), and then to move rapidly to the part of the body where its effects are needed. Psychoactive drugs must be able to cross the blood-brain barrier with ease.

The skin of the Ecuadorian tree frog contains epibatidine, a strong painkilling drug. Scientists are trying to develop a chemical analog of epibatidine.

Minor changes in the chemical structure of the drug can have major consequences on its rate of absorption into the bloodstream and passage through the blood-brain barrier, as is the case for the benzodiazepines (diazepam analogs). In general, high fat solubility promotes passage through membranes, so drugs with polar groups such as –OH and –NH$_2$ tend to act more slowly than analogs with fat-soluble hydrocarbon or halogen (–Br, –Cl, –F) groups.

Length of action

The ideal length of action depends on the application of a given drug. Hypnotics for day surgery need to have short half-lives (length of time for half the drug to be eliminated) so that the patient remains unconscious for only a short while after surgery finishes; longer half-lives are better for long-term drug therapy, since they reduce swings away from the optimal blood-plasma concentration of the drug. Slight chemical modifications can tailor the half-life of a type of drug by modifying the rate at which the body transforms a drug into inactive compounds or excretes it in waste.

Short-lived drugs tend to have reactive chemical groups that ease their biotransformation into easily excreted or inactive substances. Longer drug action is achieved by capping these reactive groups—by replacing –NH with –NCH$_3$, for example—so that an additional, slower biotransformation reaction must happen before the drug becomes inactive. Such minor changes usually produce analogs that are active in the same way as the parent drug. Consequently, therapeutic action lasts longer as the body slowly converts the analog into the parent drug.

Mimics of natural compounds

In some cases, the synthesis of analogs provides useful substitutes for natural compounds. An early example of this resulted in the development of aspirin (acetylsalicylic acid) as an analog of salicylic acid, a traditional painkilling extract of willow bark. Salicylic acid had two main problems: its bitterness (taken as a powder) and its harsh effects on the stomach lining. Aspirin, launched by the pharmaceutical company Bayer in 1899, proved to be less bitter and gentler on the stomach than salicylic acid.

Aspirin was one of the first synthetic drugs, but its applications continue to grow: recent clinical expe-

rience has shown it to reduce the risk of heart attacks, and new studies suggest it could help prevent colon cancer. It is a far from ideal drug, however, as it can cause gastric bleeding and other adverse effects. In 2001, Kathryn Uhrich of Rutgers University developed a new variant of salicylic acid that could reduce the risk of gastric bleeding. Called Poly-Aspirin, it is a polymer of around 100 salicylic acid groups per molecule linked by suberic acid molecules. The acidic groups that cause stomach irritation are bound up in the polymerization reaction, and stay that way until they reach the bloodstream. Only then does the polymer fall apart to release salicylic acid. The structure of PolyAspirin is similar to that of polyesters used to make fibers, so it is possible that fibers of PolyAspirin could be used as surgical sutures that steadily release painkiller as they dissolve.

Pharmacophores

Modifying the properties of a known drug is not simply a matter of changing any part of its molecular structure. In some cases, large portions of the molecular structure can change without losing the basic therapeutic effect of the original drug in the resulting analog. In other cases, a small change in molecular structure completely eliminates the therapeutic effect. Drug designers explain this in terms of pharmacophores, which are the fragments of a molecule's structure that produce its drug effect. As long as the pharmacophore is present in an analog, the therapeutic effect will be in force (to a greater or lesser degree). Removing any part of the pharmacophore eliminates the drug effect.

Discovering the pharmacophore of a given drug is often a case of detective work. Researchers produce a series of compounds based on the known drug, each one lacking a different feature of its molecular structure. Laboratory tests then reveal which of the variants have the desired pharmaceutical activity and which do not. The inactive compounds then reveal which parts of the structure must be present in an effective analog, and this sets the basic requirement for the development of new analogs.

Knowing the pharmacophore of a given natural drug helps in the design of synthetic analogs that are safer to use or easier to manufacture than the original drug. The search for a useful analog of epibatidine provides a good example. Epibatidine is a potent painkiller present in the skin of an Ecuadorian tree frog (*Epipedobates tricolor*). Epibatidine is interesting because it prevents pain sensations by blocking nicotinic acetylcholine receptors in the brain, rather than opiate receptors. Hence, it is potentially less addictive than opiate painkillers such as morphine. However, epibatidine also blocks similar receptors in the nerves that make muscles work, so it causes paralysis. Used on a poison dart, the epibatidine from one tree frog can paralyze a water buffalo.

By discovering the pharmacophore related to epibatidine's painkilling effect, it became obvious that the complex bridged ring in the molecular structure of epibatidine is not necessary for drug action, provided the –NH group is in approximately the same place relative to the other ring. This is good news for a synthetic chemist, since bridged rings are difficult to make industrially. More important, tests show that the analog coded ABT-154 blocks pain receptors as effectively as epibatidine but causes no paralysis because it has little affinity for receptors in nerves that control muscles. The potential for addiction to ABT-154 is as yet unknown.

Molecular modeling and drug design

The activity of a drug usually depends on how it fits into a receptor site in a protein, which is often compared to a key fitting a lock. Pattern recognition compares candidate molecules with others that have proven themselves to be good "keys" for various "locks," but does it without examining the "lock" directly. A more direct approach examines the shape of the protein receptor site—the "lock"—and calculates how well different candidate molecules fit. A good fit suggests the likelihood of an effective drug.

In some cases, the receptor site for a pharmaceutical response is well known and characterized by techniques such as X-ray crystallography, which gives a precise position for each of the atoms around the receptor. Given this knowledge, the technique of CoMFA (Comparative Molecular Field Analysis) calculates the attractive and repulsive forces between a candidate drug molecule and the receptor. The most important forces are usually hydrogen bonds, bonds that form fleetingly between loose hydrogen atoms on one molecule and electron pairs on the other. For this reason, the pharmacophores of most drugs include groups with active loose hydrogen,

---

ADDICTIVE ANALOGS

Felix Hoffmann, the chemist at Bayer who developed aspirin as a superior analog of a natural painkiller (salicylic acid), claimed he followed his instincts in his work. His instincts were not always to be trusted, however: in 1897, within a few days of producing aspirin, he made an acetyl analog of morphine—another natural extract. He intended to produce a painkiller more effective than morphine but less addictive. Bayer marketed this analog under the trade name Heroin. Only after many years of sales would it become obvious that the synthetic analog was far more addictive than morphine itself. In an ironic twist of fate, Bayer's two discoveries, aspirin and heroin, went on to become the world's most successful legal and illegal drugs, respectively.

---

such as –NH– or –OH, and groups with lone electron pairs, such as –O– and –N=.

Hydrogen bonds determine the orientation of a drug candidate at the receptor site. The drug effect can be improved by adding molecular structure that holds hydrogen-bonding groups in the best positions for interacting with their partners in the protein, or by adding hydrophobic (water-repellant) groups, typically hydrocarbon rings and chains or halogen atoms, where they will be close to similar groups in the protein structure.

Developers of haptics—the "touch" aspect of virtual reality—are currently taking an interest in CoMFA. By combining the two technologies, it will be possible to "feel" how well a drug fits a receptor by wearing force-feedback gloves and virtual reality goggles. Such a development would advance analog design in a way early experimental drug designers could never have dreamed possible.

M. CLOWES

Antidepressant Drugs

Antidepressants are prescription drugs that combat the symptoms of depression. Three main types of antidepressants are in use; they all work by increasing the concentration and action of chemicals in the brain called monoamines.

Depression is a common and debilitating illness that affects people from all sectors of society. Its principal symptom is an overwhelming feeling of hopelessness and inability to cope with life. Other symptoms can include changes in eating or sleeping patterns, inability to concentrate on tasks, tiredness, and reduced sex drive. In extreme cases, the desperation is so strong that sufferers turn to drugs to relieve their feelings or attempt suicide as a way out of their distress.

Monoamines and depression

Antidepressant drugs form one of the treatment options for depression. The development of antidepressant drugs works on the hypothesis that abnormally low concentrations of certain neurotransmitters—dopamine, norepinephrine, and serotonin—are responsible for depression. These three neurotransmitters are examples of chemicals called monoamines, and they are responsible for communication between brain cells.

Depression improves through treatment with drugs that increase concentrations of monoamines in the gaps between brain cells, while drugs that deplete those same compounds cause depression. This information was originally gathered from the effects of tricyclic antidepressants, which boost monoamine levels in general. Drugs introduced in the late 1980s that boost individual monoamine levels have given more detailed insights. Behavioral studies suggest that low levels of dopamine could be responsible for apathy and lack of enjoyment of normally pleasurable activities. Low levels of norepinephrine undermine confidence with strangers, while low levels of serotonin make people more vulnerable in stressful social situations.

Tricyclic antidepressants

Launched in the late 1950s, this class of drugs has the longest history of use in treating depression. The term *tricyclic* refers to their molecular structures, which feature three linked rings. Some have a fourth ring in addition to the characteristic tricycle.

Tricyclic antidepressants, or TCAs, work by inhibiting reuptake—one of the mechanisms that remove neurotransmitters from the gaps between brain cells. After a signal has passed across a synapse, reuptake transporters carry neurotransmitter molecules back into the neuron, ready for release when another signal comes along. Reuptake is a form of recycling that reduces the need for neurons to produce neurotransmitters. By inhibiting the reuptake of norepinephrine and serotonin, TCAs increase the background level of these neurotransmitters in synapses. Boosted neurotransmitter levels increase the activity of the brain systems that communicate using these compounds, thus relieving depressive symptoms.

While TCAs are just as effective in treating depression as more modern types of antidepressants, their weak point is that they also act on neuro-

People taking MAOI antidepressants must take care to avoid foods such as cheese and wine, which can trigger a dangerous increase in blood pressure.

transmitter systems that cause negative side effects. In particular, they block muscarinic receptors for acetylcholine. This action causes blurred vision, dryness of the mouth, constipation, and retention of urine. The effect on the urinary system is so great that imipramine is sometimes used to overcome childhood bedwetting. Other side effects include dizziness caused by a drop in blood pressure on standing; this happens because TCAs block the receptors for epinephrine that maintain blood pressure by constricting blood vessels.

Sensitivity to side effects varies from patient to patient, and doctors often prescribe different TCAs at gradually increasing dosages until they find the best course for an individual. The side effects caused by the blockade of acetylcholine receptors tend to diminish within two weeks, and the antidepressant effect begins to work within two to three weeks.

Monoamine oxidase inhibitors (MAOIs)

The second type of antidepressant drugs boosts neurotransmitter levels by knocking out the enzymes that destroy monoamines such as dopamine, norepinephrine, and serotonin. These enzymes are called monoamine oxidases (MAOs); their function in healthy individuals is to prevent monoamines from saturating the synapses and disrupting normal nerve function. In depressed individuals, reduced MAO activity can allow monoamines to rise to healthy levels that relieve depression.

The disadvantage of MAOIs is that people who take them have to be careful to avoid a wide range of foods and beverages, such as mature cheese, yeast extract, pâté, beer, and some wines. These items contain a monoamine called tyramine that MAOs in the gut would normally destroy. With MAOs inhibited, tyramine can pass into the bloodstream, where it causes the release of norepinephrine. The result is a sudden and sometimes life-threatening rise in blood pressure.

The use of MAOIs also requires caution with other drugs. In some cases, the inhibition of MAOs cuts out a major pathway for elimination of a drug, and the drug can then rise to dangerous levels even when used at the normal dosage. The same effect occurs with recreational monoamine drugs, such as amphetamine. For all of these reasons, doctors seldom prescribe MAOIs unless other antidepressants fail to work.

Selective reuptake inhibitors

The newest antidepressants have returned to the mechanism of TCAs. That is, they boost neurotransmitter concentrations by inhibiting reuptake of neurotransmitters into neurons. Such antidepressnts differ from TCAs in that they target specific neurotransmitters, thereby avoiding the side effects that result from TCAs' unwanted interference in the acetylcholine and epinephrine systems.

The most famous antidepressant of this group is fluoxetine (Prozac), which is a selective serotonin reuptake inhibitor, or SSRI. These drugs improve mood by increasing serotonin levels in the brain. They also have a beneficial blocking effect on 5-HT_{2A} serotonin receptors, whose activity has been linked to suicide.

SSRIs have some side effects due to their interactions with serotonin receptors in various parts of the body. These effects can include nausea and diarrhea, insomnia, and anxiety. Dosage must be slowly reduced at the end of treatment to avoid the possibility of withdrawal symptoms that include stomach upsets, flulike symptoms, dizziness, and sensations similar to electric shocks. These effects are most likely to occur when suddenly stopping treatment with paroxetine (Paxil or Seroxat).

Reboxetine (Edronax) is chemically similar to fluoxetine, but it selectively blocks the reuptake of norepinephrine. It is the first of a new class of antidepressants called norepinephrine (noradrenaline) reuptake inhibitors, or NARIs. Norepinephrine has a stimulant effect, so reboxetine is suited for treating patients whose depression slows down their reactions. As side effects, it can cause dryness of the mouth, insomnia, and constipation.

Venlafaxine (Effexor) is the first of a class of antidepressants called serotonin and norepinephrine reuptake inhibitors, or SNRIs. Its antidepressant action is most similar to that of TCAs, which target the same neurotransmitter systems, but it has the drawback of increasing blood pressure.

Bupropion is a selective reuptake inhibitor for norepinephrine and dopamine. Prescribed as Wellbutrin, it is effective in treating major depression and the depressive phase of bipolar depression (manic depression). Bupropion is also helpful in suppressing cravings for addictive substances such as cocaine and nicotine.

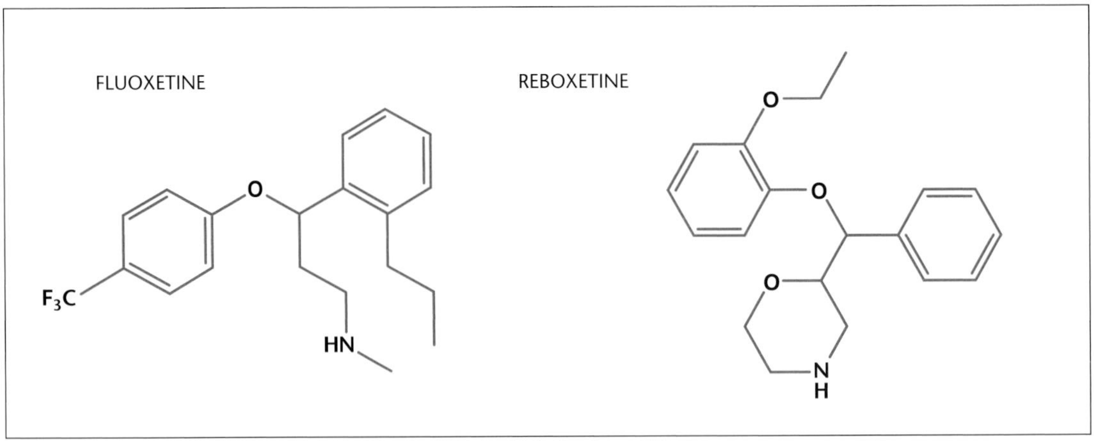

Fluoxetine and reboxetine are commonly known as Prozac and Edronax, respectively. They both selectively inhibit the reuptake of neurotransmitters by the brain's neurons. Fluoxetine inhibits the reuptake of serotonin, while reboxetine inhibits the reuptake of norepinephrine.

Depression and suicide

Autopsies of depressed patients who committed suicide consistently find low concentrations of serotonin (also called 5-hydroxytryptamine, or 5-HT) in the brain, as well as an unusually high concentration of $5\text{-}HT_{2A}$ receptors. Supporters of the monoamine hypothesis argue that a low concentration of serotonin is the principal cause of depression, and the increased concentration of this type of serotonin receptor occurs as the body attempts to compensate for the lack of serotonin in the cerebrospinal fluid. On the other hand, some researchers argue that it could be the increased number or activity of receptor sites that is the direct cause of depression.

One argument against the monoamine hypothesis is based on the fact that antidepressants would work much more quickly if the concentrations of these neurotransmitters were directly responsible for depression. Tricyclics produce an almost immediate block on neurotransmitter reuptake, for example, and MAOIs suppress the MAO system within days. Yet, in practice, these and other types of anti-depressants become effective only after two to six weeks, which would be more consistent with gradual reduction of the receptor systems in response to higher neurotransmitter concentrations.

Studies on twins have shown that a predisposition to depression is partially hereditary; in fact, genetic inheritance is a strong factor in determining whether a person is likely to suffer from depression. Genetic variations could be responsible for low neurotransmitter levels or variations in the number of receptor sites, so the contribution of genetics to depression can provide arguments both for and against the monoamine hypothesis.

A further weakness of the monoamine hypothesis is that it fails to explain why stress is the most important cause of depression after genetic inheritance. Supporters of the monoamine hypothesis generally assume that stress must somehow suppress neurotransmission by monoamines. However, recent studies on rats have shown that another process might be more directly responsible for depression. Stress causes the adrenal glands to release a hormone called corticosterone, and this hormone slows the formation of new cells in the hippocampus region of the brain. Conversely, boosted serotonin levels favor the production of new brain cells. In the future, research on humans might help clarify whether depression could be prevented by drugs that boost the production of cells in the hippocampus directly, rather than by boosting monoamine levels.

M. CLOWES

SEE ALSO:

Acetylcholine • Amphetamines • Dopamine • Drug Receptors • MAOs and MAOIs • Neurotransmission • Prozac • Serotonin • SSRIs

Aphrodisiac Drugs

An aphrodisiac is defined as any of various forms of stimulation that arouse sexual excitement. Almost all drugs regarded as aphrodisiacs, however, work by reducing sexual inhibitions rather than by arousing sexual excitement.

In every language and culture, there are numerous stories about foods, drinks, drugs, and various other substances, including scents and perfumes, that are supposed to cause sexual arousal and enhance sexual performance. The *Kama Sutra*, an ancient Indian guide to sex written sometime between the first and sixth centuries CE, recommends lovers to eat the testicles of rams or goats boiled in sweetened milk, or sparrow's eggs and rice with butter and honey. *The Perfumed Garden*, a sixteenth-century Arabic treatise on erotic arts, suggests dishes that contain onion seeds, honey, as well as peas boiled with onions and spiced with cinnamon, ginger, cardamom, almonds, and pine nuts. Writings on this theme have continued down the ages. Hot foods such as onions, ginger, and pepper have been widely thought to be aphrodisiac because they make those who consume them heat up and sweat, giving them the flushed appearance that is a symptom of sexual excitement. Other foods, such as oysters, bananas, ginseng root, and asparagus, have been considered aphrodisiacs owing to their resemblance to sexual organs.

Spanish fly

The most famous of all the reputed aphrodisiacs is in fact a lethal poison. Cantharides, commonly known as Spanish fly, is obtained from the dried and powdered remains of the blister beetle, an insect named for the intense irritant it produces as a defense mechanism. Spanish fly is taken as a powder or in solution. Cantharides contains a natural inflammatory agent that burns the mouth and throat and

This shop in a bazaar in Istanbul, Turkey, specializes in aphrodisiacs. Despite scientific evidence refuting the claims made by manufacturers of aphrodisiac drugs, many people still take them to increase sexual desire.

can cause acute abdominal pain, vomiting, diarrhea, and kidney damage even in small doses. The drug strongly irritates the genitourinary tract: in the short term, cantharides dilates the erectile tissues and causes sexual arousal, but it also badly scars the urethra. It has been used on livestock to stimulate mating, but in humans as little as one-thousandth of an ounce (28 mg) of the active chemical in cantharides is sufficient to cause kidney failure and death, making it one of the most dangerous substances associated with sexuality. Cantharides is classed as a poison and is illegal throughout the world.

Yohimbine

Yohimbine is a crystalline alkaloid substance derived from the bark of the *Corynanthe johimbe*, a tree that is native to Central Africa, particularly Cameroon, Gabon, and Zaire, where it has been used for hundreds of years to enhance sexual activity. Now marketed commercially as an aphrodisiac in two forms—yohimbe (the bark) and yohimbine (the pharmaceutical extract), the drug is supposed to stimulate the nerve centers in the spine that control erections. Although the producers and their customers proclaim yohimbine's efficacy, most scientists take the view that any resultant arousal is the consequence of the user's belief that the drug works, because stimulatory effects can be achieved only when the bark is ingested in toxic doses. An overdose of yohimbine causes heart palpitations and insomnia lasting for up to 30 hours.

Illicit drugs

Many drugs of abuse are reputed to act as aphrodisiacs, but their apparent stimulating effects on sexual drives are often the consequence of these drugs reducing inhibitions. An example of this is alcohol, which, although a depressant, may in small doses improve orgasm in women by reducing inhibitions. In larger doses, alcohol actually reduces the ability of a woman to climax. In men, although reduced inhibitions may increase arousal, this is not reflected in the ability to perform sexually, and in large doses, alcohol can induce impotence.

Similar effects are found with marijuana, but in addition to reducing inhibitions, marijuana also distorts perceptions of time. This effect can result in the user perceiving extended and more pleasurable periods of sexual stimulation, but again there is evidence to suggest that increased use of marijuana reduces the ability of a man to achieve an erection. In addition, male marijuana smokers have been shown to have reduced sperm counts and testosterone levels.

Ecstasy (MDMA) is a stimulant drug that is often reported to induce feelings of great physical and emotional openness and intimacy and a heightened awareness of sensations, producing a desire to touch and taste, a state often described as being "loved up." One negative effect of Ecstasy and also of many other drugs is that, by reducing inhibitions, the drug encourages the user to act irresponsibly and engage in risky sexual behavior, leaving him or her at increased risk of disease. Some studies also indicate that the drug depresses the immune system, leaving the user more susceptible to infections.

Another stimulant drug reported to enhance sexual experiences is cocaine, but again, it operates by reducing inhibitions rather than directly causing an increase in sexual desire. Users report heightened erotic feelings, but in the long term, frequent cocaine use actually reduces sexual desire. This is particularly true of crack cocaine. Studies on animals have shown that, when addicted to crack cocaine, an animal will choose the drug rather than an opportunity to copulate. In addition, studies have shown that humans addicted to crack cocaine have increased levels of sexual dysfunction.

Other illicit drugs, such as LSD, amphetamines, mescaline, opium, and amyl nitrate, are reputed to have enhancing effects on sexual behavior but are not themselves aphrodisiacs. The prescription drug Viagra is also not an aphrodisiac but is prescribed to treat erectile dysfunction. The only substances known to increase sexual interest, drive, and performance in both sexes are androgens such as the male hormone testosterone, which is produced naturally by both men and women. However, testosterone increases sexual desire only in individuals who have a deficiency of this androgen. In such instances, physicians may prescribe androgen therapy to increase desire and performance without causing other behavioral changes.

H. RUSSELL

SEE ALSO:
Alcohol • Club Drugs • Cocaine • Crack Cocaine •
Ecstasy • Marijuana • Plant-Based Drugs

Barbiturates

Barbiturates were once commonly prescribed by doctors for their calming effects, but their addictiveness and associated risk of overdose, both intentional and accidental, has led to a great reduction in their use.

Barbiturates are a class of sedative drugs introduced around 1900 for use as sleep-inducing agents (hypnotics). They are also effective in preventing seizures and treating anxiety. Barbiturates are central nervous system (CNS) depressants, with behavioral effects similar to those of alcohol. Their use as sleeping pills is limited by the development of tolerance to the sedative effect, and continuous use can result in dependence. Withdrawal symptoms are severe and can include seizures. Barbiturates are commonly abused; they are both psychologically and physically addictive. Overdoses can result in coma or death due to respiratory depression. The use of these drugs as hypnotic and antianxiety agents has largely been replaced by the less toxic benzodiazepines, but barbiturates are used regularly in surgical anesthesia and for seizure prevention.

Background

Barbiturates are derivatives of barbituric acid, first synthesized in 1864 by the German chemist Adolf von Baeyer. The first drug made clinically available was the hypnotic barbital, in 1903. Phenobarbital was introduced in 1912 for treatment of epilepsy and remains one of the major antiepileptic drugs used worldwide. The rapid increase in popularity of the barbiturates before 1950 was chiefly due to anti-anxiety effects, associated with feelings of relaxation and euphoria. By 1962, over 500 tons (454 tonnes) of barbiturates were sold in the United States each year, equivalent to 24 doses for every man, woman, and child in the country. Since the 1960s, barbiturate use has decreased, owing to the availability of benzodiazepines such as diazepam (Valium) and chlordiazepoxide (Librium). Less than 10 percent of all depressant prescriptions in the United States are for barbiturates.

A number of barbiturates remain in use, however. Their clinical uses are determined by how quickly the drugs are absorbed and distributed in body tissues, and how fast they are degraded and excreted. Ultrashort-acting barbiturates such as thiopental (under the brand name Pentothal) have peak levels for a few minutes and are used for the rapid induction of surgical anesthesia. Secobarbital (Seconal) and pentobarbital (Nembutal) are short-acting agents and are used for sleep induction and in anesthesia. Butalbital (in Esgic, Fiorinal, Phrenilin, and many other drugs) is a short-acting agent used in mixtures with caffeine and aspirin or acetaminophen (Tylenol) for treatment of headaches.

Amobarbital (Amytal) is a short-acting agent with only specialized uses. In a procedure called the Wada

KEY FACTS

Classification
Schedules II, III, and IV (USA), Schedule IV (Canada), Class B (UK), Schedule III (INCB). CNS depressant.

Street names
Amy's, barbs, blue angels, blue birds, blue devils, downers, goofballs, nembies, pink ladies, purple hearts, rainbows, red devils, tooies, yellow jackets

Short-term effects
Feelings of relaxation and euphoria, decreased inhibitions, coordination problems, drunken or intoxicated feeling, sleepiness progressing to coma and death (in overdose)

Long-term effects
Physical dependence requiring higher doses for the same effect. Erratic behavior and social isolation. Risk of fatal overdose increases with prolonged use.

Signs of abuse
Drunken behavior, sleepiness, shallow breathing, unresponsiveness

Actress Marilyn Monroe is just one celebrity who overdosed on barbiturates.

likely that they will talk about their problems.

Phenobarbital (Luminal) and primidone (Mysoline) are long-acting barbiturates that remain in the body for days and are used primarily to prevent seizures. These drugs are still widely prescribed, although newer anticonvulsant drugs are often more effective and cause less drowsiness and cognitive slowing.

All of these drugs have potential for abuse. Barbiturates are sometimes abused by patients who get them from physicians by prescription, and by street users who obtain them illegally. According to the Drug Abuse Warning Network, fewer than 6,000 U.S. emergency department visits in 1994 were related to barbiturate abuse. In 2001, that number had increased to more than 9,500 and fell in 2009 to 6,600. The rate of barbiturate abuse may be related to the use of stimulants such as methamphetamine and cocaine, since barbiturates counteract the excessive excitement and alertness induced by those drugs. Many users are also too young to remember the deaths of actresses Marilyn Monroe and Judy Garland and guitarist Jimi Hendrix, all from accidental or intentional barbiturate overdose.

test, patients with seizure disorders being evaluated for epilepsy surgery are injected with amobarbital into the carotid artery, which supplies blood to one-half of the brain, to determine which brain hemisphere supports language and memory. Amobarbital is also occasionally used in psychiatric interviews. After World War II (1939–1945), psychiatrists began using low doses of amobarbital or thiopental (sodium pentothal) to help soldiers with psychiatric disorders relax and reveal repressed memories and thoughts, which led to the false concept of a truth serum. In fact, the drugs do not force patients to tell the truth, but their inhibitions are decreased, making it more

Barbiturates and addiction

Barbiturates are usually taken orally, but street addicts will sometimes inject them into veins or muscles. Users who take barbiturates often take them together with other depressant drugs, including opiates and alcohol. The combined effects increase the likelihood of respiratory depression. Since tolerance develops to the sedative and euphoric effects, a user will gradually increase the amount of drug taken in order to attain the high. However, less tolerance develops for the respiratory depressive effect, and the margin of safety between a therapeutic dose and a toxic dose narrows, making a dangerous overdose more likely. A further danger is that barbiturate intoxication impairs memory, so users may take doses because they do not remember that they have already taken the drug. Barbiturates are involved in about one-third of all reported drug-related deaths.

Chemistry

The basic structure of the barbiturate molecule is shown at right. The atoms at the corners of the hexagon are carbons, except for the two labeled nitrogen. The X, Y, and Z stand for chemical side chains that determine the properties of individual barbiturates. These side chains are typically strings of hydrocarbons (or, in the case of phenobarbital and mephobarbital, a benzene ring). For thiopental, the oxygen at the upper left is replaced by a sulfur atom.

The barbiturates dissolve readily in lipids (fats), which allows them easily to cross the blood-brain barrier and enter the brain. Barbiturates accumulate in fat stores, which prolongs their presence in the body and slows their breakdown and excretion. They are metabolized by a class of liver enzymes called cytochrome P450. Over time, the drugs also induce the liver to make more cytochrome P450 enzymes, which leads to faster barbiturate metabolism and is part of the mechanism underlying tolerance to the drugs. Even short-acting barbiturates remain in body fat stores for many hours to days. The breakdown products of barbiturates are made more water-soluble by the addition of oxygen-containing groups, allowing excretion by the kidneys. In pregnant women, barbiturates can cross the placenta and affect the fetus. They are also secreted into breast milk and can cause sedation or toxicity in breast-fed babies.

Pharmacological effects

The barbiturates are depressants of the central nervous system. They work by enhancing the action of gamma-aminobutyric acid (GABA), the main inhibitory neurotransmitter, at the $GABA_A$ receptor. This receptor forms a channel through the neuron membrane that conducts chloride ions. The channel

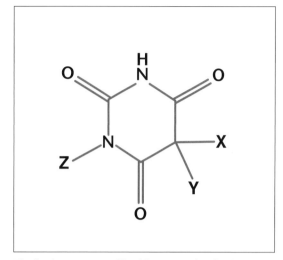

The basic structure of barbiturate molecules is a framework upon which a number of different barbiturates can be synthesized by attaching chains or rings of atoms to X, Y, and Z.

opens more efficiently in the presence of barbiturates, allowing passage of a chloride current that helps prevent neurons from sending excessive signals. The $GABA_A$ receptor is also enhanced by benzodiazepines and alcohol, which explains the similarity in their behavioral effects and the increased effects when used.

Abusers typically prefer short-acting barbiturates, which act more quickly and give a more intense high. In small doses, barbiturates cause drowsiness, disinhibition, and feelings of intoxication and euphoria. At higher doses, the user develops slurred speech, lack of coordination, and confusion. Concentration and short-term memory are impaired. Barbiturates suppress rapid eye movement (REM) sleep and dreaming. Children treated with barbiturates for epilepsy may have a paradoxical reaction in which they become hyperactive, while adults can display agitation or disinhibited aggressive behavior. Still higher doses result in unconsciousness from which the user cannot be aroused, and breathing becomes slow or may stop. If the user does not receive immediate medical attention, death will follow quickly.

Daily use of barbiturates for more than a month can result in both psychological dependence and physical addiction. Abstinence from the drug at that point causes not only craving but withdrawal symptoms, including nervousness, agitation, insomnia, tremors, and nightmares. These symptoms sometimes progress to fevers, hallucinations, and seizures. Medical treatment for withdrawal is essential, since symptoms can worsen without warning. Addiction to prescribed barbiturates is now rare but still occurs. Withdrawal symptoms can be prevented by gradually decreasing the dose of barbiturates, a process called detoxification.

Health effects

Even though drowsiness may wear off after a few hours, effects of barbiturate use can last days, with residual depression, irritability, impaired judgment, and lack of coordination. Users may be unaware that their ability to drive is impaired. Other symptoms include nausea, vomiting, dizziness, and diarrhea.

Barbiturates depress respiratory drive. A dose only three times greater than that necessary to produce sleep is enough to stop the drive to breathe. At higher doses barbiturates can alter the heart rhythm by acting on the conduction pathways in the heart and can weaken the heart muscle contraction. In the liver, barbiturates can interfere with the metabolism of other drugs that require liver enzymes for breakdown, or they can increase the metabolism of these other drugs by inducing a buildup of cytochrome P450 and other enzymes. Increased metabolism in the liver could make usual doses of medications ineffective—for example, increased breakdown of the hormones in birth-control pills could result in unwanted pregnancy. As barbiturates can cross the placenta, a baby born to a mother taking barbiturates may have reduced drive to breathe. Babies born to addicted mothers can also undergo withdrawal and require specialized care.

Barbiturate overdose or poisoning occurs in the context of accidental overdose by addicts, suicide attempts, and accidental ingestion by children. The first step in treating a possible barbiturate overdose is to call 911 or the local ambulance service. Rescue breathing, as part of cardiopulmonary resuscitation (CPR) by trained individuals, can be lifesaving. It is important to gather any pill bottles at the scene to help physicians determine what medications were taken. Medical treatment is primarily supportive and often requires mechanical respiration until the patient can breathe unassisted. Efforts are made to decrease continued absorption of ingested pills by inserting a tube into the stomach and rinsing with fluid (gastric lavage) followed by administration of a slurry of activated charcoal to absorb drugs in the gut. However, these methods cannot be used if the barbiturates have been injected. Excretion of the drug can also be enhanced by agents that increase urine output (forced diuresis). The prognosis for recovery depends on whether the patient received medical care before oxygen deprivation could cause brain or other organ damage.

Social effects

Barbiturate addicts are often also dependent on opiates and alcohol. Chronic use leads to psychological and social deterioration, with poor grooming and hygiene, lying, paranoid and bizarre thoughts, violent and erratic behavior, and suicidal tendencies. Such behavior leads to social isolation. These factors often have a severe impact on school or work performance and can lead to job termination, expulsion from school, and deterioration of the family structure. Criminal behavior to obtain barbiturates can result in arrest and imprisonment. Users undergoing barbiturate withdrawal in the absence of supporting social structures are less likely to receive medical care.

Treatment

Treatment of barbiturate addiction is often accomplished by substituting short-acting agents (like pentobarbital) for longer-acting barbiturates, and slowly withdrawing the medication at no more than 100 milligrams per day. Benzodiazepines may also be used to minimize withdrawal symptoms. Counseling is essential in rehabilitation, which is best accomplished in a medical setting where supportive medications are available and the patient has no access to addictive substances. There is a risk of delirium tremens (DTs) with agitation and hallucinations, often of bugs crawling on the skin. Such symptoms are signs of impending seizures, which can be treated with sedation and supportive therapy.

L. J. GREENFIELD JR.

SEE ALSO:

Benzodiazepines • Blood-Brain Barrier • Metabolism

Belladonna Alkaloids

Many plants naturally produce belladonna alkaloids. In small doses, these highly poisonous chemicals are used in medicines. In larger dosages, however, belladonna alkaloids induce hallucinations and can cause death.

The shiny red berries of the deadly nightshade contain alkaloids that can be fatal when eaten.

The alkaloids are an important class of organic molecules containing nitrogen in addition to carbon, hydrogen, and sometimes oxygen. Alkaloids are natural components of plant metabolism found in many different types of herbs and wild flowers; they form a major class of drug molecules. Well-known examples of plant alkaloids with potent drug properties are quinine (used to prevent malaria), morphine (a painkiller and narcotic), and nicotine (an addictive stimulant found in tobacco). The word alkaloid itself is derived from the Arabic *al kali*, meaning the ashes of the plant, a reference to the use of prepared extracts of plant material in medieval Arabic medicine.

The drug properties of the belladonna alkaloids, also known as the tropane alkaloids, have been used in the traditional herbal medicine of many cultures for thousands of years. The belladonna alkaloids are extracted from flowering plants of the nightshade family (Solanaceae), such as *Atropa belladonna* (the belladonna or deadly nightshade, sometimes known in the United States as poison black cherry) and *Hyoscyamus niger* (henbane or black henbane, sometimes known in the United States as poison tobacco). Other members of the Solanaceae family, such as *Datura stramonium* (thornapple) and *Scopola carniolica,* are also sources of these compounds.

The nightshades normally have brownish-purple flowers and berries that change from red to purple-black over the summer months. The plants are very poisonous when eaten, and their old, common English names allude to this fact. Deadly nightshade refers to the poisonous properties of *Atropa belladonna* and henbane refers to the fact that poultry are very susceptible to poisoning by seeds of wild *Hyoscyamus niger. Atropa belladonna* contains significant concentrations of tropane alkaloids in its roots, leaves, and berries, and it is still the main natural source of pharmaceutical atropine. Ingestion of extracts from any of these parts of the plant is very dangerous as they are extremely poisonous.

The name *belladonna*, Italian for "beautiful lady," refers to the fact that drops made from an extract of the plant expand the pupils of the eye, resulting in a wide-eyed, youthful, and innocent appearance. Dilated pupils are also a signal of sexual attraction. Belladonna was thus used as an early beauty treatment by men as well as women.

Medically useful compounds extracted from the nightshade plants are today marketed as the pure pharmaceuticals atropine ($C_{17}H_{23}NO_3$), scopolamine ($C_{17}H_{21}NO_4$), and the isomer of atropine, hyoscyamine ($C_{17}H_{23}NO_3$). Atropine is the most widely used tropane alkaloid in current medical use.

Atropine

Atropine competes with the neurotransmitter acetylcholine by binding to acetylcholine receptors (to which it has structural similarities) on smooth muscle, cardiac muscle, and glandular cells. This action has the effect of blocking the transmission of impulses from the nerve cells to muscles and glands. Atropine is widely used as premedication before general anesthesia to decrease bronchial and salivary secretions and anesthetize the nerve endings in the skin. Atropine is also used to decrease stomach acid production and relieve heartburn, to relax smooth muscle, control spasms, and alleviate stomach and bladder cramps. In addition, atropine is employed to treat certain cardiac conditions. By slowing the action of the parasympathetic nervous system (part of the nervous system responsible for inhibiting the action of internal organs), the actions of the sympathetic nervous system, which stimulates internal organs, are increased, thus stimulating the heart and increasing heart rate.

Atropine is available only with a doctor's prescription in capsule, liquid, or tablet form. The side effects of atropine treatment are usually associated with decreased secretion of body fluids. Particularly in older adults, common side effects of treatment with any of the belladonna alkaloids include constipation, difficulties with urination, and a dry mouth, nose, throat, and skin. Confusion, drowsiness, and memory loss are also possible side effects.

Scopolamine and hyoscyamine

The tropane alkaloid scopolamine is chemically similar to atropine, although it is usually extracted from the henbane rather than the belladonna plant. As with atropine, it has a structural similarity to acetylcholine, and administration also depresses the parasympathetic nervous system, resulting in dilated pupils, accelerated heart rate, and decreased secretion from skin, mouth, and respiratory passages.

Scopolamine is not as widely used in surgery and anesthesia as atropine, but it is used as a sedative and treatment for certain conditions causing trembling and agitation such as Parkinsonism, delirium tremens, and manic psychosis. Scopolomine is also used to suppress motion sickness. In the first half of the twentieth century, scopolamine was used in combination with morphine to induce the condition known as twilight sleep, which enabled mothers to give birth without pain. This drug combination was also used in treatment of patients in psychiatric institutions. Scopolamine and morphine anesthesia is now recognized to be too dangerous an anesthetic

KEY FACTS

Classification
Not scheduled in United States, Canada, UK, or INCB

Common names
Henbane and belladonna

Short-term effects
Alleviation of stomach or intestinal problems, sedation, dry mouth, drowsiness

Long-term effects
Dry skin, mouth, nose, and throat, constipation, and confusion or memory loss, particularly in older patients

Dangers
Real-seeming hallucinations that may lead to dangerous actions. Death at high doses.

procedure and of limited usefulness in psychiatry. However, a variety of sedatives containing scopolamine are sold over the counter, and overuse has been reported to result in dependence in some people. Scopolamine is also sometimes added to illicit drugs, such as cocaine and heroin.

Hallucinogens

When used at high levels, tropanes, such as atropine, begin to have hallucinogenic effects that may seem very real to the person taking the drug—so real, in fact, that he or she may attempt to interact with these hallucinations, with potentially disastrous effects. In addition, the quantity of a tropane necessary to induce hallucinations is very close to the amount necessary to cause death, making tropanes extremely dangerous drugs to experiment with.

Belladonna alkaloids as poisons and antidotes

Poisoning with any of the belladonna alkaloids can be fatal and there is no simple antidote. To succeed, action must be taken within two to three hours of poisoning. The patient can be treated by stomach pumping, colonic irrigation, and artificial respiration

Atropine (left) is very similar in structure and chemistry to scopolamine (right), and they are both structurally similar to the neurotransmitter acetylcholine, the action of which they block at receptor sites.

in an intensive care environment. Belladonna extracts have appeared throughout history as an easily available poison widely used in murder and assassination.

One notable exception to the rule of medical prescription and supervision of atropine use is the widespread stockpiling of the drug for military medicine and civil defense. Atropine is the best available rapid-use antidote to organophosphate nerve-gas poisoning, as it blocks acetylcholine neurotransmission and thus counteracts the effects of nerve toxins. Military personnel considered at risk of attack with nerve gas have been issued with atropine autoinjectors for rapid injection into the thigh. Atropine is also widely used in emergency room medicine as an antidote to acute opiate poisoning resulting from overdosing with narcotics, such as heroin or morphine, and to counteract mushroom and prussic acid poisoning.

Medicine men, wise women, and belladonna

The belladonna alkaloids occupy a fascinating position in the history of pharmacy and medicine. Knowledge of belladonna and henbane and the properties of prepared extracts from these common plants has passed from master to apprentice, leading to the appearance of a class of medicine men and wise women. This specialty may have occurred as early as Neolithic times. Ancient Egyptian art from at least 3,000 years ago prominently depicts plants that appear to be nightshades and other psychoactive flowers and herbs.

Humans found the properties of belladonna and henbane extracts fascinating and evolved religious and occult practices associated with their use, the effects of which were often regarded as magic. Some of the earliest accounts of using potions containing *Atropa belladonna* nightshades are found in medieval manuscripts on magic and witchcraft. In *The Book of the Sacred Magic of Abremelin the Mage* published in 1458 by a German alchemist known as Abraham the Jew, the author details how a woman he describes as "a young witch" told him of a "witches' ointment," which when rubbed into the hands and feet induced the sensation of flying. It is known that potions containing atropine can be administered through the skin and that they can induce vivid dreams, sometimes of an erotic nature, delusions, and manic excitement. A recipe containing belladonna extracts is also mentioned by another alchemist, Giovanni Batista Porta, in his *Magiae Naturalis* (Natural magick), published in 1558. There is therefore evidence that the belladonna alkaloids were used in medieval times to produce narcotic and psychedelic effects by individuals who sought, for a variety of reasons, what we would now call hallucinatory and out-of-body experiences.

D. E. ARNOT

SEE ALSO:

Acetylcholine • Hallucinogens • Jimsonweed • Plant-Based Drugs

Benzodiazepines

Benzodiazepines form a versatile class of drugs whose applications include the treatment of insomnia, anxiety, and panic attacks, as well as the suppression of convulsions. The drugs also find use as sedatives and for inducing anesthesia.

Since the introduction of chlordiazepoxide (Librium) in 1960, benzodiazepines have become the most widely prescribed group of drugs, with an estimated 15 to 20 percent of the U.S. population receiving them medicinally at any given time. The most commonly prescribed antianxiety drug is diazepam (Valium), although around 15 related compounds are also used as drugs in the United States and some 20 more are available in other countries.

The widespread use of benzodiazepines (BZs) is in part due to their breadth of application, from the treatment of anxiety and panic attacks to the treatment of convulsions in withdrawal from other drugs and the suppression of epileptic seizures. Benzodiazepines are also widely used in dentistry and

Short-acting benzodiazepines such as Valium induce light sedation for dentistry and find use in combination with anesthetics for surgery.

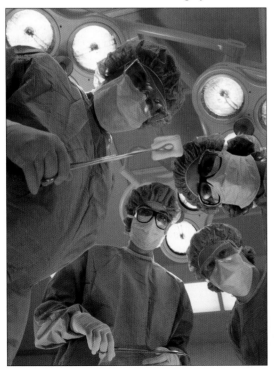

surgery to relieve anxiety, to induce anesthesia, and to ensure that the patient has no unpleasant memory of the procedure. With lethal doses around 1,000 times the therapeutic doses, the benzodiazepines are safer than the barbiturates they have replaced in many contexts. BZs are not without problems, however: patients can become dependent in a short time, and in some cases, notably for triazolam (Halcion), their use has been linked with aggression.

One nonmedical use of benzodiazepines is to counteract the aftereffects of illegal drugs such as amphetamines and Ecstasy. In such cases the drug abuser typically chooses a BZ that acts quickly and for a short time, such as temazepam. Benzodiazepines relieve anxiety and restlessness caused by the residual actions of the stimulants, thus promoting sleep. Heroin addicts also use benzodiazepines to suppress cold-turkey withdrawal symptoms when trying to come off heroin or when heroin is not available. Benzodiazepines are rarely abused for their own effects unless other substances of abuse are unavailable or too expensive.

Anxiety and panic

Benzodiazepines work by inhibiting the mechanism that our ancestors acquired to help them survive in an environment riddled with physical threats and hostile predators. Sometimes called the fight-or-flight response, it is the mechanism that prepares the body for action in the face of a hazard. The familiar symptoms of fear—racing heart, palpitations, heightened alertness, sweating, and trembling—are side effects of these preparations.

The options of fighting or fleeing fail to provide solutions to many problems of modern life, such as financial stress. Nevertheless, the human body continues to respond as if going to fight or running away will remove the threat. When the symptoms of fear occur in a short-lived but intense episode, they constitute a panic attack; longer-term or less intense symptoms constitute anxiety. Both conditions can prevent their sufferers from functioning normally and in a way that could help them resolve the origin of their stress. Hence, intervention with drugs that reduce panic and anxiety is often desirable. Once the stress symptoms are under control, counseling can help panic-attack and anxiety sufferers to reformulate their approach to problems and deal with the root causes of stress in an effective manner.

GABA

The commands that produce the fear response originate in the brain. From there, nerve impulses pass through the sympathetic nervous system—part of the peripheral nervous system that connects the brain with the rest of the body—to the appropriate organs. Under normal conditions, this system is kept in check by a substance called gamma-aminobutyric acid (GABA, or 4-aminobutanoic acid), which the body produces from substances in food. GABA can attach to specific sites, called GABA receptors.

One type of GABA receptor, called the $GABA_A$ receptor, is found in the membranes of neurons in the part of the brain responsible for the fear response. When a GABA molecule attaches to such a receptor, a nearby channel opens through the cell wall. The channel selectively allows chloride ions to flood into the cell, changing the electrical potential of the neuron relative to its surroundings. In this condition, the neuron is less likely to fire (allow an impulse to pass) in response to incoming nerve impulses. Hence, GABA has the effect of decreasing the sensitivity of the neuron. As the proportion of neurons with occupied $GABA_A$ receptors increases, so the fear response subsides.

Benzodiazepines and GABA

The benzodiazepines act by attaching themselves to receptor sites close to, but distinct from, the $GABA_A$ receptors. Once in position, they intensify the attraction between GABA molecules and $GABA_A$ receptors, which causes an increase in the number of sites occupied by GABA, and hence in the number of desensitized neurons. In this way, benzodiazepines calm the fear response by boosting the natural calming effect of GABA on nerve activity.

Studies of the human brain have found at least six different subtypes of benzodiazepine receptors near GABA receptors in different parts of the brain. It is likely that the antianxiety, sedative-hypnotic, and anticonvulsant effects of benzodiazepines each stem from different subtypes of these receptors. It is possible that future developments could yield more selective drugs—anticonvulsant benzodiazepines that have little or no sedative effect, for example.

The existence of receptors for benzodiazepines has prompted speculation that the body produces its own benzodiazepine analogs. Deficiencies of such compounds could be the underlying cause of low stress tolerance in certain individuals. Attempts to identify such natural compounds have so far failed, but a success would provide a starting point for developing new drugs.

Tolerance and dependency

As treatment with benzodiazepines progresses, the dose must be increased to maintain the drug effect, either because the activity of $GABA_A$ receptors becomes downgraded or because the body compensates for the increased activity of those receptors by reducing the GABA supply. The decrease in response to benzodiazepines with use is an example of tolerance.

Once tolerance develops, the natural ability of GABA to calm the fear response remains weak until the $GABA_A$ receptors recover their full activity or until GABA concentrations return to normal. If the drug is withdrawn, anxiety levels will increase, so a patient who has developed tolerance to BZs is also dependent on the drugs and will suffer withdrawal symptoms unless the dose is decreased at a rate that does not exceed the ability of the GABA system to recover. Tolerance and dependency are particularly problematic for short-acting BZs and can develop within a few days of starting treatment.

Chemical structure and potency

The term *benzodiazepine* refers to a double-ringed chemical structure where two adjacent carbon atoms in a benzene ring also participate in a seven-membered diazepine ring (*see* opposite). This structure is not sufficient for therapeutic activity, however; all the benzodiazepine drugs have a second ring attached to an atom in the diazepine ring.

Additional substituents, such as chloro (–Cl), nitro ($-NO_2$), and alkyl groups ($-C_xH_y$) inserted at positions W, X, Y, and Z, also have effects on the potencies of the different diazepines. The high potencies of flunitrazepam and clonazepam show how the

Chlordiazepoxide (right)

Chlordiazepoxide (Librium) was the first benzodiazepine to go on the prescription market. In common with other drugs of this class, it has a seven-membered ring fused to an aromatic six-membered ring along one bond. The second aromatic ring and the two nitrogen atoms are also present in all drugs of this class.

   This molecule is unusual in that it has an oxygen atom on the nitrogen atom closer to the aromatic side ring. Other members of the class have no atoms or groups attached at this position, but they have atoms or groups attached to the other nitrogen in the ring. This other nitrogen atom has no groups attached in chlordiazepoxide.

Diazepam and related compounds (left)

All have an oxygen atom attached to the seven-membered ring.

Name	-X	-Y	-Z	Potency*
Diazepam (Valium)	$-CH_3$	$-Cl$	$-H$	1
Flunitrazepam (Rohypnol)	$-CH_3$	$-NO_2$	$-F$	10
Flurazepam (Dalmane)	$-CH_2CH_2N(C_2H_5)_2$	$-Cl$	$-F$	0.33–0.67
Halazepam (Pixapam)	$-CH_2CF_3$	$-Cl$	$-H$	
Prazepam (Centrax)	$-CH_2(C_3H_5)$**	$-Cl$	$-H$	0.5–1.0
Quazepam (Doral)	$-CH_2CF_3$	$-Cl$	$-F$	
Clonazepam (Klonopin)	$-H$	$-NO_2$	$-F$	5–20

**cyclopropyl

Oxazepam and related compounds (right)

Name	-X	-Y	-Z	Potency*
Oxazepam (Serax)	$-H$	$-Cl$	$-H$	0.33–0.50
Lorazepam (Ativan)	$-H$	$-Cl$	$-Cl$	5–10
Temazepam (Restoril)	$-CH_3$	$-Cl$	$-H$	0.5

*The potency values cited are relative to diazepam.

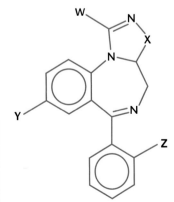

Tricyclic benzodiazepine derivatives (left)

Name	-W	-X-	-Y	-Z	Potency*
Alprazolam (Xanax)	$-CH_3$	$-N-$	$-Cl$	$-H$	10
Estazolam (ProSom)	$-H$	$-N-$	$-Cl$	$-H$	5
Midazolam (Versed)	$-CH_3$	$-CH-$	$-Cl$	$-F$	
Triazolam (Halcion)	$-CH_3$	$-N-$	$-Cl$	$-Cl$	20

introduction of a nitro group in place of a chloro group at position *Y* increases drug action, just as the presence of the additional chloro group in lorazepam makes it 10 to 30 times more potent than oxazepam. The additional ring structures in alprazolam and estazolam increase potency by factors of 10 and 5, respectively, when compared with diazepam.

Absorption and elimination

The second factor in the drug interaction—the concentration of drug in the fluids around the receptor—is determined by how quickly the drug is absorbed into the circulation, how much of it passes through the blood-brain barrier, and how quickly the drug is eliminated from the body. A related factor is whether or not the body converts the drug into substances that are themselves capable of interacting with the receptor. Such substances are called active metabolites. These aspects of drug behavior are called pharmacokinetics, and they determine how quickly a drug will start to act and how long its effects will last.

The fastest way to get a drug into the circulation is by intravenous injection of a solution. Diazepam and lorazepam can be injected as solutions in mixtures of water with cosolvents such as propylene glycol and ethyl alcohol. Chlordiazepoxide and midazolam are more basic and can be neutralized with hydrochloric acid to form water-soluble hydrochloride salts for injection. In the bloodstream, these salts revert to their parent bases, which are lipid (fat) soluble.

When swallowed in tablets or capsules, the most common method of administration, BZs pass into the bloodstream by absorption through the wall of the small intestine. Their high lipid solubility assists this process, and the most lipid soluble BZs, such as diazepam and chlordiazepoxide, can reach peak plasma levels (bloodstream concentrations) in around 30 minutes. Other BZs take a few hours to reach peak concentration. The high lipid solubility also allows the BZs to pass freely through the blood-brain barrier to reach the central nervous system, where the $GABA_A$ receptors are found.

KEY FACTS

Classification

Mostly Schedule IV (USA, Canada, UK, INCB). Exceptions are flunitrazepam (Schedule III for UK and INCB), temazepam (Schedule III for UK). CNS depressants. Anxiolytics (antianxiety drugs) and sedative-hypnotics. Some also act as anticonvulsants.

Street names

Candies, downers, tranks (general); roofies, date-rape drug (Rohypnol)

Forms

Tablets and gel-filled capsules, injectable solutions

Active ingredients

Various benzodiazepine compounds

Method of consumption

Usually swallowed. Temazepam gel sometimes injected. Rohypnol sometimes added to a person's drink without his or her knowledge to facilitate rape or robbery.

Short-term effects

Effects range from feelings of tranquility and relief of tension at low doses to drowsiness and sleep at higher doses. Some people experience dizziness, confusion, or slurred speech. Amnesia, particularly for Rohypnol.

Long-term effects

Tolerance and psychological dependence develop rapidly. Supervised withdrawal by tapered dosage reduction reduces the risk of effects such as anxiety, irritability, emotional instability, and hallucinations.

Dangers

Can cause drowsiness and impair ability to drive and operate machinery. The effects of alcohol and other CNS depressants, such as marijuana and heroin, become much more intense when combined with these drugs. Benzodiazepines reduce the lethal dose of heroin, so accidental overdose becomes more likely. Death rare unless other CNS depressants are present. Injection of temazepam gel can cause ischemia and gangrene.

The rate of elimination from the body depends on how quickly the body converts a given drug into a substance that can be excreted in urine. For conversion to occur, the drug molecule must have a chemical group that can link it to a substance in the body called glucuronic acid. The compounds that result, called glucuronides, form salts that can pass out of the kidney, whereas BZs themselves cannot.

The oxazepams already possess a hydroxy (–OH) group that can bond to glucuronic acid, so their elimination starts immediately and their effects subside after 8 to 18 hours. Even faster elimination occurs with tricyclic BZs that have a methyl group at W (see page 52). Enzymes oxidize the methyl group to a methylol group ($-CH_2OH$), which rapidly joins with glucuronic acid. Other diazepines pass through a series of conversions into active metabolites such as nordiazepams (diazepams with hydrogen at X) and oxazepams before they can be eliminated. The effect of a single dose of such a compound typically lasts more than 48 hours.

Related to the pharmacokinetics of benzodiazepines is the behavior of flumazenil. This compound shares some of the structural features of the benzodiazepines and competes to bind to their receptor. However, flumazenil fails to stimulate the interaction of GABA with its receptor. Occasional doses of this drug slow the development of tolerance in individuals on long-term benzodiazepine therapy.

Applications

The differing pharmacokinetics of the individual benzodiazepines partly determine which drug is used for a given application. Dosage schedules usually start with a low dose that increases until the best dose for the patient and condition is found. Further increases may be needed to overcome tolerance.

Anxiety and panic attacks. Diazepam (5 to 20 mg/day) is the usual treatment for short-term anxiety. The drug's quick onset ensures rapid relief from symptoms, while its slow elimination from the body helps maintain an even effect between daily doses. Such doses of diazepam and lorazepam are also helpful in reducing the anxiety created by the physical pain of an injury or acute disease. Higher doses of diazepam (up to 80 mg/day) are helpful for panic attacks, as are small doses of a more potent BZ, such as alprazolam (1 to 4 mg/day).

Sleep disorders. Sleep disorders take a variety of forms. Each responds best to a benzodiazepine whose profile of onset and elimination is most appropriate. Long-acting flurazepam (15 to 60 mg/day) helps the onset of sleep and prolongs its duration. It can also provide some daytime sedation, if desirable. The intermediate action of temazepam (10 to 30 mg/day) helps patients who have difficulty staying asleep and can help with the onset of sleep if taken two to three hours before bedtime. Faster-acting benzodiazepines such as midazolam and triazolam (0.5 to 2 mg/day) are best for patients who have trouble getting to sleep, since their effects have almost completely worn off by the next day.

Surgery. Benzodiazepines are useful in combination with anesthetics for surgery. Since rapid onset is desirable, diazepam and midazolam are used to induce anesthesia. The rapid dissipation of effects makes midazolam a better choice for outpatient surgery and simple dental procedures.

Seizures. BZs can help treat seizures for epileptics and alcoholics in withdrawal. Clonazepam is a long-term treatment for epilepsy, requiring occasional doses of flumazenil to ward off tolerance. Diazepam can treat epileptic seizures as they occur. Chlordiazepoxide, diazepam, and oxazepam act against fits caused by alcohol withdrawal.

Long-term addiction and withdrawal

Enthusiasm for the newly launched benzodiazepines in the 1960s led to their sometimes being prescribed without due regard for their ability to cause dependence. As a result, many people became trapped on ever-increasing dosages for years or even decades. The newer antidepressants, such as Prozac, are the treatment of choice for general anxiety and offer a less addictive option for people who can withdraw from BZs. The process can often be eased by putting the patient on an equivalent dose of a slow-acting and less addictive BZ before gradually reducing the dose of that drug.

M. CLOWES

SEE ALSO:

Agonists and Antagonists • Barbiturates • Gamma-aminobutyric Acid • Librium • Prescription Drugs • Prozac • Rohypnol • Valium

Betel Nut

The chewing of betel nut produces a mild stimulant effect and, if used often, results in distinctive red and brown staining on the user's lips and teeth. Regular use can also lead to addiction and a variety of health problems.

Betel nut preparations are actually ground areca nut wrapped in a leaf from the betel pepper plant.

Betel nuts are one of the most popular global stimulants. The practice of betel-nut chewing is widespread across Southeast Asia and India. It produces a feeling of mild euphoria and well-being. Over the long term, however, betel use can be addictive and may result in mouth cancer.

Betel nuts are the fruit of the areca palm (*Areca catechu*). Also called areca nuts, they are usually sold wrapped in the leaf of the betel pepper plant (*Piper betel*) together with quicklime (calcium hydroxide) from burned coral or seashells. When chewed, the wrap acts as a mild euphoric stimulant. The term *betel nut* is a misnomer, as it is the areca nut that is chewed. However, users of the drug understand *betel nut* to mean "the nut chewed with betel." Local names for the wrap include *paan* in India, *sirih* in Indonesia or Malaysia, and *plu* in Thailand.

The practice of chewing betel nuts has existed for thousands of years. Archaeologists in southern Taiwan, for example, have found 4,500-year-old human remains that have the characteristic tooth staining caused by the nuts. Betel-nut chewing is an integral part of hundreds of millions of people's lives. It is chewed while working or socializing. The nuts can also be presented as formal gifts, and the spit from chewing is used in some rituals and medicines.

Betel nut users typically chew the wrap slowly, with the chewer's saliva causing a reaction between the quicklime and nut that releases the psychoactive alkaloids. These alkaloids are absorbed through the tongue and gums, and are carried by the body's blood system to the brain. Meanwhile, the chewer produces copious amounts of bright red saliva that is spat out. After a few minutes the drug produces a feeling of mild euphoria, sweating, raised temperature, and a heightened awareness of one's surroundings. This effect lasts typically for tens of minutes, after which

55

KEY FACTS

Classification
Not scheduled in USA, Canada, UK, or INCB

Street names
Paan in India, *sirih* in Indonesia or Malaysia, and *plu* in Thailand

Short-term effects
Mild euphoria, sweating, raised temperature, and a heightened awareness of one's surroundings. Stupor and inability to stand up at higher doses.

Long-term effects
Potential to become addicted. Cancer of the mouth, tongue, larynx, and pharynx is associated with prolonged use. Other possible health effects include heart disease, diabetes, and asthma.

Signs of abuse
Dark red or brown staining of the mouth and teeth from the bright red saliva produced from betel-nut chewing. A user will typically be seen spitting this saliva onto the floor.

the chewer returns to a normal state. Betel-nut chewing is habit forming if performed regularly, with a pattern of use that includes sequential chewing.

Chemical action

The main psychoactive compound in betel nuts is the alkaloid arecoline ($C_8H_{13}NO_2$). In addition to the effects of arecoline, a range of complex chemical reactions and interactions may result from chewing betel nut. For example, quicklime changes arecoline to arecaidine, which is also psychoactive. Further, the betel leaf contains several potentially psychoactive compounds, such as aromatic phenols. The chemical properties of the betel nut are not fully understood.

Arecoline in the betel nut works in a similar manner to the neurotransmitter acetylcholine (a chemical messenger), by stimulating the brain's nicotinic receptors. The response to stimulation quickly produces a feeling of euphoria and well-being. Yet the effect can also be addictive and lead to withdrawal symptoms such as headaches and sweating. Nicotinic receptors are part of the body's autonomic nervous system, which regulates the involuntary muscles and glands not under conscious control. Because of its interaction with the acetylcholine system, betel-nut chewing also produces watery eyes, a loss of appetite, and an increase in heart rate, blood pressure, and body temperature. Too large a dose makes the user intoxicated, resulting in a dazed stupor and a need to lie down.

Another compound that stimulates the brain's nicotinic receptors is nicotine from tobacco. Many effects from the two drugs are similar: a period of well-being, and addiction and withdrawal with continued use. In many parts of the world, betel nuts are prepared with tobacco leaf, a combination that is even more addictive and also has the adverse health effects of chewing tobacco.

Adverse effects

Short-term use of the betel nut does not appear to have any harmful effects. The most obvious feature of long-term use is a red or brown staining of the teeth and gums, and often a resulting premature loss of teeth. Studies, however, have associated long-term chewing with cancer of the mouth, tongue, larynx, and pharynx (the most common form being oral squamous cell carcinoma). Oral carcinomas are the sixth most common cancer in the world—35 percent of cancers in India are mouth related. Other ailments associated with betel-nut use include cardiovascular disease, diabetes, and asthma, which have a high prevalence among Asians in the United States.

Betel nuts are legal and readily available in many parts of the world. They are legal to buy in the United States but illegal to import. The Food and Drug Administration (FDA) maintains an import alert that orders confiscation if found by Customs. Meanwhile, many Asian areas of American cities continue to have shops where betel nuts can be bought legally.

N. LEPORA

SEE ALSO:
Acetylcholine • Central Nervous System • Nicotine • Plant-Based Drugs

Blood-Brain Barrier

The blood-brain barrier is a sheath of tightly opposed cells that surrounds the blood vessels of the brain and spinal cord. It forms a protective boundary that all psychoactive substances must cross to reach and take effect on the brain.

The first person to observe evidence of a separation between the bloodstream and the cerebrospinal fluid around the brain and spinal cord was German-born bacteriologist Paul Ehrlich in 1885. He noted that injections of dyes into the bloodstreams of test animals stained almost all organs and tissues but left the brain and spinal cord unstained. At the time, he assumed that tissues of the brain and spinal cord had no affinity for the dye.

Ehrlich's assumption was disproved by his student Edwin Goldmann. In 1913 Goldmann showed that an injection of dye into the cerebrospinal fluid (CSF) of a test animal stained its brain and spinal cord but caused no coloration of other tissues. Meanwhile, in 1900, the German neurobiologist Max Lewandowsky had coined the term *blood-brain barrier* (*Bluthirnschranke* in German) while discussing the penetration of potassium ferrocyanide into the brain. Further information about the blood-brain barrier came in 1942, when researchers discovered that highly lipid-soluble (fat-soluble) dyes can enter the brain from the bloodstream.

Nature of the barrier

For any drug to produce an effect on the brain it must pass from the bloodstream to the cerebral fluid that bathes the brain cells. Blood flows around the brain through tiny blood vessels called capillaries. The walls of capillaries consist of endothelial (flattened, single-thickness) cells. These cells are encased in lipid membranes that point in toward the bloodstream and out toward surrounding tissues and fluids. In this respect, brain capillaries are similar to those elsewhere in the body.

Capillaries in the brain differ from other blood vessels in the closeness of the joints between cells in their walls: in comparison, capillaries elsewhere in the body have loose-knit walls. Also, brain capillaries are surrounded by other cells, called astrocytes. These cells have protrusions, called foot processes, that form sheaths around the capillaries. From the 1940s onward, there was much debate as to whether the

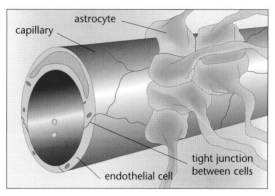

Capillaries that carry blood through the brain are characterized by the tight junctions between the endothelial cells that make up their walls, and by the surrounding sheath of astrocyte foot processes.

blood-brain barrier was caused by the tightness of the junctions between endothelial cells or the presence of the astrocyte sheath. This debate was settled in 1969, when South African neurobiologist Morris Karnovsky used an enzyme—horseradish peroxidase, or HRP—to test for permeability. After injecting HRP into the blood or cerebrospinal fluid, a second injection of diaminobenzidine and osmium tetroxide produced a precipitate that was opaque to both light and electron beams. HRP catalyzed the precipitation, so the precipitate formed only where HRP was present. Karnovsky's studies revealed that HRP did not penetrate the endothelial membrane from the bloodstream, but it did penetrate the astrocytic sheath from cerebrospinal fluid. Hence, there was final proof that the blood-brain barrier is formed by the capillary walls, not the astrocytic sheath.

Function of the barrier

The function of the blood-brain barrier is to protect delicate brain cells from potentially harmful substances in the bloodstream while allowing essential nutrients to enter the brain. These nutrients include oxygen, glucose, and amino acids. Oxygen molecules are small enough to permeate the barrier,

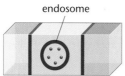
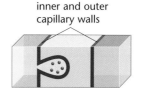

In mediated transport, the inner wall of the capillary envelopes the nutrient, then detaches and travels across the cellular fluid to fuse with the outer wall, where it expels the nutrients into the cerebrospinal fluid.

whereas glucose, amino acids, and certain other nutrients pass through the cells in the capillary walls by a process called mediated transport. This process is poorly understood at present but seems to rely on the nutrient attaching to a receptor in the capillary wall. Once activated in this way, the receptor triggers a process called endocytosis, whereby part of the cell membrane forms a pocket that swallows the nutrient. The pocket then closes up and separates from the cell wall as a bubble of membrane, or vesicle, that contains the nutrient. This vesicle is called an endosome; it can travel through the fluid within the cell to the opposite wall, where exocytosis spits out the nutrient into the CSF in a reverse of endocytosis.

Mediated transport is specific to molecules that bind to receptors in the cell walls. An example is the transport of glucose: mediated transport only works for one form of glucose, called D-glucose. The other form, L-glucose, stays in the bloodstream. In other parts of the body, such as muscles, both forms leave the bloodstream with similar ease.

Lipid-soluble substances pass through the blood-brain barrier by an entirely different mechanism. Their solubility in lipids lets them dissolve in the cell walls and diffuse through the blood-brain barrier, driven by the difference between concentrations of the substance in the blood and CSF. Since the molecules have to break through the cell walls, this process works better for small molecules than for large ones. Groups that form hydrogen bonds, such as $-NH_2$ groups, hinder the diffusion process because they increase the effective molecular size by forming hydrogen bonds with water in the bloodstream. These water molecules must be stripped off before diffusion occurs.

Lipid-soluble substances of low molecular weight that have few hydrogen-bonding sites diffuse well through the blood-brain barrier. Such substances include amphetamine, aspirin, caffeine, cocaine,

ethanol (alcohol), and heroin. These substances pass from the bloodstream to the receptors in brain cells, where they produce their psychoactive or therapeutic effects. Molecules that are too large or insoluble in lipids cannot pass through the blood-brain barrier in this way. Such compounds include proteins and molecules that are highly charged or polar and therefore have a greater affinity for water than for lipids.

Breaking through

Although the highly selective permeability of the blood-brain barrier helps protect the brain, it can sometimes hinder therapy by preventing drugs from crossing into the brain. Examples of such drugs include antiretroviral agents for HIV treatment and anticancer drugs for attacking brain tumors. While some drug researchers address this problem by trying to make lipid-soluble analogs of proven drugs, others are investigating more cunning strategies.

One experimental approach is to attach a proven drug to a substance that enters the brain by mediated transport. Docosahexaenoic acid (DHA) is an example: derived from certain fish and vegetable oils in the diet, DHA enters the brain by mediated transport and plays a role in healthy brain function. Researchers have attached drugs such as dopamine (a neurotransmitter used in therapy for Parkinson's disease), and Taxol (an anticancer agent) to DHA. The DHA portions of the resulting molecules trick mediated-transport receptors into action. Once the drug and carrier compound is in the brain, enzymes separate the drug from the DHA molecule, and both go on to perform their respective functions in the brain.

M. CLOWES

SEE ALSO:

Central Nervous System • Dopamine • Pharmacokinetics

Bufotenine

Bufotenine, an alkaloid drug extracted from toad venoms, is the subject of many myths. Despite stories about people licking toads to experience hallucinations, the drug is believed to be inactive when taken orally.

Bufotenine is a constituent alkaloid of the venom of poisonous toads and frogs of the genera *Hyla, Leptodactylous, Rana,* and *Bufo.* It can also be extracted from some mushrooms. Bufotenine was shown in 1934 to be present in significant quantities in toad venom and secretions. Clinical tests of its effects, along with those of other psychoactive drugs, were carried out in the United States in the 1950s in studies primarily aimed at investigating mental illness. The studies employed prison "volunteers" attracted by the prospect of sentence remission. Such reasearch practices are no longer considered ethical.

The experiments indicated that injected bufotenine induced hallucinations similar to those resulting from mescaline and lysergic acid (LSD) ingestion, as well as leading to a transient purple hue on the faces of recipients. These data led the Federal Food and Drug Administration (FDA) to place bufotenine in Schedule I of the Controlled Substances Act in 1967. This official classification defines a drug as being too dangerous for use in research and as having potential for abuse.

Drugs and drug abuse are the source of many modern myths. Some of the most colorful legends adhere to the supposedly hallucinatory effects of toad licking, in which an individual licks bufotenine from the skin of *Bufo alvarius,* the Sonoran Desert toad, found along the desert rivers and canyons of New Mexico and Arizona. Given the bizarre, illegal, and cultlike activity surrounding bufotenine, stories about this drug have proved a perennially popular but inaccurate media item.

Self-proclaimed Sonoran Desert shamans, claiming to use the drug as "sacred toad sweat," insist that they do not actually lick the toads but smoke small quantities of their venom, collected without harming the animals. Disentangling fact from fiction is difficult in this area, but it is known that *Bufo marinus,* the large cane toad common in California and Australia, has poisonous rather than hallucinogenic secretions. Following several severe poisonings, toad licking never became popular.

KEY FACTS

Classification
Schedule I (USA), Schedule I (Canada), Class A (UK), Schedule I (INCB). Possible hallucinogen.

Short-term effects
Hallucinations, anxiety, and psychological disturbance

Long-term effects
Largely unknown; possibly long-term psychological disturbance

Dangers
Illness and possibly death from licking poisonous toads

Chemically, bufotenine is 5-hydroxy-N,N-dimethyltryptamine, also referred to as N,N-dimethyl serotonin ($C_{12}H_{16}N_2O$). There has been a scientific debate as to whether bufotenine itself is actually psychoactive or whether the hallucinogenic activity is due to a related component of the Sonoran Desert toad's venom, 5-methoxy-dimethyltryptamine, better known as 5-MeO-DMT. This substance is probably the most potent hallucinogen found in nature, but is present only in the Sonoran toad. Research indicates that bufotenine may, like 5-MeO-DMT and other known hallucinogens such as LSD, act at the brain's serotonin receptors to induce hallucinations and dreamlike sensations via mechanisms that are not understood. The reported failure of some experiments with highly purified bufotenine to induce hallucination in human volunteers may be due to its limited capacity to cross the blood-brain barrier.

D. E. ARNOT

SEE ALSO:
DMT • Hallucinogens • Serotonin • Tryptamines

Buprenorphine

Buprenorphine is a painkilling opioid drug that has received attention as a therapeutic treatment for rehabilitation from opioid drug abuse, particularly heroin addiction.

Buprenorphine ($C_{29}H_{41}NO_4$) is a member of the opioid class of drugs and a derivative of thebaine, a natural compound found in opium poppy juice. Buprenorphine, also known by the trade name Buprenex, is a narcotic painkiller with both agonist and antagonist effects. As with other opioids, buprenorphine produces agonist effects by binding to opiate receptors in the brain, thus initiating the response that produces the normal opioid effects of feelings of euphoria and respiratory depression. However, buprenorphine is only a partial agonist because although its effects initially increase with increasing dose, they then quickly level off. This antagonistic "ceiling effect" is absent in the full agonists such as heroin, morphine, and methadone.

This difference is significant because it is the respiratory depression caused by opioid drugs that leads, in cases of overdose, to rapid cessation of breathing and subsequent death. Heroin overdoses are particularly dangerous, and several thousand deaths result from use of uncertain doses of illegal opiate drugs each year.

Buprenorphine's potential for treating opiate addiction is partially based on the fact that it is a less powerful agonist and is therefore intrinsically safer than other opiates. When administered at low doses as a substitute for an abused drug, buprenorphine has enough opioid agonist effect to occupy the brain receptors and thus help dependent individuals to give up heroin or morphine without experiencing acute withdrawal symptoms.

Clinical trials of buprenorphine as a treatment for heroin addiction showed that patients had reduced cravings for heroin during the withdrawal process. In 2002 the Food and Drug Administration (FDA) approved buprenorphine as a therapy for opioid addiction treatment, marketed as Subutex and Suboxone. Based on the clinical trial data and estimation of the overall potential of buprenorphine for creating dependence and abuse, the drug was reclassified from Schedule V to a Schedule III narcotic, available by prescription within approved programs.

There are two other areas of medical interest in the drug. Cocaine is not an opioid drug, and buprenorphine is used at present only for the treatment of opioid dependence. However, preclinical research has shown that buprenorphine also reduces cocaine self-administration in rhesus monkeys. Clinical trials are investigating possible buprenorphine-cocaine interactions and the use of the drug in cocaine abuse rehabilitation. Another possible therapeutic use may be in the treatment of severely depressed individuals who fail to improve when treated with conventional antidepressant drug therapy. Researchers have long known that some chronically depressed patients show improvement when treated with opioids, but the risk of dependence has been considered too great. Significant improvements in some patients treated with buprenorphine have been observed. Further clinical studies in this area are underway.

D. E. ARNOT

SEE ALSO:

Agonists and Antagonists • Heroin • Opiates and Opioids

KEY FACTS

Classification
Schedule III (USA), Schedule I (Canada), Class C (UK), Schedule III (INCB). Opioid.

Short-term effects
Similar to those of all opioid drugs and include constipation and occasional nausea and vomiting

Long-term effects
There is potential for dependency and abuse, particularly in those who are not opioid addicts.

Caffeine

Caffeine is a stimulant drug that is present naturally in coffee and tea and is added to many soft drinks. Used for many centuries, caffeine is one of the most popular self-administered drugs in the world.

The fruits of the coffee plant are called coffee cherries. The soft pulp of the fruit must be removed before the coffee beans (two in each fruit) can be dried and roasted.

Roughly 90 percent of the world's population uses caffeine. Found in coffee, tea, and chocolate, caffeine is consumed by more people than any other legal drug. In the United States, for example, it has been estimated that 80 percent of adults consume coffee or tea on a daily basis. Caffeine is also added to soft drink beverages such as Coca-Cola and is found in many medications, such as over-the-counter painkillers, cold remedies, and stimulants, such as Excedrin and Vivarin. The main sources of caffeine are the coffee bean, tea leaf, kola nut, and cacao pod.

Caffeine, which is known chemically as 1,3,7-trimethylxanthine, is composed entirely of carbon, hydrogen, nitrogen, and oxygen, with the general formula $C_8H_{10}N_4O_2$. Pure caffeine crystals are a white, often fleecy powder, or long silky crystals. Most of the world's purified caffeine, which is used in soft drinks and over-the-counter medicines, comes from caffeine extracted from poor-quality coffee beans and tea leaves, or is the by-product of decaffeination.

Caffeine is the best-known member of a class of drugs called the methylxanthines. The other two naturally occurring and self-administered methylxanthines are theobromine and theophylline. All three of these drugs have similar molecular structures and behavioral and physical effects. While coffee contains only caffeine, chocolate contains both caffeine and theobromine, and tea contains caffeine, theobromine, and theophylline.

It appears that caffeine is present in plants as part of their chemical weaponry to defend themselves against predators and competitors. Caffeine has potent antibiotic and antifungal effects and causes sterility in several insects. Caffeine also permeates the soil that surrounds the plants through the accumulation of fallen leaves and berries, thus inhibiting the growth of competing plants. However, in doing this, the coffee plant ultimately kills itself as well. Over many years, the accumulation of caffeine in the soil becomes so great that the toxicity level is high enough to harm the parent plant. It is this buildup that contributes to the degeneration of coffee plantations between the age of 10 and 25 years.

History of caffeine
Caffeine was first isolated and purified in 1819 by the German physician Friedlieb Ferdinand Runge. Runge isolated caffeine from some arabica mocha

coffee beans at the request of the German poet Johann Wolfgang von Goethe. In the form of drinks such as coffee and tea, however, caffeine has been used as a self-administered drug for many hundreds of years. Although the origins of coffee are not known, one persistent legend has it that coffee was discovered around 850 CE in the area known today as Ethiopia by a goat herder named Khaldi. One night Khaldi's goats did not return home. When he found his goats, Khaldi saw them dancing around a shrub with red berries (coffee beans). After Khaldi tried some of the berries, he started to dance, too. Khaldi shared this story with some monks who used the berries to make a drink and were reported to have the stamina to pray for hours and hours. From these origins coffee was born. From Ethiopia, coffee use spread to the Middle East. The Ottoman Turks brought coffee to Constantinople in 1453, and its use spread to Europe by 1600. The first English coffee house opened in Oxford in 1650 and coffee houses quickly became widespread throughout England, followed by Europe, and eventually America. Coffee use came to North America in 1668, and coffee became a favorite American beverage in 1773, when British taxes made tea unfashionable and many Americans began drinking coffee as a patriotic duty.

As in the case of coffee, there are many legends about the origins of tea. Tea was reportedly discovered by the Chinese emperor Shen Nung in 2737 BCE. Printed records show that tea was being cultivated and sold commercially in China by 780 CE. In the 1660s the Dutch started shipping tea to Europe on a regular basis, and tea drinking became popular in the Netherlands, Germany, France, and Portugal. In 1662 tea drinking became popular in England also, after Charles II married the Portuguese princess Catherine of Braganza, who introduced tea drinking from Portugal. Tea drinking became popular in the American colonies in turn about this time.

Cocoa is made from seeds of the cacao tree, which are fermented, dried, and roasted. The result is unsweetened chocolate. Cocoa was used by the Maya of the Yucatán Peninsula, the Aztecs of Mexico, and the Inca of Peru, all of whom believed it was a gift from the gods. Chocolate was reserved for the wealthy and powerful. It was believed to be an aphrodisiac and was used at wedding feasts and by wealthy men who could afford to support, and had to satisfy, many wives. Montezuma, emperor of the Aztecs, was reported to consume 50 goblets of cocoa drink a day. This concoction included maize and chili peppers but no sugar or milk. The Spanish conquistador Hernán Cortés introduced chocolate to the Spanish in 1520. To make the drink more palatable to Spanish tastes, vanilla and sugar were added. This form of chocolate eventually gained popularity across Europe. The Spanish kept the source of chocolate secret for 100 years. The Dutch, however, eventually introduced the plant to the Philippines and Ceylon (now Sri Lanka). Chocolate was introduced into Europe before coffee and tea and was briefly popular, but it was too expensive for most Europeans and eventually was replaced by coffee (except in England, where coffee was replaced by tea).

Use of caffeine

Caffeine is usually taken orally. The vast majority is taken by drinking, although some caffeine is eaten in chocolate or swallowed in medications. Caffeine is widely used throughout the world and is the most popular self-administered drug. Indeed, coffee is the world's most valuable traded commodity after oil. The average caffeine consumption of the world's population is about 70 milligrams per person per day, 90 percent of which is consumed as coffee or tea. Although estimates vary, in the United Kingdom and the United States adults consume on average between 200 and 400 milligrams per day. In the United States, 80 percent of adults consume three to five cups of coffee every day.

Caffeine is a stimulant and is consumed to make the drinker feel more alert. Thus, caffeine is used throughout the day, especially in the morning to reduce fatigue and in the evening to increase wakefulness and delay sleep.

The therapeutic uses of caffeine are minimal, and the overwhelming majority of caffeine use is self-administration for its stimulant properties. There are three therapeutic uses, however. Caffeine is mildly effective in treating headaches caused by high blood pressure and is included in some headache medications, such as Anacin. In addition, caffeine is used to treat newborn infants who show apneic episodes (periodic cessation of breathing). Because of its stimulant effects on breathing, caffeine can be life-

KEY FACTS

Classification
Not scheduled in USA, Canada, UK, INCB. Stimulant.

Distribution
One of the most widely consumed drugs in the world. Eighty percent of adults in the United States consume coffee or tea on a regular basis, with an average intake of between 200 and 400 milligrams per day.

Short-term effects
Increases feelings of mental alertness, a faster and clearer flow of thought, wakefulness, restlessness, and reduced fatigue. May enhance performance of various psychomotor tasks but causes agitation, anxiety, tremors, rapid breathing, and insomnia at higher doses. Stimulates heart, increasing blood pressure and cardiac contractility and output, and dilates coronary arteries. Increases respiration rate, enhances water excretion and stimulation of chemicals called catecholamines, which include the neurotransmitter epinephrine. Caffeine exerts the opposite effect on cerebral blood vessels—it constricts them. Thus, caffeine can relieve headaches.

Long-term effects
Chronic caffeine use may cause an increased density of adenosine receptors, leading to an increased sensitivity to adenosine. Possible effects on reproduction at higher doses. Chronic caffeine use leads to habituation and tolerance, and discontinuation may produce a withdrawal syndrome (headache, drowsiness, fatigue, generally negative moods). Cardiac arrhythmias are not uncommon, but they are rarely serious.

Dangers
Very high doses of caffeine stimulate the spinal cord, resulting in convulsions. Deaths, although rare, have occurred. Caffeine may be a risk factor for heart disease, miscarriage, and low birth weight.

Signs of abuse
Long-term ingestion of excessive amounts of caffeine can result in a condition called caffeinism, which is characterized by nervousness, restlessness, insomnia, and physiological effects such as rapid heartbeat. Higher doses of caffeine can cause more severe psychiatric effects.

saving in these patients. Also, because caffeine causes dilation of air passages, it is sometimes used for the treatment of asthma.

Pharmacological effects
Caffeine is rapidly absorbed by the stomach and small intestine, with significant blood levels reached in 30 to 45 minutes and peak concentrations achieved in 2 hours. Caffeine crosses the blood-brain and placental barriers and so is found in almost equal concentrations in all parts of the body and the brain. Most caffeine is metabolized in the liver before it is excreted by the kidneys. Only around 2 percent of caffeine is excreted unchanged. The half-life of caffeine, which is the time needed for the concentration in the blood to decrease by half, is between 2.5 to 4.5 hours in most adults. Smoking nearly doubles the clearance rate of caffeine from the body, thus decreasing the half-life. In contrast, caffeine metabolism is slowed by alcohol. Women metabolize caffeine 20 to 30 percent faster than men, although the rate of elimination depends on hormone levels. The half-life of caffeine is longer after ovulation than before ovulation. The half-life of caffeine is nearly doubled in women taking oral contraceptives compared with women ovulating naturally, and caffeine elimination is also slowed during pregnancy.

Effects of caffeine
Although the effects of caffeine are not completely understood, the primary mechanism of the action of caffeine appears to be attaching to and blocking adenosine receptors in the brain and spinal cord. In addition to other functions, adenosine acts as a neuromodulator, meaning that adenosine regulates cellular functions. Adenosine binds to specific

adenosine receptors, which has the effect of inhibiting the activity of nerve cells; it inhibits the release of many types of neurotransmitters (the brain's chemical messengers), including norepinephrine, dopamine, acetylcholine, glutamate, and GABA. Because of these effects, the overall action of adenosine is to inhibit nerve-cell firing throughout the brain and to act as a central nervous system (CNS) depressant. Caffeine, however, blocks the adenosine receptors and thus increases the activity of the neurotransmitters listed above and increases the activity of nerve cells. In humans, these effects result in increased arousal and mental alertness, reduced fatigue, and reduced sleep.

Caffeine has other effects on the body outside the CNS. Caffeine has a direct effect on muscles: striated (voluntary) muscles are strengthened and become less susceptible to fatigue, while smooth muscles tend to relax. Smooth muscle relaxation dilates the bronchial tubes of the lungs, decreasing airway resistance.

Caffeine has different effects on blood flow in different parts of the body. Caffeine constricts blood flow in the head while increasing blood flow to the rest of the body (the periphery). By decreasing blood flow to the brain, caffeine can lead to relief from headaches caused by high blood pressure, which is

why caffeine is included in some headache medications. By increasing blood flow in the periphery, caffeine increases blood pressure. Caffeine also increases breathing rate and urine output.

Higher doses of caffeine, from 12 or more cups of coffee per day, can cause more intense effects, such as agitation, anxiety, tremors, and insomnia. Huge doses of caffeine (2 to 5 grams) may stimulate the spinal cord and cause convulsions. The lethal dose of caffeine is about 10 grams, or roughly 100 cups of coffee at once. Death from caffeine is thus highly unlikely, and caffeine is considered relatively nontoxic. Moderate caffeine use does not produce toxic effects, and long-term use of caffeine, unlike alcohol or tobacco, does not cause obvious organ damage. However, overuse of caffeine can result in a clinical syndrome called caffeinism, which is characterized by CNS and non-CNS symptoms. Caffeinism generally results from doses greater than 500 to 1,000 milligrams, or 5 to 10 cups of coffee per day. The CNS effects include anxiety, insomnia, and mood changes. Peripheral effects include increased heart rate (tachycardia), high blood pressure (hypertension), irregular heartbeat (cardiac arrhythmia), and stomach problems. Decreasing or ceasing caffeine intake alleviates these effects.

This engraving shows people drinking coffee at an open-air coffee stand in France around 1815.

CAFFEINE CONTENT OF COMMON FOOD ITEMS AND DRUGS

Beverages	Caffeine content
Coffee	85 mg / cup
Decaffeinated coffee	3 mg / cup
Tea	28 mg / cup
Cocoa or hot chocolate	30 mg / cup
Red Bull	115 mg / can
Java water	89 mg / can
Jolt	72 mg / can
Mountain Dew	55 mg / can
Battery Energy Drink	47 mg / can
Coca-Cola, Diet	45 mg / can
Dr. Pepper	41 mg / can
Pepsi	38 mg / can
Coca-Cola, Classic	34 mg / can
Snapple	32 mg / can
Nestea Sweet Iced Tea	27 mg / can
7-Up, Fresca, Sprite	0 mg / can
Chocolates	
Baking chocolate	35 mg / oz.
Milk chocolate	6 mg / oz.
Analgesic drugs	
Anacin, max. strength	32 mg / tablet
Excedrin	64.8 mg / tablet
Over-the-counter stimulants	
NoDoz	100 mg / tablet
Vivarin	200 mg / tablet

The values in this table represent the amount of caffeine in standard servings, as shown.

Dependence and withdrawal

Regular caffeine use causes a physical dependence, which is apparent in most people when the caffeine intake is abruptly decreased or stopped, resulting in a caffeine withdrawal syndrome. Caffeine withdrawal results in a variety of psychological and physical symptoms, including headaches, drowsiness, fatigue, and impaired concentration and motor performance. Some people also experience mild anxiety or depression, and sometimes an intense craving for coffee. While caffeine withdrawal was first reported in people consuming large doses of caffeine (greater than 600 milligrams per day), it can also occur in people consuming as little as 100 milligrams per day, which is about one cup of coffee or three cans of caffeinated soft drinks per day. The symptoms of caffeine withdrawal begin on the first day of abstinence and continue for about two to six more days. Getting relief from these withdrawal symptoms is thought to be a major reason for chronic coffee drinking, especially the first cup each morning.

Because some people ingest excessive amounts of caffeine, and caffeine causes physical dependence, caffeine possesses some of the characteristics of an abused substance. Indeed, caffeine is reportedly reinforcing to regular users. On the other hand, caffeine is not normally associated with compulsive drug-taking patterns caused by drugs such as alcohol, cocaine, and opiates. Also, unlike these drugs, caffeine does not impair daily functioning. In addition, the reinforcing effects of caffeine are not due to an intense euphoria such as that produced by cocaine and opiates. Instead, they are probably due to a combination of performance enhancement (increased concentration and motor performance) and relief of withdrawal symptoms.

In humans, tolerance appears to occur to most of the stimulatory effects of caffeine. Chronic administration of caffeine causes an increase in the number of adenosine receptors, presumably in an attempt to overcome the effects of caffeine. Tolerance to the cardiovascular and sleep-disrupting effects of caffeine have been shown. However, it is less clear if tolerance occurs to the CNS effects of the drug. For example, only a mild tolerance has been seen to the daytime activating effects of caffeine, yet caffeine produces less sleep disruption in heavy coffee drinkers than in light coffee drinkers. One thing to keep in mind is that while these types of studies may be demonstrating caffeine tolerance, they may simply be showing that individuals who are resistant to the effects of caffeine are more likely to become heavy coffee drinkers.

J. JAWORSKI

SEE ALSO:

Chocolate • Central Nervous System • Drug Receptors

Central Nervous System

The central nervous system is composed of the brain and spinal cord. It receives and sends signals to the rest of the body. Drugs affect the nervous system by interfering with the methods that it uses to send signals.

The central nervous system (CNS) includes the neural elements contained in the skull and spinal column, including the brain and spinal cord. Those elements located outside these protective bony structures are known as the peripheral nervous system. In health, the central nervous system is the source of individuality and mental well-being. While social, personality, and genetic factors are important contributors to drug abuse, the effect that a particular drug has on the central nervous system is the main reason for the development of drug addiction.

While the brain is often discussed as if it were an organ like the heart, the brain is made up of a large number of complex circuits organized into functional regions. The cerebral cortex is the prominent convoluted part of the human brain, which is home to most of the complex mental functions. The thalamus lies beneath the cerebral cortex and is thought of as a variable relay of sensory information. Just above the upper part of the spinal cord is the brain stem, which controls the body's vital functions (such as respiration and heart rate), and the cerebellum, which coordinates movement. The uppermost part of the brain stem controls some reflex actions and is part of the circuit involved in the control of eye movements and other voluntary movements.

The spinal cord projects down from the brain through a hole in the base of the skull called the foramen magnum and extends down through the vertebral column. Nerve roots exit the spinal column through small openings along the column. The nerve roots that emanate from the spine become the nerves of the peripheral nervous system. These nerves carry motor commands from the brain and spinal cord to the individual muscles in the body, and carry sensory information to the central nervous system. The spinal cord conveys reflex responses to the stretch of tendons that allow people to stand erect without much thought, as well as responses that allow people to withdraw from sudden, painful stimuli. Motor neurons within the spinal cord send out signals for purposeful movement to the muscles. The brain exerts descending control of certain spinal activities, in some cases overriding or modulating spinal reflexes or programmed patterns of activity, such as walking or running.

The brain and spinal cord (shown in red) are the main elements of the central nervous system. Radiating from the spinal column are the nerves of the peripheral nervous system (shown in blue), which carry messages from the brain to all areas of the body and relay sensory information back to the brain for processing.

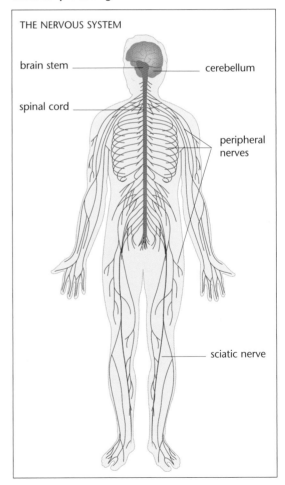

THE NERVOUS SYSTEM

brain stem

cerebellum

spinal cord

peripheral nerves

sciatic nerve

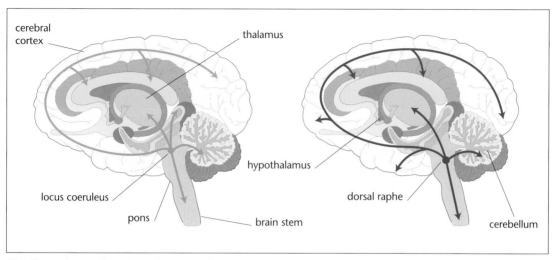

This illustration depicts the pathways of the norepinephrine (left) and serotonin (right) systems in the brain.

How brain chemicals affect the CNS

The brain stem is of particular importance in understanding the influence of drugs on the brain. The brain stem controls many CNS functions that maintain life, such as breathing, heart rate, blood pressure, and general arousal. Many of these modulatory systems (systems that make necessary adjustments) are located in the central region, or core, of the brain stem, and they can function without conscious thought. The targets of the individual neurons that make up these cell groups are widely dispersed across multiple regions of the central nervous system. Effective medical treatments for mood disorders and schizophrenia involve drugs that affect many of the modulatory systems of the brain by acting to increase brain chemicals (neurotransmitters) that are used within these systems. Although there may be overlap in the projections (nerve pathways) of these systems, each is characterized by use of a particular neurotransmitter. Many of these systems are also affected by drugs of abuse.

Norepinephrine

The locus coeruleus (from the Latin for "blue region") is the location of most of the neurons in the central nervous system that contain the neurotransmitter noradrenaline. The locus coeruleus comprises a pair of nuclei (cluster of nerve cells) located at the back of the pons, which is situated near the top of the brain stem. These blue-pigmented neurons project out into the cerebral cortex, thalamus, hypothalamus, cerebellum, midbrain, and spinal cord. The locus coeruleus is the most widely projecting modulatory system and is involved in attention, arousal, sleep, learning and memory, anxiety, pain, mood, and the metabolism of the central nervous system. Experiments in animals suggest that the locus coeruleus responds to novelty in the environment. Stimulant drugs, such as amphetamine, 3,4-methylenedioxymethamphetamine (MDMA, or Ecstasy), ephedrine, methamphetamine, phentermine, and aminorex, all cause increased levels of norepinephrine in the brain. Studies indicate that amphetamine stimulates the release of norepinephrine, and that cocaine may prolong the effect of the released norepinephrine by inhibiting its return to the neuron that released it.

Serotonin

Nine pairs of serotonin-containing nuclei are clustered around the brain stem region known as the dorsal raphe (from the Greek for "seam"). There are two main projection streams, descending and ascending. A group of serotonin neurons in the medulla send descending projections to the spinal cord, where they modulate pain signals. Centers in the pons and midbrain send ascending projections to the cerebral cortex, thalamus, hypothalamus, and cerebellum. These neurons form synapses with many of the same targets that are served by the norepinephrine-containing cells in the brain stem. Experiments in a number of animals, including primates, suggest that serotonin-containing neurons are most active during wakefulness and less active during sleep, and are involved (along with nor-epinephrine and acetylcholine) in controlling the sleeping and waking cycle. Serotonin neurons also have a role in determining mood and aggressive behavior. Certain antidepressants work by increasing the amount of serotonin in the synapses, usually by reducing the rate of removal of serotonin from the synapse. The drug Ecstasy works in part by increasing the amount of serotonin released in this circuitry. The hallucinogen LSD binds very tightly to the serotonin receptors, causing a greater than normal activation of the receptor. At high enough concentrations, it may cause mood swings, altered perceptions, delusions, and visual hallucinations.

Acetylcholine

Two regions are especially rich in the neuro-transmitter acetylcholine (the adjectival form of acetylcholine is *cholinergic*). These regions are the basal forebrain and the parabrachial pontine tegmentum region of the pons. These regions are not the only source of acetylcholine in the brain, and there are also important cholinergic neurons in the striatum and cerebral cortex. There are two key modulatory areas in the basal forebrain complex.

One is the medial septal region, whose axons course backward to the hippocampal formation and are therefore thought to be involved in learning and memory. The other is the nucleus basalis of Meynert, whose axons project diffusely to much of the cerebral cortex. The cholinergic neurons in the pons and midbrain project to the thalamus, where they excite the relay cells of the thalamus during wakefulness and dreaming sleep. These cells also project to the basal forebrain complex, where the two main cholinergic systems may interact. In addition to acetylcholine, these neurons also often contain an enzyme that makes the gaseous neurotransmitter nitric oxide. The brain stem projection helps to maintain wakefulness and arousal in humans. Certain nervous system depressants, such as barbi-turates and benzodiazepines, can counter this arousal effect by inhibiting stimulatory signals within the brain, promoting sleep. Nicotine works by binding to so-called nicotinic acetylcholine receptors that are targeted by these diffuse projections, which results in a feeling of alertness.

Dopamine

Certain regions of the central nervous system show particular sensitivity to drugs of abuse, and dopamine-containing systems stand out as a major focus of research into the effect of drugs on the central nervous system. Dopamine is contained in a

This illustration depicts the acetylcholine (left) and dopamine (right) pathways in the brain.

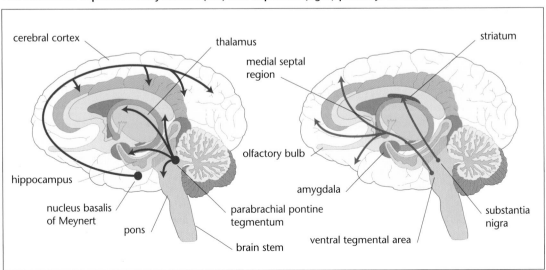

number of structures, including the retina of the eye, the olfactory bulbs (associated with the sense of smell), the hypothalamus, and the substantia nigra. The substantia nigra is part of the midbrain involved in body movement. Loss of dopamine neurons in the substantia nigra—and their links to movement circuits in the basal ganglia—produces the tremor and other movement disorders seen in Parkinson's disease. The neurotransmitter dopamine has received special attention from pharmacologists because of its role in regulating moods and in mediating motivation and reward processes.

The brain's reward circuit

An important region implicated in the effects of drugs of abuse is known as the medial forebrain bundle. In the 1950s, it was discovered that rats would, under some conditions, ignore water, food, and sex in favor of electrical stimulation to this region of fibers within the brain's reward system. The system encompasses the dopaminergic projection from cells in an area of the midbrain called the ventral tegmental area (VTA) to the ventral striatum, known as the mesolimbic dopaminergic system, as well as to other regions. When stimulated by certain behaviors or drugs, this brain circuit creates the sensation of pleasure or euphoria. Stimulation of the neurons of the VTA results in electrical impulses traveling down the nerve axons, prompting the release of dopamine at the nerve terminals. The dopamine rapidly diffuses across the tiny fluid space between nerve cells (called the synapse) to affect target neurons in the nucleus accumbens, a part of the emotional center of the brain (also called the limbic system), and in the frontal region of the cerebral cortex, part of the brain's decision-making system. After release, dopamine is quickly re-absorbed into the neuron by special molecules located at the synaptic terminals called dopamine transporters. Blocking the dopamine transporter causes accumulation of dopamine in the synapse, prolonging its effects.

Cocaine, amphetamines, nicotine, and alcohol appear to exert their major addictive effects through increasing the activity of the mesolimbic dopa-minergic system. Although each of these drugs interacts with the circuitry in a different way (and some can have effects on other regions of the brain

and the body as a whole), they all appear to increase the amount of dopamine available in the synaptic clefts of the mesolimbic dopaminergic system.

Cocaine and amphetamine are stimulants that increase the availability of dopamine in the synapse by blocking the dopamine transporter on synaptic terminals. In addition to dopamine, norepinephrine and serotonin uptake are also blocked. Ecstasy is an amphetamine that is considered a hallucinogen but does not cause typical hallucinations. In contrast with methamphetamine, Ecstasy triggers a larger increase in serotonin and a smaller increase in dopamine.

Nicotine is a drug that mimics the neuro-transmitter acetylcholine and binds to specific acetylcholine receptors on neurons in the ventral tegmental area of the brain. When nicotine binds to these receptors, an electric impulse is sent down the nerve axon, resulting in the release of dopamine at the synapse. The active drug in marijuana is delta 9-tetrahydrocannabinol (THC). THC excites dopa-mine neurons in the ventral tegmentum and substantia nigra, causing increased dopamine release in the targets of these projections.

Drugs that affect rapid communication

In addition to influencing the reward circuitry of the brain, some drugs act on brain chemicals (neurotransmitters) involved in rapid communi-cation within the brain. Two important systems of rapid neurotransmission are excitatory (using glutamate) and inhibitory (using gamma-amino-butyric acid, or GABA). In addition to increasing dopamine release in the mesolimbic system, alcohol performs the dual role of depressing excitatory neurotransmission and enhancing inhibitory neuro-transmission. Barbiturates and benzodiazepines bind to inhibitory receptors that use GABA, enhancing the effect of GABA at these receptors. Inhalant abuse (glue sniffing) may also have depressant effects on the central nervous system. Dissociative anesthetics, including phencyclidine (PCP) and ketamine, reduce the response of brain regions to glutamate.

Cognitive effects of drug abuse on the CNS

Basic research has suggested that in addition to the effect of repeated use of certain drugs on the reward pathway of the brain, there are disruptions within the frontal cortex, an area that regulates decision-making, inhibition of certain responses, planning, and memory. This disruption may occur in addition to effects of drugs on the dopamine-containing neurons of the reward pathway. There is also a basic disruption of motivational urges, sometimes called "motivational toxicity". This effect is evident in some drug addicts who neglect normal motivating influences such as food, sex, and personal achievement in order to pursue drug-related behaviors.

Other parts of the brain are also vulnerable to drug use. The active compound in marijuana, tetrahydro-cannabinol (THC), suppresses the neurons in the information-processing system of the hippocampus, the part of the brain that is crucial for learning, memory, and the merging of sensory experiences with emotions and motivation. Abuse of marijuana is also associated with impaired attention and memory. These impairments may last up to a day after the use of marijuana. Prenatal exposure to THC is associated with impaired verbal reasoning and memory in preschool children. Researchers have also found that cocaine abusers perform significantly worse than nonabusers in attention and motor skills, even one year after abstinence. Other side effects of drug abuse may involve impairment of natural physiological responses that are initiated and modulated by the central nervous system. For example, a common side effect of drug abuse is erectile dysfunction, which is associated with a number of abused drugs including cocaine, alcohol, and heroin.

Nervous system depressants may also cause powerful cognitive impairments. Alcohol use can degrade reasoning, judgment, and basic motor skills, often while imparting a feeling of denial that adverse effects of alcohol have occurred. Gamma-hydroxybutyrate (GHB), like alcohol, is a central nervous system depressant that can cause a loss of control, memory impairment, or loss of consciousness. Mixed with alcohol, GHB can cause respiratory distress, coma, and death. Rohypnol (flunitrazepam) is one of a class of drugs known as benzodiazepines. Rohypnol causes a profound form of amnesia, where experiences while under the effects of the drug cannot be remembered. A street name for Rohypnol is the "forget-me pill," and because of its properties it has been used in sexual assaults.

Sleep disruptions are also commonly reported as a consequence of drug abuse. Alcohol use may have a sedative effect that results in a drinker falling asleep faster. However, chronic alcohol abusers frequently suffer disruption in the amount and quality of sleep. Severe sleep disruptions may also contribute to a return to drinking after a period of abstinence and can last for months or years after drinking has ceased. At the other end of the spectrum, cocaine and other stimulants may cause prolonged sleeplessness.

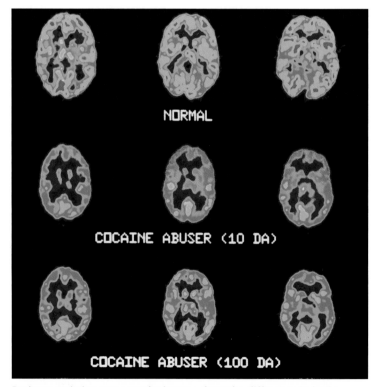

NORMAL

COCAINE ABUSER (10 DA)

COCAINE ABUSER (100 DA)

Positron emission tomography images show the difference in brain metabolism between a normal person and a cocaine abuser. The cocaine user has few red and yellow areas, indicating poor brain function. After 100 days' abstinence, there is still significant impairment.

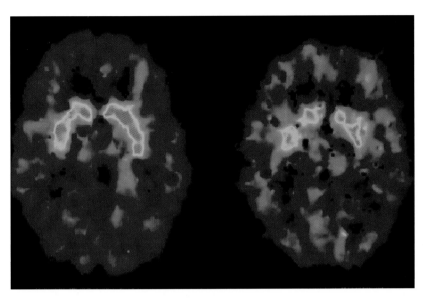

Scans of dopamine levels in a nonuser (left) and a methamphetamine user (right) show depletion of dopamine (indicated by the red areas) in the abuser. Methamphetamine is damaging to the brain and may result in long-term impairment of cognitive functions.

Drugs that damage the CNS

In addition to disruptions of neural communication and cognitive task performance, several drugs of abuse appear to cause long-term damage to nerves and brain circuitry.

Ecstasy appears to prune, or reduce in number, serotonin axons and axon terminals. Months after Ecstasy has been taken, some brain regions show significant axon pruning and regrowth as the brain attempts to rewire the damaged serotonin system. Ecstasy abuse produces psychiatric effects ranging from fear through depression to actual psychoses. Researchers have found that, many years after taking the drug, individuals may score higher on depression ratings than people who have never taken it. While the full mechanism is still being investigated, it is suspected that depression could occur because of the damage caused by Ecstasy to the serotonin neurons. The degree and behavioral significance of this damage is a matter of current investigation and debate. Methamphetamine is similar in its chemical structure to dopamine and may be taken up by dopamine-containing terminals, where it can damage the frontal cortex, amygdala, and the striatum. Decreases in dopamine levels can be seen in these regions using brain-imaging techniques.

Alcohol abuse is associated with a number of nervous system dysfunctions, such as memory loss, confusion, and movement disorders. Research has shown that alcohol kills brain cells, particularly if exposure occurs during early development. Extensive loss of brain cells is more difficult to demonstrate in adult humans, but experiments suggest that selective cell death may occur in regions such as the hippocampus. Alcohol may also produce degeneration of portions of the cerebellum, which can cause a disorder called ataxia in which the sufferer is unable to coordinate voluntary movement of his or her muscles.

Another class of drugs, known as designer drugs, can also be abused and may have many of the effects outlined above. Designer drugs are modified forms of existing drugs that are structurally very similar to a controlled substance and may even have similar cognitive and damaging effects, but may not yet be classified as controlled substances. Abuse of these drugs still poses significant health risk to the user.

The central nervous system is key to human's ability to think, remember, plan, and act. When activated by drugs of abuse, certain circuits of the central nervous system related to reward and a sense of well-being are apparently directed away from normal sources of behavioral stimulation and toward drug-seeking behaviors. Impairment of basic mental function may occur, and—depending on the drug—damage to these vital circuits may be long lasting.

D. W. GODWIN

SEE ALSO:

Acetylcholine • Blood-Brain Barrier • Dopamine • Norepinephrine • Serotonin

Chloral Hydrate

Chloral hydrate is one of the oldest sedatives still in medical use. The drug acquired a sinister reputation through its ability to induce unconsciousness when mixed with alcohol, a fact often exploited by criminals.

Chloral hydrate is a central nervous system depressant. As such, the drug interferes with the traffic of nerve impulses between the brain and the rest of the body that keep a waking person alert and coordinated in speech and actions. At lower dosages this interference results in relaxation, slurring, and sleep; overdoses impair the correct functioning of the heart and circulatory system and can lead to death.

First synthesized in 1832, chloral hydrate became the first synthetic medical sedative in 1869, when Mathias Liebreich used it to induce sleep in patients. It proved much more effective than the bromide salts previously used—a dose of 0.5 to 1.0 grams is sufficient to induce sleep in an average adult within an hour. The sleep lasts for four to eight hours, and most patients then recover with few side effects, such as mild nausea. Chloral hydrate has now largely been replaced by other sedatives, such as barbiturates, but continues to be used for the treatment of children and elderly patients and for emergency medicine.

Outside medicine, chloral hydrate became notorious for its use in knockout drops (solutions of chloral hydrate in ethyl alcohol) and Mickey Finns (alcoholic beverages spiked with chloral hydrate). In both cases, alcohol combines with chloral hydrate to make the more powerful sedative chloral alcoholate, and criminals have used these combinations to stupefy and knock out their victims—a practice called "slipping a Mickey." This practice has since been superseded by the use of other drugs, such as the benzodiazepine Rohypnol. Voluntary abuse of chloral hydrate tends to be limited to situations in which other substances of abuse are unavailable. Overdoses can be treated by oral doses of activated charcoal followed by a purgative before sedation sets in, otherwise heart monitoring and standard treatment of heartbeat irregularities are options.

The chemical name for chloral hydrate is 2,2,2-trichloroethane-1,1-diol, with the formula $CCl_3CH(OH)_2$. When pure, chloral hydrate is a colorless crystalline solid that melts at 135°F (57°C). Chloral hydrate is administered in water-based liquid preparations in gelatin capsules and suppositories, and in syrups. Typical doses are 25 to 50 milligrams per kilogram of body weight for deep sleep and 60 to 75 milligrams per kilogram for general anesthesia. Once administered, chloral hydrate starts to take effect within 30 minutes, and complete sedation usually follows in less than an hour.

The $-CCl_3$ group makes chloral hydrate highly lipid (fat) soluble, which helps its rapid distribution through the body. Alcohol dehydrogenase in the liver rapidly converts up to 90 percent of the dose of chloral hydrate into trichloroethanol, an active metabolite largely responsible for the sedative action.

M. Clowes

KEY FACTS

Classification

Schedule IV (USA). Not scheduled in Canada, UK, INCB. CNS depressant.

Street names

Knockout drops, Mickey Finn

Short-term effects

Drowsiness and mild euphoria at low doses; slowed respiration, nausea and vomiting, slurring of speech, stupor and sleep at higher doses. Danger of coma or death from irregular heart function at high doses.

Long-term effects

Moderately high potential for physical and psychological dependence to develop. Liver damage can arise with prolonged repeated use.

SEE ALSO:

Central Nervous System • Classification of Drugs • Rohypnol • Sedatives and Hypnotics

Chlorpromazine

Chlorpromazine, also known by the trade name Thorazine, has been widely used in psychiatric practice as a drug to treat schizophrenia and manic-depressive illness. The drug is also used to terminate LSD-induced hallucinations.

Chlorpromazine is an organic chemical with drug properties that is technically known as chloro-dimethyl-aminopropyl phenothiazine (formula $C_{17}H_{19}ClN_2S$). It is one of a group of aliphatic phenothiazines originally patented in 1953 by the French drug company Rhone-Poulenc. It is mainly used as a relatively mild antipsychotic drug for the treatment of disorganized, confused, and psychotic or paranoid thinking as well as hallucinations and delusions. However, chlorpromazine has a broad range of activities secondary to this action. Its first reported use was as a sedative that did not lead to loss of consciousness (narcosis). The antipsychotic action of the drug was noted later, as was its effectiveness in suppressing nausea and vomiting.

Chlorpromazine and the other phenothiazines are not addictive, habit forming, or likely to induce dependency. Chlorpromazine has been widely used for the treatment of manic-depressive illness (sometimes known as bipolar personality disorder). It has also been used to alleviate manic-phase activity and other severe behavioral problems in children. The drug also acts as a strong sedative, inducing drowsiness and somnolence, particularly when first used. Some psychiatrists believe that these sedative properties contribute, in some clinical situations, to the therapeutic usefulness of chlorpromazine.

Although its mechanism of action is not completely understood, chlorpromazine seems to exert its antipsychotic effects by blocking receptors in the central pathways for the important brain messenger molecule, or neurotransmitter, dopamine. Dopamine, like other important neurotransmitters such as acetylcholine and serotonin, is released from nerve cells after they have been stimulated by electrical nerve impulses. The releasing nerve cells are close to other cells that receive the transmitted signal via specific receptors. The dopamine pathways affected by chlorpromazine are in the mesolimbic and medullary regions of the brain.

There are also side effects of the drug that result from the additional interference of chlorpromazine with

CHLORPROMAZINE

Chlorpromazine is thought to terminate LSD hallucinations by interfering with the action of the neurotransmitter serotonin.

dopamine signaling in the basal ganglia, responsible for regulating movement. Precautions taken with chlorpromazine treatment include careful monitoring of dose and usage in patients with heart conditions, as the drug can induce increased pulse rate and hypotension in some patients. Other undesirable side effects include dry mouth, visual impairment and blurring, urine retention and constipation, and weight gain.

LSD hallucinations

Although not itself a drug of abuse, chlorpromazine has been used as a tranquilizer to attempt to terminate disturbing hallucinations induced by LSD (lysergic acid). LSD has a molecular structure that enables it to interact with the brain receptors for another neurotransmitter, serotonin, and chlorpromazine may be able to block the interaction, perhaps in a similar way to the process by which it inhibits dopamine neurotransmission.

D. E. ARNOT

SEE ALSO:

Chocolate

Chocolate is a substance that prompts strong cravings in many people. Its attractions may be linked to the discovery of cannabinoid compounds that impact the brain's pleasure circuits.

Chocolate is one of the world's widespread passions. The Swiss are the biggest consumers, eating over 21 pounds (9.5 kg) each per year. The Belgians and British consume an average of 16 pounds (7.3 kg) annually. In the United States, consumption averages 11.5 pounds (5.2 kg) per year.

History

Chocolate, in the form of cocoa, was first used by the Mayans and Aztecs of Central America and the Incas of Peru, all of whom believed it was a gift of the gods. It was drunk with powdered maize and spices; vanilla and sugar were not added until Hernando Cortés introduced chocolate to the Spanish in 1520. This sweeter form of chocolate eventually gained popularity across Europe. The Spanish kept the source of cocoa beans a mystery for a century until the Dutch discovered the secret and introduced the plant to the Philippines and Ceylon (Sri Lanka). Chocolate drinking enjoyed a brief popularity in Europe; however, it was too expensive for most people and was replaced by coffee and tea.

Source

All chocolate and cocoa comes from cocoa beans, the seedpods of a tropical tree called the cacao tree. Native to South and Central America, the cacao tree grows only within 20 degrees above and below the Equator because it requires hot and moist climates. The seedpods grow on the trunk and main branches of the tree. The ripe seedpods are picked by harvesters and split open. Each pod contains between 20 and 50 seeds, or cocoa beans. Harvesting the beans is time consuming. Roughly 400 beans are needed to make one pound of chocolate. The cocoa beans are first yeast fermented, which removes the bitter taste and activates enzymes that produce the chocolate flavor when the beans are roasted. Next, the beans are dried and then roasted. The blend of the beans determines the taste and aroma. The beans are roasted for between 30 minutes and two hours, which brings out the characteristic chocolate aroma.

The roasted cocoa beans are crushed and heated. The heat turns the beans into a liquid, which can be poured into molds. If allowed to solidify, the result is unsweetened, or baking chocolate. Otherwise, the liquid can be pressed by giant hydraulic presses that let the vegetable fat, called cocoa butter, drain away. Cocoa butter forms around 25 percent of most chocolate bars. The pressed cake left behind after the removal of cocoa butter is sifted into cocoa powder for use in dairies, bakeries, and confectionery industries. Cocoa contains around 10 percent cocoa butter. Thus, while cocoa powder is made by

The temptations of chocolate may arise from natural cannabinoids present in cocoa beans.

removing some of the cocoa butter, eating chocolate (including dark, bittersweet, or milk chocolate) is made by adding it.

Chocolate and craving

Many people get intense cravings for chocolate. In susceptible individuals, it can fuel an addiction-like desire, especially among people who over-exercise. Little is known about why chocolate causes such strong cravings. Some people see it as a "forbidden" pleasure, which makes it more appealing. Socially, chocolate is often associated with a treat or a bribe. It is also a wrecker of attempts to diet and is a cause of such negative attributes as obesity and tooth decay. These negative attributes may cause a "naughty but nice" attraction, which can cause cravings.

Cravings may also be caused by the presence of addictive substances in chocolate. Chocolate contains roughly 300 chemicals, many of which are active in the brain. The stimulant caffeine is the best known, but is present only in low quantities. A related stimulant, theobromine, is present in slightly higher quantities, and another amphetamine-related stimulant called phenylethylamine is also present. In addition, the high fat and sugar content of chocolate may also partly explain cravings. Eating high-fat foods can trigger the brain's production of natural opiates, called endorphins. These opiates play an important role in craving. Other substances in chocolate that may have possible behavioral effects include histamine, serotonin, tryptophan, and salsolinol. The problem with the idea that these chemicals can cause addiction or craving is that many of them exist in higher concentrations in other foods with less appeal than chocolate. Few studies have tested whether these chemicals are active after oral ingestion at the concentrations found in chocolate.

Chocolate and cannabinoids

Another possible explanation for chocolate cravings involves the presence of cannabinoids in chocolate. In 1994, the U.S. neuropharmacologist Daniele Piomelli and his colleagues discovered that nerve cells in the brain produce anandamide. This chemical activates the same cellular receptors as tetrahydrocannabinol (THC), the agent in marijuana smoke that causes a pleasurable high. Shortly after the brain makes anandamide, an enzyme breaks it down,

limiting the duration of anandamide's effects. As yet, little is known about what anandamide, does in the brain. However, deductions can be drawn from the effects of THC, because if anandamide is given to animals, it produces the same effects as when they are injected with THC.

In addition to anandamide, Piomelli and his co-workers discovered two more related chemicals, or analogs, that they believe could provide insights into treating ailments, such as depression. These anandamide-like compounds in chocolate— N-oleoylethanolamine and N-linoleoylethanolamine —both delay anandamide's breakdown. Compared with the low concentration of anandamide in chocolate, that of its chemical analogs is relatively high. Pleasure derived from eating chocolate probably owes less to anandamide than to its related compounds and the role they play in prolonging the pleasurable sensations associated with the body's natural production of anandamide. Together, the three chemicals may act independently of fat and sugar in their ability to enhance a sense of pleasure.

Such an indirect role in pleasure enhancement may explain why eating chocolate does not create the same euphoria as smoking marijuana. Marijuana's THC activates the brain's cannabinoid receptors to give a high. Because anandamide's analogs do not bind to cannabinoid receptors, they may be inactive unless anandamide is present. Even then, their effects may be limited to those parts of the brain where anandamide is produced naturally. These chemicals may simply be prolonging the natural and quite localized effects of the body's own anandamide.

The discovery of cannabinoids in chocolate may have therapeutic benefits. Many depressed people reach for chocolate as a form of self-medication. High-fat dark chocolate seems to combine the maximum cannabinoid concentration (two to three times as much per ounce than milk chocolate) in a form enriched with endorphin-inducing cocoa butter. Further research may lead to the discovery of more potent cannabinoids that can be used to treat people suffering from depression without the fattening consequences of chocolate.

J. JAWORSKI

SEE ALSO:

Endorphins • Marijuana • Serotonin

Classification of Drugs

Abused drugs are taken for the effects they produce on the brain. Often these substances are chemically related or affect the same receptor systems. On this basis, drugs can be classified into groups that describe their actions and effects.

Drugs can be classified in a number of different ways. One of the simplest is to divide them into the legal and the illegal. However, this distinction becomes blurred for those drugs with a defined medical use but that are classified as illegal because of their illicit use for recreational purposes. Drugs may also be categorized by their chemical properties, use in treating medical symptoms, how they work, and what effects they produce.

Drugs that are abused are generally classified by their pharmacological action in the body and the subjective effects they produce. Subjective effects are the perceptions of an individual of the effect a drug is having on his or her body. Such effects may be experienced by the majority of users or may be peculiar to the individual. For example, cocaine is widely regarded as a drug that makes a user euphoric, but in some people it can cause depression.

In the main, most types of drugs either depress or stimulate the central nervous system (CNS). Depressants include alcohol, benzodiazepines, and

the opioids. Stimulants include cocaine, amphetamines, and designer drugs such as Ecstasy. Added to these are drugs that, as well as having stimulant or depressive effects, have additional properties, such as the ability to produce hallucinations or feelings that the mind has separated from the body. Other drugs do not fall easily into any of these categories—marijuana, nicotine, and the anabolic steroids, for example.

For the purposes of this encyclopedia, drugs used for their particular effects on the brain and body are classified in the following groups: alcohol, sedatives and tranquilizers, opioids, stimulants, inhalants, nicotine, cannabinoids, hallucinogens, dissociatives, and anabolic steroids.

Alcohol

Alcohol (ethanol or ethyl alcohol) is one of the most widely used substances in the world, but it is not generally regarded as a drug in the same sense as other addictive substances. This belief is misplaced—

Alcohol is one of the most used and abused substances in the world, but it is not always viewed as a drug.

alcohol does affect the brain and body even when taken in small quantities, and drinking to excess is one of the biggest substance abuse problems in modern society. Alcohol also suffers from the perception that it is a stimulant through its association with social occasions and its use in putting people into a relaxed or confident frame of mind. Alcohol is in fact a depressant. The confusion over its description arises because of alcohol's psychoactive nature, in which the effect it has on the brain leads to changes in behavior, particularly loss of inhibition in the early stages of a drinking session. With time and continued intake, the depressant effects begin to take hold; a loss of concentration and memory, followed by more general anesthesia until the drinker falls asleep or passes into unconsciousness.

Chronic use of alcohol leads to a worsening of symptoms such as memory loss and sleep disturbances. More severe forms of brain damage become apparent, psychosis and seizures being the most common. As dependence takes hold, withdrawal symptoms increase in severity, producing shaking, convulsions, and delirium. The alcoholic's physical health also becomes compromised. Ethanol is one of the biggest causes of heart disease as it gradually weakens and damages the heart muscle. Gastric ulcers are another common result of drinking. Alcohol irritates the lining of the stomach and stimulates the production of digestive acid, which causes lesions in the stomach and intestines. The most damaging effects occur in the liver, where accumulation of acetaldehyde, the metabolic product of the breakdown of alcohol, can result in cirrhosis, an acute failure of the liver.

How alcohol impacts the brain is uncertain, as a specific receptor site has not yet been identified, but two neurochemical systems are believed to be responsible for alcohol's intoxicant and behavioral effects. Gamma-aminobutyric acid (GABA) is the brain's major inhibitory neurotransmitter (chemical messenger). When it activates appropriate receptors, GABA enhances the transport of chloride ions through the receptor, leading to a decrease in the activity of the neuron. Benzodiazepines, which produce similar effects on the CNS to alcohol, are known to affect GABA receptors in this way. It is possible that alcohol also impacts the GABA receptors, causing many of the same behavioral and cognitive effects as the benzodiazepines.

Glutamate is the other neurochemical system thought to be affected by alcohol. Glutamate is the major excitatory neurotransmitter in the brain. One of glutamate's receptors, the N-methyl-D-aspartic acid (NMDA) receptor, is inhibited by alcohol, and increasing sensitivity may account for some of the symptoms of alcohol withdrawal, such as seizures and hyperexcitability.

Another possible mechanism may lie in the opiate receptors. Naltrexone, a known opiate antagonist, has been used successfully in treating some of the symptoms that lead to alcoholic relapse, suggesting that alcohol shares a similar action to the opiates.

Sedatives and tranquilizers

As their names suggest, the sedatives and tranquilizers are another group of central nervous system depressants. Chief among this group are the benzodiazepines and the barbiturates. These drugs interact with GABA receptors to reduce the brain's electrical activity, particularly the circuits responsible for wakefulness. Depending on the dose and the drug used, this class of drugs can be used to treat a range of medical symptoms from mild anxiety to panic attacks, epileptic seizures, and sleep disorders. These drugs are rarely used for their own effects; instead they are used to counteract stimulants or the withdrawal effects of opiates.

Continuous use of sedatives can lead to tolerance of their effects, which may prompt users to increase the dosage. With barbiturates, increased dosage can result in a lowering of the toxicity threshold, and many people have died accidentally as a result of respiratory depression. Benzodiazepines are much safer and less likely to be abused, but can still be lethal when taken in combination with alcohol or opioids.

Many people using sedatives become dependent rather than addicted and show withdrawal symptoms if medication is stopped abruptly. For this reason, use is reduced gradually over a long period. Symptoms include insomnia, tremors, excitability, and in the case of sudden stoppage, seizures or convulsions.

Opioids

The opioids are a family of compounds derived from the juice of the opium poppy seedhead. The natural compounds found in the juice, including morphine and codeine, are generally referred to as opiates,

Cocaine's powerful stimulatory effects have made it a popular drug with people who like to party and who use it to provide energy and euphoria.

irritability, goose bumps, and tremors, accompanied by nausea, diarrhea, depression, and muscle spasms and seizures. It is the unpleasant nature of withdrawal that makes opioid users reluctant to quit. Untreated, withdrawal usually lasts about seven to ten days. Methadone, a less potent but longer acting opioid, is often used to treat patients with an addiction to morphine or heroin, as its withdrawal symptoms are milder. If necessary, patients can be maintained on methadone indefinitely.

Stimulants

Drugs classed as stimulants have a common range of efffects including elevation of mood, euphoria, and increased alertness and energy. Among the more popular stimulants are caffeine, cocaine, and the amphetamine family. Caffeine is a legal substance in all parts of the world and is found in a wide range of beverages, such as tea, coffee, and cola drinks. It begins to reach the body tissues within five minutes of ingestion and produces a number of mild changes in the metabolism, including increased temperature, breathing, urination, and levels of fatty acids in the blood. In the brain, caffeine enhances mental alertness and decreases fatigue and drowsiness. With larger doses, headaches, insomnia, restlessness, and an abnormally rapid heartbeat can result. Unlike some of the stronger stimulants, caffeine's long-term effects are relatively minor, but physical dependence can develop to regular intakes of more than 350 milligrams per day (three or four cups of coffee), and interrupting use can produce withdrawal symptoms of severe headache, tiredness, irritability, and anxiety.

Cocaine is much more powerful than caffeine in its stimulant effects. These appear very quickly after it is taken into the body, chiefly as a feeling of acute pleasure and euphoria. This feeling can be accompanied by talkativeness, energy, and improved mental agility, although some users experience anxiety, panic, or depression. Physically, the heart rate accelerates, and temperature and blood pressure increase. Higher doses, especially when the drug is taken as part of a binge, can cause sharp mood swings, twitching, blurred vision, chest pains, convulsions, and even coma. With long-term exposure to cocaine, achieving euphoria becomes more difficult, and users may instead develop restlessness, excitability, paranoia, hallucinations, and delusions. Psychologi-

whereas the artificial morphine derivatives, such as heroin and fentanyl, are known as opioids, although the latter term is also used for the whole family. The opioids are powerful painkillers and anesthetics. Their effects are produced by binding to specific opiate receptors in the brain that stimulate the production of dopamine. Dopamine is the neurotransmitter associated with the pleasurable sensations experienced in the limbic system of the brain.

When an opioid is taken into the body, particularly by a fast method of administration such as smoking or injection, an intense warm sensation spreads through the body, lasting around one minute. This initial "kick" is followed by a dreamlike state, or high, that may last for several hours. Continuous use of opioids can lead to the rapid development of tolerance to their effects—part of the reason they are highly addictive substances.

Suddenly stopping opioid use results in the onset of withdrawal symptoms that vary in severity according to the type of substance and the individual. During the first 12 hours of withdrawal, the user may have a chronic runny nose and watery eyes and may sweat excessively. The syndrome progresses and intensifies with feelings of restlessness and cal dependence to cocaine manifests itself as powerful cravings that are satisfied only by taking more of the drug. Abrupt withdrawal results in a "crash," followed by anxiety, insomnia, and depression.

Amphetamines and related substances, such as Ecstasy, methamphetamine, and Ritalin, have subjective and physiological effects similar to cocaine. Long-term heavy users can develop a psychosis resembling paranoid schizophrenia and become violent and irrational. Users often turn to depressant drugs to combat these effects, resulting in a cycle of "uppers and downers" and dependence on both types of drug.

Stimulants increase the amount of dopamine in various parts of the brain, particularly the limbic and cortical regions. They prevent the reuptake (reabsorption) of dopamine into the neurons by blocking the mechanism by which it is transported. This blockade results in large amounts of dopamine in the spaces between the neurons, which continue to be stimulated until the dopamine is broken down. However, because the dopamine is not reabsorbed, the neurons become depleted and cannot respond as quickly to new nerve impulses. This depletion causes the crash and results in feelings of depression. With amphetamines and methamphetamine, the neurons may be damaged permanently.

Smoking is one of the fastest ways to deliver a drug to the brain, as the vapor is rapidly absorbed into the bloodstream from the lungs.

Inhalants

Inhalants are gases or solvents that are breathed into the body through the nose or mouth. Among the substances generally described as inhalants are anesthetics, glues, paint thinners and strippers, gasoline and lighter fuel, felt-tip pens, and nail polish remover. Inhalants enter the bloodstream very quickly via the lungs and are then transported to the brain and liver. Initial feelings of euphoria are accompanied by exhilaration, lightheadedness, and vivid hallucinations. These sensations last only a few minutes, so users seek to maintain the high by inhaling repeatedly for several hours. Physically, inhalants can cause coughing and sneezing, nausea, muscle weakness, and slow reflexes. A particular danger is the delusion that the user is invincible, which can lead to reckless behaviors. In the long term, continued exposure to inhalants produces weight loss, bloodshot eyes, nosebleeds, tremors, depression, confusion, and paranoia.

Because inhalants have different constituents, they vary in their action on the brain. Most depress the central nervous system and can induce anesthesia and unconsciousness when large amounts are inhaled. As with other drugs that depress the CNS, inhalants affect the dopamine system, which is responsible for pleasurable feelings. By contrast, the alkyl nitrates dilate the blood vessels and increase the heart rate. Nitrates are believed to enhance sexual performance and are abused for the feelings of heat and excitement they produce rather than any intoxicating effects.

Inhalants are highly toxic and can cause long-term, irreversible damage to the brain and nervous system, kidneys, liver, and lungs. The heart can also be damaged. Prolonged sessions can result in sudden sniffing death, in which the heartbeat becomes irregular and then stops within minutes of inhalation.

Nicotine

Nicotine is a highly addictive drug found in tobacco. Inhaling the smoke from cigarettes or cigars is an efficient method of delivering nicotine to the bloodstream, enabling it to impact the brain within seconds. The kick that is experienced is caused by nicotine stimulating the adrenal glands to produce epinephrine, which increases the heart rate and blood pressure. The initial stimulant effect is followed by pleasurable feelings as nicotine indirectly prompts a

Research into cannabinoids suggest that there may be specific receptors for these compounds in the brain. Substances related to cannabinoids have also been found in chocolate.

release of dopamine into the limbic system of the brain. Some people experience a sedative effect instead. Nicotine also interacts with receptors in the acetylcholine neurotransmission system, which is thought to trigger the craving to smoke.

Regular smokers find that smoking makes them feel mentally alert and reduces feelings of irritability or aggression. Women especially may smoke because nicotine decreases weight gain by depressing appetite, which in itself acts as an incentive to keep smoking. However, because nicotine's subjective effects wear off within minutes, smokers must take in regular doses throughout the day to maintain its pleasurable effects and prevent withdrawal symptoms from appearing. Withdrawal is characterized by feelings of irritability, poor sleeping patterns, increased appetite, and lack of concentration. The craving to smoke is very strong and can last for six months or more. During this time, anything that a user associates with smoking, such as the sight or smell of a cigarette, or a situation in which the user habitually smokes, can trigger craving. While the physiological symptoms can be helped by the use of nicotine patches or gum, cravings for the drug persist.

The link between smoking and coronary heart disease is well established. Smokers typically risk

heart attacks, strokes, and vascular diseases as a result of their habit. Smoking is also responsible for 90 percent of all lung cancer cases and is associated with a host of other lung problems, including bronchitis, emphysema (acute shortness of breath), and asthma attacks. Nicotine is extremely toxic at high doses and is used as an insecticide. Poisoning by accidental ingestion can result in convulsions, vomiting, and death from paralysis of the lungs.

Cannabinoids

Chief among the group of compounds known as the cannabinoids is tetrahydrocannabinol (THC), which is the main active ingredient in marijuana leaves and flowers. Little is known about exactly how the cannabinoids impact the brain, but the discovery of natural cannabinoids in the body suggests that there may be specific receptors for these chemicals or that they affect known receptors in a particular way.

Marijuana is usually smoked or eaten. Feelings of euphoria and relaxation are the immediate effects, but they are accompanied by a lack of coordination and short-term memory loss. At higher doses or with prolonged use, feelings of mellowness are replaced by increasing incidence of anxiety, paranoia, and hallucinations, and it becomes harder to achieve a high. Regular use of marijuana can produce the symptoms of amotivational syndrome, in which apathy, loss of interest in personal regard and achievement, and impaired judgment are prevalent.

Marijuana is addictive, and tolerance to the drug's negative effects can develop. However, withdrawal is mild compared with other drugs. Symptoms range across feelings of restlessness and irritability, chills, sleeping problems, and weight loss.

Hallucinogens

The hallucinogens are a wide group of compounds that are taken to change the user's mental state. Many are natural substances obtained from plants; others are synthetic and have been designed to create specific effects. Among the natural compounds are mescaline, psilocybin, dimethyltryptamine (DMT), and ibogaine. Synthetics include LSD and the designer phenethylamines, such as Nexus and 2C-I. Most hallucinogens have a chemical structure similar to serotonin and produce their effects by disrupting the brain's serotonin system. These effects can vary from mild distortions in the user's perception of reality to visions, heightened awareness of sounds or colors, and ecstasy. However, these effects can depend on a variety of factors, including frequency of use, the emotional state of the user, and the amount taken. Reactions to this class of drugs can change each time the drug is used and may be unpredictable. If the user is relaxed and in a good mood, the effects may be pleasant; if tense or anxious, the experience may be disturbing and even terrifying. Hallucinations are most likely to occur at high doses.

Physically, the hallucinogens produce symptoms that include increased heart rate and blood pressure, sweating, headache, nausea, dizziness, tremors, and numbness. Tolerance can develop within days, but the hallucinogens do not appear to cause physical dependence, although some users become psychologically dependent. Regular users of this type of drug prefer to space out their "trips" to prevent tolerance from developing. Unlike other types of abused drugs, the hallucinogens produce no obvious withdrawal symptoms. However, users may experience unexpected flashbacks years after use has ceased. Another long-term effect, particularly with LSD use, is persistent psychosis. Symptoms range from acute mood swings to mania, depression, hallucinations, and vivid visual disturbances.

Dissociatives

The dissociatives are a diverse group of substances that include the opiate dextromethorphan (DXM), and the anesthetics ketamine, nitrous oxide, and phencyclidine (PCP). Dissociatives, so-called because of the out-of-body effect they produce, are some of the most dangerous drugs used illicitly. Most have a restricted use as surgical and veterinary anesthetics, but DXM is a common ingredient in cough medicines. All the dissociatives work by blocking the NMDA (N-methyl-D-aspartic acid) receptors, which usually attach the excitatory neurotransmitter glutamate. By doing so, the dissociatives block the body's response to pain and affect cognition and emotion.

PCP is the most potent of the dissociatives, but its effects are also the most unpredictable. Onset begins within seconds if the drug is smoked, and at low doses induces rapid increases in temperature, heart rate, and breathing. Doses above 10 milligrams cause

blurring of vision, nausea, and muscle contractions that lead to uncoordinated movement. Very high doses can result in convulsions, coma, and death. PCP users report feeling detached from reality and can experience feelings of panic and anxiety. Some may feel invincible and perform risky actions. Others become violent or suicidal. Reactions to ketamine are similar and have been likened to a near-death experience, often referred to as "being stuck in a K-hole." DXM is the least potent, and the effects plateau with increasing doses, ranging from mild stimulation and distorted visuals to a complete out-of-body sensation.

Heavy use of dissociatives is very dangerous, as the affected neurons become unable to repair themselves and die, which can result in permanent brain damage. Some people feel jolts when they move their eyes, and there is a high risk of seizures. Addiction to dissociatives is largely psychological. However, some users suffer withdrawal symptoms if use is stopped, suggesting that physical dependence may also occur.

Anabolic steroids

The anabolic steroids differ from the substances described above in that they are not abused for the effect they have on the brain but to build up muscle and improve performance in sports. Steroid abuse is habit forming and predominant among men, but it is increasing among young women. Anabolic steroids are synthetic substances related to the male hormone testosterone. Users take these drugs in cycles that they believe cause more muscle to be built. Physically, steroids upset the hormone balance, causing acne, aggression, baldness, breast development, and shrinking of the testicles in men. Steroid use by adolescents can also stunt growth. Users are at great risk of heart attacks and strokes through the buildup of cholesterol in the blood, and they can also suffer from cysts and tumors in the liver.

W. A. HORAN

SEE ALSO:

Alcohol • Amphetamines • Anabolic Steroids • Barbiturates • Benzodiazepines • Cocaine • DXM • Hallucinogens • Inhalants • Ketamine • LSD • Marijuana • Nicotine • Opiates and Opioids • PCP • Plant-Based Drugs • Sedatives and Hypnotics

Clonidine

Clonidine is a drug that can control the release of the neurotransmitter norepinephrine from neurons. This property makes clonidine useful in treating some of the symptoms of opiate withdrawal.

Clonidine is a drug used in the treatment of opiate addictions to alleviate certain withdrawal symptoms. When combined with the opioid antagonist naltrexone, clonidine can be used to shorten the period of detoxification and reduce the incidence of cramps, sweating, and high blood pressure.

Clonidine is an interesting drug because it was one of the compounds used to define a novel receptor, the alpha$_2$-adrenoceptor, which significantly altered the thinking about how chemical neurotransmission works. Norepinephrine as well as other alpha-adrenoceptor agonists are able to inhibit the release of norepinephrine from neurons, whereas alpha-adrenoceptor antagonists increase the release. This discovery was the first clear example of a neurotransmitter modifying its own release by using a type of feedback control to prevent excessive neurotransmitter release when neurons are firing rapidly. Because the norepinephrine was controlling its own release, the receptor was termed an autoreceptor, and because the receptor was present on the neurons releasing the neurotransmitter, the receptor also became known as a presynaptic autoreceptor.

The behavior of this receptor was clearly different from the already known alpha-adrenoceptor found on the postsynaptic neuron; consequently the new autoreceptor was designated the alpha$_2$-adrenoceptor and the original alpha-adrenoceptor was designated the alpha$_1$-adrenoceptor. Clonidine is an agonist at the alpha$_2$-adrenoceptor (that is, it mimics the action of norepinephrine and therefore inhibits further norepinephrine release), while having no action at alpha$_1$-adrenoceptors. The concept of autoreceptors took time to gain acceptance, but many autoreceptors have since been discovered for other neurotransmitters.

Uses of clonidine

The first clinical use of clonidine related to its action on the cardiovascular system. Clonidine given orally produces a sustained decrease in blood pressure, and this effect has been used in the treatment of hypertension (high blood pressure). The site of action is the cardiovascular control center in the brain stem, where activation of alpha$_2$-adrenoceptors reduces the output of sympathetic nervous activity from the brain. The major disadvantages of clonidine are sedation and dry mouth. These symptoms initially affect about half the patients. Although symptoms may diminish after several weeks, some patients are unable to tolerate them. With the advent of newer treatments for lowering blood pressure that have fewer side effects, clonidine is rarely used for hypertension. Instead, clonidine is given in situations where a combination of sedation and antihypertensive effects can be used to advantage, for example, in patients undergoing intensive care. Clonidine has also been used as a preventive treatment against migraines but its effectiveness is doubtful.

The sedative and analgesic effects of clonidine have been used as a premedication before surgery, where it reduces the doses of anesthetic and analgesic agents required. Clonidine and opiate analgesics, such as morphine, produce additive analgesic effects by activating two separate receptor mechanisms, both of which suppress the transmission of pain impulses. The interaction of opiate and alpha$_2$-adrenoceptors is also used to treat opiate withdrawal in dependent individuals. One characteristic of opiate withdrawal is the effects it has on the sympathetic nervous system, which result in sweating, hypertension, nausea, vomiting, and increased heart rate. These symptoms are alleviated by clonidine. Clonidine has also been used to reduce the withdrawal effects of other drugs of dependence, including alcohol, nicotine, and cocaine. The drug has also been used in treating obsessive-compulsive symptoms, attention deficit disorder, mania, and other anxiety-related disorders.

R. W. HORTON

SEE ALSO:
Agonists and Antagonists • Drug Receptors • Heroin • Naltrexone

Club Drugs

Many young people regard the taking of mood-altering drugs as an essential part of a good night out. While drugs may seem to get the party spirit going, the ramifications of their effects may not be felt until years afterward.

The term *club drugs* refers not to a particular chemical or functional class of drugs but rather to those drugs commonly abused in dance clubs and at raves. The drugs themselves are diverse in terms of chemistry and pharmacology, as well as mental and emotional effects, but the grouping together of these drugs is useful because they are likely to be used within the same social and cultural milieu, often in combination, and by the same individuals. Because the club culture is by its nature looking for novelty, any list of club drugs rapidly becomes out-of-date and is therefore incomplete. However, several drugs are consistently included in any discussion of the subject. Those drugs are MDMA (Ecstasy), Rohypnol, methamphetamine, GHB, ketamine, and LSD. Until fairly recently, most of these drugs were viewed as acceptably safe by their users compared to drugs such as cocaine and heroin, which were abused by a previous generation of partygoers. However, the safety of the new generation of club drugs is no greater than that of the so-called hard drugs.

Trends in drug use

Drug use can be a fashion and, as such, has cycles. This is especially true of youth drug use, which tends to be more peer driven and excitement oriented than the drug use of the confirmed adult addict. It is instructive to recall that most users of cocaine in the 1960s and 1970s regarded it as a fairly safe drug, although by the late 1980s many were more wary. Most people were unaware that the same cycle of apparently harmless cocaine use, followed by burgeoning evidence of harm, began in the early 1900s and ended in the 1930s. Heroin followed a similar course, as have amphetamines, which were often the drug of choice of the postwar Beat generation but which had gained a bad reputation by the 1970s. MDMA, which might be said to be the prototypical club drug (it emerged at the same time as the birth of rave music in the 1980s), and GHB are newer drugs, but the cultural history of drug use

would suggest that they too will show problematic effects, as research has now begun to confirm.

MDMA—called 3,4-methylenedioxymethamphetamine by pharmacologists and "X," "rolls," "Ecstasy," or "E" by its users—is a modified amphetamine with some hallucinogenic properties. It is also referred to as an empathogen because of the emotional and physical closeness that users often feel toward those around them. MDMA acts by increasing levels of serotonin and dopamine in the brain, which in turn produce feelings of increased well-being and euphoria in users. On the negative side, users have arrived at hospitals suffering from seizures and hyperthermia as well as kidney and heart failure. Ecstasy has been associated with thousands of visits to emergency rooms in the United States over the past decade or so of use and several hundred deaths. Studies in animals have shown that even moderate exposure can destroy the neurons responsible for the manufacture of serotonin and dopamine, and a growing body of evidence suggests that human users may be burdening themselves with long-term mental and emotional deficits. Methamphetamine (meth, speed, or crystal) is chemically similar to MDMA, but its effects are more restricted to the neurochemical dopamine, which produces an alert, euphoric state lasting several hours. Long-term use can produce addiction, neurotoxicity, and psychosis, as well as cardiovascular and liver damage.

Dance-floor dangers

Rohypnol, or roofies, and other drugs of the benzodiazepine class, such as Xanax or Valium, have legitimate medical uses as treatments for anxiety and for sedation. As recreational drugs they have gained a reputation as "date-rape drugs" because of their ability to sedate and cause blackouts and memory loss in their victims. When combined with alcohol, these effects are even more pronounced and can progress to unconsciousness, respiratory depression, and death. These drugs also share with alcohol an association with increased violence in some users.

Taking drugs to enhance moods and feelings is a key element of the club experience for some clubbers.

GHB, or gamma-hydroxybutyrate, and analogs such as GBL (gamma-butyrolactone) and 1,4-butanediol have also been used as a chemical aid to sexual assault. GHB is more commonly used for its euphoric and sedative effects and as an anabolic aid in body building. GHB is known to increase the risk of seizures, especially when combined with amphetamines. By itself or in combination with alcohol, it can cause unconsciousness and, in some cases, death. Studies have shown that as many as half of GHB users have overdosed, and even first-time users have died from GHB ingestion. GHB also produces rapid dependence in some users, with profound withdrawal symptoms, much like the delirium tremens of alcohol withdrawal.

Ketamine, or special K, is a dissociative anesthetic used in animals and humans. Ketamine works in essentially the same way as PCP, or angel dust. Both drugs can produce a state similar to psychosis, including hallucinations and a dissociation from bodily sensations, which may make users ignore pain or danger. Higher doses can produce a near-deathlike experience (referred to as "being stuck in a K-hole") as well as vomiting, rapid heartbeat, and amnesia. Flashbacks seem to occur more commonly with ketamine than with other hallucinogens. While the long-term effects of ketamine in humans are unknown, in animal studies persistent cognitive problems have been observed.

LSD, lysergic acid diethylamide, or simply acid, is perhaps the best known of the hallucinogenic or psychedelic drugs, although it has been little studied owing to restrictions placed on its use by most governments. First popular in the 1960s, LSD is an extremely potent drug: less than 0.1 milligrams is required to produce its effects of perceptual and mood alteration. These effects may be frightening or unpleasant to many users, resulting in "bad trips" that may cause users to panic or injure themselves. LSD also produces hallucinogen perceptual disorder, or flashbacks, like many other hallucinogens. Few other long-term effects can be definitively associated with LSD use, although more research is needed before this can be stated with certainty.

Future of club drugs
Club drugs are beginning to lose some of their aura of harmless fun as more research is done and public awareness of adverse consequences increases. These drugs are likely to be used for some time to come, however, often in combination with one another as well as with nicotine and alcohol, leading to any number of possible outcomes. Given the probable long-term effects of some club drugs, it is also likely that some veterans of the club scene may eventually find themselves frequenting psychiatric clinics, though like many participants in previous waves of drug use, most will probably move on to more moderate pastimes.

R. G. Hunter

See also:
Designer Drugs • Ecstasy • GHB • Ketamine • LSD • Methamphetamine • Rohypnol

Cocaethylene

The human liver produces cocaethylene whenever cocaine and alcohol are taken together. Cocaethylene has a stimulant action similar to that of cocaine but acts for a longer period and is a possible factor in deaths by sudden heart failure.

cocaine   + C_2H_5OH (in the liver)   cocaethylene

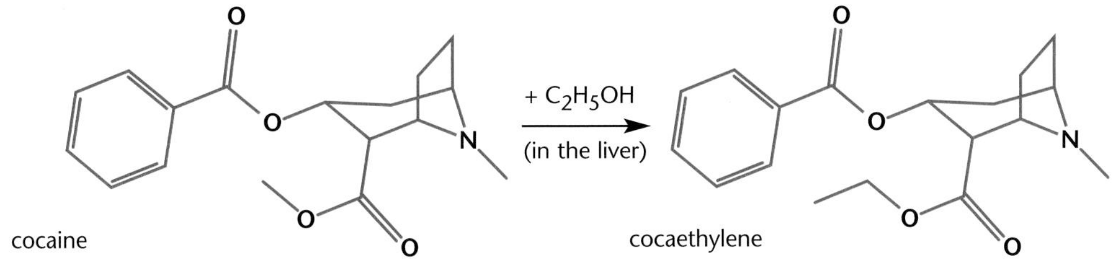

In the liver, cocaine is transformed into cocaethylene by an enzyme that replaces a methyl group (CH_3) with an ethyl group (C_2H_5) from ethanol (C_2H_5OH). Addition of an ethyl group changes cocaine's effect on neurotransmitter transporter systems and can increase the risk of sudden death.

Many recreational drug users take combinations of drugs with the intention of playing the effects of one against those of another. The combination of alcohol and cocaine is popular, with alcohol reducing the edginess of a cocaine high or cocaine putting off the stupor of an alcoholic binge. The same combination is also a risky one, however, being implicated in a large proportion of drug-related deaths by sudden heart failure.

In 1990 toxicologists at the Medical Examiner's Department of Miami-Dade County, Florida, found that 62 percent of cocaine-using sudden-death victims had the compound cocaethylene in their liver and brain tissues and blood. It was notable that some of those victims whose samples contained cocaethylene had taken less cocaine than would normally be expected to cause heart failure.

On hearing about the discovery at the morgue, researchers at the University of Miami School of Medicine set about exploring the action of cocaethylene on neurotransmitter (chemical messenger) systems in the brain. They found that, like cocaine, cocaethylene blocks the reabsorption of dopamine from the synapses (spaces) between neurons. The accumulation of dopamine that results causes a pleasurable rush and can lead to dependency on cocaine.

Unlike cocaine, cocaethylene fails to block the reuptake of serotonin, probably because the ethyl group prevents it from attaching to the transporter proteins responsible for serotonin reuptake. Since serotonin in synapses moderates the effects of dopamine, the fact that cocaethylene has little impact on serotonin reuptake makes it a potential cause of heart failure. Cocaethylene also blocks the action of acetylcholine at muscarinic receptors, and drugs that do this cause irregularities of heart rhythms.

A third potential reason for cocaethylene fatalities is the longer period of action of cocaethylene relative to cocaine. Whereas the blood concentration of cocaine halves after around 45 minutes, cocaethylene takes around 2.5 hours to fall by 50 percent.

Cocaine and cocaethylene each contain two ester linkages (–CO–O–), and one or both of these linkages must be broken to form inactive metabolites that the body can then eliminate. It seems that the presence of ethanol (alcohol) inhibits the enzymes that promote this process, thus maintaining the concentration of cocaine. Enzymes in the liver form cocaethylene by replacing the methyl group in cocaine with an ethyl group from ethanol. This change makes cocaethylene difficult to break down by other enzymes, so prolonging its action.

M. Clowes

SEE ALSO:

Acetylcholine • Alcohol • Cocaine • Crack Cocaine • Dopamine • Ethanol • Metabolism • Potentiation • Serotonin

Cocaine

Cocaine is a highly addictive and widely used stimulant drug derived from the leaves of the coca plant. Although the drug produces pleasurable feelings, it also has a range of harmful effects on the body and mind.

Cocaine is a central-nervous-system stimulant that produces feelings of euphoria and excitement and increased motor activity. However, it is also a powerfully addictive substance that has deleterious effects on the brain and emotions. Cocaine was first extracted from leaves of *Erythroxylon coca*, a plant widely cultivated in Bolivia, Peru, Ecuador, and Colombia. Evidence of cocaine use has been found in Chilean mummies dating from 2000 BCE to 1500 CE. Cocaine is classified as a Schedule II drug in the United States, owing to its high potential for abuse, but medical personnel may administer it for legitimate medical uses such as local anesthesia for minor surgery.

How cocaine is used

There are four basic routes of cocaine administration and intoxication:

Oral. Traditionally, coca leaves have been chewed for social, medicinal, and religious purposes. Native South Americans who live in the foothills of the Andes chew coca leaves to relieve the negative effects of high altitude and provide energy for daily work.

Intranasal. Snorting is a process of inhaling cocaine powder through the nostrils, where it is rapidly absorbed into the bloodstream through the nasal tissues. Cocaine is inhaled in the form of cocaine hydrochloride, a white crystalline powder that has a bitter taste and numbs the tissues.

Intravenous. Injecting cocaine involves using a needle to release the drug into the bloodstream. The onset of the drug's effects is so instantaneous that in the case of an overdose the person may experience a heart attack or seizure with the needle still attached to the vein.

Inhalation. Smoking involves inhaling cocaine vapors that enter the lungs, from where absorption into the bloodstream is rapid. *Freebasing* is the term used for smoking purified cocaine, of which crack cocaine is one form. Smoking allows extremely high doses of cocaine to reach the brain within seconds and delivers intense but brief feelings of pleasure followed by a depressive mood.

In the early 1900s, cocaine was an ingredient in numerous elixirs and tonics.

Pharmacology of cocaine

Cocaine is metabolized (broken down) by enzymes in the blood and liver into nearly a dozen pharmacologically inactive substances (metabolites), the most important being benzoylecgonine, ecgonine, and ecgonine methyl ester. Norcocaine is the active metabolite of cocaine and produces similar effects in the body. Approximately 20 percent of the drug is excreted unchanged into the urine. Both cocaine and its metabolites may be detected in urine up to 15 days after last administration by a chronic user.

Different routes of consumption of cocaine produce different patterns and levels of cocaine concentrations in the blood. The most rapid absorption and the highest blood concentrations of cocaine are obtained following intravenous injection and smoking. The rate by which cocaine is cleared from the blood varies considerably among individuals. The estimates of elimination of cocaine, measured by its half-life, the time required for the plasma concentration of cocaine to decrease by half, range from 16 to 90 minutes. Rapid elimination of cocaine may explain the intense craving to repeat the drug experience after a single intravenous or smoked dose of cocaine.

Mechanism of action

Cocaine's principal mode of action is to block transporter proteins in the brain. The transporters operate like pumps that allow neurotransmitters to go in and out of the neurons. Cocaine blocks transporters responsible for reuptake, or return, of serotonin, norepinephrine, and most important, dopamine to the neurons. Dopamine is the brain chemical that makes humans feel pleasure. In the normal communication process, dopamine is released by neurons into the synapse (the space between adjoining neurons) and then recycled back into the transmitting neuron by dopamine transporters. Cocaine interferes with this process and prevents the neuron from reabsorbing dopamine, thus producing an increase in the amount of dopamine present in the synapse. While the resulting overload of dopamine produces feelings of extreme euphoria, the inability of the brain to reabsorb dopamine results in lower stocks in the neurons and is associated with the severe depressive mood that occurs after cocaine has been eliminated.

Research studies devoted to understanding the mechanisms by which cocaine produces euphoric feelings have demonstrated that all types of pleasurable stimuli, including food, water, sex, and many drugs of abuse, increase neuronal activity and dopamine levels in the region of the brain called the nucleus accumbens. When a pleasurable event takes place, it is accompanied by a large increase in the amount of dopamine in the nucleus accumbens. Likewise, when high doses of cocaine are taken via faster routes of administration, large quantities of released dopamine in the pleasure region produce vivid memories of euphoria from the drug. Because of its ability to imitate key pleasurable stimuli,

KEY FACTS

Classification
Schedule II (USA), Schedule I (Canada), Class A (UK), Schedule I (INCB). Stimulant.

Street names
Coke, Charlie, snow, Big C, flake, Bolivian marching powder, nose candy

Short-term effects
Euphoria, increased levels of energy, talkativeness, and mental alertness, although some people experience the opposite. Raises heart rate, temperature, and blood pressure. Large amounts can cause twitching, tremors, paranoia, restlessness, anxiety, and irritability.

Long-term effects
Highly addictive drug that can quickly lead to loss of control over how much is taken. Bingeing can lead to mood disorders, auditory hallucinations, irritability, paranoid psychosis. Risk of heart disease, stroke, seizures, and bowel gangrene.

Dangers
Risk of sudden death on first use or as a result of sensitization even to small doses. Intravenous users can experience severe allergic reactions. Mixing with alcohol is the most common form of multiple-drug-related death.

Signs of abuse
Short-lived periods of euphoria and alertness followed by dramatic changes in mood. Evident weight loss and malnourishment. Track marks in intravenous users or chronic runny nose and nosebleeds in inhalers.

cocaine "instructs" the brain to remember the experience as something worth pursuing, and cocaine is taken again and again. This compulsion to repeat the experience is the hook that catches the addict. As cocaine abuse continues over time, tolerance often develops, and higher doses and more frequent use of cocaine are necessary for the brain to

THE LURE OF COCAINE

Cocaine was regarded as a miracle drug of great medicinal value in the nineteenth century. Psychiatrists prescribed cocaine to relieve symptoms of depression and for the treatment of physical and psychological exhaustion. Cocaine was also prescribed as a substitution therapy for morphine addicts. Patent medicines such as Coca-Bola chewing gum and coca lozenges were very popular treatments for fatigue and exhaustion. A very fashionable method of cocaine consumption was in the form of wine. The even more potent cocaethylene was produced by mixing cocaine with ethyl alcohol. One famous cocaine wine was Vin Mariani, named after its developer, Angelo Mariani. When Mariani tried his wine on a depressed actress, she reportedly made a spectacular recovery. The Atlanta-born discoverer of cola drinks, John Pemberton, made yet another coca-based beverage. His original drink was based on Vin Mariani. However, during the alcohol prohibition era, Pemberton had to replace the wine in his recipe with sugar syrup. His "wine cola" became the world-famous Coca-Cola. Cocaine was removed from Coca-Cola in 1904. During the same period, cocaine was commonly used as a local anesthetic in dentistry and minor surgeries. However, it was soon replaced with less harmful but equally potent anesthetics, such as novocaine.

Cocaine's popularity peaked in the 1980s. Smoking crack cocaine was cheap, and it brought users immediate euphoria. In addition to smoking cocaine, millions of drug-naive Americans were introduced to "decocainized" coca tea from South America. The mixture, named "Maté de Coca," was advertised as "the divine and magic plant of the Incas." This tea possesses invigorating and mood-enhancing properties, but despite being "decocainized," the average bag of maté de coca contains 5 milligrams of cocaine.

experience the same amount of pleasure experienced during initial use. Cocaine addicts frequently increase the dose to intensify and prolong its euphoric effects. While tolerance to the high develops, some users may become more sensitive to cocaine's anesthetic and convulsant effects without increasing the dose taken. This increased sensitivity may explain sudden deaths occurring even after low doses of cocaine.

Effects of cocaine use

In the short term, cocaine produces subjective effects that can include euphoria, increased self-confidence, talkativeness and sociability, increased energy, heightened sexual interest, and extreme mental alertness. How long these immediate euphoric effects last depends upon the route of administration. The faster the absorption, the more intense the high and the shorter duration of action. The high from snorting is slow to begin but it can last up to 30 minutes, compared with that from smoking, which lasts only 5 to 10 minutes. The use of cocaine in a binge, when the drug is taken repeatedly and in increasingly higher doses, produces negative effects including irritability, exhaustion, incoherent speech, and delusion. Bingeing may lead to a state of paranoid psychosis, in which the individual loses touch with reality and experiences auditory hallucinations. The long-term use of cocaine can lead to addiction, irritability and mood disturbances, auditory hallucinations, paranoia, and restlessness.

Physiologically, the cocaine user may experience temporary relief of fatigue, increased heartbeat and blood pressure, constricted blood vessels, local anesthesia, increased temperature, and dilated pupils. Mentally, chronic cocaine use also leads to a reduction in performance for tasks requiring manual dexterity, memory, problem solving, and mathematical skills.

Addiction to cocaine

Scientific evidence suggests that the stimulant and addictive properties of cocaine are related to its ability to inhibit the reabsorption of dopamine by nerve cells. This mechanism also appears to be involved in the addictive properties of every other major drug of abuse. Cocaine, especially crack (freebase cocaine), can hook some users with their first experience of the drug. In scientific studies of addiction, when rats or monkeys are taught how to self-administer the drug, the animals will do virtually nothing else. They stop eating and sleeping, and they keep pushing the lever that delivers the drug as long as they are physically capable of doing so. Unlimited access to cocaine leads to death within a month.

The apparently compulsive nature of cocaine self-administration reflects its high addictive potential in both animals and humans. Even when the supply of cocaine is discontinued, animals become very excited at the sight of the lever associated with cocaine intake. This is termed an *addiction cue* and is commonly encountered in human addiction to cocaine. When a human cocaine addict encounters a cue associated with cocaine, such as a place, particular music, a crack pipe, or a hypodermic needle, he or she experiences an increase in heartbeat accompanied by feelings of intense craving and a compulsion to repeat the pleasurable experience. The stimulating effects of addiction cues and cocaine itself are powerfully reinforcing and compel addicts to seek cocaine.

Cocaine can exert toxic effects on the brain as well as on other organ systems. Several complications associated with cocaine abuse range from seizures to vascular disorders and intracerebral hemorrhage. Although these events lead to the death of brain cells, cocaine does not seem to damage neurons directly except at very high doses, as revealed by histological (microscopic) examination of cocaine-treated animals.

Medical consequences of cocaine use

The most frequent medical complication of cocaine use involves cardiovascular problems. Cocaine can produce chaotic heart rhythms, accelerated breathing, and an increase in blood pressure and body temperature. Physical symptoms such as blurred vision, muscle spasm, convulsions, and coma may also occur. Cocaine affects the respiratory system and produces chest pain and respiratory failure. Neurological effects include stroke, headaches, and seizures. Gastrointestinal complications can manifest as abdominal pain and nausea.

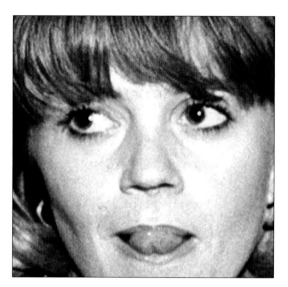

Snorting cocaine can dissolve the cartilage of the nose, which may require plastic surgery to repair.

Different routes of administration can produce different adverse effects. Ingested cocaine can produce bowel gangrene due to reduced blood flow. Snorting cocaine can lead to loss of smell, problems with swallowing, chronically inflamed runny nose, and damage to the septum (the cartilage that divides the nostrils). People who administer cocaine intravenously may experience kidney failure. Cocaine can disturb the menstrual cycle and produce reproductive system damage, leading to sexual dysfunction in both sexes. Cocaine taken during pregnancy can cause miscarriage, premature delivery, stillbirth, or low birth-weight babies.

Psychologically, use of cocaine has been linked to mood disorders, depression being the most commonly diagnosed coexisting condition. Cocaine addicts may develop depression due to physical and psychological damage associated with cocaine use, and patients suffering from depression may become addicted to cocaine to relieve depressive symptoms in an attempt to self-medicate. Research has demonstrated that therapy for the mood disorders alone has a positive effect on treatment of cocaine abuse.

A. VICENTIC

SEE ALSO:

Cocaethylene • Coca Leaf • Crack Cocaine • Dopamine

Coca Leaf

The coca plant is native to mountainous regions of South America, where its leaves have been chewed and made into tea for thousands of years. The leaves are a natural source of cocaine, which is highly addictive when refined.

The tropical shrub *Erythroxylon coca,* or coca, has vivid green leaves that resemble bay leaves, and small white flowers that give way to bright red berries once a year. Coca originated in the tropical reaches of the Andes Mountains in South America. The leaves of the coca plant contain numerous alkaloids, notably cocaine—a powerful stimulant.

Coca grows best in the warm, damp conditions of forest clearings, but the leaves grown in these sheltered conditions contain as little as 0.1 percent cocaine by weight. By contrast, leaves of plants grown on drier hillsides can contain 0.9 percent cocaine. The leaves are ready for harvesting when they snap on folding between the fingers.

Heritage

Coca has enormous significance in the culture and lives of the indigenous peoples of the Andes. Archaeologists have found evidence for at least 5,000 years of coca cultivation and use. For the Aymara-speaking peoples and Quechua of the region, coca is a sacred plant that carries the spirit of *mama coca.* As such, coca leaves are burned in offerings to the deities of Earth and Sun in religious practices that the Aymara inherited from the Tiahoanaco people and

that the Quechua inherited from their Inca forebears. Coca leaves also play traditional roles in the rites of local shamans, fortune tellers, and magicians.

Mama coca also has many practical virtues, which are now attributed to the nutritious and pharmacologically active contents of the coca leaf. The natives of the Andes have traditionally chewed coca leaves to boost their stamina for long treks and arduous labor at high altitude, and to stave off hunger and provide energy when food was unavailable. When Spanish invaders arrived in the sixteenth century, they tried to stamp out the use of coca, thinking it satanic because of its use in native religions. They soon changed their minds when they found that the forced laborers in gold and silver mines were less productive when deprived of coca.

In the 1860s, shortly after cocaine had been found to be largely responsible for the properties of coca, entrepreneurs and druggists started to use coca extract in various tonic preparations. One such preparation was Vin Mariani, a mixture of Bordeaux wine and coca extract that found favor in Europe and North America; another was Coca-Cola.

To this day, coca is legally marketed in Peru and Bolivia in products as diverse as tonic wines, tooth-

IS THERE COKE IN A COLA?

The best-selling soda in the United States takes its name from two psychoactive plant products: the coca leaf and the kola nut. Coca-Cola started out in 1886 as a general tonic and hangover remedy. Invented by Atlanta druggist John Pemberton (1831–1888), the original formulation was a sugar-based syrup whose ingredients included cocaine from the coca leaf, caffeine from the kola nut, and alcohol. A dose of syrup would be made up to 7 ounces (0.14 liters) by adding carbonated water from a soda fountain. Each glass contained around 9 milligrams of cocaine.

In 1887 U.S. drugstore owner Asa Candler (1851–1929) bought the formula and became the first president of the Coca-Cola Company. Being a teetotaller, Candler set about taming the formulation by drastically reducing its alcohol content and eventually using decocainated coca leaves. Historians believe that the inclusion of cocaine in Coca-Cola was abandoned in 1904, and in 1906 the absence of cocaine was confirmed when the Pure Food and Drugs Act required manufacturers to list habit-forming or otherwise harmful ingredients in their products.

pastes, and soothing ointments. The most widespread way of consuming coca is in the form of *maté,* a tea made by infusing boiling water with coca leaves. Visitors to La Paz International Airport are greeted with coca tea to help them avoid altitude sickness.

The chewing of coca leaves is also prevalent. The user first crushes one or two leaves between his or her teeth, then adds *llipta,* a pasty mix of cereal ash with salt or sugar or other flavorings. The user then rolls the mixture into a ball placed between the teeth and cheek and gradually sucks out the juice that forms.

Composition

Analysis of the coca leaf reveals it to be more nutritious weight-for-weight than staple foods such as cereals; this is somewhat misleading, however, since the coca leaf is only chewed and not swallowed, and the amount chewed by even a heavy user is much less than a typical portion of food. Nevertheless, the leaf and *llipta* contain vitamins and minerals, such as calcium, iron, and phosphorus, that are valuable supplements when food is lacking.

The principal effects of coca are due to its alkaloids, and the *llipta* encourages their absorption by making the saliva alkaline. Cocaine is one of these alkaloids; its stimulant and anesthetic properties boost endurance. Another is ecgonine, which maintains blood sugar levels by increasing the rate at which the body metabolizes carbohydrates—a process slowed by the lack of oxygen at high altitude. Globuline acts as a heart tonic, and inuline promotes the production of red blood cells. Other alkaloid effects open up airways and blood vessels. These actions explain how coca fights altitude sickness, which is caused by scarcity of oxygen.

Coca-based ointments take advantage of the analgesic-anesthetic effects of cocaine, cocamine, and conine and the skin-healing effects of benzoin and papain. Coca toothpaste helps prevent tooth decay by the presence of quinoline in coca extract.

Coca paste

The coca leaf products mentioned above are unlikely to cause dependence because the cocaine hit is so slow and mild. The story changes dramatically for *pasta de coca,* or coca paste—the product of the first stage in cocaine refining. This substance is highly addictive when smoked because of the intensity of the hit.

A farmer samples a coca leaf near La Paz, Bolivia. The crop goes to the production of coca tea, which helps drinkers endure life at high altitude.

Because the concentration of cocaine in coca leaves is low, it takes up to 1,100 pounds (500 kg) of leaves to produce 2.2 pounds (1 kg) of cocaine. The process starts by mashing the leaves by foot in a plastic tank with kerosene, acetone, and sulfuric acid. After several days of digestion in this way, filtration and evaporation produce a paste of cocaine sulfate with acid and kerosene. The first people to sample the paste are the workers, who smear it on cigarettes that they smoke to kill the pain of the ulcerated burns that the acid causes on their feet. They rapidly become dependent on the drug. The remaining paste goes to the slums of South America and to processing centers in Colombia, where clandestine operators convert it into pure cocaine hydrochloride.

M. CLOWES

SEE ALSO:
Cocaine • Crack Cocaine

Codeine

Codeine is an easily available pain relief product that can be misused, leading to drug dependency problems. Derived from the opium poppy, codeine is high on the list of abused over-the-counter and prescription drugs.

Codeine, or methyl morphine, is one of the most commonly used opiate agonists and is employed as a sedative and painkiller in both prescription and over-the-counter (OTC) pharmacy products throughout the world. Codeine produces its analgesic painkilling and sedative effects primarily by being converted to morphine by enzymes in the liver. The drug is present in the opium directly harvested from poppies but occurs at rather low concentrations of between 0.7 to 2.5 percent, depending on the source. Codeine was first isolated by the French chemist Pierre-Jean Robiquetin in 1832; its chemical formula is $C_{18}H_{21}NO_3$. Today, codeine is usually synthesized from morphine itself, by methylation of the 3-hydroxyl group on the second nonaromatic ring of the morphine molecule.

When injected intramuscularly or taken in tablet form as a sodium or phosphate salt, codeine produces an analgesic response of less than 10 percent that of morphine. Codeine is thus safer and less addictive than morphine, which has led to its widespread incorporation into prescription and OTC drugs used outside hospital settings, where it is used for mild-to-moderate pain, dry cough, and relief of diarrhea.

Codeine is a common ingredient of cough syrups and is frequently mixed with the nonnarcotic analgesics acetaminophen (paracetamol), aspirin, and ibuprofen, as well as caffeine, in prescription painkillers for headaches and muscle pain. While its dependency potential is moderately low, codeine-containing products are some of the most commonly abused prescription and OTC drugs and are usually the agents being referred to in media reports of individuals, often sports stars or actors, being addicted to prescription painkillers.

Process of addiction

As with all opiates, codeine prevents naturally produced endorphins from binding to the body's pain receptors. Constant exposure to opiates will eventually result in the body decreasing its own production of endorphins. With continued overuse

of the codeine product, lowered natural endorphin production results in "empty" pain receptors and heightened perception of pain. Increasing consumption of painkillers can then lead to physical and psychological dependency on codeine.

Habitual use of codeine can lead to a variety of ill-effects, including tolerance, addiction and dependency, headaches, nausea, liver malfunction, depression, constipation, and mood swings. Withdrawal can be difficult and is similar to the process required to reverse other opiate dependencies, such as heroin addiction. Unsupervised, overabrupt cessation of habitual codeine use can result in a milder form of cold turkey withdrawal than that associated with other opiate dependencies and can lead to *status epilepticus*, a syndrome involving successive violent fits.

D. E. Arnot

SEE ALSO:
Endorphins • Morphine • Opiates and Opioids • Pharmacy Drugs • Prescription Drugs

Cognitive Impairment

Drugs that affect the central nervous system have effects on the mind's thought processes. Some drugs have positive effects, but others produce temporary or permanent impairments in a variety of ways.

One of the consequences of using drugs or alcohol can be a general disruption of thought processes known as a cognitive impairment. This condition can include difficulties with such cognitive processes as memory, attention (ability to concentrate), motor (movement) control, planning ahead, ability to make decisions, and visual-spatial performance (locating and reacting to objects) in such tasks as driving an automobile or playing chess. Some drugs cause only temporary cognitive impairments that disappear as soon as the drugs wear off or shortly afterward, but drugs such as alcohol can produce long-term (and sometimes permanent) cognitive impairments that have a damaging effect on people's lives.

Types of cognitive effects

All drugs, by definition, have some effect on the body while they are present in a significant concentration. Drugs that work by affecting the central nervous system typically have cognitive effects (they alter the way people think). Stimulants such as the caffeine in coffee or the nicotine in cigarettes can help people to concentrate and think more clearly; these are short-term cognitive improvements. Other drugs such as alcohol, barbiturates (tranquilizers), and marijuana can produce short-term cognitive impairments. People who are under the influence of any of these drugs should not drive automobiles, because their ability to concentrate and motor control may be badly affected.

Alcohol and marijuana are among the drugs that can produce permanent cognitive impairments. Long-term, moderate-to-heavy alcohol use can lead to severely impaired memory, planning, problem-solving, and other cognitive impairments in a type of irreversible brain damage known as Wernicke-Korsakoff's syndrome (WKS). The poor memory and reduced attention span that marijuana users experience during intoxication are sometimes irreversible. Although these can become long-term cognitive impairments, they are usually much less severe than the problems caused by alcohol abuse.

Alcohol and marijuana have been used as drugs for thousands of years, and their cognitive effects are relatively well known. Newer drugs such as methamphetamines (fast-acting stimulant drugs) are much less clearly understood. The lasting effects of the club drug Ecstasy (3, 4-methylenedioxymethamphetamine, or MDMA) are not well understood, but they are believed to include moderate-to-long-term cognitive impairments such as memory problems and a greater risk of psychiatric problems such as mood disorders.

Not all drugs produce long-term cognitive impairments. Opiates and hallucinogenic drugs are believed to cause little or no cognitive damage. Some prescription drugs can actually cause long-term cognitive improvements, especially where they relieve the symptoms of psychiatric or neurological conditions. Some of the newer antipsychotic drugs that are used to treat schizophrenia, such as clozapine and risperidone, can produce dramatic long-term cognitive improvements. Older antipsychotic drugs, including neuroleptics such as haloperidol, do not have such beneficial effects.

Psychological tests can indicate cognitive problems with memory or learning among drug users.

While people can generally choose whether they want to risk the long-term cognitive impairments associated with such drugs as alcohol, the cognitive impairments produced by some essential medications are unavoidable side effects. People who suffer from bipolar disorder (manic-depressive psychosis) experience great swings in mood between mania (out-of-control, overexcited behavior) and depression (a debilitating mental illness characterized by profound feelings of sadness that sometimes lead to suicide). Unless they take regular doses of a mood-stabilizing drug such as lithium, they are unable to lead normal lives and are at a very high risk of committing suicide. However, the side effects of lithium include such cognitive impairments as forgetfulness, mental slowness, and poor coordination.

Drugs produce different cognitive impairments in different types of people. The elderly are typically more likely to experience cognitive impairments such as memory loss when they take tranquilizers. Drug-induced cognitive impairment in the elderly ranges from a type of acute confusion known as delirium, which often stops when the drug is discontinued, to a more permanent form of impairment called dementia. Adolescents may also be at higher risk of long-term cognitive impairment through repeated binge drinking or heavy marijuana use because their brains are still developing.

Causes and effects

Drugs can cause permanent cognitive impairments when they lead to irreversible changes in the brain's structure or mechanisms. Alcoholism can lead to various changes in the brain, including reduced blood flow, altered electrical activity, and reduced brain tissue. Damage is usually concentrated in the frontal cortex (the outer layer that controls cognitive functions) and cerebellum (a deeper structure in the brain that controls movement), which explains why alcoholics show a range of cognitive impairments and a type of poorly controlled, staggering movement sometimes known as cerebellar gait. Not all drugs cause cognitive impairments in the same way, however. Increasingly, studies of long-term Ecstasy users suggest that this drug can cause cognitive impairments by damaging neurons that transmit serotonin (a neurotransmitter that helps to regulate memory, sleep, pain, and moods).

Psychologists once believed that people become addicted to drugs because the brain's "pleasure centers" provide a reward for continuous drug use. In much the same way that a pigeon will learn to peck a lever constantly to obtain pellets of food, so humans can learn to take drugs continuously to ensure constant pleasure. This is termed a *behaviorist theory;* it assumes that people are compelled to take drugs by reasons that have nothing to do with rational thought processes. However, the use of brain imaging studies has revealed that some marijuana and cocaine addicts have damage to the frontal cortex of the brain and, as a result, are worse at making decisions and lack motivation. Some psychologists believe these cognitive impairments are a key cause of continued addiction, as well as one of its effects. Studies such as these suggest that theories of addiction must take into account cognitive processes as well as behavioral ones; in other words, how addicts think is just as important as how they behave.

Treating cognitive impairments

Some cognitive impairments disappear altogether or become less severe when the cause (the drugs or alcohol that produced the impairment) is removed. Alcoholics, for example, may find a steady improvement in their cognitive abilities for several months to a year after they stop drinking.

Not all cognitive impairments are reversible, however. People who suffer permanent brain damage through drug and alcohol abuse may have to learn coping strategies, such as writing things down to help them remember, or may become increasingly reliant on family and friends to help them with certain tasks. Behavioral problems linked to cognitive impairments can be improved with psychotherapies, such as cognitive behavior therapy. One of the biggest problems caused by cognitive impairments, however, is the way they can undermine this kind of therapy: people with impaired memories, planning skills, and motivation may have difficulty remembering their treatment and persevering through its course.

C. WOODFORD

SEE ALSO:
Central Nervous System

Controlled Substances

A controlled substance is a drug covered under the Controlled Substances Act (CSA), which is the basis for the U.S. government's classification of a drug as an illegal substance and the legal foundation of federal drug-law enforcement.

The Controlled Substances Act has its roots in the attempt to regulate the use and distribution of drugs in the early part of the twentieth century. Many drugs that are now illegal were once available in items that were easily obtained. The first real regulation of drugs in the United States took the form of legislation called the Harrison Narcotics Act of 1914, which was driven in part by American missionary groups in East Asia. The lobbying efforts to pass the legislation used racial prejudice and degrading stereotypes to persuade passage of the legislation. The Harrison Act was, at its core, a piece of tax legislation that authorized stiff penalties for nonprescribed medical use of cocaine. However, after 1914, treatment of addiction by prescription of cocaine was not deemed a legitimate medical use, and cocaine was made an illegal substance.

Other laws followed the Harrison Narcotics Act in response to newly perceived threats from marijuana and amphetamines. Significant increases in drug use in the 1960s and early 1970s led to the decriminalization of marijuana in some areas and inconsistencies in the legal drinking age. In attempting to adapt to changing perceptions of drugs, as well as to respond to their scientifically demonstrated dangers, 55 federal drug laws and numerous state laws enacted before the 1970s carried an inconsistent mixture of punishments that ranged from fines to the death penalty.

A system of classification

In order to structure drug enforcement law under a consistent set of penalties, the U.S. Congress passed the Comprehensive Drug Abuse Prevention and Control Act in 1970. All potentially dangerous drugs are now covered by a consistent legal policy governing manufacture and distribution, as well as the chemicals used in the production of controlled substances. The Controlled Substances Act (CSA), which is part of the Comprehensive Drug Abuse Prevention and Control Act, provides a classi-

fication of drugs according to their abuse and addiction potential, potential medical value, and danger. The drugs are grouped into categories called schedules, which rank from Schedule I (those drugs that are most addicting, dangerous, and with the least medical value) to Schedule V (the least addicting).

Adding and reassigning drugs

The CSA also provides a system of petition procedures for substances to be added to a schedule, transferred between schedules, and removed from a schedule. The Drug Enforcement Administration (DEA) is responsible for enforcing the controlled substances laws and regulations of the United States. The DEA will initiate an investigation of a drug either in response to a formal petition by private individuals or industry (for example, a drug company developing a new medicine), or in response to information received from the law enforcement community or from Health and Human Services (HHS), the principal agency charged with protecting the public health.

The evaluation of the petition requires the DEA to collect information about the drug from a number of sources, including the HHS. The HHS provides an evaluation of the biological effects of the drug, the potential medical uses of the substance, and its abuse potential. Part of this procedure involves soliciting the opinion of the National Institute on Drug Abuse (NIDA), one of the National Institutes of Health, which sponsors scientific research on the effect of drugs on human health. In addition, the opinion of the Food and Drug Administration (FDA) is also sought. The FDA, which is responsible for protecting public health by assuring the safety and effectiveness of drugs and medical devices, renders an opinion based on its body of expertise. The HHS may also obtain opinions from scientists and doctors outside these agencies.

After collecting the data and opinions of experts, the HHS makes a specific recommendation to the

DESIGNER DRUGS

Structural similarities explain how drugs fool the brain and illustrate how some criminals have tried to fool the Drug Enforcement Administration. Nearly all drugs that act on the brain affect nerve cells, often by mimicking chemicals (neurotransmitters) that brain cells use to communicate with one another. Neurotransmitters can be thought of as keys that fit a particular receptor, or lock, on the brain cell. On the left are two naturally occurring neurotransmitters, dopamine and norepinephrine. Many illicit drugs, known as analogs, because they have a similar structure, are able to act within particular pathways of the nervous system. Makers of designer drugs exploit this known chemical similarity by attempting to modify existing drugs to create new licit drugs that achieve similar effects on the brain. Drug enforcement agencies must constantly monitor the introduction of such drugs and assess whether they should be criminalized. Shown on the right is amphetamine and its chemically modified form, methamphetamine. The drug Ecstasy (not shown) is a modified form of methamphetamine that was synthesized in the 1950s. Ecstasy was criminalized in the United States in 1985.

dopamine

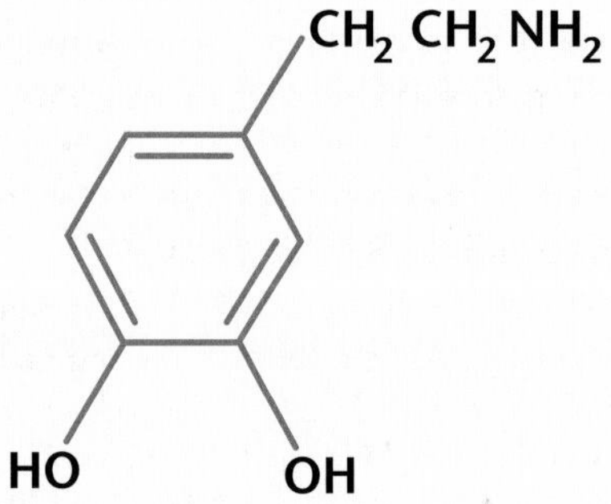

$CH_2 CH_2 NH_2$

HO   OH

amphetamine

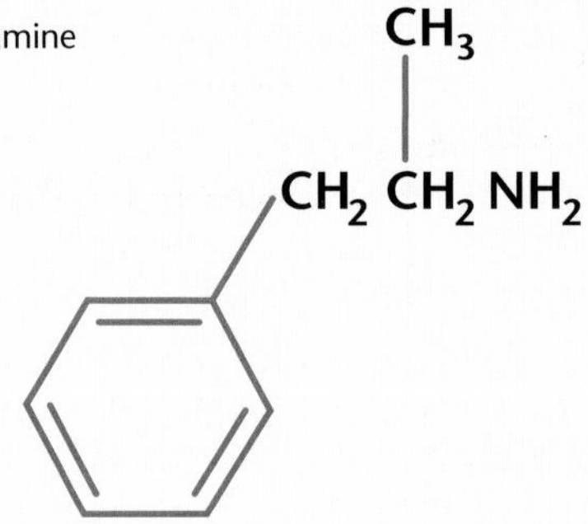

CH_3

$CH_2 CH_2 NH_2$

norepinephrine

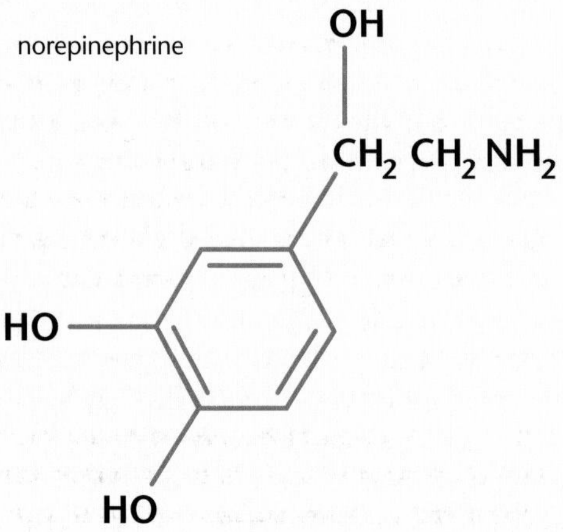

OH

$CH_2 CH_2 NH_2$

HO

HO

methamphetamine

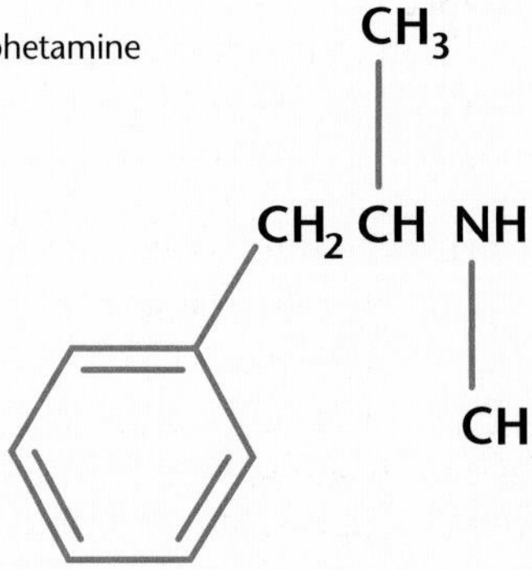

CH_3

$CH_2 CH NH$

CH_3

U.S. LAW CONTROLS DRUGS THROUGH FIVE SCHEDULES

Schedule I	Schedule II	Schedule III	Schedule IV	Schedule V
Beta-hydroxyfentanyl (China White)	Amphetamine	Amobarbital	Alprazolam	Codeine preparations— 200 mg/100 ml or
Codeine methylbromide	Coca leaves	Anabolic steroids	Barbital	100 gm
Gamma hydroxybutyric acid (GHB)	Cocaine	Barbituric acid derivatives	Butorphanol	(Robitussin A-C)
Heroin	Codeine	Dihydrotestosterone	Chlordiazepoxide	
Ibogaine	Methadone	Ketamine	Clonazepam	Difenoxin preparations
LSD	Methamphetamine	LSD precursors	Diazepam	
Marijuana	Methylphenidate	Testosterone	Fenfluramine	Opium preparations—
MDMA (Ecstasy)	Morphine		Flunitrazepam	100 mg/100ml or gm
Mescaline	Opium		Phenobarbital	(Parepectolin,
Peyote	Pentobarbital		Triazolam (Halcion)	Kapectolin PG)
	Phencyclidine (PCP)			

$\longleftrightarrow$

Most controlled, no medical use	Have approved medical uses but also have potential for addiction	Least controlled, some sold over the counter

This table shows representative drugs that are controlled according to specific schedules under the Controlled Substances Act. The above table represents the most commonly abused drugs found in the listed schedules.

DEA. This recommendation includes an evaluation of the medical and scientific issues related to the drug's safety, medical use, and addiction potential. The recommendation also specifies the schedule in which the drug should be placed (in the case of adding or transferring a drug), or whether the drug should be removed. HHS decisions are binding on the DEA. The DEA cannot control the drug if the HHS recommends against it.

Transfer procedures are an important feature of the CSA, because new data may require the addition or reassignment of new substances. Amphetamine and methamphetamine, for example, were transferred from Schedule III to Schedule II in 1971, and in the 1990s the narcotic analgesic butorphanol was removed, then rescheduled later in the decade. In 1995 Jon Gettman and *High Times Magazine* petitioned to move marijuana from Schedule I to a schedule where it may be prescribed by physicians for medical use. The petition was ultimately denied in 2001 by the DEA (this decision was published in the *Federal Register*, volume 66, page 20,038).

The CSA also prescribes a system of controls for the handling of scheduled drugs (the "Control" part of the CSA). Authorized persons, including physicians, pharmacists, veterinarians, researchers, and drug companies, must be registered by the DEA to handle controlled substances. Once registered, the registrant must keep accurate records of inventories and transactions involving the controlled drug, as well as being responsible for the secure storage of the drug. In Canada, the Controlled Drugs and Substances Act performs much the same function as the U.S. law but uses six schedules instead of five.

Designer drugs

Designer drugs are chemical modifications of a controlled substance, some of which were originally made to mimic the biological effects of other controlled substances in an attempt to bypass the enforcement laws. In the mid-1980s designer drugs were added to the list of controlled substances. One example of a designer drug is methamphetamine, which is an analog (a chemical that is structurally very similar to another chemical) of amphetamine. Designer drugs are formulated in illegal labs, with little attention to the safety or purity of the product. Consequently, such drugs can be highly toxic and their effects potentially deadly.

Penalties

The penalties for drug trafficking and possession of illicit drugs can be severe. The Controlled Substances Act categorizes the specific penalties according to the addictive nature of the drug, the amount of drug, and whether the offense is the first or second. Penalties for subsequent convictions are twice as severe. If death or serious injury results from the use of a controlled substance that has been illegally distributed, a person convicted on federal drug-distribution charges faces a mandatory life sentence and fines of up to $8 million. People convicted on federal charges of drug trafficking within 1,000 feet (300 m) of a school or university face penalties of prison terms and fines that are twice as high as the regular penalties for the offense, with a mandatory prison sentence of at least a year.

A federal conviction on charges of possessing any controlled substance can result in penalties of up to one year in prison and a mandatory fine of no less than $1,000, up to a maximum of $100,000. Second convictions are punishable by 15 days to 2 years in prison and a maximum fine of $2,500. Subsequent convictions are punishable by 90 days to 3 years in prison and a minimum fine of $5,000. Special provisions for possession of crack cocaine impose a mandatory prison sentence of between 5 and 20 years and a fine of up to $250,000.

International drug law

The CSA is part of a network of international drug regulations and laws. The United Nations International Drug Control Programme is part of the United Nations Office on Drugs and Crime (UNODC). The UNODC was established to enable the United Nations to provide the legal foundation for action against drug-related offenses. The three major international drug control treaties are the Single Convention on Narcotic Drugs of 1961 (amended in 1972); the 1971 Convention on Psychotropic Substances; and the United Nations Convention against the Illicit Traffic in Narcotic

Drugs and Psychotropic Substances, 1988. The United States, United Kingdom, Canada, and Mexico are all party to these treaties. Just as the CSA protects the use of substances that have medicinal and scientific value, in addition to regulating illicit trafficking and drug abuse, these UN conventions seek to ensure the availability of narcotic drugs and psychotropic substances for medical treatment and scientific research while preventing them from reaching illegal distribution. UNODC's Office of Treaty and Legal Affairs coordinates with member countries in their implementation of United Nations' treaties and resolutions, advises member countries on the drafting and adoption of drug control legislation, and assists governments in ratifying the international drug control conventions. The United Nations may also provide information that could influence the scheduling of substances in member countries. After discussing U.S. obligations to respond to scientific data reported by the United Nations as to the danger presented by a drug or substance, the CSA allows the United States the right to have the international status of a drug or substance reviewed and possibly amended.

The Controlled Substances Act lies at the core of the efforts by the federal government to strike a balance between the need to prevent illicit drugs from falling into the hands of drug abusers, and the legitimate need for some of these scheduled substances in a medical or research context. There are ongoing debates about whether certain substances should be included, and the scheduling provisions allow for transfer or removal of substances. There is also a significant decriminalization debate. Proponents of decriminalization argue that the money spent in enforcement efforts could be better used elsewhere. However, in 1999, the United States spent over $17 billion on drug control, including enforcement, prevention, education, and treatment—a fraction of the yearly costs resulting from the abuse of drugs and alcohol, which top $246 billion each year.

D. W. GODWIN

SEE ALSO:

Classification of Drugs ● Designer Drugs ● Drug Laws ● Legalization Movement ● Prohibition of Drugs

Crack Cocaine

Crack cocaine is an impure form of the freebase of cocaine. It is manufactured from powder cocaine by chemical transformation that makes it more volatile than cocaine. Crack smoking is a highly dependence-forming habit.

Crack or rock cocaine is quite a recent development in the cocaine trade, having been available on the streets only since around 1984. Prior to its introduction, the volume of the illegal cocaine trade had been dwindling. The more intense high of crack smoking compared with cocaine snorting reversed the trend and created a new type of addict with a strong craving for the drug and a determination to obtain supplies regardless of consequences.

There is a minor chemical difference between powder and crack cocaine that makes a big difference in how the two drugs are used. Powder cocaine is a hydrochloride—a salt formed by reacting cocaine alkaloid with hydrochloric acid. It vaporizes at 383°F (195°C) but also decomposes at that temperature. Crack cocaine contains the freebase of cocaine, rather than the salt, and this form of cocaine vaporizes at 208°F (98°C) with little decomposition.

Traffickers first produced freebase cocaine in the 1970s when checking the quality of their supplies. The process started by dissolving cocaine hydrochloride in water to leave behind any water-insoluble impurities. Addition of an alkali such as sodium hydroxide then produced water-insoluble base cocaine that was dissolved in ether to leave behind

This picture shows "rocks" of crack cocaine approximately 0.5 to 2 inches in width seized by agents of the U.S. Drug Enforcement Administration.

water-soluble impurities. Evaporating the ether solution yielded solid cocaine base without any other alkaloid impurity. Smoking the base in a pipe would then reveal the quality of the goods.

The procedure was risky, because ether is both volatile and highly flammable. Many accidental fires started as a result of clandestine freebase production. Freebase cocaine produced in this way was sold on the drug market for a while, but the risks inherent in its manufacture limited its availability.

Crack manufacture cuts the risk of fire and explosion by eliminating the flammable solvent. The alkali that converts the hydrochloride into freebase is baking soda (sodium bicarbonate, $NaHCO_3$) in water. Heating completes the reaction and then boils off the water to leave a solid that consists of freebase cocaine, sodium chloride from the acid-base reaction, and any remaining baking soda. The solid is then broken into lumps for sale without purification of the freebase. If the manufacturer wants to reduce the purity to increase profit, he or she simply adds an adulterant before the drying stage.

Crack users consume the drug by heating it in a pipe using a flame. The remaining baking soda crackles as it gives off carbon dioxide gas, and this is the origin of the name *crack*.

Crack and crime

Since its appearance on the illicit drug market, crack cocaine has been a major cause of concern for parents, drug workers, and authorities. The problem stems from the tendency of crack users to become aggressive and paranoid while high. These symptoms occur because cocaine blocks the reuptake of the

WHY IS CRACK SO ADDICTIVE?

When people use crack, the drug that gets them high is cocaine. It is exactly the same drug that produces a high when people snort "lines" of cocaine, and their bodies dispose of it in exactly the same way. Given these facts, it might seem odd to say that crack is more addictive than cocaine. In fact, it is more accurate to say that cocaine becomes much more addictive when smoked in the form of crack cocaine.

Inhalation of fumes or vapor is an extremely effective way of rapidly delivering any psychoactive drug to the brain and acts only marginally slower than intravenous injection. The inhaled drug passes readily through the lungs and into the bloodstream, then crosses the blood-brain barrier to work its effects on the brain. Inhalation delivers effects in a matter of seconds, and for this reason it has long been used to deliver nicotine from tobacco as well as for marijuana, opiates, and other drugs.

The rate of increase of the blood-cocaine concentration determines the intensity of the rush. In the case of crack smoking, the amount of cocaine in the bloodstream typically rockets to more than 900 micrograms per liter within a few seconds of inhaling the cocaine vapor. This rate of increase compares to a peak cocaine concentration of 150 to 200 micrograms per liter that occurs around 30 to 40 minutes after snorting powder cocaine.

These figures show why smoking crack produces a much more intense rush than snorting cocaine. Also, since cocaine acts on dopamine—the neurotransmitter most closely associated with euphoria—the rush is intensely pleasurable.

After either method of administration, the blood cocaine concentration halves every 45 minutes unless the user takes another dose. The stimulation of dopamine receptors diminishes with falling blood cocaine concentrations, and the result is a rapid "crash" back to normality. For crack users, the crash is so much more brutal when compared with the initial high that they are unlikely to resist smoking more crack as long as it is available.

With repeated crack use, the dopamine system becomes numb to abuse and the body gets rid of cocaine more rapidly. Maintaining a high becomes more and more difficult to achieve, so the frequency of crack smoking and the amount consumed tend to increase. If this happens, the crack user has become dependent on the drug.

neurotransmitters (chemical messengers in the brain) dopamine, norepinephrine, and serotonin. The action on the dopamine system produces the intense pleasure of the crack high (see box opposite), but the effects on the norepinephrine and serotonin systems fire up the fight-or-flight response and cause paranoia and lack of judgment. This combination of effects underlies the tendency to violence.

The need to acquire money to maintain a crack habit of typically $200 to $300 per week drives addicts to theft and prostitution. In some cases, a dependent user provides sexual services for money or crack in premises where dealing and consumption of the drug take place. These "crack houses" range in character from rooms in derelict buildings to rented units in otherwise respectable apartment buildings.

A second form of crack-related criminality stems from rivalry between suppliers. In major urban centers, the street-level suppliers are often members of organized gangs Members of these gangs resort to armed violence to defend and increase the territories in which they hold monopolies of crack sales. Victims of this violence include bystanders caught by stray bullets, law enforcers, and gang members themselves.

Crack-related gang violence reached its peak in cities such as New York and Los Angeles in the late 1980s and has since subsided there to some extent due to constant law-enforcement efforts. Monitoring such as the U.S. Drug Enforcement Administration's Pulse Check program show that the early 2000s saw a spread of the crack trade and associated gang violence to smaller cities and some rural areas of the United States.

Keeping perspective

The link between crack and the crime wave of the late 1980s and early 1990s provoked a strong reaction that verged on hysteria in some sectors of society. An extreme reaction is seldom a good way to address a problem, and it can distract from other emerging issues. For this reason, it is wise to view crack in the context of the drug scene as a whole.

There is no doubt that crack is highly addictive, but claims that a single crack experience will cause instant addiction are untrue and are also likely to enhance the appeal of the drug to a self-destructive rebel. A study of 308 established drug users in Miami found that 90 percent of them had tried crack, but

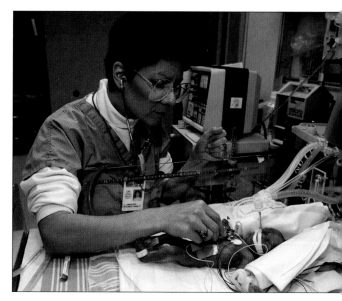

Babies born to crack-addicted mothers are often premature and may require a period of intensive care to overcome exposure to the drug.

only 29 percent used the drug on a daily basis and most of that subgroup took no more than one or two hits per day. A few individuals indulge in regular crack "runs" that can last days, and they are most likely to develop crack dependence in a short time.

In 2002 a National Institute on Drug Abuse survey of high school seniors revealed that 6.7 percent had tried methamphetamine compared with the 3.8 percent who had tried crack. Given that methamphetamine also gives an intense rush when smoked, it is potentially just as addictive as crack.

The notion of crack babies who are born addicted to crack is a myth. It is true that crack can cause complications in pregnancy, stillbirth, and premature birth of underweight babies. Also, a baby born to a crack-using mother will inevitably suffer disturbed sleeping and feeding patterns when cut off from the cocaine supply of its mother's blood, but these are short-lived effects, not signs of addiction. What is more important for the child's health is to protect it from exposure to cocaine fumes and from neglect or abuse due to crack use where it grows up.

M. CLOWES

SEE ALSO:
Cocaine • Methamphetamine

101

Cutting Drugs

Cutting is the mixing or diluting of a particular drug with another substance. It is usually carried out to add bulk to a drug and thus increase its cost, but drugs are also sometimes cut to enhance their effect.

The cutting, or adulteration, of street drugs happens when a manufacturer, trafficker, or dealer adds substances to the drug other than what the buyer might expect it to include. The other substances are generally cut (mixed) into the drug in such a way that the buyer will be unaware of the adulteration. For this process to be successful, substances that have a similar appearance, texture, and even taste may be used to disguise the fact that cutting has taken place. Consequently, rather than simply buying heroin, cocaine, or Ecstasy, users may in fact buy heroin plus one, two, or more other substances mixed in with the drug. Because of the lack of formal quality controls in the illicit drug marketplace, users cannot therefore be fully confident that what they are using is wholly or even partly the drug they thought it to be.

Why drugs are cut

The main reason that street drugs are cut relates to profit. If a seller has a kilo of cocaine and adds a kilo of another substance to it before selling it, effectively doubling the amount of drug, the seller can then double his or her profit. In the 1960s and 1970s this type of cutting seems to have taken place at each stage of the chain of distribution. In other words, an initial pure shipment of drugs would first be cut by the importer; whoever then bought the drugs would also cut the drugs before selling to others, and so on right down to the dealer on the street, who would again cut the drug before selling to the user. The extent to which drugs are cut may vary widely over time. In the 1960s in New York City, street-level heroin often consisted of little more than 3 percent heroin. Street-level heroin in New York in the 1990s and since has consisted of around 50 to 60 percent heroin.

Not all cutting is done purely for dilution purposes, however. Forensic research has found that some commonly added substances appear in relatively small proportions and can actually increase the potency of the drug being used. Whereas dilutants such as sugar reduce the quality of the drug, certain other additives, for example, strychnine, appear to be cut into drugs such as heroin to enhance the effect. It may also be the case that certain substances are cut into a drug because of the preference of users rather than for dilution purposes.

Substances used to cut drugs

Many different substances have been found cut into drugs. Some are active, such as quinine and caffeine, which are formally called adulterants; some are inactive, that is, they do not have any psychoactive effect, and these are known as diluents. The more inclusive term *cutting agents* encompasses both types.

In the United States the most common cutting agents found in heroin are various sugars, such as mannitol, lactose, dextrose, and glucose. Other cutting agents include starch, quinine, procaine, diphenhydramine, caffeine, and acetaminophen. By and large these substances are comparatively harmless (in relation to the drug itself) or are found in proportions that render them so. Some years ago the presence of the poison strychnine was common in a particular type of heroin known as Heroin No. 3, or China White, but it was not found at levels considered to be harmful, nor was it put there for increasing the product's bulk. It actually enhanced the product for heroin smokers (chasers) by increasing the amount of heroin available and thus added to rather than detracted from the heroin being sold. Similarly, quinine (a substance also currently added to some soft drinks such as tonic water) is added to heroin in the North American market, where its addition appears to relate to the preference of users who are familiar with the bitter taste it provides. Not including quinine as a cutting agent would for some users indicate less, not more, quality.

Although drugs in powder form, such as heroin and cocaine, are most commonly associated with cutting, drugs that come in tablet form, such as Ecstasy (MDMA), may also be cut with other, usually psychoactive, substances.

Incidence of cutting

In the 1960s and 1970s some drugs were cut so extensively that little of the actual drug was left. However, since the 1990s, largely due to increased and more open competition in the illicit drug market, much less cutting takes place. While some drugs have small amounts of other substances present prior to importation, forensic evidence reveals that much of the heroin that is sold in the United States, the United Kingdom, Australia, and many other markets is comparatively free of cutting agents. Although some cutting still takes place, it appears that drugs are not routinely cut at each stage of the chain of distribution. Many dealers argue that they would not cut the drugs they sell because of a desire to protect their reputation for selling quality drugs.

One factor that often confuses the issue of cutting relates to the way in which levels of purity are reported. If a heroin seizure is only 50 percent pure or even 30 percent pure it does not mean that the rest of the sample is made up of cutting agents. A sample of only 30 percent purity (particularly Mexican Brown Tar Heroin) may in fact have no cutting agents present at all. Poor manufacturing processes can result in a low concentration of pure heroin among high concentrations of impure by-products. Incorrect storage of the heroin can also lead to high levels of degradation and a consequent reduction in the diamorphine (heroin) content.

Dangerous drug adulteration

One of the commonplace beliefs about drug cutting is that dealers ruthlessly cut the drugs they sell with anything at hand, and that drugs therefore contain substances such as rat poison, scouring powders, talcum powder, brick dust, and even ground-down glass lightbulbs that will eventually kill the user. It is also assumed that this is a common, not rare, practice. A range of forensic and investigative research, however, has shown that this widely believed notion has almost no basis in fact. Analysis of seized drugs over many years and in a number of countries fails to reveal the presence of substances such as ground glass, scouring powders, and brick dust. Rat poison in the form of strychnine is sometimes used in small amounts in an effort to improve the quality of heroin. Substances that are found, such as talc and chalk, tend to be in relatively small quantities; thus it is unlikely they were used to dilute or add bulk. Talc and chalk are additives that are found in many over-the-counter drugs such as acetaminophen (paracetamol); since acetaminophen is a common cutting agent in heroin, the presence of talc and chalk in small amounts is most likely explained by their original inclusion in the acetaminophen. Talc, a natural product, is not the same as perfumed talcum powder, although the two are often confused. Overexposure to substances such as talc by intravenous drug users may cause significant harm over a number of years (talc can block the veins), but it does not seem to present itself as a consistent problem, especially when compared with the other dangers, such as infectious diseases or collapsed veins, associated with the injection of drugs.

There are also some logical reasons that dangerous drug adulteration is extremely rare, if indeed it even happens. Drug dealers rely on their clients for their income. There is little reason for them to endanger intentionally the lives of their customers, many of whom they know personally, when harmless additives are just as available and are often cheaper. Qualitative research has also found that drug dealers often are concerned about their reputation for selling quality drugs (which can sell for higher prices and attract repeat customers), that many are often fearful of their clients and as such would not risk upsetting them, and that they have alternative means to increase profit, such as selling in smaller units or selling a little under weight.

Occasionally the market sees the emergence of a drug combination that causes specific problems for the drug-using population. In the late 1990s in New York, the adulteration of heroin with a prescription drug (scopolamine) caused a number of fatal and nonfatal reactions. The occurrence itself, however, was very limited, and the availability of this particular form of heroin soon declined. While such occurrences demonstrate that mixing drugs such as heroin with other drugs can be dangerous, there is little evidence to suggest that the harmful consequences of mixing drugs are intentional.

R. COOMBER

SEE ALSO:
Ecstasy • Heroin • Potentiation

Designer Drugs

Designer drugs are chemical analogs of established drugs. They were originally made to avoid antidrug legislation. Now they continue to be made for other motives, despite changes in drug laws that outlaw them.

When pharmaceutical researchers embark on the development of a new drug, they commonly begin with an existing drug that is known to work. Legitimate scientists then consider chemical modifications that could lead to similar compounds, called analogs, which could have pharmaceutical properties similar to or even better than those of the existing drug. Clandestine drug developers use the same approach, but their motives are somewhat different.

Early drug legislation specified the substances to be controlled. Any drug whose composition was unlisted in the regulations was legal. As a result, a clandestine drug developer could make a minor change in the chemical structure of an existing street drug and create an entirely legal new drug. These compounds were the original designer drugs—substances formulated to slip through gaps in loose legislation. Confusion reigned as legislators tried to plug loopholes in the law to keep up with the emergence of new drugs from clandestine sources.

The cat-and-mouse game between legislators and drug developers ended with the introduction of a new type of drug-control legislation in 1977 in the United Kingdom and 1986 in the United States. The new laws applied not only to known psychoactive substances but also to substances that resembled them in structure or action. The opportunity to evade the law by formulating new designer drugs was over.

Meanwhile, it had become apparent that some designer drugs had stronger or more unusual psychoactive properties than the drugs they had been intended to mimic. Since the market for illicit drugs is constantly seeking a new or more intense high, each new drug offered its dealers a competitive edge over their rivals. Hence, designer-drug development continued even after the change in legislation.

Another reason for the development of new drug analogs was the introduction of restrictions on raw materials crucial for the standard methods of making drugs. One such material is P2P (phenyl-2-propanone), a raw material used to synthesize amphetamine. If restriction makes illicit supplies of P2P impossible to obtain, clandestine amphetamine manufacturers can produce an amphetamine analog from phenyl-2-butanone, which is chemically similar to P2P. The product is alpha-ethylphenylethylamine.

Stimulants and hallucinogens

The broadest group of psychoactive analogs is based on structures that have an aromatic ring system attached to an ethylamine group. These compounds fall into two groups: phenethylamines and tryptamines. The enormous scope for producing compounds based on these structures was explored under license by the U.S. pharmacologist and chemist Alexander "Sasha" Shulgin (1925–). The books *Pihkal: A Chemical Love Story* and *Tihkal: The Continuation*, written by Shulgin and his wife Ann, document his work in the field of analogs.

Phenethylamines. In *Pihkal* (*P*henethylamines *I Have Known and Loved*), Shulgin reports the syntheses of 179 phenethylamine derivatives, with brief descriptions of their psychoactive effects. While Shulgin's interest in these substances was based on their potential as psychotherapeutic agents, many phenethylamines have also reached the illicit drug market. Some members of this group are mainly euphoriant stimulants, including amphetamine and methamphetamine. Others are hallucinogens and often have methoxy groups ($-OCH_3$) or similar substituents on the phenyl ring; examples are mescaline (3,4,5-trimethoxyphenethylamine), a natural hallucinogen in peyote cactus, and TMA (3,4,5-trimethoxyamphetamine). Other phenethylamines are termed *empathogens* and *entactogens*, which cause a desire to communicate with others and an enhanced emotional state. An early example of this class was the 1960s "Love Drug" MDA (3,4-methylenedioxyamphetamine). Ecstasy (3,4-methylenedioxymethamphetamine) is an MDA analog.

Tryptamines. The book *Tihkal* (*T*ryptamines *I Have Known and Loved*) covers the syntheses of 55 tryptamines. They differ from phenethylamines by having a bicyclic (two-ringed) group in place of the phenyl ring of phenethylamine. This group of chemicals includes serotonin (5-HT, or 5-hydroxytryptamine) and natural hallucinogens such as bufotenine, psilocybin, and psilocin. The potent synthetic hallucinogen LSD also has the tryptamine structure in a polycyclic compound.

Opioids

In 1979 medical examiners started to report deaths by apparent heroin overdose but found no trace of heroin or its breakdown products in the bodies. In time, it emerged that the culprit was an analog of fentanyl, a potent surgical anesthetic. Called China White in the illicit drug market, alpha-methylfentanyl was the first of around 12 fentanyl analogs to reach the street. All have the same effects on mind and body as heroin but are hundreds of times more potent. Such high potencies were the likely cause of accidental overdoses in users accustomed to impure samples of heroin.

Other narcotics that mimic heroin include analogs of meperidine (Demerol, or pethidine), a Schedule II narcotic. One such drug is MPPP (1-methyl-4-phenyl-4-propionoxypiperidine).

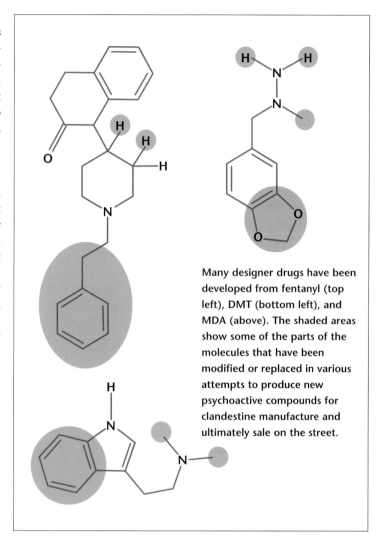

Many designer drugs have been developed from fentanyl (top left), DMT (bottom left), and MDA (above). The shaded areas show some of the parts of the molecules that have been modified or replaced in various attempts to produce new psychoactive compounds for clandestine manufacture and ultimately sale on the street.

This drug is particularly hazardous because an impurity that forms during manufacture, MPTP, causes irreversible brain damage. The symptoms of this damage include muscle spasms and tremors, rigidity, and drooling; the syndrome resembles severe Parkinson's disease.

High risks

Even pure drugs produced by competent chemists and pharmaceutical companies are toxic if used at higher than safe doses, but the risks with analogs made in illicit laboratories are much higher. First, the clandestine chemist is likely to try to improve the yield by reducing the purity of the compound, so there is a risk of contamination with a harmful impurity such as MPTP. Second, the effects of each analog vary from user to user, so there is a chance of unexpected adverse reactions to an analog even if a user tolerates the original drug well. Given these extra risks, the use of designer drugs is a particularly hazardous activity.

M. CLOWES

SEE ALSO:
Amphetamines • Analogs • Bufotenine • Ecstasy Analogs • Fentanyl • Hallucinogens • LSD • Meperidine • PCP Analogs • Phenethylamines • Psilocybin and Psilocin • Tryptamines

Disulfiram

Disulfiram is a prescription drug that helps recovering alcoholics stay sober by inducing an unpleasant reaction to alcohol. To be effective, disulfiram must be used in conjunction with other treatments such as psychotherapy.

Alcohol is more widely used than any other psychoactive substance, with the possible exception of caffeine. The widespread availability of alcohol and the variety of social circumstances where its consumption occurs present formidable hurdles to people who are fighting alcoholism. Disulfiram (trade name Antabuse) can provide valuable help to alcoholics who have decided to quit drinking but are aware that their self-discipline might fail them. Disulfiram works by producing acetaldehyde poisoning whenever alcohol is taken. This effect is called the alcohol-disulfiram reaction; it occurs because disulfiram disrupts the bioconversion of alcohol.

Physiological action

When a person drinks an alcoholic beverage, its ethanol (ethyl alcohol) content passes rapidly into the bloodstream and works its way into the central nervous system. At the same time, two distinct enzymes in the liver start to convert ethanol first into ethanal (acetaldehyde), then into ethanoic acid (acetic acid). The enzyme responsible for the first stage of conversion is alcohol dehydrogenase (ADH); acetaldehyde dehydrogenase (ALDH) completes the conversion into acetic acid. Whereas acetic acid is relatively harmless and is easily excreted in the kidneys, acetaldehyde is a poison whose effects include skin flushing, nausea and vomiting, throbbing headaches, heart palpitations, and sweating.

In a normal person, ALDH usually converts acetaldehyde at a sufficient rate to prevent it from reaching toxic concentrations. In a patient who takes disulfiram, the drug renders ALDH inactive by binding strongly to the site responsible for bioconversion of acetaldehyde. If the patient then drinks alcohol, the bloodstream concentration of acetaldehyde soars to between 5 and 10 times that of a normal drinker, and symptoms of acetaldehyde poisoning ensue.

The alcohol-disulfiram reaction is sometimes described as an instant hangover because of the throbbing head and nausea that occur. This description is misleading, since true hangovers result not only from acetaldehyde but also from a combination of factors that include accumulations of breakdown products of methanol and other impurities in alcoholic drinks, as well as dehydration and low blood sugar.

Therapeutic use

Disulfiram discourages alcoholic relapses partly because the prescribing physician warns the patient of the effect an alcoholic drink will have, and partly because patients who drink despite taking disulfiram soon experience the unpleasant effects of acetaldehyde poisoning. Disulfiram requires patient cooperation, so it is only effective for alcoholics who have resolved to stop drinking and want to put that resolve into effect by taking the drug.

Therapy can only start when the patient has spent at least 12 hours without drinking, as bioconversion of residual alcohol in the bloodstream can trigger the alcohol-disulfiram reaction. Dosage starts with one or two weeks of once-daily 500 milligram doses to rapidly establish an effective bloodstream concentration of the drug. Subsequent doses of around 250 milligrams per day then maintain that concentration for as long as is necessary. While taking disulfiram, the patient must take care to avoid even small quantities of alcohol in such forms as sauces, cough syrups, mouthwash, and colognes.

Disulfiram therapy is not an adequate treatment for alcoholism when used alone; it must be accompanied by treatment of withdrawal symptoms and psychotherapy that addresses any issues that reinforce the dependency-forming nature of alcohol. Nevertheless, disulfiram is useful in keeping willing patients away from alcohol until their circumstances have changed to such an extent that the drug is no longer necessary to prevent problem drinking.

M. CLOWES

SEE ALSO:
Acetaldehyde • Alcohol

DMT

Dimethyltryptamine (DMT) is a naturally occurring hallucinogenic drug that occurs in a number of plant species, including the shrub *Psychotria viridis* and the *Phalaris* grasses, and in trace amounts in the human nervous system.

DMT is the major active ingredient in a number of hallucinogenic snuffs, such as *yage, yopo* or *epena*, as well as the brew ayahuasca, which are all used by the indigenous peoples of South America for ritual purposes. The drug is not commonly used in the West except for certain groups interested in drug taking for spiritual reasons. A major reason for this lack of popularity is the pharmacological effects of DMT, which can be severe.

The effects of DMT are unusually intense when compared with those of drugs such as LSD used at normal recreational doses. Unlike LSD, which typically produces visual geometric illusions rather than true hallucinations, DMT often produces a trancelike state with auditory hallucinations and powerful visual experiences. A substantial number of DMT users also report contacts with hallucinatory beings, which appear to be intelligent, although they are generally described as highly alien. This combination of effects, coupled with the tendency to produce either anxiety or flattening of emotions, makes DMT an unattractive drug for most users. Some users of the drug regard its effects as a spiritual experience, providing an opportunity to commune with the spirits of the otherworld and for purposes of personal transformation.

Pharmacologically, DMT is distinct from more commonly used drugs such as LSD or psilocybin in that it is very short acting (lasting only 5 to 30 minutes). It also produces little tolerance to subjective effects. Traditionally, DMT-containing powders were snorted or, with the addition of plants containing enzymes to break down the DMT, drunk as a tea. In a recreational context, either of these methods may be used, but smoking the drug sprinkled on tobacco or mint leaves is also common. Intramuscular injection is also used on occasion. Beside its effects on the perceptions of users, DMT also increases heart rate and blood pressure and stimulates the release of certain hormones such as cortisol and growth hormone.

The short but intense effects of DMT have made it something of a cult drug in the West. Its nickname, the businessman's trip, is said to refer to its suitability for consumption in, say, a lunch hour. Most recreational users, however, are warned off by the intensity of the effects.

DMT is also naturally present in the human nervous system, which has led some investigators to suggest that the drug may be involved in psychotic disorders, particularly schizophrenia.

R. G. HUNTER

SEE ALSO:
Hallucinogens ● Harmine and Harmaline ● MAOs and MAOIs ● Serotonin ● Tryptamines

KEY FACTS

Classification
Schedule I (USA), Schedule III (Canada), Class A (UK), Schedule I (INCB). Hallucinogen.

Street names
45-minute psychosis, businessman's trip, fantasia; snuffs and teas containing DMT include *yage, yopo, epena,* and ayahuasca.

Short-term effects
Intense rapid-onset hallucinogenic "trip," usually lasting less than 30 minutes. Can be frightening or anxiety producing due to the speed at which the drug takes effect and its effects on the cardiovascular system. Can cause a complete loss of contact with external reality.

Long-term effects
No long-term effects, although the fear and anxiety sometimes experienced when using DMT can cause psychological trauma in certain individuals.

Dopamine

Dopamine is one of the neurotransmitters that takes part in communications between neurons. It is implicated in the reward mechanism that drives basic urges and addictions, as well as in Parkinson's disease and schizophrenia.

Dopamine—3,4-*dihydroxyphenethylamine*—is one of a class of compounds that act as chemical messengers in the brain. Such compounds are called neurotransmitters; other examples are gamma-aminobutyric acid (GABA), norepinephrine, and serotonin. Neurotransmitters diffuse across synapses —the junctions between neurons—when an electrical nerve impulse arrives at the end of its passage along a neuron. The transmitting neuron is described as presynaptic, in reference to its position relative to the synapse along the signal path. Neurons that produce, store, and release dopamine during normal functioning are described as dopaminergic.

Neuroscientists currently recognize 16 distinct types of dopaminergic neurons at various locations in the brain and body, and there are five known subtypes of dopamine receptors. The cell responses associated with the stimulation of these receptors by dopamine fall into two categories. D1 and D5 receptors stimulate the production of cAMP (cyclic adenosine monophosphate), whereas D2, D3, and D4 receptors inhibit cAMP production.

Since cAMP activates enzymes by adding phosphate groups to the appropriate proteins, dopamine release and bonding to receptors have indirect effects on various enzyme-promoted processes. These include processes that generate energy and control movement and emotions, as well as those that enable sensations such as pleasure, craving, and pain.

Reward system

In the context of drugs and addiction, the role of dopamine in the sensations of pleasure and craving is most relevant. The neurons that participate in these sensations occur primarily in the mesolimbic pathway of the ventral tegmental area (VTA) of the brain. This

The dopamine systems in the brain are important in establishing the reward mechanism that drives addiction. The neurons that make up these systems of pathways project forward into the frontal lobe of the brain and into the limbic system, releasing dopamine when stimulated and producing a feeling of pleasure and well-being.

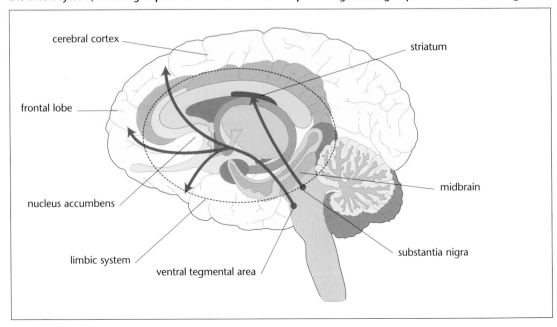

pathway projects onto regions of the brain such as the nucleus accumbens, which is part of the emotional control center of the brain, and the frontal lobe, where decision making occurs.

The dopaminergic reward system probably evolved as a mechanism for the continuation of the species by creating urges to eat and mate. These activities prompt the release of dopamine in the reward system, and this release results in a pleasant emotional state. Hence, dopamine provides an emotional reward for activities that are essential for survival and procreation.

Drugs that cause addiction also cause an increase in dopamine levels, so they create dependencies by subverting the reward system. In the case of amphetamine, the drug causes stores of dopamine and other neurotransmitters in neurons to dump their contents into synapses; on the other hand, cocaine blocks the reuptake mechanism that clears dopamine and other neurotransmitters from synapses and returns them to storage. In either case, rapidly increasing concentrations of synaptic dopamine cause pleasurable sensations courtesy of the dopamine system. Alcohol also causes pleasure by mechanisms that stimulate dopamine release, but the slower rate of intoxication causes a milder high.

Studies of drug-dependent individuals commonly reveal excitement at images related to consumption of the drug of their dependency, even if there is no real prospect of taking the drug in the immediate future. This excitement could be a physiological sign of the priming peak of dopamine that occurs in anticipation of drug consumption. It is possible that a drug that would diminish the priming peak of dopamine could help drug-dependent individuals by reducing the cravings that nurture their addictions.

Psychosis

Psychosis is one of the acute problems that can occur from taking large amounts of substances such as amphetamine and cocaine. Drug-induced psychosis is indistinguishable from psychotic episodes associated with conditions such as schizophrenia.

Abnormalities in dopaminergic neurons seem to be the link between drug-induced psychosis and psychotic episodes of schizophrenia. For cocaine or amphetamine psychosis, there is a known increase in dopamine levels in synapses. To treat psychosis related to mental illness, drugs that block dopamine

receptors prove effective. The first generation of antipsychotic drugs were found to be dopamine antagonists at D2-type receptors, and this was thought to be their mode of action. (An antagonist is a chemical that blocks the action of another substance by attaching itself to that substance's receptor but without activating the receptor.)

One of the side effects of typical antipsychotics such as haloperidol is their tendency to cause lethargy and dulled emotions. More modern atypical antipsychotics such as risperidone have more affinity for D4 receptors than for D2. They have fewer side effects than older drugs, yet they are just as effective in reducing the incidence of psychotic episodes. This suggests that D4 dopamine receptors, rather than D2, might be responsible for psychosis.

Parkinson's disease

One of the major dopaminergic neuron pathways is the nigrostriatal pathway, which starts in the substantia nigra region of the brain and projects onto the striatum. This pathway participates in the control of movement, and its degeneration is the cause of Parkinson's disease, or Parkinsonism. It has both D1-type and D2-type dopamine receptors.

Parkinson's disease causes a collection of symptoms that include muscular rigidity and tremors, a shuffling gait and distorted posture, and slurred speech. These symptoms occur most often in elderly people whose brains have lost a significant proportion of dopamine-generating neurons in the substantia nigra. The deficit causes an imbalance in a system of neurons that are excited by acetylcholine receptors and inhibited by dopamine D2 receptors.

The imbalance between acetylcholine and dopamine causes an impairment of voluntary muscle control that can be alleviated for up to two years by treatment with levodopa. This drug gets converted into dopamine after passing through the blood-brain barrier, which dopamine itself cannot do. Other therapeutic agents include selective D2 agonists and monoamine oxidase inhibitors (MAOIs) that slow the breakdown of dopamine.

M. CLOWES

SEE ALSO:

Drug Control Policy

The creation of drug control policy is the result of a complex interrelationship of ideas and beliefs about the causes and effects of drug abuse. Such policies vary over time, reflecting changes in public and official attitudes toward drugs.

Governments control and attempt to control the production, distribution, and use of illicit drugs through a wide variety of policies. "Illicit drugs" refers to psychoactive substances (substances that affect sensations, perceptions, cognition, and emotions) that are illegal for the general public to possess, purchase, manufacture, or sell. In most cases this list includes narcotics, stimulants, depressants, hallucinogens, and marijuana, and may include some of the chemicals used in the production of such drugs. Decisions on what makes a drug illicit are often based on known medical uses, as well as the potential for abuse of the substance. Policies are also shaped by political values as well as the ways in which different groups define particular drugs as problematic.

A brief history of drug control policy

Human use of psychoactive substances stretches back to ancient history. Many of the substances that we now try to control grow naturally (in some form) throughout the world—opium poppies in Asia, coca leaves in South America, and marijuana as a weed throughout the world. Human beings have learned how to extract psychoactive chemicals from these plants, cultivate them to increase their psychoactive chemical potency, and create new synthetic drugs from readily available chemical precursors. Since the world has become a global trading village, drugs can be distributed as rapidly as any other product.

In the nineteenth and early twentieth centuries, what are now illicit drugs were an important part of extensive, legitimate, lightly regulated global trade. For example, coca products were sold to increase energy, and opium was often a key ingredient in advertised cure-all elixirs. These powerful substances were advertised in the major retail catalogs of the late nineteenth and early twentieth centuries. Policies toward these drugs began to change as part of major social reform movements. In the United States these movements included efforts to provide voting rights to women, improve working conditions and food quality, and control the distribution of psychoactive drugs. While each nation has taken a unique path in its drug policy process, policy changes in the United States can be used as an example of the steps involved in moving from historically non-regulated drug markets to present-day international treaties and nation-specific policy environments.

Concern about the increasing number of drug users in the United States, as well as reported harms associated with drug use, led to early attempts to control the patent medicine industry. The Pure Food and Drug Act of 1906 required the patent medicine industry to list all ingredients in its products. Thus, for the first time, consumers could see what substances they were actually using when taking various medicines. During this era, perceptions of drug use became more and more negative, until such behavior came to be seen as individually deviant and culturally dangerous unless it occurred under the supervision of a physician. Over time, even medical usage of some drugs came to be viewed as inappropriate. The Harrison Narcotics Act of 1914 and the Marihuana Tax Act of 1937 essentially made personal use of cocaine, opium, and marijuana illegal and discouraged medical use. The result of these initiatives was to move the United States from a policy of very little regulation to strict prohibition of the production, distribution, or possession of specific drugs. Individuals who used these substances were viewed as dangerous and hopelessly enslaved to substance use; penalties for use or sale of illegal drugs were severe.

The movement to prohibition was relatively rapid, and over the following decades there appeared to be strong international support for this approach. In 1961 the United Nations Single Convention of New York was signed, forming the basis for international drug control. Although updated and revised since then, the Single Convention remains the framework for international efforts to reduce illicit drug use. Major demographic and cultural changes occurred during the 1960s and 1970s. Many parts of the world experienced a cultural revolution led by youth that severely questioned traditional definitions of norms, values, and laws. Included in that cultural revolution was the use of a wide variety of prohibited drugs, including heroin, LSD, cocaine, and marijuana. The extent of drug use caused a rethinking of drug control policy around the world. Many policy advocates argued that drugs such as marijuana could not be compared with others, such as heroin or cocaine. Arguments were made for the decriminalization or legalization of some drugs, and for treatment instead of incarceration of drug users.

From the 1970s onward, nations have struggled to define the most successful drug policy while remaining within international treaties and internal societal and cultural expectations. Different approaches and policy positions have grown out of this process. These policies differ in what level of legal access to drugs is allowed, as well as in the severity of sanctions. Policy positions theoretically range from prohibition to decriminalization to legalization. Policies may also incorporate elements that result from defining drug abuse as a public health problem or as a purely medical problem. Finally, within policy positions, the consequences of breaking the law may vary based on the type of substance and the type of behavior involved. Drug policy is therefore a complex combination of various policy positions and penalties for different substances and activities.

Prohibition

Prohibition, at its most extreme, is a policy that prohibits individuals from using, possessing, selling, or manufacturing a specific substance for any reason. Prohibition of some form has been the official policy of the United States for all illicit drugs since 1914. It is also a common international policy. Many Islamic countries, for religious reasons, have remained strongly prohibitionist toward the use of illicit drugs as well as alcohol. Severe punishment for drug offenses is often part of prohibitionist approaches. In the United States, drug law violations are often punished by mandatory imprisonment. In some other countries, drug law violations may result in capital punishment. Supporters of prohibition argue that the individual and social harms associated with drug use and abuse (such as crime, violence, and economic costs) require strong deterrence to limit drug availability and use. Proponents point to lower levels of drug use in the United States since 1980

that seem to coincide with efforts to strengthen prohibition.

Critics of prohibition note that overall illicit drug use rates in the United States are often significantly higher than in other nonprohibitionist countries, and that the risk of severe punishment does not appear to lower drug-use rates among addicts. Critics also raise concerns about the erosion of basic civil rights and legal due process that may accompany strongly prohibitionist policies, citing research that indicates that the harms resulting from drug use do not justify the severe punishments imposed. The number of individuals imprisoned for nonviolent drug law offenses has grown tremendously over recent years in the United States. From this perspective, strict prohibition with an emphasis on incarceration for drug law violations has been a costly and ineffective policy.

Decriminalization

Decriminalization essentially means that, although a policy of prohibition remains in place for behaviors such as selling or manufacturing illicit drugs, individual use or possession of a substance has no or minimal criminal penalties or is subject only to civil penalties, such as fines. While there are those who argue for the decriminalization of personal use of nearly all currently illegal drugs (Portugal adopted this policy in 2001), the focus has usually been on marijuana. Arguments for marijuana decriminalization are largely based on what is perceived to be the limited harm associated with marijuana use and the high degree of harm caused by prohibiting a substance used by a large proportion of the population. Increases in the number of individuals imprisoned in the United States have been credited largely to marijuana-related arrests. It is argued that decriminalizing marijuana would alleviate prison overcrowding—and its associated high costs—without endangering the public. Further arguments are that prohibiting the use of a substance that may be less harmful than other legal substances, such as alcohol, is illogical and undermines respect for law and basic human rights.

Decriminalization for possession of small amounts of marijuana has occurred in Belgium, Spain, and some states in Australia. In 2004 Great Britain reclassified marijuana from a Class B to Class C

Governments around the world are eager to promote events that deter young people from taking drugs. Here, U.S. president Bill Clinton takes part in a 1996 rally warning teenagers of the dangers of smoking.

substance (a category carrying minimal penalties for possession). However, in 2009, marijuana was reclassified again as a Class B drug. The Netherlands has a unique system of nonprosecution for both possession and sales of small quantities of marijuana. In the United States, Alaska, California, and Massachusetts have decriminalized the possession of small amounts of marijuana with other states having minimal penalties for the possession of small amounts of marijuana.

Many of the arguments used in campaigns against decriminalization have focused on the harm that marijuana intoxication can cause (for example, accidents from distorted perception, problems with memory and learning, lowered cognitive ability, and neurological problems from prenatal exposure) and the gateway hypothesis. The gateway hypothesis holds that marijuana use leads to use of harder and more dangerous drugs such as heroin and cocaine.

Legalization

Legalization is a broad and mostly theoretical policy position. Essentially, this position would not only take away penalties for illicit drug use but also provide a regulated framework for the production and distribution of these drugs. Such frameworks could take several forms, as summarized by policy researchers Robert MacCoun and Peter Reuter: a free market with no restrictions for any users; a limited adult market (no use for minors); a negative adult license (available for any reason to adults unless they violate eligibility requirements); or a positive adult license (available only to adults who have obtained a specific license for use). Virtually all proponents of a legalization approach reject giving young people access to illicit drugs. Also, as with decriminalization, the focus of most legalization arguments has been on marijuana. Advocates of legalization point out that, even if decriminalized, illicit drugs would continue to have no regulations for quality, potency, or access. Thus, health consequences—such as the spread of infections through shared injection equipment, overdoses from the use of substances of unknown quality or potency, or deaths from substances laced with dangerous substitutes for the real drug—would remain a concern. Those who advocate legalization and regulation also argue that a regulated market would do away with the violence associated with illegal drug distribution, increase the tax base through revenue generated from sales, protect civil rights, and provide more effective control of use through measures such as taxes to push up the price of drugs so as to deter young people. A major marijuana legislation effort failed in a 2010 California ballot initiative.

Critics of the theoretical discussions of legalization have argued that current heavy regulation of legal substances such as alcohol and tobacco has not stopped use among young people, or abuse and addiction among both young people and adults. They argue that without the perceived stigma of illegality, use rates would increase. Further, opponents have expressed concern that if illicit drugs were legalized, advertising and marketing efforts would probably dramatically increase use of many illicit substances that currently are used only by a relatively small proportion of the population.

Policy decisions

Policy decisions are influenced by what individuals, advocacy groups, and policy makers perceive to be the underlying cause of a societal problem. Drug policy is no exception. The drug policy approaches discussed so far have dealt with restricting access to illicit drugs. However, implicit in the level of access is a corresponding understanding of what drives and affects the underlying phenomena of drug use itself. For strongly prohibitionist policies with severe penalties, drug use is viewed as deviant behavior based on rational choice, which is best dealt with by the criminal justice system through punishment. For open-market legalization policies, drug use can be understood as a form of consumer behavior driven by market forces. However, there are types of prohibitionist policies, as well as some versions of decriminalization and conceptualized legalization policies, that incorporate the unique perspectives of public health and medicalization.

Public health

The public health perspective defines illicit drug use and abuse as a public health problem best dealt with through education, prevention, and best practice treatment rather than punishment. The argument for this approach rests on the conclusion that severe deterrence punishment is simply not an effective means of reducing or stopping drug abuse or addiction and its associated harms. From this perspective, the best approach is one that provides the following: a strong emphasis on education that accurately describes substance-use consequences, education on the least harmful methods of use, prevention of the underlying causes of use, and quality

Many people who protest drug control policies argue that imprisoning people for nonviolent violations of drug laws is an ineffective and expensive way of dealing with the problem.

treatment-on-demand that recognizes that drug addiction is a chronic reoccurring disease. Treatment instead of incarceration has considerable support in many countries, including the United States, most often for nonviolent offenders and those not involved in selling or drug trafficking. Such approaches often incorporate an option whereby individuals arrested on drug charges who meet certain eligibility requirements have the option of choosing a treatment program over incarceration. If an offender successfully completes the treatment program and does not commit any further offenses, he or she is released; no further involvement with the criminal justice system is required. There is some recognition across political ideologies that punishment does not work to prevent drug abuse and is very expensive. However, the harm-reduction aspect of the public health perspective (the element that argues for the importance of teaching less harmful use practices, including safe needle use or safer methods of using Ecstasy) has been very controversial and has often undermined attempts to build broad support for this policy alternative.

Medicalization

Those who advocate the medicalization of drug policy argue that drug abuse and addiction are diseases that are best addressed solely by the medical profession through treatment. Such treatment may take the form of maintenance (for example, heroin users participating in methadone maintenance programs) or adversarial and interference approaches, in which individuals take a substance that either suppresses the effects of a drug or actually reacts against certain drugs. Supporters point out that drug use and abuse, as physical conditions, cannot be dealt with through either criminal justice systems or market forces. Proponents for medicalization also call for physicians to have greater access to illicit drugs in order to treat a variety of human mental and physical problems. Medical marijuana policy provokes the most discussion concerning medicalization. Support for the medical use of marijuana is based on claims that the drug helps with appetite stimulation, controlling nausea and vomiting, neurologic and movement disorders, pain relief, and glaucoma. In the United States, fifteen states plus the District of Columbia have some form of medical marijuana laws that permit (or do not prohibit) some type of medical marijuana use. Supporters of such initiatives argue that physicians must have the right to prescribe drugs that provide significant pain relief, and that patients must have rights for access to the best available medicines that can alleviate disease or pain.

Arguments against medicalization include doubts that many of those currently abusing drugs would willingly seek treatment and questions about how such treatment would be paid for and evaluated. Critics of medical marijuana laws are concerned that young people will perceive marijuana to be less problematic if the medical profession is allowed to prescribe the substance. Furthermore, current policies have not clearly resolved issues of access for medical marijuana. Physicians are often unwilling to violate federal laws prohibiting marijuana possession; when such prescriptions are made, problems remain about legally obtaining the drug. Some states (such as Hawaii) have permitted the personal cultivation of a few marijuana plants for one's own medicinal use. However, issues of purity, potency, and dosage level for specific medical conditions remain predominantly unresolved. Clashes between the U.S. federal and state governments on medical marijuana have occurred, and the final outcome of such policies is unknown.

Drug policy complexity and future directions

Reviews of drug policy positions across the world, or even in different states in the United States, are very confusing. All sides make assertions that seem more consistent with ideological beliefs than logic or science. At times, policy seems to be going in opposite directions for different substances. For example, while punishments for marijuana possession and use have tended to decrease in the United States, punishments for manufacturing, possession, or sale of methamphetamine have increased. The policy position that seems to have the broadest base of support internationally is general prohibition for the production, sales, and distribution of illicit drugs with some interest in decriminalization for individual possession of small amounts of drugs, particularly marijuana. Within the United States, there seems to be broad support for treatment as an alternative to incarceration for nonviolent drug offenders. On all sides of the political spectrum there is some recognition that drug addiction is not simply a rational choice that can be addressed by a singular emphasis on punishment for deviant behavior. As research continues to show that treatment can be effective and—most important—cost effective, agreement is being reached that using scarce resources to incarcerate nonviolent drug offenders is not in the public's best interest. Efforts to develop successful drug policies are highly complex, politically charged, and difficult. Human suffering from the effects of drug abuse and addiction must be measured against individual freedom of choice as well as the need for public safety, the desire to reduce drug-related crime, and acknowledgement of the economic costs associated with promoting a particular policy.

D. McBride, Y. Terry-McElrath

SEE ALSO:

Drug Laws • Legalization Movement • Prohibition of Drugs

Drug Laws

Many of the drug laws instituted at national and international levels were created to prevent the illegal use of controlled substances. Others may relate to more local concerns or reflect different attitudes toward the effects of drug use.

National laws and international conventions on the use of drugs have been in a process of evolution and diversification since the middle of the nineteenth century. Current legal practice regulating illicit drugs exists within an international framework based on bans or limitations of the use of particular drugs. This approach was pioneered by the U.S. Controlled Substances Act, originally passed in 1970 in an effort to control and limit the use of certain drugs. The aim was to balance the therapeutic medical value of drugs against known dangers to health and the risks of abuse and addiction. Essentially, all countries subscribe to the United Nations Convention against the Traffic in Narcotic Drugs and Psychotropic Substances (Vienna, 1988). However, the national antidrug legislation that works in conjuction with the current international conventions has often been enacted many decades earlier, under particular local, social, and political pressures. This has led to persistent criticism that many drug laws are archaic, ineffective, and in need of reform.

Landmark drug legislation in the United States

For complex reasons, in part related to the social and political stresses generated by a fast-growing society open to immigration from many cultures, the United States has been at the forefront of societal concern about drug abuse. Global drug legislation has thus tended to be strongly influenced by legal precedents in the United States. In 1875 the first legal regulation of drug use was enacted in San Francisco to ban opium smoking by Chinese immigrants. This was a local rather than a federal law, and it did not affect the rapidly growing and completely unregulated patent medicine industry. Many products were of dubious medical value, and by the early twentieth century, opiate addiction in the United States was strongly associated with consumption of patent medicines, the most popular of which contained significant quantities of morphine.

A significant development in drug legislation was the landmark Pure Food and Drug Act passed by the U.S. Congress in 1906. This act was not a piece of criminal legislation, but it created a set of trading standards, enforced by a federal Food and Drug Administration (FDA) in Washington, whose approval was required before any food or drug could be sold for human use or consumption. The specific contents of foods and drugs were also required to be included on the label. Patent medicines containing morphine and tonics containing cocaine were not approved by the FDA, and these ceased to be legally marketed, thus greatly reducing, although not criminalizing, the accidental addiction and abuse common at the time.

In 1914 continuing concerns about drug use led to the passage of the Harrison Narcotics Act, the first federal criminal law regulating the medical use and, for the first time, criminalizing the nonmedical use of opium, morphine and its derivatives (including heroin), and cocaine and its derivatives.

At that time the prevalent states' rights constitutional doctrines held that the U.S. Congress did not have the right to regulate professions or pass general criminal laws. Therefore, the Harrison Narcotics Act required doctors to pay a small annual fee for a stamp that would permit validation of prescriptions for opiates or cocaine. It also taxed all nonmedical exchanges of opiates and cocaine heavily. Thus, possession of these controlled substances opened the possessor up to criminal tax-evasion charges enforced by the Treasury Department. In 1922 these criminal sanctions were strengthened by the Narcotic Drug Import and Export Act, intended to eliminate all nonmedical use of *narcotics*, a word that soon became widely used to describe all illegal nonmedically prescribed drugs. Somewhat unscientifically, narcotics include cocaine and marijuana, which are different classes of drugs from the opiate narcotic and sedative painkillers. The Heroin Act of 1924 banned the manufacture of heroin, the potent morphine derivative.

The smoking of marijuana (also known as cannabis or hashish) was essentially unknown in western Europe and the United States before the twentieth century, although it was used in Africa, the Middle East, South America, and Mexico. The hemp plant itself was widely grown for use in rope making, notably by George Washington at his Mount Vernon farm, where it was the main cash crop. The first state antimarijuana laws were passed in Utah in 1915. They targeted the habit of marijuana smoking that had been introduced by Mormon groups returning to Utah after unsuccessful attempts to establish a settlement in Mexico. Subsequently a further 27 states, mainly in the Rocky Mountains and the Southwest, criminalized this practice, then popularly associated with Mexican migrant laborers. Marijuana use was also criminalized in New York State during a brief popularity of "tea shops" selling the drug, after the saloons and liquor stores of the city were closed by the federal prohibition of alcohol sales in 1920. National marijuana prohibition was instituted following the passage of the Marijuana Tax Act in 1937, and the outlaw status of all cannabis extracts—marijuana, hashish, and cannabis oil—was confirmed by their classification as narcotic drugs under both Schedule I and IV

of the 1961 United Nations Convention on Narcotic Drugs.

Current regulation of drugs in the United States

The United States operates a policy of deterrence toward the use of all illegal drugs. State police and federal agents are empowered to arrest and prosecute those found to be manufacturing, distributing, selling, or using controlled substances. However, there are few areas where the diversity established in the U.S. constitution is more apparent than in the varied interpretation and amendment of federal drug laws in state legislatures.

The description and definition of an illegal drug is based on guidelines established in 1970 in the federal Controlled Substances Act (CSA), which regulates the manufacture and distribution of narcotics, stimulants, depressants, hallucinogens, and anabolic steroids. The key innovations in the 1970 law were the creation of five schedules, based on a drug's potential for abuse, likelihood for dependence, and currently accepted medical use. Schedule I contains those controlled substances that have a high potential for abuse and few or no known medical uses. The

The sale of drug paraphernalia, such as bongs and opium pipes, is regulated by state criminal laws in the United States. Some businesses require a license to sell drug equipment, and advertising is banned.

Switzerland is one of several European countries that has a harm-reduction approach to drug use. In an attempt to cut crime and drug use in public areas, the authorities allowed this railroad station in Zurich to be used by heroin addicts but closed the site in 1995 when the policy was deemed to have failed.

seriousness of legal sanctions for possession and use declines until Schedule V, which contains those controlled substances with very low potential for abuse and proven therapeutic use.

While U.S. federal law applies to all states, state laws have developed some significant variations in controlled substance guidelines, and individual states have reclassified specific drugs within the original five schedules. Alaska, Arkansas, North Carolina, and Virginia have created a six-schedule system, while Tennessee has increased this to seven. South Dakota has reduced the schedules to four. By creating their own versions of the 1970 schedules, states have maintained a degree of autonomy and flexibility in the implementation of federal law and treatment of drug offenses in state courts. In practice, this autonomy has created considerable variation between sentencing decisions for similar drug offenses in different state courts. Thus, while 37 states endorse the 1970 CSA by listing marijuana with heroin and cocaine as a Schedule I drug, six states (Colorado, Georgia, Illinois, South Dakota, Virginia, and Wisconsin) do not schedule marijuana at all.

There are also significant differences between states in the penalties for breaches of the drug laws. Sentencing is usually based on the amount of a drug someone possesses. Greater amounts trigger heavier sentences, although the relationship between quantity of possession and likely sentence varies among the states. Maximum and minimum fines and severity of jail sentences associated with first and repeat sale and possession offenses also vary considerably from state to state. This is particularly true for offences involving possession of such drugs as marijuana, cocaine, and methamphetamine. Heroin offenses are treated more uniformly and severely.

Most notably, the eleven states of Alaska, California, Colorado, Maine, Minnesota, Nebraska, North Carolina, Mississippi, New York, Ohio, and Oregon decriminalized possession of marijuana in the 1970s. In doing so, some 35 years of complete national marijuana prohibition effectively ended. Again, no uniform legal standard was adopted. Although all of the eleven became known as "decriminalized states" with reduced penalties for possession of small amounts of the drug and no prison terms for punishment, four states (California, Minnesota, North Carolina, and Ohio) retained statutes defining marijuana possession as a misde-meanor. By 1990, the distinction between the original decriminalized states and those that did not pass such measures had become blurred as other states passed marijuana "depenalization" laws, which abolished imprisonment for many marijuana-related offenses.

In 1996 a second wave of state legislation on marijuana further challenged the original 1970 scheduling of this drug. California and Arizona passed the first laws permitting the use of marijuana for medical purposes; specifically mentioned uses included chronic pain relief of neurodegenerative diseases, such as multiple sclerosis. However, the federal government has not changed its official position of denying that marijuana has any legitimate medical role. The constitutionality of the California and Arizona state laws has not been challenged outright in federal courts. However, a 2001 Supreme Court ruling prevents these state laws from applying to any organization that seeks to distribute marijuana to patients (*United States v. Oakland Cannabis Buyer's Cooperative*, 2001).

A recurrent feature of drug legislation is that it has had to include successive new laws regulating both newly popular drugs and newly created synthetic chemical compounds. In 1986 the U.S. Congress passed the Analogue (Designer Drug) Act, which made illegal the use of substances that were chemically different from existing illicit drugs but had similar overall chemical structure and drug effects. The Anabolic Steroid Control Act came into force in 1991. It classified 27 different steroid mole-cules as Schedule III substances within the CSA.

There are also instances in which a particular drug may be relatively easy to classify and ban but related substances with similar effects can pose problems. Gamma-hydroxybutyrate (GHB), a central-nervous-system depressant, was banned by the FDA in 1990. The reasons were suspected low-level toxicity and lack of pharmacological or medical advantage in efficacy over other compounds of this type. GHB can generate feelings of intoxication and euphoria. It became a popular, albeit illegal, club and "rave" drug in the 1990s. GHB has been used in sexual assaults because it can render the victim incapable of resistance and without clear memory of the assault,

thus making prosecution of perpetrators difficult. The Hillory J. Farias and Samantha Reid Date-Rape Prohibition Act of 2000 made GHB a Schedule I drug under the CSA.

However, another drug, flunitrazepam (trade named Rohypnol), has somewhat similar effects and has become even more notorious as a "date-rape drug" than GHB. Rohypnol causes the victim to experience short-term memory loss after ingestion with alcohol. This drug is neither made nor approved for medical use in the United States. However, Rohypnol is widely manufactured and sold in Europe and South America as a hypnotic for short-term treatment of insomnia and as a preanesthetic medication. It is thus more difficult to ban Rohypnol than GHB, at least in part, because banning it could criminalize tourists and travelers with legitimate medical prescriptions. Thus Rohypnol is currently a Schedule IV substance in 38 states and in the CSA. Yet it is a Schedule I substance in six states and is unscheduled in four states.

The search for effective drug-control measures
A possible way to improve drug-control measures is to experiment with different legal regimes for drug control. In the United States this is achieved to some extent by the existence of different legal frameworks in different states. However, there is another multistate confederation that has tended toward a different philosophy of legal regulation of drugs than that of the United States—the member states of the European Union. It would be inaccurate to state that Europe has a more lenient view of drug addiction and trafficking than does the United States. Many European states and regions are less tolerant of marijuana use than parts of the United States. In fact, there have been European cases in which the possession of small amounts of marijuana has been treated more severely than the possession of small quantities of heroin. Heroin users have, on occasion, been treated more leniently since they might be considered victims of their addiction, while marijuana users are not generally considered addicts. This scenario would be most unlikely in U.S. courts. However, the European Union member states are generally in agreement that harm-reduction policies are more effective than criminal sanctions against drug users.

The European experiments

All European Union members, candidate members, and close associates, such as Norway and Switzerland have incorporated the provisions of the 1988 U.N. Convention. However, several European nations have decentralized their policy and have implemented more radical decriminalization measures than any U.S. state. One underlying difference between the two approaches is the European view that drug addiction is a medical problem rather than a crime. This is particularly true for the classification of heroin users, who are seen as having a medical condition, opiate addiction.

Many, but not all European states, have relaxed their drug laws without directly violating the international conventions. In the Netherlands in particular, the extent of the liberalization has caused concern in neighboring countries. Decriminalization is not the same as legalization. In the Netherlands, where marijuana is sold for use in licensed premises (the famous "coffee shops"), which are forbidden to sell alcohol, marijuana possession is not legal but is officially tolerated by the authorities. The United Kingdom reclassified cannabis from Class B to Class C of the Misuse of Drugs Act (1971) in 2003. Minor possession was thus decriminalized, but attempts to open Dutch-style "coffee shops" were prevented by the police. In 2005 the British government referred the reclassification of cannabis back to its Scientific Advisory Council on the Misuse of Drugs. In 2006, the council decided not to recommend reclassification to Class B, but the government did so in 2008. The chairman of the advisory council was then dismissed for protesting the government's decision, leading to the resignation of five members from the council and an open split between the government and its scientific advisors.

Some of the European focus on harm reduction has been driven by the rapid spread of HIV, the virus that causes AIDS, since the early 1980s. Measures have included free needle exchange programs and provision of clinic-style drug consumption facilities, particularly for heroin users. While the ultimate goal has been rehabilitation, maintenance treatment (in which doctors supply drugs to registered addicts) has been provided in several countries, such as Germany and Switzerland, to regulate drug use in those who are unwilling to enter traditional treatment programs. Although there has been some international criticism of Switzerland's heroin distribution program for addicts, the Swiss public overwhelmingly voted for the continuation of the program in a 1999 national referendum.

Conclusions

The debate on drugs is conducted at an emotional pitch, and this probably inhibits moves toward more just and effective laws. On one side of the debate, critics of current drug laws maintain that prohibitions do not protect individuals from murder, theft, fraud, libel, or persecution, as many laws do, but instead express social disapproval and seek to preserve certain social and moral values. As such, prohibitions are intrinsically authoritarian and can be directed against an outcast or minority community identified as users of the prohibited substance.

Supporters of drug-control legislation point out that illicit drug use is associated with real and negative health and social consequences. In particular, there are a significant number of drug-related deaths as well as a clear relationship between drug use and crime. A frequently quoted example of the latter comes from the monitoring of drug use in arrestees in U.S. cities in the 1990s. This research indicated that more than two-thirds of felony arrestees tested positive for recent use of an illicit drug.

It is clearly possible to see validity in the arguments of both sides and at the same time to sympathize with the difficult decisions that face elected lawmakers. They must seek to steer an intellectually and morally consistent path between protecting the inexperienced and vulnerable and maintaining and developing individual freedom within a just society that respects its own laws. Research, education, and open debate in democratic societies remain the only secure foundation for managing the risks and benefits of drugs. Some form of medicolegal scheduling process appears logically unavoidable, as does the application of some form of sanction to deter unregulated profit from the sale of substances that can harm their users.

D. E. ARNOT

SEE ALSO:
Controlled Substances • Legal Controls

Drug Receptors

Receptors are the molecular sites on cells at which naturally occurring chemicals or drugs in the body act to produce a response. Drugs can mimic or prevent the actions of these chemicals at receptors in the brain.

Most drugs target specific protein molecules in the body. These so-called drug receptors normally interact with naturally occurring substances, such as neurotransmitters (chemical messengers) and hormones. The ability of a drug to recognize a specific receptor protein is often described in terms of a lock and key. The drug (the key) recognizes a specific receptor protein (the lock), and this match provides for a certain degree of specificity of drug action.

The concept of a "receptive substance" for drug action developed long before the molecular nature of receptors was discovered. All original drugs were natural substances and were used for their presumed curative or mind-altering properties. Opium, an extract from the poppy *Papaver somniferum*, had been used for thousands of years to reduce pain and to promote sleep and a feeling of well-being. Derivatives of opium continue to be used in pain management, but it is now known that opiates produce their analgesic effects by acting on specific receptors that exist in the brain and spinal cord.

By the late nineteenth century, scientists were beginning to study the mechanistic basis for drug action, and the scientific discipline of pharmacology was born. Modern pharmacology is directed toward placing drug action in a rigorous chemical context. The development of the "receptor concept" owes much to the achievements of some early physiologists. These include Paul Ehrlich (1854–1915), a German scientist, often considered to be the founder of chemotherapy. Ehrlich showed that certain dyes (or drugs) stained specific cells and that this staining depended on the chemical nature of the dyes. This discovery suggested a specificity of drug action that could perhaps be explained by science. At the same time, John Langley (1852–1925), working at Cambridge University, independently demonstrated that there were interactions between different drugs such as curare and nicotine acting on mammalian muscle. These observations could only be explained by the existence of a specific receptive substance on the muscle cells. In the 1930s, A. J. Clark, at

University College, London, continued to examine these observations and began to quantify the relationship between drug concentration and tissue response, thus pioneering the theories of drug-receptor interactions.

Discovery of receptors

Major advances in protein biochemistry during the 1970s led to the first purification and characterization of receptor molecules. During the 1980s, techniques in molecular biology were developed that made it possible to identify the genes directing creation of particular receptors and to glean information from the sequencing of the deoxyribonucleic acid (DNA) that encodes the different receptors. It is now known that thousands of different receptors exist and that there are multiple variants, or subtypes, within a single receptor family. Nicotine, for example, does not interact with a single type of receptor protein. It interacts with a number of related, but structurally different, receptors in the peripheral nervous system and the central nervous system.

So, what are the implications of drug interactions with specific receptor molecules? First, most target receptors are located on specific cells or cell types. A receptor that is abundant in cardiac muscle may be lacking in the smooth muscle of the bronchial airways. This variation provides for tissue selectivity in drug action, meaning that drugs will target cells that carry the receptor of interest. Some drugs may bind to one receptor subtype more tightly than another, that is, they have higher affinity for some receptors. This mechanism provides for receptor selectivity, making it possible to design a drug that binds more tightly to a receptor in the heart than to a related protein in bronchial smooth muscle. Receptors also show a distinct distribution in the cell. For example, some steroid receptors are found in the cytoplasm; any drug that is targeted to these receptors must be able to cross the cell membrane. Many drugs are too fat-insoluble to cross the

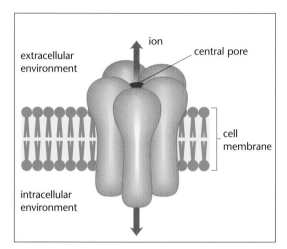

Ligand-gated ion channels are composed of five structurally similar protein subunits that assemble to form a central pore. This pore may be either cation (Na⁺) or anion (Cl⁻) selective.

cell membrane, so these drugs must be able to interact with receptors on the cell surface. Thus, drugs may alter the ability of a receptor to produce an intracellular response, a process known as signal transduction.

Drugs and neurotransmitters

Drugs themselves fall into several categories depending on how they affect the interaction of their targeted receptor with its naturally occurring substance, such as its neurotransmitter or hormone. One of the best-characterized receptor proteins is the receptor in skeletal muscle that responds to the neurotransmitter acetylcholine. This receptor is the prototypical nicotinic acetylcholine receptor (nAChR). Normally, acetylcholine (ACh) is released from the motor nerve that supplies the muscle; ACh binds to its receptor protein, and that causes the receptor ion channel to open, resulting in the flow of Na⁺ ions into the cell. This influx causes a change in membrane potential that provides the trigger for muscle contraction. ACh is thus the natural neurotransmitter that plays the crucial role in muscle contraction. Nicotine, a plant alkaloid, can mimic the actions of ACh by binding to the receptor and inducing the ion channel to open. Nicotine is referred to as an agonist because, like the natural neurotransmitter, it can induce a receptor response.

Its mimicking of ACh effects led to the naming of this receptor as a "nicotinic" receptor. Other drugs bind to the nAChR but do not induce a response; however, because they block the sites to which ACh normally binds, they antagonize, or oppose, the response to the natural agent, leading to their description as antagonists. An example of an antagonist is curare, originally used as an arrow poison by South American Indians. Curare binds to the nAChR and blocks the response to ACh, making the muscles relax and causing paralysis.

Ionotropic receptors

The nAChR is a member of a large family of ligand-gated (opened by small molecules) ion channels, also known as ionotropic receptors. These proteins are found throughout the brain, spinal cord, and in excitable cells, such as muscle. They mediate fast synaptic transmission and are a very important class of receptors because they control, in a precise and highly regulated fashion, the delicate balance between neuronal inhibition and excitation. Specific subtypes of receptors for acetylcholine (nAChR), gamma-aminobutyric acid (GABA$_A$R), glycine (GlyR), and serotonin (5-HT$_3$R) belong to this family. These ligand-gated ion channels are large protein complexes composed of five subunits that are arranged in such a way that they form a central pore. When the neurotransmitter binds to its

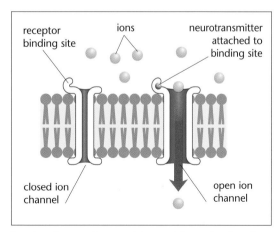

Ionotropic receptors are triggered by molecules of neurotransmitter binding to their surface, which changes the shape of the receptor and opens the channel, allowing ions to pass through.

121

receptors, it elicits a change in the conformation, or shape, of the protein, which allows the central ion channel to open and enables ions to flow across the membrane. This, in turn, excites (depolarizes) or inhibits (hyperpolarizes) the cell, depending on the type of ion being conducted and the direction in which it flows. These channels can be grouped as anionic (GABA, glycine) or cationic (nAChR, 5-HT_3R) because they result in a flux of chloride, or sodium or calcium ions, respectively. $GABA_A$ and glycine receptors are the major inhibitory neurotransmitter receptors in the brain and spinal cord, while nAChR and 5-HT_3R play important roles in excitatory neurotransmission.

To date, many different classes of subunits that make up the ligand-gated ion channels referred to above have been identified. The inclusion of specific subunits within their respective receptors often confer unique pharmacological properties. The distribution of the different subunits varies according to brain region and stage of development, which suggests that each subunit plays a very highly specialized role in the body. Many of these proteins have also been implicated in a number of diseases or conditions. The $GABA_A$ receptor has, for example, been implicated in anxiety, panic disorder, and epilepsy. Due to its central role in brain function and these disease states, the $GABA_A$ receptor is the specific target for a number of drugs, including the benzodiazepines, barbiturates, general anesthetics, and some steroids. The 5-HT_3R plays a role in the vomiting response, and drugs that block the function of this receptor are used in the treatment of vomiting associated with chemotherapy and radiation therapy in cancer. Neuronal nACh receptors, which are activated by nicotine, are important in the psychopharmacology of smoking addiction. Mutations in the structure of muscle-type nAChR have been implicated in myasthenia gravis, an autoimmune condition in which patients suffer from muscle weakness.

Metabotropic receptors

A second important class of membrane-bound receptor is the G-protein-coupled receptor, or metabotropic receptor. Examples of metabotropic receptors include those for norepinephrine, dopamine, and peptide hormones. Unlike ligand-gated ion channels, metabotropic receptors operate on a

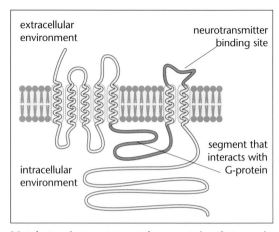

Metabotropic receptors are long proteins that pass in and out of the cell membrane seven times. Binding of a neurotransmitter causes a change in shape that allows the receptor to interact with a G-protein.

slower timescale and involve changes in intracellular processes through activation or inhibition of so-called second-messenger processes. Activation of these receptors by a neurotransmitter or hormone causes a change in the shape of the receptor, which leads to a subunit of the G-protein splitting off from the cytoplasmic surface of the receptor. This, in turn, alters the activity of an effector element, often an enzyme or ion channel, and subsequently the concentration of additional intracellular second messengers. For example, in the case of epinephrine, activation of the beta$_2$ subtype of adrenergic receptors (adrenergic means responsive to epinephrine and norepinephrine) leads to separation of the G-protein subunit from the receptor, and the subunit then acts on a membrane-bound enzyme (adenylate cyclase) that converts adenosine triphosphate (ATP) to cyclic adenosine monophosphate (cAMP). The cAMP, in turn, stimulates another intracellular enzyme, protein kinase A, which plays a role in phosphorylation (yet another metabolic process). While this is only one example of the many second-messenger systems that have been discovered, it illustrates that intracellular cascades are able to amplify the original signal several hundredfold.

Hormones

Hormones, unlike neurotransmitters, exert their effects by interaction with intracellular receptors.

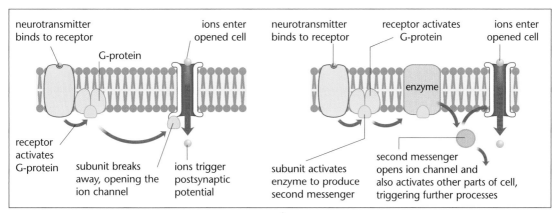

Metabotropic receptors do not trigger a postsynaptic potential directly. Instead, they cause a G-protein to trigger a response at an ion channel (left) or an enzyme (right). If an enzyme is activated, then the response can be amplified hundreds of times through the formation of second-messenger systems that react within the cell.

The lipophilic nature of steroids allows them to cross the plasma membrane and to activate receptors within the cell cytoplasm. This, in turn, causes the steroid-receptor complex to be translocated to the nucleus, where the complex binds to elements of DNA that may lead to an increase or decrease in the transcription (copying) of a particular gene. Since these processes tend to be slow, it explains why natural or synthetic steroids have a characteristic lag time before their pharmacological effects are achieved and the effects of these drugs persist after drug withdrawal. Examples of drugs that bind to intracellular receptors include corticosteroids, mineralocorticoids, vitamin D, sex steroids, and thyroid hormones. The abuse of steroids by athletes is a major problem and has led to the development of ever increasingly sophisticated tests for their detection in blood and urine samples.

Tolerance and dependence

Irrespective of the site of action, the effects of drugs on neurotransmission are obviously complex. Prolonged exposure to any drug may lead to a reduced responsiveness over time. Reduced responsiveness, or tolerance, requires that a person take increasingly higher doses of a drug to achieve the same initial effect. This, in turn, can cause physical or psychological dependence on the drug being taken. Dependence is characterized by withdrawal symptoms that occur when a patient stops taking a particular drug. The molecular mechanisms underlying the development of tolerance and dependence phenomena are poorly understood; however, two possible mechanisms may account for their development. The increased responsiveness of a receptor after prolonged drug exposure is called desensitization. Desensitization is a rapid and reversible process that develops over time and does not result in a decrease in the number of receptors on the cell surface. The effect is most apparent in the study of ligand-gated ion channels where sustained application of a neurotransmitter leads to a decrease in the response of the receiving cell. Alternatively, chronic exposure to a drug may produce a more pronounced change in the number of receptors within the body. This process, called down-regulation, involves a loss of the number of receptors from the cell surface. Down-regulation is believed to account for the development of tolerance to narcotic analgesics, such as morphine. Finally, some drugs alter the phosphorylation state of the receptor. Phosphorylation refers to the addition of phosphate groups to specific amino acids by enzymes called kinases. Phosphorylation can alter receptor function by altering, among other factors, the speed and magnitude of the response. Desensitization, phosphorylation, and down-regulation all represent important elements of regulation of receptor function by drugs.

J. G. NEWELL, S. M. J. DUNN

SEE ALSO:

Acetylcholine • Central Nervous System • Dopamine • Gamma-aminobutyric Acid • Norepinephrine • Serotonin

DXM

In the United States more than 125 over-the-counter products contain the cough suppressant DXM, or dextromethorphan. It has become a drug of abuse among the nation's youth, especially those involved in the club scene.

Dextromethorphan (3 methoxy-17-methylmorphinan) is a nonnarcotic opioid agent used to relieve a dry, nonproductive cough caused by a cold, the flu, or other conditions. It is the active ingredient in many popular commercial cough remedies in the United States. Although it is a derivative of morphine, DXM has no pain-relieving qualities. When used at the recommended dosage, DXM is a safe and effective cough suppressant. However, when used in high doses, it can depress the central nervous system. As such, a person using this drug may experience difficulty regulating body temperature, which could result in reduced sweating and increased body temperature, putting the person at risk of heatstroke. Other effects may include euphoria, blurred vision, hallucinations, delusions, nausea, abdominal pain, vomiting, irregular heartbeat, increased blood pressure, numbness of fingers and toes, headache, loss of consciousness, and, rarely, death.

Approved by the Federal Drug Administration in 1954, DXM has been widely available since the 1960s. It was developed as an alternative cough suppressant that would be less addictive, have fewer side effects, and be more readily available than codeine, which had been the treatment of choice until that time.

Abuse of nonprescription products containing DXM has become a problem among adolescents and young adults, particularly those who are part of the club scene, where it is often passed off as Ecstasy. In fact, DXM is more like ketamine, producing an out-of-body sensation at high doses. Products containing the drug are available over the counter and without a prescription, making them relatively inexpensive and easy for adolescents to obtain. Pharmacies and other retailers have become aware of this trend, however, and many have begun regulating the availability of DXM preparations. Customers often must request the products from the pharmacist, and logs are sometimes kept of purchases.

Dextromethorphan is administered as capsules, lozenges, and syrups. Pills and capsules illicitly

KEY FACTS

Classification
Not scheduled in USA, Canada, UK, or INCB. Opioid.

Street names
Dex, DXM, robo, skittles, triple C, tussin, vitamin D

Short-term effects
Mild stimulation with distorted visual or auditory perceptions and euphoria in lower doses; drowsiness, vertigo, restlessness, respiratory depression, irregular heartbeat, high blood pressure, nausea, abdominal pain, vomiting, constipation, dry mouth, and complete dissociation from one's body at higher doses. Seizures and coma are rare effects of larger doses.

Long-term effects
Tolerance. Possibility of brain damage.

produced in clandestine laboratories may also be used in dance clubs or other places. Typical therapeutic oral doses for adults are 10 to 20 milligrams every 4 hours or 30 milligrams every 6 to 8 hours, not exceeding 120 milligrams daily. Once administered, the onset of effects is rapid, often beginning 15 to 30 minutes after ingestion. Peak concentrations occur between 1.5 to 2 hours, or around 6 hours for sustained release products. Taken recreationally, effects plateau with increasing doses, starting at mild stimulation and eventually reaching full dissociation. Some DXM preparations contain acetaminophen, which can kill at high doses.

P. L. TORCHIA

SEE ALSO:
Illicit Manufacturing • Ketamine • Opiates and Opioids • Pharmacy Drugs

Ecstasy

Ecstasy is the street name for preparations that contain the drug MDMA, or methylenedioxymethamphetamine. MDMA is a phenethylamine that has some hallucinogenic properties and also stimulates the central nervous system.

Certain drugs have intimate links with specific phases of popular culture. LSD was a seminal drug of the psychedelic hippie movement of the 1960s, for example, just as cocaine was associated with the disco movement of the 1970s. Ecstasy became the signature drug of the rave culture that emerged in the late 1980s.

In its early days, Ecstasy acquired a reputation among some recreational drug users as being a "clean" and sociable drug. It promoted empathy and affection between users, rather than the aggression associated with alcohol or the violence of crack and heroin. Ecstasy enthusiasts welcomed the fact that the feelings of well-being and heightened perception of an Ecstasy trip were accompanied by seemingly unlimited energy to enjoy the experience—a marked contrast to the lethargy often induced by marijuana. Other users preferred Ecstasy because they found its mild hallucinogenic activity less intimidating than the overwhelming psychedelic experience of an LSD trip.

Ecstasy in decline

The reputation of Ecstasy soon became tarnished. Ecstasy dealers, eager to increase their profits, started using adulterants in their products. Cheaper substances, such as amphetamines, ketamine, and caffeine, partially or completely replaced MDMA—the active ingredient of true Ecstasy. Some pills contained analogs of MDMA that had a different range of effects.

It was almost impossible to know the true composition of a pill sold as Ecstasy, and the nature of the trip that followed consumption was frequently disappointing or an unpleasant surprise. However, it seems that pills rumored to contain heroin were, in fact, more likely to contain ketamine. To date, no analysis of Ecstasy seized in law-enforcement agency raids has revealed the presence of heroin.

The reputation of Ecstasy was damaged further by high-profile media reports of hospitalizations and deaths caused by MDMA itself or by its analogs. Many of these cases were caused by heatstroke and dehydration or, paradoxically, by drinking too much water to avoid dehydration (*see* box, p. 127).

In fact, the U.S. Substance Abuse and Mental Health Services Administration (SAMHSA) data for 2001 report only 9 deaths in which MDMA was the sole intoxicant and 67 further deaths in which MDMA had been consumed with other intoxicants, notably opiates and cocaine. British studies report remarkably similar results. For the same year, the number of MDMA-related visits to U.S. emergency rooms was dwarfed by the number of cocaine-related

Ecstasy manufacturers are notable for their subversion of marketing techniques. Clandestine factories stamp pills with distinctive logos, often imitating those of popular brands to create distinctive products that encourage loyalty among users. However, there is no regulation to ensure consistent quality of a brand.

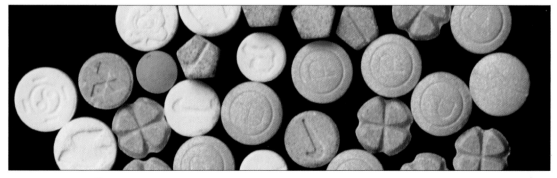

incidents and was comparable with numbers of emergency visits related to LSD and legal drugs such as fluoxetine and aspirin (*see* table, below right).

The U.S. Drug Enforcement Administration reports that Ecstasy consumption has declined since 2001. Although the SAMHSA figures suggest that MDMA is less dangerous than other drugs, there is evidence that it is addictive. There is also persistent concern about subtle and possibly long-term effects on brain cells. This concern is better understood with some knowledge of how MDMA acts in the brain.

MDMA in the brain

The active ingredient of true Ecstasy is MDMA, or 3,4-*methylenedioxymethamphetamine*. As its full name suggests, MDMA is closely related to amphetamine. Indeed, the stimulant and euphoriant effects of MDMA are caused by the release of dopamine and norepinephrine from neurons (nerve cells), as happens with other amphetamines. However, the principal effect of MDMA is to release serotonin from neurons, and this effect is the cause of the mild hallucinogenic activity of the drug as well as the characteristic "loved-up" sensation.

MDMA causes serotonin release by hijacking the reuptake mechanism that reabsorbs serotonin into transmitting neurons. Reuptake occurs through channels in the cell membranes of neurons. MDMA passes into these channels, then makes them pump serotonin out of, rather than into, the neuron. The fluid that surrounds the neurons suddenly becomes rich in serotonin, which can then bind to the various receptors around the brain that cause the characteristic effects of an Ecstasy high. Because the reuptake transporter is blocked by the MDMA, the neuron becomes severely depleted of serotonin within a matter of hours but returns to near normal levels within 24 hours.

The mechanism of action of MDMA has consequences for people on antidepressants. Selective serotonin reuptake inhibitors (SSRIs) diminish the effect of MDMA by impeding its entry into the reuptake channels. In direct contrast, monoamine oxidase inhibitors (MAOIs) exaggerate the effect of MDMA by incapacitating the enzymes that mop up excess serotonin, dopamine, and other neurotransmitters. The interaction between MDMA and MAOIs is potentially life threatening.

KEY FACTS

Classification
Schedule I (USA), Schedule I (Canada), Class A (UK), Schedule I (INCB). Stimulant and mild hallucinogen.

Street names
Ecstasy (XTC), E, Adam, pills, rolls. Some names—dove, for example—refer to embossed logos on pills.

Form
Pure MDMA is a bitter-tasting white crystalline solid. Typical street preparations are off-white powders and pills that may contain psychoactive adulterants as well as inactive bulking agents. In some cases, cheaper stimulants such as caffeine, pseudoephedrine, and amphetamine completely replace MDMA.

Short-term effects
Psychological effects include short-term anxiety followed by a euphoric "rush." Users feel at ease with themselves and those around them, and tend to have enhanced appreciation of sensory stimulations such as lights and music. Physical effects include increased energy, racing heartbeat, loss of appetite, jaw clenching, increased body temperature, and sweating.

Dangers
Risk of heatstroke and dehydration if taken during energetic activity. However, drinking too much water can cause collapse and swelling of the brain.

U.S. EMERGENCY DEPARTMENT VISITS IN 2007	
LSD	3,561
Ecstasy (MDMA)	**12,748**
Stimulants	85,043
Heroin	188,162
Marijuana	308,547
Cocaine	553,530

Source: Office of Applied Studies, SAMHSA, Drug Abuse Warning Network, 2007.

ECSTASY, DEHYDRATION, AND WATER INTOXICATION

The effects of Ecstasy use include increased body temperature (hyperthermia). Also, users often feel they have limitless stamina and can dance for hours. As a result, they sweat large volumes of water, and their temperatures can soar as MDMA suppresses the regulation of body temperature. The result can be hospitalization for heat stroke or dehydration and, in extremely few cases, death.

The dangers of failing to replace water lost in sweat were recognized in the early years of rave culture. Responsible event promoters and club owners reacted by making sure their bars had stocks of drinking water. Less scrupulous promoters disconnected the water supplies in bathrooms to ensure sales of bottled water. Many venues also started to provide chill-out areas—cool and quiet rooms offering a break from the heat of the dance floor to allow ravers to cool off.

A rarer but more insidious problem is water toxicity, or hyponatremia. In addition to water, sweat robs the body of electrolytes (salts) that are vital for many key body functions. Ideally, these salts could be replaced by drinking isotonic sports drinks that have the ideal balance of salts and water to compensate for sweating.

Plain drinking water contains practically no salts. Consequently, drinking plain water reduces the concentration of salts in the body fluids. Under normal circumstances, the kidneys would attempt to restore a healthy salt concentration by eliminating excess water in urine. The normal excretion capacity of healthy kidneys is 0.6 to 0.8 liters per hour, but this can easily be overwhelmed when a person obsessively drinks water with the intention of preventing dehydration.

MDMA worsens the situation by making the body secrete a hormone that reduces urination. Eventually, the concentration of salts in the body drops below healthy levels and causes symptoms such as muscle tremor, confusion, vomiting, and diarrhea. Excess fluid causes the brain to swell and can cause brain damage, paralysis, and even death.

Ecstasy aftermath

In the short term, the brain responds to MDMA by slowing down serotonin production and by desensitizing the neurons that respond to serotonin. This "turning down" of the serotonin system often causes a temporary depression around two days after taking Ecstasy. Mood usually returns to normal within a few days as the brain replenishes its serotonin stores. Animal studies suggest that the full sensitivity of human serotonin receptors may take several weeks to return to normal, but the relevance of such studies to people is uncertain.

More serious is the potential for long-term or permanent damage to serotonin neurons. Animal studies suggest that serotonin-depleted neurons are prone to invasion by dopamine through reuptake channels. Enzymes inside such neurons recognize the dopamine molecules as alien and potentially toxic. The products of the enzyme attack on dopamine include toxic substances such as free radicals. These substances can cause serious damage to serotonin neurons, and some neuroscientists fear that this damage could be irreparable, raising the prospect of permanent mood depression and lack of muscle control as occurs with Parkinson's disease. There is evidence that MDMA use leads to impairment of verbal and nonverbal memory functions.

Some studies suggest that a dose of an SSRI, such as Prozac, could reduce harm by blocking the influx of dopamine into serotonin neurons. Other sources recommend the use of nutritional anti-oxidants such as vitamin C, vitamin E, or zinc supplements.

The true long-term effects of Ecstasy will only become apparent over the next few decades. In the meantime, it is worth noting that even advocates of MDMA for therapeutic use recommend a maximum of four moderate doses in any year.

M. CLOWES

SEE ALSO:
Amphetamines • Club Drugs • Designer Drugs • Ecstasy Analogs • Phenethylamines • Serotonin • SSRIs

Ecstasy Analogs

Ecstasy analogs are psychoactive compounds whose molecular structures are similar to that of Ecstasy (MDMA). These compounds find use as recreational drugs, and some are being tested for potential use in psychotherapy.

The basis of many drug actions is the interaction between individual drug molecules and sites on the surfaces of cells called receptors. In the case of recreational drugs, drug effects include the "high" sought by users of the drug as well as undesirable side effects that users tolerate during their drug experience. Ecstasy analogs provide the opportunity to modify the effects of Ecstasy by altering the positive effects of the drug. Inevitably, the negative side effects of the experience also vary from one analog to another.

Analog effects

In common with most other drugs, Ecstasy (MDMA) and its analogs produce their positive and negative effects by drug-receptor interactions at various sites in the brain and elsewhere in the body. The principal effect of Ecstasy is to trigger the release of serotonin from neurons that use it as a neurotransmitter, although it also releases dopamine, norepinephrine, and other neurotransmitters. Once released, these substances trigger the neurons that respond to them. This action begins the cascade of processes that produce an Ecstasy high.

The various aspects of the effects Ecstasy produces correlate to stimulation of different neuron receptors, in particular different subtypes of 5-HT receptors. (5-HT is the abbreviation for 5-hydroxytryptamine, an alternative name for serotonin.) Neuroscientists have clarified the origins of certain effects of Ecstasy by using drugs to block or activate individual receptor types in a selective manner. They found that 5-HT_{2A} receptors contribute to the mild hallucinogenic activity of MDMA, while some 5-HT_{1B} receptors instill serenity and elevate mood by promoting further serotonin release. Other 5-HT_{1B} receptors cause euphoria by stimulating the release of dopamine. In contrast, activation of 5-HT_{1A} and 5-HT_{2C} receptors increases anxiety.

The character of an Ecstasy trip evolves as each set of receptors experiences elevated neurotransmitter concentrations. Consequently, an initial phase of anxiety and sometimes nausea is followed by

MDMA: 3,4–methylenedioxymethamphetamine

MDA: 3,4–methylenedioxyamphetamine

MDEA: 3,4–methylenedioxyethamphetamine

MBDB: N–methyl–1–(1,3–benzodioxol–5–yl)–2–butanamine

A comparison of molecular structures of Ecstasy (MDMA, at top) and its principal analogs. All have the same basic structure, but the groups that attach to the asterisked carbon atom give each compound slightly different properties and effects.

euphoria as the dopamine effect becomes stronger. One of the means by which Ecstasy analogs modify the Ecstasy reaction is by activating different systems of neurons that contribute to the high.

Other differences with analogs stem from differences in the rate at which different analogs get through the blood-brain barrier on the way in and out of the brain, and the rate at which enzymes convert active drugs into active and inactive metabolites before the body excretes these substances. Each analog exhibits further differences between the psychoactive properties of its two mirror-image forms, called enantiomers or stereoisomers. The two forms are the *S* (or *dextro*) enantiomer and the *R* (or *levo*) enantiomer.

Comparisons

Much of the study of Ecstasy analogs relies on the use of rats trained to distinguish hallucinogens such as LSD from stimulants such as amphetamine. The responses of such rats to different analogs helps classify each drug on a spectrum between purely hallucinogenic activity and purely stimulant activity. Drugs that occupy this spectrum of psychoactivity are sometimes called *entactogens*—a term that implies an ability to get in touch with an inner self.

Other research techniques include functional magnetic resonance imaging to observe brain activity in human subjects using different analogs. The book *PiHKAL: A Chemical Love Story* by U.S. pharmacologist Alexander Shulgin (1925–) also provides accounts of the effects the author and friends experienced with MDMA and its analogs.

MDMA (Ecstasy, Adam). The usual street form of the prototype of these drugs is a racemate—an equal mixture of *R*- and *S*-MDMA. Careful preparation from appropriate starting materials allows the two forms to be tested separately, however, and that is when differences in properties become apparent. *S*-MDMA acts faster and is more stimulating than the *R* form. Furthermore, pharmacological studies show that the body transforms *S*-MDMA into MDA more rapidly, as well as producing potentially neurotoxic substances faster and in greater quantities.

MDA (Love Drug). Popular in the 1960s, this drug has a stronger psychedelic effect than MDMA. The absence of the *N*-methyl group compared with MDMA suggests that this methyl group somehow impairs the interaction of the drug with serotonin neurons that stimulate the 5-HT$_{2A}$ receptors. The result is that Ecstasy has a less hallucinogenic effect compared with MDA. Once again, the *S* enantiomer is more stimulating than the *R* form.

MDEA (Eve). MDEA is less stimulating than MDMA, and greater doses are necessary to achieve a comparable effect. Even then, Eve produces less

chattiness, and users report feeling more "stoned" than they would on Ecstasy. Separate evaluations of *R* and *S* forms of MDEA in humans reveal that the pure *S* form is mood lifting, while the *R* form causes depression. The combined action of the two forms in street MDEA could explain the more subdued nature of the Eve experience.

MBDB (Eden). MBDB is essentially free of hallucinogenic activity but still creates feelings of well-being and empathy. For this reason, some researchers claim it to be the model entactogen.

Medical uses

Ecstasy analogs were considered for nonrecreational uses long before they were classified as controlled substances. The Merck company of Darmstadt, Germany, showed interest in these compounds when it applied for a patent for their synthesis in 1912. The goal at that time was to produce vasoconstricting compounds to stop bleeding.

More sinister uses were explored in the early 1950s, when the U.S. Central Intelligence Agency investigated the potential of MDMA as a truth drug and incapacitating agent. By the end of the same decade, the SmithKline French pharmaceutical company started to look at the possible use of MDA as an antidepressant or even to reduce appetite. MDA was too psychedelic for these uses, but it would soon pass into street use under the name "Love Drug."

A potential, although not yet established, use for MDMA analogs lies in their ability to help psychotherapy patients explore and address memories that would otherwise be highly distressing. In 1967, Chilean psychiatrist Claudio Naranjo experimented with MDA as a replacement for the LSD that had been used in previous experiments. Many psychotherapists began to use less hallucinogenic MDMA in the mid-1970s. Classification as a Schedule I drug put a halt to this research in 1985, but 2004 saw the Drug Enforcement Administration grant permission for small-scale trials of MDMA for treatment of trauma victims. This decision may herald a new prospect of Ecstasy analogs as psychological healing agents.

M. CLOWES

Endorphins

The body produces chemicals that have the same effects as morphine and heroin. These substances, called endorphins, reduce pain and can provide a euphoric high in response to emotional or physical stress.

Endorphins are opiatelike substances found in the brain that act in a similar manner to neurotransmitters (chemicals that transmit messages). The word *endorphin* comes from *endogenous* (meaning within) and *morphine*. Though most commonly known for their painkilling properties, endorphins are also involved in other important body functions.

Endorphins were first detected in the 1960s but were overlooked until the discovery of opiate receptors in the mid-1970s motivated researchers to look for a natural substance that would activate them. Endorphins are classified into three major categories. Beta-endorphin was one of the first to be found. It has a distinct pathway in the brain leading from the hypothalamus and also occurs in the pituitary. Enkephalins occur throughout the brain and appear to act as modulators for other systems. Dynorphins were the last to be discovered and are distributed throughout the central and peripheral nervous systems. They are thought to play a key role in promoting spinal analgesia (pain relief).

Endorphins are involved in a number of behaviors and functions, including regulation of feeding behavior and digestion, sexual behavior, pregnancy, and the release of stress hormones. The so-called runner's high experienced by long-distance runners is also thought to be the result of endorphins flooding the body in response to stress and pain. The effects produced by opiates, including euphoria and dysphoria, sedation, dilation and contraction of pupils, respiratory depression, a drop in heart rate and blood pressure, tolerance, and withdrawal symptoms are also produced by endorphins acting in their natural capacity.

Endorphins are peptides made from amino acids. The endorphins were among the first peptides to be associated with behavior. This discovery at first created problems because endorphins did not fit the criteria of a neurotransmitter. The discovery that peptides can be involved in behavior helped create the explosion, beginning in the 1990s, in the understanding of how the brain works.

How endorphins work

For an endorphin or morphine to create an effect, it must fit into a receptor. This mechanism is like a lock and key, with the endorphin (or an opiate, such as morphine) as the key and the receptor as the lock. The endorphin fits into the lock through chemical bonds. When opioid receptors were first discovered, it was thought that only one type existed. Just as there are several kinds of endorphins, there are also several kinds of receptors, and each mediates a specific response. For example, the mu_1 receptor is involved in pain and euphoria, while the mu_2 receptor is associated with the respiratory depression caused by opiate drugs.

Opioid peptides are thought to have two mechanisms of action. The first mechanism exerts their action at the synapse (nerve cell junction) as a neurotransmitter or neuromodulator. Another mechanism acts through presynaptic receptors that modulate the release of a neurotransmitter or another peptide. There is some debate about whether endogenous opioids are addictive. Evidence suggests not, since endorphins are quickly broken down by enzymes in the synapse so they are never in contact with receptors long enough to develop tolerance or dependence. Also, no withdrawal symptoms are felt when endorphins are not being produced.

The discovery of the endogenous opioids has led to considerable optimism that an understanding of the biochemistry and physiology of the endogenous opioid system will lead to a greater understanding of drug addiction and medications for its treatment and prevention. Clearly there are genetic and physical characteristics that make some people more vulnerable to addiction; however, since addictive disorders comprise environmental, behavioral, and psychological components, finding the cause and treatment will not be uncomplicated.

J. S. WOODS

SEE ALSO:
Drug Receptors • Opiates and Opioids

Ephedrine

Ephedrine is often an ingredient in herbal products, dietary supplements, and cold remedies. It was once regarded as a mild stimulant, but ephedrine has come under increasing regulation as severe side effects have become apparent.

The ephedra plant, also called ma huang, is a shrub that grows in desert regions, primarily in Asia and North America. The plant produces six alkaloid compounds, including ephedrine, which stimulates both the cardiac and central nervous systems.

Chinese herbalists have used ephedra for thousands of years to treat bronchial asthma, colds, hay fever, and sinusitis. Chemically synthesized ephedrine is used in over-the-counter and prescription drugs for treating allergies, asthma, nasal congestion, and related upper-respiratory symptoms. Ephedrine is also the active ingredient in methamphetamine and methcathinone, powerful and addictive synthetic stimulants that can easily be made using over-the-counter cold medications and other common household products.

Various dietary supplements containing herbal ephedra or synthetic ephedrine have been marketed to promote weight control, boost energy and endurance, and enhance athletic performance. These supplements often contain caffeine or other stimulants that might interact with ephedra's effects. Energy drinks marketed to students, athletes, and other active young people sometimes contain ephedra, again in combination with caffeine. These beverages advertise a wide range of appealing but unverified effects, such as greater endurance, faster reaction time, and keener mental awareness. Ephedra is also the primary ingredient in "herbal ecstasy," a product commonly sold on the Internet.

Prevalence of use

Research on prevalence of use is largely limited to the United States. In 2001 the Behavioral Risk Factor Surveillance System (BRFSS) reported that around 1 percent of adults (aged 18 years and older) in Florida, Iowa, Michigan, West Virginia, and Wisconsin reported use of an ephedra-based weight-loss product. Based on this finding, the researchers estimated that approximately 2.5 million American adults had used an ephedra-containing product during the previous three years. Another research

> ## KEY FACTS
>
> **Classification**
> Not scheduled in USA, UK, or INCB. Schedule VI in Canada. Stimulant.
>
> **Street names**
> Herbal ecstasy, ma huang, Mormon tea
>
> **Short-term effects**
> Alertness, mild euphoria, insomnia, increase in blood pressure and heart rate, dizziness, tremor, headache
>
> **Dangers**
> High doses may cause heart attack, stroke, seizures, paranoia, hallucinations

team surveyed adult health club patrons, finding that 25 percent of men and 13 percent of women reported having used an ephedra-containing product within the past three years.

Estimates of youth usage rates come from a 2003 telephone survey conducted by a health care insurance group. Fully 7 percent of the respondents, a nationally representative sample of youth aged 12 to 17, reported knowing a peer who was using ephedra, compared with zero percent in 2001. Ephedra use among young athletes appears to be especially high. In 2001 the National Collegiate Athletic Association (NCAA) conducted a national study of drug and supplement use by college athletes. More than 21,000 student athletes completed the survey. Nearly 4 percent reported having used ephedra within the previous 12 months. Reasons for using these products included improving athletic performance (24 percent), as an appetite suppressant (22 percent), for health reasons (22 percent), and to improve appearance (20 percent).

Adverse effects

Ephedra-containing products can induce headaches, insomnia, tremors, nerve damage, rapid or irregular heartbeat, high blood pressure, strokes, heart attacks, seizures, brain damage, and even death. The *Annals of Internal Medicine* published a study in 2003 suggesting that ephedra accounted for 64 percent of all adverse reactions from herbal products in 2001, while representing just over 4 percent of industry sales during that same year.

A study published in the *New England Journal of Medicine* in 2000 examined 140 health incidents related to ephedra products. The researchers concluded that 43 cases (31 percent) were "definitely" or "probably" related to the use of dietary supplements containing ephedrine alkaloids. Among these cases, three people died, seven became permanently disabled, and four required continuing medical treatment. The researchers concluded that another 44 cases were possibly related to ephedra-containing products.

The RAND Corporation, in a 2003 study commissioned by the U.S. National Institutes of Health, conducted an analysis of controlled trials of ephedra or ephedrine use for weight loss or enhanced athletic performance. Evidence suggests that short-term use of ephedra or synthetic ephedrine, either with or without caffeine, does promote modest weight loss. However, there are no data available regarding maintenance of weight loss once the use of these products is discontinued.

The researchers found that there have been no clinical trials on the impact of ephedra use on athletic performance. Studies of synthetic ephedrine have involved small numbers of participants, administration of a single dose, and varying outcome measures, which makes cross-study comparisons very difficult. No studies have tested the impact of repeated use on athletic performance.

However, safety data from 50 trials indicated that use of these supplements increases the risk of heart palpitations, psychiatric symptoms, autonomic hyperactivity, and gastrointestinal symptoms by 2.2 to 3.6 times. The data also revealed a trend for increased blood pressure, but the increase was not statistically significant. Most of the dietary supplements that were tested also contained caffeine, so it was not possible to separate out caffeine's contribution to these events.

The RAND researchers also screened more than 16,000 case study reports of adverse events associated with prior ephedra or ephedrine consumption. They identified 5 deaths, 5 heart attacks, 11 cerebrovascular accidents, 4 seizures, and 8 psychiatric cases in which ephedra was identified as the precipitating factor. About half of these cases involved people aged 30 years or younger.

In the United States, ephedrine gained notoriety after the death in 2003 of Steve Bechler, a professional baseball pitcher with the Baltimore Orioles, who, according to the coroner's report, died after taking ephedrine alkaloids. Ephedrine was also blamed in the deaths of college football players at a number of U.S. universities. These high-profile cases led to renewed calls for government regulatory action against ephedra-containing dietary supplements.

Government regulation

In December 2003 the U.S. Food and Drug Administration (FDA) advised consumers to stop using ephedra products. The agency also took enforcement actions against firms making unsubstantiated claims about enhanced athletic performance for their ephedra-containing dietary supplements. Products advertised on that basis were removed from the market.

In April 2004 the FDA banned the sale of dietary supplements containing ephedrine alkaloids, declaring that these products present a significant or unreasonable risk of illness or injury under ordinary conditions of use. The FDA's ruling was due primarily to the substance's effect in raising blood pressure and stressing the circulatory system, reactions that are linked to heart ailments and strokes.

If manufacturers continue to market ephedra-containing dietary supplements, the FDA can prohibit the products from being sold. Some ephedra-containing products are not covered by the ban, including traditional Chinese herbal medicines and herbal teas. Also not covered are approved medications containing chemically synthesized ephedrine, which are regulated as drugs.

W. DeJong

SEE ALSO:
Illicit Manufacturing • Methamphetamine • Methcathinone • Norepinephrine

Epinephrine

Epinephrine, which is known as adrenaline in many parts of the world, is a hormone that is secreted from the body's adrenal glands in times of stress. It is also released by the sympathetic nervous system, preparing the body for danger.

Epinephrine plays an important role in survival since it prepares the body for a "fight or flight" response to conditions that are perceived to be threatening. It is released directly into the bloodstream and it achieves its effects rapidly, generally within a few minutes. Hans Selye (1907–1982), a physiologist at the University of Montreal in Canada, devoted his career to the study of the general adaptation syndrome, which he described as the response of the body to a stressful environment. Selye was the first to describe how exposure to hostile conditions results in a series of coordinated responses that promote increased chances of survival. This response depends primarily on the release of large amounts of epinephrine from the adrenal glands as a result of stimulation of a specific branch of the nervous system, the sympathetic nervous system.

Everyone experiences stressful situations, and the effects of a sudden rise in epinephrine levels are familiar to most people. Heart rate and blood pressure go up, the airways dilate to allow for improved breathing, the pupils widen to give better distance vision, metabolic rates rise to provide an immediate source of energy, and the blood vessels in skeletal muscle dilate to accommodate the greater blood flow that may be required for physical action. Redirection of blood flow from the skin results in a characteristic pallor, and nonessential activities such as digestion and urination are suppressed. These effects are what constitute the feelings associated with a rush of adrenaline; this, in turn, appears to motivate some people to engage in thrill-seeking behaviors.

Chemistry and effects on the body

Epinephrine belongs to a class of structurally related chemicals called catecholamines, which are derived from the amino acid tyrosine. Other chemicals in this class include the neurotransmitters dopamine and norepinephrine. However, unlike these neurotransmitters, which play important roles in the brain, epinephrine exerts most of its effects on the periphery, that is, outside the brain and spinal cord.

Some people thrive on activities that produce a rush of epinephrine; whether they can become addicted to its effects is a matter of debate.

Epinephrine will act on all cells in the body that carry protein targets for this hormone. These targets, called adrenergic receptors, or adrenoreceptors, were identified more than fifty years ago. They are broadly classified into two groups, alpha and beta receptors. While epinephrine does not show a strong preference for any of these receptors, its actions appear to be more prominent on beta receptors in the heart, blood vessels, and smooth muscle. Since epinephrine induces such wide-ranging effects, it is not surprising that drugs that affect its action have great utility in medicine. Epinephrine itself is a very effective agent in the treatment of acute asthma because of its ability to dilate bronchial smooth muscle. However, it cannot be given orally because it is rapidly destroyed in the gastrointestinal tract. There are, however, naturally occurring and synthetic analogs of epinephrine that are less liable to break down and which, to varying extents, can mimic its actions. These include the plant product ephedrine, which is a major component of many prescription and over-the-counter drugs used in the treatment of respiratory disorders. Other drugs (adrenoreceptor antagonists) inhibit the actions of epinephrine. These include the beta-blocker propranolol, which is widely used to block the effects of epinephrine in the treatment of cardiovascular diseases such as hypertension and angina. Propranolol is also prescribed for social phobias such as the fear of public speaking, for example. In such cases, blocking the effects of epinephrine prevents peripheral symptoms, including the increased heart rate and trembling, that make these situations uncomfortable for many people.

Anaphylactic shock
One emergency situation in which the use of epinephrine is indicated is in the treatment of anaphylactic shock. This is a potentially life-threatening allergic reaction that occurs in about 30 out of every 100,000 people. Common allergens that provoke this response are peanuts, insect stings, latex, drugs, shellfish, and dairy products. Anaphylaxis usually occurs within seconds to minutes but may take hours to develop. It is characterized by flushing of the face, hives, difficulty breathing, swallowing, or speaking, changes in heart rate, severe asthma, abdominal pain, nausea, vomiting, or a severe drop in blood pressure. The exposure to the allergen stimulates production of antibodies, which then cause the release of histamine from cells.

The front-line treatment for anaphylactic shock is administration of epinephrine by intramuscular injection into the thigh. People who suffer from severe allergies must carry epinephrine preparations and administer them when required. While these injections can alleviate the early symptoms, patients must still seek emergency medical assistance, as other forms of support may be necessary.

The effect of drugs
Since epinephrine plays such an important role in normal physiological responses, an understanding

of its interaction with other drugs is crucial. In this respect, it is important to consider some recreational drugs, in particular methamphetamine (which is structurally related to epinephrine) and nicotine.

Methamphetamine (also known on the street as crystal, speed, ice, or crank) was originally used for the treatment of obesity but became widely used as a club drug. This drug stimulates the release of dopamine and epinephrine from nerve cells in the brain, resulting in the elevation of both mood and body movements. Consequently, the effects of methamphetamine include wakefulness, increased physical activity, decreased appetite, hyperthermia and euphoria; adverse effects include insomnia, confusion, tremors, anxiety, paranoia, repetitive behavior, and convulsions. Blood pressure and heart rate may be increased to the point that the drug can cause irreversible damage to vessels in the brain, leading to stroke, cardiovascular collapse and, ultimately, death. It has also been established that methamphetamine use during pregnancy may result in premature delivery of the fetus.

Nicotine is one of the most heavily used drugs in the United States. Cigarette smoking has been the most popular method of taking nicotine since the beginning of the twentieth century. In 1989 the surgeon general of the United States issued a report that concluded that cigarettes are addictive. Nicotine acts as both a stimulant and a sedative to the central nervous system. The ingestion of nicotine results in a kick or high because it causes a discharge of epinephrine from the adrenal glands, resulting in stimulation of all of the effects of epinephrine described above. Stimulation is then followed by depression and fatigue, leading the smoker to try to reverse the situation by seeking more nicotine. The nature of nicotine addiction is undoubtedly complex. The adrenaline rush may play a part. Some people do appear to get high under dangerous conditions and revel in, for example, extreme sports. Whether this can be described as an addiction remains to be established.

J. G. NEWELL, S. M. J. DUNN

Erythropoietin

Erythropoietin is a natural hormone secreted by the body to stimulate the production of red blood cells. The synthetic version of erythropoietin has been abused by athletes in an attempt to improve their performance.

Erythropoietin is a hormone that stimulates erythropoiesis, the process by which the body produces red blood cells. The hormone itself is a polypeptide chain made up of 165 amino acids and with four sugars attached to its structure. It is synthesized primarily in the kidneys and is excreted into the bloodstream.

Synthetically produced erythropoietin was approved by the Food and Drug Adminstration in 1988 for the treatment of anemia (a low level of red blood cells) in patients with chronic renal failure or cancer patients receiving chemotherapy. In these situations, erythropoietin therapy is used to stimulate red blood cell production, leading to a noticeable improvement in feelings of fatigue and lethargy by the patient.

The primary illegal abuse of erythropoietin is as a doping agent by endurance athletes. The goal of these athletes is to increase their red blood cell count to above-normal levels, thereby raising the oxygen-carrying capacity of the blood and improving performance. These benefits are most beneficial to athletes competing in endurance events such as long-distance running, cross-country skiing, and bicycle racing. Owing to these performance-enhancing characteristics, the International Olympic Committee has placed erythropoietin on the list of banned substances.

In response to accusations of widespread abuse of the drug during the 1990s, the World Anti-Doping Agency engaged scientists to develop a reliable test to determine the presence of synthetic erythropoietin in an athlete's blood. Such a test was pioneered by Australian scientists and introduced at the 2000 Olympics in Sydney. The test has since undergone significant improvements, and an additional test has been developed using a sample of the athlete's urine.

In the years since testing began, a number of endurance athletes have been caught illegally using erythropoietin. The true extent of erythropoietin abuse is difficult to determine, as the test is only able to reveal use within the preceding 4 to 7 days.

Erythropoietin is manufactured as a sterile, colorless liquid. It is injected either directly into the

Distance runners have been known to take injections of erythropoietin to improve their stamina.

bloodstream or under the skin. In both methods, noticeable effects are seen after five or more days, and desirable levels are often reached after two weeks to a month of treatment. The dangers of erythropoietin abuse involve potential problems associated with a thickening of the blood from an increase in red blood cells. A person abusing erythropoietin is more likely to suffer from blood clots as well as potentially deadly heart attacks and strokes. Blood may be further concentrated when a person becomes dehydrated. This is a particularly deadly combination, given that most abusers of erythropoietin are athletes competing in endurance events in which dehydration is common.

The social consequences of erythropoietin abuse are numerous. At the core of modern sports events, such as the Olympics, lies the notion that all players are competing without the use of chemical aids such as erythropoietin. France became the first nation to pass laws making the use of doping agents such as erythropoietin illegal on the grounds that the abusers are attempting to defraud the athletes against whom they compete.

M. Spigelman, M. Nadel

See also:
Hormonal Effects

Ethanol

Ethanol, or ethyl alcohol, is the main intoxicating ingredient of all alcoholic beverages. It has immediate and chronic effects on the brain and many other parts and functions of the human body, notably the heart and liver.

Ethanol is a colorless volatile liquid with a pungent aroma; its formula is C_2H_5OH. It forms through the fermentation of sugars under the action of yeasts, as well as in numerous industrial chemical processes. Practically all ethanol for human consumption comes from the natural fermentation of sugars present in fruits or derived by the breakdown of more complex carbohydrates in grains and starchy vegetables.

The molecular simplicity of ethanol contributes to its ability to spread throughout a human body after ingestion. In particular, ethanol is highly efficient in getting across the blood-brain barrier to work its effects on mood, judgment, and coordination, as well as on the brain mechanisms that maintain wakefulness, breathing, and reflexes.

Physiological effects

The effects of consuming alcoholic beverages are modulated by the rate of absorption of ethanol into the bloodstream, by the rate of distribution to sites of action around the body, notably in the brain, and by the rate at which the body eliminates ethanol or converts it into inactive compounds. This set of parameters forms the pharmacokinetics of ethanol.

Absorption. Ethanol passes into the bloodstream through all parts of the gastrointestinal tract, but it does so most rapidly through the walls of the small intestine. Carbon dioxide, which forms the bubbles in sparkling drinks and mixers, promotes the passage of stomach contents into the small intestine and accelerates the absorption of alcohol. High concentrations of ethanol in spirits also speeds absorption, so the combination of a spirit and a carbonated mixer gets ethanol into the bloodstream much faster than the same dose of alcohol in a flat beer. Furthermore, the relatively low concentration of ethanol in beer puts a tighter limit on the dose of ethanol that can be ingested without discomfort due to bloating.

In contrast to carbon dioxide, milk and fatty foods cause a reflex closing of valves that control the passage of stomach contents to the small intestine. This reflex helps ensure adequate digestion, but it

KEY FACTS

Classification
Unscheduled central nervous system (CNS) depressant. Retail sale is restricted and subject to payment of duty on drinkable alcohol-containing products.

Form
Almost always in drinks: beers, wines, spirits, liqueurs, and cocktails. Present in some household products, including mouthwashes and perfumes.

Short-term effects
Dose-dependent CNS effects range from apparent stimulation due to reduced inhibition through impaired coordination and reflexes, to sedation, coma, and death as respiration fails or if an unconscious user inhales vomit. Disinhibition and impaired reasoning can lead to physical and verbal confrontations, as well as injuries and deaths due to accidents while driving or operating machinery while intoxicated.

Long-term effects
Malnutrition and obesity due to high caloric value and lack of nutrients in alcoholic drinks. Chronic heavy drinking causes liver diseases such as fatty liver, alcoholic hepatitis, and cirrhosis. Neurological and mental effects include damage to peripheral nerves, depression, and psychosis. Heavy drinking can cause heart disease and promote some cancers, and can cause fetal alcohol syndrome if pregnant.

Drug interactions
Ethanol modifies the body's response to many drugs in both the short and the long term. Prescription drug users should always obey accompanying information and seek medical advice before drinking alcohol. Can produce fatal reactions with some illicit drugs.

also slows the progress of ethanol to the small intestine. Furthermore, the presence of food reduces the concentration of ethanol and further slows its absorption into the bloodstream. Hence, wine taken with a meal causes much slower intoxication than spirits taken on an empty stomach.

Distribution. Ethanol is unusual in that it has high affinities for both water-based fluids, such as the plasma in cells, and lipid-based materials, such as cell membranes. Ethanol even passes with ease through the blood-brain barrier, so there is a rapid distribution of ethanol throughout the whole body via the circulation of ethanol-laden blood.

Elimination. Breath contains a concentration of ethanol in direct proportion to the blood-alcohol concentration (BAC), so there is a slow elimination of ethanol in exhaled breath. Also, the kidneys excrete some ethanol in urine. Even so, these two elimination routes account for no more than 2 to 10 percent of the total load of alcohol. The majority of ethanol is bioconverted by liver enzymes into ethanal (acetaldehyde) then ethanoate (acetate).

The amount of ethanol consumed in a drinking session is sufficient to saturate the enzymes that metabolize it. In other words, these enzymes work at bioconverting ethanol at a fixed rate that does not depend on the BAC. This rate is around 8 to 10 grams per hour for normal adult liver function.

Regular drinkers become more competent at metabolizing ethanol as the liver produces more enzymes in response to the regular presence of ethanol. This process, called enzyme induction, has consequences for the effectiveness of other drugs that degrade under the influence of the same enzymes. If a regular drinker abstains during treatment with such a drug, the increased number of liver enzymes will eliminate the drug at an unusually high rate that might make an increased dosage necessary.

If the same patient persists with drinking during treatment, ethanol will impede bioconversion of the drug by competing for enzymes; so the amount of drug in the body may become undesirably high. Chronic alcoholism causes liver damage that reduces the ability of the liver to convert ethanol and other drugs, so reduced dosages may be necessary.

One form of treatment for alcoholism uses disulfiram, a drug that blocks the enzyme that converts ethanal into ethanoate. If a patient drinks while on this drug, the first stage of bioconversion turns ethanol into ethanal as usual, but the conversion to ethanoate is impeded. Hence the blood concentration of ethanal rises and causes unpleasant effects such as nausea, hot flashes, and headaches.

Behavioral effects

Recreational drinkers consume alcohol to benefit from its disinhibiting and relaxing effects, often during a social event. Excessive drinking in a single session can cause rowdiness and aggression or stupor, while chronic heavy drinking usually causes dependence. All these effects occur as a result of the effects of alcohol in the brain.

At high doses, ethanol has anesthetic properties, and indeed was used as an anesthetic in early surgery. One theory of the anesthetic effect is that small molecules such as ethanol disrupt neuron membranes and cause a general but reversible disruption of their activity, resulting in loss of consciousness. Ethanol is not safe as an anesthetic, since the median lethal dose (LD_{50}) is only six times greater than the median effective dose (ED_{50}) for anesthesia. Hence, there is a significant risk that a dose that is too

Bar rituals such as those that surround the drinking of tequila shots usually increase the rate of drinking and hence the total amount of ethanol consumed.

ALCOHOLIC AMNESIA

One of the risks of a drinking binge is the failure to remember events that happened while under the influence. For many years, this memory loss was vaguely blamed on general brain damage caused by ethanol. In recent years, scientists have found a more specific way in which the presence of ethanol blocks the formation of new memories.

In a 1995 study, Scott Swartzwelder of Duke University Medical Center, Durham, North Carolina, discovered that ethanol blocks a subtype of glutamate receptors, called NMDA receptors, in the hippocampus of the rat brain. This receptor participates in memory formation, and a second study revealed that rats intoxicated with ethanol were unable to learn tasks that sober rats in a control group learned with little difficulty.

Swartzwelder extended his testing to humans in 1998. The human test consisted of an examiner reading a list of words to test subjects and determining how easily the subjects spotted words from the list after 20 minutes. The ages of the test and control subjects ranged from 21 to 30, and the results showed that while all test subjects fared worse than the control subjects, memory impairment by alcohol was worse for younger members of the test group. This is consistent with the fact that NMDA receptors become less abundant and less influential in the formation of memories with increasing age.

Ethics prevented Swartzwelder from testing memory impairment in candidates younger than 21. Nevertheless, he warned of the likelihood that a greater abundance of NMDA receptors in younger people would make them more prone to impaired learning and memory functions through the action of even small amounts of alcohol.

little to cause anesthesia in one person will be sufficient to kill another person.

At lower doses, ethanol has more subtle effects caused by its influence on neurons that communicate via GABA (gamma-aminobutyric acid). Ethanol molecules strengthen the interaction between GABA and its receptors, so a given GABA concentration near a receptor causes greater stimulation of that receptor. There is growing evidence that ethanol also boosts the release of GABA from neuron stores. This would further boost neurotransmission by GABA.

The behavioral effects of ethanol occur because of the inhibitory role of neurons that use GABA for transmission. They moderate brain activity by opposing the excitatory effects of glutamate neurons. This is particularly important in the reticular activating system (RAS), a part of the brain that governs self-control, motivation, wakefulness, and coordination of physical activity and movements.

A low but rising ethanol concentration has an apparently stimulant effect because enhanced GABA neurotransmission reduces social inhibition. This effect occurs because the mental processes that maintain restraint and "proper" behavior are among the first to be knocked out by enhanced GABA neurotransmission. It is important to note the different senses of inhibition here: social inhibition is restraint and conformance to a learned and accepted code of taboos and standards of decency; neuronal inhibition is the suppression of the activity of one set of neurons by some influence, in this case GABA.

Behavioral changes at this stage depend also on circumstances: a drinker whose social inhibition is diminished typically responds to a stimulating social environment by becoming more chatty, rowdy, or daring than usual. At the same stage of intoxication, a lone drinker at home might turn up the music without regard for sleeping neighbors.

While a limited degree of social disinhibition may be useful for breaking the ice between people, too much disinhibition and impaired reasoning at higher levels of intoxication can result in behavioral undercontrol, a state in which a drinker becomes prone to uncharacteristically rash actions and decisions that can have negative consequences. Such actions include gambling and getting into physical or verbal conflicts; there is also an increased likelihood of drinkers making or accepting sexual advances they would otherwise think inappropriate. The blood-alcohol concentration at which behavior can become problematic varies from person to person.

As ethanol concentration continues to rise, other functions governed by the RAS become increasingly impaired by GABA inhibition. Symptoms include staggering, slurred speech, and lack of coordination. Vision can become blurred, and the drinker starts to lose the ability to follow conversations. Further inhibition of RAS activity causes incontinence, vomiting, drowsiness, and stupor.

Overdose

Extreme ethanol intoxication can cause coma and even death as the impeded RAS fails to maintain breathing. Some deaths occur when unconscious drunks inhale vomit and fail to clear their airways because ethanol suppresses the coughing reflex.

The greatest risk of overdose occurs when a drinker combines alcohol with other drugs that promote activity of GABA neurons. Notable examples are barbiturates and benzodiazepines. The effect of one drug amplifies that of the other, so the stupefying effects of ethanol occur at a lower dose and can take the drinker by surprise. The time taken for alcohol to enter the bloodstream means a drinker can remain conscious long enough to consume a lethal dose of alcohol without knowing it. Stupor, coma, and death then follow as the BAC continues to rise.

Dopamine

Dopamine is another major neurotransmitter implicated in the behavioral effects of alcohol. It seems that dopamine release is stimulated by increased activity of some GABA neurons. Rising dopamine levels cause the euphoria of amphetamine and cocaine highs, so dopamine release could partly explain the stimulant effect at the start of ethanol consumption. Falling dopamine levels after the last drink of alcohol could also explain why identical BACs are stimulating at the start of a drinking session but soporific after drinking stops.

Long-term neurological effects

Chronic use of alcohol reduces the activity of GABA neurons as the brain adjusts to the frequent presence of ethanol. This down-regulation of the GABA system enables a drinker to tolerate more ethanol in his or her bloodstream, but it also leads to symptoms of anxiety and jitteriness if the drinker abstains. The down-regulated GABA neurons fail to moderate the excitatory effect of glutamate neurons in the RAS.

Brain scans reveal that the brain shrinks as neurons are destroyed through chronic alcohol use. There is a corresponding drop in the ability to concentrate, solve problems, and memorize facts. A slow but only partial recovery happens when former alcohol abusers quit drinking for at least a few months.

Other physical effects

Ethanol affects many sites apart from the RAS. It irritates the stomach, which can result in nausea and vomiting in the short term and can cause gastritis in chronic drinkers. Alcohol blocks vasopressin, an antidiuretic hormone, so it stimulates urination in proportion to the quantity of ethanol consumed. This can cause dehydration, one of the main causes of hangovers, unless the drinker compensates by taking nonalcoholic beverages after drinking.

Ethanol causes blood vessels to dilate. The resulting boost in blood circulation near the skin can cause flushing, which gives the impression of alcohol having a warming effect. In fact, heat is being carried away from the core of the body and can heighten the risk of hypothermia in exposure victims. Ethanol also blocks the reflex constriction of lower-body blood vessels after standing up. This mechanism usually maintains a healthy blood supply to the brain, so its failure can cause the drinker to become dizzy and even pass out just seconds after standing up.

Men who drink can have erectile problems caused by ethanol. These sometimes occur transiently after a single drinking bout, but more persistent erectile problems become a risk for chronic drinkers.

The long-term physiological effects of drinking include severe and sometimes fatal liver and heart diseases. Also, a woman who knows she is pregnant or could become pregnant should consider the risks of alcohol, which can cross the placenta, to her baby.

M. CLOWES

SEE ALSO:

Acetaldehyde • Alcohol • Barbiturates • Disulfiram • Gamma-aminobutyric Acid

Fentanyl

Fentanyl is a potent opioid painkiller that is also used as an anesthetic. It is significantly stronger than morphine or heroin and has been implicated in an incident that killed more than a hundred people in Russia.

Fentanyl is an opioid drug and thus is classed as a narcotic. Fentanyl acts on the brain and spinal cord at specific subtypes of opioid receptors (the mu receptors) on certain nerve cells that inhibit the sensation of pain. It is also powerful enough to cause anesthesia. Like morphine, fentanyl has medical uses, but it can also be a drug of abuse. Fentanyl is around a hundred times more potent than morphine and is faster acting. Fentanyl (1-phenethyl-4-N-propionylanilinopiperidine) belongs to the phenylpiperidine chemical class of synthetic opiates; several chemically related compounds (for example, alfentanil and sufentanil) are also used as extremely potent narcotics.

There are several clinical uses of fentanyl. It can be used as an anesthetic for surgery when small doses (typically 100 micrograms) are injected intravenously. This causes an almost immediate anesthetic effect that lasts for 30 to 60 minutes. Fentanyl is also used for pain relief. Skin patches containing fentanyl are used for transdermal delivery of the drug to provide continuous pain relief for up to 72 hours. In addition, a candylike preparation in which fentanyl is absorbed through the lining of the mouth is used to treat severe cancer-related pain. This dosage can be fatal to children and teenagers.

Like other opioid drugs, fentanyl has characteristic side effects for which it is abused. These include central nervous system effects, such as changes in mood, euphoria, and a greater sense of well-being. Beyond the euphoric feeling, other side effects of fentanyl include depressed breathing (which can be fatal in an overdose), nausea and vomiting, constipation, dizziness, and constriction of the pupils of the eyes. Fentanyl, being much more potent than morphine or heroin, requires significantly lower amounts of the drug to produce euphoric effects. Abusers of fentanyl are known to intravenously inject the drug, but it can be smoked, snorted, or swallowed to get the desired effect. Traditionally, abuse of fentanyl had been confined to those with access to the drug, such as the medical professions;

KEY FACTS

Classification
Schedule II (USA, Canada, INCB), Class A (UK). Opioid.

Street names
Apache, China girl, China white, dance fever, goodfellas, jackpot, king ivory, murder 8, Tango and Cash

Short-term effects
Euphoria, nausea and vomiting, drowsiness, confusion, constipation, anesthesia. Can be fatal if overdosed.

Long-term effects
Tolerance to the analgesic effect, physical and psychological dependence (after repeated use). Withdrawal symptoms if drug is stopped, skin rashes (with transdermal patch).

however, there is now a greater potential for misuse with availability of the painkiller as transdermal patches for outpatients. The patches, even after use, can contain a large amount of the drug, and this can be a source of fentanyl for abuse and overdose.

Compounds related to fentanyl have veterinary use for anesthetizing large animals. Russian military forces allegedly used a fentanyl-based gas to end a hostage situation inside a Moscow theater in 2002. The incident caused significant casualties as a result of the gas being pumped into a confined space, which was compounded by the failure of the military to provide an antidote (naloxone) to the gas's effects and to inform doctors of the nature of the substance.

J. Derry, A. Kapur

SEE ALSO:

Analogs • Designer Drugs • Morphine • Naloxone • Opiates and Opioids

Gamma-aminobutyric Acid

Gamma-aminobutyric acid, or GABA, is a neurotransmitter that inhibits the excitation of nerves. Its diverse roles include the production of mental calm and the suppression of seizures.

Gamma-aminobutyric acid (4-aminobutanoic acid, $H_2N \cdot (CH_2)_3 \cdot COOH$) is one of the most versatile chemical messengers of the nervous system. It interacts with receptor proteins to reduce the excitation of nerve cells, and as such is an inhibitory neurotransmitter. Neurotransmitters such as GABA counter the effects of excitatory neurotransmitters, such as glutamate (glutamic acid), acting as throttles on a system that otherwise would rapidly burn out through constant overstimulation.

GABA forms by the action of an enzyme (glutamic acid decarboxylase) on glutamate in certain neurons. It resides in vesicles (minute pouches) in the synaptic terminal—the "output" end of a neuron—which is where the action potential (nerve impulse) ends up when the neuron fires. The arrival of the action potential increases the concentration of calcium ions (Ca^{2+}), and this change effects the release of GABA into the synapse—the junction between the "output" end of one neuron and the "input" end of another. The released GABA molecules then bind to receptors before biotransformation and reuptake mop them up. In biotransformation, an enzyme (GABA transaminase) makes GABA inactive by converting its amino group ($-NH_2$) into an aldehyde ($-CHO$) group. In reuptake, transporter proteins recycle GABA by taking it back into a neuron.

GABA receptors

GABA produces its effects by binding to ionotropic and metabotropic receptors on a variety of cells. The interaction with each type of receptor is subtly different and subject to modification by other chemicals—natural or synthetic—that happen to be present. This multitude of contributing factors accounts for how so simple a molecule can play so complex a role in living systems. Examples of the diversity of GABA-related processes include the management of stress and sleep, and the development of muscles.

The known GABA receptors currently form three classes, called subtypes. These are the $GABA_A$, $GABA_B$, and $GABA_C$ receptor complexes. $GABA_A$ and $GABA_C$ receptors consist of five protein subunits. At least 15 $GABA_A$ receptors with different subunit combinations have been identified to date. Although structurally similar, $GABA_A$ and $GABA_C$ receptors respond to different GABA agonists and antagonists, and each receptor has its own response profile. Also, $GABA_C$ receptors respond more intensely but slowly to the arrival and departure of GABA molecules. Strikingly different from $GABA_A$ and $GABA_C$ receptors, the $GABA_B$ receptors consist of two protein subunits and they respond to their own set of GABA agonists and antagonists.

The inhibitory mechanism shared by $GABA_A$ and $GABA_C$ receptors also differs from that of the $GABA_B$ receptors. When GABA binds at $GABA_A$ and $GABA_C$ receptors, the neuron that carries the receptor becomes less likely to respond to incoming stimuli. In contrast, when GABA binds to $GABA_B$ receptors, the neuron that carries the receptor becomes less likely to release a neurotransmitter.

GABA can therefore reduce the traffic of nerve impulses in two ways: it can weaken the chemical signal from an excited (transmitting) neuron by binding to a $GABA_B$ receptor at a presynaptic site, or it can reduce the sensitivity of an excitable (receiving) neuron by binding to a $GABA_A$ or $GABA_C$ receptor at a postsynaptic site. An estimated 60 to 80 percent of central nervous system (CNS) neurons have GABA receptors, and what happens at any given GABA-sensitive neuron depends on its receptor type.

Stress, relaxation, and sleep

The GABA receptors that have received the most attention in pharmaceutical research are the $GABA_A$ receptors of the amygdala—part of the limbic system of the brain. The amygdala processes feelings such as fear, anxiety, pleasure, and excitement, and it governs emotional expressions, including aggression.

The amygdala also participates in the reward pathway, which forms mental associations between pleasurable experiences and the actions that cause

GABA_A COMPLEX

The GABA_A receptor complex consists of five protein subunits around a channel that allows the passage of chloride ions (Cl⁻) when open. In addition to the receptor for GABA itself, there are barbiturate and benzodiazepine receptor sites that enhance GABA activity when activated by appropriate compounds.

A further receptor site produces an anesthetic effect when stimulated by neurosteroids that are produced by the body itself. Picrotoxin—a convulsant drug present in fishberry seeds—produces a stimulant effect by blocking GABA activity and is an antidote for barbiturates.

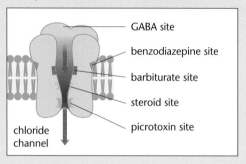

GABA site

benzodiazepine site

barbiturate site

steroid site

chloride channel

picrotoxin site

them. Stimulation of the reward pathway is one of the mechanisms that leads to drug dependency; substances that stimulate GABA_A receptors can therefore be highly addictive.

Insufficient GABA activity in the amygdala results in anxiety and panic episodes. These symptoms can be alleviated by the use of benzodiazepines, such as diazepam (Valium). The benzodiazepines boost the effect of GABA by binding to their own sites on GABA_A receptors and increasing the strength of the interaction between GABA and its respective binding site. This makes the benzodiazepines effective in reducing anxiety and promoting sleep, although they are dangerously dependency forming if used repeatedly. It is possible that selective GABA_C agonists could be developed to attack anxiety and insomnia with less risk of side effects and dependency.

Alcohol, barbiturates, benzodiazepines, and certain anesthetics (halothane, for example) act on GABA_A receptors at various sites in the brain to cause depression of the CNS. (Here, the term *depression* refers to reduced stimulation as a result of the inhibitory effect of activated GABA_A receptors.) Symptoms of this CNS depression range from relaxation and mild euphoria through impaired coordination and diminished emotional inhibition to stupor, sleep, coma, and, in extreme cases, death.

Some people use substances such as alcohol or barbiturates to relieve tension or induce euphoria by stimulating GABA_A receptors. The potential for dependency is high, however, and there is a risk of unpredictably strong effects when using combinations of substances that act on the GABA_A receptors, such as alcohol and barbiturates.

Convulsions, fits, and mania

Epileptic fits, manic episodes of bipolar disorder, and certain types of seizures are all characterized by repetitive firing of neurons causing undue excitation of the neurons they stimulate. Such conditions improve when stimulation of GABA_B receptors increases, thereby reducing the output of excitatory neurotransmitters and calming brain activity.

Some therapies that focus on GABA_B stimulation work by increasing the availability of GABA. Progabide does this by crossing the blood-brain barrier (which GABA does badly, if at all) then decomposing to form GABA in the CNS. Gamma-vinyl-GABA (Vigabatrin) increases concentrations of GABA by binding irreversibly to GABA transaminase, an enzyme that destroys GABA. The resulting complex is unable to catalyze the bioconversion of GABA to inactive compounds. Tiagabine (Gabitril) inhibits reuptake by binding to the proteins that carry GABA back into neurons.

Gabapentin, although structurally similar to GABA itself, does not act at GABA receptors; rather, it is thought to stimulate GABA production. In contrast, baclofen acts as an agonist at GABA receptors and can be injected into the spine to reduce muscular rigidity caused by multiple sclerosis without affecting receptors in the brain.

M. CLOWES

SEE ALSO:

Alcohol • Barbiturates • Benzodiazepines • Blood-Brain Barrier • Drug Receptors • GHB

GHB

Gamma-hydroxybutyrate and its precursors are club drugs that are sometimes used as date-rape drugs. These drugs have been marketed as food supplements for bodybuilders despite their potential for causing dependency.

GHB, or gamma-hydroxybutyrate, is an analog of the neurotransmitter gamma-aminobutyric acid (GABA) in that it has a hydroxy group (–OH) in place of the amino group ($-NH_2$) of GABA. It crosses the blood-brain barrier with ease—GABA itself does not—and partially transforms into GABA inside the brain. Since the early 1960s, researchers have discovered natural GHB in various parts of the body, including the brain, as well as GHB-sensitive receptors.

GHB inhibits the central nervous system in a similar way to alcohol, at least in part because it boosts activity in inhibitory GABA neurons. Hence, the presence of GHB leads to relaxation and a reduction in social inhibition, followed by poor coordination at moderate doses. A slight increase in dose can cause deep sedation for a few hours. The user often wakes up feeling fine but with little or no memory of events just prior to falling asleep. While sedated, the user is prone to rape or robbery. Higher doses can cause coma and death, especially if GHB is taken with alcohol, benzodiazepines, or barbiturates.

In the short term, GHB blocks the release of dopamine, a neurotransmitter that causes the habit-forming rush of a cocaine high. This characteristic lies behind the mistaken belief that GHB has a low potential for addiction. In fact, tolerance to GHB rises rapidly, and regular users become dependent as they need more GHB to prevent withdrawal effects, which are similar to those of alcohol addiction.

In the 1980s, GHB was popular with bodybuilders because it causes the release of growth hormone (GH), which stimulates muscle formation and reduces body fat. A rebound release of dopamine after GHB wears off causes a feeling of vitality ideal for training. When the United States classified GHB in its schedule of controlled substances in 1990, manufacturers of GHB food supplements turned to gamma-butyrolactone (GBL) and 1,4-butanediol (BD). These compounds are precursors that are turned into GHB by enzymes in the liver; they are potentially as harmful as GHB itself.

M. CLOWES

KEY FACTS

Classification
Schedule I (USA), Schedule III (Canada), Class C (UK), Schedule IV (INCB). CNS depressant.

Street names and some supplement names
GHB: G, GBH, liquid Ecstasy, Renewtrient. GBL: Blue nitro, Rest-Eze, Regenerize. BD: SomatoPro, Enliven.

Form
GHB: usually as the sodium salt dissolved in water at various concentrations; these solutions may be colorless or dyed. Occasionally pure as a white or off-white powder with a salty taste. GBL and BD: colorless liquids or solutions unless dyed; capsules.

Method of consumption
Voluntarily taken as capsules or liquids. Involuntarily taken dissolved in strong-tasting drinks that conceal the taste of the intoxicant from the intended victim.

Dangers
The response to a given dose of this drug varies greatly between individuals, and a small overdose can result in profound sedation and even coma or death. Emergency room staff may give inappropriate treatment if unaware of the true intoxicant.

Precautions
Do not accept drinks from strangers or provide opportunities for strangers to contaminate drinks. Some users write "G" or "GHB" on their palms to alert health care staff if taken to a hospital.

SEE ALSO:
Club Drugs • Ethanol • Gamma-aminobutyric Acid • Rohypnol

Glutethimide

Glutethimide is a sedative and hypnotic drug with potential for abuse, notably in combination with codeine preparations. Other drugs with better safety records have now superseded glutethimide in medicinal and recreational uses.

Glutethimide was introduced in 1954 as a safer alternative to barbiturates for people suffering from insomnia, a sleep disorder. Such an alternative had long been sought because barbiturates were far from ideal for long-term or unsupervised therapy. Barbiturates cause effects similar to alcohol hangovers, often leaving patients groggy, disorientated, and slightly queasy for hours after waking. These side effects thereby negated the effects of the good night's sleep that the drugs otherwise enabled.

Patients on regular doses of barbiturates rapidly became tolerant to the drug and the required increases in dose. At the same time, users became dependent on the drugs and would suffer a range of symptoms, including tremors, anxiety, seizures, and even heart attacks, if the drugs were withdrawn. To make things yet worse, it was easy to overdose on barbiturates, especially when taken with alcohol or opiates.

Glutethimide shares some of the chemical structure typical of barbiturates, and it was hoped at first that it would inherit their useful properties while being relatively free of side effects. This was not to be. As time passed, it became clear that glutethimide caused tolerance and dependency in a similar manner to barbiturates, and its overdoses were difficult to treat. In addition to common features with barbiturates, glutethimide suppresses the appetite, and long-term users suffered unhealthy degrees of weight loss.

Within a few years of its introduction, the track record of glutethimide had been sufficiently sullied to discredit it as a viable alternative to barbiturates. When new central nervous system (CNS) depressants such as the benzodiazepines and methaqualone were launched in the early to mid-1960s, they rapidly replaced glutethimide as replacements for barbiturates in treating insomnia.

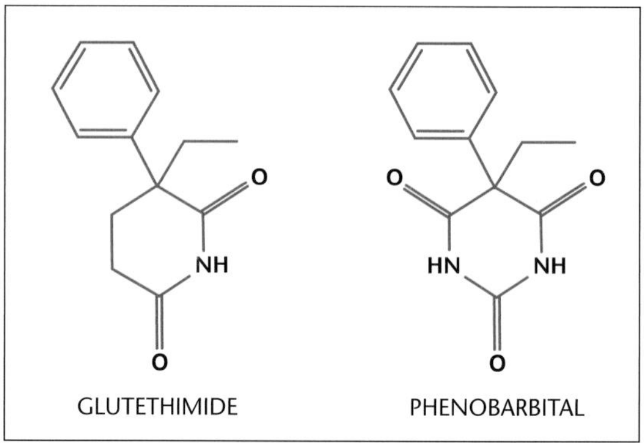

Recreational use

In its time, glutethimide had the same recreational appeal that benzodiazepines, such as Valium and temazepam, have today. All three drugs work by increasing the attraction between gamma-aminobutyric acid

A comparison of structures shows glutethimide to be a close analog of phenobarbital. This structural similarity underlies parallels between the activity and side effects of glutethimide and the barbiturates.

(GABA) and its receptors. As GABA is the neurotransmitter (chemical messenger) that inhibits the neural activity responsible for alertness, these drugs can calm or induce sleep. The exact effect depends on dosage and other active substances in the user's body.

A popular combination for glutethimide was with codeine in over-the-counter medicines. This combination acquired the name "fours and doors" after the brand names Tylenol 4 and Doriden. Codeine, the opiate in Tylenol 4, modified the effects of glutethimide in Doriden to produce an experience similar to a dose of heroin. The likelihood of fatal overdoses was increased by the combination of two CNS depressants and by liver toxicity due to the acetaminophen content of Tylenol 4.

A spate of fatal overdoses led to glutethimide being placed in Schedule II of the U.S. drug schedules in 1991. Since then, glutethimide production has ceased in most parts of the world, and the drug is no longer a significant recreational substance.

M. CLOWES

SEE ALSO:
Barbiturates • Benzodiazepines • Gamma-amino-butyric Acid • Methaqualone • Prescription Drugs

144

Hallucinogens

The psychedelia of the 1960s was inspired by the use of hallucinogenic drugs. Used throughout history to produce altered states of consciousness, hallucinogens change how a person sees, hears, and interacts with the world.

Hallucinogens are substances that produce unique psychoactive (mind-altering) effects. Although compounds in this class, such as LSD, were most popular among young people during the late 1960s and early 1970s, they continue to be used. These drugs have been placed into Schedule I of the Controlled Substances Act, the most restrictive category of all drugs. This classification makes it difficult to carry out research on hallucinogens because of legal restrictions. Their Schedule I classification is based largely upon the fact that hallucinogens have no accepted medical value and have been widely used as recreational drugs. Although Western society was largely unaware of these substances until the latter part of the twentieth century, their use extends far back into history and was well documented in many early societies, where hallucinogens were often used during religious occasions or by tribal shamans to induce altered states of consciousness.

There are a number of naturally occurring hallucinogens, including mushrooms from northern South America in the Psilocybe genus, which contain psilocybin, a tryptamine-type hallucinogen, and the peyote cactus, *Lophophora williamsii*, which contains mescaline, a phenethylamine-type hallucinogen. *Psilocybe* mushrooms, often referred to as "magic mushrooms" or sometimes simply as "shrooms," were used by the Aztecs, who knew them by the name *teonanacatl*, which essentially translates as "flesh of the gods" or "food of the gods." The peyote cactus was also used by the Aztecs and was known as *peyotl*. In modern times, peyote is used as a sacrament by the Native American Church, where it is eaten during all-night religious services, accompanied by singing and prayer. The Aztecs also used *ololiuqui*, the crushed seeds of a flower in the morning glory family that contain lysergamide, an alkaloid with a structure very similar to LSD, a semisynthetic molecule containing a tryptamine fragment within its structure.

The term *hallucinogen* often has been rather loosely applied and is sometimes associated with types of drugs that one would not normally include with the classic hallucinogens. For example, jimsonweed, *Datura stramonium*, contains the alkaloids atropine and scopolamine. These alkaloids block receptors for a neurotransmitter called acetylcholine. Ingestion of the leaves or seeds of jimsonweed can produce disorientation, visual and auditory hallucinations, severe disruption of consciousness, and even death in overdose. Phencyclidine, known as PCP, blocks a type of brain glutamate receptor and has effects similar to those of atropine. PCP overdose has sometimes been misdiagnosed as acute paranoid schizophrenia. Even tetrahydrocannabinol (THC), the active component in marijuana, can cause disorientation and hallucinations when taken in very large doses. Therefore, it is often the case that drugs that produce disorientation, hallucinations due to toxic overdose, or symptoms resembling schizophrenia may be referred to as hallucinogens, but the formal definition includes only compounds with a mechanism of action similar to the natural products psilocybin and mescaline.

Hallucinogens and psychedelics

The name *hallucinogen* implies that these substances produce hallucinations. At ordinary doses, however, that does not occur. Hallucinations are visual and perceptual events that are indistinguishable from reality. By contrast, users of hallucinogens are usually aware that the perceptual and emotional changes that occur are related to consumption of the drug, and are therefore not real. Hallucinogens have also been called other names. In the 1960s, the term *psychotomimetic* was popular, a word that suggests these substances produce psychosis, or a schizophrenia-like mental state. Following the discovery in 1943 of the most well-known of the hallucinogens, a substance commonly known as LSD (or LSD-25), it was thought that this drug produced effects resembling schizophrenia. Thus, *psychotomimetic* first became popular as the name of the class including LSD and similar drugs.

Hallucinogens are particularly known for the visual effects they can produce, especially the explosion of colors and patterns that inspire the work of many contemporary artists.

Hallucinogen gradually replaced *psychotomimetic* as the preferred term in scientific circles and remains most accepted today. The term *psychedelic* gained early popularity in nonscientific circles and is still widely used in popular culture. This term has a positive connotation, suggesting that these drugs bring forth desirable properties of the mind that are not ordinarily accessible. There are many instances in modern culture in which the term psychedelic is used, for example, to describe brightly colored or fluorescent patterns, or fractal designs on artwork or fabrics, because they are similar to the visual effects induced by hallucinogens. A more recent term that has emerged for this class is *entheogen*. This name implies that these substances can produce spiritual feelings or allow a connection with the divine.

Hallucinogenic effects

How can one class of drugs produce such a variety of effects, for example, induce a schizophrenia-like state, cause hallucinations, bring forth beneficial qualities of the mind, and allow divine inspiration?

Hallucinogens are truly unique among all of the drugs that affect the brain and are most remarkable in their effects. They have not been easy to understand, and much literature has been written in attempts to explain how these drugs affect the brain, and why their actions can be so variable.

One thing that is known, however, is that the effects of hallucinogens very much depend on two important factors known as set and setting. Set is the mental expectation of the person who uses the drug, and setting is the environment in which the drug is taken. When these substances were used in experiments designed to provoke a religious experience, the effects were seen to be indistinguishable from those that occur in a spontaneous mystical experience, such as a mystic might describe. On the other hand, when these substances are used recreationally, with no understanding of how powerful they can be and no care taken to manage the environment, the effects can be disastrous. The expressions "bad trip" and "bummer" come directly from the description of a bad experience that has resulted from taking a hallucinogen.

HALLUCINOGEN FAMILIES

There are two main types of chemicals that produce hallucinogenic effects: the tryptamines and the phenethylamines. All of these compounds are organic, and a number of them occur naturally in plants and seeds. More rarely, some compounds are made by animals—DMT has been found in human cerebrospinal fluid, and bufotenine is secreted by toads. The tryptamines and phenethylamines are related to certain neurotransmitters, with which they share a similar chemical structure. The tryptamines have an indole structure, which is a benzene ring connected to a five-sided ring containing nitrogen. Serotonin is a member of the tryptamine family. The phenethylamines also have a benzene ring with an ethylamine (C_2H_6N) tail. Dopamine and norepinephrine are two neurotransmitters that share this structure.

There are hundreds of compounds in these two families. Substituting different chemical groups at various points around the benzene ring makes the compound more psychedelic in effect; adding them to the tail produces more stimulant effects. Amphetamines are members of the phenethylamine family and are mainly stimulants. However, the addition of a dimethoxy group to the benzene ring of amphetamine results in the more psychedelic effects found in Ecstasy and MDA.

Tryptamine structures	Phenethylamine structures
Serotonin	Dopamine
Psilocybin	Norepinephrine
LSD	Mescaline
DMT (dimethyltryptamine)	Ecstasy (methylenedioxymethamphetamine)
Bufotenine	MDA (methylenedioxyamphetamine)
5-MeO-DMT (5-methoxy-DMT)	Nexus (2C-B)

Although there is no good definition for this class of substance, one of the most authoritative texts on pharmacology has described them as substances that produce changes in consciousness that otherwise occur only during dreaming or at times of religious exaltation. This description clearly would be applied when the experience with one of these drugs was a positive one, and also reflects the origin of the term *entheogen*.

These drugs do not reliably produce positive effects, however. In fact, the same dose of the same drug taken by the same person on different occasions can lead to two very different experiences. On some occasions, these drugs might produce a hellish experience, with extreme paranoia, panic, and fear that one is going insane. These effects would comprise a so-called bad trip. Some drugs, such as LSD and mescaline, remain active for 8 to 12 hours, so such an experience could be very long-lasting and emotionally painful. Worse yet, in certain individuals who have a predisposition to mental illness, it

appears that hallucinogens can precipitate psychiatric disorders that may be long-lasting or even permanent. Such events are rare, but they do occur. Although there is no evidence to suggest that this type of effect occurs in most people, long-lasting adverse effects can be produced that resolve only over several months.

Leo Hollister described a clinical syndrome produced by hallucinogens that might include the following effects:

- somatic symptoms—dizziness, weakness, tremors, nausea, drowsiness, paresthesias (sensations on the skin), and blurred vision.
- perceptual symptoms—altered shapes and colors, difficulty in focusing on objects, a sharpened sense of hearing, and sometimes synesthesias (such as "feeling" colors).
- psychic symptoms—alterations in mood (happy, sad, or irritable at varying times), tension, distorted time sense, difficulty

in expressing thoughts, depersonalization, dreamlike feelings, and visual hallucinations (depending on drug and dose).

Colorful visual patterns may be produced, colored patterns may appear that move in time with music or other sounds, hearing may be altered, and the sense of time can be distorted so, for example, a few minutes may seem like hours. Emotions and feelings also change throughout the trip.

Action on the brain

The effects of hallucinogens are thought to arise following activation of a particular type of serotonin receptor called the serotonin 2A receptor, usually abbreviated as the $5\text{-}HT_{2A}$ receptor. Serotonin is one of the neurotransmitter chemicals in the brain that regulate a number of important functions, including mood, hunger, sensory processing, sex drive, and others. There are 14 known types of serotonin receptors. They are all proteins and vary in their amino acid composition and structure, as well as by the biochemical changes that are produced inside the neuron when the particular receptor is activated. The $5\text{-}HT_{2A}$ receptors that are the targets of hallucinogens are expressed at high levels on cells in the prefrontal cortex at the front of the brain. These brain neurons, called pyramidal cells, are involved in integrating the sensory information and emotional characteristics of every situation that a person experiences and somehow making it into a coherent whole. That is, the things that humans see, hear, touch, feel, and think at any given moment arrive from different parts of the brain, and it is largely the responsibility of the frontal cortex to take all that information and make it into a conscious perception that makes sense, and which can be understood and acted upon.

Hallucinogens also stimulate serotonin $5\text{-}HT_{2A}$ receptors in parts of the brain that are active when someone is awake and quiet when asleep, as well as in parts of the brain that become alert when novel things occur in the environment. Serotonin $5\text{-}HT_{2A}$ receptors also appear to be located in an area of the brain (the thalamus) that is responsible for deciding which of the things being experienced at any given moment are important enough to focus attention. Thus, when a hallucinogen activates

$5\text{-}HT_{2A}$ receptors in the brain, a number of important changes occur in the way the brain processes and interprets incoming sensory information.

Tolerance and dependence

In contrast to many other drugs of abuse, such as cocaine or heroin, hallucinogens have very low toxicity and do not produce dependence or addiction. No overdose deaths have been produced by LSD, psilocybin, or mescaline, and the amount required to produce toxic effects is very much greater than the dose necessary to produce subjective effects. With hallucinogenic drugs it is impossible to produce the kind of tolerance that is seen

"Magic" mushrooms contain the mild hallucinogenic drug psilocybin. Hallucinogens interact with serotonin receptors to affect sensory and emotional processing, often resulting in distorted perceptions of sounds, colors, and textures.

with addictive drugs such as heroin. On the other hand, the dose of a hallucinogen needed to produce an effect increases dramatically, so by the third or fourth day of continuous use, hallucinogens fail to induce any effect at all. This very rapid tolerance with loss of effect is called tachyphylaxis, and it can be "transferred" among hallucinogens. Such transference is called cross-tolerance. For example, if a person takes LSD every day for three days, by the fourth day it would require a huge dose of LSD to have any effect at all. If on this fourth day the person were to take a dose of mescaline or psilocybin that would ordinarily be effective, it too will be found to be almost without effect. Thus, tolerance to LSD can lead to cross-tolerance to mescaline or to psilocybin. Tachyphylaxis, or tolerance, to hallucinogens is quite different from tolerance to drugs that produce addiction, such as amphetamines, cocaine, or heroin. Continuous use of addictive drugs causes the drug effect to become weaker, but the dose can simply be increased to compensate for tolerance and allow the drug effect to be experienced. Therefore, people dependent on addictve drugs will seek to obtain and administer larger and larger amounts in order to achieve the desired drug effect. With hallucinogens, however, the effect of virtually any dose simply disappears after a few days of use.

Potency and activity

Most hallucinogens are taken orally, but their potencies vary widely. With LSD, for example, the most potent of the hallucinogens, the typical dose is 0.1 milligrams or less, and the effects may last as long as 10 to 12 hours. Mescaline is the least potent of the hallucinogens, with an effective dose being typically between 250 to 400 milligrams, and the effects also last 10 to 12 hours. The dose of psilocybin is 6 to 15 milligrams, but with the effect lasting only 4 to 6 hours. There are a number of synthetic mescaline analogs that have appeared on the illicit drug market, generally referred to as hallucinogenic amphetamines, and they too are orally active, with a duration of action that is typically 10 hours or more.

There are two naturally occurring hallucinogens in the tryptamine family that are not active when taken orally. N,N-dimethyltryptamine (DMT) is produced in many plants, and must be smoked or used as a snuff to be active. The effective dose of DMT is 75 to 100 milligrams, and although the effects are very intense, they are brief, with a duration of 30 to 45 minutes. In the past, DMT was sometimes referred to as the "businessman's lunch" because of its brief action. A related compound is 5-methoxy-DMT, also found in nature, which must be smoked or used as a snuff to be active. The dose for this compound is 10 to 20 milligrams, and its effects are also extremely intense, again with the duration of action being very short, typically 15 to 30 minutes.

Although hallucinogens are not directly toxic to the body, they can lead to a number of serious adverse effects. There have been many accidents when people using hallucinogens in unsupervised settings have injured themselves. For example, there are documented cases of users jumping off high cliffs because they believed they had the power to fly, drowning while attempting to swim, or severely damaging their eyes by staring into the sun while intoxicated with LSD. Attempting to drive, swim, or even walk in dangerous environments (for example, next to highways, or in areas where rockslides can occur) can lead to serious or fatal accidents. These drugs powerfully distort perception, reduce the sensation of pain, and can grossly impair judgment. Hallucinogens also produce powerful effects on mood and emotion, and can precipitate depression, psychosis, or other serious and sometimes long-lasting psychiatric aftereffects. Suicide following LSD-induced depression is not unknown. The most widely known adverse reaction is called a flashback, in which the drug effect reappears at some later time when the user has taken no drug at all. The official medical designation for flashbacks is "hallucinogen persisting perception disorder" (HPPD). Although this adverse reaction is rare, there is no effective treatment for it. Flashbacks occurred only very rarely in supervised clinical research settings but are more likely to happen when used in recreational and unsupervised settings.

D. E. NICHOLS

SEE ALSO:

Bufotenine • DMT • Jimsonweed • LSD • Mescaline • Phenethylamines • Psilocybin and Psilocin • Serotonin • Tryptamines

Harmine and Harmaline

Harmine and harmaline are constituents of an ancient South American brew called ayahuasca. There is some doubt over the properties of the harmala alkaloids, but they are known to help the activity of the hallucinogen, DMT.

Harmine and harmaline are known as beta-carboline alkaloids and occur naturally in a number of plant species, including Syrian rue, *Peganum harmala*, from which they derive their names. Although it was believed that harmaline had hallucinogenic properties, today it is generally thought that this idea resulted from an incomplete understanding of the nature of the composition of a South American decoction known as ayahuasca (huasca). Ayahuasca, also known as *caapi* and *yage*, is a beverage that has a long and documented history of use in the Amazon valley of South America as a psychoactive preparation that has served as the focus of various rituals. The most commonly used name is *ayahuasca*, from the Quechua name meaning "vine of the souls." This name has been applied both to the beverage and to one of the plants used in its preparation, *Banisteriopsis caapi*.

In more modern times, ayahuasca has been incorporated into the rituals of at least two religions. Although both had their origins in South America, they have spread into the United States and Western Europe. A central feature of these churches is their use of ayahuasca as a sacrament, which they believe provides for them a primary religious experience and a direct connection with God.

Following the ingestion of ayahuasca, effects begin within 35 to 40 minutes, and last approximately four hours. The subjective effects of ayahuasca include phosphene imagery seen with the eyes closed, dreamlike reveries, and a feeling of alertness and stimulation. Peripheral autonomic effects such as changes in blood pressure, heart rate, and so on, are usually minimal. In most individuals, nausea and vomiting may occur, although this effect does not uniformly occur in everyone.

The preparation of ayahuasca involves a plant extract, or decoction, from two plants. The first is *Banisteriopsis caapi*, a large vine. The bark and stems of this plant are beaten to break down their structure, and then placed into water. Banisteriopsis is the plant that contains the beta-carboline alkaloids harmine

and harmaline. A second plant is also essential, usually from the genus *Psychotria*, most commonly *P. viridis*. This plant contains a hallucinogen known as *N,N*-dimethyltryptamine, or DMT. Leaves of *P. viridis* are added with the *Banisteriopsis caapi* to the water, and the two plants are then soaked or boiled together to extract their active principles. These two ingredients are essential to the psychoactive properties of ayahuasca, although other plants are sometimes added to the mixture, depending on the shaman who is preparing the material.

In 1957 the principal beta-carboline alkaloids in ayahuasca were determined to be harmine, harmaline, and tetrahydroharmine. A study in 1972 analyzed a sample of ayahuasca and determined that a typical 200 milliliter dose of ayahuasca would contain 25 milligrams of DMT and 40 milligrams of a mixture of beta-carboline alkaloids. Neither harmine nor harmaline have significant intoxicating effects. Harmine was briefly used under the name

KEY FACTS

Classification
Not scheduled in USA, UK, INCB. Schedule III, Canada. Possible hallucinogen. Status of ayahuasca not defined.

Street names
Ayahuasca, *caapi*, vine, *yage*

Short-term effects
Initial nausea and vomiting, followed by dreamlike state, alertness, and visual effects

Dangers
Harmala alkaloids taken in conjunction with some antidepressant drugs and certain foods may cause unpleasant and dangerous effects.

The preparation of ayahuasca involves boiling bark, stems, and leaves of at least two different plants to produce a brew that is drunk as a religious sacrament.

"banisterine" to treat Parkinson's disease in the late 1920s. It produced a modest beneficial effect but was ineffective in relieving tremor. One report indicated that an oral dose of 40 milligrams or 30 milligrams subcutaneously produced predominantly restlessness, with no effect on consciousness. There is no evidence that harmaline has hallucinogenic activity, although very high doses have been reported to possess psychoactive effects.

If the hallucinogen DMT is given orally, it has no activity because it is broken down by an enzyme in the liver called monoamine oxidase (MAO). It is presently believed that the admixture of DMT with harmala alkaloids contained in ayahuasca leads to activation of the DMT because the harmala alkaloids inhibit the function of the MAO in the liver and elsewhere that would ordinarily destroy orally administered DMT.

After ayahuasca is ingested, the psychological effects peak about 100 minutes later, a time that corresponds to the maximum concentration of DMT in the blood. In all published studies, psychological effects have been shown to parallel blood plasma concentration levels of DMT. It is not proven, however, that all of the psychological effects of ayahuasca are simply the result of oral administration of DMT. On the basis of interaction studies between beta-carbolines and DMT in rats, the unique effects of ayahuasca may be due to factors in addition to an increase in bioavailability of orally ingested DMT. Thus, the psychological state produced by ayahuasca may not be completely attributable to the simple combination of DMT with beta-carbolines but may be more complex as a consequence of the ingestion of other alkaloids contained in the ayahuasca, even if those alkaloids are present only in minor amounts.

The principal recognized pharmacology of the beta-carbolines themselves is as reversible inhibitors of monoamine oxidase (MAO inhibitors). Although MAO inhibitors were initially used to treat depression, they had serious side effects, including interactions with certain foods containing tyramine that caused serious and even fatal increases in blood pressure. Those early MAO inhibitors, however, chemically reacted with MAO and essentially destroyed the enzyme. People who have used ayahuasca on a regular basis have not suffered similar toxicity problems, however, probably because the beta-carbolines do not chemically combine with MAO and are relatively short-acting substances.

D. E. NICHOLS

SEE ALSO:
DMT • Hallucinogens • MAOs and MAOIs

Heroin

When it first appeared, heroin was regarded as a benign substitute for morphine. It soon became obvious, however, that heroin was not only as addictive as morphine but was a far more potent drug.

Diacetylmorphine, better known as heroin, is made from morphine by adding two acetyl groups. Pure heroin is a white, odorless powder with a bitter taste. Most illicit heroin, however, varies in color from white, pink, beige, to dark brown because of impurities left from the manufacturing process or the presence of additives. In fact, the purity of a bag of street heroin can range from 1 percent to 90 percent, with an average purity, in North America, of around 50 percent. So, a bag may contain 100 milligrams of powder, but not all of the content is heroin; the remainder could be sugars, starch, quinine, or, more probably, the by-products of poor manufacture. Street heroin is sometimes cut with small quantities of the poison strychnine to enhance heroin's effect. Because heroin users do not know the actual strength of the drug or its true contents, they are at risk of overdose or death. Street names associated with heroin include smack, H, diesel, and mud. Other names may refer to types of heroin produced in a specific geographical area, such as Mexican black tar.

History

The name heroin comes from the German word *heroisch*, which means "heroic". Diacetylmorphine, also known in some countries as diamorphine, was first invented in 1874 by the British chemist C. R. Wright. However, it was Heinrich Dreser, a chemist working for the German chemical company Bayer, who first realized the commercial potential of heroin. He was in charge of testing the efficacy and safety of new drugs, including nonaddictive substitutes for morphine, which at that time was widely used as a painkiller and for treating respiratory diseases.

Diacetylmorphine was first synthesized by Bayer in 1897. By early 1898, Heinrich Dreser had tested heroin on a wide range of animals and some of Bayer's employees, who said it made them feel "heroic." *Heroisch* was also the term used by German chemists to describe any strong drug, and heroin was significantly stronger than morphine. Heroin thus became Bayer's brand name for diacetylmorphine.

Dreser presented heroin to the Congress of German Naturalists and Physicians in November 1898, claiming that it was 10 times more effective as a cough medicine than codeine but had only a tenth of its toxic effects. At that time, finding a good cough medicine was important, since tuberculosis and pneumonia were the leading causes of death. Dreser also showed that heroin was more effective than morphine as a painkiller and argued that, unlike morphine, it was not habit forming.

By 1899, Bayer was producing about a ton (0.9 tonnes) of heroin a year and exporting the drug to 23 countries. The drug was incorporated into a range of products, including pastilles, cough lozenges, tablets, water-soluble salts, and an elixir.

Worrying rumors about the drug began to surface as early as 1899. Patients developing tolerance and consuming inordinate quantities of heroin-based cough remedies were identified. French and American researchers were also reporting cases of what was described as "heroinism," or addiction.

In 1906 the American Medical Association approved heroin for medical use, but with strong reservations about its addictive potential. Around the same time, there was a huge increase in heroin-related admissions at hospitals in New York and Philadelphia, and in East Coast cities a substantial population of recreational users was reported. Bayer eventually halted heroin production in 1913, by which time its addictive qualities had become obvious and irrefutable.

Absorption and excretion

Heroin is a fast-acting opiate drug. In fact, because heroin is highly fat soluble, it can cross the blood-brain barrier very quickly and enter the brain more readily than morphine. However, soon after administration, heroin is rapidly hydrolyzed to 6-monoacetylmorphine (6-MAM), which in turn is hydrolyzed to morphine. Therefore, most of the chemical reactions of heroin are caused by 6-MAM and by morphine rather than by the compound itself.

When injected, heroin reaches the brain in 7 to 8 seconds. Smoking or snorting the drug is slower, the effects peaking after 10 to 15 minutes. Experienced heavy users will inject or smoke between two and four times per day. Heroin's intense high lasts only a few minutes. The effect of heroin wears off in three to five hours, depending on the dose. Heroin is mainly excreted in the urine, largely as free morphine or morphine combined with another salt.

Site of action

Heroin and its metabolites morphine and 6-MAM mimic the action of the brain's natural opioids (called endorphins) at opioid receptors. A so-called activity at the mu-receptors is primarily associated with the induction of pain relief, cardiovascular and respiratory depression, and other neuroendocrine effects. The brain's limbic system contains a high density of opioid receptors, and their activation by heroin is believed to produce feelings of happiness, relaxation, and fearlessness.

Acute effects

Taking heroin results in a euphoric rush of warm pleasurable feelings that seem to start in the abdomen and then spread throughout the body. This effect peaks after a few minutes and subsides into a period of tranquility ("on the nod"), lasting up to an hour; during this period, time may appear to slow down for the user. After taking heroin, some people feel protected and emotionally self-contained, while others feel stimulated and sociable. Gradually the user subsides into a dreamy and relaxed state that may last another four hours. At high doses the user may lapse into a semi-conscious state.

With heroin, the rush may be accompanied by nausea, vomiting, and severe itching. Also, cardiac and breathing functions are slowed, sometimes with fatal results. Overdosing is a particular risk with street heroin, especially if an unusually pure batch of the drug is in circulation.

Chronic use

Tolerance to the effects of heroin develops fairly rapidly. As a result of tolerance, users tend to increase their daily dosage, sometimes leading to an extraordinary escalation of intake over time.

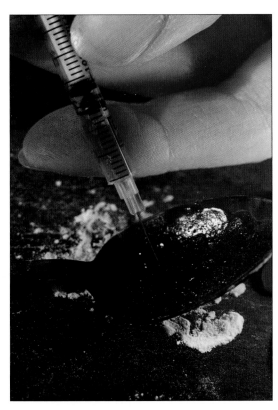

The stigma and fear of injecting has been a major factor in preventing people from using heroin. Increasing purity has persuaded many to try smoking or snorting heroin, but the drug is equally addictive in these forms.

Heroin can be smoked, snorted, or injected. Injection is the most common method of taking low-purity heroin, which is dissolved in water before being injected either into a vein, under the skin ("skin-popping"), or into a muscle. Injecting the drug is an efficient method of administration, the intravenous route providing the greatest intensity and most rapid onset of drug effects. With the increased availability of high-purity heroin, however, snorting or smoking are now as popular. There is a misconception among younger users that smoking or snorting heroin is less addictive—that is not true, although these methods do not have the same health risks associated with injection. Heroin smoking, in which the drug is heated on foil and the vapor inhaled through a straw or tube, is referred to as "chasing the dragon." Snorting is most common in areas where high-purity heroin is easy to obtain.

Tolerance is usually accompanied by physical dependence, which represents an adaptation of the body and brain to the chronic administration of heroin, and it manifests itself as intense physical and psychological disturbances. These disturbances, which are collectively known as withdrawal or abstinence syndrome, regularly emerge after a period of abstinence from heroin (for example, after a night's sleep), and they comprise an array of physiological and psychological effects that are essentially opposite to the acute effects of heroin. Heroin addicts constantly oscillate between periods of euphoria and periods of withdrawal. Symptoms of withdrawal include muscle and bone pain, insomnia, restlessness, diarrhea, vomiting, shivers and gooseflesh, jerky leg movements, abdominal cramps, dilated pupils, depression, anxiety, and other nervous reactions. Although heroin withdrawal is not considered life-threatening and often resembles a severe flulike condition, clinical evidence suggests that the psychological distress associated with withdrawal is extremely aversive, and avoidance of this state motivates heroin-dependent individuals to self-administer more of the drug. Withdrawal symptoms peak between 48 and 72 hours after the last dose of heroin and subside after about a week. However, some people display persistent withdrawal signs for many months, often as a result of exposure to heroin-related stimuli. Heroin withdrawal is rarely fatal unless the addict has another serious health problem, but babies born to pregnant addicts require special care to manage their withdrawal symptoms.

Physical dependence and the emergence of withdrawal symptoms were once believed to be the key features of heroin addiction. It is now recognized that this may not be the case entirely, since cravings and relapse often occur weeks and months after withdrawal symptoms have subsided. It is also known that patients with chronic pain who need opiates to function sometimes become dependent on them but have few, if any, problems giving them up after their pain is resolved by other drugs. This incongruity may arise because the patient is seeking relief from pain and not the emotional rush sought by the addict.

Medical complications
Chronic heroin abuse leads to a number of medical problems, often as a result of poor hygiene when

KEY FACTS

Classification
Schedule I (USA), Schedule I (Canada), Class A (UK), Schedule I (INCB). Opioid.

Street names
Big H, bin Laden, black pearl, brown sugar, Charley, China white, chip, hero, horse, poison, rambo, smack, stuff, tiger, tootsie roll, white junk, witch hazel

Short-term effects
Intense feeling of euphoria lasts only a few minutes, subsiding into dreamlike state. Accompanied by nausea, vomiting, itching, mental impairment.

Long-term effects
Tolerance to increasing doses leads to dependency. Risk of collapsed veins, infections, liver disease, lung diseases, constipation. Withdrawal causes muscle pain, restlessness, diarrhea, gooseflesh, insomnia.

Dangers
Respiratory failure and death due to depressant effect on central nervous system. Risk of contracting HIV and other diseases through dirty needles. High potential for overdose because of uncertain purity.

Signs of abuse
Disorientation, alternating drowsy or wakeful state, reddening of whites of eyes, constricted pupils, dry mouth, shallow breathing. Needle marks or scarring and bruising of veins.

injecting or the inclusion of contaminants in street drugs. Among these complications are bacterial infections of the blood vessels, heart valves, and soft tissues, scarred or collapsed veins, and liver or kidney diseases. Conditions such as pneumonia and tuberculosis may result from the poor health of the user as well as from heroin's depressant effects on respiration. Substances cut into street heroin may include materials that do not readily dissolve, such as talc and other pill-filling agents, which can clog

PERCENTAGE OF STUDENTS WHO HAVE USED HEROIN IN THE PAST YEAR

	2006	2007	2008	2009
8th grade	0.8	0.8	0.9	0.7
10th grade	0.9	0.8	0.8	0.9
12th grade	0.8	0.9	0.7	0.7

Source: NIDA, *Monitoring the Future Study*, 2010.

the blood vessels that lead to the lungs, liver, kidneys, or brain. Contaminants can also cause immune reactions, including arthritis and rheumatic problems. Other consequences of heroin addiction arise from addicts sharing or not sterilizing injection equipment. Users can contract a variety of blood-borne diseases, such as hepatitis B and C, and HIV from contaminated needles. These diseases might then be passed on to sexual partners or children.

Withdrawal and relapse

Heroin withdrawal is typically treated in two ways. The first consists of substituting heroin with a prescription opiate drug and then gradually reducing dosage. The drug of choice in this case is usually methadone because of its long half-life, which reduces the need for frequent doses to prevent symptoms from appearing. The second approach involves the use of clonidine. Clonidine is an alpha$_2$-adrenergic agonist that, because it inhibits the release of norepinephrine, effectively decreases many of the symptoms of heroin withdrawal, such as nausea, vomiting, cramps, sweating, rapid heartbeat (tachycardia), and high blood pressure. However, clonidine does not reduce the generalized hypersensitivity to pain and the extreme feelings of being unwell in the withdrawing addict.

Management and treatment of withdrawal, however, is not a cure for heroin addiction, which is a chronic relapsing disorder in which the potential of returning to compulsive drug use is extremely high. It is believed that relapse can be caused by three factors. First, relapse can be initiated by exposure to drug-related cues, which induce conditioned responses. The abstinent addict,

therefore, may start using again as a result of experiencing cravings for the positive effects of heroin, or may start using again to alleviate a state of discomfort. Second, relapse can be initiated by reexposure to heroin itself (a lapse), even if taken in small amounts. The abstinent addict may convince him- or herself that, this time, heroin use will be controllable. However, reexposure to a small dose of heroin will "prime" an addict to crave and seek more heroin, and will thus lead to a rapid escalation of intake and consequent loss of control over drug use. There is evidence, however, that not all lapses lead to relapse. The third and final cause of relapse is the experience of negative emotional states, or exposure to stressful events. A significant component of psychotherapy in addicts is thus aimed at teaching effective strategies for coping with negative moods or stressful events.

Because of the elevated potential for relapse, successful treatment of heroin addiction often requires stabilization on methadone or other long-acting opiate drugs such as levo-alpha-acetyl methadol (LAAM). Patients maintained on methadone do not experience the alternation of emotional and physiological states that are typical of heroin addiction. In fact, methadone maintenance eliminates symptoms of withdrawal and, because of cross-tolerance, it reduces the effects of heroin, if used. Patients become tolerant to the sedative effects of methadone and eventually are capable of conducting a normal life.

F. LERI

SEE ALSO:
Clonidine • Cutting Drugs • Endorphins • LAAM • Methadone • Morphine • Opiates and Opioids

Hormonal Effects

The functioning of the body depends on a delicately balanced system of chemical messengers. Hormones, like neurotransmitters, can be influenced by the introduction of drugs that interfere with the way in which they work.

Hormones are natural substances that control and regulate the body's systems and organs. They are secreted by glands in various parts of the body and act as chemical messengers, instructing other tissues and organs to produce a response. Chief among these glands are the pituitary and hypothalamus in the brain, the thyroid and parathyroid in the neck, the adrenal glands above the kidneys, the pancreas, and the sex organs, particularly the ovaries and testes.

Hormones are responsible for the coordination of four main regulatory functions in the body: energy production, growth and development, control of internal processes, and the reproductive system. Under normal circumstances, hormonal systems are finely balanced, producing the right amount of hormones at the right time to give the required response at the target tissue or organ. The intake of drugs and alcohol can interfere with many hormonal processes and have a profound effect on how they work. Gender differences in reactions to drugs may also have implications for how addiction takes hold and the reasons for starting substance abuse.

Alcohol

As one of the most commonly abused and studied substances, the effects of alcohol on hormone systems are well known. One of alcohol's biggest impacts is on the metabolism of glucose, vital for energy to power the body and the maintenance of brain function. The body obtains glucose from three sources: the digestion of food; the breakdown of glycogen, which is stored in the liver; and manufacture by other bodily systems. Two hormones, insulin and glucagon, secreted by the pancreas, are responsible for regulating the amount of glucose in the blood. The concentration of glucose is especially important for the brain, which cannot make or store its own supply. Too little glucose in the blood (a condition called hypoglycemia), even for short periods, can lead to brain damage.

One of the main consequences of heavy drinking is the effect it has on nutrition. Many alcoholics neglect to eat or do not eat well, depriving their bodies of glucose. Natural production of glucose can also be inhibited while alcohol is being processed, leading to hypoglycemia. Diabetics who drink are at particular risk since they do not produce enough insulin. Insulin lowers the concentration of glucose in the blood, while glucagon increases it. Alcohol interferes with the balance between these two hormones and medications used by diabetics to keep blood glucose levels even. As a result, diabetics can suffer episodes of both hypoglycemia and hyperglycemia (too much glucose) if they drink alcohol. Even well-nourished nondiabetic people who binge drink are at risk of upsetting the delicate balance between too much and too little glucose in the blood.

The reproductive system is also affected by alcohol. The ovaries and testes produce a number of hormones that regulate primary sexual functions, such as the production of sperm, and secondary characteristics including control of the menstrual cycle and maintenance of a pregnancy. Heavy-drinking men are subject to reductions in testosterone levels, which can lead to impotence and feminization of sexual characteristics, for example, growth of the breasts. Alcohol may also damage sperm and affect their motility. Women who drink may find that their menstrual cycle becomes irregular or ceases. Ovulation can be suppressed, preventing women from conceiving, or an early pregnancy may be spontaneously aborted. Effects may show in women who drink only socially (up to three drinks a day). Alcoholic women may also go through menopause early, leaving them at risk of cardiovascular disease and osteoporosis (brittle bones). Postmenopausal women who drink heavily while taking hormone replacements are also in greater danger of developing breast cancer than those who consume only one drink a day. However, postmenopausal women who consume between three and six drinks a week can actually reduce their risk of cardiovascular disease without increasing their chances of developing osteoporosis or breast cancer.

the impact on the sexual and reproductive systems. Although most of the steroids taken by bodybuilders are related to the male hormones testosterone and androsterone, both of which help to masculinize the body, too much can have adverse effects on the sexual organs. In men, the testes can shrink and the prostate gland can enlarge, which can make urination difficult. Sterility can also occur, although most of the effects of anabolic steroids reverse if the user stops taking them. Testosterone in men can also be converted to the female hormone estrogen, which can lead to breast development and the formation of lumps that may require surgical removal.

Women who take steroids can acquire male characteristics, such as growth of hair on the face and chest as a result of elevated levels of testosterone. Steroids may also interfere with the menstrual cycle, causing irregular periods and an inability to conceive. The breasts

Female bodybuilders who take anabolic steroids face a number of risks as a result of using substances related to male hormones. The shape of the body can become masculinized and the breasts can shrink as fat is lost and the muscles become more defined.

Osteoporosis is caused by alcohol disrupting the hormones that control calcium levels and its distribution around the body. Heavy drinking causes a deficiency of parathyroid hormone, which leads to an increase in the amount of calcium lost to the body in urine. The nutritional problems incurred by heavy drinking can lead indirectly to a lack of vitamin D in the body. This vitamin is responsible for the absorption of calcium (which may also be lacking in the diet) into the bones and teeth. Bone-forming cells in the marrow are directly inhibited by alcohol, which prevents them from functioning properly.

Anabolic steroids

Anabolic steroids have a direct effect on the hormonal systems, because some steroids are hormones and others act on the body's natural hormones to produce or suppress their effects. One of the most direct effects of steroids in both men and women is

often shrink, the voice can deepen, and the clitoris can become enlarged. Unlike with men, not all of these symptoms reverse after stopping steroid intake. Both sexes also find that the desire for sex can increase or decrease with steroid use.

Adolescents who have not yet reached puberty and who take steroids may not reach full height. The presence of high levels of testosterone signal that puberty has been reached, preventing the bones from growing any further. Other effects that may affect steroid users include acne, muscle twitches, sleep apnea (in which a person momentarily stops breathing during sleep), and premature baldness. Some users try to reduce symptoms of steroid use by taking nonsteroidal hormones. For example, human chorionic gonadotropin is injected to stimulate the testicles to produce more testosterone and prevent shrinkage, and drugs that block estrogen production are used to stop breast enlargement.

Nicotine

The main reason that many people continue to smoke is the initial feeling of alertness that is prompted by the intake of nicotine. Nicotine causes a rapid release of epinephrine (adrenaline) from the adrenal glands. This hormone prepares the body to face a threat or shock. The effect it produces is an increase in heart rate and blood pressure, and rapid, shallow breathing that would help the individual fight or flee a threatening situation. Nicotine also prompts the release of hormones that control an individual's reactions to stressful situations.

Another effect of epinephrine is that it tells the body to dump glucose into the bloodstream, so the muscles can react quickly to the perceived threat. However, nicotine is believed to inhibit the release of insulin, which prevents glucose levels from rising too high. The result can be hyperglycemia, which could explain why nicotine seems to curb the appetite—the body believes it already has enough sugar and inhibits the release of hormones that signal hunger.

Marijuana

There is a great deal of debate about whether marijuana affects hormonal systems. Some research has suggested that it can damage male fertility by interfering with sperm production. While there is evidence that marijuana can actually increase sperm motility, there is concern that the sperm may "burn out" before they reach the egg and may be unable to penetrate and fertilize the egg. Other research has indicated that the active ingredient in marijuana, tetrahydrocannabinol (THC), can prevent sperm from binding to an egg. Reports that marijuana can also lead to feminization by reducing testosterone production suggest another area of uncertainty, although such effects are believed to be reversible if marijuana use stops. In women, THC is thought to increase the amount of testosterone in the body, producing an increase of body hair and a decrease of fat in the breasts and buttocks. The menstrual cycle may also be interrupted and fertility affected.

Cocaine

Cocaine's influence on hormones varies between men and women. Cocaine's effects on the female reproductive system are an important area of research, in particular the way that it disrupts the menstrual cycle. Little is known about how cocaine affects luteinizing hormone, which is responsible for stimulating the ovaries to produce eggs. On the other hand, there is an increased chance of becoming pregnant in women who use cocaine. Sustaining a pregnancy is also more problematic; cocaine is known to constrict blood vessels, which can have implications for blood flow to the placenta while a fetus is developing. Increases in blood pressure and heart rate have been observed in fetuses exposed to cocaine. There is evidence in animals that cocaine can pass from the mother to the baby through the placenta and the umbilical cord and possibly through the amniotic fluid. There is also an increased risk of miscarriage and premature labor.

Cocaine may make users more susceptible to infections by lowering the amounts of hormones that regulate the production of immune system regulators called cytokines. These proteins regulate the body's response to stress, injury, and infection. Cocaine users who indulge in risky behaviors, such as intravenous injection or unsafe sex, may unknowingly be putting themselves at a greater risk with cocaine because it prevents the immune system from responding adequately to infection.

Stress

Stress is an important factor in drug abuse; it is believed to be associated with relapse in established users and may be a reason that some people initiate drug use. There are three hormones involved in the stress cycle: corticotropin-releasing factor (CRF), which is released by the hypothalamus in response to a perceived stress event; adrenocorticotropin (ACTH), produced by the pituitary gland in response to the CRF signal; and cortisol, produced by the adrenal glands. Cortisol is triggered by a rise in ACTH in the bloodstream and travels throughout the body, including to the hypothalamus and pituitary. If the original source of stress has abated, the cortisol inhibits the release of CRF and ACTH and the cycle stops. If stress is ongoing, the cortisol fails to inhibit the production of more CRF, and the cycle continues until the stress stops.

Other chemicals that inhibit the production of CRF are endogenous opioid peptides, which are chemically similar to morphine and heroin. People who take opiate drugs add to the inhibitive effects of

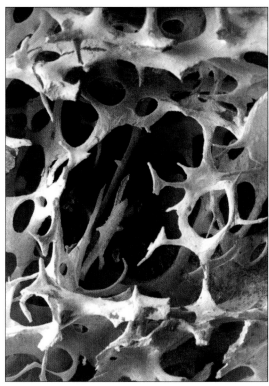

Osteoporosis is a condition in which the interior supporting structure of the bone thins and becomes brittle, making a person prone to broken bones. Women alcoholics are particularly at risk as alcohol negatively affects female hormones that help maintain bone density.

opioid peptides, which may be a factor in starting to use such drugs. If a user is struggling with stressful emotions, the combined effect of the peptides and the opiate drug can blunt the effect of stress hormones and thus set up a reward pattern. However, when the effect of the drug begins to wear off after four to six hours and the user goes into withdrawal, the stress hormones surge and may retrigger the emotions that caused the user to take the drug. The user takes more of the drug and the cycle begins again. The constant cycling of opiates and stress hormones can result in the user becoming hypersensitive to stressful situations.

Cocaine also stimulates the production of stress hormones, but instead of dulling the response, it is heightened and perceived as part of the rush associated with taking cocaine. The rush is part of the pleasurable feelings that encourage people to continue to take cocaine. When the user goes into withdrawal, the stress hormones are triggered again, but this time their activation is perceived as being unpleasant. Because these hormones are triggered both by taking and withdrawing from cocaine, the user quickly becomes hypersensitive to their effects.

Stress hormones can produce other effects if they are circulating at high doses around the body. Thyroid and adrenal hormones can induce psychotic mental symptoms, such as restlessness, excitability, and irritability. Cortisone, which is also used to treat allergies and inflammation, can cause mood-related hallucinations and swings from elation to depression.

Gender differences

The balance of sex hormones that are present in men and women may explain why women have a different motivation to take drugs. The female hormone estrogen has been found to affect the levels of dopamine released in response to sexual activity and addictive drugs. Stimulant drugs, such as amphetamines and cocaine, may also produce a different reaction depending on where a woman is in her menstrual cycle when she takes them. Research into the effects of cocaine have shown that women become dependent more quickly and after taking smaller doses compared with men. Female motivation to take the drug also differs from men; women take the drug to self-medicate when feeling depressed or unhappy, whereas men tend to take cocaine to heighten the effect when they are already feeling good. Experiments have shown that estrogen can also make female rats become more sensitized to the effects of cocaine and exhibit greater behavioral responses than female rats not exposed to estrogen. There are similar effects with nicotine. Women smoke to regulate their mood, whereas men smoke to improve their performance at work, lessen feelings of aggression, and for pain relief. Hormone differences may also explain why nicotine replacements are less effective in women than in men. Women often find antidepressants and psychotherapy more helpful.

W. A. Horan

See also:
Anabolic Steroids • Metabolism

Human Growth Hormone

Human growth hormone is a natural chemical that promotes growth and builds protein and fat into muscle. It is used illicitly by some athletes and bodybuilders to develop their muscles and help the body heal after injury.

Growth hormone, also called somatotropin, is produced by the pituitary gland. This hormone stimulates the metabolism of protein and helps the body use stored fat. It also helps the body maintain blood glucose within a normal range and thus is important in the metabolism of carbohydrates. Growth hormone's role in converting food into muscle has made it attractive to some athletes, who take it to enhance performance and prevent injury.

Certain genetic conditions or acquired diseases can cause either excessive growth hormone secretion or a deficiency. An excess can result in giantism. The world's tallest man, Robert Wadlow, had giantism. By the time he was five years old, he was 5 feet 4 inches (1.6 m) tall. As an adult, he grew to almost 9 feet (2.7 m). Giantism is a very rare disorder. By far the most common problem is a deficiency in human growth hormone.

Deficiency problems

Deficiencies in human growth hormone result in retardation in growth in children or even dwarfism. When children are of "pathologically short stature," it is common to treat them with growth hormone. It is estimated that 10,000 to 15,000 children in the United States fall into this category. A child with a deficiency in growth hormone is often small and has an immature face.

Children diagnosed as having stopped growing can be treated with injections of growth hormone. Some children receive three or four injections a week, and some receive daily injections. Patients usually respond within three to four months, when an increase in growth rate is typically observed. The overall treatment usually takes several years and ceases when the child reaches an acceptable adult height.

Use and abuse

There are three major issues related to the use of human growth hormone. Prior to 1985, growth hormone could only be obtained from human brains when a person died. However, the U.S. Food and Drug Administration approved a synthetic version that is now readily available. This availability has led to a proliferation of advertisements and companies promoting the benefits and sale of growth hormone. The question of abuse has been raised. Since human growth hormone can enhance athletic performance by stimulating protein synthesis and building muscle, its use can provide an unfair advantage. Anabolic steroid use is similar, and has been banned in major sports. Evidence that growth hormone is being used by athletes is anecdotal because abuse of the drug is as yet undetectable, but thefts from manufacturers and retailers suggest there is a substantial illicit market. Growth hormone is sometimes used by teenage athletes to overcome the height-limiting effect of some anabolic steroids while their bodies are still growing. There is also a belief among athletes that growth hormone can strengthen tendons and prevent stress fractures, thus decreasing risk of injury. Scientists are attempting to find a way to test whether an athlete has used growth hormone. A related issue regards the safety of such use and some uncertainty regarding long-term effects on the body.

A final issue lies in a field known as bioethics, which examines the ethics associated with use of medical and scientific breakthroughs. Some have questioned the use of growth hormone for children who are not of pathologically short stature. If parents decide that their normal-stature child should be taller, one must consider the ethics of such a decision. The medical profession is debating this issue, and most pediatricians do not approve of growth hormone use in a normal-height child. Nevertheless, nonprescription sources are plentiful, making it relatively easy to obtain the drug.

As with many new medical breakthroughs, the bioethics regulating use are still being debated.

J. L. Johnson

SEE ALSO:
Anabolic Steroids • Hormonal Effects

Hydromorphone

Hydromorphone is a powerful semisynthetic narcotic analgesic with a potency estimated at two to eight times that of morphine. It is manufactured under the trade names Dilaudid and Hydromorph Contin.

Hydromorphone is one of a range of narcotic analgesics introduced by pharmaceutical companies to deal with different levels of pain, from mild to severe. Inevitably it was promoted as a safe, non-addicting substitute for morphine—a claim quickly disproved by experience. Hydromorphone is usually prescribed for postoperative pain, cancer, burns, bone fractures, and the acute coughs of colic, tuberculosis, bronchitis, and pleurisy. Processed into a fine, white, odorless, water-soluble crystalline powder, hydromorphone is available as an injectable fluid, rectal suppository, cough syrup, soluble tablet, or powder for compounding. In hospitals, the drug is most often injected under the skin. The dosage for medical treatment of pain is 2 to 4 milligrams every four to six hours. Misusers have been known to take up to 100 milligrams a day.

The tablets are intended to be swallowed whole and are available in strengths of between 1 and 8 milligrams. When abused, Dilaudid tablets are somtimes crushed and then snorted, or dissolved in water and "cooked" for intravenous injection.

Pharmacology and effects

Hydromorphone is a hydrogenated ketone of morphine with the formula $C_{17}H_{19}NO_3$. A ketone is a substance containing the carbonyl group (C=O) attached to two carbon atoms. The main effects of hydromorphone are to control pain with mild euphoria and general lethargy and relaxation. A moderate dose alleviates pain in about 15 minutes, often placing the pain-free patient in a euphoric daze for between five to six hours. As the dose increases, so does the euphoria, but not to the intensity produced by heroin or morphine.

In the short term and at low doses, hydromorphone may cause nausea and vomiting. At higher doses, concentration is impaired and breathing and heart rate both slow down. At very high doses, there is a risk of overdose. The symptoms of overdose include respiratory depression, extreme somnolence progressing to stupor or coma, cold and clammy

KEY FACTS

Classification
Schedule II (USA), Schedule I (Canada), Class A (UK), Schedule I (INCB). Opioid.

Street names
Big D, dillies, drugstore heroin, little D

Short-term effects
Euphoria, pain relief, dizziness, drowsiness, sedation, and nausea. Side effects include blurred vision, cramps, palpitations, involuntary eye movements, fainting, flushing, and disorientation.

Long-term effects
Development of tolerance to analgesic effect. Physical dependence can occur after a few days of use, but more usually after several weeks. Withdrawal produces symptoms similar to those of heroin withdrawal.

skin, and sometimes bradycardia (slow heart rate) and low blood pressure.

Over the longer term and with chronic use, tolerance and dependence can develop. Withdrawal symptoms are very similar to those experienced with heroin withdrawal—sweating, yawning, runny nose, stomach cramps, insomnia, itching, and restlessness. Hydromorphone withdrawal is not life threatening, and the symptoms subside over a period of seven days. Other symptoms may include mood swings, reduced libido, menstrual irregularity, and acute constipation.

H. SHAPIRO

SEE ALSO:

Heroin • Morphine • Narcotic Drugs • Opiates and Opioids

Ibogaine

Ibogaine is a hallucinogenic drug that has been used for hundreds of years by members of an African religious group. It has been suggested that ibogaine may have a potential use as a treatment for some types of drug addiction.

Ibogaine is a naturally occurring chemical from an African shrub that is traditionally used by West and Central African groups for its dreamlike effects. In recent years, Western scientists have been investigating its use as a medicine to combat dependence and withdrawal from a variety of addictive drugs.

Ibogaine is a psychoactive drug found in the root bark of the African shrub *Tabernanthe iboga*. Some African people take the drug in its natural root bark form, although in the West it is more commonly available as ibogaine hydrochloride, an off-white powder that has either been made in a laboratory or chemically extracted from the plant. Local African names for the root bark include *iboga* and *eboka*.

The traditional users of ibogaine are the Bwiti, a West-Central African religious group predominant among the people of Gabon and Cameroon. Bwiti members consume the *iboga* root bark as part of an initiation ritual when they reach puberty. Ibogaine enables them to experience dreamlike visions that are believed to spiritually integrate the individual into the group. This practice appears to date back several centuries and may have originated somewhat earlier in the Congo basin. Some Africans also use smaller doses of the root bark to stay alert and to help them recover from illness.

The Bwiti consume ibogaine by eating the *iboga* root bark in the presence of a priest, who supervises the appropriate dose. Western users usually take the drug for recreation by swallowing a capsule of its pure hydrochloride form. A normal dose is around 10 milligrams per kilogram of body weight, although opiate addicts, such as those who take heroin or methadone, often need more to experience an effect. The dose of ibogaine is absorbed through the digestive system into the blood, by which it is carried to the brain. Typically, a user will feel the initial dreamlike effects of the drug around an hour after taking it, and then enter an introspective phase that starts after a few hours and lasts for about half a day.

Chemistry and effects

Chemically, ibogaine is a psychoactive indole alkaloid with the chemical name 12-methoxy-ibogamine ($C_{20}H_{26}N_{20}$). Purified ibogaine occurs as a crystalline solid that dissolves in alcohol and other organic solvents. Its hydrochloride salt is also solid at room temperature but dissolves in both water and alcohol. Although the human body's reaction to the drug is not fully understood, scientists have discovered that it is metabolized in the liver into the related chemical noribogaine.

Users of ibogaine typically take the drug as a one-time single dose. Its immediate effects are to cause a relaxed dreamlike state, with amplified senses, difficulty standing, and a tendency for introspection. The pharmacological method by which ibogaine achieves these claimed effects seems to be very complicated. Scientists have found that

---

KEY FACTS

Classification
Schedule I (USA and Canada). Not scheduled in UK or INCB. Hallucinogen.

Street names
Iboga and *eboka* in West and Central Africa

Short-term effects
Dreamlike state followed by an introspective feeling. Also accompanied by amplified sounds and light, ataxia (difficulty standing), nausea, and hallucinations.

Long-term effects
Claimed to aid the treatment of drug addiction by alleviating the withdrawal symptoms and craving for other drugs.

the drug activates several receptor cells in the brain that are associated with drug addiction, such as opiate, serotonin, and dopamine receptors. In addition, the metabolite noribogaine has similar effects but stays in the body much longer; hence, rather than ibogaine, it may be the metabolic products of the drug that are responsible for the claimed long-term effects on addiction.

Yet many people also report unpleasant side effects from taking ibogaine. It can cause muscle tremors, nausea, and vomiting, while some users suffer from feelings of anxiety or paranoia. A number of deaths have occurred after taking it, both in the West and in Africa. When used in the West, however, ibogaine is often given to people with dangerous drug habits, so some of these deaths may have been attributed to other drug use.

Ibogaine as an addiction treatment

Ibogaine has received some notoriety among drug users in the West as a potential treatment for drug addiction. In the early 1960s, Howard Lotsof, a former heroin user, took ibogaine as a new recreational drug and found that afterward he had virtually no heroin withdrawal symptoms. Later, in the 1980s, he set up a company to patent ibogaine as a treatment and to investigate its effects. Since then, there have been several scientific reports supporting ibogaine's ability to reduce both withdrawal symptoms and cravings for addictive drugs.

Research from the early 1990s suggests that ibogaine is a potential treatment for addiction to heroin, cocaine, methadone, alcohol, and possibly tobacco. When used to treat addiction, ibogaine is typically given as a single dose that is meant to last for a month or more. In addition to helping relieve the symptoms of drug withdrawal, there are reports that it also decreases the desire to use addictive drugs for several weeks. After a long period of abstinence from other drugs, while using ibogaine, many people do not return to their former habit. However, practitioners of ibogaine treatment caution that it is no quick fix for drug addiction but should be accompanied by drug rehabilitation, counseling, or lifestyle changes as part of a comprehensive treatment program.

While ibogaine is approved for clinical trials in the United States, it is otherwise illegal, and unauthorized possession can lead to imprisonment.

Bwiti rituals represent a journey to the land of the dead, hence the painting of participants' faces with a white powder. The drug ibogaine is taken to enhance communications with the spirit world.

There have also been difficulties finding funds for laboratory testing. Problems supporting research have been partially attributed to the fact that ibogaine is a naturally occurring drug, so it is difficult to secure a return on investment. Some tests have been carried out in the Netherlands, but these were halted after the death of a young heroin addict. At present, ibogaine treatment is legal in two countries, Panama and St. Kitts, although only in expensive, private clinics. Meanwhile, many people seek illegal ibogaine treatment elsewhere, which is usually provided by unqualified individuals and could therefore be dangerous.

N. LEPORA

SEE ALSO:

Hallucinogens

Illicit Manufacturing

The setting up of laboratories to produce illegal drugs is an increasing trend, particularly in rural areas. Manufacturing is usually carried out in makeshift conditions, which creates a variety of health, safety, and environmental problems.

Manufacturing of illicit drugs has increased in the United States within recent decades. The U.S. Department of Health, Office of Environmental Health and Safety, and many individual states run programs designed to detect the operation of clandestine drug laboratories and apprehend the manufacturers. The U.S. government defines an illegal laboratory as one set up to produce illicit drugs such as methamphetamine or Ecstasy. Illegal labs have been found in storage units, apartments, motel rooms, trailer parks, vehicles, and houses. Makeshift labs can be small enough to fit into a suitcase; bigger operations can be easily disassembled and transported to a different location. It does not require a lot of people to operate a lab. It is estimated that the average producer teaches ten other people per year how to make illicit substances. The relative ease of manufacturing and the chance to make quick profits have contributed to the rise in the existence of these labs.

Synthetic drugs

Production of synthetic drugs such as methamphetamine is relatively easy. Most illicit drug recipes have little understanding of chemistry, which accounts for poor manufacturing techniques and results in impurities and contaminants. A few hundred dollars in over-the-counter medications and chemicals can produce thousands of dollars worth of methamphetamine. Manufacturers combine precursor substances to produce methamphetamine and other illicit drugs, such as methcathinone. A precursor substance is one that may be inactive when used alone but produces a different effect when combined with other precursors. Precursor medications and chemicals include cold and asthma medications, red phosphorus, hydrochloric acid, drain cleaner, battery acid, brake cleaner, lye, antifreeze, cat litter, and lantern fuel.

The variety of chemicals used in the production of methamphetamine include solvents, metals, salts, explosives, and corrosives. Thus, production processes and the effects on the individual can be hazardous. Often, the first indication the authorities have of the presence of an illegal laboratory is a call to emergency services to deal with an explosion or fire.

Another drug that is illegally manufactured is methylenedioxymethamphetamine (MDMA), also known as Ecstasy. MDMA was first synthesized in 1912 as a possible appetite suppressant. Since 1985, Ecstasy has been classified as a Schedule I substance due to its doubtful medicinal benefits and high abuse potential. Most of the worldwide supply of Ecstasy is produced in illegal laboratories in the Netherlands. According to the U.S. Department of State, production of Ecstasy has been on the rise in Belgium, Poland, and the Middle East. Southeast Asia has also been a source for Ecstasy production.

In 2000 it is estimated that approximately 80 percent of the Ecstasy entering the United States came from or through the Netherlands. The United States has imposed strict domestic controls on the precursor chemicals used to manufacture Ecstasy, and is working with other countries to control access to such chemicals. In 2001 the United Nations Commission on Narcotic Drugs outlined measures governments can take to identify and control the use of Ecstasy and other synthetic drug chemicals. Thus, controlling the production of Ecstasy has become an international endeavor.

A major problem with the manufacturing of illicit drugs is that the drug that is sold on the street may contain a variety of substances that are toxic or have little to do with the substance the buyer believes he or she is purchasing. Since these drugs are illegal, there is no regulation regarding their production, and unscrupulous producers are not concerned about the health effects of their product. This fact has not necessarily affected the demand for illicit drugs. To remedy this problem, purchasers in the Netherlands can have a street drug tested at government-sponsored agencies prior to using it.

Coca processing is a large-scale operation requiring vast amounts of chemicals. Many coca processors suffer chemical burns to their hands and feet as a result of mashing the coca with sulfuric acid.

In the United States, purchasers risk criminal prosecution and no such agencies exist. There are many instances of drug users experiencing acute negative reactions and even death from ingestion of illicitly manufactured products that contain toxic chemicals.

Coca and opium processing

Some cultivated drugs also have to undergo several types of chemical processing to make them more potent or suitable for use in a different form. Leaves from the coca bush are mashed in a tank with kerosene, acetone, and sulfuric acid. The mixture is then allowed to stand for several days before being evaporated and filtered. The resulting paste is then treated with hydrochloric acid to turn it into cocaine hydrochloride, which can be dried and ground to a powder. Coca processing labs are usually hidden deep in the South American jungles, near the fields where the coca is grown. However, vast quantities of chemicals are needed to produce cocaine. Private planes have been used by the drug cartels to ship in supplies, but better monitoring of air traffic has led the cartels to switch to using

local waterways instead. Turning cocaine powder into crack requires another processing step. Because crack is too bulky to smuggle in any quantity, this operation is often carried out in smaller-scale labs near the customer base. The process is comparatively cheap and easy, which makes it harder to trace illegal labs.

Opium is another drug that undergoes various processing stages to turn it into other chemicals, such as morphine or heroin. Extracting morphine usually happens near the poppy fields and requires simple chemicals, such as calcium hydroxide, hydrochloric acid, and ammonium chloride. As morphine constitutes only 10 percent of the raw opium weight, it is easier to transport to heroin laboratories, which are often located in remote areas. Conversion of morphine to heroin is also comparatively simple. The pungent fumes from the solvents used in the acetylation process can give away the location of the processing labs.

Marijuana

Production of marijuana in many Western countries is increasingly switching to indoor cultivation as

165

eradication campaigns successfully target illegal outdoor crops. Hydroponic techniques and special lighting rigs have enabled illicit growers to set up operations in all types of buildings, from garden sheds and attics to farm buildings and warehouses. Careful breeding has increased the potency of cannabis plants, and their growth has been further enhanced by use of special fertilizers, plant hormones, and insecticides. Often these cannabis-growing operations are only discovered by neighbors, who notice that windows have been blacked out or that their own homes have suddenly become much warmer, due to the large amount of heating and lighting required to grow cannabis. Another clue is a sudden rise in demand for water, gas, and electricity at a particular address.

Hazards of manufacture

Producing illicit drugs is not a risk-free process and can be damaging to health. With synthetic manufacturing of illegal drugs, fumes and bodily contact with the substance can be toxic. Contact can occur through breathing, accidental injection, skin absorption, or eating. The risk of injury depends on the particular chemical, concentration, quantity, and whether the exposure is acute or chronic.

An acute exposure occurs over a short period of time and may cause chest pain, dizziness, shortness of breath, and coughing. It could also result in chemical irritation and burns, and lack of coordination. When police locate a lab and plan apprehension of the producers of illicit drugs, they proceed with extreme caution. Acute reactions can occur immediately after the drug bust, before the lab has been adequately ventilated. In addition, exposure to the solvents can cause problems with the central nervous system such as shakiness, dizziness, and motor problems. Solvents also present a fire hazard, since they are highly flammable. Police officers receive special training for the investigation of labs to help minimize or avoid the negative effects of contact with the substances. Protective clothing and respiratory equipment may also be necessary.

People who work in illicit manufacturing may also suffer health problems as a result of chronic exposure to the chemicals over the course of months or years. Due to their clandestine nature,

ENVIRONMENTAL HAZARDS

Illicit drug-manufacturing operations present a significant enviromental problem. Many of the chemicals used to make methamphetamine are toxic, but empty chemical drums and residues from processing are frequently dumped in woods, waterways, and fields, where they can kill wildlife, destroy trees and plants, and pollute rivers and aquifers. Dumping large quantities of chemicals into sewers can cause the formation of dangerous gases or can shut down small treatment facilties. In buildings, the chemical vapors can permeate the walls and floors, rendering buildings uninhabitable.

Cleaning up these sites is costly and usually requires specialized waste contractors. Costs range from $5,000 to as high as $20,000 to clean up each methamphetamine lab and dump site.

little is known regarding chronic health effects of working in these labs over time. However, continued exposure to the chemicals used in these labs can cause cancer, brain damage, liver and kidney damage, birth defects, and miscarriages. It is clear that working in one of these illicit labs has health as well as legal ramifications.

Demand for illegal drugs and the huge profits they render has led to a sharp increase in the number of small-scale labs producing easy-to-manufacture substances such as Ecstasy and methamphetamine. Deterrent efforts focus on regulation of the supply and transportation of precursor substances on both domestic and international fronts. Further, there are severe criminal charges for anyone apprehended and convicted of drug manufacturing. Although profitable in the short term, the long-term deleterious health effects and probability of criminal apprehension make illicit drug manufacturing a hazardous activity.

J. L. JOHNSON

SEE ALSO:
Controlled Substances • Designer Drugs

Inhalants

Inhalants are volatile substances that produce vapors that, when inhaled for abuse, result in mind-altering effects. The unpredictability of inhalants' effects puts them among the most dangerous of substances abused by young people.

Inhalant abuse is the deliberate inhalation of vapors or gases with the intention of producing enjoyable mind-altering effects. Many abusers of inhalants are adolescents who have ready access to substances that can be abused in this way, but who may be little aware of the hazards of such abuse. This fact makes inhalant abuse a matter of particular concern.

Inhalant abuse is by no means a modern phenomenon. Inhalants such as ether and laughing gas (nitrous oxide, N_2O) were used recreationally in the nineteenth century, and there are historical references to the deliberate inhalation of substances to produce intoxication dating from ancient Greek civilizations. In recent decades, however, since the mid-twentieth century, there has been a worrying trend in the prevalance of inhalant abuse, with growing numbers of people abusing inhalants.

Prevalence

Inhalant abuse is most prevalent among adolescents aged 12 to 17. Their abuse is usually short term, although some continue to abuse inhalants for up to a year. Surveys have reported that almost 10 percent of young people in the United States have experimented with inhalants at least once by the time they enter eighth grade. In 2008, 2 million Americans age 12 and older abused inhalants.

Inhalants tend to be abused by adolescent males, often as a group activity. The rate of inhalant abuse is frequently highest among children with a single-parent background, or where the father is unemployed. High rates of solvent abuse also occur among young Native Americans living in reservations, and rates of abuse are higher in Hispanics and whites than in African Americans.

Abuse of inhalants leads to a transient high caused by increased activity in the central nervous system (CNS). The initial high is shortly followed by a decrease in the activity of the CNS. This translates to a feeling of euphoria followed by blurring of vision, slurring of speech, impaired judgment, headache, and abdominal pain.

An adolescent inhales aerosol propellant from a bag. Inhalant abuse such as this can be lethal at any time.

The most serious consequence of inhalant abuse is death, which may occur due to inhaling vomit or accidental trauma arising from risky behavior. Other causes of death include irregular heart rhythm and a lack of oxygen leading to slowing of the respiratory rate (asphyxia). As many as 50 percent of deaths related to inhalants may be attributed to "sudden sniffing death" syndrome. This syndrome occurs when an intoxicated inhalant abuser is startled or engages in a strenuous activity, such as fighting. Sudden stress prompts the release of large amounts of epinephrine, norephinephrine, and other chemicals that may cause disturbances of the rhythm of the heart (arrhythmias). These arrhythmias reduce the ability of the heart to pump blood around the body and may lead to rapid fatality. The syndrome is a frequent cause of death in first-time users.

There are also many chronic side effects that occur as a result of repeated inhalant abuse. Brain damage often occurs in chronic abusers, leading to impaired ability to think and reason, poor balance, and difficulty walking. Inhalant abuse by pregnant women can also increase the risk of spontaneous abortion. Specific side effects also occur, depending on the chemicals that are inhaled. The effects caused by the depression of the CNS are similar to those produced by alcohol; however, the possible effects of inhalants are far less predictable and more dangerous.

The side effects of inhalant abuse may occur at any time, whether on first usage, or after many years of side effect–free abuse. The unpredictability of the onset of the side effects of inhalant abuse makes them one of the most dangerous of abused substances.

Methods of inhalation

There are several different ways in which these chemicals may be inhaled; some of the methods of inhalation increase the dangers to the user. The two major methods of inhalant abuse are "bagging" and "huffing." Bagging involves decanting the substance into bags. Huffing is the application of the substance to a cloth, which is then placed over the mouth and the fumes breathed in. As both of these methods bring the inhalants close to the nose and mouth, characteristic red crusty spots may form around the mouth and nose, known as erythematous lesions.

Some inhalants may be inhaled by the placing of a bag over the head and inhaling the substance from that bag. That is a particularly dangerous method of inhalation because of the danger of suffocation.

The inhalant of choice for most users tends to be the inhalant to which they have the easiest access. Inhalants can be found in many common and cheap household products, and may often be abused by people from poorer backgrounds who do not have the means of obtaining other drugs. The most commonly abused inhalants by young people aged 12 to 17 are gasoline and butane, followed closely by glue and toluene. The wide variation between the inhalants makes them difficult to classify. However, they can be arranged into four broad categories, based on the form in which they are usually found.

Volatile solvents

Volatile solvents are liquids that vaporize at room temperature. They are constituents of a wide range of commonly available products, such as glues, gasoline, paint thinners, lighter fuel, and degreasing compounds. This classification encompasses a wide range of chemicals and effects.

Toluene is an aromatic hydrocarbon, that is, a compound consisting of carbon and hydrogen atoms in the form of a ring. Another prominent aromatic compound is benzene. Toluene is often found in gasoline, glues, some paints, correction fluid, and nail polish. Historically, toluene has been the most highly used substance in the setting of inhalant abuse, and it can be found in the home, at school, and in the workplace.

Because of its chemical properties, toluene is easily absorbed by the lungs, heart, brain, liver, and reproductive organs. These tissues may take up and store toluene, so shortly after inhalation the concentration in the brain may be ten times the level in the blood. Chronic toluene abuse is associated with serious damage to the brain. Scans of the brain may show a decreased brain mass, as well as loss of white matter leading to impairment of cognitive functions, difficulty walking, and a lack of coordination. This brain damage may be due to the breakdown of the myelin sheath that surrounds the nerve cells in the brain, causing nerve-cell death. In particular, toluene may damage the nerves that relay sound and vision to the brain, leading to losses of sight and hearing.

Toluene can interfere with the rhythm-regulating system in the heart, causing a sudden and unexpected disturbance of its rhythm. This may decrease the ability of the heart to pump oxygenated blood around the body and may lead to sudden death. Serious lung and kidney damage has also been reported as a side effect of toluene abuse. Reproductive toxicity may also occur with toluene abuse, and this has wide-ranging effects: chromosome damage, abnormal pregnancies, premature birth, fetal malformation or death, and mother-child adjustment disorders, including an increased prevalence of child abuse.

Gasoline is a mixture of different hydrocarbons. The universal availability of gasoline makes its abuse particularly prominent in rural settings where other drugs may not be available.

Gasoline contains both aromatic and aliphatic (straight-chained) hydrocarbons. The aromatic hydrocarbons include benzene and toluene. The hydrocarbon components of gasoline are mainly responsible for the intoxication produced by gasoline abuse. This intoxication, with purposeful abuse, may last up to five or six hours, though it reaches its peak within three to five minutes. Many additives are present in gasoline, and these compounds aggravate the toxicity of the major hydrocarbons involved.

Components in gasoline may interfere with the rhythm of the heart and produce arrhythmias. Benzene can cause serious injury to the bone marrow, reducing the function of the immune system and possibly predisposing a user to leukemia. Benzene is a major carcinogen in humans and may also act as a reproductive toxin, in the same manner as toluene.

Gasoline is a highly flammable substance. When young people whose judgment is impaired by intoxication combine gasoline inhalation with smoking of tobacco or marijuana, the possibility of serious burn injuries is vastly increased.

Trichloroethylene and 111-trichloroethane are examples of chlorinated hydrocarbons—chains of carbon and hydrogen atoms with some of the hydrogen atoms swapped for chlorine atoms. These chemicals are often included in household products such as antifreeze, paints, glues, and sealants. They had a historic use as general anesthetic agents and dry-cleaning fluids, although they are no longer used for those purposes.

The chlorinated hydrocarbons are another group of inhalant chemicals associated with sudden sniffing death syndrome. Further studies are needed concerning the other possible dangers of abuse of these compounds, though some evidence suggests that they may be associated with heart-muscle damage, cirrhosis of the liver, and reproductive complications, especially miscarriage. Studies of the offspring of pregnant rats exposed to trichloroethylene have demonstrated growth retardation and skeletal and soft-tissue abnormalities. Prolonged exposure to these chlorinated chemicals may also cause dermatitis.

Aerosols

Spray cans deliver aerosols—fine airborne mists—when a volatile propellant drives a product through

---

KEY FACTS

Classification
Generally not scheduled in USA, Canada, UK, INCB
Hallucinogens or anesthetics, depending on type.

Street names
Aroma of men, huff, locker room, hippie crack, moon gas, oz, poor man's pot, poppers, rush, snappers, spray, Texas shoe shine, tolly, toncho, whippets

Short-term effects
Initial feelings of stimulation and euphoria last only a few minutes. Loss of inhibition and control. Continuous use leads to unconsciousness.

Long-term effects
Can result in permanent brain damage and other irreversible effects, including loss of hearing, limb spasms, peripheral nerve damage, liver and kidney damage, bone marrow depletion, and lowered oxygen levels in the blood.

Dangers
Sudden sniffing death due to heart failure, which can occur in first-time users as well as experienced users. Risk of suffocation or choking on vomit. Users of nitrites risk exposure to HIV and sexual diseases.

Signs of abuse
Similar to alcohol—slurred speech, dizziness, lack of coordination, disorientation, inattentiveness. Smell of chemicals on breath or clothes. Paint stains. Red marks and crusty sores around mouth and nose.

---

a spray nozzle and then evaporates. The vapors of many propellants are potential substances of abuse. In fact, some of these propellants include many of the volatile substances, such as butane or propane. Examples of such spray products include spray paint, hair spray, and deodorant.

These substances include the most volatile of the inhalants, since they remain in liquid form under pressure in the can. Their high volatilities enable them to produce greater concentrations in air than the solvents in liquid glues, for example. In some cases, the aerosol preparations are capable of producing almost pure inhalant vapor. Since aerosols may contain a mixture of chemicals, their use is almost always a multitoxin hazard, making the side effects and the risks all the more unpredictable.

Butane and propane are often found in paint sprays, hair sprays, air fresheners, fuel gas, and lighter fluid. They are abused by young people because of their ready availability, especially when packaged as butane lighter fluid or as fuel canisters. The high flammability of these substances combined with smoking tobacco or other illicit drugs often leads to serious burns.

Direct inhalation from the canister can cause severe damage to the respiratory tract, even without taking into account the effects of the substance being inhaled. As the gas is released from the pressurized aerosol, it expands rapidly, causing a sharp decrease in temperature, which may cause frozen-tissue injury to the mouth and throat. Under certain circumstances, it may even stop the heart. The high pressure release of gas from the aerosol my also be great enough to rupture the lining of the lung, leading to a possibly life-threatening collapsed lung.

Anesthetics

Gases that are or were used as medical anesthetics can be abused as inhalants. Some have lost favor with the medical profession because of the major side effects that can occur with their use. Although anesthetics are not commonly abused substances because of the relative difficulty in obtaining them, they are still taken by some inhalant users.

Chloroform ($CHCl_3$) was the first general anesthetic to be used during surgery. It has now lost favor in medical use because of the irritation that it can cause to internal organs both by inhalation and ingestion. Exposure to alcohol may increase these toxic effects. Chloroform has been shown to cause cancer in laboratory animals, and it is now listed as a probable human carcinogen. Chloroform is also classified as a skin irritant, and prolonged contact may lead to a rash. Chloroform may also cause reproductive damage.

Ether was previously used widely as an anesthetic. It is now used only rarely and has a long history as a drug of abuse. Ether's anesthetic properties are characterized by rapid absorption and distribution in the central nervous system, and the quick onset of short-term effects. Ether is capable of producing euphoria and hallucinations, and these effects were reported around 40 years before its potential as an anesthetic was noted.

Although ether abuse was common in the nineteenth and early twentieth centuries, it is now uncommon as a drug of abuse. The main toxic effects of ether are respiratory irritation, nausea, and vomiting. Ether also poses an explosion risk.

Nitrous oxide (N_2O) is a colorless and almost odorless gas. First synthesized as an anesthetic, it is often known by the name "laughing gas," and it is the most abused of the anesthetic gases. Loss of consciousness can occur at high concentrations, though deep anesthesia is difficult at atmospheric pressure. Consequently it is rarely used alone in modern medicine, but often with other agents, because it decreases the concentration of the other agent that needs to be administered. The biggest source of N_2O that is found on general sale is as a propellant gas in aerosols of whipping cream, also known as "whippets."

The main features of N_2O inhalation are euphoria, analgesia, and possible loss of consciousness; however, inhalation of high concentrations of N_2O can lead to reduced oxygen delivery to the tissues, leading to asphyxiation. Prolonged exposure to N_2O can also lead to a form of anemia, through its inhibition of an enzyme required for DNA and protein synthesis. Due to inhibition of a vitamin B_{12}-dependent enzyme, use of nitrous oxide can also lead to degeneration of nerve fibers, leading to neurological problems. It is possible for a user to develop tolerance to N_2O, and thus for the euphoric properties to be reduced. However, in the setting of occasional abuse, this is unlikely to happen.

Nitrites

Amyl nitrite and butyl nitrite belong to a family of compounds known as alkyl nitrites. They were previously used to control heart conditions, such as angina, because they relax the smooth muscle around the blood vessels and cause a reduction in blood pressure, rapid heartbeat (tachycardia), and flushing. The alkyl nitrites have now been replaced by more

This illustration depicts Charles Thomas Jackson (1805–1880) under anesthesia. A graduate of Harvard Medical School, Jackson experimented with the use of ether as a surgical anesthetic.

modern drugs that have fewer side effects. However, as alkyl nitrites have lost popularity within medicine, they have gained popularity as a drug of abuse and are commonly known by the names "poppers" or "snappers," which derive from the sound of an ampule being broken open.

Poppers initially gained popularity as a sex-enhancing product, particularly among gay men. However, nitrites also became popular as a club drug. When inhaled, poppers produce a transient, dizzy high that lasts for a few minutes. Nitrites have also been reported to heighten the pleasure of sex. This association with sex can also have an unfortunate result in that users become less careful about safe practice and are at risk of contracting HIV and other sexual diseases.

As well as their more desirable effects, poppers can also cause a wide range of undesirable side effects. Skin rashes often occur around the mouth and the nose, which take the form of crusty lesions. Poppers decrease the blood pressure by dilating blood vessels, which leads to a reflex increase in the heart rate to maintain normal blood flow. People with heart problems should therefore be wary of using poppers.

Butyl nitrite temporarily converts a proportion of the blood's hemoglobin into methemoglobin, which is far less able to carry oxygen around the body than is hemoglobin. This results in symptoms similar to those of anemia: headache, breathlessness, blue lips and tongue, and hemorrhaging. In serious cases, this condition can lead to coma and death. Some people can suffer a potentially life-threatening red-cell breakdown, called hemolysis, if they are carriers of certain hereditary disorders.

There have been reported cases of death due to using poppers. However, many of these have been attributed to people ingesting rather than inhaling the drug or to the preexistence of heart problems.

Impact of inhalants

The side effects of inhalants can be major and occur at any time, placing inhalants among the most unpredictable of drugs of abuse. As well as the acute side effects that may occur with inhalant abuse, there is also a wide range of side effects that occur with more chronic usage, ranging from impairing the ability to think to chronic liver damage.

With many inhalants, long-term abuse may lead to tolerance, which then requires greater amounts of the substance to be inhaled to produce the same effect, further increasing the risk to the user's health. Chronic inhalant abuse may also lead to symptoms of psychological and physical withdrawal. A withdrawal syndrome may be experienced by the user upon suddenly stopping inhalant abuse. Other psychological effects may include mood swings and personality changes.

Inhalants are among the most dangerous drugs abused by young people. In many countries, age restrictions are placed on buying certain products, but the vast number and usefulness of volatile solvents make them all too readily available for abuse.

G. FITZPATRICK

SEE ALSO:
Classification of Drugs

Jimsonweed

Jimsonweed is one of a group of plants that contain compounds known as belladonna alkaloids. These chemicals act on the acetylcholine system, producing hallucinations and affecting nerves that control muscle function.

Jimsonweed, or *Datura stramonium*, a plant native to Asia, is now spread throughout most of the world. Growing in pastures, waste areas, and roadsides, jimsonweed can reach as high as 5 feet tall (1.5 m), with large white or lavender funnel-shaped flowers and large green, irregularly lobed leaves. The jimsonweed plant bears prickly fruit containing black seeds. All parts possess active substances, specifically two drugs classified as belladonna alkaloids, atropine and scopolamine.

The history of jimsonweed dates back to ancient Greek legends that describe its use by priests of Apollo at the temple of Delphi to induce visions of the future. In North America, Native American shamans, or spiritual leaders, used jimsonweed as a mind-altering component of spiritual ritual. The most popular case of jimsonweed use occurred in the late 1600s in Jamestown, Virginia. British soldiers stationed there to stop a rebellion were fed the leaves of this plant and experienced the effects for approximately one week after ingestion, remembering nothing afterward.

The active components of jimsonweed—atropine and scopolamine—are both muscarinic receptor antagonists. Both drugs prevent the neurotransmitter acetylcholine, which plays an important role in various muscle systems, from binding to muscarinic receptors in the parasympathetic nervous system. The parasympathetic nervous system controls heart contractions, movement of the gastrointestinal tract, aspects of breathing, and different parts of the brain. When a drug such as jimsonweed is consumed, acetylcholine cannot perform its normal functions, and there is a change in heart rate, breathing, vision, and thinking.

Jimsonweed is ingested through smoking, by brewing it into a tea, or through the skin. The toxic substances easily pass through mucous membranes of the skin, in the gastrointestinal tract, and the lungs. The drug begins to take effect within 30 minutes if smoked or drunk as tea, or one to four hours if plant materials or seeds are eaten. Jimsonweed's duration of action lasts up to 48 hours; however, some reports cite symptoms lasting up to two weeks. The toxicity of jimsonweed is unpredictable because different parts of the plant have varying concentrations of the active components.

Jimsonweed use occurs accidentally or recreationally. Users are often unprepared for the effects and may require hospitalization. Treatment includes placing the patient in a nonstimulating environment while monitoring vital signs, stomach pumping, and administration of physostigmine, which increases the amount of acetylcholine in the patient's system and helps reverse jimsonweed's effects.

D. MITRANO

KEY FACTS

Classification
Not scheduled in the USA, Canada, UK, or INCB. Hallucinogen.

Street names
Devil's trumpet, Jamestown weed, locoweed, mad apple, sacred datura, stink weed, thorn apple

Short-term effects
Dry mouth; dilation of pupils; hot, dry, flushed skin; blurred vision; increase in body temperature and heart rate; hallucinations; in some cases, euphoria

Long-term effects
The adverse effects of the drug usually discourage repeated use. High doses of the drug can result in fatal arrhythmia, cardiovascular failure, or coma.

SEE ALSO:
Acetylcholine • Belladonna Alkaloids • Hallucinogens • Plant-Based Drugs

Ketamine

Ketamine is an anesthetic that has acquired some popularity as a club drug. It causes hallucinations and a dissociated state in which users feel temporarily disconnected from the surroundings and their own bodies.

Ketamine was developed in 1962 during a search for a less problematic replacement for phencyclidine (PCP), an anesthetic that had gained notoriety for inducing hallucinations and psychosis. Ketamine is useful in human and veterinary medicine because it induces anesthesia while reducing breathing and heart functions to a lesser extent than other anesthetics.

The main drawback of ketamine as an anesthetic is its potential for causing vivid hallucinations, irrational behavior, and agitated states as the concentration of ketamine in the blood falls and the patient starts to emerge from anesthesia. In severe cases, patients can become psychotic. Anesthetists often give diazepam (Valium) with ketamine to reduce the risk of disturbing side effects.

Recreational use

The hallucinatory state that can occur on emergence from ketamine anesthesia is similar to the state that many recreational users of ketamine seek to attain. Although there are variations between individuals, an oral dose of around 1 milligram per pound of body weight causes a hallucinatory state in 5 to 30 minutes, while an intramuscular (IM) injection of around 0.4 milligrams causes similar effects in 1 to 5 minutes. Snorted doses and response times are intermediate between those for oral and IM doses. Fully anesthetic doses are around 4 milligrams per pound (oral) and 1 milligram per pound (IM); light doses cause euphoria and rushes of energy without causing full-blown hallucinations. Larger doses can cause vomiting, convulsions, and oxygen starvation to the brain. One gram can cause death.

Below the fully anesthetic dose, ketamine causes an unusual state—dissociative anesthesia—in which the user retains some degree of consciousness but the brain's ability to process sensory inputs is disturbed. Hallucinations at this stage include the sensations of leaving the body, flying through a tunnel toward a light, and encountering familiar people or divine entities. Similarities between ketamine trips and near-death experiences are striking, and it seems that

both sensations occur by the same mechanism—the blockade of NMDA (N-methyl-D-aspartate) receptors for glutamate. The experience is often referred to as "being stuck in a k-hole."

Some ketamine users report feeling a profound connection with the universe as a result of their experience. This can lead to feelings of superiority and egocentrism, or it can cause paranoia if the user feels he or she is the target of malign forces. Although fatalities due to ketamine are rare, ketamine trips are too extreme to be approached lightly.

M. CLOWES

SEE ALSO:

Classification of Drugs • Club Drugs • Ecstasy • Hallucinogens • PCP • PCP Analogs • Valium

Khat

The stimulant drug cathinone occurs in the leaves of khat, a shrub native to hot climates. It is used as a social drug in its native lands, but prolonged use of khat can lead to dependence and can have serious physical effects.

Khat (*Catha edulis*) is a large, flowering evergreen shrub that can reach heights of 20 feet (5 m) and is native to Africa and the Arabian Peninsula. The leaves are glossy and crimson-brown and resemble withered basil on the shrub. Harvested khat leaves turn yellow-green in color and have a leatherlike texture.

The history of khat is rooted in social and cultural use, for example, religious ceremonies and marriages in Africa and throughout the Middle East, in particular Somalia, Kenya, Ethiopia, and Yemen. Its use in these countries is seen as being similar to the use of caffeine or tobacco in North America. It is not comparable to stimulant abuse of cocaine or methamphetamine.

Khat acts as an amphetamine-like stimulant on the body. It excites or speeds up the central nervous system. Khat can produce feelings of mild euphoria, elation, excitement and alertness, and induce talka-tiveness, loss of appetite, insomnia, dilated pupils, and increased blood pressure and heart rate. The effects commonly last between one and three hours but have been reported to last up to 24 hours.

The pharmacological effects of khat are believed to parallel those of amphetamine, although there is need for further research. Some common physical side effects of use include stomach irritation, constipation, and increased blood pressure. With repeated use and at higher doses, khat use may lead to compulsive and psychological dependence, manic behavior, paranoia, hallucinations, anorexia, aggressive behavior, brain hemorrhage, heart attack, and pulmonary edema (lung congestion). Withdrawal symptoms following prolonged use include lethargy and depression, nightmares, and tremors.

Fresh khat leaves contain the stimulant cathinone. Its shelf-life is approximately 48 hours, after which the leaves deteriorate and the cathinone is converted to cathine, a much milder stimulant. Cathinone and cathine, sometimes referred to as khatamines, are the known main constituents that contribute to khat's stimulant effects, though there may be others that have yet to be identified. Methcathinone is a synthetic form of cathinone made in illegal laboratories.

How it is used

Khat is most commonly used by chewing the leaves or by keeping a wad of leaves in the cheek, as is done with chewing tobacco. Typically, khat leaves are chewed intermittently to release the active components. When chewed, there is a strong odor, and an intense thirst is generated. Young plants and leaves are more potent. Dried khat (in the form of crushed leaves, powder, or chewable paste) is smoked, brewed in tea, and sprinkled on food. To preserve freshness, khat is typically packaged in plastic bags or wrapped in moist banana leaves for transportation.

C. A. DELL

SEE ALSO:
Amphetamines • Methcathinone

KEY FACTS

Classification
Schedule I (USA), Schedule III (Canada), Schedule I (INCB). Not scheduled in UK. Stimulant.

Street names
Abyssinian tea, African tea, African salad, bushman's tea, catha, chat, gat, kat, oat, miraa (Kenya), qat (Yemen), and tschat (Ethiopia)

Short-term effects
Alertness, mild euphoria, insomnia, increase in blood pressure and heart rate

Long-term effects
Dependence, paranoia, aggression, hallucinations. Increased risk of heart attack and lung problems.

LAAM

LAAM is a synthetic opiate that can be used in the treatment of opiate addictions. Its long period of action gives it advantages over methadone, but LAAM has been replaced by substitutes that do not have its side effects.

LAAM, levacetylmethadol, also known as levomethadyl acetate and by its brand name, Orlaam, is a long-acting opioid analgesic (narcotic pain medication) that can be used as a treatment for heroin and other opioid dependence. Manufacturing of Orlaam was discontinued in the United States in 2003. Previously LAAM was dispensed only through opioid addiction treatment programs approved by the Food and Drug Administration (FDA), Drug Enforcement Administration (DEA), and designated state authorities. Use of LAAM in such programs was subject to treatment require-ments stipulated in federal regulations. The use of pharmacotherapy for opioid dependence should be carried out in conjunction with other therapies that address the person's substance dependence in a comprehensive manner.

LAAM is a mu-opioid receptor agonist that acts in a similar manner to morphine-type opioids, produces cross-tolerance to the effects of opioids, including the subjective high, and can reduce withdrawal symptoms in people physically dependent on opioids. These actions decrease the addicted person's desire for and use of other opioids, which reduces the harmful effects to the individual and society that accompany illicit injection drug use. As an agonist, LAAM also produces characteristic opioid effects, including analgesia, respiratory depression, sedation, constriction of the pupils of the eyes, and physical dependence.

Treatment regime

LAAM was developed in the 1940s as a possible alternative to morphine in pain treatment, but the slow onset and long duration of action made it poorly suited for pain management. These properties, however, are advantageous in the treatment of chronic opioid-dependent persons who would benefit from less frequent dosing require-ments and more stable medication levels. The FDA approved the use of LAAM for the treatment of opioid dependence in 1993 as an agonist therapy (opioid substitution) alternative to methadone.

LAAM is taken orally as a liquid solution, and it takes about two to four days for half of the ingested amount to be eliminated from the body. LAAM is metabolized to nor-LAAM and dinor-LAAM, both of which have active agonist effects and half-lives also on the order of two to four days. It takes several days for the opioid effects to reach a stable, steady state.

The main advantage that LAAM has over methadone is that LAAM is given three times per week (usually Monday, Wednesday, and Friday, with a higher dose given on Friday to last three days) while methadone is given daily. Fewer clinic visits can enable some patients to resume a more normal life. Because of the longer elimination rate, a missed dose of LAAM is also tolerated better than a missed dose of methadone. However, LAAM's slower onset of action makes dose adjustments take longer and increases the risk that a person will experience drug craving, withdrawal symptoms, or relapse during early treatment. One strategy to reduce this risk is to first establish a therapeutic dose with methadone and then convert to LAAM.

The effects of LAAM can be blocked by mu-opioid receptor antagonists (such as naloxone, naltrexone, nalmefene) or partial agonists (such as buprenorphine). Concurrent use with these medications can precipitate acute withdrawal symptoms, but these medications may be necessary to treat an overdose of LAAM in an emergency.

A critical disadvantage with LAAM is its suspected potential to cause severe heart problems, including fatal arrhythmias (irregular heartbeats) and cardiac arrest. This, and the availability in 2003 of buprenorphine as a treatment for opioid dependence, has led to the discontinuation of the availability of LAAM.

J. P. Reoux

See also:

Agonists and Antagonists • Buprenorphine • Methadone • Naloxone • Naltrexone • Opiates and Opioids

Laudanum

Opium has been used as a medicine for thousands of years. Its mixture with alcohol as a remedy for pain made laudanum popular with the Victorian upper classes until its doubly addictive effects became obvious.

Laudanum is a mixture of alcohol and opium that was used from the fifteenth to nineteenth centuries as a painkiller in medicine. In Victorian times it became a popular drink, but because of its highly addictive nature was banned for nonmedicinal use in the early twentieth century.

Laudanum is an opium solution dissolved in alcohol. Other than intoxication from the alcohol, its main pharmacological effect is caused by the powerful narcotic morphine in the opium. Opium is a milky extract from the pods of the opium poppy *Papaver somniferum*, which, when treated chemically, produces a wide variety of compounds, including heroin. Other names for laudanum are "wine of opium" and "tincture of opium," a tincture being a dilute alcohol solution containing a medicine.

Although opium has been used for thousands of years, laudanum was first introduced into Western medicine in the sixteenth century by Paracelsus (1493–1541), a professor at the University of Basel in Switzerland. For several hundred years it was prescribed as a painkiller, or analgesic, to treat ailments from headaches to tuberculosis. However, in Victorian times laudanum became used habitually across large parts of European and American society. While initially popular among the working classes—being a medicine, it was not taxed and was thus cheaper than gin and wine—it soon became the drug of choice for the upper classes. Many literary figures, such as Lord Byron (1788–1824), Samuel Taylor Coleridge (1772–1834), and Mary Shelley (1797–1851), took laudanum regularly. In the early twentieth century, Europe and the United States banned nonprescription opium-based products, and the use of laudanum has since almost completely died out.

Laudanum is taken as a drink, from which the morphine is slowly absorbed through the small intestine and then carried by the blood system to the brain. Typically, a fluid ounce of laudanum mixture contained one-tenth of an ounce of opium and equal parts of alcohol and water. Morphine is the main pharmacologically active chemical in laudanum and

Laudanum was once essential in every medicine cabinet, but few realized its addictive properties.

constitutes about 10 percent by weight of dried opium powder. Opium also contains the weaker analgesics codeine and thebaine, and the muscle relaxant papaverine.

The main effect of morphine and other opiates is to suppress pain, which they achieve by mimicking endorphins, the body's natural painkillers. Other effects of opiates include sedation, relaxation, drowsiness, and loss of anxiety. Physiologically, they also depress breathing and heart rate, and relax involuntary muscles such as those of the gastro-intestinal tract. Users quickly become tolerant to opiates, and progressively larger doses are needed to obtain the same effect. Prolonged use leads to addiction, with withdrawal symptoms that include weakness, depression, anxiety, diarrhea, and vomiting. Too large a dose of opiates can slow breathing, potentially causing death.

A regular opium habit causes general deterioration of the body and mind. Further, its use while pregnant results in an addicted baby that must endure withdrawal after being born.

N. LEPORA

SEE ALSO:
Morphine • Opiates and Opioids • Opium

Legal Controls

Many governments employ legal restrictions to regulate the use of legal and illegal drugs. Such interventions in the supply and demand aspects of drug use can have a significant impact on the costs and availability of drugs.

The use of recreational drugs, such as marijuana, cocaine, heroin, alcohol, tobacco, and various other drugs, diminishes normal capacities for self-control through either intoxication or addiction. This decrease in self-control can be associated with substantial harm to both users and nonusers alike. It is the deleterious effects of drug use that induce governments to place legal controls on the manufacture, distribution, purchase, use, and possession of recreational drugs. Around the world, widely different regulatory approaches are employed to deal with drug problems.

Government policies regulating drug use can be broadly categorized as either supply-side interventions or demand-side interventions. Supply-side interventions are policies that attempt to decrease the supply of drugs available for consumption. Advocates of supply-side interventions postulate that it is primarily the supply of drugs that determines drug use, and that decreasing drug availability and increasing costs will result in fewer individuals using drugs. Demand-side interventions are policies that attempt to decrease the quantity of drugs demanded for consumption. Advocates of demand-side interventions argue that if the demand for drugs does not exist, the quantity of drugs supplied will have no impact because no one will purchase them. Described below are some of the most common demand- and supply-side legal controls in use around the world. They are by no means exhaustive, but rather illustrate the variety of different policies used to decrease drug use.

Supply-side interventions

Prohibition of drugs (that is, making it illegal to produce, distribute, sell, purchase, use, and possess drugs) is one of the most common supply-side interventions used by governments around the world. Many governments devote enormous amounts of money and labor to enforce bans and prosecute offenders. Individuals found guilty of violating a drug prohibition often face large fines and lengthy jail terms. Yet, despite the vast resources devoted to prohibiting drug use and the possibility of monetary loss and incarceration, significant evidence indicates that substantial amounts of drugs continue to be purchased and sold in illegal markets, often referred to as black markets.

Prohibition increases the costs associated with supplying drugs to the market. These costs are a consequence of suppliers attempting to avoid detection by law enforcement officials when manufacturing, distributing, and selling drugs. These increased costs translate into higher drug prices and consequently less use than if the drugs were sold legally in a free market. However, in an article in *Social Research* in 2001, the researcher Jeffrey Miron pointed out that black market suppliers are able to offset the increased costs of prohibition to a certain extent because they are evading tax laws and regulatory policies (such as environmental and health requirements) and avoiding advertising costs by selling illegally. Despite this offset, current research suggests that the net costs of supplying drugs increases substantially under prohibition.

Although prohibition strategies are thought of as supply-side interventions, they are also likely to influence the demand for drugs. Prohibitions will decrease the demand for drugs directly through the imposition of fines and incarceration and indirectly through the stigma placed on illicit drug use. The decrease in demand may be partially offset by the forbidden nature of drug consumption, that is, prohibition may stimulate demand, particularly by the young, simply because it is an illegal activity.

Researchers have attempted to quantify the impact of prohibitions on drug consumption. In general, the findings from these studies indicate that prohibitions have a moderate negative impact on use. Some of the best evidence comes from the prohibition on alcohol in the United States during the 1920s. In a 1993 article titled "Drug Policy: Striking the Right Balance," Goldstein and Kalant reviewed the previous research on this topic and concluded that

Seizures of large quantities of illicit drugs, such as this 1989 shipment of cocaine seized in Mexico, can have a major impact on the supply chain by pushing up prices to users, who may resort to crime to fund their habit or may switch to a more available drug.

the prohibition not only decreased consumption of alcohol but also decreased problems related to alcohol abuse, such as liver cirrhosis.

Jeffrey Miron also pointed out that while prohibitions are likely to decrease drug consumption, they are likely to have other consequences as well. Prohibitions change criminal behavior through various mechanisms. Violent crimes tend to increase because there are no legal mechanisms to resolve disputes. Courts have no authority to enforce illegal contracts or resolve disagreements regarding illegal activities. Instead, discrepancies between buyers and sellers often result in violent resolutions. Income-generating crimes are also likely to increase during prohibitions. By decreasing drug supply, prohibitions increase the transaction price for obtaining drugs. In order to pay for higher priced drugs, drug users require additional income and often commit crimes such as robbery, theft, and prostitution to obtain supplementary income. Prohibitions also have the potential to decrease criminal behavior. Decreasing the use of a banned drug through prohibition might decrease violent crime if using the substance causes violent behavior. Alternatively, an increase in criminal violence may result if drug users replace the banned drug with a more readily available violence generating drug.

Prohibitions may also change the potency and quality of drugs. Suppliers have an incentive to transport the drug in a concentrated fashion to better conceal it from policing authorities. The concentrated drugs are of higher potency and require dilution before consumption. If the dilution is not conducted properly, then there exists an increased potential for overdoses under prohibitions. As there is no legal retribution for low-quality illicit drugs, buyers of illicit drugs are likely to face a greater variance in the quality of their purchases than in legal markets. This greater variance in quality under prohibition can result in a larger number of overdoses.

A final effect of prohibitions is to redistribute wealth from law-abiding citizens to those who violate the prohibitions. Governments spend a significant amount of money enforcing prohibitions. To pay for the enforcement, governments are likely to raise taxes and reduce spending in other important areas. Suppliers of illicit drugs are likely to make significant profits on the sale of their products and do not pay taxes. Therefore, prohibitions redistribute wealth from society as a whole to criminals supplying illicit drugs.

Sin taxes

An alternative supply-side intervention that is widely used around the world is to legalize the use of a drug and place a tax on the sale of that drug. The imposition of a tax increases the purchase price for the drug by decreasing the quantity of drugs supplied at each price level. One of the most fundamental principles of economics is the law of demand. The law of demand states that as the price of a good increases, the quantity demanded of that good will decline, assuming all other factors are constant. Given the addictive nature of most drugs, many researchers once believed that drug consumption would not adhere to the economic law of demand. However, empirical research has shown that the consumption of cigarettes, alcohol, cocaine, heroin, marijuana, and other drugs is inversely related to price.

While sin taxes will yield reductions in drug use, they are likely to yield other consequences as well. A benefit to the implementation of a tax on drugs is increased government revenue. As opposed to a prohibition, which redistributes wealth from law-abiding citizens to criminals, sin taxes redistribute wealth from the drug users to governments.

Moreover, the costs associated with enforcing the tax are likely to be substantially less than the costs associated with enforcing a prohibition. However, sin taxes can also create a loss to producers and consumers from decreased trade associated with the implementation of a tax. Another potential negative consequence of sin taxes is that they may be regressive. In other words, the tax may be disproportionately paid by lower-income individuals if they have higher drug prevalence rates than do higher-income individuals. However, given the inverse relationship between drug prices and drug use and the inverse relationship between drug use and health, sin taxes may actually be progressive from a public health standpoint. Finally, the imposition of a sin tax on one drug will decrease the relative price of other drugs and make them more attractive from a fiscal standpoint. If users switch to more (or, alternatively, less) harmful drugs, both the user and society may be worse (or better) off.

Other supply-side interventions

Numerous other forms of supply-side interventions exist worldwide. In general, these interventions attempt to decrease the availability of drugs to potential users by banning or limiting purchase, use, possession, sale, and distribution under certain specified conditions. Among the most popular policies are age restrictions that ban the use of substances to individuals under a certain age. These policies have been found to be effective in decreasing use and problems associated with use. For example, Alexander Wagenaar of the University of Minnesota wrote in 1991 and 1993 that increasing the minimum legal drinking age for alcohol to 21 in the United States decreased alcohol consumption, alcohol-related deaths and injuries, and other problems related to alcohol.

Another supply-side intervention is to ban the use of drugs in certain locations. For example, the World Health Organization estimates that more than half of the countries in the world have laws to control tobacco use in public places. In an article in the *British Medical Journal* (2002), Caroline Fichtenberg and Stanton Glantz reviewed 26 studies on workplace smoking bans in Australia, Canada, Germany, and the United States. They concluded that workplace smoking bans decrease smoking prevalence and average cigarette consumption.

Demand-side interventions

Treatment and rehabilitation of drug users is a common demand-side intervention used around the world. Treatment programs generally employ a variety of approaches in an attempt to restore drug addicts to productive members of society. Because drug abuse and addiction constitute a threat to public health and because drug treatment can be expensive, many governments have chosen to subsidize treatment programs in an attempt to increase enrollment by defraying some of the costs. Also, because drug abuse decreases productivity, many employer-subsidized health plans may also provide coverage for drug treatment. Evidence from numerous countries suggests that treatment of drug users is effective in reducing drug use. For example, using 2003 data from the National Treatment Outcomes Research Study in the United Kingdom, Michael Gossop and colleagues found significant reductions in drug use and related problems even years after treatment concluded.

Mass media campaigns

Mass media campaigns attempt to change social norms associated with drug use by reaching large segments of the population. Many types of messages have been employed, including demonstrating the negative consequences of drug use and the positive consequences of drug abstinence, educating and empowering individuals to reject drugs, changing perceptions about the types of people using drugs, changing beliefs on the prevalence of drug use, and various others. Mass media campaigns have used a variety of media to reach individuals, including television, radio, newspaper, and magazine advertisements, billboard messages, Web sites, music videos, and various others. While mass media campaigns have generally been found to increase the public's knowledge about drugs, the findings with respect to drug use have been mixed.

School education programs

Many country and local governments and school boards have invested large sums of time and money into school drug-education programs. These programs have used a variety of techniques in an attempt to prevent or delay the onset of drug use and to minimize the harm associated with drug use.

Advertising warning of the negative impacts of drug use is a common method of reducing demand for legal substances, such as alcohol and nicotine. There is some evidence that these methods help educate people about potential dangers.

One type of strategy is to provide students with factual information about drugs and the potential consequences of use. Evaluations of information-only programs generally find these programs to be insignificant determinants of drug use and drug-related outcomes. However, a few studies found that by increasing students' awareness of drugs, information-only programs had a detrimental impact on drug-related outcomes. Another strategy is to improve students' resistance in avoiding drug use by teaching them how to cope with peer pressure and how to react to media influences. A third technique is to provide students with skills to reduce the potential for harm to occur and to decrease the severity of the harm if harm does occur. Previous studies have found some support for both resistance and harm-reduction skill training; however, most of these studies were conducted on North American prevention programs, which focus more on non-use and delayed use than on harm reduction.

Other demand-side interventions

Many other forms of demand-side interventions are used worldwide. For example, many countries place strong warning labels on drugs that are sold legally in an attempt to inform the public (and sometimes to scare them) about the harms associated with drug use. Some countries ban advertising for legal drugs in an effort to decrease the demand for those products. In an attempt to prevent injuries and increase productivity among workers, many companies around the world have implemented drug-testing strategies in the workplace. Limited evidence suggests that all three of these demand-reducing strategies have a negative impact on drug-related outcomes.

Conclusion

A vast number of interventions are used throughout the world to reduce the consumption of recreational drugs and mitigate the adverse consequences associated with using and supplying drugs. Researchers and policy makers seem to agree that a portfolio of both supply-side and demand-side interventions is required. Choosing the optimal mix of interventions, however, is a complex decision, with which governments from around the world have struggled for centuries. Debates both within countries and across countries ensue each year on the optimal allocation of resources across interventions.

An optimal drug-intervention portfolio for one country may not be appropriate for another country. There is a great deal of disagreement on the morality of drug use among individuals and governments around the world. There is also vast disagreement on the harmful effects of drug use. For example, individuals and governments disagree over whether or not internal costs of drug use, such as harm caused to drug users, necessitate government action. Further, the effectiveness of alternative drug-control strategies may differ greatly in different countries due to different societal and cultural attributes. Country-specific empirical research cannot resolve differences in opinion about drug use morality, but it can be effective in decreasing the aggregate damage caused by drug use and supply and can significantly contribute to the development of more effective policies in the future.

J. TAURAS

SEE ALSO:
Drug Laws • Prohibition of Drugs

Legalization Movement

Some people view the prohibition of drug use as an unnecessarily harsh reaction to uncontrolled use by a minority of the population. The lobby to make drugs legal continues to put forward its case for reform of the drug laws.

Ever since drug use became popular among white middle-class students in the 1960s, there have been calls for the laws on drugs to be relaxed or removed altogether. Most of this effort has been focused on marijuana. The U.S. poet Allen Ginsberg was an early campaigner, and in the United States, the movement became more organized with the founding of the National Organization for the Reform of Marijuana Laws (NORML) in 1970, which boasts hundreds of thousands of members across the country. The other main legalization lobby in the United States is the Drug Policy Alliance, based in Washington, which argues for the legalization of all drugs.

There has been separate campaigning calling for the legalization of marijuana for medical uses. There is strong medical evidence that marijuana relieves the symptoms of a number of medical conditions, including glaucoma (a disease of the eye), the pain associated with multiple sclerosis, and the nausea caused by chemotherapy treatment for cancer. However, attempts to make medical marijuana legal have met with mixed success in many states, and the Food and Drug Administration refuses to approve its use until the risks have been fully assessed.

In the United Kingdom, the pro-marijuana movement has been less well organized, with small groups coming and going since the late 1960s. The leading groups include the Legalize Cannabis Alliance and the U.K. Cannabis Internet Activists, although, as in the United States, there are a number of local and national politicians, judges, police officers, newspaper editors, media celebrities, and others who have called for a reform of the law. Some want outright legalization, others suggest that the penalties should either be reduced or that marijuana use should be taken out of the criminal justice system altogether, with penalties no more serious than receiving a parking ticket. Other groups want to go much further, such as Transform, which, like the Drug Policy Alliance, is pressing for the legalization of all drugs. There are similar groups in other countries, including the Italian-based Radical Party.

How would drugs be controlled?

Advocates of legalization argue that prohibitions on selling drugs have created an unregulated criminal market that puts users at risk (*see* box, p.183). Legalizers identify a number of models for legitimate control of the use and distribution of drugs, which would probably vary for different drugs, depending on how dangerous they were thought to be:

- Unlicensed sales—similar to buying ordinary produce in a supermarket. This method would seem the least acceptable form of legal distribution, although legalizers argue that the current illegal market, which is unregulated and uncontrolled, is exactly the same.
- Licensed sales—in which the shopkeeper would need to have a special license to sell the drugs, in the same way that a license is required to sell liquor. It might even be that the government would have a monopoly on sales so that drugs could only be purchased from government-owned shops.
- Pharmacy sales—whereby certain drugs are available from the pharmacist.
- Prescription—whereby certain drugs could be obtained on prescription from a doctor.

The legalization movement acknowledges that the legalization of all drugs may not reduce drug misuse, but it might reduce some of the harms of banning drug use, such as using adulterated drugs or having a school or work career ruined by being convicted of a drug offense. The movement also says that organized crime would not disappear, but as drugs constitute such a large proportion of criminal income, it would take a long time to find similar profits elsewhere. Proponents also acknowledge that legalization would not deal with the root causes of chronic drug problems, such as poverty, urban deprivation, and social circumstances.

No government has taken the step of legalizing any drug that is currently the subject of

Marijuana is a main focus for the legalization movement because marijuana is considered safe by its advocates. However, some groups would like to see all drugs made legal, arguing that such a policy would cut crime and violence and assure that supplies were safe and use regulated.

circumstances the police have chosen not to enforce the law, such as when a small amount of marijuana is bought and smoked on the premises of a so-called coffee shop. The Dutch government does not believe that cannabis use leads to heroin use, but it does argue that having an outlet for the permissable supply of marijuana helps to protect young people from coming into contact with drug dealers who might want to sell them other drugs. The statistics seem to show that the Dutch heroin-using population is getting older, with fewer young people coming in at the other end—although whether this has anything to do with the policy on marijuana is unclear.

Even so, there is controversy over whether or not the Dutch government is breaking the international treaties it has signed. In order to get so many countries to agree, any United Nations treaty is often worded quite generally, so as not to infringe on national sovereignty. With the treaties on drugs, a number of countries have interpreted the statutes as giving each state room to maneuver in deciding how to interpret the law. So, for example, in a number of European countries, including Italy, Spain, Portugal, and Belgium, little or no action is taken against a person caught in possession of a small amount of any drug that is intended for personal use. A number of countries have also adopted various public health, harm reduction measures. These are measures taken to reduce the accompanying damage caused by drug use as part of a realization that simply stamping out drug use is not possible. Such measures include needle exchange programs, the prescribing of heroin to users, and the provision of consumption rooms under medical supervision.

international controls under various United Nations treaties. Although many people think that the Netherlands has legalized marijuana, this is not the case. The law against marijuana is still in place, it is simply that under certain special

ARGUMENTS FOR THE LEGALIZATION OF DRUGS

Many legalizers would like drugs, such as Ecstasy, marijuana, and cocaine, controlled and regulated in ways similar to the controls on alcohol and tobacco. What are the arguments in favor of legalizing drugs?

- Legalizers say that the "war on drugs" does not work. People cannot be prevented from wanting to take drugs. Laws against drug use only serve to put vast sums of money into the pockets of organized criminals, who bring violence and corruption to the use of drugs.
- The state should not be interfering with the rights of the citizen to use drugs in private.
- It is hypocritical to have laws against some drugs when tobacco and alcohol are legal and cause far more health damage, especially when a number of expert reports have suggested that moderate use of marijuana is no more of a health risk than either of these legal drugs.
- If drugs were legal, then the government would be able to levy taxes on them, which would benefit all of society. The extra funds could be used to help those with health problems caused by drugs.
- By making drugs legal, a major source of criminal income would be reduced. People would not have to steal to pay for drugs and, as a consequence, the profits of organized crime would collapse.
- Having legal products would ensure proper quality control. People would not have to

use unsafe drugs inexpertly manufactured in illegal laboratories or cut with dangerous additives.
- Whatever the harms of drugs, the drug laws make everything worse. Aside from the risks of contaminated drugs, violence, and corruption, otherwise law-abiding citizens are made into criminals, and they lose respect for the law.
- The costs of prohibition in terms of actual policing and the costs of crime to society worldwide run into billions of dollars every year, including the cost of keeping large numbers of people in prison for minor drug offenses.
- The climate of prohibition stigmatizes users and their families and is a disincentive to seeking treatment.
- It is not necessarily the case that making drugs legal would result in more people using them. During the 1970s, 11 U.S. states reduced the penalties for possession of marijuana, and use did not rise dramatically. The only reason these initiatives were abandoned was because the political climate changed with the presidency of Ronald Reagan beginning in 1981.
- If drugs were legalized, it would be easier to promote a more effective drug-education program. For example, young people would be encouraged to drink alcohol sensibly, with some government guidance regarding both drinking levels and the dangers of mixing alcohol with other drugs.

As with any official policy, drug policy can change along with the political climate of the day. For example, in the 1970s, 11 U.S. states decriminalized cannabis possession down to a misdemeanor. These decisions were reversed during the administration of President Ronald Reagan, not because of escalating drug use, but under threat of the withdrawal of federal funding and the promotion of the "Just Say No" campaign. After 1998, 15 states and the District of Columbia enacted laws allowing use and sale of marijuana for medical purposes.

H. SHAPIRO

SEE ALSO:
Drug Control Policy • Drug Laws • Legal Controls • Marijuana • Prohibition of Drugs

Levorphanol

Levorphanol is a potent narcotic analgesic similar to morphine in its actions but four to eight times more potent. It is manufactured under the trade name Levo-Dromoran.

Levorphanol is one of a range of synthetic opioid analgesics introduced by pharmaceutical companies to deal with moderate to severe levels of pain. Levorphanol is chemically similar to morphine and belongs to a small group known as the morphinans. It occurs as a mixture of two mirror-image molecules, levorphanol and dextrorphan, of which levorphanol is more powerful than dextrorphan or the mixture (racemorphan). Levorphanol is used medicinally as a tartrate salt, which is a white crystalline powder soluble in water and ether.

Pharmacological effects

Levorphanol is an agonist that acts at mu-opioid receptors in the brain and spinal cord to alter the transmission and perception of pain signals. Like morphine or meperidine, it produces euphoria and general lethargy and relaxation. However, it has a longer half-life than morphine, which makes it suitable for chronic pain relief, such as for treating cancer patients and in postoperative care.

The therapeutic oral dosage for pain is 2 to 3 milligrams every 6 to 8 hours. There also is an extended-release (long-acting) product that is taken every 6 to 24 hours as needed. Dosages for intravenous or intermuscular use are lower, generally between 1 and 2 milligrams. As with other opioids, tolerance develops with continuous use, and larger doses become necessary to achieve pain relief.

Health effects

In the short term and at low doses, use of levorphanol may cause constipation, itching, dizziness, drowsiness, stomach upset, nausea, flushing, and difficulty urinating. At higher doses, concentration is impaired, and breathing and heart rate both slow down. The biggest risk of overdosing occurs when the initial dose is too large, or if other nervous system depressants, such as alcohol or sedatives, are being used. The symptoms of overdose include respiratory depression, extreme somnolence progressing to stupor or coma, cold and clammy skin, and sometimes bradycardia (very slow heart rate) and hypotension (low blood pressure).

Over the longer term and with chronic use, tolerance and dependence can develop. Withdrawal symptoms are very similar to those experienced with other opioids—sweating, yawning, runny nose, stomach cramps, insomnia, gooseflesh, and restlessness—but withdrawal is not life threatening, and the symptoms subside over a period of seven days. There may be mood swings, reduced libido, menstrual irregularity, and acute constipation.

H. SHAPIRO

SEE ALSO:
Meperidine • Morphine • Opiates and Opioids

KEY FACTS

Classification
Schedule II (USA), Schedule I (Canada), Class A (UK)
Schedule I (INCB). Opioid.

Short-term effects
Euphoria, analgesia, palpitations, sweating, dry mouth, nervousness, itching, lethargy, nausea and vomiting, constipation, difficulty urinating

Long-term effects
Tolerance and physical and psychological dependence may develop. Withdrawal effects include restlessness, irritability, stomach cramps, chills, muscle aches and spasms, sleeplessness.

Dangers
Acute risk of overdose if initial dose is too high or too frequent in users with no opioid tolerance. Pills contain talc, which can clog veins if injected.

Librium

Librium is a member of the benzodiazepine family of tranquilizers. Initially popular in the 1960s as an anxiety treatment, Librium's addictive effects became apparent when withdrawal produced the anxiety it was trying to prevent.

Librium is the trade name of chlordiazepoxide. It was the first of an important group of drugs called benzodiazepines. They are also referred to as "minor tranquilizers," a rather misleading term because their effects are certainly not minor. Librium is used to treat anxiety disorders, withdrawal symptoms in alcoholics, and preoperative anxiety, and the drug is usually supplied in capsule form.

Although benzodiazepines have similar pharmacological properties, they differ in their duration of action. Librium is classified as a long-acting benzodiazepine, in part due to the fact that the parent compound has a long biological half-life, and in part because Librium is metabolized in the body through a series of active intermediates, which also have long biological half-lives.

Sedation is an adverse effect of Librium when it is used to treat symptoms of anxiety but is clearly the basis of its use as a hypnotic. Common adverse effects of Librium include slowing of reaction time, impairment of concentration, and reduced performance in carrying out skilled tasks. Because of the long half-life of Librium, these effects may be significant the day following use of Librium as a nighttime hypnotic (termed the "hangover" effect). Subjects taking Librium are routinely advised against driving motor vehicles or operating machinery that may be a hazard to themselves or others. Librium normally makes people feel calm and relaxed. However, in a small proportion of people there is a paradoxical increase in hostility and aggression. Benzodiazepines also have the potential to depress respiration. This is normally insignificant for healthy individuals but can become significant in subjects whose respiration is compromised.

The most important drug interactions of Librium are its additive effects with other drugs that suppress activity of the central nervous system, such as barbiturates or opiates. Small amounts of alcohol in combination with clinical doses of Librium produce sedative effects that are greater than the sum of the individual effects. Taken alone, high doses of benzo-

KEY FACTS

Classification
Schedule IV (USA), Schedule IV (Canada), Class C (UK), Schedule IV (INCB). Sedative and anxiolytic.

Street names
Lib, mother's little helper

Short-term effects
Relaxation, intoxication, mild drowsiness, slurred speech, confusion, lack of coordination

Long-term effects
Physical and psychological dependence, confusion in elderly patients. Withdrawal symptoms include tremor, cramps, vomiting, insomnia, and sweating.

diazepines are rarely fatal. However, in combination with excessive amounts of alcohol, emergency intervention is necessary to prevent fatal respiratory depression. Flumazenil can be given as an antidote to benzodiazepines in cases of overdosage.

Tolerance and dependence have long been recognized as a problem when benzodiazepines are taken in large doses for long periods of time. Withdrawal results in a distinct syndrome, the symptoms of which include anxiety. This syndrome helps maintain dependence because users feel they cannot cope without the drug. Symptoms may take up to two weeks to develop and may persist for up to six months. However, Librium, with its long half-life and relatively low potency, has a lower dependence potential than many other benzodiazepines.

R. W. HORTON

SEE ALSO:
Benzodiazepines • Valium

LSD

LSD is famous for its association with the 1960s counterculture. When LSD's use for therapeutic treatment was banned in 1966, its influence diminished, only to see a revival in the 1990s by a new generation of drug users.

LSD (lysergic acid diethylamide) is an artificial hallucinogenic drug originally manufactured from ergot, a parasitic fungus that grows naturally on rye and other grasses. LSD comes in various forms. Most common are stamps or blotters, made by impregnating a sheet of paper with a solution of LSD in alcohol. Each paper usually has its own brand design covering the whole sheet or just one dose, usually ¼ by ¼ inch (7 mm by 7 mm). The designs change with time and have included lightning flashes, rainbows, smilies, strawberries, and buddhas. Apart from brand names based on designs, general street names for LSD are acid, tabs, and trips. LSD can also be bought as microdots or in its liquid form. Microdots are small grains of LSD about 2 millimeters long. The liquid form is usually sold in a small pipette bottle containing tens or even hundreds of doses.

Background

LSD was discovered in 1938 by Albert Hofmann, a chemist at Sandoz Pharmaceuticals in Switzerland. The drug was first made in the course of an attempt to prepare new therapeutic drugs from ergot. The work had been the main concern of Sandoz's Natural Products Division since the discovery of ergotamine in 1918. LSD was the 25th compound (hence its factory name LSD-25) in a series prepared from lysergic acid, the original aim being to make a new stimulant drug. Disappointing tests on animals resulted in further work on the compound being halted until 1943, when, on a hunch, Hofmann decided to prepare a fresh quantity. During these later tests, Hofmann unwittingly ingested a tiny amount and triggered the first ever LSD "trip."

Suspecting LSD was the cause of his strange experience, Hofmann began a series of experiments on himself and colleagues. Confirmation was swift. With only a minute dose of LSD needed to produce an effect, Hofmann had stumbled upon one of the most potent mind-altering hallucinogenic drugs ever developed.

LSD was made available by Sandoz, and later by SPOFA of Czechoslovakia, to supply a growing research and medical market throughout the 1950s and early 1960s. Beginning as early as 1950, LSD was used extensively in the treatment of alcohol and drug addiction, for those with disturbed personalities and severe mental health problems, and with terminally ill patients to alleviate pain and help them cope with facing death. LSD was valued for its ability to deliver what one writer called "a big bang" to the memory of a repressed neurotic, releasing a stream of buried recollections and suppressed responses.

Medical opinion remained divided on the efficacy and safety of LSD psychotherapy. A British expert report published in 1970 concluded that LSD had a real, if limited, therapeutic value and recommended licensing of "approved and responsible practitioners" for a continuation of LSD's clinical and experimental

KEY FACTS

Classification
Schedule I (US), Schedule III (Canada), Class A (UK), Schedule I (INCB). Hallucinogen.

Street names
Acid, California sunshine, Lucy, tabs, trips

Short-term effects
Strong visual hallucinations and auditory distortion, perception of time slows, anxiety and fear in naive users may lead to panic attacks

Long-term effects
Possible psychological disturbance in those with existing or latent mental illness, flashbacks, occasionally use leads to psychological dependence. Does not produce withdrawal effects.

use. However, by then the drug had leaked out into the general student population in the United States and the United Kingdom and was banned in both countries in 1966. Sandoz withdrew from the clinical market, which in turn helped to shut down further research into LSD's therapeutic applications.

LSD also attracted the U.S. military and intelligence services as a potential brainwashing or truth drug and a substance that could disable an army without destroying weaponry, buildings, and general infrastructure. Military personnel were given the drug without being told, and a few committed suicide in the belief that they had gone mad. These tests were eventually abandoned in the 1960s. In the process, some of the United States' most prestigious universities and hospitals had played host as test centers using volunteer students and graduate assistants. One such hospital was attached to Harvard University. Students and academics began feeding back their experiences. These tests attracted the attention of two Harvard psychologists, Timothy Leary and Richard Alpert.

Leary and Alpert conducted their own experiments on the nature and value of the "psychedelic" experience (a term first coined in 1957 by Humphrey Osmond, a pioneer LSD researcher). They thought LSD was a chemical that could open up the mind to new experiences of self-awareness and enlightenment. As such, Leary and Alpert believed that LSD could benefit the whole human race. By making his opinions public, however, Leary donned the mantle of public crusader under the banner "turn on, tune in, and drop out." The university authorities became alarmed and subsequently fired both Leary and Alpert. Leary was later to renounce his earlier stance as naive and became a devotee of cyberspace as the great liberalizing force for humanity.

Leary's legacy was to catapult LSD into the public domain. Through the endeavors of underground chemists, LSD circulated freely among students, intellectuals, artists, and musicians, and the idea of LSD as a means to self-improvement caught on.

Inevitably, use of LSD spread to a wider and predominantly younger age group who were not so interested in "finding themselves" but simply liked using the drug. Consequently the drug came under wide public scrutiny. Concerns were expressed about LSD's health impact. Fears ranged from brain damage, deformed babies, psychosis, homicide and suicide, to a mistaken belief in one's ability to fly.

The designs for LSD blotters have became an underground art form. Favorite subjects include cartoon characters, Warhol paintings, and religious symbols. This blotter celebrates an anniversary of Hofmann's discovery of the effects of LSD, which he experienced while riding his bicycle home.

Some of these dangers were real, others were without foundation. However, publicity over these concerns elevated LSD to the status of a media horror drug, much as cannabis had been in the 1930s, heroin in the 1950s, phencyclidine (angel dust or PCP) in the 1970s, and crack in the 1980s and 1990s. It is hard to disassociate the cultural phenomenon known as "the sixties" without the effect of LSD on the musicians, filmmakers, artists, fashion designers, photographers, and writers who reinterpreted their LSD experiences into the explosions of sound and color that defined the period.

During the 1970s, interest in LSD diminished considerably as the supporting ideology faded away. However, with the advent of the "New Age" movement, there was a revival of interest in LSD, magic mushrooms, and other hallucinogenic drugs. Use of LSD resurfaced in the later 1980s as part of the general rise in recreational drug use, often alongside the use of marijuana and club drugs such as Ecstasy. However, forensic scientists who test seized substances to ascertain if they are controlled drugs report that they rarely see LSD.

In the United States, government figures on the numbers of new users every year were relatively stable through the 1980s and early 1990s. In association with the rave culture of the late 1990s, new users rose to a peak unseen since the late 1960s. Since then numbers have declined, in part due to the demise of the rave, or acid, culture and the dropping in price and increase in availability of other drugs such as Ecstasy, amphetamine, and cocaine.

Use of LSD

LSD is effective in doses as small as 25 micrograms (25 millionths of a gram), although the average dose for a full-blown psychedelic experience is 100 to 150 micrograms. A trip begins about 30 minutes to 1 hour after taking LSD, peaks after 2 to 4 hours, and fades out within 8 to 12 hours, depending on the dose. Exactly what happens when a drug is taken is often determined by what the user expects to happen and the situation in which the drug is used (for example, alone or with a group of trusted friends). This is especially true of LSD. Once a trip is underway, there is no way to stop it, even if the experience turns out to be unpleasant.

Chemistry and pharmacological effects

The full chemical name for LSD is 9,10-didehydro-N,N-diethyl-1-6-methylergoline-8-carboxamide and its chemical formula is $C_{20}H_{25}N_3O$. LSD is structurally similar to the neurotransmitter serotonin, and its effects are thought to arise from its interaction with serotonin receptor sites, particularly those in the raphe nuclei region of the brain stem. There is much debate about how LSD acts at serotonin receptors, variously being described as an agonist, antagonist, and partial agonist according to the concentration of the drug, the response from the different subtypes of receptor, and whether it is binding to presynaptic or postsynaptic neurons. LSD is also thought to interact with receptors for acetylcholine, dopamine, histamine, and norepinephrine. The main site for norepinephrine cells is also situated in the brain stem and, like the serotonin projections, its neuron pathways extend throughout the brain. Norepinephrine is involved in the regulation of attention, arousal, and the sleep-wake cycle, while one of serotonin's functions is thought to be protection of the brain from sensory overload. LSD's effects probably arise from its inhibition of this sensory protection mechanism and its enhancement of the norephinephrine system to sensory stimulation.

Users of LSD often report visual effects such as intensified colors, distorted shapes and sizes, and the movement of stationary objects. Distortions of hearing occur, as do changes in sense of time and place. Generally the user knows these effects are unreal. True hallucinations (that is, those the user believes to be real) are relatively rare. Physical effects are so slight (for example, dilation of pupils, slight rise in body temperature, goose bumps) compared with psychological or emotional effects that they are of little importance.

There is no physical dependence with LSD, but tolerance to the drug builds up rapidly. After 24 hours, a much larger dose is necessary to achieve the same initial effect. After 3 to 4 days of increasing the dosage, a limit (approximately 200 micrograms) is reached whereby the drug will not produce any of its subjective effects. A break of around three days would be required for LSD sensitivity to return. Only a small minority of those who have ever used LSD become psychologically dependent.

Health effects

Emotional reactions to LSD vary but may include heightened self-awareness and mystical or ecstatic experiences. Feelings of dissociation from the body are commonly reported. Unpleasant reactions are more likely if the user is unstable, anxious, or depressed and may include anxiety, depression, dizziness, disorientation, and sometimes a short-lived psychotic episode including hallucinations and paranoia, commonly known as a "bad trip."

The same person may have good and bad trips on different occasions, and good and bad periods within the same trip. While the LSD experience is variable compared with many other drugs, it is also relatively more open to the user's intentions and to the suggestions of others. Hence friendly reassurance is an effective antidote to a bad trip. Experienced users steer the trip toward the area they wish to experience or explore.

It is difficult to combine a trip with a task requiring concentration, and driving will almost certainly be impaired. Suicides or deaths due to LSD-induced beliefs or perceptions, although much publicized, are rare. Fatal overdoses were unreported in the literature until as recently as 1985, when twice the amount ever found at postmortem was detected in a subject's body with no other drug present.

A bad trip can be very frightening and may induce fear, anxiety, and paranoia. This phenomenon is more likely with high doses and when the user already feels anxious. People who experience a bad trip can usually be calmed by the reassurance of others.

There are no known physical dangers attributable to long-term LSD use. In particular, there is no reliable evidence that LSD causes brain damage or reproductive damage. Adverse psychological effects are possible after one trip but are more common in regular users. For some users, the experience of hallucinating can be acutely distressing and include feelings of paranoia, phobia, and delusion. These effects take time to subside.

Case studies of prolonged, serious adverse psychological reactions are reported in the literature but appear to be rare. Reactions to LSD use can be psychotic, but this usually only occurs among users who already have existing or latent mental illness. Psychosis is more common after repeated LSD use, when LSD has perhaps acted as the final straw

At the Acid Test Graduations, held in warehouses in San Francisco in the 1960s, users of LSD met to talk and dance while under the influence.

leading to a breakdown. Among drug users, such individuals are marked out as "acid casualties"—those who have taken so much LSD over a period of time and spent so much time tripping that they never quite come back to normal cognitive function.

A number of LSD users report flashbacks—short-lived, vivid reliving of a past trip without use of the drug. Among LSD's media scare tactics were claims that LSD users could have flashbacks lasting days or even weeks. In truth an LSD flashback (which can occur months or years later, even after using the drug only once) normally lasts only a few minutes and is rarely dangerous, although it can leave the person feeling anxious, disorientated, or distressed, especially if he or she is unaware that flashbacks can happen. Flashbacks are most likely to happen in situations reminiscent of past LSD experiences, or sometimes when a past user is smoking cannabis or using other drugs.

H. SHAPIRO

SEE ALSO:
Hallucinogens • Serotonin

MAOs and MAOIs

Monoamine oxidases (MAOs) are enzymes that control the effect of hormones and neurotransmitters in the body and chemicals taken into the body through food and drugs. Monoamine oxidase inhibitors (MAOIs) block the action of the MAOs.

A monoamine oxidase is an enzyme that catalyzes the oxidation of monoamine molecules, which include neurotransmitters and hormones. This process is often part of a series of reactions that culminate in substances the body can eliminate with ease in waste.

Many monoamines have affinities for receptor sites where they trigger or inhibit cell responses, and oxidation often converts such monoamines into substances that have no affinity for receptor sites. Hence, an MAO can convert a pharmacologically active substance into an inert substance, or it can turn a toxic substance into a benign substance. Monoamines that occur naturally in the body include the neurotransmitters dopamine and serotonin. Monoamines that are taken into the body include psychoactive drugs such as phenethylamines and food constituents such as tyramine.

MAO subtypes
MAO-catalyzed oxidation requires a monoamine to form a temporary attachment to an active site in the MAO molecule. The ease with which this happens depends on the fit between the monoamine and the structure of the enzyme around the active site. Hence, the effectiveness of MAO catalysis depends on the shape of the monoamine molecule.

MAOs in the human body fall into two subtypes—A and B—according to how well they catalyze oxidation for different monoamines. MAO_A is more effective for norepinephrine and serotonin, while MAO_B is the better catalyst for oxidation of phenethylamine and dopamine. Even so, if serotonin occurs where MAO_B abounds and MAO_A is absent, MAO_B replaces MAO_A in catalyzing the oxidation of serotonin. Such substitutions occur because the two types of MAO are selective but not fully specific for different monoamines.

MAO functions
One of the functions of MAOs is in destroying neurotransmitter molecules after their release from neurons. If these substances were to accumulate, they

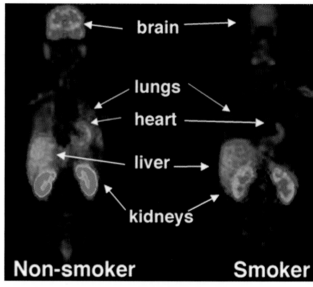

Researchers at the Brookhaven National Laboratory, Upton, New York, used compounds labeled with radioactive carbon-11 to bind to MAO_B molecules in smokers and nonsmokers. PET (positron emission tomography) scans revealed reduced levels of MAO_B throughout smokers' bodies. The highest concentrations of labeled MAO_B are red in the above scan, the lowest are purple.

would saturate their receptors, and neurotransmission would cease. In effect, the receptors would be jammed in the "on" position, whereas they need to alternate between "on" and "off" to carry signals.

The combination of selectivity and distribution of the two types of MAO in the central nervous system determines that MAO_A mops up dopamine, norepinephrine, and serotonin, while MAO_B deals only with dopamine. Norepinephrine and dopamine also degrade through the action of another enzyme, COMT (catecholamine O-methyl transferase).

Another important function of MAOs is to destroy monoamines in food that would otherwise prompt a release of norepinephrine around the body, leading to a hypertensive crisis: a catastrophic increase in blood pressure. Tyramine presents the greatest liability in this respect, since it is present in mature cheeses, many dried and pickled foods, as well as in many types of beers and wines. Under normal circumstances, MAO_A in the gut destroys tyramine before it can cause a hypertensive crisis.

MAO inhibition for therapeutic uses

Certain health conditions can be improved by the administration of drugs that reduce or completely halt the action of MAOs. These drugs are the monoamine oxidase inhibitors, or MAOIs.

MAOIs work by stealth to disable MAOs. In the absence of MAOIs, monoamines bond to the MAO, undergo oxidation, and the oxidation products then drift away to leave the MAO molecule free to accept another monoamine for oxidation. When a MAOI is present, it approaches the active site of the MAO but then forms a bond that prevents the active site from interacting with other monoamines.

The first manufactured MAOIs were used to treat depression. By knocking out MAO activity in the brain, they caused levels of norepinephrine, dopamine, and serotonin to rise and thereby improved mood. However, the same drugs also prevented gut MAO_A from destroying tyramine, so patients had to follow a strict diet that excluded sources of tyramine. Accidental tyramine ingestion could cause severe headaches and even brain hemorrhages. Patients who ceased taking these drugs had to wait weeks before returning to a normal diet while the body replaced its MAO molecules.

More recent developments have led to reversible MAOIs that reduce the risk of tyramine reactions by hindering but not completely deactivating MAOs. Also, selective MAO_B inhibitors such as selegiline treat parkinsonism by boosting dopamine in the brain while leaving gut MAO_A alone.

Drug interactions

MAOIs can cause negative drug interactions by deactivating liver enzymes that would normally destroy other drugs. This slows the elimination of the other drug from the body, and the prescribing doctor has to reduce its dosage to compensate.

More serious problems occur when a patient whose MAOs have been disabled by MAOI therapy takes a drug that boosts neurotransmitter levels by other means. An example would be a selective serotonin reuptake inhibitor (SSRI), such as Prozac. The combined effects of the drugs can result in serotonin syndrome, the symptoms of which include fever, confusion, agitation or drowsiness, heatstroke, kidney and liver failure, and coma. Serotonin syndrome is fatal in 10 to 20 percent of cases.

An even greater risk occurs with recreational drugs whose users may be unaware of their interaction with MAOI medication. Amphetamines, Ecstasy, and cocaine all produce their effects by boosting the levels of neurotransmitters around neurons, and this increase can combine with MAO inhibition to result in serotonin syndrome. Also, MAOs help eliminate these drugs from the body, so MAO inhibition can result in dangerously intense and prolonged highs.

Natural MAOIs

A number of plant species contain substances that are active MAO inhibitors. These substances include harmaline and harmine, and they are based on a compound called beta-carboline. Plants that yield these substances include the ayahuasca vine *(Banisteriopsis caapi)* and Syrian rue seeds *(Peganum harmala)*.

Some people who consume preparations from these plants report psychedelic experiences, but it is doubtful that the natural MAOIs alone could cause these effects. A better indication of the function of these compounds comes from observing the traditional preparation of ayahuasca by shamanic sects in the Amazon basin. Their method is to boil the ayahuasca vine together with chacruna *(Psychotria viridis)* leaves. The shaman filters the liquor from this process and boils it down to form a concentrate for drinking in rituals.

Chacruna leaves contain the psychedelic *N,N*-dimethyltryptamine (DMT), and this is the likely source of psychoactivity. The MAOIs in ayahuasca enable DMT to take effect by deactivating gut MAO that would otherwise destroy DMT before it entered the bloodstream. A similar effect occurs when extracts of Syrian rue seeds are taken with mushrooms that contain psilocybin.

M. CLOWES

Marijuana

Marijuana is the most widely used illicit drug in the world. Many believe that it is not addictive, but repeated use can lead to tolerance and a range of physical and behavioral problems, including decreased learning abilities.

Marijuana (occasionally spelled marihuana) refers to the material produced by drying the plant *Cannabis sativa*. Cannabis grows in a variety of climates and has been cultivated for both commercial and pharmacological purposes. The fibers in the stem of cannabis plants have been used to produce a rope-like material, known as hemp, which is used in a variety of products, including clothing and paper. The seeds also have commercial value, serving both as a source of oil that is used in different products, including paint and varnish, as well as birdseed. In addition to these commercial uses, the plant generates chemical compounds called cannabinoids that engender a variety of physiological and behavioral effects. Some of these compounds, principally delta-9-tetrahydrocannabinol (THC), are responsible for the nonmedical use of marijuana.

Marijuana is the most commonly used illicit drug in the United States. In 2009, based on results from the National Survey on Drug Abuse and Health, 2.4 million Americans aged 12 or older used marijuana for the first time within the previous year, and 16.7 million reported using marijuana in their lifetime, and slightly less than 5 percent (fewer than 10 million) reported using it during the past month. It is estimated that slightly less than half of all high school seniors have used marijuana in their lifetime, and that approximately one in five use marijuana at least once a month. The reasons for the initiation of and continued nonmedical use ·of marijuana are complex, as are the medical and social consequences of marijuana use. An understanding of the interrelationship between marijuana and human behavior requires an analysis of many issues, including the history of marijuana, its physiological, neurochemical, and behavioral effects, as well as the social and medical consequences of its use.

The cannabis plant

Many different varieties of *Cannabis sativa* have been described. These varieties differ with respect to growing height, amount of cannabinoid production,

THC occurs in all parts of the cannabis plant. The highest concentrations are contained in young leaves and the sticky resin exuded by the flowers.

and region of growth, although most varieties are sufficiently hardy to grow in any region. Different varieties have slightly different appearances that are related to varying concentrations of pigments in addition to green chlorophyll, such as xanthophylls, carotenoids, and anthocyanins. The flowering tops of female plants from different varieties also display varying colors, including white, yellow, green, red, or purple. During sun drying, a typical step in the preparation of marijuana for commercial production, the green color of the plant is lost as the chlorophyll pigments contained in the living plant tissue are broken down. The relative concentrations of other pigments influence the final appearance of the dried leaves and stems. This color is sometimes used

KEY FACTS

Classification
Schedule I (USA and INCB), Schedule II (Canada), Class C (UK). Marijuana is not easily designated within any single drug classification (for example, sedative, hypnotic, stimulant, analgesic, hallucinogen).

Street names
Bhang, charas, ganja, grass, hemp, herb, kif, Mary Jane, pot, reefer, skunk, weed, and many others

Short-term effects
The magnitude and extent of short-term effects depends on the potency, or amount of THC. Effects are variable and can include an altered state of consciousness, mild euphoria, pleasant sensations, relaxation, loss of coordination, altered judgments, reduced learning and memory efficiency, increased appetite, impaired driving ability, and increased heart rate. Higher doses can cause anxiety and panic.

Long-term effects
Repeated use results in tolerance to the short-term effects of THC, as well as both physical and psychological dependence. Studies suggest that regular users perform less well on tests of cognitive ability. Repeated exposure to marijuana smoke increases risk for respiratory and immune system disorders and lung cancer.

Signs of abuse
Red, bloodshot eyes, sweet fruity smell of smoke on clothes or hair, giggliness, lack of coordination, poor concentration

derived, the relative concentration of flowering tops and young leaves contained in the product, growing conditions at the time of harvest, which is related to the degree of resin production, and storage length and conditions. THC concentrations in samples of marijuana confiscated through law-enforcement efforts suggest that potency has escalated during the past 20 years.

Many different chemical compounds (around 400) have been found in cannabis plants. Individuals who swallow marijuana are exposed to all of these chemicals. Many of the chemicals are released in smoke when marijuana is burned, and several new compounds are also produced as marijuana is heated. The amounts of various chemical compounds in smoke derived from marijuana depend on a number of factors, including the source of the marijuana, the relative contribution of various portions of the plant contained in the marijuana, the age of the marijuana, and the processes used to prepare the drug. The chemical content of samples of marijuana obtained from street sources varies markedly, and this variability has often contributed to confusion regarding marijuana and the effects it produces.

As mentioned earlier, compounds that are primarily associated with the behavioral and physiological effects engendered by marijuana are called cannabinoids. The concentrations of cannabinoids determine the strength (potency) with which marijuana produces its effects. THC is the cannabinoid that produces the most potent behavioral effects, although others, such as cannabinol, cannabidiol, and delta-8-tetrahydrocannabinol, also produce behavioral and physiological effects. More than 60 different cannabinoids have been identified. Many other chemical compounds, such as proteins, sugars, alcohols, simple and fatty acids, hydrocarbons, terpenes, and phenols are also present in the cannabis plant. Many of these substances are also in the smoke produced by burning marijuana, as well as additional toxic substances, including carbon monoxide. Several known carcinogens are also present in marijuana smoke.

History of use
Nonmedical use of marijuana throughout the history of North America and western Europe has been well documented. However, until early in the twentieth century, most of the marijuana used for recreational

in street names to identify different varieties of marijuana (for example, Acapulco Gold or Panama Red).

The concentration of cannabinoids, primarily THC, determines the potency of the behavioral and physiological effects produced by marijuana. Potency can be affected by several factors, including the variety of plant from which the marijuana was

HASHISH

The concentration of delta-9-tetrahydrocannabinol (THC), which is the primary psychoactive compound in marijuana, varies among different parts of the cannabis plant. Leaves contain higher concentrations than stems, and the flowering tops of the female plant contain even higher concentrations. Marijuana consisting largely of the flowering tops of the unpollinated female cannabis plant is called sinsemilla (from the Latin for "without seeds"). The female cannabis plant also produces a sticky resin material that serves several important functions for the plant, including moisture retention, protection, and to help with fertilization. This resin also contains the highest concentration of THC produced by the cannabis plant. Hashish refers to this resinous material, or to marijuana that contains a high concentration of this resin. THC can also be extracted from hashish and other cannabis materials through distillation or chemical extraction. The resulting tarlike liquid is called hash oil.

- Marijuana: 5 percent THC
- Sinsemilla: 9–25 percent THC
- Hashish: 9–19 percent THC
- Hash oil: 19–27 percent THC

purposes was introduced by travelers and soldiers returning from southwestern Asia and Africa. Reports of enjoyable effects resulting from the consumption of cannabis products (for example, hashish) were not infrequent, but these descriptions often included accounts of the cultures from which the drugs were imported, as well as exotic tales of effects that the drugs engendered. There does not appear to have been a clear association between the marijuana imported from southwestern Asia and Africa for recreational use and that grown locally for commercial hemp production. Unlike widespread use patterns observed in southwestern Asia and Africa, recreational consumption of marijuana products appears to have been limited to small social groups, such as artists and writers. In fact, even during the early 1900s in North America, when opium, morphine, and alcohol use was quite prevalent in the general population, marijuana use was relatively infrequent.

Controls on marijuana

In the nineteenth century, reports of medical benefits associated with marijuana began to emerge in North America and western Europe from research conducted in southwestern Asia. Although readily available without prescription, marijuana products never gained popularity with the medical community. THC was not water soluble, so dose administration and regulation was a problem. The drug was only available in oral preparations of unknown and inconsistent quality, and the onset of action following oral administration was slow (1 to 2 hours). In comparison, following the invention of the hypodermic needle, other drugs, such as morphine, could be administered in controlled amounts that produced instantaneous effects. Reports of variable clinical response following marijuana administration, even in the same patient on different occasions, were prevalent. Marijuana also produced unpredictable and undesirable side effects, including intoxication, hallucinations, and delusions. Finally, the passage of the Marihuana Tax Act in 1937 increased the cost and inconvenience of the medical use of marijuana (*see* box page 198).

Nonmedical use of marijuana was rare in the United States until early in the twentieth century and developed approximately simultaneously in two separate groups, rural Southwestern migrant workers and urban jazz musical communities. Southwestern migrant workers, consisting largely of immigrants from Mexico and South America, brought pre-existing patterns of marijuana use into the United States. Marijuana use also escalated with the emergence of the jazz musical communities located primarily in large metropolitan cities, such as New York and New Orleans. Social concerns in these communities were also highly publicized, resulting in

Marijuana for medical use is being tested in several countries. Genetically modified strains have been developed to reduce some harmful effects and provide consistent levels of tetrahydrocannabinol.

an association between marijuana use and social problems. Overly dramatized reports of sexual promiscuity and violence following marijuana use, sales of marijuana to children, and marijuana-induced escalation use to opiates and other drugs were emerging. In response to growing public concern, several states, including New York, California, Texas, and Mississippi, passed laws banning the possession or use of marijuana for nonmedical purposes. Federal drug control agencies began to focus on marijuana, and in 1937 the Treasury department in collaboration with the Bureau of Narcotics passed the Marihuana Tax Act. The act sought to control marijuana use through taxation ($1 per ounce for approved medical use, and $100 per ounce for nonapproved uses). Penalties for use included substantial fines and prison terms for tax evasion. In 1951 Congress imposed mandatory prison sentences for violations of the marijuana legislation, and in 1956 the length of the prison term for violations involving the sale of marijuana to minors was substantially increased. In 1969 the United States Supreme Court declared the Marihuana Tax Act unconstitutional due, in part, to the requirement that suspects incriminate themselves by paying taxes on their marijuana use, a violation of the Fifth Amendment. Today, marijuana possession is regulated by the Comprehensive Drug Abuse Prevention and Control Act of 1970. This act enabled the comprehensive federal enforcement and prosecution of illegal drug possession.

Effects of THC on the body

The physiological and behavioral effects of marijuana are dependent primarily on the concentration of THC that is absorbed into the bloodstream. Other cannabinoids that are present in marijuana also produce effects, but in general THC is the most potent of these compounds. Cannabinoids can be absorbed in one of two ways. First, they are efficiently absorbed into the bloodstream through the capillaries of the lungs when marijuana smoke is inhaled, with blood levels increasing almost instantaneously and producing immediate effects. The second method is through oral consumption of marijuana, in which absorption occurs more slowly and the onset of effects does not begin to appear until 30 minutes later, peaking after several hours. Once absorbed, THC readily binds to lipid membranes (fatty tissues) that are prevalent throughout the body. This results in the rapid removal of substantial amounts of THC from the bloodstream. When individuals use marijuana regularly, increasing amounts of THC accumulate in the body until the fatty tissues become saturated with the drug. THC is also removed from the system through liver metabolism. The potency with which THC produces acute effects once it reaches the bloodstream is regulated by both lipid binding and by its rate of metabolism.

Because of lipid binding, it takes a long time to eliminate THC from the system. For example, it takes approximately three days to eliminate half of the total amount of THC present in individuals who have had no prior exposure. Individuals who are daily users can continue to have small amounts of THC in their bloodstreams for many weeks after discontinued use, resulting from a slow and continuous release of the accumulated lipid-bound drug. Sophisticated biochemical techniques have been developed to detect the presence and amount of THC and its metabolites in biological samples, such as blood, hair, and urine. These techniques vary in accuracy, expense, and reliability. Urine testing occurs in many settings, including schools, the workplace, drug-treatment programs, research laboratories, and correctional facilities. Testing procedures have also been used to determine the involvement of drug use in public-safety incidents, such as highway, railroad, or airplane accidents. However, care must be taken when interpreting test results. A number of variables can influence drug and metabolite concentrations in urine, which is the most common source for drug testing. Passive exposure to marijuana smoke, for example, will produce detectable levels of THC metabolites in the urine of nonusers. The gradual release of THC bound to lipid membranes can result in extended intervals in which metabolites can be detected in urine samples, even under conditions of complete abstinence. All of these factors must be considered when interpreting the results of urine tests. Urinalysis is useful for detecting the presence of THC metabolites; however, THC concentrations in urine are not reliable indicators of either the time or the amount of marijuana use or of the behavioral consequences of that use.

Physiological effects

Among the physiological effects of marijuana, perhaps the most pronounced effect is the increase in heart rate. Increases of between 30 and 50 beats per minute are common after marijuana smoking, and increases of up to 160 beats per minute have been reported. Marijuana also produces a characteristic reddening of the eyes, resulting from dilation of the blood vessels in the whites of the eyes, although no discomfort or visual distortion is associated with this effect. Marijuana also reduces pressure within the eye, and has been suggested as a possible medication for managing the symptoms of glaucoma. Vasodilation (expansion of the blood vessels) also occurs throughout the body following marijuana smoking. Peripheral dilation of the blood vessels produces a warming sensation but paradoxically also decreases core body temperature. Dilation of the bronchioles of the lungs also occurs following THC administration. Smoking marijuana, however, exacerbates the problems of asthma and other breathing disorders, since repeated exposure to marijuana smoke will result in a deterioration of lung capacity and increased airway resistance. THC alters endocrine function in a complex manner. Research with animal models indicates that both acute and chronic THC administration can alter hormones that regulate reproduction, metabolism, and stress. THC has also been shown to impair the normal function of the

PERCENTAGE OF STUDENTS WHO HAVE USED MARIJUANA IN THE PAST YEAR						
	2005	2006	2007	2008	2009	2010
8th grade						
Lifetime	16.5	15.7	14.2	14.6	15.7	17.3
Annual	12.2	11.7	10.3	10.9	11.8	13.7
Daily	1.0	1.0	0.8	0.9	1.0	1.2
10th grade						
Lifetime	34.1	31.8	31.0	29.9	32.3	33.4
Annual	26.6	25.2	24.6	23.9	26.7	27.5
Daily	3.1	2.8	2.8	2.7	2.8	3.3
12th grade						
Lifetime	44.8	42.3	41.8	42.6	42.0	43.8
Annual	33.6	31.5	31.7	32.4	32.8	34.8
Daily	5.0	5.0	5.1	5.4	5.2	6.1

Source: *Monitoring the Future Study*, University of Michigan, 2010.

immune system. This fact is particularly troublesome, given that use of the compound is also associated with high-risk behavior, such as risky sexual behavior. The use of THC by individuals engaged in high-risk behaviors could increase the risk for contracting AIDS and other life-threatening diseases.

Rapid scientific advances in understanding marijuana's effects have occurred since the 1970s. Cannabinoid receptors have been identified, and their roles and functions are being clarified. High densities of these receptors occur in the brain's cerebellum, cerebral cortex, and hippocampus. Analyses of receptor systems associated with drugs of abuse have proven to be very successful for enhancing understanding of the neurobiology of behavior and have proven useful for the development of new medical advances. Soon after the discovery of the receptor, a naturally occurring compound in the body that interacts with these receptors, anandamide, was identified. The role of this compound is the focus of ongoing research. Studies have also begun to demonstrate the neurochemical pathways through which cannabinoids exert their effects. THC

interacts with the nervous system pathways that are associated with the effects of other drugs of abuse, such as cocaine, amphetamine, alcohol, and heroin. As understanding of the roles of different receptors and neurotransmitter systems in the control and regulation of behavior continues to emerge, the interactions of the neurochemical, physiological, and behavioral effects of THC become more apparent. Understanding the mechanisms by which THC produces these effects can stimulate the development of medications having beneficial THC-like effects without the adverse long-term risks and side effects. For example, medications blocking the effects of THC and the natural substances in the body that work at these receptor sites have been developed and are being evaluated in clinical trials for the treatment of marijuana abuse and for other therapeutic applications.

Behavioral effects

The behavioral effects of marijuana have been a focus of research since the start of the twentieth century. The abuse liability of marijuana (that is, the likelihood of the nonmedical use of the substance in the

Marijuana is an easy plant to grow in indoors, which makes it ideal for illicit producers to conceal their operations. However, sophisticated lighting, watering, and heating systems are necessary for large-scale commercial production of the drug. Unusually high utility bills are often the only clue to an illegal operation.

MEDICAL MARIJUANA

The diversity of effects produced by marijuana has driven efforts to isolate the chemical agents associated with these effects. These compounds have potential for therapeutic applications. In fact, the Food and Drug Administration (FDA) has approved a pill form of delta-9-tetrahydro-cannabinol (THC), as well as nabilone, which is chemically similar to THC, for use in treating nausea and loss of appetite. However, side effects similar to those associated with the use of marijuana limit the widespread use of these drugs. Other medical conditions that have been identified as potential targets for medical marijuana include glaucoma, pain management, respiratory disorders, neurological disorders, including migraines, multiple sclerosis, spastic disorders and epilepsy, and in the management of psychiatric disorders. To date, the FDA has not approved marijuana for use in the treatment of any medical condition, as available scientific evidence suggests that the risks to endocrine and immunological systems outweigh the potential medical benefits, and that the beneficial effects of marijuana are not superior to approved medications in respect of their side effects and long-term risks.

Arguments supporting the development and further testing of marijuana as a medicine began to appear in a number of prominent locations, including the New England Journal of Medicine and the Wall Street Journal, in the late twentieth century. Beginning in 1997, states began to enact laws permitting individuals to use marijuana under a physician's care, and commercial industries supporting medical marijuana emerged. By 2010, 16 states had passed medical marijuana laws despite the sale of marijuana remaining illegal under federal law. Adverse social consequences associated with the expanded availability of medical marijuana have emerged, and some states are considering the repeal of medical marijuana legislation.

general population, as well as the degree of behavioral impairment or adverse medical consequences associated with its use) has been well documented. Marijuana is used more frequently in the general population than any other illicit drug. The adverse behavioral and medical consequences of marijuana, while not completely understood, have been demonstrated repeatedly. Repeated use of the drug promotes tolerance to the behavioral effects of THC, as well as physical and psychological dependence. It has also been shown to lessen powers of concentration and learning.

Factors associated with the onset and maintenance of regular marijuana use and dependence have also been examined extensively. Studies of marijuana users indicate that THC is the primary component of sustaining use of the drug. As is the case with most drugs of abuse, THC functions as a reinforcer and produces feelings of well-being and euphoria. As described above, THC engenders a variety of physiological effects that, in turn, can influence behavior. Following repeated administration of THC, toler-ance and physical dependence can also develop. When physical dependence develops, the presence of the drug is required to maintain normal functioning. An array of uncomfortable experiences, called a marijuana "withdrawal syndrome," such as feelings of restlessness, loss of appetite, shaky hands, and trouble sleeping, have been documented when regular users initiate abstinence. With repeated use, cues in the environment become associated with THC effects and, in turn, begin to trigger physiological and psychological effects independent of marijuana. These cues can also engender withdrawal-like experiences and sometimes play a prominent role in relapse and reinstatement of marijuana use. Treatment of marijuana abuse and dependence must address a complex array of physiological, behavioral, and social factors maintaining regular marijuana use.

T. H. KELLY

SEE ALSO:
Legalization Movement

Meperidine

Meperidine is a synthetic opium derivative that has similar actions to morphine and is a high-potency painkiller. The drug has a rapid action but its analgesic effects do not last for long, which limits meperidine's uses for pain relief.

Meperidine was first synthesized in 1939 as a drug to treat muscle spasms. It was accidentally discovered to have analgesic (pain-relief) properties. Meperidine was initially considered to have advantages over morphine, including less liability for drug dependence. However, it is now known that meperidine shares the addictive effects of morphine. Like other opiates (morphinelike drugs), meperidine acts in the brain and spinal cord at the mu-opioid receptors to inhibit signals carrying pain impulses and to cause other actions.

The chemical name of meperidine (known in the United Kingdom and Canada as pethidine and also by the trade name Demerol), is ethyl-1-methyl-4-phenylpiperidine-4-carboxylate. Meperidine hydrochloride occurs as a fine, white, crystalline powder that is readily soluble in water and has a bitter taste.

The main clinical uses of meperidine are for moderate to severe pain relief. It is widely used for control of labor pains and postoperative pain. It is also used for preoperative sedation and as a supplement to anesthesia. This drug can be given by injection (intramuscular or intravenous) and can be taken by mouth. Meperidine is preferred over morphine for the rapid control of acute pain as it acts faster; however, it has a less potent and shorter analgesic effect. Its analgesic effect lasts for two to four hours, warranting repeated administration, which makes the drug unsuitable for long-term pain management. The usual adult dose for pain relief is 50 to 150 milligrams by mouth or 25 to 100 milligrams by injection every four hours.

Meperidine shares the undesirable toxic effects of opiates. The frequently observed problems include depressed breathing (potentially fatal in overdose situations), lightheadedness, sedation, nausea, dry mouth, vomiting, and dilation of the pupils of the eyes (mydriasis). Since meperidine crosses the placenta and is distributed into milk, unwanted effects can appear in the unborn or newborn. It also has stimulatory effects on the central nervous system that include euphoria, hallucinations, disorientation, and tremors. Meperidine is transformed in the liver into an active by-product (normeperidine) that has significant hallucinogenic and convulsant effects. Although a known antidote for opiate overdose exists (naloxone), it does not reverse the hallucinogenic effects of meperidine. Traditionally, physicians and nurses addicted to narcotics preferred meperidine due to the ease of its availability, shorter duration of action, and lack of the giveaway sign of constricted pupils (seen with most opiates). The euphoric effects and dependence liability of meperidine are similar to morphine. The withdrawal symptoms appear more rapidly than morphine and are of shorter duration.

A. KAPUR, J. DERRY

KEY FACTS

Classification
Schedule II (USA), Schedule I (Canada, INCB), Class A (UK). Opioid.

Street names
D, dillies, dust, juices, smack

Short-term effects
Analgesia, euphoria, respiratory depression, dilated pupils, nausea, dry mouth

Long-term effects
Tolerance, physical and psychological dependence, seizures, agitation, irritability, tremors, nervousness, twitching, hallucinations

SEE ALSO:
Designer Drugs • Morphine • Narcotic Drugs • Opiates and Opioids • Prescription Drugs

Meprobamate

Meprobamate was developed as a safe replacement for barbiturates. However, meprobamate proved to have the same pharmacological effects and also led to dependence. Although rarely used medically, it is still a drug of abuse.

In the 1950s the barbiturate group of drugs, which includes phenobarbital, amobarbital, and seco-barbital, were still considered the most useful and versatile drugs for the treatment of anxiety and insomnia. However, the problems of tolerance and dependence and toxicity in overdose were already recognized. It was against this backdrop that in 1955 the Czech pharmacologist Frank Berger introduced meprobamate (marketed under the trade names Miltown and Equanil) as a non-barbiturate agent for the treatment of anxiety and insomnia. Within two years the drug became widely prescribed, partly because of an effective advertising campaign and partly due to the desire by many doctors for a nonbarbiturate agent. Its pharmacological actions proved to be very similar to the barbiturates. Its prominent sedative and hypnotic properties made it popular as a treatment for insomnia, but made it difficult to achieve a selective treatment for anxiety without significant sedation. Meprobamate also has pronounced muscle-relaxant properties, resulting in its use in a number of skeletal-muscular disorders in which muscle spasm is thought to be involved. Meprobamate also has anticonvulsant properties. Unlike barbiturates, it is effective against primary generalized epilepsy with absences (petit mal) but may make tonic-clonic seizures (grand mal) worse.

Meprobamate is well absorbed following oral administration. It has a moderately short half-life and is largely excreted as hydroxymeprobamate glucuronide. Long-term use of meprobamate is commonly associated with a number of dermato-logical and allergic reactions and is more rarely associated with a variety of blood disorders.

Unfortunately, mepromabate's similarity to barbiturates extends to tolerance and dependence. Animal experiments have demonstrated cross tolerance and cross dependence between barbiturates and meprobamate. Meprobamate withdrawal in dependent subjects produces tremors, hallucinations, and epileptic seizures. This withdrawal syndrome is difficult to distinguish from barbiturate withdrawal.

KEY FACTS

Classification
Schedule IV (USA), Schedule III (Canada), Class B (UK), Schedule IV (INCB). Sedative.

Street names
Happy pills, soma (carisoprodol)

Short-term effects
Sedation, unsteadiness, drowsiness, dry mouth, blurred vision, allergic reactions

Long-term effects
Dependence, cross tolerance with barbiturates, withdrawal symptoms

The onset of withdrawal occurs 12 to 48 hours after last use and lasts for a similar length of time. Acute ingestion of large amounts of meprobamate results in loss of consciousness, marked lowering of blood pressure, respiratory depression, and death. Crushing or chewing extended-release capsules can be dangerous as it may cause an unexpected overdose. Meprobamate in combination with other drugs that depress brain and respiratory function, such as benzodiazepines, barbiturates, and alcohol, is a lethal cocktail. Meprobamate abuse has continued despite the fact that the drug is now rarely used clinically. Another muscle-relaxant drug, carisoprodol, is partially metabolized to meprobamate in the liver and carries a similar risk of dependency. Unlike meprobamate, which is a Schedule IV drug in the United States, carisoprodol is unscheduled.

R. W. HORTON

SEE ALSO:
Barbiturates

Mescaline

Mescaline, a substance obtained from the peyote cactus, is one of the oldest known hallucinogens. It was used in religious rituals by various Native American peoples to communicate with their gods.

Mescaline is one of a small number of substances that are classified as hallucinogens (subtances that induce hallucinations). Although mescaline remained fairly obscure until the mid-1950s, its isolation in 1897 marked the beginning of the modern era of knowledge and understanding of these types of drugs. Indeed, peyote can be considered the prototype of New World hallucinogens, and pure mescaline is the prototype of one of the two chemical classes of hallucinogens, the phenethylamines. Early studies of structurally related substances often used mescaline as the benchmark for potency, for example ranking compounds as "twice the potency of mescaline," "four times as potent as mescaline," and so on. It was not until the 1943 discovery of the effects of LSD-25 by the Swiss chemist Albert Hofmann, however, that the significance of mescaline and other hallucinogens began to be appreciated by the Western world.

Mescaline is a small alkaloid molecule that is the psychoactive component of the *peyote* cactus, *Lophophora williamsii.* Peyote grows in the deserts of central and northern Mexico and the adjacent part of southern Texas and occurs extensively in the area near the Rio Grande valley. The crowns are light green to gray, about 1 to 3 inches (2.5–7.5 cm) in diameter, and grow close to the ground from a long taproot. Peyote was known as peyotl by the South American Aztecs, and was one of the earliest discovered and certainly the most spectacular vision-inducing plant to be encountered by the sixteenth-century Spanish conquerors in Mexico.

Although mescaline is produced by other species of cacti, peyote is the most well-known example. This cactus grows wild in the southern United States and northern Mexico. Mescaline occurs to the extent of about 1 percent of the total dry weight of the cactus. Mescaline was first identified as the active component of the peyote cactus in a series of the experiments carried out at the turn of the twentieth century by German scientist Arthur Heffter. The definitive experiment was carried out on November 23, 1897, when Heffter self-administered 150

The peyote cactus has long been used in religious rituals. The dried tops of the cactus, known as buttons, are chewed or made into a tea and ingested as part of a formal group experience.

milligrams of mescaline hydrochloride to confirm that this alkaloid was the active principle. The correct structure of mescaline was then shown to be 3,4,5-trimethoxyphenethylamine by its chemical synthesis in 1919 by the Austrian chemist Ernst Späth. Subsequent studies of mescaline have generally employed the synthetic material.

Peyote contains at least 40 other minor alkaloids in addition to mescaline, and it has been suggested that the effects produced by the cactus are not identical to those resulting from the administration of pure mescaline. Although no experiments have been carried out to test this hypothesis, studies of the other alkaloids found in peyote have failed to reveal any that have effects resembling peyote. Therefore, although it is possible that the other alkaloids may alter the effects of mescaline in some subtle way, it is certain that mescaline is the principal psychoactive alkaloid in peyote.

Pharmacological effects

The dosage of pure mescaline is 200 to 400 milligrams (as the sulfate salt), or about 180 to 260 milligrams (as the hydrochloride salt). Effects following oral dosages of mescaline begin to appear within about 30 to 40 minutes, often with an initial period of nausea or vomiting. The nausea typically disappears with the onset of the psychological effects. Some autonomic effects typically also occur, such as a slight decrease in blood pressure, extensive pupil dilation, sometimes a feeling of being cold, as well as changes in consciousness that can include states of intense introspection, changing moods and emotions, and a markedly altered sense of time. The visual phenomena produced by mescaline are particularly vivid and characteristic of this drug, especially with the eyes closed, and typically comprise vibrantly colored and rapidly changing patterns. The visual and emotional effects peak about four hours after ingestion, and gradually taper off over the next six to eight hours. Sleep is generally not possible until the effects have completely worn off. The most widely cited modern description of the effects of mescaline is probably Aldous Huxley's book *The Doors of Perception,* which describes a 1953 self-experiment conducted by Huxley prior to the legal prohibition against these drugs.

As with all of the hallucinogens, the toxicity of mescaline is very low. One case report documents the ingestion of 8 grams of mescaline without ill effect. There have been no genetic or neurological abnormalities observed in members of the Native American Church who may use peyote ceremonially up to 35 times per year. The relatively long action of mescaline is consistent with studies using radioactive substances, where the biological half-life in humans was found to be about six hours, with about 60 percent of the mescaline being excreted unchanged, and 87 percent of the total radioactivity excreted into the urine within 24 hours. None of the hallucinogens, including mescaline, has caused overdose death or leads to drug dependence or addiction. Rapid tolerance occurs upon repeated administration of mescaline, such that after three or four days of repeated use, the drug loses its psychoactive effect.

Historical and religious use

The use of peyote for religious purposes was firmly established by the time of the Spanish conquest in the sixteenth century, and radiocarbon dating of materials from shelters and caves in Coahuila, Mexico, has shown that peyote was used as long as 8,000 years ago. As with many other aspects of South American indigenous culture, the Christian missionaries made radical efforts to destroy the peyote religion of the native inhabitants. Fearing that peyote use was spreading not only among converted Christians, but possibly among Spaniards as well, the church brought the Inquisition to bear against peyote in 1620 and issued an edict forbidding the use of peyote or of its administration to any other person, with the threat that disobedience would lead to the same punishments taken against people suspected of heresy. Though hearings from this edict occupied the church for the next two hundred years, the use of peyote was so ingrained among the Native Americans, and the power of peyote so respected, that during the U.S. Civil War (1861–1865) its use was still known and began to spread among the Plains Indians of the United States. Several tribes adopted the peyote religion and incorporated elements of Christianity, ultimately leading to the organization known as the Native American Church, formalized in Oklahoma in 1880 and now representing more than 250,000 members. In the years since incorporation of the church there has been intense opposition by non-Native

KEY FACTS

Classification
Schedule I (USA), Schedule III (Canada), Class A (UK), Schedule I (INCB). Hallucinogen.

Street names
Beans, buttons, cactus, mescal, mese, peyote, topi

Short-term effects
Often initial nausea or vomiting, followed by marked changes in consciousness and perception. Colorful alterations of the visual field. Sleeplessness, loss of appetite, weakness, tremors.

The vivid yarn paintings made by the Huichol Indians depicting animals, plants, people, and gods are inspired by the visions seen while using peyote.

Americans to the use of peyote, which has generated stiff resistance and numerous legal battles by the church's members.

Today, peyote is legally used as a sacrament in religious services by members of the Native American Church. The peyote is harvested by cutting off the exposed tops of the cactus, leaving the root to produce new growth. The small, dried, brown, disk-shaped tops, or crowns, of the cactus are called buttons, and are consumed during the ceremony, with three to 12 typically being ingested. Although there are some variations in the ceremony, depending on the tribe, the service typically consists of an all-night ritual led by a guide, with chanting, singing, meditation, and prayer, that usually ends in the morning with a communal meal.

Nevertheless, the use of peyote by Native Americans remains controversial in certain circles. The American Indian Religious Freedom Act (AIRFA), passed in 1978, had acknowledged prior infringement on the right of freedom of religion for Native Americans. AIRFA clearly stated that federal laws passed for other purposes were not meant to restrict the rights of Native Americans to believe, express, and exercise their traditional religions. Even

so, in 1990 the U. S. Supreme Court ruled that the State of Oregon could enforce antidrug laws against members of a Native American sect who had used peyote as part of their religious practices. This decision led to passage of the Religious Freedom Restoration Act (RFRA) of 1993 by Congress, with the specific intent of protecting the free exercise of religion unless the government had a compelling interest and reason to interfere with a specific religious practice. Subsequently, the principles of AIRFA were reaffirmed in a general policy statement regarding American Indian religious freedom:

> …henceforth it shall be the policy of the United States to protect and preserve for American Indians their inherent right to freedom to believe, express, and exercise the traditional religions of the American Indian, Eskimo, Aleut, and Native Hawaiians, including but not limited to access to sites, use and possession of sacred objects, and the freedom to worship through ceremonial and traditional rites [42 United States Code (U.S.C.) 1996].

In June 1997 the U.S. Supreme Court held that Congress lacked the authority to pass the RFRA to supersede state and local laws. Thus RFRA is no longer applicable to other minority religions, although AIFRA still provides protection for the use of peyote by bona fide members of the Native American Church.

Although a verbal description of the visual effects of mescaline (or peyote) is difficult, Huichol Indian shamans create yarn paintings that attempt to convey certain aspects of the peyote experience. The Huichol Indians are a small tribe of approximately 15,000 living in central Mexico near Ixtlan in the Sierra Madre Mountains. They have attempted to maintain their pre-Columbian traditions. The yarn paintings are made on large wooden squares that are first covered with beeswax. Individual strands of brightly colored yarn are then pressed into the wax to form the designs. Intricate and bold patterns of symbols and color are combined in an attempt to depict the visions encountered during the peyote-induced experience.

D. E. NICHOLS

SEE ALSO:
Hallucinogens • Phenethylamines • Tryptamines

Metabolism

Metabolism is an important factor that controls the levels of drugs in the body and how quickly they are broken down and eliminated. Without metabolism, drugs would accumulate in the body and become toxic.

Drugs and medicines produce their effects for variable lengths of time. The major factor in determining this duration is how long the active form of the drug remains in the body. A minority of drugs and medicines are removed from the body without being chemically changed. For example, almost all of the antibiotic penicillin G and two-thirds of a dose of Ecstasy is removed unchanged. However, the majority of drugs and medicines undergo enzyme-mediated reactions that convert the parent compound into different chemical entities. These processes are termed drug metabolism, or biotransformation.

Drug metabolism can be divided into two distinct phases. Phase I reactions involve insertion or modification of an active group in the parent molecule. This is usually (but not always) associated with a decrease in pharmacological activity of the metabolite compared with the parent compound.

Phase II reactions involve the conjugation of the drug or metabolite with a normal body constituent. The conjugate is usually of lower pharmacological activity and of greater water solubility than the drug and is thus more easily removed from the body. Phase I reactions are often referred to as preconjugation reactions because they produce products that are suitable compounds for phase II or conjugation reactions. Although many compounds undergo both phase I and phase II, some compounds are able to undergo phase II reactions directly without the need for phase I reactions.

Phase I reactions

The most important site of drug metabolism is the liver, although other organs, for example the lungs, may also be involved. Enzymes present in blood can also be important for the metabolism of some drugs.

The most important of the phase I reactions is oxidation. Oxidation is carried out mainly in the liver by a superfamily of enzymes known as the cytochrome P450 mixed function oxidase system. These are iron-containing proteins, and their name is derived from the

fact that they combine with carbon monoxide to form a pink (hence P) colored compound with maximal spectral absorption at wavelengths of 450 nanometers. The P450 enzymes are bound to membranes within liver cells called the smooth endoplasmic reticulum (SER). The SER is also referred to as the microsomal fraction. The P450 combines the drug with molecular oxygen, one atom of which is transferred to the drug molecule while the other oxygen atom is reduced to water. Unlike most enzyme-catalyzed reactions, these enzymes are able to break down many different substances. There are, however, many chemically distinct but functionally similar enzymes, which have different but overlapping patterns of preference. Drugs of abuse that undergo oxidation by P450 enzymes include cannabinoids, amphetamines, and barbiturates.

A number of medicines and environmental agents are able to alter the activity of liver P450 enzymes. Several medicines used to treat epilepsy, for example carbamazepine and phenytoin, increase levels of P450 enzymes and so increase the rate of metabolism of other medicines and drugs metabolized by the same enzyme system. Alcohol and smoking also increase P450 enzymes. On the other hand, some medicines inhibit P450 enzymes and thus decrease the metabolism of other medicines and drugs. Cimetidine (the anti-ulcer drug), some drugs used to treat depression, and some antibiotics selectively inhibit the working of P450 enzymes.

Other phase I reactions that do not involve the enzymes associated with the SER include some oxidations, reductions, and hydrolysis. The oxidation of ethanol (ethyl alcohol) is the most important non-SER oxidation. Alcohol is almost completely metabolized, mostly in the liver; the remainder (5 percent) is excreted unchanged in urine. The soluble enzyme, alcohol dehydrogenase, becomes saturated (that is, working as fast as it can) at low concentrations of alcohol. Thus the activity of this enzyme limits the clearance of alcohol from the body to around one unit of alcohol per hour.

Hydrolysis involves the splitting of a molecule by

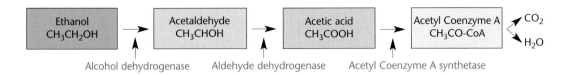

The metabolism of alcohol involves a series of reactions catalyzed by enzymes (shown in red). Alcohol is eventually metabolized to carbon dioxide and water. A small amount of unmetabolized alcohol is excreted in urine. The rate of breakdown can be affected by genetic differences in enzyme levels that can lead to a toxic buildup of acetaldehyde.

the addition of water. Cocaine, an ester of benzoic acid and methyl ecgonine, is hydrolyzed and inactivated by pseudocholinesterase, an enzyme present in blood as well as in the liver. In contrast, heroin (diacetylmorphine) is rapidly hydrolyzed to 6-monoacetylmorphine and morphine. These two compounds are responsible for the pharmacological actions of heroin. Thus, these two examples illustrate one drug being inactivated by hydrolysis and another drug being activated by hydrolysis.

Phase II reactions

Phase II, or conjugation reactions, are enzyme-mediated conjugations of a drug with an endogenous biochemical (a chemical that exists within the body). The most common conjugation is glucuronidation (combination with glucuronic acid, which is derived from glucose). Addition of glucuronide makes many drug metabolites soluble so they can be excreted by the kidneys in urine. For conjugation to take place, the drug must contain the appropriate functional group. Hydroxyl (–OH), carboxyl (–COOH), amino (–NH$_2$), and sulfhydryl (–SH) are suitable groups for glucuronidation. The endogenous biochemical also requires activation. With glucuronidation this involves combination with the high-energy phosphate UTP (uridine triphosphate) to form UDP (uridine diphosphate) glucuronic acid (the activated form). Other conjugation reactions include acetylation, methylation, and amino and sulfate conjugation.

Benzodiazepines are extensively metabolized to glucuronides. The short-acting benzodiazepines, such as oxazepam and temazepam, are conjugated directly to glucuronides without prior phase I reactions, while the longer-acting benzodiazepines, such as diazepam and chlordiazepoxide, undergo extensive phase I reactions prior to glucuronide formation. The benzo-

diazepine glucuronide complexes are pharmacologically inactive, and that is the general rule for phase II products. An important exception is morphine. Morphine undergoes glucuronide formation at the 3- and 6-OH groups. Morphine 6-glucuronide is a more potent analgesic agent than morphine itself.

There is wide individual variation in the ability of individuals to metabolize drugs. Factors such as age, liver disease, and genetics are important. Within the population, basal levels of drug-metabolizing enzymes approximate to a normal distribution curve, and thus the ability of individuals to metabolize a particular drug may differ by as much as threefold. For some enzymes there are specific genetically determined differences. The ability of the population to acetylate various drugs can be divided into two distinct groups, slow and fast acetylators. Slow acetylators have a low amount of the enzyme N-acetyltransferase and are at risk from toxic effects of drugs that are metabolized by this route, such as caffeine and nitrazepam. In Asia 10 to 20 percent of the population are slow acetylators, while in Europe and the United States as many as 55 to 60 percent of the population are slow acetylators.

The metabolism of an individual drug often gives rise to a number of metabolites, the proportions of which may differ markedly between individuals. While some of the metabolites will be eliminated quickly, some may remain in the body and be detected for days or even weeks after initial exposure to the drug and long after its pharmacological actions have disappeared. Smoking cannabis produces a large number of cannabinoids, some of which can be detected in the body for as long as two weeks.

R. W. HORTON

SEE ALSO:
Acetaldehyde • Pharmacokinetics • Potentiation

Methadone

Methadone has been the frontline treatment for opiate addiction for many years. Its benefits include a long period of action and the reduction of withdrawal symptoms. However, methadone itself can be addictive.

Methadone is a long-lasting synthetic opioid agonist that was developed during World War II (1939–1945). The circumstances surrounding its development have been associated with various myths. Some people have argued that methadone was developed in response to an order by Adolf Hitler to create an alternative to morphine, which was in short supply during World War II. Consistent with this origin, others have argued that methadone was developed when the Allies cut off the supply of opium to Germany. Nazi opium addicts, including Hermann Göring (commander-in-chief of the Luftwaffe), needed to avoid withdrawal, so German drug companies were instructed to produce a completely synthetic opiate drug. These myths have been widely expanded and even describe one of methadone's first trade names, Dolophine, as a derivation of Adolf. Some have even argued that it was originally called Adolophine, and that the "A" was dropped after the end of the Nazi regime.

Methadone actually was discovered by the chemical company IG Farbenindustrie at Hoechst-am-Main, in Germany, during the development of novel analgesic and spasm-relieving compounds with less addictive properties. The name Dolophine was created as a trade name after the war by the U.S. pharmaceutical company Eli-Lilly. It was probably derived from the French words *douleur* ("pain") and *fin* ("end"), or from the Latin root *dolor*, which has been used in medicine to measure pain (1 dol = 1 unit of pain).

Discovery and clinical application of methadone
In 1939, Otto Eisleb and O. Schaumann, scientists working for IG Farbenindustrie, discovered an effective opiate analgesic drug, which they called Dolantin. This marked the discovery of meperidine (pethidine), which constitutes the active ingredient in the drug sold under the trade name of Demerol. Meperidine was produced commercially by 1939, and at the height of the war, in 1944, annual production had risen to 3,500 pounds (1,600 kg).

At the same time, other scientists at IG Farbenindustrie, Max Bockmühl and Gustav Ehrhart, were working on compounds with a similar structure to Dolantin. They hoped to discover a water-soluble hypnotic substance that would slow down the gastrointestinal tract to facilitate surgery, that would have strong analgesic properties, and that would be structurally dissimilar to morphine and thus, in theory, nonaddictive.

The result of their work was the creation of a fully synthetic substance, which was initially called "Hoechst 10820" and then polamidon. However, because the two-dimensional structure of this compound bore no resemblance to morphine, its painkilling potential was not recognized. Furthermore, because IG Farbenindustrie conducted tests using exceedingly high doses, the researchers concluded that the clinical use of polamidon was

Methadone is usually given out in limited doses to prevent addicts from selling it to others. Users may be required to attend a clinic to obtain their supply and to consume it on the premises.

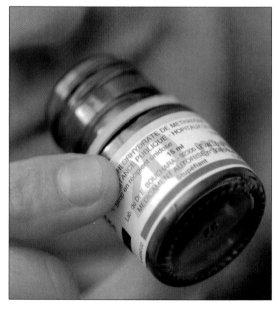

limited by its severe side effects. In the autumn of 1942, after having clearly established that polamidon was both an analgesic and relieved spasms, the drug was handed over to the military for further testing and was given the code name Amidon.

All German patents and trade names, including those for polamidon, were appropriated by the Allies after World War II ended. The IG Farbenindustrie factory was in a U.S. occupation zone and, therefore, came under American administration. The U.S. Foreign Economic Management Department sent an industrial intelligence committee to investigate the wartime work at Hoechst and, in 1945, the U.S. Department of Commerce published a report that included a description of the structure and pharmacological effects of polamidon.

The formula was distributed around the world and was exploited by many companies, so it has many different names, including amidone, miadone, butalgin, diadone, and methadone. Eli-Lilly and other American and British pharmaceutical companies quickly began clinical trials and commercial production of methadone. In these early clinical trials, methadone was demonstrated to be an effective painkiller and was recommended for use in the control of severe pain.

Pharmacology

In most countries, methadone is available as a mixture of two mirror-image isomers, levo-methadone and dextro-methadone. The painkilling activity of the mixture is almost entirely attributable to the levo isomer, which is 8 to 50 times more potent than the dextro isomer. Dextro-methadone is less likely than levo-methadone to cause respiratory depression, has a lower addiction liability, and is able to suppress coughing.

Methadone is available in many forms and strengths: liquid mixtures (orange, yellow, green, or clear), tablets, and ampoules for injection. Methadone is most frequently mixed at 1 milligram per milliliter concentrations. Liquid methadone is designed to be taken orally and is mixed with an irritant to deter injection. Tablets are also designed to be taken orally, but some users grind up tablets and inject them. Concentrated 50 milligram per milliliter ampoules are intended for subcutaneous or intramuscular use.

KEY FACTS

Classification
Schedule II (USA), Schedule I (Canada), Class B (UK), Schedule I, INCB. Opioid.

Street names
Amidone, dollies, done, fizzies, frizzies, jungle juice, meth, metho

Short-term effects
Reduces cravings for opiates and prevents symptoms of withdrawal. May cause drowsiness, weakness, dizziness, constipation, nausea, and allergic reactions.

Long-term effects
Tolerance to drug's effects may lead to physical dependence. Withdrawal symptoms may be more severe than for heroin. Risk of kidney failure and seizures. Overdose may cause death.

Orally administered methadone is first metabolized in the liver to a product that the body can use. This yields a metabolite that acts in a similar manner to morphine. Methadone and its metabolites are mainly excreted in feces. Unmetabolized methadone excretion in the urine accounts for less than 11 percent of the administered dose. Excess methadone is also stored in the liver, bloodstream, and brain, which explains why it is slow to act and why it has a long half-life. The higher the dose, the more methadone is stored. As a result, patients on blockade doses (70 milligrams/day or more) are able to go for a day or two without their medication.

Methadone as an addiction medication

The earliest accounts of the clinical use of methadone in the United Kingdom were from papers published in *The Lancet* in 1947, which described it as "at least as powerful as morphine, and 10 times more powerful than pethidine." Early advertisements claimed that Physeptone (the drug company Wellcome's trade name for methadone) carried "little risk of addiction," and the consensus was that methadone was a better analgesic than morphine.

In the early 1960s, the number of opiate addicts in the United States and the United Kingdom increased dramatically, mostly as a result of young people taking opiates for pleasure rather than as part of medical treatment. Heroin first overtook morphine as the most well-known drug of addiction in the United Kingdom in 1962 and, by 1966, there were six times more heroin addicts than morphine addicts.

The British approach to this problem was to set up specialized drug clinics, which began operating in 1968. These clinics were set up to provide a legal supply of drugs, to bring heroin users into contact with physicians, to interfere with the illicit drug market and the crime associated with illicit drug use, and to help people get off drugs altogether. In their initial years, drug clinics prescribed drugs that the clients were already taking, mostly in injectable form.

During the 1970s, the incidence of heroin use continued to rise, and clinics began to doubt the efficacy of prescribing the client's drug of choice as a way of producing change. At this point, clinics moved toward the prescription of oral methadone because it was more therapeutic to prescribe a noninjectable drug, and because such a long-acting drug needed to be administered once daily rather than every few hours.

The idea of treating heroin addiction by substituting methadone for heroin, however, originated in the United States, as a result of the pioneer work of a team of clinicians in New York composed of Vincent P. Dole, Marie E. Nyswander, and Mary Jeanne Kreek. In the early 1960s, Nyswander and Dole had found that they could not stabilize heroin users on morphine without continually increasing the morphine doses. They reviewed the medical literature in search of possible alternatives to morphine and pioneered the radical step of prescribing methadone, which was effective orally and was long acting. They soon found that once adequate treatment doses were reached, people could be maintained on methadone for long periods.

From this research, Nyswander and Dole developed the methadone maintenance treatment (MMT) program. Their experiments with this approach began with treatment of patients in a locked ward with elaborate security procedures. It was soon realized that this level of security was unnecessary, and it was gradually abandoned by moving first to an open ward, and then having patients reside in the ward though they were released during the day to work.

Dole, Nyswander, and Kreek based their therapeutic approach on the theory that opiate addicts

Addicts withdrawing from heroin in clinics are often given methadone to prevent symptoms that might cause them to relapse. Once stabilized, addicts can attend daily outpatient clinics to obtain methadone.

suffer from a metabolic disorder, similar in principle to metabolic disorders such as diabetes, in which the normal functioning of the endogenous opioid system is disrupted. Therefore, just as insulin normalizes the dysfunction in diabetes, so methadone was proposed as a means of normalizing endogenous opioid dysfunctions caused by addiction. As a consequence of methadone maintenance, therefore, patients would neither experience withdrawal nor cravings for opiates. In addition, it was recommended to use large doses of methadone (80 to 150 milligrams) in order to establish a "narcotic blockade" against the effects of heroin. Based on cross-tolerance between methadone and heroin, this blockade would prevent the experience of heroin-induced euphoria in methadone-maintained individuals.

It is now recognized that because of the high morbidity and mortality associated with opiate dependence, it is of major importance that methadone is used at an effective dosage in maintenance treatment—at least 60 milligrams per day, but typically between 80 to 100 milligrams per day. However, because individuals may differ in intensity of opiate addiction, some patients benefit from methadone dosages of more than 100 milligrams per day. Furthermore, there can be a 17-fold variation in methadone blood concentration for a given dosage beween individuals, mainly as a result of genetic variations in the levels of the cytochrome P450 enzyme found in the body, which breaks down opiates into metabolites. Since methadone probably also displays differences between individuals in its pharmacodynamics, methadone treatment must be adapted to each patient on an individual basis.

Methadone's fast rate of absorption into the body and long half-life make it an ideal drug for outpatient maintenance of opioid addiction. While these characteristics would seem to also make it an ideal analgesic for chronic pain, the large differences in its action among patients, in addition to its variable painkilling potential, complicate its effective and safe dosing.

For opiate detoxification, methadone is administered under close supervision. During detoxification, a patient may receive methadone when symptoms of opiate withdrawal emerge. Then, after several days of stabilization, the amount of methadone is gradually decreased. The rate at which methadone is decreased depends on the reactions of the individual.

The most common side effects of methadone are drowsiness, lightheadedness, weakness, euphoria, dry mouth, urinary retention, constipation, and slow or troubled breathing. Some occasional side effects are allergic reactions, skin rash, hives, itching, headache, dizziness, impaired concentration, a sensation of drunkenness, confusion, depression, blurred or double vision, facial flushing, sweating, heart palpitation, nausea, and vomiting. The least common side effects of methadone are anaphylactic reactions, low blood pressure (causing weakness and fainting), disorientation, hallucinations, unstable gait, tremor, muscle twitching, and myasthenia gravis (a weakness of the skeletal muscles). The risks include kidney failure and seizures. Symptoms of overdose are marked drowsiness, confusion, tremors, convulsions, stupor leading to coma, clammy skin, low blood pressure, bradycardia (slow heart beat), and death.

Methadone addiction
Methadone used to control narcotic addiction is occasionally encountered on the illicit market and has been associated with a number of overdose deaths, especially when taken by individuals who are not experienced with opiates. Subcutaneous administration of methadone (10 to 20 milligrams/kilogram) produces euphoria similar in duration to that caused by morphine. In fact, the behavior of addicts who inject methadone is similar to that of morphine addicts, but many former heroin users maintained on oral methadone display no overt behavioral effects.

Tolerance develops to many effects of methadone, but at a slower rate than to morphine. As with other opiates, physical dependence on methadone also develops with long-term use, and a withdrawal syndrome typically follows cessation of daily use. Some former heroin users have claimed that heroin withdrawal is far less painful and difficult than withdrawal from methadone. Due to the addictive nature of methadone, alternative drugs, such as LAAM and buprenorphine, have also been used to treat opiate addiction.

F. LERI

SEE ALSO:
Agonists and Antagonists • Buprenorphine • LAAM • Meperidine • Opiates and Opioids

Methamphetamine

Methamphetamine is a chemical derivative of amphetamine that is more powerful and longer-acting. These properties make methamphetamine useful in medicine but increase its potential for causing dependency.

Methamphetamine, or *N*-methylamphetamine, is a close relative of amphetamine both in terms of its chemical structure and its activity as a stimulant in the central nervous system and throughout the body. Its chemical name is similar to that of MDMA (Ecstasy), but its effects are markedly different. In particular, recreational doses of methamphetamine provide a rush of energy and confidence, but there is none of the "loved-up" empathogenic effect typical of MDMA. The mildly hallucinogenic effect of MDMA is absent in methamphetamine, but paranoid delusions and some hallucination can occur if amphetamine psychosis develops.

How it works

Methamphetamine works by promoting the release of neurotransmitters (chemical messengers) from their stores in neurons, as is the case with amphetamine. Norepinephrine and dopamine are released in the greatest quantities, and these are the agents that produce the effects of the amphetamines. Norepinephrine stimulates the mind and body by firing up the fight-or-flight mechanism, while dopamine provides a pleasurable rush by fueling the reward system of the brain.

The *N*-methyl group in methamphetamine makes it more fat soluble than amphetamine, so its passage through the blood-brain barrier is easier and its effects are more rapid. The same group makes methamphetamine more difficult for the body to bioconvert for excretion, so the drug stays in the body longer than amphetamine. Also, one of the main bioconversion reactions produces amphetamine, so the drug works a second time as a stimulant.

In total, the methamphetamine high lasts around 6 to 8 hours before the effects lessen. The user starts to feel tired and despondent as dopamine and norepinephrine levels subside, and the temptation to take another dose of methamphetamine is strong.

Redosing never achieves the high, of the original dose, however. Dopamine and norepinephrine reserves are reduced after the initial high and their receptors have become less sensitive. Nevertheless,

KEY FACTS

Classification
Schedule II (USA), Schedule II (Canada), Schedule II Class B (UK), Schedule II (INCB). Stimulant.

Form
Prescription tablets (Methedrin, Desoxyn); off-white powder containing methamphetamine hydrochloride cut with various adulterants to 10 percent purity or less; white crystals of pure methamphetamine (ice).

Street names
Crank, crystal meth, ice, speed, tweak, yaba

Method of consumption
Intravenous injection and smoking provide the most rapid effects (within 2 minutes). Snorting is slightly slower (within 10 minutes). Swallowed doses take from 20 minutes on an empty stomach to more than an hour.

Short-term effects
Euphoria, excitement, and confidence for the user; others may find the user annoyingly verbose, agitated, and prone to grandiose thinking. Heart palpitations, nausea and vomiting, stomach cramps and diarrhea.

Immediate risks
Risk of heart attack or stroke, particularly in people with cardiac or circulatory conditions. Hepatitis or HIV infections through shared needles or unprotected sex.

Long-term dangers
Paranoia, psychosis, and damage to dopamine and serotonin systems in the brain, causing permanent psychological problems. Malnutrition caused by prolonged suppression of appetite. Liver damage and sometimes fatal kidney and lung conditions.

HISTORY AND USAGE PATTERNS

The first recorded synthesis of methamphetamine occurred in 1919, more than 30 years after the first amphetamine synthesis. Neither drug was used medicinally or recreationally until the 1930s, and methamphetamine then tended to follow where amphetamine had become established.

Medical uses derive from the fight-or-flight responses caused by the amphetamines: increased focus and alertness, increased heart rate and blood pressure, appetite suppression, and dilation of the airways. Hence, these drugs have been used to treat asthma and breathing difficulties, obesity, narcolepsy (sudden catatonic sleep episodes), and attention deficit hyperactivity disorder (ADHD).

Legal amphetamine production soared during World War II (1939–1945), when these drugs were issued to troops. When the war ended, the producers of these chemicals sold them to the growing market for pep pills and diet pills. Sales were legal without prescription, and the amphetamines became favorites of truck drivers, cramming students, and other people who worked long hours or were seeking to lose weight. Awareness of growing abuse and dependency led to prescription-only sales being enforced in 1956.

Methamphetamine went on to become one of the chief drugs of the 1960s biker culture, principally around San Diego, California. Many pills were diverted from legitimate use by unscrupulous doctors selling prescriptions or by prescription holders selling their drugs to others. Crackdowns on diversion of methamphetamine led to an upsurge in clandestine laboratories making the drug from over-the-counter decongestants.

Methamphetamine consumption has spread since the late 1980s, with the government estimating past month users at 502,000 in 2009. Clandestine labs have proliferated during this time, particularly in rural areas. The explosive and toxic chemicals used in manufacturing the drug have caused a heavy toll in human casualties and environmental damage, adding to the health dangers and increased criminality associated with the use of methamphetamine and dependency.

a user can keep going for a run of two to three days or more by redosing, and that is when the risk of amphetamine psychosis becomes great.

Psychosis

Amphetamine psychoses closely resemble the psychotic episodes of paranoid schizophrenics. Violent mood swings and aggressive behavior often accompany delusions, and paranoid belief in shadowy figures pursuing the user make him or her far more likely to carry weapons.

The cause of amphetamine psychosis seems to be excessive dopamine in the brain. Dopamine-blocking antipsychotics, such as chlorpromazine, provide rapid relief from the harrowing symptoms.

Dependency potential

The potential of methamphetamine for causing dependency varies according to how it is taken. Regular low doses of methamphetamine prescribed for medical use show little or no tendency to cause dependency, while smoking and intravenous injections present the greatest hazard.

In the latter case, large doses of methamphetamine reach the brain within seconds and cause extreme highs as dopamine levels rocket. Exactly the same phenomenon occurs through crack smoking, which has a similarly high potential for causing dependency.

People who snort or swallow methamphetamine experience less extreme highs, and the potential for causing dependency is correspondingly lower. Nevertheless, dependency can still occur as the infrequent and light user becomes able to function only with heavier and more frequent doses.

M. CLOWES

SEE ALSO:

Amphetamines • Amphetamine Sulfate • Chlorpromazine • Club Drugs • Crack Cocaine • Dopamine • Ephedrine • Norepinephrine

Methanol

Methanol, methyl alcohol, and wood alcohol are all names for a potentially toxic substance present in small amounts in alcoholic beverages. Methanol can cause blindness and death if drunk in sufficient quantities.

Methanol is the simplest of all alcohols. Its formula (CH_3OH) shows that it is only one $-CH_2-$ group away from ethanol (C_2H_5OH), yet this small structural difference makes a great difference in its properties. Methanol is less effective than ethanol in producing the pleasurable symptoms of moderate drinking, for example, but it is much more toxic if drunk in sufficient quantities.

In fact, methanol itself is only moderately harmful. The real dangers associated with methanol arise when human enzymes oxidize it first to methanal (formaldehyde, HCHO) and then to methanoic acid (formic acid, HCOOH). Methanal is a carcinogenic aldehyde that has unpleasant properties in its own right, but it is present only briefly before turning into methanoic acid. This acid is the irritant of stinging ants and the main culprit in methanol poisoning.

SOURCES OF METHANOL

	Methanol (mg/l)	Ethanol (g/l)
Beer	1–10	30–50
White wine	20–40	60–100
Red wine	60–100	70–110
Brandy	200–300	300
Vodka	1–100	300–400
Whiskey	80–200	300–320
Fruit schnapps	1,000–4,000	300–320
Orange juice*	10–160	0

Sources: Institute of Forensic Medicine, University of Cologne; *U.K. Government Food Standards Agency.

Acidosis

Methanoic acid causes a condition called acidosis, which disrupts the normal functioning of cells and gradually kills them. The effects of acidosis are strongest where there are enzymes to oxidize methanol circulating in the body. One such site is the retina, the light-sensitive lining of the eye that participates in sight. The retina has enzymes that convert retinol (vitamin A) into retinal. These enzymes also convert methanol into methanal, thereby assisting the formation of methanoic acid that destroys nearby cells and can cause blindness. Four grams of methanol is enough to cause blindness.

The most frequent cause of death by methanol poisoning is failure of the kidneys and liver. These organs have enzymes for methanoic acid formation, so they are prone to acidosis. Ten grams of methanol can cause death by damage to kidney and liver cells.

Treatment

The main treatment for methanol poisoning is therapy with ethanol. This works because the affinity of ethanol for dehydrogenase enzymes is around 100 times greater than that of methanol. Intravenous infusion of ethanol keeps these enzymes busy and prevents them from turning methanol into its toxic metabolites. Meanwhile, unchanged methanol gradually leaves the body in breath and urine.

Methanol in drinks

The amount of methanol in drinks is minor—even in the roughest moonshine—and its potential for harm is limited if ethanol is present. Severe methanol poisoning only occurs through drinking concoctions based on methanol or denatured alcohol (ethanol with enough methanol to make it undrinkable).

Mild methanol toxicity is a likely contributor to hangovers, since dehydrogenase enzymes work on methanol after ridding the body of ethanol. An alcoholic drink at this point can provide some relief by switching the enzymes back to ethanol, but the hangover symptoms will return as soon as the concentration of ethanol diminishes.

M. CLOWES

SEE ALSO:

Acetaldehyde • Alcohol • Ethanol • Illicit Manufacturing • Naltrexone

Methaqualone

Quaaludes, one of the trade names for methaqualone, were a popular drug of the 1960s. Promoted as a safe alternative to barbiturates, methaqualone was in fact just as addictive and dangerous if overdosed.

Methaqualone was developed in India during the 1950s by researchers looking for a cure for malaria. Its sedative qualities led to its production by a number of U.S. pharmaceutical companies looking for a replacement for glutethimide, itself a supposedly nonaddictive replacement for barbiturates. Methaqualone appeared on the U.S. market in 1965 under a range of different trade names, including Sopor, Optimil, Mandrax, and Quaaludes. These drugs became very popular on student campuses and in the music business where "luding out" with methaqualone and alcohol became a common pastime. In the 1970s there were nightclubs in New York entirely devoted to Quaalude parties, where the only drink available was fruit juice. However, the partying came to an end when reports of overdoses and deaths began to come in, first from countries like Japan and Germany and then the United States. By 1983, the drug had been taken off the market. Attempts are still made to produce these drugs illicitly, but the process is difficult, and underground chemists based in Mexico or Colombia usually make the analog mecloqualone, which has a similar effect, by mistake.

India, where the drug was first discovered, remains the world's largest source of illicit methaqualone, and major drug seizures are not uncommon. In September 2000, more than 2.2 tons (2 tonnes) of Mandrax powder was seized near Hyderabad. In February 2001, 1.5 tons (1.4 tonnes) of tablets were seized in Bombay. Much of this production finds its way to South Africa, which has a serious problem with methaqualone, as do other countries in the region.

Use and effects

Methaqualone is usually swallowed as a tablet, but it has been known for the drug to be injected. The daytime sedation dose was 75 milligrams up to four times a day; for sleep, the dosage ranged from 150–300 milligrams. When the drug was being abused, it was not unusual for a tolerant user to ingest 1,000–2,000 milligrams a day.

KEY FACTS

Classification
Schedule I (USA), Schedule II (Canada), Class B (UK), Schedule II (INCB). CNS depressant.

Street names
Ludes, mandies, quacks, sopes, wallbangers

Short-term effects
Drowsiness and lack of coordination, similar to being drunk. Sense of well-being and loss of inhibition. Side effects include hangover, stomach pains, and sweating.

Long-term effects
High risk of overdose, tolerance, and dependence. Can induce paranoia, anxiety, loss of muscle control, and loss of erectile function in men. Cross-tolerance can develop to other sedative drugs.

The desired effects occur at low doses—a dreamy state of calm relaxation—and last up to four hours. Users report feeling mellow; self-confident, and sociable. Libido may increase as the drug reduces inhibition.

As the dose goes up (or if the drug is taken with alcohol), so do the risks. There is a marked lack of coordination and motor ability, which makes driving very dangerous. High doses can induce delusions and general disorientation. Overdosing is common and often causes death. It was quickly demonstrated that methaqualone was just as dependence producing as the barbiturates and that withdrawal requires care to prevent acute respiratory depression.

H. SHAPIRO

SEE ALSO:
Barbiturates • Glutethimide

Methcathinone

Methcathinone is a synthetic drug that is related to the active ingredient in khat. Its street name of "bathtub speed" reflects its relative ease of manufacture in illegal backstreet laboratories.

Methcathinone is an artificial stimulant that can be easily manufactured from common medicines and household chemicals. Its effects are very similar to the drug amphetamine, such as making the user energetic and euphoric while possibly leading to addiction and mental illness. Chemically, methcathinone is similar to cathinone, a naturally occurring substance that is found in the khat plant *Cathula edulis*. Typically bought as a white powder, methcathinone is easily manufactured in illegal laboratories. Other names for methcathinone include bathtub speed, cat, and ephedrone.

German chemists first synthesized methcathinone in 1928, after which it was used in the Soviet Union as an antidepressant until the late 1940s. American scientists also investigated the medicinal properties of methcathinone in the 1950s but concluded that it was unsafe and had severe side effects. Methcathinone was then largely forgotten until 1989, when a student working at a pharmaceutical company accidentally found details of its manufacture and some samples of the drug. These details became well known, and significant amounts of methcathinone began to be manufactured and sold as a recreational drug. In response, the United States government made methcathinone a Schedule I restricted substance in 1992.

Powdered methcathinone is typically snorted through the nose, although it can also be dissolved in a liquid and then drunk or injected. Its immediate effects are similar to the stimulant amphetamine, such as alertness, euphoria, increased heart rate, faster respiration, and loss of appetite. At large doses it can also produce unpleasant side effects, which include anxiety, paranoia, restlessness, insomnia, impotence, and hallucinations or delusions in some people. Methcathinone is addictive, and habitual use can lead to both tolerance and withdrawal symptoms upon ceasing the drug. Long-term use can also cause physical damage of the nasal cavities and potential heart problems. Further, after a methcathinone binge, users experience a crash that leaves them feeling exhausted and depressed.

The most common illegally synthesized form of methcathinone is its water-soluble hydrochloride salt. Methcathinone hydrochloride can be manufactured from common household ingredients. Drug enforcement agencies are increasingly worried about the availability of the drug. While methcathinone makes up less than 1 percent of illegal drug sales, in recent years police have found many illegal laboratories and have attributed several house fires and explosions to its manufacture.

N. Lepora

KEY FACTS

Classification
Schedule I (USA, Canada, INCB), Class B (UK). Stimulant.

Street names
Bathtub speed, cadillac express, cat, ephedrone, goob, Jeff, mulka, speed, the C, wildcat

Short-term effects
Alertness, euphoria, increased heart rate and respiration, and loss of appetite. At large doses also anxiety, paranoia, restlessness, insomnia, impotence, and hallucinations or delusions in some people.

Long-term effects
Addiction, with tolerance and withdrawal. Also damage to the nasal cavities and potential heart problems. Possibility of mental illness.

SEE ALSO:

Amphetamines • Illicit Manufacturing • Khat • Methamphetamine

Morphine

Morphine, one of the most potent narcotic analgesics, plays a major role in the management of moderate to severe pain, especially in cancer patients. However, the drug also has a high potential for abuse and dependence.

Morphine is a naturally occurring substance found in the seedhead of the opium poppy, *Papaver somniferum*. Because of the relative difficulty in synthesizing morphine in the laboratory, the drug is still produced by extraction from opium. Of the medically useful alkaloids found in powdered opium, morphine is the most concentrated.

In the 1800s, morphine was widely used as a painkiller, especially during the U.S. Civil War. Indiscriminate use of the drug led to a widespread problem of morphine addiction and dependency during and after the war. It was not until the latter part of the century, with the discovery of heroin in 1874, that the problem of morphine addiction was replaced to a certain extent by the abuse of heroin.

Morphine is available medically in many different formulations. It can be taken intravenously, subcutaneously, intramuscularly, intrathecally (into the spinal cord), or orally. Dosages can range from only 1 or 2 milligrams to gram quantities depending on the route of administration and the tolerance of a patient to opioids. Morphine has a relatively short half-life of only two hours and a duration of action of approximately five hours. Therefore, when used to relieve pain, morphine is usually given by a constant intravenous infusion or at frequent intervals if given by a different route of administration. Morphine produces its analgesic effect primarily through its effect on the mu-opioid receptor in the brain.

Action of morphine

The pharmacological effects of morphine, however, are extremely diverse. In addition to producing pain relief, morphine's effect on the central nervous system can also result in drowsiness, mood changes, and difficulty concentrating. The pupils of the eyes become constricted and vision may be blurred. The cough reflex may also be suppressed; at one time morphine was used as a cough remedy. If given in high enough doses, morphine causes sleepiness. Other effects may include nausea and vomiting. Morphine can also change the equilibrium point of the mechanism for temperature control such that body temperature may fall slightly. Another effect of morphine is to depress respiration. When death occurs from a morphine overdose, the cause is usually a cessation of breathing or respiratory arrest. Morphine depresses respiration by reducing the effect of carbon dioxide on the respiratory centers in the brain stem. Normally, when carbon dioxide increases in the bloodstream, a signal is sent to the brain stem that respirations need to be increased in order to exhale the increased carbon dioxide. This response is blunted by morphine, producing less frequent and shallower breathing. Morphine also has potential effects on the cardiovascular system. The drug can cause dilation of the peripheral blood vessels and inhibition of pressure sensitive reflexes. The result of these effects can produce a decrease in blood pressure on standing, with the resulting possibility of fainting.

KEY FACTS

Classification
Schedule II (USA), Schedule I (Canada), Class A (UK), Schedule I (INCB). Opioid.

Street names
M, Miss Emma, morph

Short-term effects
Drowsiness, restlessness, constipation, diminished breathing

Long-term effects
Increased tolerance, dependence

Signs of abuse
Constricted pupils, track marks, shallow breathing, lethargy

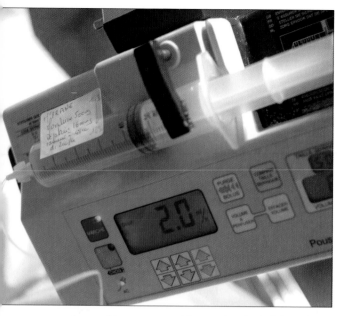

A morphine pump enables continual administration of the drug to hospital patients by feeding small amounts through a drip.

Morphine can also have significant effects on the gastrointestinal tract. It usually decreases the secretion of hydrochloric acid in the stomach. Morphine also has the ability to decrease gastric motility, thereby causing food or other drugs to stay in the stomach longer than usual, which may be problematic when patients are taking other medications orally. In the small intestine, morphine decreases the secretions from the pancreas, gall bladder, and small intestine itself. The movement of food through the small intestine is slowed, thus allowing for more water absorption through the intestine. Similarly, in the large bowel, motility is diminished, resulting in delayed passage of the bowel contents, leading to severe constipation. Morphine can also cause constriction of the sphincter of Oddi in the common bile duct, which may result in abdominal pain or biliary colic. Other smooth muscle, such as that in the ureter and bladder, may be affected by morphine. Morphine can inhibit the urinary voiding reflex, making it difficult to urinate. Morphine may also prolong labor, as the drug may decrease the frequency and strength of uterine contractions. The effect of morphine on the skin includes dilation of the blood vessels, resulting in flushing, especially over the upper half of the body. In addition, sweating and itching may occur after the administration of morphine. Thus, morphine, in addition to its therapeutic uses, has a host of potential effects on a wide variety of organ systems in the body.

Dependence and withdrawal

As with other opioid analgesics, tolerance and physical dependence occur with repeated use of morphine. Any person who takes the drug for a period of days to weeks will require increased doses to achieve the same analgesic effect, and sudden withdrawal of morphine may produce certain symptoms such as restlessness, irritability, cramps, nausea, anxiety, or muscle aches. The phenomena of physical dependence and withdrawal, however, need to be distinguished from that of abuse. While physical dependence and withdrawal occur in virtually all people who take morphine for a protracted period of time, relatively few patients will go on to abuse the drug or take it for nonmedical reasons.

However, abuse of morphine occurs and can have profound physical, psychological, and social effects, including death. The diverse pharmacologic effects of morphine imply that abuse of the drug can lead to a wide variety of problems. These include not only the physical aftereffects of morphine use, but the attendant social and economic problems of attaining what is usually an illegal supply of the drug. Overdosage with morphine will typically produce a clinical syndrome in which the patient is in a coma and has pinpoint pupils and with depressed breathing. One specific way to diagnose an opioid narcotic overdose is by the use of the opioid antagonist naloxone. The effects of naloxone can be dramatic, although one must be careful in giving the appropriate doses to reverse respiratory depression without precipitating a full-blown withdrawal syndrome. Withdrawing drug abusers from physical dependency on morphine is relatively easy through graded decreases in administration of a narcotic with minimal euphoric effects. However, the treatment of the addiction itself, so that there is no further desire to abuse the drug, is much more difficult.

M. Nadel

SEE ALSO:
Naloxone • Opiates and Opioids • Opium

Naloxone

Naloxone is a drug derived from a chemical in opium poppy juice. Unlike most other opium compounds, naloxone does not produce euphoric effects and can be used to treat symptoms of addiction.

Naloxone is a synthetic opioid drug that is used to reverse the effects of an overdose of other opioids, such as heroin, morphine, or fentanyl. It is made by substituting an allyl group ($-CH_2CH=CH$) for the methyl group ($-CH_3$) on the nitrogen atom of oxymorphone, a compound derived from the opium alkaloid thebaine. Naloxone is generally classed as an opioid antagonist and typically has little effect when administered to individuals who do not take opiate drugs.

Although acute administration of naloxone will have few effects in individuals who do not take opiates, if the body's natural opioid systems have been activated by pain or by stress, some consequences will be observed. In these cases, naloxone antagonizes the action of natural opioid peptides known as endorphins, which are segments of amino acids that act as neurotransmitters. This may explain why naloxone can reduce the painkilling effects of placebo medications and of acupuncture. Also, because certain hormones secreted by the hypothalamus are inhibited by natural opioid peptides, acute administration of naloxone can increase the secretion of gonadotrophin- and corticotropin-releasing hormones, enhancing the concentrations of sex and stress hormones. Such an effect on hormonal regulation may account for the action of naloxone on feeding (reduced food intake) and energy metabolism (increases in energy expenditure).

Treating opiate overdose

Naloxone can effectively block various actions of opiates and therefore reverse their effects. The onset of the antagonistic action of naloxone is quite rapid (one to five minutes), making it the treatment of choice for opiate overdose. Furthermore, antagonism of acute opioid effects by naloxone is often followed by "overshoot" phenomena. Thus, for example, the rate of respiratory depression caused by opioids is briefly elevated when compared with rates prior to the period of depression. In general, the duration of the antagonistic effects of naloxone is one to four hours, depending on the dose.

In individuals dependent on opioids, such as heroin, morphine, or oxycodone, a small dose of naloxone (0.5 milligrams) will precipitate opioid withdrawal. The symptoms, and their intensity, closely resemble the withdrawal syndrome that is typically experienced as a result of abstinence from opioids. The major differences are that naloxone precipitates withdrawal within minutes after administration, and the symptoms subside after around two hours. The intensity and the duration of precipitated withdrawal will vary according to how dependent the patient is on opioids, and the dose of naloxone. The lack of agonistic activity and short duration of action also make naloxone suitable for reversing potentially lethal respiratory depression caused by opioid overdose in dependent individuals. Further, if naloxone is administered slowly in small intravenous doses, respiratory depression can be brought back to normal without precipitating withdrawal. However, because of its short duration, naloxone is less useful for treating opioid addiction because the frequency of supervised drug administrations would become impractical for the patient.

Naloxone has little or no abuse potential and can be administered over long periods, even at high doses, without inducing physical dependence. Thus, discontinuation of naloxone is not followed by a recognizable withdrawal syndrome. However, there is evidence that long-term administration of naloxone can lead to an opioid addict becoming hypersensitive to the effects of opioids if he or she goes back to taking opioids.

F. Leri

SEE ALSO:

Endorphins • Hormonal Effects • Naltrexone • Opiates and Opioids

217

Naltrexone

Naltrexone is a long-acting opioid antagonist medication used in the treatment of both recovering heroin addicts and alcoholics to help them remain drug free. A third use is for detoxification from heroin or methadone.

Naltrexone is used as part of the treatment and rehabilitation programs for heroin addicts and alcoholics. It is prescribed only when the patient has been completely detoxified and the addictive drug is no longer present in his or her body. For heroin addicts, this process may take 7 to 10 days. When naltrexone is taken as prescribed, it blocks the effects of heroin or morphine, so the individual will not feel high if he or she uses the narcotic. In the United States and Canada, naltrexone is produced under the brand name of ReVia as 50-milligram tablets. An earlier brand name was Trexan. In the United Kingdom, an implant containing naltrexone that lasts for about six weeks is available.

Naltrexone, like heroin and morphine, is an opioid but is classified as an opioid antagonist. Opioid antagonists block opiate receptors in the brain and elsewhere in the body, preventing such drugs as heroin or morphine from linking up with these same receptors. Therefore, if a recovering addict uses heroin or morphine while he or she is taking naltrexone, the illegal drug's desired effect will not occur. Because using the drug no longer produces a high, reinforcement of the drug-taking behavior does not occur. Lack of reinforcement leads to the cessation (extinction) of the drug-taking behavior in people who use the medication as prescribed. In other words, the urge to seek the drug has decreased.

In the case of alcoholism treatment, naltrexone's actions on opioid receptors also serve to block the enjoyable effects of alcohol. Because a high is not felt when alcohol is consumed, the craving for more alcohol is diminished. It is important to add that naltrexone will not prevent impairment of functioning (including slowed reaction time, problems with judgment, and so on) from drinking alcohol.

Naltrexone was derived from another narcotic antagonist, naloxone, by scientists in the federal government. The U.S. Food and Drug Administration (FDA) approved naltrexone for use as a narcotic antagonist in 1984. In 1995 the FDA approved its use to help formerly alcohol-dependent patients—the first new drug treatment for alcoholism in 50 years.

The advantage of this medication is that it has no potential for abuse. A person cannot become physically dependent on naltrexone, and it does not produce euphoria. Joseph R. Volpicelli, a naltrexone researcher, refers to it as an "antipsychoactive drug" since it blocks the effects of psychoactive drugs like heroin and alcohol. However, while naltrexone helps recovering addicts, it does not cure heroin or alcohol addiction but must be used as part of a comprehensive treatment program.

Treatment with naltrexone

In order to live a drug-free life successfully, people who are addicted to alcohol or drugs almost always require a comprehensive treatment approach. After detoxification from the drug or drugs to which the individual is addicted, addiction professionals generally recommend the use of both psychotherapeutic help (individual, family, and group counseling and education) and support systems (including family, friends, and organizations such as Alcoholics Anonymous and Narcotics Anonymous). Naltrexone can provide a valuable third form of assistance. Together, these approaches provide a biopsychosocial approach to recovery.

In the United States, naltrexone is available as a 50-milligram tablet. The average weekly dose prescribed is 350 milligrams. To treat narcotic addiction, some physicians prescribe patients one pill a day, while others divide the total dose over 3 to 6 days during the course of a week. (Each pill lasts about 24 hours.) Such a schedule can enable medical staff to monitor patient compliance more easily. To treat alcoholism, one tablet per day is recommended. Dose and frequency for those under 18 years old must be decided by the patient's physician in cases of drug addiction or alcoholism.

Motivation is a major issue when success depends on the patient's willingness to take an oral medication. After all, it is simple to just stop taking a pill

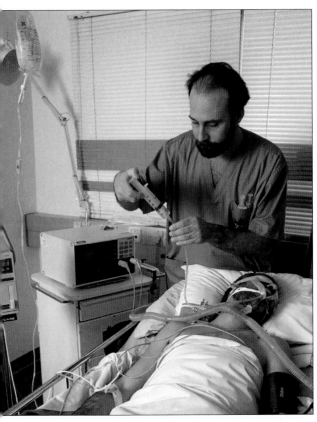

Naltrexone can be used as an inpatient treatment to help speed up detoxification in heroin addicts. This procedure is dangerous unless carried out by doctors.

when one wants to drink or use narcotics. For this reason, many experts feel that naltrexone is most effective with highly motivated patients. Such patients include addicted professionals (such as physicians, nurses, pharmacists, and lawyers) who are at risk of losing their licenses to practice their professions and those in the criminal justice system (who are at risk of going to prison).

Two new developments promise to improve compliance for less motivated patients. One approach being investigated at Yale University School of Medicine awards vouchers that can be exchanged for goods and services to patients who take their medication or test negative for drug use. These patients did much better than those receiving the standard naltrexone treatment. A second innovation, being studied at New York State Psychiatric Institute and Columbia University, is the

development of a "depot" formulation of naltrexone. With this approach, the medication is injected under the person's skin, from where it is released slowly over a period of one month. Reducing a patient's need to decide whether or not to take naltrexone to a monthly choice allows the patient to focus on other aspects of the treatment program.

About 10 percent of people taking naltrexone experience side effects. These effects include nausea, difficulty in sleeping, anxiety, nervousness, abdominal pain or cramps, vomiting, low energy, joint and muscle pain, and headaches. Large doses of naltrexone may cause liver failure; people with hepatitis or other liver diseases face an increased risk of side effects. A person taking naltrexone should never take a large dose of heroin or any other narcotic. Death or coma can result. Small doses of opioids or alcohol, as noted above, will produce no effect at all. However, tolerance for narcotics may decrease after beginning naltrexone therapy and sensitivity may increase.

In addition to its use in the treatment of narcotic addiction and alcoholism, naltrexone can be used along with other drugs to speed up detoxification from heroin or methadone. Such procedures must be closely medically supervised. Naltrexone causes withdrawal symptoms if narcotics are still present in the patient. Patients are often treated with naloxone initially to block effects of opioids present in the body. Because a person must have no narcotics in his or her body to benefit from naltrexone, the health care provider may use a "challenge" dose of naltrexone to confirm that a person is no longer in withdrawal. Finally, it is very important for the health care provider who may prescribe naltrexone to know whether any narcotic-containing medications are being used.

The use of naltrexone for helping heroin addicts and alcoholics in conjunction with other treatment methods holds great promise. By blocking the effects of narcotics and decreasing the craving for alcohol, this medication uses the body's biochemistry to help addicted people concentrate on developing a drug-free lifestyle using a variety of supports.

M. NADEL

SEE ALSO:
Agonists and Antagonists • Naloxone • Opiates and Opioids

Narcotic Drugs

The term *narcotic* has had a variety of meanings over the centuries. Primarily used to describe opiates, its definition has been expanded to cover all sleep-inducing addictive drugs, and even the stimulant cocaine.

Medicine, pharmacology, neuroscience, and law have somewhat different systems of drug classifications and the law in particular struggles to keep abreast of scientific knowledge. This has led to some confusion about the categorization of certain drugs. A common question, such as which drugs are narcotics, can be answered in different ways, according to the different systems of drug classification.

The term *narcotic* comes from the Greek word *narkotikos*, which means "benumbing." According to definitions given in older medical dictionaries, narcotics are "drugs which induce sleep or cause loss of feeling, and may be of medical value when rightly used but with overuse are the cause of an unbalanced condition of the mind, the loss of normal powers, a serious tendency to become unconscious, and possibly convulsions and death." Another definition is "those pain-relieving drugs which make a patient sleep, such as barbiturates, cocaine, and opiates."

Differing views

In laws passed in the early decades of the twentieth century, opiates and cocaine were classified as narcotics, and marijuana was added to this class of prohibited drugs in the late 1930s. Responsibility for suppression of the trade in these drugs was given to the Treasury Department's Federal Bureau of Narcotics. Illegal distribution of these drugs became notorious as "the narcotics trade," combated by police narcotics squads in major cities. Special agents, known in the parlance of detectives and criminals as "narcs," tended to play to their media image as an elite group of tough guys who kept the streets safe. Populist politicians were eager to serve on special commissions denouncing this criminal vice.

Medical specialists in addiction research and treatment have never been enthusiastic supporters of this perspective. They have tended to stress that the problem of drug abuse is more complex than politicians generally recognize. They have also drawn attention to the fact that improved scientific understanding of the chemical structures of drugs and of drug action on the nervous system has undermined the legal definitions of what constitutes a narcotic drug.

Opiates such as morphine, heroin, and codeine relieve pain and induce sleep. So do high doses of marijuana and alcohol. These similar effects stem from the fact that all these substances are central nervous system depressants that slow neurotransmission. However, cocaine is a central nervous system stimulant, which speeds up neurotransmission and counteracts sleep (although its derivatives, such as the local dental anesthetic novocaine, have painkilling properties).

The fact that alcohol can, by virtue of some definitions, come close to being considered a narcotic may seem unrealistic, although the anti-alcohol lobby used this argument to support Prohibition, as did the 1930s antimarijuana campaigners. However, cocaine is clearly not a narcotic, and marijuana is not as dangerously addictive in the same way that opiates and alcohol can be.

By the mid-twentieth century all dangerous, addictive, or otherwise undesirable drugs had become labeled as narcotics, but a better understanding of drug actions has led to a progressive shift away from the use of the term. The Bureau of Narcotics first added "and Dangerous Drugs" to its name, but by 1973 reorganization of the federal antidrug effort included dropping the word "Narcotics" from the title of the new Drug Enforcement Administration. By now redolent of a bygone era, the word had become too imprecise to be legally useful. The more specific term *narcotic analgesic,* however, remains in use to describe the pharmacological action of opiates and opioids.

D. E. ARNOT

SEE ALSO:
Classification of Drugs • Cocaine • Marijuana • Opiates and Opioids • Psychotropic Drugs • Sedatives and Hypnotics

Nexus

Nexus is a synthetic substance that is chemically related to mescaline, Ecstasy, and amphetamine. Nexus is sometimes sold as Ecstasy, but its effects are more psychedelic, and it can cause problems in the digestive system.

Nexus, also known as 2C-B (4-bromo-2,5-dimethoxyphenethylamine), is a member of the phenethylamine family of chemicals. It was synthesized in 1974 by the U.S. pharmacologist Alexander Shulgin during his investigations into analogs of amphetamine and mescaline. Structurally, Nexus is similar to mescaline, with a bromine atom substituted at the C2 position on the benzene ring.

Nexus first came to prominence when Ecstasy was scheduled in 1985. Its similar properties to Ecstasy, to which it is chemically related, and its unregulated legal status made it easy for dealers to substitute it for Ecstasy. Nexus was eventually scheduled in the United States in 1993 as a Schedule I substance, and it has since been similarly regulated in most countries around the world. Although rarely available, Nexus and its close relation 2C-I (4-iodo-2,5-dimethoxyphenethylamine) have made a number of reappearances since 2000, again usually sold to the unwary as Ecstasy.

The subjective effects of Nexus are regarded as being a milder psychedelic experience (at low doses) than LSD or magic mushrooms, having less of a dissociative and mind-expanding effect and a shorter period of duration. Users may experience open- and closed-eye visual patterns, with color shifts and wavering movement at higher doses. Nexus also has positive mood stimulant effects like those of Ecstasy but is said to be less forceful, with less of a crash as the drug wears off. Effects last between four and six hours when taken orally in doses ranging between 10 and 40 milligrams. Nexus is sometimes snorted for a faster effect, but this is not advised as it is extremely painful to the nasal lining. The drug is also described as having a heavy "body load" in that it makes users very aware of the effect it is having on the body, particularly as it can upset the digestive system, producing stomach cramps, gas, and mild diarrhea in some users.

Nexus is not reported to cause physical or psychological dependence, although its lack of availability makes it less likely to be taken on a

regular basis. As with other psychedelics, Nexus produces an increasing tolerance if taken on consecutive days, such that an increase in dose produces no effect after several days. A break of five to seven days restores the drug's effect. Nexus is dangerous if taken in combination with monoamine oxidase inhibitor antidepressant medications, such as Nardil, Prozac, or Manerix. Psychedelics are known to trigger emotional and psychological problems, so Nexus is especially dangerous for anyone with a family history of mental illness.

W. A. HORAN

SEE ALSO:
Club Drugs • Hallucinogens • MAOs and MAOIs • Mescaline • Phenethylamines

Nicotine

Nicotine is the active chemical in cigarettes and other tobacco products. It is a highly addictive substance, and smoking delivers nicotine to the brain in a rapid manner that quickly leads to tolerance of its effects.

Nicotine is a drug extracted from the leaves of the plant *Nicotiana tabacum*, more commonly called the tobacco plant. Nicotine acts as a mild stimulant on the central nervous system and has an array of pharmacological effects. Although it has other uses, nicotine is primarily consumed through tobacco products by individuals desiring its drug effects. This article will explore the history of nicotine and examine its uses, active properties, pharmacological effects, and addictiveness.

The history of nicotine

The tobacco plant is grown on every continent except Antarctica. Long before Columbus arrived in the New World, tobacco was being cultivated in Latin America. It is believed that nicotine played an important role in indigenous Native American culture for more than 5,000 years. Ancient native art depicts its use in both religious and medicinal rituals. In the 1500s, early explorers to the New World encountered native people in the Caribbean smoking tobacco and decided to take tobacco with them back to Europe. Sailors aboard these ships came to like smoking tobacco and began to plant it at various ports of call so they could have easy access to the plant on their travels. In Europe, Walter Raleigh was said to have planted tobacco plants along with potatoes on his estate in Ireland. However, it was the French diplomat Jean Nicot who distributed the seeds around Europe, leading the taxonomist Carolus Linnaeus to name the tobacco plant Nicotiana to honor him. Nicot's distribution of tobacco seeds led to the worldwide distribution of tobacco. Yet, it was the turn of the twentieth century that saw the greatest increase in tobacco's popularity. The advent of the cigarette-rolling machine, the safety match, improved tobacco blends, and advertising have all led to the tremendous growth of tobacco smoking, especially through cigarettes, and hence tobacco production. By the beginning of the twenty-first century, approximately 79 million people in the United States regularly used various types of tobacco products, the most popular of which were cigarettes.

Nicotine is a psychoactive chemical that occurs in the leaves of the tobacco plant. Nicotine is poisonous and was once used as an insecticide.

Obtaining nicotine from tobacco plants

Nicotine is a chemical that grows naturally in the leaves of tobacco plants. When directly extracted from the leaves, particularly the tips where nicotine concentrations are highest, pure nicotine is highly poisonous. To create an ingestible form of nicotine, the leaves of the tobacco plant must be cured through a series of complex biochemical events. During the curing process the leaves are fermented, browned, and dehydrated. Moisture is extracted from the tobacco leaves, drastically reducing their water content. The processed dried leaves are then chopped up and mixed with a large number of additional ingredients to make cigarette, cigar, snuff, or chewing tobacco.

How nicotine works

Nicotine is a mild stimulant that affects the central nervous system. Nicotine acts on receptors in the brain that are part of the cholinergic system, a main neurotransmitter system in the brain that affects body functioning—both thinking and movement. The cholinergic system is made up of acetylcholine receptors, a subset of which will bind with nicotine and are therefore called nicotinic receptors. When nicotine enters the brain and binds with a nicotinic receptor, it can initiate an action potential, or firing of the cell. However, over time, these receptors become less sensitive to nicotine. Gradually, more and more nicotine is needed in order for individuals to get the same nicotine effects they initially gained with a small dose. This change is called tolerance. The process of tolerance has also been implicated as a reason for the development of nicotine dependence, because tolerance requires ever increasing amounts of the drug to be consumed in order to maintain the same effects from tobacco use. Tolerance can easily explain the pattern of escalation in the amount and frequency of smoking during the first few years after starting to smoke. This escalation may eventually lead to the regular use of a large quantity of a tobacco product, for example, smoking a pack of cigarettes a day.

Nicotine can act upon nicotinic receptors in a variety of cells throughout the brain and the rest of the central nervous system. Therefore, such cell action underlies a wide array of complex behavioral and physiological effects. These include physiological effects such as increases in heart rate, blood pressure, and respiratory activity. In extremely high doses, nicotine can lead to respiratory distress, seizures, and hypothermia (a dangerous drop in body temperature). While these physiological effects are well known, the effect of nicotine on cognitive and behavioral activity is more controversial. There is some evidence that nicotine might enhance concentration, attention, and task performance, and that it might act in reducing appetite, anxiety, and pain perception. However, these effects have not been clearly shown in individuals who are functioning normally. Effects of nicotine on improving performance tend to occur in smokers only when they have not smoked recently and are experiencing withdrawal, or when they are performing poorly

NUMBER OF PEOPLE IN THE UNITED STATES USING VARIOUS TYPES OF TOBACCO	
Cigarettes	58.7 million
Cigars	13.3 million
Chew/Snuff	8.6 million
Pipes	2.1 million

Source: *Results from the 2009 National Survey on Drug Use and Health.* Substance Abuse and Mental Health Services Administration (2010).

for other reasons, such as fatigue or as the result of a cognitive disorder.

Nicotine withdrawal is the body's reaction to no longer having nicotine in the system after a period of time when nicotine was regularly administered, as is the case when someone engages in daily tobacco use. Some of the symptoms of withdrawal are short-term declines in cognitive functioning, including such symptoms as difficulty concentrating, irritability, negative mood, and cravings. Withdrawal can begin to occur even after brief abstinence from nicotine, for example, within a few hours. Using tobacco again relieves withdrawal, and these symptoms disappear, including problems with cognitive functioning. Thus, nicotine does not seem to improve cognitive functions beyond normal capability under optimum conditions. Rather, nicotine might prevent these functions from declining over time (such as a loss of concentration or a rise in irritability) due to nicotine withdrawal, fatigue, or similar factors.

How nicotine reaches the brain

The most popular methods of nicotine delivery are through cigarette, cigar, and pipe smoking, as well as chewing tobacco and, less commonly, snuff. Multiple ways exist for getting nicotine to the brain due to the body's ability to absorb nicotine through both the pulmonary system (through the lungs, as is done by smoking) and the mucous membranes (through the mouth and nose, as with chew and snuff). Nicotine can also be absorbed transdermally, through the skin, as with the nicotine patch. These different methods of nicotine delivery differ in the speed with which they get nicotine to the brain.

NICOTINE AS A MEDICINE

The fact that nicotine alone is not particularly harmful to the human body has led scientists to determine its potential medicinal value. One commonly known therapeutic use of nicotine is as a smoking cessation aid. However, nicotine has been examined as a potential treatment to relieve cognitive symptoms of neurodegenerative disorders, such as Alzheimer's and Parkinson's disease. Patients with these dementia disorders were found to have fewer nicotinic receptors in the brain. Having fewer nicotinic receptors is associated with lower levels of acetylcholine, a neurotransmitter, or brain chemical, necessary for proper memory and cognitive brain function. Nicotine use leads to the generation of nicotinic receptors, thereby allowing for increased production of acetylcholine. Increasing this memory-related neurotransmitter might prove beneficial to those with specific deficits related to acetylcholine. Similarly, nicotine has been examined, with some success, as a treatment for reducing tics among patients with Tourette's Syndrome, a disorder also linked to neurotransmitter deficits.

Of the tobacco products available, cigarettes provide the quickest method of getting nicotine to the brain by smoking. Pulmonary absorption, which occurs with smoking, is at least as quick a method of getting nicotine to the brain as injecting nicotine directly into a vein, as is done with drugs like heroin. When tobacco smoke is inhaled, it bypasses the venous system and enters the arterial blood system through the lungs. It quickly crosses the blood-brain barrier and reaches the brain in approximately 10 seconds. Nicotine absorption through the nasal cavity is second quickest, followed by absorption through the mucous membranes of the mouth, both of which take several minutes or longer.

Is nicotine addictive?

The speed with which nicotine gets to the brain is a key factor in its addiction potential; the quicker nicotine crosses the blood-brain barrier, the more likely it is to be addictive. Additionally, the doses at which nicotine is taken have an impact on its addictiveness, with larger doses usually being more addictive than smaller. For these reasons, tobacco products offer a particularly addictive form of nicotine delivery.

To explain this, consider that the average smoker will be exposed to 1 milligram of nicotine per smoked cigarette. The actual amount of nicotine per cigarette is higher than that, approximately 6 to 8 milligrams, but only around 1 milligram is absorbed through smoking. The rapid rate at which this dose of nicotine enters the brain increases the addictive potential of nicotine. The rest is lost in sidestream smoke, which is the smoke that a smoker does not inhale, or that is left in the cigarette butt. On the other hand, chewing tobacco is a comparably slow method of getting nicotine to the brain. However, a typical pinch of chewing tobacco delivers at least as much nicotine as a cigarette. Therefore, although not as expedient as smoking, chewing tobacco is an addictive method of getting nicotine to the brain due to the large dose provided with each use.

Another addictive product that delivers nicotine rapidly and in large doses is the bidi. Bidis are small unfiltered, flavored cigarettes made in India. Some people wrongly believe that because bidis are sometimes sold in health food stores and rarely have a surgeon general's warning on the label, they are a healthy alternative to cigarettes. In truth, bidis have higher carbon monoxide, nicotine, and tar levels than regular cigarettes. Another common misconception about tobacco products is that cigarettes described as "light" are healthier than regular ones. This is not the case, as the only difference between the two is that the tobacco in light cigarettes is not packed as tightly and the paper around their filters is porous, meaning it has tiny holes in it. Most smokers easily compensate for this design by dragging harder on light cigarettes, taking more puffs, putting their mouth over the holes, or simply smoking more cigarettes a day. Not surprisingly, people who smoke light cigarettes have the same risk of tobacco-use-related diseases as those who smoke regular cigarettes.

Understanding how the dose and speed of absorption determine nicotine's potential addictiveness helps explain why nicotine replacement products are not particularly addictive. The nicotine gum and lozenge (which are absorbed in the mouth), the patch (which is absorbed through the skin), and the nicotine spray (which is absorbed nasally) are all slower means of getting nicotine to the brain. These methods take many minutes, or even up to an hour, to deliver nicotine to the brain, compared with a few seconds for smoking. Also, replacements typically provide lower doses of nicotine than tobacco products. Therefore, although replacement products still get nicotine to the brain and thereby help relieve the withdrawal symptoms that occur when an individual is trying to stop using tobacco, they do not expose the individual to quick enough or large enough doses of nicotine to be addictive.

The question "Is nicotine addictive?" is thus incomplete. Rather one must ask, "Is nicotine, when absorbed quickly or in large doses, as with cigarettes or other tobacco products, addictive?" The answer to that question is decidedly "yes."

Is nicotine dangerous?

More than 400,000 Americans die each year from tobacco-related diseases. Smoking, in particular, features in approximately one-fifth of all deaths in

Only a small amount of the nicotine in a cigarette is inhaled by smoking. The rest is lost in sidestream smoke or is absorbed by the filter.

the United States and is the leading cause of lung cancer, chronic bronchitis, and emphysema. Smoking also increases mortality due to other causes and increases risk of heart disease and stroke. While it is clear that nicotine is the addictive component of tobacco and thus plays a key role in perpetuating the use of tobacco products, nicotine itself is not particularly dangerous to health. As stated before, nicotine in its pure form is a poison, and high doses are lethal to humans. When it was used as a pesticide, nicotine poisoning was a relatively common occurrence. However, most individuals come in contact with nicotine only through processed tobacco or medicinal aids, in which nicotine concentrations are low. At ordinary doses, nicotine may briefly affect immune function and lead to heart arrhythmias, which are episodes of unstable heart rhythm. However, there is no evidence that nicotine by itself increases risks of cancer or other serious diseases, including those clearly associated with smoking and other tobacco product use. For this reason, nicotine medications to help smokers quit, such as gums and patches, are safe.

What are dangerous to human health are the compounds and additives of tobacco products other than nicotine. When tobacco is processed, it is mixed with a variety of ingredients. In addition to dried tobacco leaves, tobacco products contain more than 500 additives. Many of these ingredients are relatively harmless, such as sugar, honey, menthol, and licorice. Such additives enhance tobacco's flavor and aroma, even more so when the tobacco is burned. However, the burning of tobacco also creates tar and carbon monoxide, along with 4,000 other compounds, which are then inhaled during smoking. Tar is the most carcinogenic (cancer-causing) component of smoking, but it is not the only one. In fact, tobacco products contain several dozen compounds, such as benzene, formaldehyde, cadmium, lead, and nickel. These carcinogens have also been implicated in the development of reproductive problems. Therefore, it is the many other ingredients of tobacco, and not nicotine, that makes the use of tobacco products the cause of serious negative health consequences.

C. A. CONKLIN, K. A. PERKINS

SEE ALSO:
Acetylcholine ● Tobacco

Nitrous Oxide

Nitrous oxide gas is used as an anesthetic, a whipping agent for cream, and a performance enhancer for internal-combustion engines. Its tendency to cause giggles when inhaled earned it the nickname "laughing gas."

The intoxicant property of nitrous oxide (N_2O) was discovered in 1799 by British chemist Humphry Davy. Noting the ability of nitrous oxide to induce fits of giggles, he coined the name "laughing gas." Davy discovered the anesthetic property of nitrous oxide around the same time and suggested it could be useful for surgery, but it would be another 44 years before U.S. dentist Horace Wells demonstrated its use. Meanwhile, nitrous oxide inhalation became a regular pastime at Davy's high-society parties and soon became a feature of traveling shows.

Anesthesia

Nitrous oxide continues to be used in anesthesia, since its painkilling properties are good and its toxicity low if given with oxygen. Nitrous oxide requires additional sedation to cause complete loss of consciousness, otherwise the patient remains in a dissociative state similar to that caused by ketamine.

Despite its long history of use, little is known for certain about how nitrous oxide works. It is known to act as a neurotransmitter (chemical messenger) in the brain. The sequence of uninhibited excitement followed by disorientation and stupor resembles the effects of alcohol in a shorter time frame, which implies a possible interaction with gamma-aminobutyric acid (GABA) receptors. The fact that nitrous oxide can help in opiate and alcohol withdrawal also suggests an interaction with opiate and GABA receptors.

Recreational use

Nitrous oxide is relatively safe because its action is short and wears off rapidly once the user starts breathing normal air again. The whole experience of giddiness, giggles, mild hallucinations, and possible blackout is over in a matter of seconds. There is a danger of death by suffocation if the user passes out with a strap-on mask attached. Also, at least 50 percent of inhaled gas must be nitrous oxide for intoxication to occur, so there is partial oxygen starvation unless the gas is mixed with some

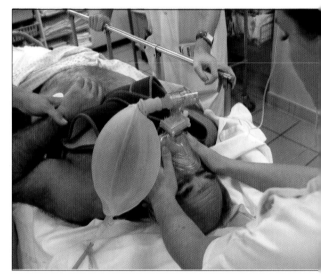

Anesthetists have appropriate equipment and training for the safe use of nitrous oxide in surgery.

pure oxygen. Some neurologists warn that repeated oxygen starvation could cause significant brain damage in the long run. Chronic heavy use can also cause nerve damage by depleting vitamin B_{12}.

Apart from injuries that occur when people pass out and fall onto fires or through windows, there have been cases of frostbite and other injuries when people have inhaled high-pressure freezing-cold gas directly from cylinders. It is safer to release the gas into a balloon or other container before inhaling.

Another source of danger comes from contaminants. Unlike the medical-grade gas, whipped cream canisters contain mineral oil, which forms a mist when the contents are released. Far more dangerous are recipes for making nitrous oxide by chemical means, since the nitrous oxide produced is likely to contain toxic or corrosive contaminants.

M. CLOWES

SEE ALSO:

Ethanol • Gamma-aminobutyric Acid • Inhalants • Ketamine • Naloxone

Norepinephrine

Norepinephrine is the major neurotransmitter that stimulates the sympathetic nervous system. Key to the fight-or flight response, norepinephrine is also implicated in the addictive properties of some drugs.

Norepinephrine, also known as noradrenaline, is a chemical that acts as a neurotransmitter and a hormone. Norepinephrine is released from two main sites: the adrenal glands, situated above the kidneys, and the locus coeruleus in the brain stem. Together with epinephrine (adrenaline), to which it is chemically similar, norepinephrine is released from the adrenal glands in response to a stressful stimulus as part of the fight-or-flight response. Both chemicals stimulate the sympathetic nervous system and prepare the body to cope with danger by increasing the rate and force of heart contractions, thus raising the blood pressure and breathing rate. They also prompt cells to dump glucose and fatty acids into the bloodstream to provide fuel for the muscles.

The locus coeruleus is a pair of nerve clusters situated near the top of the brain stem. The neurons in this region have a blue color and project bilaterally to the cerebral cortex, limbic system, cerebellum, and spinal cord. The wide reach of these modulatory neurons has an effect on many brain systems, particularly those associated with learning and memory, sleep, mood, arousal, and anxiety. In a normal, unstimulated state, the neurons of the locus coeruleus rarely fire. When a stimulus is perceived by the sensory cortex, it is relayed to the thalamus and from there to the brain stem, where it prompts the release of norepinephrine in the locus coeruleus. The individual becomes more attentive to what is happening in the environment around him. If the stimulus continues and becomes perceived as more threatening, a more prolonged release of norepinephrine occurs, activating the sympathetic nervous system. Some of the nerve endings of the sympathetic system act directly on the heart, breathing centers, and blood vessels, and the release of norepinephrine at these sites prepares the body for action.

As with other neurotransmitters, norepinephrine acts at a number of receptor sites known as adrenoceptors. There are two main classes of each type of receptor, alpha and beta, although these are thought to have as many as ten subclasses. Of these, the $alpha_1$, $alpha_2$, $beta_1$, and $beta_2$ receptors are the best studied and have differing effects. $Alpha_1$-adrenoceptors are responsible for mediating the contraction of smooth muscle, particularly that of the blood vessels. $Alpha_2$-adrenoceptors are found on presynaptic nerve terminals, where they act as autoreceptors. Autoreceptors have an inhibitory effect and prevent too much neurotransmitter from being released into the synapse. $Beta_1$-adrenoceptors are found in the heart muscle and increase the rate and force of the heart when the body is under stress, while $beta_2$-adrenoceptors relax smooth muscle. Both types of beta receptors are involved in the conversion of fat and carbohydrate stored in liver and muscle cells into usable fuels. Alpha receptors respond strongly to norepinephrine and only weakly to epinephrine, while beta receptors respond equally strongly to both.

Action of drugs

A number of drugs can stimulate or inhibit the release of norepinephrine from nerve terminals. Stimulants, including amphetamine, Ecstasy, ephedrine, and methamphetamine all increase levels of norepinephrine in the brain, which causes feelings of excitement and leads to an increase in heart rate. Chronic abuse leads to tolerance, and higher and more frequent doses are needed to gain the same high. Amphetamine and methamphetamine can cause psychosis to develop in which the addict suffers from auditory and visual hallucinations, paranoia, and aggression. Cocaine is also believed to increase levels of norepinephrine by preventing its reuptake into the presynaptic neuron. Drugs that act as agonists at $beta_1$ receptors are used to treat cardiac diseases such as angina, high blood pressure, and irregular heartbeat. However, because most of these drugs also act as antagonists on $beta_2$ receptors, they may cause unwanted side effects such as difficulty breathing and cold hands and feet. Beta-

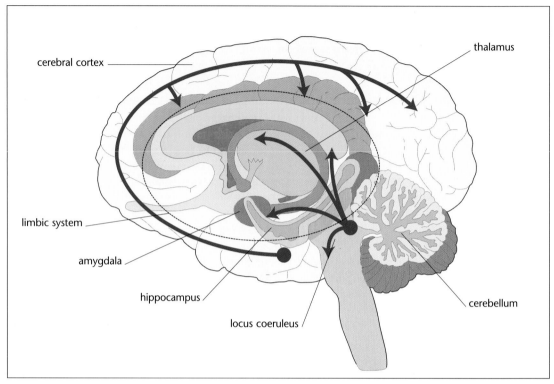

cerebral cortex

thalamus

limbic system

amygdala

hippocampus

locus coeruleus

cerebellum

The norepinephrine system is spread widely through the brain and targets a large number of structures involved in learning, memory, the sleep-wake cycle, and sensory organs that respond to environmental signals.

adrenoceptor antagonists are also used for controlling muscle tremors and anxiety.

Drugs that target the alpha$_2$ receptors can work in different ways, depending on whether they act as agonists or antagonists. Agonists, such as clonidine, can be used to treat migraine and high blood pressure. Clonidine inhibits the release of norepinephrine from sympathetic nerves and acts on centers in the brain that control blood pressure. Antagonists are also used to lower blood pressure and treat cardiac failure as they block the ability of norepinephrine to constrict the blood vessels, causing them to relax and dilate.

Effects on cognitive processes
Studies have shown that norepinephrine plays a key role in sensory processing in the brain and its response to stimulation. Less is known about its effects on behavioral and cognitive processes. There are indications that the norepinephrine pathways may be involved in the reward and drug-seeking behaviors of

people who use amphetamines and cocaine. It has also been suggested that the norepinephrine system may play a role in cognitive and affective disorders, such as attention deficit hyperactivity disorder, posttraumatic stress disorder (PTSD), anxiety, and depression, by increasing norepinephrine levels in the prefrontal cortex regions that control working memory and attention regulation. Further investigations into norepinephrine's role in the formation and retrieval of certain types of memories in the amygdala and hippocampus may explain the recurrence of the disturbing flashbacks experienced by people with PTSD, who show high levels of norepinephrine in cerebrospinal fluid. With depression, memories can be difficult to retrieve. Again, norepinephrine may play a key role in this condition in determining how and what memories are stored.

W. A. HORAN

SEE ALSO:
Central Nervous System • Clonidine • Epinephrine

Opiates and Opioids

The classes of drugs known as opiates and opioids include a wide and diverse range of natural and synthetic chemical compounds derived from opium. Some opioids are produced naturally in the human body.

The opiates are a class of drugs that are collectively known as narcotic analgesics. These drugs have been used for centuries for the purpose of reducing pain. In fact, opium, an extract from the *Papaver somniferum* poppy, is one of the oldest medications. It was known for its behavioral effects and its ability to relieve pain and diarrhea as long ago as 4000 BCE in Sumeria (present-day Iraq). Initially, opium was administered as a vapor through smoking or through punctures in the skin but, because of the variability of the opium content, casualties from respiratory depression were common. The medical potential of opium was greatly improved when its main active ingredient, morphine, was isolated in 1803.

Basic opiates

Although the *Papaver somniferum* can be successfully cultivated in most temperate zones, the majority of the world's supply comes from Afghanistan and Southeast Asia. Opium is first collected as a milky juice that exudes from cuts made on the seed capsules of the poppy. The juice is then dried, yielding a powder that contains more than 25 alkaloids. The most important of these are morphine (10 percent), codeine (0.5 percent), thebaine (0.3 percent), papaverine (1 percent), narcotine (6 percent), and narceine (0.2 percent). Of these natural alkaloids, morphine and codeine have the widest clinical and nonclinical uses. Morphine, the prototypical opiate drug, produces a variety of pharmacological actions, and scientists have been actively investigating the mechanisms that underlie these actions. The activities on the central nervous system that are most explored include relief of pain (analgesia), mood changes (euphoria), reinforcement of behavior, tolerance, and physical and behavioral dependence. In some vulnerable individuals, physical and behavioral dependence make up the major undesirable side effects of the opiate drugs, namely, narcotic addiction. Opiates also act on the gastrointestinal tract, which can result in constipation. The drugs also affect the autonomic nervous system in various ways that reduce respiration, heart rate, and the diameter of pupils (miosis).

The determination of the chemical structure of morphine in 1925 marked the beginning of attempts to produce morphinelike compounds with non-addictive properties, a goal that has yet to be achieved. Nevertheless, much has been learned about the different properties of the opiates. Codeine, which is identical to morphine except for the substitution of a methoxy group ($-OCH_3$) for a hydroxyl group ($-OH$), has reduced hypnotic properties and moderate analgesic effects, making it an ideal compound for the alleviation of mild to moderate pain. A small modification of the morphine molecule (the addition of two acetyl groups, $-OCOCH_3$) produces diacetylmorphine, also known as heroin. The pharmacological effects of heroin and morphine are identical because, once in the brain, heroin is quickly metabolized to monoacetylmorphine and then to morphine. Heroin, however, is around 10 times more potent than morphine because the diacetylation makes it more lipid soluble, thus enhancing its ability to cross the blood-brain barrier and reach specific receptors in the brain.

The basic structure of the morphine molecule can be changed to produce a wide range of compounds with differing properties, effects, and potencies.

OPIOID FAMILIES BASED ON CHEMICAL STRUCTURE				
Morphines	**Morphinans**	**Benzomorphans**	**Phenylpiperidines**	**Diphenylpropyl-**
Acetorphine	Butorphanol	Metazocine	Fentanyl	**amines**
Codeine	Buprenorphine	Pentazocine	Loperamide	Alphamethadol
Heroin	Dextromethorphan		Meperidine	LAAM
Naloxone	Levorphanol			Methadone
Oxycodone				Propoxyphene

Apomorphine, also prepared from morphine, is a potent emetic and dopaminergic agonist. Hydromorphone, oxymorphone, hydrocodone, and oxycodone are also made by modifying the morphine molecule.

Synthetic opiates

In addition to morphine, codeine, and the semisynthetic derivatives of the natural opium alkaloids, there are several classes of clinically useful synthetic drugs with pharmacological activity similar to morphine: the diphenylpropylamines (for example, methadone), the 4-phenylpiperidines (meperidine), the 6,7-benzomorphans (pentazocine), and the morphinans (levorphanol). Although structurally diverse, these compounds all share a piperidine ring or contain a critical part of the ring structure. Additionally, most have a methyl group attached to the ring as well as a variety of other bulky groups. These similarities to morphine are believed to account for the effectiveness in producing analgesia, respiratory depression, gastrointestinal spasms, and physical dependence. Nevertheless, the various structural modifications can change affinities for particular brain receptors, altering opiate activity as agonist or antagonist, and affecting lipid solubility and resistance to metabolic breakdown.

The substitution of an allyl group ($-CH_2CH=CH$) for the methyl group on the nitrogen atom of morphine produces the antagonists naloxone and nalorphine. Although similar to morphine, these compounds do not produce the same physiological response. Furthermore, because of their ability to occupy the same brain receptors at which morphine acts, these antagonists prevent and reverse the effects of opiates. In dependent individuals, administration of naloxone results in sudden displacement of opiates from their receptors, leading to the rapid appearance of withdrawal symptoms. Physical dependence represents an adaptation of the body and brain to the chronic administration of opiates, and it manifests itself as intense physical and psychological disturbances. These disturbances, which are collectively known as withdrawal syndrome, regularly emerge after a period of abstinence from opiates (such as after a night of sleep), and they comprise an array of physiological and psychological effects that are essentially opposite to the acute effects of opiates. Thus, whether induced by abstinence from opiates or by administration of antagonists, the dependent individual will experience enhanced responses to pain (hyperalgesia), negative mood (dysphoria and depression), diarrhea, hyperventilation, pupillary dilation (mydriasis), and a variety of other reactions representing extreme emotional arousal. Although opiate withdrawal is not considered life threatening, and often resembles a severe flulike condition, clinical evidence suggests that the psychological distress associated with withdrawal is extremely aversive, and avoidance of this state motivates opiate dependent individuals to self-administer more of the drug.

The acute effects of opiates are dose dependent. At low to moderate doses (5 to 10 milligrams), the principal effects include analgesia, relaxation, drowsiness, muscle relaxation, mental clouding, and general decreased sensitivity to stimulation. Higher doses, especially if administered intravenously, lead to the experience known as a rush, which is described as a sudden flush of warmth in the stomach. This effect, however, depends on the amount of previous exposure to the drug and on the state of the individual during administration. In fact, pain-free,

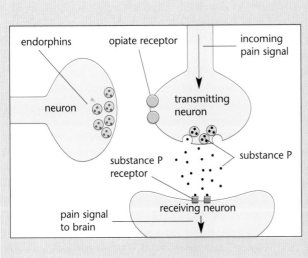

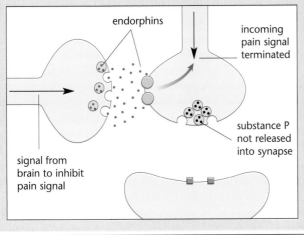

PAIN AND THE BRAIN

One way in which pain signals are deactivated is through natural opioids in the brain. Pain signals are transmitted to the central nervous system by special sensory nerves and small fibers called C fibers. Scientists have discovered that these fibers and some neurons contain a peptide called substance P, which is released into the synapse when a pain signal activates the neuron. Substance P binds with receptors on the receiving neuron and transmits the pain signal to the next neuron in the chain.

When the brain receives the pain signal, it sends out another signal to a neighboring neuron that tells it to release endorphins. The endorphins bind with opiate receptors on the transmitting neuron. By doing so, the endorphins change the chemistry of the transmitting neuron and prevent the vesicles containing substance P from discharging into the synapse, and the pain signal is stopped. When opioids such as morphine or heroin bind with opiate receptors, they produce the same response as endorphins, so they are used extensively in medicine as painkillers.

nondependent individuals may report restlessness, anxiety, and even dysphoria. Nausea is produced at both low and high doses, and occurs in both dependent and nondependent people. Very high doses of opiates lead to respiratory depression, unconsciousness, and death.

Morphine is readily absorbed through most mucous membranes and thus it can be injected subcutaneously, ingested, or snorted. Other routes of administration are common for related compounds, such as heroin or opium that is smoked. The half-life of opiates varies considerably depending on their chemical structures, ranging from 2 hours for morphine to 27 hours for methadone. The kidney is the principal route of excretion; most of the administered drug is found in the urine within 24 hours of administration. Although some morphine is excreted unchanged, a large proportion is metabolized, and there is clear evidence that some of the metabolites (for example, morphine-6-glucuronide) are pharmacologically active.

Opioid peptides and receptors

The search for nonaddictive analgesic drugs conducted in the 1940s and 1960s yielded a number of scientific discoveries, including the discovery that many of the effects of opiates depend on whether the molecule is right- or left-handed. Many of the opiates exist in mirror-image forms that determine the activity of the compound. The left-handed version is usually active, while the right-handed version is essentially inactive. This finding suggested the interesting possibility that the brain contains very specific receptors for opiates. These receptors were eventually identified in animal and human brains by the mid-1970s. This discovery led to the subsequent question of why most animal species would contain receptors for opiates that responded to the activity of the compound. It was postulated that natural opiatelike substances might exist in the brain, and between 1974 and 1975, novel peptides (chains of amino acids) isolated from animal brains were shown to exhibit these properties. The term *opioid* was therefore used to refer to these natural opiatelike substances, and the term *opioid receptor* was used to refer to those receptors that are activated by both opiate drugs and by natural opioid peptides.

Three major types of opioid receptors exist: mu, kappa, and delta. These receptors are widely distributed throughout the brain and spinal cord, with limbic and limbic-association areas in the brain displaying the highest concentrations. All three receptors occur together in some brain regions, although other regions contain only one type. Surprisingly, the distribution of opioid receptors tends to be similar from species to species, although some important differences have been found.

The mu receptor, so-called because it was identified using morphine, has high affinity for morphine and related opiates, and its activation is associated with the induction of analgesia, positive emotional states, cardiovascular and respiratory depression, and other neuroendocrine effects of opiates. Two different mu-opioid receptor subtypes have been identified (mu_1 and mu_2), and they appear to have a differential role in opiate analgesia and opiate dependence. Morphine has greater affinity for the mu_1 receptor. The kappa receptor was identified using ketocyclazocine, an opiate analog that produces hallucinations and dysphoria. The kappa receptor appears to have a role in intestinal motility, pain perception, and neuroendocrine functions. Studies have identified two subtypes of kappa receptors, $kappa_1$ and $kappa_2$, although some scientists have postulated the existence of a $kappa_3$ and a $kappa_4$ receptor. Activation of kappa receptors leads to hallucination, fear, anxiety, and extreme dysphoria, suggesting a possible role of this receptor

in psychosis. The delta receptor (so-called because it is concentrated in the vas deferens), appears to be involved in the sense of smell, motor integration, and cognitive functions. Various subtypes of the delta receptors have been identified ($delta_1$ and $delta_2$), and one of these receptor subtypes has been shown to interact with mu receptors to modulate analgesia.

Endogenous opiates

The brain produces its own natural (endogenous) opioids. The first endogenous opioid peptides were identified in 1975 and were called enkephalins from the Greek word *enkephalin*, "in the head." Two similar pentapeptides were then sequenced and called met-enkephalin and leu-enkephalin, respectively. Shortly afterward, endorphins (from *endo-*, signifying endogenous, and *-orphin*, from the common suffix in the names of opiates) were discovered, followed by the dynorphins. Since then, a large number of different polypeptides with activity at opioid receptors have been identified.

The role of these substances in the body is unclear, but it is thought that they are active in relieving pain and adapting behavior when the body is under stress. By relieving pain, endorphins enable a wounded animal to escape from a threat that would endanger its survival. As such, natural opiates are believed to have played a crucial part in the evolutionary process.

Natural opiates and the receptors to which they bind are located along the pathways in the brain that respond to pain signals from different parts of the body. All endogenous opioid peptides produce a variety of pharmacological effects, including analgesia, respiratory depression, reinforcement, and, depending on the dose, catatonia. These effects are very similar to the effects observed after administration of opiate drugs. Natural activation of opioid peptides is also involved in complex psychological and behavioral functions such as feeding and social bonding. Deregulation of endogenous opioid systems has also been implicated in stress, mood, and mental illnesses, including affective disorders, schizophrenia, autism, and addiction.

F. LERI

SEE ALSO:
Drug Receptors • Endorphins • Morphine • Narcotic Drugs • Opium

Opium

Opium is the base drug for the production of a wide variety of compounds. Obtained from a wild poppy, opium contains morphine, codeine, and thebaine and has been used and abused for its painkilling properties for centuries.

The opium poppy, *Papaver somniferum,* belongs to the Papaveraceae family. It is a hardy annual plant and can endure most climates except extreme cold. The main stem of a mature plant is 2 to 5 feet (0.6–1.5 m) in height. The plant flowers after about 90 days growth. Eventually the petals fall to reveal a round, green seed pod, which contains the opium. The farmer collects the opium by scoring down each pod with a knife so that the sticky gum oozes out and dries on the surface of the pod. The dried gum is then scraped off the pod and shaped into balls or blocks. The raw opium is roasted over a flame and can then be used for smoking. Alternatively, the opium is processed to produce morphine by adding chemicals, such as calcium hydroxide and ammonium chloride, and taking the mixture through a number of heating and cooling stages. To produce heroin from morphine requires additional chemicals and further heating, cooling, and filtration processes. The manufacture of heroin will differ depending on whether the end product is for smoking or injecting.

Background

As an unrivaled painkiller, opium was known across the ancient world. It was first described in detail in the early third century BCE, and 4,000 years before that in Sumeria (present-day Iraq), the image representing the poppy in the Sumerian picture alphabet conveyed the meaning "joy plant." Because of its magical powers to relieve pain and suffering, opium featured significantly in the mythology of ancient Greece. Fertility rites were often associated with opium because the sleep of the poppy was so deep that people appeared to be dead before they awoke; death and rebirth were images associated with the growing seasons and crop cultivation.

Opium was carried eastward to India by traders and reintroduced back into western Europe by the Christian crusaders, who had learned of its powers from Arab doctors. Originally confined to the world of potions and sorcery, by the early sixteenth century opium's value as a medicine was rediscovered. In 1520 Paracelsus, the foremost medical authority of his day, concocted a drink made of opium, wine, and spices, which he named laudanum, "a drink to be praised." For the next 400 years, most opium would be consumed in this form. Opium retained its preeminence down the centuries because medical knowledge was slow to develop. In 1680 the English doctor Thomas Sydenham wrote, "Among the remedies which it has pleased Almighty God to give man to relieve his suffering, none is so universal and so efficacious as opium." Even in the nineteenth century, doctors underwent the minimum of textbook training, had no idea of hygiene or infection, nor any notion of the genesis of diseases. They could do little to relieve suffering other than to turn to practices such as blood letting. The most distressing symptom for patients was pain, and for that there was opium.

Opium as a recreational drug

The smoking of opium for recreational purposes began in China after the introduction of tobacco smoking in the seventeenth century, but the practice did not become endemic until British-owned Indian opium flooded into the country in the nineteenth century. During this time, opium was also the key ingredient for a wide array of patent medicines that came onto the British and American markets, allowing ordinary people who could not afford doctor's fees to self-medicate to relieve pain. The U.S. patent medicine industry was worth some $80 million a year by the end of the nineteenth century.

The most public display of opium use came during the U.S. Civil War (1861–1865). It has been estimated that 10 million opium pills and more than 2 million ounces of other opiate products were distributed to the Union forces alone. Opium was swallowed to kill pain or rubbed into wounds as an anesthetic. Toward the end of the war, morphine injections became common following the invention of the syringe, but injecting led to a rapid rise in opiate addiction.

Opiate use on both sides of the Atlantic was virtually unregulated—what laws were in place had hardly any impact on availability. However, concerns were raised in the pages of the medical press about excessive use of what are now known to be potentially harmful drugs. For example, there were cases of children accidentally overdosing on the "soothing syrups" administered by parents to keep their offspring quiet and, more generally, those who had become dependent on their medication were in a debilitated state. These were clearly reasonable concerns. However, the public health agenda was overlain by a moral argument, which suggested that those who had a drug habit were not simply ill or weak but morally degenerate and in some cases evil. The argument coalesced into an antidrug campaign forged from a loose coalition of organizations and individuals who made up the social reform movements in the United Kingdom and the United States.

Collecting opium is a labor-intensive process. The pods are scraped to release their milky sap, which is then dried and processed.

Chemistry and use

Raw opium contains a number of natural opioid alkaloids. Chief among these are morphine, codeine, and thebaine. Almost all morphine is derived from opium, as it is difficult and expensive to synthesize. Codeine can also be crystallized out as a pure compound. Thebaine has none of the opioid properties that make morphine and codeine useful in relieving pain. It is, however, the source material for manufacture of many of the semisynthetic painkillers, including oxycodone and naloxone.

Opium is rarely used for medicinal purposes in modern times, although tincture of opium (a concentrated alcoholic extract of opium) can be used for acute diarrhea. Even this has been replaced by paregoric, a camphorated tincture of morphine in alcohol that does not cause analgesia or euphoria but that can lead to dependence if used excessively, although the taste tends to put people off. Opium eating is still practiced in countries where poppies are grown, such as India and Afghanistan. Here is it used for its traditional medicinal purposes as a remedy for pain and other ailments.

Sources of opium

For much of the period from 1920 through the 1970s, Turkey was one of the main suppliers of opium for the production of heroin. The raw opium was shipped to Lebanon for processing to morphine, then to the heroin laboratories of Marseille and on to the United States. This chain was known as the French Connection. Once this chain was exposed, production switched to Southeast Asia and the region of Myanmar (Burma), Laos, and Thailand known as the Golden Triangle. Most of the heroin produced there is bound for the United States, although opium from Colombia and Mexico is increasing in market share. The highest opium yields are from Afghanistan, which produces some 75 percent of the world market and 90 percent of the European market.

H. SHAPIRO

Oxycodone

Oxycodone is a prescription opiate used for the treatment of moderate to severe pain. It has been abused as an alternative to heroin, particularly among younger users who may have access to it in the home.

Opium yields a number of alkaloids, including morphine, codeine, papaverine, and thebaine. Thebaine itself has little analgesic effect, but it is a precursor to several important compounds, including the semisynthetic opiate oxycodone.

Oxycodone is typically made into the salt form, oxycodone hydrochloride, a white, odorless crystalline powder that is highly soluble in water and slightly soluble in alcohol. Its half-life in serum following oral administration is quite short, ranging from 3 to 4 hours, which also corresponds to the duration of its analgesic action.

As with other opiates, the most dangerous potential side effect of oxycodone is respiratory depression by direct action on the brain stem respiratory centers. Oxycodone also depresses the cough reflex, constricts the pupils of the eyes, and produces some degree of nausea, vomiting, and slower diges-

tion. Headache, dry mouth, constipation, somnolence, itching, sweating, dizziness, and weakness are also reported by a small percentage of patients.

Oral 5-milligram oxycodone formulations have been available in the United States since the 1950s, typically combined with a coanalgesic agent such as aspirin (Percodan) or acetaminophen (Percocet, Tylox, Roxicet). In large doses, however, aspirin and acetaminophen can be toxic to the liver, stomach, and kidneys. Since the 1990s, single-entity oxycodone products have been available as 5-milligram tablets (Roxicodone, Percolone, OxyIR) and liquid formulations (Oxyfast). These products removed the potential for aspirin or acetaminophen toxicity, but the problems of frequent dosage persisted because of the short half-life of oxycodone.

OxyContin is the brand name of a 12-hour slow-release formulation of oxycodone, available in 10-, 20-, 40-, 80-, and 160-milligram dosage forms. Controlled-release oxycodone is effective in the control of pain caused by cancer, osteoarthritis, major surgery, and degenerative spine disease.

The clinical usefulness of OxyContin, however, has been obscured by its abuse liability, especially in its highest dosage forms. OxyContin abusers either crush the tablets and ingest or snort it, or dilute it in water for injecting. Oral and nasal routes of administration are more common because extra purification steps are required to prepare OxyContin for injection. Regardless of the route of administration, crushing or diluting the tablets disarms the timed-release action of the medication and causes a quick, powerful high, which is liked by users and often preferred to the high produced by heroin, although it is of shorter duration. In some areas of North America, the use of heroin has been overtaken by the abuse of OxyContin.

F. LERI

KEY FACTS

Classification
Schedule II (USA), Schedule I (Canada), Class A (UK), Schedule I (INCB). Opioid.

Street names
Cotton, hillbilly heroin, kicker, O.C., oxy, oxycotton

Short-term effects
Analgesia (pain relief), euphoria, nausea and vomiting, slowed breathing, constipation. Risk of overdose if OxyContin is crushed and injected.

Long-term effects
Tolerance to the analgesic effect and physical dependence. Withdrawal symptoms include muscle spasms, gooseflesh, restlessness, insomnia, diarrhea, and vomiting.

SEE ALSO:

Morphine • Opiates and Opioids • Prescription Drugs

Paraldehyde

Paraldehyde was one of the earliest sedatives to enter medical use. Its effects are similar to those of the barbiturates and benzodiazepines that have replaced its use in surgery and the treatment of agitation and seizures.

Paraldehyde entered medical usage as a sedative in the late nineteenth century. It provided a safer alternative to the bromide salts and chloral hydrate that until then had been the alternative sedatives to alcohol and opium. Paraldehyde was notably useful in calming mentally ill patients whose condition made them agitated or aggressive, and it made the use of physical restraints redundant in most cases. Other applications included the induction of sleep and the treatment of alcohol withdrawal.

In common with other central nervous system depressants, paraldehyde works by increasing the affinity between gamma-aminobutyric acid (GABA) and its receptors. These receptors dampen the neural activity stimulated by glutamate receptors, so paraldehyde has a calming and sedating effect.

Alcohol withdrawal

For many years, paraldehyde was the treatment of choice for alcohol withdrawal. In a landmark article about Alcoholics Anonymous in *The Saturday Evening Post* of March 1, 1941, Jack Alexander described the aroma of paraldehyde in the psychiatric ward of Philadelphia General Hospital as resembling a mixture of alcohol and ether. The aroma would be due to paraldehyde on the patients' breath.

Paraldehyde forms when three molecules of ethanal (acetaldehyde, CH_3CHO) condense together in the presence of sulfuric acid. Despite the suggestion in its name, it is an alcohol rather than an aldehyde.

The role of paraldehyde in alcohol withdrawal was to reduce the incidence and severity of seizures by stimulating the GABA system—a role now overtaken by benzodiazepines. Such intervention is necessary because the GABA receptors of chronic heavy drinkers become desensitized to compensate for the constant presence of alcohol in the brain.

Once alcohol levels start to fall during withdrawal, the blunted GABA system fails to provide sufficient regulation for excitatory nerve impulses, and seizures can result. Paraldehyde provides the necessary stimulation of GABA activity in the place of alcohol and must be withdrawn gradually as the GABA system slowly returns to a healthy level of activity.

Disadvantages

Paraldehyde has a strongly unpleasant odor and taste, which are problematic because much of the drug leaves the body through the lungs. Paraldehyde is an irritant, so injection sites often became inflamed and painful. For this reason, paraldehyde was usually given as a mixture with vegetable oil to be swallowed or deposited in the rectum by syringe. Above all, there is potential for creating paraldehyde dependency in those who are treated with the drug.

The introduction of barbiturates displaced paraldehyde from most applications in the first decade of the twentieth century. In the late twentieth century the introduction of benzodiazepines and major tranquilizers further reduced the need for paraldehyde. Even so, its use continued in a minority of psychiatric hospitals until the end of that century.

Paraldehyde is no longer available for prescription in the United States, where it is a Schedule IV controlled substance. It continues to be a raw material in the manufacture of certain plastics.

M. Clowes

See also:
Alcohol • Barbiturates • Benzodiazepines • Chloral Hydrate • Gamma-aminobutyric Acid

PCP

PCP is a dissociative drug that was tested as a human anesthetic before becoming a street drug. It has potential for causing powerful hallucinations and occasional psychotic behavior in patients and recreational users.

Pharmaceuticals company Parke, Davis developed phencyclidine in the 1950s as a safer alternative to barbiturates for human anesthesia. Its alternative name, PCP, is an abbreviation of the chemical name for phencyclidine: 1-(1-*phenylcyclohexyl*)*p*iperidine.

An alternative anesthetic was desirable because of the tendency of barbiturates to suppress breathing at anesthetic dosages. Early clinical trials indicated phencyclidine to be an effective anesthetic for use alone or with a reduced dosage of barbiturate. Furthermore, it produced its effects without hindering respiration. By the end of the 1950s, Parke, Davis had patented phencyclidine and created the Sernyl brand of phencyclidine anesthetic.

Anesthetic properties

Human trials revealed PCP to produce a state of anesthesia in which the patient was conscious but unaware of pain, free of distress, and unable to move voluntarily. This condition was called a cataleptoid state at the time of early trials, but later became known as dissociative anesthesia. In this state of anesthesia, the patient's conscious mind is isolated from signals from the body that supports it. Complete unconscious sedation for surgery can be achieved by increasing the dosage above that for dissociative anesthesia or by additional use of other medications. However, the state of untroubled, pain-free wakefulness was considered potentially useful for childbirth and some surgical procedures.

Negative effects

Phencyclidine revealed itself to be far from ideal for anesthesia in 1957, during the first trials on humans. The principal problems with phencyclidine were due to patients emerging from anesthesia in distressed and agitated states, sometimes suffering from delusions, hallucinations, or psychotic episodes. Slow elimination caused these symptoms to last for several hours and sometimes days. Over time it became clear that these side effects made PCP unsuitable for human use, and Parke, Davis withdrew Sernyl in

---

KEY FACTS

Classification
Schedule II (USA), Schedule I (Canada), Class A (UK), Schedule II (INCB). Dissociative hallucinogen.

Form
As the hydrochloride salt in powders, pills, capsules, or solutions. Impregnated into or sprinkled over leaves of kitchen herbs, marijuana, or tobacco for smoking.

Street names
Angel dust, embalming fluid, peace pill, rocket fuel, wack. Mixed with marijuana: crystal supergrass, killer weed, KJs (killer joints, krystal joints). Mixed with crack: space base. PCP is also sold as other drugs, notably as pure THC (tetrahydrocannabinol).

Short-term effects
Mild doses cause euphoria, increased breathing and heart rate, sweating, nausea, and vomiting. Moderate doses numb physical and emotional pain and can cause out-of-body sensations and other hallucinations. Delusions of extreme physical strength are common, as are anxiety, aggression, lack of reasoning, paranoia, and psychotic behavior. Speech becomes garbled. Some users fall into an unresponsive state of catatonia. High doses kill by stopping heart and lung functions.

Dangers
Self injury is likely owing to failure of judgment and the inability to feel pain. Accidents are the principal cause of death through PCP use. Paranoia, aggression, and feelings of strength can exacerbate problems in encounters with law enforcers. Potential exists for irreversible brain damage and changes in behavior and mental capacity. Pregnant users risk fetal brain damage leading to mental retardation of their children.

1965. Having failed for humans, phencyclidine reappeared in 1967 as Sernylan, a veterinary anesthetic that persisted on the market for over a decade.

PCP use in the 1960s

As far as is known, the first wave of recreational PCP use occurred in 1967 and was based around the Haight Ashbury district of San Francisco. The reception of PCP on the drug scene was mixed, since it was nearly impossible to judge the outcome of any given PCP experience. The most usual format was in pills that took full effect after around 30 minutes, by which time the user was committed to the effects of whatever dose he or she had taken.

Users seeking the euphoria of a light dose often became overwhelmed by sinister and powerful hallucinations with distortions of their own body images. Some believed they had died, some had hallucinations of traveling through a dark tunnel toward a light—a typical near-death hallucination. Inevitably, many recreational users also suffered the psychoses that occurred in clinical trials.

While a few recreational users enjoyed the feeling of mind separating from body and the profundity of hallucinations on PCP, the widespread opinion was that it was an unpredictable and risky drug. Upbeat

street names such as peace pill and angel dust failed to boost the popularity of PCP in the recreational drug community, and its bad reputation practically killed off its street use by the end of the 1960s.

1970s to 1990s

Undaunted by failure in the 1960s, drug dealers began to reintroduce PCP in the early 1970s. This time the emphasis was on PCP-containing solutions and powders that could be injected, snorted, or mixed into materials for smoking. These methods deliver the drug to the brain much more quickly than swallowing a pill that has to break down in the stomach and be absorbed into the bloodstream, so the full effects were felt in three minutes or less, compared with half an hour or more for a pill.

The change in format made it easier to reach the desired level of high by taking multiple small doses and waiting for effects. In theory, this change might have improved sales by making the drug seem more controllable. Also, the euphoric rush of a small dose would be greater as its effects took hold more rapidly. In practice, the reputation of PCP was so bad that few people would knowingly buy it when more reliable highs were available from other drugs.

In another ploy, dealers sold PCP under the guise of another street drug with a better reputation. The most frequent ruse was to sell PCP as "pure" tetrahydrocannabinol (THC), the main active compound in cannabis products. Alternatively, PCP was soaked into poor-quality marijuana or dried leaves of other plants with no psychoactivity to then be sold as marijuana leaves. Some PCP was sold as hallucinogens such as LSD, psilocybin, and mescaline, or mixed with the authentic products as a cheap but potent filler. Only a small proportion of the all PCP in street trade was sold as PCP itself. As a result, many casualties of the PCP trade took the drug in the belief that it was another substance whose effects were familiar to them, and subsequently became overwhelmed by the potent effects of PCP.

Dealers made such efforts to market PCP because it is potent yet cheap and easy to make, and hence has great potential for making profit. When Parke, Davis withdrew the drug in 1978, clandestine factories were already capable of supplying the street.

PCP JARGON

The nature of PCP's subjective effects varies greatly, depending on dosage and user sensitivity. Various terms have arisen to describe different states of PCP intoxication, and four of these terms have been adopted by researchers.

"Buzzed" refers to a mild stimulant high that occurs at low doses and does not interfere with senses or actions. "Wasted" is the state when coordination and senses start to fail; the user has odd sensations, such as the feeling of walking on spongy ground. "Ozoned" is when the still-conscious user can hardly move or communicate sensibly. "Overdosed" is when the user loses consciousness; in this context, the term usually refers to having taken too much PCP to be able to enjoy its psychoactive effects.

MEDIA FRENZY

Lurid reports of bizarre and dangerous behavior caused by drug use are standard media fare. It is no surprise that PCP is a good target for such reporting, since it has a well-documented ability to cause psychotic states in clinical trials.

In 1980 the *Journal of Psychedelic Drugs* published a study by John Morgan and Doreen Kagan of media coverage of PCP. The authors found 323 articles on PCP in a selection of U.S. newspapers between 1958 and 1979. Of this total, 247 articles appeared in 1978; a fall to 42 articles in 1979 showed that the main swell of media interest in PCP had passed by that year.

The flood of PCP horror stories followed in the wake of interviews with R. Stanley Burns in the journal *Emergency Medicine* (1976) and on the television show *60 Minutes* (October 23, 1977). Burns was coauthor of a clinical report on PCP in 1975, but it was in the subsequent interviews that he mentioned murders, suicides, and accidental deaths by burning and drowning while under the influence of PCP. Burns formed a corporation offering PCP-related advice and treatment with Steven Lerner, who contributed PCP horror stories in the *60 Minutes* interview, and Ronald Linder. Lerner went on to make several appearances in topical television programs and to act as a PCP consultant to popular television dramas.

Many of the PCP-related horror stories that went into print featured different locations and people but were substantially similar, suggesting that a single story had become distorted by retelling. The story that recurred most often was that of a person—usually male—who gouged out his or her own eyes while in custody after arrest. Some versions specified a male Baltimore college student, in one case the son of a Massachussetts member of Congress, who had been arrested for indecent exposure.

In their report, Morgan and Kagan identified a police case from 1971 that they suggested to be a possible origin of the oft-cited PCP story. The subject of this case was Charles Innes, a college dropout living in Baltimore who was the son of a state legislator from Massachusetts.

During a police raid at his home, Innes swallowed a drug that was later identified as LSD. No test for PCP was performed. Four days later, Innes was arrested after an incident of public nudity and subsequently blinded himself in jail. Innes claimed he had taken PCPA (para-chlorophenylalanine), a street drug completely unrelated to PCP despite the common initials. On this basis, it seems feasible that the most popular "PCP" story of the late 1970s was in fact a retelling of an old story related to a different drug.

Despite the initial unpopularity of PCP, some people became regular users of the drug. Its popularity peaked in the 1980s but declined into the mid 1990s as a result of users perceiving the potential of PCP for causing long-term brain damage. Clinical tests suggest that long-term PCP use might indeed cause neurological problems with symptoms such as poor memory, depression, and psychosis.

Current status

Reports suggest that PCP use has declined since 2001, when the U.S. National Institute on Drug Abuse (NIDA) listed PCP as an emerging drug after an upsurge in PCP-related deaths and emergency room (ER) admissions. In 2008, 99,000 Americans age 12 and older had abused PCP at least once during the previous year, according to the National Survey on Drug Use and Health. Other data suggest that early adolescents usually lose interest in the drug by the end of their teens. Nevertheless, the proven contribution of PCP to accidental deaths and the possible risk of cumulative brain damage through long-term PCP use are cause for concern.

M. CLOWES

SEE ALSO:

Cutting Drugs • Illicit Manufacturing • Ketamine • PCP Analogs

PCP Analogs

PCP analogs are chemical relatives of phencyclidine that share at least some of its psychoactive properties. The analogs include medical anesthetics, illicit drugs, and experimental compounds for research into the brain and addiction.

When a chemical compound has clear physiological or psychoactive effects, the testing of related compounds is a routine approach to studying how the parent compound works and searching for new compounds with better therapeutic effects or fewer side effects.

One reason for the study of PCP analogs is that this otherwise useful anesthetic has an ability to cause psychotic and catatonic states that are hard to distinguish from symptoms of schizophrenia. Hence, many related compounds have been produced in the search for an anesthetic that is less likely to cause such disturbances.

The search for alternative anesthetics led to the development of eticyclidine (PCE), rolicyclidine (PCPy), and tenocyclidine (TCP)—all of which are now INCB Schedule I drugs—as well as ketamine and tiletamine. Ketamine is still used as a human and veterinary anesthetic, and tiletamine is used in conjunction with a benzodiazepine as an anesthetic for large animals. All these drugs have similar effects to PCP and have also been manufactured illicitly for sale as recreational drugs.

General patterns

The structural unit responsible for activity, or pharmacophore, seems to be cyclohexylamine with an aromatic ring attached to the same carbon atom as carries the nitrogen atom. At least 30 variants on this structure have been sold as street drugs, and the potencies of these variants follow certain trends.

An increase in activity occurs when a thienyl group replaces the phenyl group of PCP, as is the case for TCP. Activity drops when there are additional groups on the phenyl group, such as the chloro (Cl–) group in ketamine. The strongest effects occur when the nitrogen atom is part of a ring system such as piperidine (as in PCP) or pyrrolidine (as in PCPy). If a straight hydrocarbon chain replaces a ring, the loss of potency is least for an ethyl group (C_2H_5–),

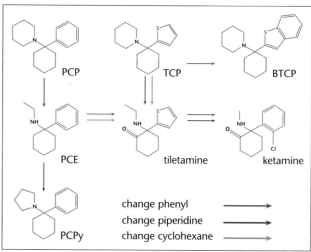

as in PCE and tiletamine. Compounds with other numbers of carbon atoms have reduced potency.

Experimental drugs

PCP affects many neurotransmitter systems. Its characteristic interaction is with sites near NMDA glutamate receptors, but it also interacts with dopamine, serotonin, and norepinephrine systems—targets for cocaine and other stimulants—as well as with acetylcholine, endorphin, and sigma receptors.

PCP analogs vary greatly in their interactions with different types of receptors, and some have effects that are not typical of PCP. In particular, BTCP has interactions that resemble those of cocaine. This PCP analog can quell a dependent's craving for cocaine without creating a habit. As such, it has potential for use in treating dependency. On the other hand, it is also possible that clandestine chemists will find other PCP analogs that they can manufacture as cheap but powerfully addictive substitutes for cocaine.

M. Clowes

Pentazocine

Pentazocine is a synthetic opioid drug that is used as a painkiller and is abused for its mood-altering effects. To prevent the drug from being used intravenously, many pentazocine formulations are made with a built-in antidote.

Pentazocine belongs to the class of drugs called opioid analgesics (narcotic painkillers). It is a synthetic benzomorphan compound that has effects similar to morphine. Narcotic drugs act at specific sites on nerve cells in the brain and spinal cord called opioid receptors, which reduce the sensation of pain. There are different types of opioid receptors, and most narcotic painkillers act at the mu-receptor to cause their effects. Pentazocine has a weaker effect through the mu-receptors and, if taken with a drug that fully activates mu-receptors (for example, morphine), it will compete and can antagonize the effects of the more powerful drug. This effect can cause withdrawal symptoms in patients dependent on drugs that act via the mu-receptors.

Pentazocine is used for the relief of moderate to severe pain. The analgesic effect occurs with very small doses (as low as 25 milligrams) and lasts for approximately three hours, necessitating repeated doses for long-term pain management. It is most commonly taken by mouth, though preparations for injection are available for hospital use. Another property of the drug is that it causes sedation, which can be useful in patients prior to surgery.

Beyond the clinically useful analgesic properties of pentazocine, it has characteristic adverse effects. These include some of the typical side effects of opioid drugs, such as changes in mood, excessive sedation, nausea, and depression of breathing. Hallucinations and thought disturbances are occasionally seen with pentazocine use, effects possibly due to the drug acting at the sigma-receptor.

Pentazocine, like other narcotic analgesic dugs, has a known abuse and dependence liability due to its mood-altering effects. However, the liability for drug dependence is reportedly less than with patients taking morphine, and consequently, withdrawal symptoms are generally less severe. It is commonly abused in the pill form, but injection of the contents of crushed pills is another method of taking the drug. For this reason, certain pill formulations of pentazocine (Talwin NX) include small doses of

---

KEY FACTS

Classification
Schedule IV (USA), Schedule I (Canada), Class B (UK), Schedule III (INCB). Opioid.

Street names
One and ones, poor man's heroin, T's and B's, T's and R's, Talwin

Short-term effects
Analgesia (pain relief), sedation, changes in mood (for example, euphoria), respiratory depression

Long-term effects
Tolerance to the analgesic effect, physical and psychological dependence (after repeated use, but less than with morphine), withdrawal symptoms if drug is abruptly stopped

---

naloxone, an opioid antagonist (antidote). If taken by mouth, the antagonist is not absorbed and therefore does not interfere with the painkiller. However, if the pills are crushed and injected intravenously, naloxone can counteract the effects of pentazocine. These preparations are designed to reduce the drug's abuse potential. Pentazocine is often abused in combination with certain stimulants (such as Ritalin) or antihistamines to enhance the effects on mood, giving a greater rush to the user. Known on the street as "poor man's heroin," these drugs in combination reportedly mimic the effects of heroin taken with cocaine.

J. DERRY, A. KAPUR

SEE ALSO:

Agonists and Antagonists • Morphine • Naloxone • Opiates and Opioids

Pentobarbital

Pentobarbital is a barbiturate, one of a class of sedative drugs that are also effective in preventing seizures and treating anxiety. It is a central nervous system depressant, with behavioral effects similar to those of alcohol.

The barbiturates were introduced at the turn of the twentieth century for use as sleep-inducing agents. The popularity of pentobarbital was related in part to its accompanying feelings of relaxation and euphoria. With the introduction of benzodiazepines, barbiturate use declined markedly, and pentobarbital is now rarely used to aid sleep.

As an intravenous medication, pentobarbital is used for induction of surgical anesthesia due to the extremely rapid loss of consciousness. Pentobarbital also reduces brain metabolic activity and decreases brain swelling after injury, leading to its use by neurosurgeons to help the brain recover after a severe trauma. Pentobarbital is used by addicts for its antianxiety and euphoric effects, or as a "downer" by polydrug abusers to reduce the anxiety and unpleasant side effects of repeated stimulant use.

Use and abuse

Barbiturates work by enhancing the action of the inhibitory neurotransmitter GABA at its receptor on brain neurons. Pentobarbital acts as a central nervous system depressant, slowing reaction times, dulling the senses, and causing "drunken" incoordination and slurring of speech before inducing sleep. Tolerance develops quickly and contributes to the addictive potential. A typical adult oral dose of pentobarbital for sleep induction is 100 milligrams, though abusers may take several pills once tolerance develops. The respiratory depressive effect persists, hence the risk of a dangerous overdose increases with prolonged use. Street addicts will sometimes dissolve the contents of the capsule in water and inject pentobarbital intravenously, a dangerous practice since the drug passes quickly through the blood-brain barrier: an overdose can kill within minutes. Pentobarbital is often taken together with other depressant drugs, including the opiates and alcohol, which increases the likelihood of respiratory depression. Barbiturate intoxication also impairs the memory, so users may forget that they have taken it and take additional doses. The drug is metabolized in

the liver, and prolonged use induces the liver to synthesize more enzymes, leading to faster breakdown and contributing to tolerance.

Dependence on the drug manifests initially as insomnia, but later can result in a severe withdrawal syndrome beginning 8 to 12 hours after the last dose, consisting of anxiety, muscle twitches, tremors, nausea and vomiting, delirium, and seizures. These symptoms last up to 5 days and can be fatal. Pentobarbital addiction is usually treated by decreasing the dose by 10 percent per day. Alternatively, it can be replaced by substituting phenobarbital, a longer acting barbiturate, which prevents withdrawal but no longer causes a "high," and gradually reducing the dose.

L. J. GREENFIELD, JR.

SEE ALSO:

Amobarbital • Barbiturates • Secobarbital • Sedatives and Hypnotics

242

Pharmaceutical Industry

Many of the drugs that people abuse started out as therapeutic drugs to alleviate symptoms such as pain and depression. Developing drugs is expensive, but the market for pharmaceuticals is enormous and still growing.

The pharmaceutical industry's origins lie in the use of herbal potions and wound dressings by "wise women" and "medicine men" in early human society. The earliest written references to a trade in drugs are from the Sumerian culture of Mesopotamia (modern Iraq) where the opium poppy, known as *hul gil,* the "joy plant," was cultivated; opium, the dried resin secreted from incisions made in the unripe seed pod, was exported to Egypt.

By the classical period in the Mediterranean basin (500 BCE–400 CE), a professional class of physicians and apothecaries were trading proprietary concoctions for the cure of various ills. The decline of the Roman Empire inhibited development, although the rise of Islamic medicine preserved classical works on pharmacy through the European Dark Ages. These works provided a basis for renewed research into drugs in early modern Europe. Around 1527, the apothecary and scientist Paracelsus is credited with inventing laudanum, a solution of unrefined opium dissolved in concentrated alcohol obtained via the recently invented pot-still distillation process.

The commercial history of the early pharmaceutical industry is one of individual entrepreneurs marketing patent or proprietary medicine. Patrick Anderson's "Scotch Pills" were widely sold in Britain from the 1630s, and an opium solution, "Sydenham's Laudanum," was first marketed in England in 1680. Many patent medicines contained high levels of poisons such as antimony and mercury. Nonetheless, self-medication was cheaper than consulting a physician. Rising prosperity led to manufacturing and marketing improvements and increased sales of laudanum, popular sedatives, and restoratives such as Dr. Solomon's brandy- and herb-based "Balm of Gilead" and the many brands of "digestive" pills.

Development of pharmaceutical chemistry

Infusions of cinchona tree bark and raw opium poppy resin were known to be effective treatments for malaria and pain before it was understood that such plant products contained active drug

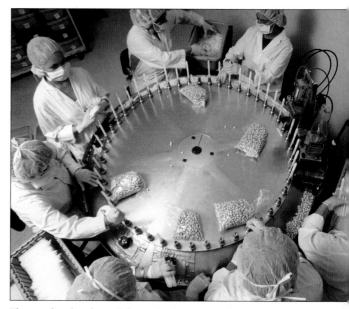

The market for drugs is huge. In 2000 more than $317 billion was spent on pharmaceutical products globally, nearly half of this by U.S. consumers.

compounds, which could be purified to give more reproducible effects. Advances in analytical chemistry in the late eighteenth century stimulated efforts to isolate pure drugs, and in 1803 the German pharmacist Friedrich Sertürner discovered that a single alkaloid chemical was the active ingredient of opium, comprising 9 to 15 percent of unrefined opium. He named it morphine, after Morpheus, the Greek god of dreams.

In 1820 two French chemists, Pierre-Joseph Pelletier and Joseph-Bienamié Caventou, purified quinine from the bark of the cinchona tree. Within a few years pure quinine was available to treat malaria. In 1856 William Perkins, an 18-year-old English chemist, attempted to synthesize quinine in the laboratory. Perkins failed to synthesize quinine but he did synthesize "mauve," the first water-fast synthetic textile dye and the catalyst for the rapid expansion of a chemical dye manufacturing industry.

The nineteenth-century dye industry was the progenitor of the modern pharmaceutical industry. It recruited highly trained chemists into the first industrial research laboratories and had close links to university laboratories, particularly in Germany. In 1889 the German medical researcher Paul Ehrlich noticed that the synthetic dye methylene blue stained microscopic malaria parasites inside human blood cells. He reasoned that because the dye stained the parasites, it might also kill them. In 1891, in the first clinical trial of the first synthetic drug ever used in humans, Ehrlich cured two patients of malaria with methylene blue. German dye manufacturers such as Friedrich Bayer began to diversify into profitable new pharmaceutical ventures, recruiting research teams to develop new drugs such as synthetic antimalarials, using methylene blue as a prototype compound.

Aspirin and the modern pharmaceutical industry

Around 400 BCE the Greek physician Hippocrates prescribed extracts of the white willow tree, *Salix alba,* for the relief of pain and fever, particularly in pregnant women. In 1828 Johan Andreas Buchner purified an extract of willow bark and named it "salicin." By 1859 the chemical structure of salicylic acid was derived by Hermann Kolbe of Marburg University. His student, Friedrich von Heyden established a business in Dresden, manufacturing salicylic acid to reduce fevers and relieve rheumatic stiffness and pain.

Salicylic acid has an unpleasant taste and causes stomach irritation. To improve the prototype, in 1897 a Bayer chemist, Felix Hoffmann, synthesized acetylsalicylic acid, a derivative with reduced side effects, effective as an analgesic, anti-inflammatory and fever-reducing drug. Bayer registered this compound in 1899 as aspirin. Aspirin was originally marketed as a powder but was quickly formulated by Bayer into a stamped tablet, to standardize dosage and prevent adulteration. Aspirin remains the most consumed drug in history, more than 100 billion tablets being taken per year.

Two interesting twists that were to exert significant influence on the twentieth-century pharmaceutical industry can be added to the story of aspirin. Aspirin was not only a major commercial and medical success, it was seen as a demonstration of the scientific and industrial might of an increasingly nationalistic

Germany in a politically unstable world. During World War I (1914–1918) both the United Kingdom and the United States seized German assets, including Bayer's New York aspirin factory and its patents, licences, and trademarks. The bitterness this caused contributed to the exacerbation of normal commercial rivalries in the postwar pharmaceutical industry, which became organized on decidedly nationalistic and somewhat cartelized lines. In 1986, 61 years after their confiscation, Bayer AG of Germany paid $800 million dollars for the right to use their name and the "aspirin" trademark in the United States to Sterling Drug.

The second twist is that Bayer's management was initially cool toward Hoffmann's work on aspirin and much more interested in another of their research laboratory's discoveries, diacetylmorphine, which was seen as a promising treatment for coughs in an era when lung diseases such as pneumonia and tuberculosis were the leading causes of death. Thought to be nonaddictive, indeed useful in suppressing morphine addiction and withdrawal symptoms, this compound was marketed with the brand name "Heroin." Unfortunately, heroin itself proved to be dangerously addictive and rapidly became the most notorious illegal narcotic in history.

The age of chemotherapy

The truly important age of pharmaceutical advancement was ushered in by Paul Ehrlich's discovery of Salvarsan in 1909. Marketed by Hoechst, Salvarsan was the first effective cure for syphilis, a hitherto incurable degenerative venereal disease transmitted by the bacteria-like spirochete *Treponema pallidium.* Sulphonamide, the first of the class of drugs now referred to as "antibiotics," was developed in 1934 by May & Baker, a British subsidiary of the French pharmaceutical combine Rhone-Poulenc.

World War II (1939–1945) forced the pace of drug development, particularly the search for effective antimalarials such as mepacrine and paludrine. Chloroquine, a novel synthetic derivative of quinine, was to play a major role in the eradication of malaria from Europe and North America in the early 1950s.

There were spectacular advances in disease treatment. The most famous was penicillin—a "miracle" drug effective against a broad spectrum of bacterial infections, including wound infections,

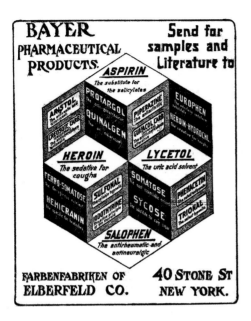

An early advertisement for two of Bayer's most famous products—aspirin and heroin.

venereal diseases, and respiratory tract infections. Several British and American firms, now household names, owed their early success to penicillin sales. The 1950s saw the development and mass production of new classes of antibiotics, such as tetracycline, chloramphenicol, and erythromycin, all major medical and commercial successes. With the development in the 1950s of effective combination antibiotic treatments for tuberculosis, using drugs such as rifampicin, streptomycin, and isoniazid, many once common diseases nearly disappeared from the developed world. By 1970 the United States surgeon general declared that infectious disease was no longer a significant health problem in the United States.

Sedatives, stimulants, and the relief of depression

The commercial success of the sedative-hypnotic barbiturates, such as veronal (introduced in 1903) and phenobarbitol (introduced in 1912), encouraged development of new sedatives and sleeping pills. Stimulant drugs such as the amphetamine benzedrine were also developed and introduced in the 1920s and 1930s, initially for the treatment of asthma and lung congestion. These were widely used by all sides during World War II to counter exhaustion in fighting men.

Problems with addiction and recreational use (also a problem with amphetamines) led to a gradual replacement, in the 1960s, of barbiturates with non-barbiturate "tranquilizers," such as diazepam (Valium) and chlordiazepoxide (Librium). Although heavily prescribed and extremely profitable to their manufacturers (principally Hofmann-LaRoche), by the end of the 1970s the side effects and dependence induced by tranquilizers reduced their popularity, although they remain as widely prescribed as mood-altering drugs.

Research to find safer antidepressants led to the discovery of the specific serotonin reuptake inhibitors (SSRIs). Marketed by Eli Lilly in 1987 as Prozac, SSRIs have proven very successful in relieving anxiety and depression. The wide prescription of Prozac, particularly in the United States, has ensured its commercial success, but it remains to be seen if the SSRI drugs will avoid following the same path as the barbiturates and tranquilizers from enthusiastic reception to ultimate disillusion.

Regulation of pharmaceutical products

Morphine was first marketed as a painkiller and cure for opium addiction. Its sale was completely unregulated. However, its use as an anesthetic and for dysentery treatment during the U.S. Civil War (1861–1865) led to the creation of the so-called army disease—morphine addiction—suffered by half a million veterans. By 1890 the United States had started to legislate to control narcotic drugs, initially by imposing a tax on opium and morphine sales. In 1905 the U.S. Congress banned the sale of opium and in 1906 passed the landmark Federal Pure Food and Drug Act. This law required all pharmaceutical products and patent medicines to have an accurate description of their complete contents on the label.

The 1906 act was concerned solely with drug purity but was amended in 1937 to impose product safety standards. These required analysis of product toxicity to be submitted to the Food and Drug Administration (FDA) before approval for marketing could be granted. Further regulation was introduced in the 1960s in both Europe and the United States following the thalidomide scandal. Thalidomide, a sedative-hypnotic with no advantage over existing products, was introduced in Europe but not the United States, where it had not been licensed. It caused severe birth defects after prescription to pregnant women for morning sickness. The 1962 Harris-Kefauver amendment to the Pure Food and Drug Act introduced stringent new standards of pharmacologic and toxicological testing before any drug could be tested in humans and required that proof of superior efficacy be demonstrated for new drugs.

Globalization of the pharmaceutical industry

The FDA system of approval has been copied throughout the world and has driven consolidation of the pharmaceutical industry. The costs of research and development (R&D) and regulatory compliance have driven the evolution of "Big Pharma" such that a few large companies now dominate the global market. In order of sales in 2009, the biggest drug companies are Johnson & Johnson (U.S.) and Pfizer (U.S.). The 12 largest corporations sell around half of all drugs sold globally and had combined revenues of around $440 billion. Mergers and acquisitions occur frequently in this highly competitive industry. In 2009 Merck acquired Schering-Plough ($41 billion), Pfizer acquired Wyeth ($68 billion), and Roche acquired Genentech ($47 billion).

In 2007, the United States spent $287 billion on pharmaceutical drugs out of total health costs of $2.6 trillion. This was around 10 percent of the total U.S. health expenditure, which comprises 16 percent of Gross Domestic Product. An average of around $700 was spent on prescription drugs by each American, while Japan spent around $450 per person annually and the United Kingdom around $250. The developing world, including China and India, spent less than $30 per person annually.

Problems and challenges

Individual drug companies face a less certain future. It has proved impossible to predict whether scientific ideas can be translated into safe and effective medical treatments. More than 75 percent of the 5,000 candidate drugs under current development will fail to be approved for marketing, and even approved drugs are sometimes recalled following new revelations of risks to users. Drug companies are spending an average of $800 million and 15 years on each drug that reaches the market. Patent protection from legal copying of a drug by "generic" manufacturers with no R&D costs is limited to 20 years from the date of

filing the first patent application. As a result of these costs and time frames, despite increased research expenditure, companies are experiencing diminishing returns and are thus introducing fewer new drugs.

Conditions remaining without cures are more complex than those tackled at an earlier stage in the industry's development. A major problem is the new wave of infectious disease. In 1984 a new disease was recognized, the acquired immunodeficiency syndrome (AIDS), caused by the rapidly mutating human immunodeficiency virus (HIV) transmitted through blood products and sexual contact. A huge effort by the pharmaceutical industry has succeeded in delivering new antiviral drugs that delay the onset of severe manifestations of the infection.

Antiretrovirals have saved many lives, but they have severe side effects and have to be taken for the rest of the patient's lifetime. Compared with the antibiotic miracle cures of the past, this is a partial success. Furthermore, the ethics of a situation in which HIV-positive Westerners have access to expensive drugs while poor Africans and Asians frequently do not, are now hotly debated. In a more educated and skeptical world, laboratory success has not brought the public admiration that was accorded to the early pioneers of the pharmaceutical industry.

These factors have contributed to a crisis in the pharmaceutical industry. If highly successful drugs emerge from 5 percent of research projects, then a company needs to support 20 projects to ensure profitability. The model breaks down, however, if the rate of success falls and costs per project rise, as has occurred. Attempts to pass increasing development costs on to consumers have led to media criticism and political opposition, notably in the case of HIV therapy costs in Africa. It remains to be seen whether scientific advances into genomic medicine, bioinformatics, and computerized chemistry can be combined with changes in the business model, such as the trend toward "biotech start-up" companies, thereby renewing the smaller flow of curative drugs and the confidence of the industry.

D. E. ARNOT

SEE ALSO:

Pharmacokinetics

For drugs to work in the body, they must overcome a number of physiological barriers to reach their site of action. The study of how drugs are taken into, metabolized by, and eliminated from the body is called pharmacokinetics.

Pharmacokinetics is the study of how drugs are taken into the body (absorption), distributed among body tissues (distribution), broken down or changed by body organs (metabolism), and eliminated from the body (excretion). These factors differ markedly between drugs and are critical determinants of how drugs behave in the body. The ultimate effect of a drug depends on its interaction with receptors, which are proteins in the cell membrane with sites where the drug binds tightly, changing the shape of the protein and resulting in chemical or electrical signals within the cell. These factors will be considered in more detail below. However, the ability of the drug to reach its receptor, and how long it stays there, can be equally important in determining a drug's effect. For example, heroin and morphine are both drugs that act on opioid receptors in specific areas of the brain, causing narcotic effects including pain relief, sleepiness, euphoria, and respiratory depression. They differ only by the presence of two acetate (CH_3CO) groups on heroin that make it more lipid (fat) soluble. The increased lipid solubility helps heroin cross cell membranes, enabling rapid transport across the blood-brain barrier. As a result of this pharmacokinetic property, high drug levels occur quickly in the brain and produce the rush desired by addicts, which may increase its addictive potential relative to morphine. Understanding the pharmacokinetics of a drug is key to knowing how abusers will get it into their bodies and how it will behave when it gets there.

Routes of administration

Use of mind-altering substances like alcohol, opium, cocaine, and marijuana has occurred since prehistoric times, and a variety of methods have been devised for taking in these and more recently discovered substances. Specific routes of administration are used for individual drugs, often defined by social customs that vary over time. Psychotropic substances were initially discovered by chewing, eating, or drinking natural products, and this mode is still used for both traditional, unrefined substances (for example, peyote, coca leaves, betel nuts) and highly purified pharmaceuticals.

Smoking of tobacco, opium, and marijuana dates back 2,000 to 4,000 years. Burning the drug-bearing plant matter suspends microscopic organic particles in air, where they can be inhaled into the lungs and rapidly absorbed through the thin alveolar lining into

For administration routes other than intravenous, drugs have to pass through a number of biological membranes before they reach the blood plasma. Once in the plasma, they are taken to their site of action or can be transferred to other extravascular body fluids that surround the target receptors. Waste products and metabolites are removed from the body by excretion.

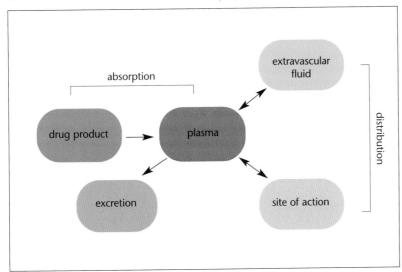

lung capillaries. Smoking is an efficient method for getting drugs into the bloodstream; nicotine reaches the brain within eight seconds of being inhaled. However, smoking also generates more than 4,000 gaseous and particulate compounds, including tar (composed of aromatic hydrocarbons that are often carcinogenic), carbon monoxide, nitrogen oxides, hydrocarbons, sulfur-containing compounds, ketones, alcohols, and aldehydes. Inhalation can also be used for volatile hydrocarbons (such as toluene) that are used as solvents for plastic glues (sniffing glue, or "huffing"), a dangerous practice that can be fatal if the user loses consciousness, can no longer pull away from the source of fumes, and suffocates.

The mucous membranes lining the nasal passages are another available site for drug absorption, traditionally used for cocaine, heroin, and tobacco (snuff), and more recently for crushed tablets of methylphenidate (Ritalin) or slow-release oxycodone (OxyContin). Snorting the crushed tablets defeats the slow-release mechanisms that make these drugs effective for chronic use and that limit their abuse potential. Users who snort drugs avoid the social stigma of injection and the fear of acquiring syringe-borne diseases such as HIV/AIDS and hepatitis. However, repeated snorting can damage mucous membranes and cause severe nosebleeds.

The hypodermic syringe was invented by Thomas Wood in 1853 and rapidly gained popularity as a means of introducing drugs into the body. The tip of the needle can be placed under the skin for sub-cutaneous injection (known as "skin popping" when heroin is injected in this fashion), into a muscle for intramuscular injection, or directly into a vein. Absorption from subcutaneous and intramuscular injections occurs over minutes to hours, hence most injection drug users prefer the intravenous route. Veins have relatively thin walls relative to arteries, and will collapse unless venous return of blood to the heart is blocked. A rubber con-striction band is used above the injection site to allow the veins to fill

with blood so that the drug can be injected. Repeated injections cause the major veins to collapse and sclerose (harden), forcing addicts to seek new sites and creating tracks of injection scars along the veins of the arms or legs.

Opiates accounted for the vast majority of substance abuse treatment admissions in the United States for injection drug abuse, followed by amphetamines and cocaine. Substances must be in liquid form and are usually placed in a spoon with water and heated over a flame to help the drug melt or dissolve. A small wad of cotton is used as a filter for particulate impurities, but cellulose, talc, and other substances frequently end up in the lungs and other tissues of injection drug users. Although most diseases, including hepatitis and HIV, could be prevented by sterile needle exchange or cleaning injection paraphernalia with bleach, injection drug abuse accounted for 19 percent of HIV cases in the United States according to a 2010 report by the U.S. Department of Health and Human Services.

Absorption

Drugs are poorly absorbed across the multiple cell layers of skin but are more readily exchanged across the mucous membranes lining the gastrointestinal, nasal, and respiratory passages. Drugs that are lipid

Drugs administered orally will survive the harsh environment of the stomach longer if they are weak acids (HA), as this will prevent them from splitting into ions (H$^+$ and A$^-$) until they have crossed the mucosal barrier. Once in the neutral pH of the plasma, the drug ionizes and becomes trapped until it reaches its site of action.

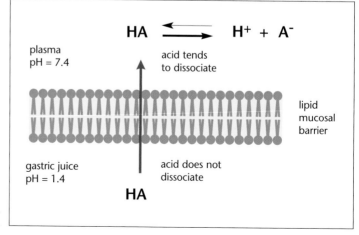

soluble can be absorbed by passive diffusion across mucous membranes. However, many drugs are weak acids or bases that exist in solution in equilibrium between ionized (charged) and non-ionized (neutral) forms. The non-ionized form distributes fairly quickly across lipid mucosal membranes, while ionized forms do not. The distribution between charged and uncharged forms depends on the pH at which H^+ ions dissociate from the drug, known as the pKa. For a drug that is a weak acid (HA) with a pKa of 4, the drug will exist primarily in the non-ionized state in the acid environment of the stomach (pH 1.4), promoting transport across the stomach mucosal membrane (*see* diagram at left). When that drug crosses into the blood plasma, the neutral pH (pH 7.4) favors dissociation to H^+ and A^-, trapping the drug in the plasma and promoting absorption of the drug from the stomach. Some drugs are transported across the mucosal membrane by specific molecules known as carriers, either by energy-dependent processes (active transport) or by using the electrochemical gradient generated by cellular ion pumps (facilitated diffusion). These carriers exist to aid absorption of essential amino acids and nutrients, and many drugs are sufficiently similar in chemical structure to these compounds that they can use the same transport mechanisms.

Oral ingestion is the most common and convenient method of drug administration for conventional pharmaceuticals, but some drugs are poorly absorbed by this route, destroyed by stomach acid, or metabolized extensively by the liver just after absorption ("first pass effect"). Drugs in solution are readily absorbed after subcutaneous or intramuscular injection, while intravenous injection bypasses the absorption process and leads directly to the next phase of pharmacokinetics, drug distribution.

Distribution

Once the drug enters the bloodstream, it initially travels with venous blood toward the heart, where it makes a pass through the lungs before being distributed via the arterial system to body tissues. A large proportion of the cardiac output of blood is directed to the major organs, including the brain, liver, and kidneys, while distribution to muscles, skin, and fat is slower. Blood passes through smaller and smaller end arteries until it reaches capillaries,

where only a single cell layer separates the drug-containing plasma from the end-organ tissues. Blood is a mixture of cellular elements (red and white blood cells, platelets) and soluble proteins; the latter contain binding sites for many drugs. The binding of drugs to plasma proteins limits the distribution to tissues, since only the unbound fraction ("free drug") is available to distribute across cell membranes into tissues. The lipid solubility and pKa are important in determining how drugs partition into different organs; highly lipid-soluble drugs accumulate in fat stores, and to a lesser extent in the brain and liver, where the concentrations of lipid membranes are high. In obese people, the fat content of the body can exceed 50 percent of body weight, and drugs such as the highly lipophilic barbiturates may accumulate in the fat within minutes to hours after administration. In fact, redistribution of such drugs from the brain or heart into fat stores is the initial means of terminating their actions in these tissues, since it lowers end-organ drug concentrations rapidly.

Distribution of drugs into the brain is different from other end organs, because the cells lining brain capillaries are joined by tight junctions, creating the blood-brain barrier (BBB). The more lipophilic the drug, the more likely it will pass through this barrier. Specific uptake transporters also assist in getting some drugs across the BBB. Other proteins, particularly the P-glycoprotein, actively transport some drugs out of the brain. Brain infections (for example, meningitis or encephalitis) or tumors can increase the permeability of the BBB. A similar but less restrictive barrier is present in pregnant women between the uterus and the placenta that feeds the developing fetus; this barrier is easily permeated by lipid-soluble drugs. Hence, many drugs taken by pregnant drug users are also exposed to the fetus, and dependence on such drugs as cocaine, opiates, barbiturates, or benzodiazepines can result in withdrawal symptoms after delivery.

Metabolism, clearance, and elimination

Drugs are eliminated from the body either unchanged or after modification by various enzymes, most often in the liver. Charged or polar compounds (which have no net charge but have a positive and a negative orientation) are more easily excreted than those with high lipid solubility. The kidney is the chief organ for excretion of drugs and their metabolic products. Drugs unabsorbed after oral ingestion are excreted in the feces, along with some drug metabolites excreted by the liver into the bile. Some drugs are secreted into breast milk, which can expose the nursing infant to their toxic effects. Inhalants can be excreted through the lungs into the exhaled air.

The kidneys excrete body waste products, toxins, and drugs by three processes: filtration of the blood in capillary structures called glomeruli, followed by active secretion of ions and charged drug metabolites in the proximal renal tubule, and finally passive reabsorption of sodium ions and water in the distal tubule. Multidrug transporters assist in the excretion of many drug metabolites. In the case of drug overdose, weak acids or bases are sometimes given to make the urine more acid or alkaline, which traps the drug in the excreted fraction and hastens elimination. The speed at which a drug is removed from the body is known as the clearance rate.

More lipophilic drugs require biotransformation to more polar and less biologically active forms before they can be excreted by the kidneys. These reactions are performed by several classes of liver enzymes. Phase I reactions create a new functional group on the drug, which can then actively combine with other compounds to produce water-soluble conjugates. Many of these reactions are mediated by a large family of enzymes known as the cytochrome P450 system. Phase II conjugation reactions link a functional group on the drug (or its Phase I metabolite) to water-soluble compounds, including glucuronic acid, sulfate, glutathione, amino acids, or acetate. The most important of these enzymes is uridine diphosphate glucuronosyltransferase (UGT),

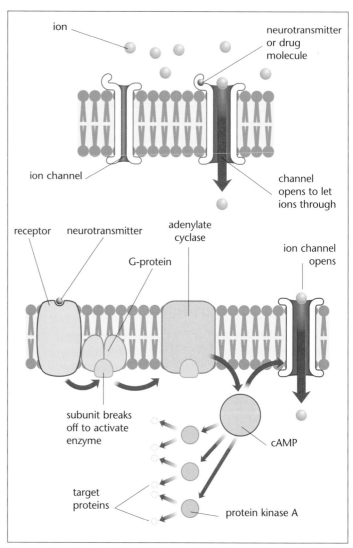

Drugs can bind to the receptors for endogenous neurotransmitters that activate ion channels (top) or to G-protein–coupled receptors (bottom). The latter are coupled to second messenger systems such as adenylate cyclase, which makes cyclic AMP (cAMP). This in turn activates protein kinase A molecules, enabling these molecules to phosphorylate a number of other target proteins, thus propagating the initial signal many times over.

which adds a glucuronate group to oxygen, nitrogen, or sulfur atoms on a number of compounds. The conjugates are usually biologically inactive and readily excreted in the urine. There is significant variation in the degree of metabolism and hence the rate of drug elimination between individuals, likely due to genetic differences (polymorphisms) in the enzymes involved. Some of these enzymes differ among individuals by single nucleotide changes in the genes encoding them, known as single nucleotide polymorphisms (SNPs). Such differences may lead to the development of individualized drug therapies based on a person's genetic makeup.

Pharmacodynamics

Pharmacodynamics is the study of the biochemical and physiological mechanisms of drug actions. These actions result from the binding of drugs to receptor proteins in the brain, heart, or other organs. The receptors for many drugs are also receptors for neurotransmitters (chemicals that nerve cells secrete to transmit electrical signals from one cell to the next) or hormones (chemicals secreted by endocrine glands into the bloodstream to regulate body functions) and mimic, enhance, or inhibit the function of those signaling molecules. For example, benzodiazepines, barbiturates, alcohol, and inhaled anesthetics bind to and enhance the function of the GABA type A receptor, a chloride channel activated by the inhibitory neurotransmitter gamma-aminobutyric acid (GABA). The opiates bind to several classes of opioid receptors, which are the target of endogenous opioid peptides that generate chemical signals called "second messengers" in their target cells. Other drugs act elsewhere in signaling systems, binding to neurotransmitter transporters, the enzymes that synthesize or degrade them, voltage-gated ion channels that mediate electrical signaling, or other enzymes that mediate or modify intracellular chemical signals. Hence, drug receptors are binding sites that affect cellular biochemistry and physiology in a number of different ways. A schematic view of some of these mechanisms is shown in the diagram on page 672.

Drugs that bind to the same sites as endogenous transmitters and hormones can have several possible effects. Those that mimic the endogenous agent are called agonists. Such drugs may be equally effective in activating the receptor as the actual transmitter (full agonists), or less effective (partial agonists). A drug may have no efficacy at all, but it can block the action of the endogenous neurotransmitter when it binds to the transmitter's binding site, making it a competitive antagonist. Other drugs known as allosteric agents affect receptor function without affecting the transmitter binding site, since they bind at different sites on the receptor molecule. Allosteric agents can either enhance or inhibit the function

of the receptor by changing its shape or activity. For example, the benzodiazepines allosterically enhance GABA$_A$ receptor function at a benzodiazepine binding site distinct from the place where GABA binds (*see* diagram below). The benzodiazepines are considered agonists at this site. Drugs that bind to the benzodiazepine site and have no effect are termed benzodiazepine antagonists. A third class of allosteric agents binds to the benzodiazepine site and inhibits GABA$_A$ receptor function; these are called inverse agonists. The most prominent example of inverse agonists are certain beta-carbolines, benzodiazepine-like compounds that bind to the benzodiazepine site on the GABA$_A$ receptor and inhibit its chloride channel function. Another class of drugs, which includes picrotoxin and penicillin, block the GABA$_A$ channel directly.

The GABA$_A$ receptor has a number of sites where other chemicals can attach that can change the shape or activity of the receptor, inhibiting or enhancing its ability to send signals.

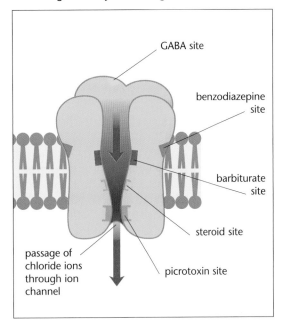

While some membrane ion channels are activated by binding neurotransmitters or hormones, others are activated by changes in the voltage across the membrane. These are also the targets of some drugs. The local anesthetics bind to voltage-gated sodium channels that are opened when the neuron's membrane potential is depolarized, preventing the neuron from firing action potentials. Part of the effect of cocaine is as a local anesthetic, though it also acts at adrenergic (norepinephrine emitting) nerve terminals to block reuptake of norepinephrine, increasing the amount of that transmitter in the synaptic junction. The barbiturates enhance $GABA_A$ receptor function but also inhibit voltage-gated sodium channels, blocking repetitive action potentials. Other drugs target channels that carry potassium or calcium ions.

Besides operating ion channels, neurotransmitters can also trigger chemical signaling in the target cell. Some receptors interact with GTP-binding proteins ("G-proteins"), resulting in activation of intracellular second messenger systems, like the enzyme adenylate cyclase that makes cyclic AMP from the energy molecule, ATP (see diagram, p. 250). Cyclic AMP then activates another enzyme called protein kinase A that attaches phosphate groups to certain target proteins, altering their function. A large number of kinases, phosphatases (enzymes that cleave off the phosphate groups), and other signaling proteins have complex and interacting pathways with multiple targets for drug action. In some cases, ions themselves act as second messengers after entry through voltage or transmitter-gated channels; most notably, calcium can activate a variety of kinases and phosphatases. As noted above, some drugs can interact at multiple binding sites and have several mechanisms of action.

Pharmacokinetic and pharmacodynamic tolerance

Repeated or continuous exposure to a drug often results in tolerance, defined as decreased drug effect with same amount of drug. Along with tolerance, some drugs also induce dependence, a state in which failure to take the drug results in a withdrawal syndrome. Tolerance can result from several different mechanisms. Pharmacodynamic tolerance results when receptors produce a smaller signal for the same drug concentration. This can be due to

desensitization, which can occur when the receptor is modified (for example, the beta-adrenergic receptor undergoes phosphorylation) or enters an inactive state (as occurs with many ion channel receptors). Heterologous desensitization occurs when a second messenger system shared by several receptors becomes less responsive, such that any receptor that works through that system is affected. Long-term drug exposure can also change the number or type of receptor molecules expressed by the target cell by changing the pattern of receptor processing at the protein or RNA level; receptor proteins may be degraded more quickly, or the number of mRNA molecules encoding the receptor may be reduced. Drugs such as cocaine and methamphetamine that act at presynaptic terminals can cause depletion of the endogenous neurotransmitter, making subsequent doses less effective; this process is called tachyphylaxis. In addition to these mechanisms, a drug may also cause pharmacokinetic tolerance by increasing the synthesis of enzymes that metabolize it in the liver, increasing the number of transporters that keep it out of the brain, or increasing processes that assist in its excretion. All of these mechanisms have the same final result—increased drug doses are needed to achieve the same effect.

Tolerance and dependence can result from several of these mechanisms at once. For example, chronic alcoholics metabolize alcohol much more quickly than naive subjects due to induction of alcohol dehydrogenase in the liver. However, they also develop decreased sensitivity to high alcohol concentrations that would be fatal to people who had never used alcohol before. Similar mechanisms apply to the opiates and barbiturates. The escalation of drug doses is not just more expensive for the addict; it also increases the risk of death. For barbiturates and opioids, tolerance to the somnolence, incoordination, and euphoric effects may be greater than tolerance to respiratory depression, making fatal overdose more likely with chronic use.

L. J. Greenfield, Jr.

Pharmacy Drugs

Many people think that drugs that can be bought without a prescription are legal and safe to use. Although this may be true when used properly, these drugs are still dangerous if abused or taken in excess.

Pharmacy, or over-the-counter drugs (OTC), are substances that are sold without a prescription and can be easily bought at pharmacies, drugstores, gas stations, and grocery stores across the country. Because of their legal status and easy accessibility, there is a heightened risk of self-medication and intentional abuse of OTC drugs. Abuse of OTC drugs is becoming an increasing problem among teenage and young adult populations.

Individuals who self-medicate or intentionally abuse OTC drugs commonly misperceive that because OTC drugs are so prevalent and legal, they are also safe. Abuse of these types of drugs, however, can lead to a variety of serious health problems, including death. Preventive methods like supply control are usually not successful because it is difficult to restrict OTC drugs. The Internet is becoming an increasingly important source of information on how to abuse certain types of OTC drugs to get high. The Internet is also becoming a key source for the legal purchase of OTC drugs through online pharmacies, even among teenagers and young adults. As a result, restricting access to these drugs is very difficult.

Medications that are abused

Although the majority of OTC users are responsible users, a small number of users do intentionally self-medicate and abuse. Three of the commonly cited reasons include weight control, weight loss, and getting high.

Commonly abused OTCs related to weight control or weight loss include laxatives, ipecac, and diet pills. Abuse of laxatives entails taking laxatives too frequently or using multiple types at once. Many abusers, mostly misguided dieters and individuals with eating disorders, believe abuse is safe because of the legal status and easy accessibility of these drugs. Misguided dieters include those individuals who do not have eating disorders but still use laxatives with the idea that it will prevent weight gain. Laxatives are available at any grocery store or convenience store, and this availability offers unlimited opportunities for self-medicating. Self-medicating can become very dangerous when an individual is using the drug for the wrong reasons, or is intentionally overusing the drug.

Two types of commonly abused laxatives include stimulant-type and bulk agents. Stimulant-type laxatives are more likely to be abused than bulk types and include products like Ex-Lax, Correctol, and Feen-a-mint. Bulk agents include products such as Metamucil and Colace. Individuals who abuse either type of laxative often do not understand the effects of laxatives. For example, many abusers believe that taking laxatives will move food through the body faster, preventing calorie absorption. However, calorie absorption occurs in the small intestine, and laxatives only stimulate the large intestine. Any weight loss that does occur is actually related to the loss of water. This weight is usually regained when the body rehydrates itself, but a person who continually abuses laxatives can suffer from severe dehydration.

Dehydration is not the only negative health risk associated with laxative abuse. Other negative effects include deterioration of the colon, bleeding (which may result in anemia), impaired bowel function, electrolyte abnormalities, abdominal pain, tremors, kidney damage, and, in severe cases, death. Laxative abuse is also habit forming. If an individual continually uses laxatives the body may become dependent on the drug to function properly.

Ipecac abuse is another way individuals may attempt to control or lose weight. Ipecac is sold as a product that induces vomiting and is used by those who have ingested poison or overdosed on medication. To induce vomiting, ipecac stimulates the central nervous system and stomach. Individuals with eating disorders abuse ipecac as a way to facilitate purging. Once again, abusers may believe that using ipecac is harmless because it is so easy to buy. However, abuse of ipecac can lead to serious health complications, including seizures, shock, blackouts, high blood pressure, respiratory complications, dehydration, electrolyte abnormalities, hemorrhaging, cardiac arrest, and death.

Another commonly abused OTC drug related to weight control and weight loss is diet pills. Diet pills, like the previously mentioned OTC drugs, are easily accessible and are sold at grocery, health food, and convenience stores. Diet pills are composed of stimulants such as ephedrine, caffeine, and phenyl-propanolamine, which stimulate the central nervous system. Although diet pills are used as an appetite suppressant to facilitate weight loss, they are also used and abused for a number of other reasons. For example, diet pills are often used by adolescents in high school and young adults in college as a way to stay awake and study. Truck drivers also use diet pills to stay awake, and athletes often use them to improve energy and strength.

As with laxative and ipecac abuse, there are a number of negative health effects associated with prolonged use and abuse of diet pills. These effects include seizures, heart palpitations, high blood pressure, dizziness, anxiety, insomnia, paranoia, menstrual irregularities, cardiac arrest, and death.

Cold remedies

OTCs commonly abused for psychedelic effects are cough and cold medicines. Abuse of cough suppressants or syrups usually involves adolescents looking for a cheap and legal alternative to more serious drugs. Although there are no formal statistics kept on the rate of cough-suppressant abuse, it is a very dangerous form of drug abuse because it occurs in unpredictable waves. Most drug abuse among young people usually follows a trend pattern. However, information about abusing cold remedies is mostly passed from student to student, school to school, by word of mouth. As a result, it is very difficult to predict where it is becoming a problem. Most towns are not aware that this type of drug abuse is a problem until a number of students experience hallucinations or overdose while at school.

Two common cough and cold medicines include Robitussin cough syrup and Coricidin cold-relief pills. Cough and cold medications are sold in a variety of forms, including tablets, capsules, lozenges, and syrups. Just like other commonly abused OTC

drugs, cough and cold medicines are cheap and easily accessible. Teenagers abuse these types of medicines for the ingredient dextromethorphan (DXM). DXM is used in more than 125 over-the-counter medicines. It is a synthetic drug related to opiates and is chemically similar to morphine. It was approved by the FDA in 1954 and in the 1970s was put in cough medicines as a substitute for codeine.

Taken in appropriate doses, cough suppressants containing DXM have no serious negative side effects, but in large doses its effects mimic PCP or ketamine. Desired effects include sensory enhancement, heightened perceptual awareness, hallucinations, and perceptual distortion. Street names include skittles, Triple Cs, and robo, and using DXM is often referred to as "robotripping," "dexing," or "robodosing." Negative effects of DXM include confusion, blurred vision, slurred speech, loss of coordination, paranoia, high blood pressure, impaired judgment, loss of consciousness, irregular heartbeat, seizure, panic attacks, brain damage, addiction, coma, and death. Abusing DXM can result in serious negative health effects; however, a number of these are the result of abusing a combination of drugs. Using in combination can occur in two ways. A user can mix cough syrup use with alcohol or other drugs, which increases the dangers. There is also increased physical danger with the mix of medicines in the syrup itself. For example, many cough and cold medicines also contain acetaminophen. Acetaminophen is a painkiller, commonly found in Tylenol. Consuming large quantities of acetaminophen can cause liver damage and, in severe cases, liver failure.

Since there are no legal restrictions on DXM, it is very difficult to regulate. A wide variety of cough medicine is available in a range of stores, and DXM is therefore very easy to acquire. In areas across the United States most directly affected by cases of youth abuse of DXM, drug stores are putting DXM products behind the counter so people must request them. Another technique designed to prevent the purchase of this type of drug by youth involves packaging. The manufacturers of Coricidin increased the package size of their products containing DXM to make them more difficult to steal. However, there is another easy source: the family medicine cabinet. Many teenagers do not need to step out of

More than 700 medicines that were previously available only by prescription can now be bought over the counter. Global sales of these products exceed $47 billion per year. More than three-quarters of Americans take OTC remedies to deal with minor ailments, saving them billions of dollars each year in doctors' fees, prescription costs, and time lost from work.

the house to find an OTC medicine that contains DXM. The powdered form of DXM is also available through a variety of sources.

Painkillers

Analgesics for the relief of headaches and moderate pain, particularly those containing codeine, are another abused OTC product. Codeine converts to morphine in the body, giving the characteristic opiate high. Because the amount of codeine in these products is low, large quantities are taken to produce the desired effect. Other ingredients in these formulations include aspirin or acetaminophen, which can both cause organ damage or overdose when taken in large quantities. Restrictions are sometimes placed on how many can be bought without a prescription, but this does not prevent people from going from shop to shop or ordering online to build up a supply. Taking OTC drugs at the same time as prescription drugs can also be dangerous.

Conclusion

Not all abuse of OTC drugs is related to getting high. The factor that links all forms of OTC drug abuse is the incorrect belief by many abusers that these drugs are safe because of their legal status and easy accessibility. Many abusers may be ill informed about the real effects of OTC drug use and abuse, especially DXM abuse; techniques of abuse are often passed around by word of mouth.

Prevention of OTC drug abuse is clearly very difficult. The most important tool in preventing OTC drug abuse is education. For example, if abusers of laxatives were educated on proper use, they would know that laxatives do not prevent calorie absorption. In terms of DXM abuse, the role of the Internet poses a serious problem. Web sites that educate people about negative effects also inform readers about exceeding the appropriate dosage to experience a high. Online pharmacies are also very difficult to regulate, especially when the drug of concern is legal. With potential abusive drugs within easy reach, increasing awareness and education among teenagers, young adults, parents, and teachers should be considered the primary defense in the prevention of OTC drug abuse.

E. J. Farley, D. J. O'Connell

See Also:
DXM • Prescription Drugs

Phenethylamines

Phenethylamine is a simple compound that occurs in a multitude of plants and animals. Its chemical derivatives include neurotransmitters as well as natural and synthetic substances used in medicine and abused for recreation.

A phenethylamine molecule consists of a phenyl ring (C_6H_5-) linked to an amino group ($-NH_2$) by a chain of two carbon atoms, each with a pair of hydrogen atoms attached. Diverse chemical groups can replace one or more hydrogen atoms on any of the eight carbon atoms or the nitrogen atom of this molecule. Such substitutions form a myriad of compounds that qualify as phenethylamines or, more precisely, as derivatives of phenethylamine.

Phenethylamines form and participate in the life processes of plants and animals. They pass through food chains as one species ingests another and absorbs them, and their ultimate fate is to be excreted or destroyed by enzymes. Enzymes that destroy phenethylamines in humans and other animals include monoamine oxidases (MAOs) and catechol-ortho-methyltransferases (COMTs).

Neurotransmitters

The phenethylamine structure is present in three of the principal chemicals that convey signals between neurons in humans and other animals. These are the neurotransmitters dopamine and norepinephrine, and the neurohormone epinephrine.

Dopamine is phenethylamine with hydroxy groups ($-OH$) in place of hydrogen atoms at the 3 and 4 positions of the phenyl group. Norepinephrine has a further $-OH$ group at the beta position of the

The diagram of phenethylamine below has labels in parentheses that identify positions where chemical groups can substitute hydrogen atoms to form phenethylamine derivatives. The *1* position of the phenyl group is occupied by ethylamine and cannot be substituted. The two hydrogens on the nitrogen (N) atom can be substituted. Dopamine, norepinephrine, and epinephrine are examples of natural phenethylamines; the hydroxy groups at the *3* and *4* positions of the phenyl ring specify them as catecholamines.

ethylamine chain, and epinephrine is similar to norepinephrine but has a methyl group in place of one of the hydrogens on the amino group.

Dopamine, epinephrine, and norepinephrine stimulate neural activity when they attach to receptors that fit them. The consequences of that stimulation in the brain include exhilaration, alertness, anxiety, paranoia, and outright psychosis. The same compounds have stimulant effects in the body that include increased heart rate and blood pressure, and dilation of the pupils and airways.

Many other phenethylamines have effects on the mind and body because of their structural similarity to neurotransmitters. Some phenethylamines directly mimic the effects of such compounds by stimulating receptors that respond to them; some act indirectly by causing the release of natural neurotransmitters. Alternatively, phenethylamines can reinforce the effects of neurotransmitters by blocking the entities that deactivate them. These entities are reuptake channels that return neurotransmitters to storage vessels in neurons, and enzymes that convert neurotransmitters into inactive compounds.

Structure and activity

The physical shape of a molecule plays a key role in its drug activity, as does the presence or absence of charge variations around a molecule. Polar molecules have regions of positive and negative charges that attract other polar molecules by electrostatic forces; they have much less affinity for nonpolar molecules such as those that constitute the lining of the small intestine and the blood-brain barrier.

Groups such as $-OH$ and $-NH_2$ tend to contribute polarity. Molecules that have such groups have difficulty entering the bloodstream when swallowed, and even more difficulty getting into the brain from the bloodstream. The polarity of these groups reduces when methyl groups replace hydrogen atoms to form $-OCH_3$, $-NHCH_3$, or $-N(CH_3)_2$ groups. Such modifications improve absorption into the bloodstream of such drugs and can also increase their activity in the brain. They also hinder enzymes that attack polar groups, so they keep the compound active for longer.

The dependence of activity on structure also makes for differences in the drug activities between isomers—compounds that have the same chemical

Chocolate contains phenethylamine, up to around 2 percent by weight. The presence of this compound has been cited as a potential contributor to the mood-elevating property of chocolate, but it is likely that enzymes destroy phenethylamine before it has a chance to work its effects in the brain.

formula but different structures. In some cases, a small difference in structure can have major consequences for drug activity.

The effect of isomerism is perhaps easiest to understand for positional isomerism, whereby the same chemical groups attach to different parts of a core structure. The presence of the phenyl ring in phenethylamines offers plenty of scope for positional isomerism, and changes in the positions of groups attached to this ring cause enormous variations in the therapeutic or recreational properties of drugs.

Stereoisomers

Stereoisomerism is the existence of pairs of mirror-image molecules that are distinctly different. It has consequences for drug activity because nature tends to use only one of the pair of possible molecules, so the drugs that correspond to the natural isomer are more active than their mirror-image counterparts.

Stereoisomerism becomes a possibility when chemical groups replace one or more hydrogen atoms on the carbon atoms of the ethylamine chain. A carbon atom attached to four different chemical groups is a source of asymmetry that leads to the existence of mirror-image pairs.

The formation of stereoisomeric pairs can be visualized by considering the successive addition of four different groups to a carbon atom. Once the first two groups are in place, the second two can be added in either of two distinct configurations. Each configuration results in a different stereoisomer, denoted *R* or *S* according to the arrangement of chemical groups around the carbon atom in question.

Another naming system uses *d* (dextro) and *l* (levo) to distinguish between stereoisomers according to how they rotate the plane of polarization of light that has passed through a polarizing filter. The interaction with light is the reason that this type of stereoisomerism is sometimes called optical activity. The rotation of polarized light as it passes through a solution provides a useful means of testing for and identifying the stereoisomers present.

Stimulant phenethylamines

A number of natural and synthetic phenethylamines increase alertness, chattiness, and euphoria without causing hallucinogenic or psychedelic effects. These are the stimulant phenethylamines, as typified by amphetamine. Members of this group increase heart rate and blood pressure; they also relieve congestion and symptoms of asthma by dilating the airways, and their ability to reduce appetite gives them potential as antiobesity drugs.

The negative properties of the stimulant phenethylamines include their potential for causing dependency and psychosis. Malnutrition can also occur as a result of prolonged appetite suppression, and they can cause strokes or heart attacks in people who are vulnerable to such diseases. Because of these negative effects most stimulant phenethylamines appear in the strictest schedules of drug legislation. A few exceptions have recognized uses in the treatment of breathing difficulties, obesity, and attention deficit disorder.

Stimulant phenethylamines typically have no additional substituents on the phenyl ring of phenethylamine, but they are otherwise close relatives of dopamine, epinephrine, and norepinephrine. The absence of hydroxy groups on the ring is crucial to their activity, since their polarity prevents molecules that carry them from crossing the blood-brain barrier. Also, the absence of ring hydroxy groups makes these compounds less attractive targets for destruction by COMT enzymes, so they remain active for longer.

One of the principal stimulant phenethylamines is ephedrine, an active principal in the traditional Chinese medicine ma huang. This substance is present in the stems of the ephedra shrub, and it is largely responsible for the effectiveness of ma huang in treating congestion and asthma as well as providing energy by burning fat deposits. Ephedra also contains pseudoephedrine, which produces a milder effect similar to that of ephedrine.

Ephedrine and pseudoephedrine both have a phenethylamine core with methyl groups attached to the nitrogen and beta-carbon atoms, and a hydroxy group on the alpha carbon. The alpha and beta carbons are both sources of stereoisomerism, so two pairs of mirror-image isomers are possible. Both compounds

This diagram represents an ephedrine molecule docked to matching regions in a receptor. The strength of the interaction has three major sources. First, there is an affinity between the hydrophobic phenyl ring of ephedrine and a hydrophobic region in the receptor. Second, there is hydrogen bonding at the hydroxy group. Third, there is ionic attraction between a negatively charged region in the receptor and the positive charge of the nitrogen.

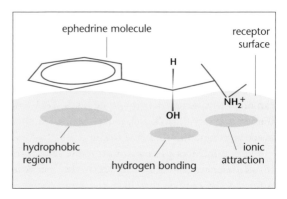

have *S* configurations at the alpha carbon, and the difference of configuration at the beta carbon is what separates ephedrine and pseudoephedrine.

Ephedrine has the *R* configuration at the beta carbon, as do the natural forms of epinephrine and norepinephrine. This resemblance makes for a good interaction at receptors. Pseudoephedrine has the *S* configuration and is much less active. Nevertheless, its reduced cardiovascular side effects make it safer for use in decongestant medicines.

Ephedra also contains small amounts of norephedrine and norpseudoephedrine, which differ from their parent compounds by having no methyl groups on their nitrogen atoms. These are also stimulants. Norephedrine also has the name cathine, which stems from its presence as the main active compound in *Catha edulis* (khat), a stimulant shrub.

Ephedrine, pseudoephedrine, and cathine all have pronounced effects on breathing and heart rate, but they have relatively little effect in the brain. The polarity of their beta-carbon hydroxy groups is sufficient to ensure they stay mainly on the blood side of the blood-brain barrier.

Psychostimulant phenethylamines

Amphetamine and methamphetamine are close chemical relatives of the ephedra stimulants, but they lack the polar hydroxy group. Chemical reduction of either ephedrine or pseudoephedrine produces methamphetamine and is the main clandestine source of this drug; the same reaction converts cathine into simple amphetamine.

This removal of the hydroxy group has two consequences. First, it produces compounds that get into the brain with relative ease; second, these compounds have chemical structures more closely related to that of dopamine. Thus, it is no surprise that these compounds produce their characteristic rush by interfering with the normal functioning of dopamine neurons in the brain.

The amphetamines have mirror image isomers because they have methyl groups at the alpha carbon. Their *dextro* or *S* forms are responsible for the amphetamine rush, while the *R* isomers are much less potent. Careful reduction of natural ephedra stimulants produces the desired *S* isomer of methamphetamine rather than its less effective *R* isomer counterpart.

Seen here in his laboratory, Alexander "Sasha" Shulgin synthesized more than 200 phenethylamines between the mid-1960s and the withdrawal of his DEA license in 1994. He also tested many of these compounds on himself and a group of scientists to evaluate their psychoactivity. Some people call him the "godfather of Ecstasy" despite the fact that MDMA was synthesized many years before Shulgin started his research. Shulgin's purpose was to explore the potential use of phenethylamines in psychotherapy.

Cathinone is a psychostimulant phenethylamine that accompanies cathine in khat. It has a ketone group at the beta position, and this again is less polar than the hydroxy group in cathine. Hence, cathinone has similar psychoactive effects to amphetamine.

Just as cathinone is the substance that would result from the oxidation of cathine, methcathinone or ephedrone is the oxidation product of ephedrine or pseudoephedrine. Methcathinone became a drug of abuse in the former Soviet Union, where it was prescribed as an antidepressant, but it does not have much history of recreational use elsewhere.

Psychedelic phenethylamines

While stimulant phenethylamines tend to have plain phenyl rings, psychedelic phenethylamines have diverse substituents for hydrogen atoms on the phenyl ring. These chemical groups provide the principal cause of psychedelic effects. Substituents on the ethylamine chain modulate the potency and length of action of phenethylamines. The presence of one or two methyl groups at the nitrogen atom usually removes psychedelic activity.

Mescaline. The natural prototype of the psychedelic phenethylamines is mescaline, and it is one of the benchmarks for comparisons of the action of psychedelics. Mescaline gets its name from mescal, a peyote cactus that contains it, and its chemical name is 3,4,5-trimethoxyphenethylamine.

The presence of three methoxy groups on the phenyl ring of mescaline makes its molecular shape significantly different from that of phenethylamine. A consequence of this change is that mescaline and related phenethylamines interact with serotonergic neurons—those that respond to serotonin. These interactions are responsible for psychoactive effects ranging from hallucinations to the "loved-up" empathogenic state associated with Ecstasy and its analogs. Serotonergic neurons can also cause nausea and vomiting when these drugs are taken.

DOM. The mid-1960s saw synthetic psychedelics start to emerge from research laboratories. Some of these compounds revealed themselves to be extremely potent; an example is DOM, also named STP after an unrelated gasoline additive. This amphetamine derivative proved to be an effective hallucinogen at doses of a few milligrams, compared with the hundreds of milligrams in mescaline doses.

The amphetamine core of DOM makes stereoisomerism possible, and U.S. pharmacologist Alexander Shulgin (1925–) made and tested the two stereoisomers for psychoactivity. He found that the *R* isomer produced hallucinogenic effects, while the *S* isomer was inactive as a hallucinogen. This result contrasts with the pattern for stimulant phenethylamines, whose *S* isomers are more active. It suggests that the two types of phenethylamines act at different receptors that have different geometries.

Other hallucinogens. Intrigued by the potential for self-exploration during mescaline experiences, Shulgin embarked on a search for similar or superior psychoactivity in other phenethylamines. He generated several series of compounds that varied by positions of chemical groups and lengths of alkyl chains, and he substituted such entities as bromo (–Br), iodo (–I), methyl (–CH$_3$), and methylthio (CH$_3$S–) groups onto the phenyl ring.

In 1991, Shulgin and his wife, Ann, published the results of this work in *PiHKAL: A Chemical Love Story,* where "PiHKAL" is an acronym of "phenethylamines I have known and loved." The first part of *PiHKAL* is semi-autobiographical, but the second half lists the synthesis and testing of 179 phenethylamines. Some of these compounds proved to have neutral or unpleasant psychoactive effects; others became popular recreational hallucinogens. The latter group includes DOM and Nexus (2C-B).

Entactogenic phenethylamines

Shulgin produced a third class of phenethylamines whose effects differ from those of both the stimulant and the hallucinogenic phenethylamines. The prototype of this group is the 1960s "love drug" 3,4-methylenedioxyamphetamine, or MDA; the *N*-methyl derivative of this drug is MDMA, the active component of genuine Ecstasy. The characteristic chemical group of these compounds is the methylenedioxy (–O–CH$_2$–O–) bridge between the 3 and 4 positions of the phenyl ring.

In common with the stimulants and in contrast to the hallucinogenic phenethylamines, the more active forms of drugs in this group are the *S* isomers. Also, these compounds have pronounced stimulant effects that suggest some similarities to the amphetamines. However, the effect of these drugs is characterized by heightened contentment and empathy for others, which are the opposite of the typically "edgy" amphetamine effects. The term *entactogen* was coined for these drugs and refers to their ability to make users feel more in touch with themselves and others. Drugs in this class also have a mild hallucinatory action that contributes to their popularity for use in club environments.

M. CLOWES

SEE ALSO:

Amphetamines • Dopamine • Ecstasy • Ecstasy Analogs • Ephedrine • Epinephrine • Mescaline • Nexus • Norepinephrine

Placebos

Placebos are medications used to test the efficacy of new drugs. Despite the fact that placebos do not contain an active ingredient, some patients claim relief from their symptoms, which suggests that expectations play a role in a drug's effects.

A placebo is a substance or treatment believed to be inert or to have no known therapeutic effect. A placebo could be a sugar or starch pill or even "fake" surgery. Currently the only known and accepted use for a placebo is in research experiments; when a new drug (medicine) is being tested for efficacy, or a drug that has an established use is being tested for a new condition, then placebos are used. A drug is usually tested by administering it to people suffering from the condition that the drug has been designed to cure. If, after taking the drug, the subjects show an improvement in their condition, the drug is deemed to be effective. In fact, it is not that simple.

When designing experiments, scientists attempt to control the environment as much as possible in order to eliminate other possible explanations. According to this principle, if all possible alternative explanations are eliminated, then the one that is left must be true. So, if people are given a drug and they get better, what other explanations might there be? One explanation could be that the condition would have improved in time, without medication. One way to control for this outcome might be to give a second group of subjects a placebo. If all subjects, those taking the drug and those taking the placebo, improve, then the explanation is probably that drugs are not required. If only the subjects who are given the drug improve, then the drug is probably effective for this condition. This is the most common use of the placebo, to test the effect of other drugs.

In the 1950s researcher H. K. Beecher coined the phrase "placebo effect" to describe a strange phenomenon. In a number of studies, he noted that a substantial number of subjects given a placebo were improving in a similar manner to those given the real drug—people were getting better even though they had not been given any active medication. Over the years, a number of explanations have been suggested for this phenomenon.

One explanation was that the subjects improved because they were never actually clinically ill. Since they suffered from an imaginary illness, an imaginary cure would suffice. Opponents of this theory point to the finding that the phenomenon has been observed with visible illnesses; for example, it has been found that warts can react to a placebo ointment. Hence, some suggest the effect may be produced by chemicals, such as endorphins, being released in the body. Indeed, there is an ongoing debate over whether or not antidepressants have any pharmacological effect or whether they have a placebo effect. Finally, others have suggested that the healing process is more than just the administration of a pill and that the effect, whatever it may be, could be triggered by the climate of caring that surrounds the patient. Whatever the explanation, healing appears to be based on the deception that the subject is taking beneficial medication. Thus, the person believes that he or she will get better. This finding also has relevance for the abuse of alcohol and other drugs.

Chemical effects and learned behaviors

Until the end of the 1960s, it was widely believed that alcohol and other drugs had certain predictable effects and that those effects were purely a function of the chemical properties inherent in the drugs. These are known as the pharmacological effects. However, in 1969 researchers McAndrew and Edgerton published a book called *Drunken Comportment*. This cultural and anthropological study demonstrated that people of different cultures and nations consumed alcohol in different ways, experienced different effects, and behaved differently (the "drunken comportment" of the book's title). It would appear that the differences between the groups were cultural; for example, some cultures became more violent, while others became more friendly. McAndrew and Edgerton argued that the effects of alcohol must owe more to cultural learning than to pharmacological effects. Indeed, when the behaviors were examined, only three universal effects, called the "three S's," were found: impaired gait (staggering), impaired speech (slurring), and drowsiness (sleeping); all other effects were learned.

THE BALANCED PLACEBO EXPERIMENT

The balanced placebo experiment is an elegant and powerful experimental design that allows researchers to distinguish between the pharmacological (purely chemical) and the learned or psychological effects of alcohol. The design of the experiment is quite straightforward. If 100 people were taking part in the experiment, 50 of them, chosen at random, would be told that they would be given alcohol (conditions 1 and 2). The remaining 50 would be told that they would be given a soft drink (conditions 3 and 4). Of the first 50, half would be given an alcoholic drink (usually vodka and orange juice) and the other half would be given a placebo, a drink that looks and smells like an alcoholic drink but contains no alcohol—usually a glass of orange juice that has had vodka rubbed on the rim of the glass. The second group of 50 are treated the same—half are given straight orange juice and the other half are given vodka and orange juice.

All subjects are then given some task to perform, for example, filling in questionnaires or watching films. Researchers observe the subjects and take measures to gauge the effect. If all subjects who have consumed alcohol (conditions 1 and 3) behave similarly and different from those subjects who did not consume alcohol (conditions 2 and 4), then any effect or behavior can be explained by the pharmacological effect of alcohol. However, if all subjects who believe they have consumed alcohol (conditions 1 and 2) behave similarly, and different from those subjects who believe they have consumed a soft drink (conditions 3 and 4), any effect or behavior is then explained by the mere belief of drinking alcohol and not by any pharmacological effect.

Researchers in the 1970s and 1980s became interested in this "learning" explanation of intoxication and started to investigate it using a design called the balanced placebo experiment (*see* box above). Using this experiment, they found that learning explained the majority of intoxicated behaviors; for example, aggression, sexual arousal, and social facilitation could all be explained by the placebo effect of alcohol. Researchers studying alcoholism found that some firmly held views such as the priming effect (if an alcoholic takes one drink, then loss of control and drunkenness will inevitably ensue) and craving were again culturally learned behaviors. Thus, new questions were asked about the validity of viewing alcoholism as a disease. The learned effects of alcohol have been found to be powerful motivators to initiate and continue drinking and indeed appear to have a greater influence on relapse in dependent drinking than the effects of alcohol itself. It has been found that people drink to achieve the effects that they expect, and that this is true of both social and dependent drinkers. Among the commonly expected effects are:

- Global positive change (things are generally better after a drink)
- Sexual enhancement (more attractive to opposite sex, more sexually accomplished)
- Social facilitation (can mix better at social functions)
- Relaxation, both physical and emotional
- Assertiveness
- Aggression.

Finally, it should be obvious that the placebo effect applies as well to other recreational and illicit drugs. Thus, much of the effect of drug use that people experience is learned, much of it depends on the individual's metabolism, and the rest is governed by pharmacology. An examination of the effects of drug use must therefore take into account the individual and the environment as well as the drug.

J. McMahon

SEE ALSO:
Pharmaceutical Industry • Pharmacokinetics • Pharmacy Drugs • Prescription Drugs

Plant-Based Drugs

Plants have been used to treat diseases in all cultures for centuries. As well as treating illnesses, plants have been and continue to be used in their natural as well as manufactured forms for their hallucinatory, stimulative, or sedative effects.

The natural world contains many drug-producing plants. People in the West and other societies often use these drugs in social situations, for medicine, or as part of their cultural rituals. This article covers a variety of such naturally occurring drugs.

Many plants contain natural substances that affect the brain's chemistry; these substances may have a stimulating, sedating, or hallucinatory action. Once these properties are discovered, people with access to such plants make use of them in various ways.

In Western society, for example, there are several well-known legal and illegal drugs that are derived from plants. For example, alcohol is a product of the fermentation of yeast and sugar; the stimulant caffeine comes from coffee beans; the powerful painkiller morphine is from the opium poppy; and tetrahydrocannabinol (THC) in marijuana is found in hemp leaves. Alcohol and caffeine are used by millions of people every day, marijuana is smoked illegally, and morphine is an important analgesic used in medicine.

There are many more plant-based drugs that are not widely used in modern Western society but that were used in the past or were used by other cultures. A wide range of natural substances work as drugs in the body because the chemical messengers in the human brain are sometimes similar to compounds found in plants. For example, nicotine in tobacco is a poison used by the plant to deter pests, but it also reacts with acetylcholine receptors in the brain because its chemical structure is similar to acetylcholine, a natural body chemical.

Fly agaric mushroom

Amanita muscaria, known more commonly as fly agaric, is a brightly colored mushroom that contains several hallucinogenic substances and organic poisons. It is around 6 inches (15 cm) tall and has a distinctive appearance, with a bright red or yellow-orange cap covered with white spots. The main psychoactive effects of eating Amanita mushrooms are from muscimol, which is metabolized by the body from ibotenic acid in the mushroom. A few mushroom caps at first produce nausea, then a dreamy relaxed feeling, and finally hallucinations for several hours. However, some people also find the experience distressing. *Amanita muscaria* is legal to pick and grows widely over the Northern Hemisphere.

Several cultures use *Amanita muscaria* in their religious rituals, including Siberians, Native Americans, and the Sami of Scandinavia. In these rituals, the hallucinogenic dreams are often interpreted as visions. The Western name, fly agaric, comes from a traditional use of the mushroom in flypaper.

Yopo

The seeds from the yopo tree (*Anadenanthera colubrina*) contain a powerful psychoactive drug, which tribes in Colombia, Venezuela, and parts of Brazil use to make a hallucinogenic snuff called *yopo*.

The story book appearance of fly agaric is deceptive; if eaten these mushrooms are very poisonous.

Typically, the seeds are dried, ground, and then snorted through a bamboo tube. The main active chemical in the snuff is dimethyltryptamine (DMT). A regular dose of around 30 milligrams of DMT has a similar hallucinogenic effect to LSD, but DMT begins to wear off after only half an hour. Many plants containing DMT can be grown legally, although its purification is illegal.

Yopo is relatively unknown but has been popular among native South Americans for centuries. For example, almost one in five Mayans regularly took *yopo*. Many tribes in South America also use similar plants to make other snuffs.

Hawaiian baby woodrose

Seeds from the clambering vine Hawaiian baby woodrose (*Argyreia nervosa*) contain several hallucinogenic chemicals called ergot alkaloids. Of these psychoactive alkaloids, the main active chemicals—chanoclavine, lysergol, ergotmetrine, and ergine—are all members of the lysergic acid amide (LSA) family of chemicals, which are closely related to LSD. Ergot alkaloids naturally occur in several plants. Hawaiian baby woodrose, like many bright red or yellow-orange plants that contain LSA, can be grown legally. The seeds of Hawaiian baby woodrose were not traditionally used as a psychoactive drug, although in recent times they have become popular for their LSD-like effects.

Absinthe

Wood from the absinthe (*Artimisia absinthium*) shrub, more commonly known as wormwood, is a main ingredient of the alcoholic beverage absinthe. Called green fairy, or *la feé verte* in French, this drink is also flavored with licorice, fennel, and aniseed, and it gets its distinctive green coloring from chlorophyll in the wood. In addition to its alcohol content, wormwood contains a psychoactive drug, thujone, that has a similar effect to the active chemical tetrahydrocannabinol (THC) found in marijuana. The combination of thujone and alcohol can result in extreme intoxication, while excessive use is associated with addiction, hallucination, and mental deterioration. It is illegal to sell absinthe in the United States, although it is legal to possess the drink.

A French doctor named Pierre Ordinaire invented the recipe for absinthe in 1792. Soon after, the Swiss distiller Henri-Louis Pernod acquired the recipe and began large-scale commercial production. Absinthe was a popular drink throughout the nineteenth century, and was often drunk to excess by artists such as Edouard Manet (1832–1883) and Vincent Van Gogh (1853–1890), who believed it helped their creativity. Because of worries about its adverse health effects (thujone is toxic and can cause seizures), many countries banned absinthe at the beginning of the twentieth century.

Ergot

Claviceps purpurea, more commonly known as ergot, is a fungus that infects grains such as rye and some wild grasses. Because the fungus is both toxic and psychoactive, it causes an unpleasant disease called ergotism in cattle and humans. Symptoms include a burning sensation, convulsions, hallucinations, and black, gangrenous limbs, all of which originate from a large amount of ergot alkaloids in the fungus. Ergot is also an abortifacient (causes abortions).

The main chemicals ergotamine, ergotine, and ergotoxine are derivatives of lysergic acid and are also collectively termed lysergic acid amides (LSA). Similarly to LSD, these alkaloids induce hallucinations, while ergotamine constricts the body's blood vessels, causing gangrene.

In the European Middle Ages, there were periodic plagues from ergot infestation of crops. Other than causing gangrene and hallucinations, ergotism is accompanied by a burning feeling, which led to its name *ignis sacer*, or "holy fire." In modern times, ergot is used to treat migraines and is the main ingredient used to illegally manufacture LSD.

Ma huang

Ephedra equisetina, or ma huang, is a Chinese herb that has several pharmacological effects. The active chemicals in ephedra are ephedra alkaloids, of which the most important is ephedrine.

Usually taken as an ingredient in traditional Asian medicine, ephedra has a stimulating effect that is stronger than caffeine but weaker than amphetamine. Ephedra also suppresses appetite and is a natural decongestant. Asian medicine has used ephedra for over five thousand years to treat asthma and weight problems. In more recent times, ephedra has been sold as "herbal Ecstasy" preparations, which have a recreational use similar to Ecstasy (MDMA) and amphetamines. Ephedra has now been banned by the U.S. Food and Drug Administration because of its recreational use as a stimulant and unreliable claims about its medicinal properties.

Kola nut and guarana

Both the kola nut and guarana are natural sources of the stimulant caffeine, and are used by some cultures in a similar way to coffee in the West. Kola nuts grow on the *Kola vera* tree, a North American member of the cocoa family; guarana seeds come from the guarana shrub, which is native to Brazil. Coffee beans typically contain 1 to 2 percent caffeine, while the kola nut has around 2 to 3 percent and guarana 4 to 8 percent. Caffeine stimulates the central nervous system and is used to stay alert; too much can cause nervousness, irritability, and sleeplessness.

At one time the kola nut was an ingredient in American colas, although now it is replaced by synthetic flavorings that mimic its taste. Meanwhile, South American tribes have used guarana for thousands of years as a stimulant in many foods and drinks. Today guarana is used in many energy drinks and is a main ingredient of guarana soda, a popular beverage in Brazil.

Mimosa

The sweet-tasting flowers of the Chinese herb mimosa (*Albizia julibrissin Durazz*), or he huan hua, are used in traditional Asian medicine for their calming effects. Commonly referred to as Chinese herbal Prozac, mimosa flowers are used as an antidepressant, to relieve anxiety, and as a sleeping aid. Although there is little research on the pharmacology of the flowers, their sedative action is thought to be from quercitrin, a drug found in the flowers. Another compound, tetracosanoic acid, is also present, but its effects are currently unknown.

Nutmeg

Myristica fragrans, the common nutmeg, is a tree native to the Indonesian spice islands. When dried and ground, the seeds are called nutmeg. Around 10 to 20 ounces (280–560 g) of nutmeg produces an intense hallucinogenic effect that is often accompanied by vomiting, diarrhea, and an extremely dry mouth. Its effects start after a few hours, last for up

The common culinary spice nutmeg is also a hallucinatory drug when taken in large amounts of more than one pound.

to a day, and are usually described as very unpleasant. The main psychoactive chemical in nutmeg is myristicin, also called methoxysafrole. European and North American cooks have used nutmeg as a spice since the sixteenth century in cakes, savory dishes, and mulled wine. Its psychoactive effects have been well documented for most of its modern history. Some cultures use nutmeg as a medicine; a Hindu pharmacopoeia mentions it as a treatment for fever, asthma, and heart disease.

Reed canary grass

Phalaris arundinacea, more commonly known as reed canary grass, is a tall, reddish green grass that grows on marshy land and contains small amounts of the psychoactive chemical dimethyltryptamine (DMT). There is too little DMT in the grass to have a direct

The flowers of mimosa are used in traditional Asian medicine to relieve insomnia, depression, and anxiety.

effect, although it can be chemically extracted, then snorted in its pure form. Pure DMT is illegal, but legislation against the plants is impossible because they are common around the world.

Reed canary grass is sometimes used in traditional South American brews called ayahuasca, which are drinks that have hallucinatory effects. The plant has been used as a source of illegally obtained DMT.

Kava

The roots of the kava shrub (*Piper methysticum*), a pepper plant from the islands of the South Pacific, are dried and ground to make a mood-altering herbal remedy. Typically, the powdered roots are boiled in water and taken as a drink, although kava can also be eaten in its natural form or as tablets. Its main pharmacologically active chemicals are kava lactones, which produce relaxation and sharpen the senses.

One of the properties of kava is the relief of anxiety; it is also a muscle relaxant. Kava is one of the most popular herbs bought from health food stores in the United States.

Pacific islanders have grown kava for thousands of years, using it at social gatherings, religious ceremonies, and in many other ways. More recently, kava has been sold in the West as a health food remedy for a variety of ailments. Kava is banned in some countries, such as the United Kingdom, because of safety concerns.

Diviner's sage

Salvia divinorum, or diviner's sage, is a shrub native to southern Mexico. It is probable that the native Central Americans used *Salvia divinorum* in religious rituals. The leaves of the plant contain a powerful psychoactive chemical called salvinorin. Salvinorin is a drug that is traditionally imbibed by chewing pairs of leaves, although the plant can also be dried and smoked. Salvinorin is a powerful hallucinogen, which when smoked lasts for around half an hour; if it is chewed, its effects last longer. Users do not become tolerant to salvinorin. However, many people find the hallucinations unpleasant and choose not to repeat the experience.

N. LEPORA

SEE ALSO:
Belladonna Alkaloids • Betel Nut • Coca Leaf • DMT • Jimsonweed • Marijuana • Mescaline • Psilocybin and Psilocin • Tobacco

Potentiation

Potentiation is the enhancement of the physiological activity or psychoactivity of one substance as a result of the action of other substances. Potentiation can occur through a wide variety of mechanisms as a drug passes through the body.

The term *potentiation* applies to a diversity of mechanisms that enhance the effects of a substance that is either psychoactive or physiologically active in some other way. Targets for potentiation include hormones and neurotransmitters naturally present in humans, as well as synthetic or natural substances taken for recreational or therapeutic purposes.

In the case of a psychoactive drug, effects such as distorted perception, euphoria, drowsiness, or social disinhibition are manifestations of cascades of nerve impulses that originate when the drug binds to receptor sites on neurons. Potentiation occurs when one or more secondary substances increase the availability of a drug at an active site. Alternatively, a potentiating agent can enhance the interaction of the drug with its receptor so as to make a given concentration of a substance more effective.

Improved absorption

The path of a drug through the body starts with the administration method, such as injection, sniffing, smoking, or swallowing. In all cases but injection, the drug must pass through a tissue membrane in order to reach the bloodstream. This is the first opportunity for potentiation to occur.

In the traditional use of coca, leaves from the plant are chewed and mixed together with ash in a wad. The ash provides alkalinity that frees the cocaine base from its salts. When the user squeezes the wad between cheek and gums, cocaine freebase passes through the lining of the cheek more readily than cocaine salts would. Hence, ash potentiates the effect of cocaine from coca leaves by keeping it in a form that favors its absorption into the bloodstream.

Cytochrome P450 inhibition

After absorption, drugs have to contend with enzymes that catalyze their bioconversion into substances that often have no activity. This assault is part of the process that helps prevent accumulations of potentially toxic compounds. Nevertheless, such enzyme action can hinder the effects of psychoactive drugs if enzyme activity eliminates a compound before enough of the drug crosses the blood-brain barrier to produce effects.

Substances that inhibit enzyme-mediated destruction of active compounds potentiate by increasing the length of time an active compound stays in the body. The same mechanism also increases the maximum drug concentration when gradual absorption of a drug from the intestine is at least as fast as the rate of elimination of the drug.

One of the major families of enzymes that destroy drugs are the cytochromes P450, or CYPs. The different members of this family are identified by codes such as 3A4 and 2C19. The CYPs reside mainly on cells in the liver and small intestine. These locations are ideal for eliminating drugs from the bloodstream and even from the contents of the intestine before they reach the bloodstream.

The nature of enzyme action provides a basis for potentiation because an enzyme molecule can only process one molecule at a time. Also, each type of

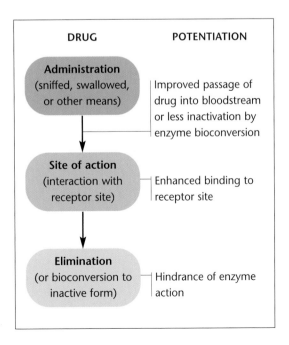

267

CYP enzyme promotes a specific bioconversion reaction in a given type of chemical compound. Thus there can be competition between different substances that degrade under the influence of a given enzyme, and one substance can impede the degradation of another by monopolizing an enzyme. A curious example is the potentiation of certain drugs by grapefruit juice, which is due to the presence of a compound called bergamottin in grapefruit. Bergamottin degrades by the action of CYP3A4 and CYP1A2; these enzymes also catalyze the degradation of benzodiazepines, cannabinoids, cocaine, codeine, fentanyl, methadone, and various tricyclic antidepressants. A glass of grapefruit juice contains enough bergamottin to interrupt normal metabolic processes, thus distorting the effects of both prescription and nonprescription drugs. The activity of some drugs can be inhibited by eating broccoli.

Another CYP enzyme, type 2D6, degrades drugs such as amphetamines, methadone, morphine, and oxycodone. Substances that potentiate these drugs by inhibiting CYP2D6 include cocaine, antidepressants, antipsychotics, and HIV drugs.

Monoamine oxidase inhibition

Recreational drugs such as amphetamines, phenethylamines, and tryptamines all belong to a class of compounds called monoamines. Such substances are prone to degradation by enzymes called monoamine oxidases (MAOs); there are two broad classes of these enzymes—MAO_A and MAO_B.

MAO_A occurs in dopamine and norepinephrine neurons as well as in the liver and gut. MAO_B occurs in serotonin neurons and on blood platelets. Hence, these enzymes can attack monoamine drugs in the gut before they are absorbed, in the bloodstream as they circulate, and in the brain where they act.

A class of drugs called MAO inhibitors (MAOIs) reduces the activity of MAOs by binding to the site where monoamines attach in the first stage of their bioconversion. Drugs such as phenelzine (Nardil) form permanent bonds to MAOs, and their inhibition is irreversible. Thus the body must produce new MAO molecules after MAOI treatment has finished before normal MAO activity returns. Other MAOIs form reversible bonds with MAOs, so their effect gradually wears off as they detach from MAO molecules and the body eliminates them.

The clinical use of MAOIs is in the treatment of depression, since they boost the activity of neurotransmitters such as serotonin and norepinephrine, whose reduced activities are implicated in depression. However, MAOIs can sometimes cause dangerous potentiation of recreational and therapeutic drugs by knocking out an enzyme system that degrades both the drugs and the neurotransmitters they cause to be released.

Some natural compounds are able to inhibit MAO activity and have traditional use together with natural extracts that contain psychoactive monoamines. An example of such a concoction is ayahuasca, which contains MAO-inhibiting harmine and psychoactive DMT and is a tool in shamanic rituals in South America. Harmine is essential for the brew's effects, since MAOs would otherwise destroy much of the DMT (N,N–dimethyltryptamine) before it had a chance to produce effects in the brain.

Potentiation at GABA receptors

A broad class of central nervous system (CNS) depressants reduces anxiety and can induce sleep by potentiating gamma-aminobutyric acid (GABA)—a neurotransmitter that has a calming effect on brain activity. Substances that act in this way include benzodiazepines, barbiturates, and alcohol.

This potentiation mechanism differs from others in that it occurs directly at the receptor. When CNS-depressant molecules attach to sites on GABA receptors, they induce changes in the shape of the receptor that are favorable for stronger interactions with GABA molecules. Hence such drugs strengthen the effects of a given concentration of GABA.

There is a risk of fatal overdose when two different types of CNS depressants work together. This is particularly true for mixtures of alcohol and barbiturates. Both depressants have different bonding sites on GABA receptors, and one drug amplifies the potentiation caused by the other. In this way, doses that would be tolerable for either drug on its own can be fatal in combination.

M. CLOWES

SEE ALSO:
Alcohol • Barbiturates • Benzodiazepines • DMT • Gamma-aminobutyric Acid • MAOs and MAOIs • Phenethylamines • Tryptamines

Prescription Drugs

Almost everyone has taken a prescription drug at some point in his or her life. While millions take these drugs safely, some drugs are potentially addictive. Misuse can lead to intentional or unintentional dependence.

Prescription drugs come in many forms and can successfully help people cope with ailments ranging from severe pain to insomnia to attention deficit disorder (ADD). While prescription drugs can increase the quality of life for many people if taken responsibly, if misused or abused they can also pose a very serious health problem. Consequences of misuse and abuse include overdose, addiction, and even death. The misuse of prescription drugs has always caused concern, but the rapid increase in the nonmedical use of prescription drugs among youth and young adults has alarmed practitioners, policy makers, and the general public alike. What are the problems, and how alarmed should we be?

Many factors must be considered when trying to understand prescription drug misuse and abuse. The belief that a pill exists for every illness or problem is pervasive in modern society. Reliance on prescription drugs for a wide range of physical and psychological ailments easily creates an opportunity for misuse and abuse among users. There are unintentional and intentional pathways to prescription drug misuse and abuse. Many people with legitimate prescriptions may begin using their medications properly. Yet prolonged self-medicating behaviors may lead to unintentional physical dependence. In 2003 Rush Limbaugh, the radio personality, admitted that he had developed an unintentional dependence on prescription painkillers. When he announced to the public that he was addicted, he claimed his addiction arose out of a legitimate prescription given for serious back pain. As his tolerance grew, he began to self-medicate by increasing his dosage of OxyContin and other drugs and, as a result, became addicted. The intentional abuse of painkillers with the objective of getting high is also a serious problem among the young. Understanding the pathways into prescription drug abuse, how it varies by age, race, and gender, and the various negative consequences are key to fully grasping the effects of prescription drug abuse. It is also an important factor in creating effective preventive, educational, and treatment programs.

Advice on side effects and the proper use of drugs is available from the pharmacist. The elderly are often unaware of the potentially addictive effects of some prescription drugs.

Prescription drugs of abuse

There are a number of categories of substances that fall under the category of prescription drugs. The most abused are stimulants, depressants, and pain relievers.

Stimulants. Stimulants, such as amphetamines, are prescribed for numerous conditions, including depression, ADD, obesity, and narcolepsy. Stimulants can increase alertness, attention, and energy. Common prescription names include Ritalin, Adderall, and Dexedrine. Prolonged use of these medications can develop a tolerance to the drug, and tolerance can lead to taking higher doses. This pattern of prescription use can lead to addiction.

Depressants. Central nervous system depressants are commonly used to treat sleep disorders, tension, panic attacks, and anxiety. Two categories of depressants are barbiturates and benzodiazepines. These types of medicines slow brain activity, resulting in a calming effect for the user. Though both types are depressants, drugs considered tranquilizers are mainly of the benzodiazepine family, and drugs considered sedatives are mostly barbiturate preparations. Common prescription names include Xanax and Valium. Long-term consequences are similar to those of stimulants, in that a person is at risk for developing a tolerance, which then can lead to addiction.

Pain relievers. The pain relievers most at risk of abuse belong to the narcotic analgesic family of drugs derived from opium poppies. Opioid drugs elevate dopamine levels in the brain and trigger feelings of pleasure. Drugs derived from opioids are used to relieve moderate-to-severe chronic pain. Common brand names include OxyContin, Vicodin, Percocet, Darvon, and Demerol. Users of narcotic analgesics can develop a tolerance over a prolonged period of use. This tolerance may lead to higher dosage, which in turn may lead to addiction. Opioid drugs have the ability to elevate dopamine levels in the brain, but prolonged use or misuse has the potential to permanently change the brain in fundamental ways. Among the various pain relievers, OxyContin (also called "hillbilly heroin" owing to its initial emergence as a serious health problem within rural areas across the United States) has been receiving greater attention due to dramatic increases in abuse.

Size of the problem

Uncovering and learning what types of prescription drugs are being abused and misused is very difficult. Prescription drug abuse is not always easy to detect. For example, it may not be obvious that someone is physically dependent until he or she runs out of medication and begins to experience withdrawal symptoms. However, national surveys and various research studies focusing on prescription drug abuse have elucidated the extent of this

type of substance abuse within the United States. In general, the majority of research studies reveal that the population most likely to abuse prescription drugs includes the elderly, whites, females, and, increasingly, adolescents and young adults.

According to the 2009 National Survey on Drug Use and Health (NSDUH) report, there were 7.0 million (2.8 percent) persons in the United States aged 12 or older who currently used prescription-type psychotherapeutic drugs nonmedically. Of this group of users, an estimated 5.3 million persons used pain relievers nonmedically in the past month, 2.0 million used tranquilizers, 1.3 million used stimulants, and 370,000 used sedatives.

In terms of lifetime use among respondents in 2009, 51.8 million persons (20.6 percent) aged 12 and older reported nonmedical use of a psychotherapeutic drug. The largest group of drugs used was pain relievers, with 35 million persons (13.9 percent) aged 12 and older reporting lifetime use. As a group, more people reported using Vicodin, Lortab, and Lorcet than any other group (22 million, 8.8 percent of the 12 and older population), followed by Darvocet, Darvon, or Tylenol with codeine (19 million users, 7.5 percent); Percocet, Percodan, and Tylox (13 million users, 5.4 percent); hydrocodone (9.6 million, 3.8 percent); and OxyContin (5.8 million, 2.3 percent). While the overall trend in lifetime use of nonmedical prescription drugs has

Self-reported use of prescription drugs for nonmedical reasons (age 12 and above).

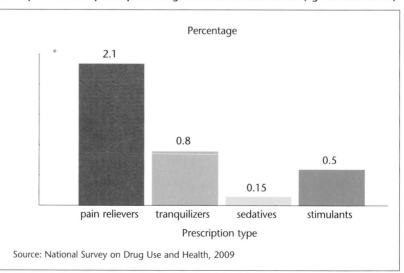

Source: National Survey on Drug Use and Health, 2009

remained relatively stable, the use of OxyContin has substantially increased since 2002 (the earliest year with comparable data). There were 1.9 million users in 2002 (.08 percent of the over 12 population). The number increased to 5.8 million in 2009 (2.3 percent of the population.)

NSDUH findings for 2009 reveal important age differences in prescription drug abuse. For example, among respondents aged 12 to 17, 10 percent reported past month illicit drug use, 3.1 percent reported using prescription-type drugs for nonmedical reasons, while 7.3 percent reported monthly marijuana use. The highest rate of general illicit drug use was that of young adults aged 18 to 25 (20.3 percent). Nonmedical use of prescription-type drugs was reported by 6.3 percent of young adults and, similar to the younger age group, nonprescription drug use was second only to marijuana (18.1 percent). Among adults aged 26 or older, 6.3 percent reported current illicit drug use, 2.1 percent reported current prescription drug use, and 4.6 percent reported current marijuana use.

New initiates concerning the abuse of pain relievers are an important topic to address. According to the NSDUH, pain relievers had the highest number of new users in 2009, with 2.1 million new users versus tranquilizers with 1.2 million, stimulants with 702,000, and sedatives with 186,000. To put this in perspective, there were an estimated 2.3 million new marijuana users and 617,000 new cocaine users in 2009. In terms of the first substance used by persons 12 years old and above in 2009, psychotherapeutics as a category accounted for 28.6 percent, including 17.1 percent for pain relievers, 8.6 percent for tranquilizers, 2.0 percent for stimulants, and 1.0 percent for sedatives. Such first use was exceeded only by marijuana, which was the first drug used among 59.1 percent of new initiates.

Other than age, 2009 NSDUH findings do not reveal many other significant demographic differences. Although other research studies have revealed that females are more likely than males to abuse prescription drugs, NSDUH finds no gender differences in the rate of any nonmedical prescription use (3.1 percent for males against 2.4 percent for females). However, there are other equally important national surveys to compliment those conducted by the NSDUH. Another commonly cited resource is the Drug Abuse Warning Network (DAWN).

DAWN collects information on drug-related hospital emergency room episodes. DAWN defines a drug episode as an emergency room visit related to the use of an illegal drug (or combination of drugs), or the nonmedical use of legal drugs (specifically for patients aged 6 to 97 years old). A drug mention is defined as the mention of a substance (up to four) during an emergency room episode. In terms of nonmedical use of legal drugs, DAWN records emergency room episodes that involve the intentional abuse of prescribed or legally obtained pharmaceuticals. However, these numbers do not account for accidental overdoses. In the DAWN data from 2007, 1.9 million of 116 million total emergency department episodes involved some form of drug misuse. Of the 1.9 million visits associated with drug misuse or abuse in 2007, 855,838 involved nonmedical use of prescription or over-the-counter drugs. This figure is up 60 percent from 2004 (536,247 episodes). Thirty-one percent of 2007 episodes involved nonmedical use of pharmaceuticals only, 10 percent involved alcohol with nonmedical use of pharmaceuticals, 8 percent involved illicit drugs with any pharmaceuticals, and 4 percent involved illicit drugs with pharmaceuticals plus alcohol.

The main detailed breakdowns utilized by DAWN are psychotherapeutic agents and central nervous system agents. Psychotherapeutic agents include antidepressants, stimulants, and sedatives. As a category, psychotherapeutic agent episodes increased 43 percent from 2004 to 2007. Within the category, abuse of stimulants increased significantly in emergency departments from 2004 to 2007 by 89 percent (9,801 to 18,561). Episodes involving benzodiazepines, a type of depressant, increased significantly by 52 percent during the same period, from 143,546 to 218,640. Episodes involving central nervous system agents, including opiates, increased 47% from 2004 to 2007, from 282,296 to 415,354. By far the largest portion of these involved pain medications, which increased 51 percent from 241,578 in 2004 to 363,621 in 2007.

DAWN has shown a long-term increase in opioid mentions since 1995, being driven largely by oxycodone preparations (for example, OxyContin) and hydrocodone (Vicodin). However, these drugs are not always reported alone. Many of the various prescription drugs discussed are also reported in combination with other drugs or medications. For example, three-quarters of emergency room visits that involved the mention of oxycodone and hydrocodone also mentioned other drugs.

From 2004 to 2007 the mentions of hydrocodone (Vicodin) increased 65 percent, mentions of oxycodone combinations (OxyContin) increased 84 percent, and mentions of unspecified narcotic analgesics increased 117 percent. These findings have alarmed both medical practitioners and law-enforcement officials alike.

Oxycodone has become the leading cause of episodes involving pain medication, eclipsing hydrocodone. According to DAWN findings, hydrocodone mentions used to be twice as high as oxycodone; however, this gap has shrunk significantly since the 1990s, with the rate of oxycodone dramatically increasing. For example, there were over 10,000 more oxycodone combination episodes than hydrocodone episodes in 2007. Looking back, there were only 4,000 mentions of oxycodone in 1994. In 2002 there were 22,000, and in 2007 there were 76,587. This is a 1900 percent increase. In 1994, there were 9,300 mentions of hydrocodone and in 2002 there were 25,000. In 2007, there were 65,734. This is a 700 percent increase. Attention should not be completely invested in oxycodone abuse because hydrocodone remains the more popular pain reliever drug of choice, and overall, pain medications are the most commonly abused prescription drug.

According to DAWN 2007 findings, 70 percent of all prescription drug episodes involved persons who were white, 12 percent involved persons who were African American, and 9 percent involved Hispanic/Latino persons. Also, according to DAWN 2007 findings, there were no significant gender differences in emergency department episodes.

Drugs and the elderly

An important and underexamined population that is extremely vulnerable to prescription drug abuse is the elderly. Although reports on nonmedical prescription drug use among youth and young adults have increased steadily since the 1990s, the population most likely to misuse prescription drugs

DOCTOR SHOPPING

Doctor shopping involves a person feigning an illness or pain to obtain a prescription. A person feigning an illness will visit as many doctors as possible to get numerous prescriptions and build up a large supply of a drug. If these prescriptions do not go through insurance companies, doctor shopping is very difficult to detect. Many doctors may not be aware that they are one of many writing a pain reliever prescription for the same person.

is the elderly. The elderly (aged 65 and above) consume one-third of all prescription drugs, although they represent only 13 percent of the population. National surveys may not detect the amount of prescription drug abuse among this population is because the elderly are difficult to monitor. Some refer to prescription drug abuse among the elderly as an invisible epidemic because the phenomenon is largely undiagnosed and undertreated. This is becoming an increasing concern because adults aged 65 and older are the fastest-growing sector of the American population.

Common risk factors for prescription abuse among the elderly include social isolation, chronic physical illness, being female, having a history of psychiatric hospitalization, and past alcohol abuse. Benzo-diazepines and opiates are the most commonly abused prescription drugs among the elderly. Prescription drug abuse causes unique and serious complications for the elderly. As a result of the fragile medical conditions of most elderly populations, abuse of prescription medications increases the likelihood of serious negative health consequences and, in turn, emergency room visits.

Prevention and treatment

There are many components involved in preventing prescription drug abuse. These components include monitoring the medical community, educating the public and prescription drug users, adequately monitoring prescription use, and the early detection of misuse.

From the perspective of education and detection, it is the primary health care physicians, pharmacists, and nurse practitioners who become the first line of defense in preventing prescription drug abuse. General practitioners should critically evaluate the need to prescribe strong medication. There are many people suffering from severe or chronic pain who legitimately need narcotic pain relievers; however, there is still a large population of people who may not need them. Once a prescription is written, general practitioners and nurse practitioners should closely monitor their patients' use. Pharmacists also have the opportunity to advise users on how to use the medication appropriately. They also have the ability to detect prescription fraud by being watchful for altered or false prescription forms.

However, most prevention techniques may fail when the doctor is intentionally writing unnecessary prescriptions for nonexistent medical problems. There are many doctors who are misled by dishonest patients who are "doctor shopping", and there are other doctors who sell prescriptions for money. Prescription drug abuse is difficult to enforce because a large proportion of prescription abusers are getting their drugs legitimately through a doctor's prescription. A key prevention technique entails ensuring that doctors are writing prescriptions for patients who rightly deserve them.

Another important component of prevention is raising public awareness of the dangers of misusing and abusing prescription drugs. In 2001 the National Institute for Drug Abuse (NIDA) and the Federal Drug Administration (FDA) joined forces to create a new initiative to educate the public about prescription drug abuse, specifically abuse of oxycodone.

For those who are already abusing prescription drugs, there are various types of treatment options available today. Treatment may vary depending on the type of prescription drug that is being abused, but two common treatment techniques include behavioral and pharmacological treatment. The first step in treatment is usually detoxification, ridding the body of the drug and managing any withdrawal symptoms.

Behavioral treatments educate abusers about how to function without the drug, how to manage cravings, and how to avoid or deal with relapse. Behavioral treatments may include group, family, or individual counseling. Pharmacological treatments, on the other hand, treat addiction with medications. These medications can decrease the physical signs of withdrawal and counteract the effects of the drug on the brain. There are no medications that treat stimulant addiction, so behavioral treatment is used. Owing to the potentially serious negative consequences of detoxification, treatment for depressant addiction should always begin with closely supervised detoxification. Successful detoxification is usually followed by behavioral treatments, such as cognitive behavior therapy or counseling. Opioid or painkiller addiction can be treated with various types of medications, depending on the patient. Medications include methadone and naltrexone. The FDA added another drug, buprenorphine, to the list of treatment medications for opioid addiction in 2002.

For the elderly, behavioral treatment and counseling are two of the most important ways of treating prescription drug abuse. One of the risk factors for prescription abuse among this population is social isolation. Important elements of treatment for this vulnerable population include the creation of a network of friends and family who will visit on a regular basis and increasing the opportunity to socialize with peers who are healthy. Physical withdrawal for the elderly is obviously a complex treatment conducted on a case-by-case basis.

Final note

Prescription drug abuse is an important issue to address across many different types of populations. Gender is obviously a complex yet important factor in understanding prescription drug abuse and will require more critical attention and analysis. Although risk factors that lead different populations to abuse prescription drugs may vary, an important line of defense for the general public—for both those who intentionally and unintentionally abuse—is the primary physician. Not only does the general public need increased awareness and education about the dangers of prescription drug abuse, but so do doctors.

E. J. FARLEY, D. J. O'CONNELL

SEE ALSO:
Pharmacy Drugs

Prohibition of Drugs

Prohibition of drug use is not a recent phenomenon—it has been going on for thousands of years. The arguments for controlling drug availability range from public health concerns to preventing more widespread use.

In 1854 James Johnson, professor of chemistry at the University of Durham in England, wrote about drugs, "from the most distant times…the craving for such indulgence…[is] little less universal than the desire for…consuming the necessary materials of our common food."

It is not only humans that seek to alter their moods through the use of drugs (including alcohol, tobacco, and caffeine). The African elephant will travel miles to seek out the fermenting fruit of a particular tree simply to get drunk. Cats love catnip; in the laboratory, monkeys will self-administer cocaine for as long as the researchers let them. It would seem that this desire for intoxication is innate for many animals as well as humans. At the same time, this desire can cause society immense problems—and the history of prohibition has been the history of the tension between what seems to be a basic human instinct and the need to control intoxication in society.

Concerns about intoxication go far back into ancient history. There are Egyptian hieroglyphs condemning those who fall down drunk in the street, and in Rome it was against the law to be drunk when in charge of a chariot. Women and slaves were forbidden to drink alcohol for fear that it would lead to sexual impurity in the former and loss of productivity in the latter. In general, the ancient world and tribal societies (both ancient and modern) have never had much of a problem with the substances that those societies successfully assimilated. For example, tribal societies in South America use very powerful hallucinogenic plants as part of their rituals and ceremonies. Because there are strict religious and social taboos about how and when these drugs are used, the tribe is able to contain any problems. By contrast, when Native Americans first encountered strong liquor from white traders, it caused serious problems within their communities.

From the sixteenth century onward, major changes in Western society made people much more receptive to the use and overuse of an increasing range of drugs. Life was becoming more urbanized, large numbers of people were crammed together, and drug-using behaviors were able to spread more quickly among societies that had been broken up and dislocated from their traditional rural existence. Scientific progress led to the processing of more powerful drugs through the distilling of whiskey and gin and the extraction of morphine and cocaine from opium and coca. More efficient ways of taking drugs were also developed, for example, the cigarette and the hypodermic syringe.

The World Health Organization estimated that in 2004 1.1 billion people smoked cigarettes, on average every person over 15 consumed 1 to 3 gallons of alcohol (5–10 liters) during the year, and that nearly 5 percent of the total world population has tried an illegal drug.

Reasons for prohibition

Why are some drugs illegal? Though the answer may seem obvious, it is more complex than might first appear. One answer, of course, is that drugs such as heroin, cocaine, or methamphetamine can be dangerous. Consequently, there is a public health imperative that demands that society makes some substances as hard to obtain as possible. Medical concerns raised by doctors about drugs go back to a time in the nineteenth century when drugs such as morphine, opium, and cocaine were perfectly legal ingredients for a wide range of medicines. As newer, safer drugs became available, the case for the legal supply of these and other drugs diminished and contributed to their final control under the law.

That, however, is not the whole story. Everybody knows how dangerous alcohol and tobacco can be, yet they remain legal. So too are a range of painkillers that can be lethal in overdose or least cause permanent damage to the liver. In fact, all drugs have the potential to be dangerous if misused. So there must be other factors in determining which drugs are legal and which are banned. One of the most influential is the degree to which society finds a particular drug acceptable or has managed to assimilate it into the culture. For example, alcohol can cause enormous damage not only to the individual but also to society through drunk driving and violence. Yet the attempt to control alcohol consumption in the United States through Prohibition (1919–1933) failed, mainly because the majority of people did not support it. By contrast, many Muslim countries, some of which have a long tradition of opium and marijuana smoking, ban alcohol. Certain types of drug use may also be tolerated among ethnic populations within a larger community. The importation and chewing of khat leaves by immigrant groups from some East African countries is permitted in the United Kingdom despite its amphetamine-like effects. As yet there are few concerns about khat because its use is largely confined to small populations, but any increase in problematic use among its native users or a spread in

Although illegal drug use is prohibited in many parts of the world, efforts continue to prevent any relaxation of drug laws that might make drugs more freely available to a wider population.

use to the wider community may eventually see khat placed on the schedule of controlled substances.

Commercial interests have long played a part in the decision to prohibit or legalize substances. The nineteenth century demand for patent medicines provided a buoyant market fueled by the easily available and highly addictive nature of many of its products. It was only when public concerns grew that the U.S. government decided to decommercialize drug distribution and put drug use in the hands of the medical profession, which it did by making drug sales subject to registration, taxation, and criminal penalties. Taxation has long been a method of controlling substance use. James I of England was vehemently against smoking but needed tobacco revenues for the financial good of the country. Both alcohol and tobacco sales continue to bring in substantial revenues to government treasuries all over the world. There is also the power of vested interests. The tobacco and alcohol industries have been very effective in maintaining their profits and position through their political influence. However, health concerns about passive smoking have created a growing backlash, leading to bans on smoking in public places in many parts of the world; these bans may yet have financial implications for the tobacco industry and the licensed premises that traditionally allowed smoking.

Religious and moral groups have also been able to influence policy. In the nineteenth century in Britain, but even more so in the United States, powerful middle-class temperance (anti-alcohol) and antidrug groups campaigned to have substances banned because they believed that intoxication of any sort was morally wrong and that it undermined progress in society by distracting people away from healthy pursuits and employment. This approach was not limited to capitalist economies— communist countries took a similarly dim view of drugs and alcohol as undermining the aims of the collective society.

Racism, too, has played its part in that the association of certain drugs with different ethnic groups in society has prompted selectively draconian responses. The backlash against the use of opium in the Chinese community in the United States during the latter part of the nineteenth century is one example.

ARGUMENTS AGAINST LEGALIZATION

Some of the main arguments for the maintenance of the laws against drugs are as follows:

- Drug use can cause significant harm to individuals, so the state has a duty to protect its citizens, even from themselves.
- Laws against drugs send out the message from government that intoxication can have harmful effects on society at large.
- To legalize drugs would make the drug situation far worse because those who are currently discouraged from drug use by the law would experiment, and those who are already using would probably use more.
- It is unrealistic to think that with so much money at stake, organized crime would cease if drugs were legalized. Criminals would find another way to be involved and make profits from selling drugs to undercut the legal price or overcome age restrictions. In any case, a drug such as marijuana can be grown anywhere, so there is every chance that the illicit market would thrive because the legal market would be heavily taxed.
- Those who want to legalize drugs have not answered some key questions. What drugs would be available? Who is going to have access to which drugs? Given how hard it is to regulate the markets for alcohol and tobacco —especially stopping young people from using—what controls can be effective against the use of a far wider range of drugs?
- People who use illegal drugs know the risks they are taking. People have to take responsibility for their own actions. Some of the reform options, such as decriminalization, would make matters worse. It would do nothing to undermine the illicit market while encouraging more widespread use.
- Legalizers say that legal and widely available alcohol and tobacco cause far more deaths and damage than drugs. How much more damage would there be if drugs such as heroin and cocaine could be obtained more easily? If alcohol and tobacco were currently illegal, it is unlikely they would now be made legal.
- There is no demand from the majority of the population for drugs to be legalized. Most people strongly oppose legalization. In some countries, experiments with decriminalizing certain drugs in some countries were rescinded once the consequences were felt by the wider community.

All of these factors and others came together between 1914 and 1939 to establish the national and international control system that is largely in place today. During that period, the production, manufacture, supply, and possession of the major plant-based drugs—opium, coca, and marijuana—and their derivatives were all severely controlled with stiff penalties. From the 1960s onward, as new drugs moved from legal or medical use to street drug, the law has intervened; LSD, amphetamines, barbiturates, and Ecstasy have been added to lists of controlled substances as their addictive or psychoactive properties have become perceived as a problem to society. Other than for established cultural uses, the majority of governments around the world prohibit recreational drug use and have a range of enforcement agencies in place to deal with illegal drugs and those who supply and possess them. There are also highly vocal and organized lobby groups, such as the Partnership for a Drug-Free America and Drug Watch International, that campaign against attempts to legalize or decriminalize drug use and support approaches aimed at prevention, education, law enforcement, and treatment.

H. SHAPIRO

SEE ALSO:

Drug Control Policy • Drug Laws • Legal Controls • Legalization Movement

Prozac

Hailed as the "happiness pill," Prozac has been prescribed to millions of people worldwide. It undoubtedly alters mood but it has limited effectiveness in drug abuse treatment.

Pharmacological studies have provided powerful evidence that the imbalance of a natural brain chemical called serotonin (5-HT) is linked to depression. During the 1960s, scientists discovered that certain drugs that block the reentry of 5-HT into the nerve cell (5-HT reuptake), could improve depressive moods and behavior. Since then, much effort has been put into developing antidepressant drugs called selective serotonin reuptake inhibitors (SSRIs), which increase the availability and utilization of 5-HT in the brain. Among SSRIs, the drug fluoxetine, under the trade name Prozac, has become the most widely prescribed antidepressant. Prozac acts by blocking the reuptake of 5-HT, which in turn increases extracellular levels of 5-HT, thereby stimulating positive behavioral and physiological functions mediated by this neurotransmitter. Another effect that underlies the antidepressant action of Prozac is the suppression of 5-HT neuronal firing, which decreases 5-HT synthesis and turnover and leads to overall enhancement of serotonergic transmission.

Prozac has a long half-life of one to four days, and its active metabolite has a half-life of about one to two weeks. The antidepressant effect of Prozac increases with time and repeated doses, so it may take several weeks of treatment before symptoms lessen.

Clinical indications for use of Prozac

Prozac is the first line of therapy for patients suffering from depressive illnesses. It is also effective in the treatment of depressive, methadone-maintained opioid addicts. Although Prozac appears to be moderately effective in the treatment of some depressed cocaine addicts, current evidence does not support its use in the treatment of cocaine addiction and dependence. Controlled clinical studies have demonstrated that Prozac reduces symptoms of obsessive-compulsive disorder, and it has also been successful in the treatment of panic and anxiety disorders, either alone or in combination with a benzodiazepine drug, alprazolam. Prozac significantly

---

KEY FACTS

Classification
Unscheduled (United States, Canada, UK, and INCB)

Short-term effects
Quickly relieves depression

Long-term effects
Appetite loss, weight loss, nausea, anxiety, rashes, insomnia, loss of libido, and sexual dysfunction

---

decreases binge-eating and purging activity in bulimia nervosa, but in the long-term treatment of obesity has been mainly unsuccessful. Prozac reduces alcohol consumption, and this may have an application for heavy drinkers.

Side effects of Prozac

In clinical trials, adverse effects commonly reported were complaints of the central nervous system, including insomnia, drowsiness, fatigue, sweating, and tremor, and gastrointestinal problems, such as nausea and diarrhea. Less common were allergic or toxic reactions such as rash, urticaria, and chills. A few patients experienced chest pain, hypertension, arrhythmia, and tachycardia; others reported bronchitis, rhinitis, and yawning. Urogenital problems were related to painful menstruation, sexual dysfunction, and urinary infections. Because of the long half-life of Prozac, active substances may be present for two months, even when no longer being taken, which could prolong the side effects.

A. VICENTIC

SEE ALSO:
Antidepressant Drugs • Prescription Drugs • Psychotropic Drugs • Serotonin • SSRIs

Psilocybin and Psilocin

Certain species of mushrooms contain the psychoactive compounds psilocybin and psilocin. While considered less powerful than LSD, these mushrooms can produce uncomfortable feelings in anyone unprepared for their effects.

The plant kingdom is a rich source of psychoactive drugs; marijuana, cocaine, and opioids all have their origins in plants. Fungi are no exception, their effects giving rise to the name "magic mushrooms." Mushrooms belonging to the *Psilocybe* genus contain two hallucinogenic compounds, psilocybin and psilocin, chemically related to the neurotransmitter serotonin (5-HT) and to LSD. Although there are many species within the genus, *Psilocybe semilanceata* (the liberty cap) is the most widely available and the most reliable in terms of drug content. These compounds produce similar effects to LSD but have only about 1 percent of the activity of LSD. Psilocin is 50 percent more active than psilocybin. The *Amanita* genus of mushrooms, which includes *Amanita muscaria* (fly agaric), contains different psychoactive compounds.

The mushrooms of the *Psilocybe* genus can be eaten raw, cooked, or steeped with hot water to form an infusion. They can be dried or frozen for later use. Estimating a suitable dose is not easy. It depends on the size and freshness of the mushrooms and the subject's weight and stomach contents. Two to four mushrooms produce effects of relaxation and mild euphoria: 20 to 30 may be required for a full psychedelic experience, including euphoria, hallucinations, and overlap of sensory impressions ("seeing" colors and "hearing" sounds). The speed of onset of effects is determined by the method of consumption. Effects may begin within five minutes of an infusion, but are likely to be delayed 30 minutes or longer if the mushrooms are eaten. The desired psychoactive effects may be preceded by activation of the sympathetic nervous system, resulting in flushing, dry mouth, and increased heart rate. The psychedelic experience may last 4 to 8 hours but is much milder and less frenetic than with LSD. Bad trips are possible but less frequent than experiences with LSD. However, there is always a risk with mushrooms, particularly dried mushrooms of unknown origin, of poisoning and sudden death. Tolerance to the psychoactive effects develops rapidly (3 to 4 days of daily use), as does cross-tolerance to chemically similar drugs, such as LSD and dimethyltryptamine (DMT). There is no evidence of physical addiction, but psychological dependence may occur.

There is very little direct evidence on the mechanism of action of psilocybin and psilocin. The similarity of their effects to those of LSD is the most compelling evidence for a similar mechanism. Thus the ability of psilocybin and psilocin to mimic the actions of serotonin (5-HT) is generally accepted as the underlying mechanism. However, LSD's interaction with 5-HT receptors (and therefore by implication that of psilocybin and psilocin) is complex and incompletely understood. An agonist action at the subtype of receptors termed 5-HT_2 is the most generally accepted explanation of the hallucinogenic effects.

R. W. HORTON

KEY FACTS

Classification
Schedule I (USA), Schedule III (Canada), Class A (UK), Schedule I (INCB). Hallucinogen.

Street names
Boomers, magic mushrooms, musk, sherm, shrooms, Simple Simon

Short-term effects
Nausea, feeling cold, open-eye visuals, distortions of time, feelings of spiritual and emotional sensitivity. At high doses, users may become fearful and anxious over repressed memories. Closed-eye visuals and a feeling of "waking up" from everyday life are common.

SEE ALSO:
DMT • Hallucinogens • LSD • Tryptamines

Psychotropic Drugs

Chemicals that alter mental activity or behavior are known as psychotropic substances. A wide range of legal and illegal drugs fall into this category; they are used for medical and nonmedical purposes precisely for such effects.

Psychotropic drugs are chemical compounds that affect human behavior and mental state through their pharmacological action on the brain and central nervous system. This definition broadly includes all mood-altering drugs with hallucinogenic, stimulatory, or depressant effects. However, the term *psychotropic* is more frequently applied to prescription psychiatric medications such as Prozac.

There are around 150 psychotropic pharmaceuticals used in the treatment of anxiety, depression, and behavioral problems. Perhaps another 50 psychotropic drugs are illegally produced or diverted into illicit traffic from legitimate manufacture. Notable illegal psychotropics include the hallucinogens such as lysergic acid (LSD) and the widely used club drug Ecstasy (MDMA). Ecstasy has been shown to damage serotonin and dopamine-producing neural cells and, in rare but well-documented cases, to lead to a severe and fatal toxicity syndrome. Such drugs cannot be registered as safe and medically useful. Their undoubted popularity among some groups thus creates a major dilemma for scientists, drug policy makers, and law enforcement. The international legal framework for the control of these drugs was last updated in 1988 in the United Nations Convention Against Illicit Traffic in Narcotic Drugs and Psychotropic Substances.

Psychotropic drug treatment of mental illness

The most widespread use of psychotropic compounds is in the treatment of depression, for which more than 65 million prescriptions are written annually in the United States. The first major specifically psychotherapeutic drug was lithium, whose beneficial effects on bipolar (manic-depressive) patients were reported in 1949. In 1952 chlorpromazine was introduced for the treatment of schizophrenia, and Iproniazid was licensed in 1957 for the treatment of depression. Imipramine, the first of the tricyclic antidepressants, introduced around 1960, did not have the side effects of jaundice occasionally produced by Iproniazid and largely replaced this drug.

Analogs of Iproniazid and Imipramine were synthesized to improve their safety and activity; however, drugs with specific effects on neurotransmission that could pass strict clinical trials of safety and efficacy in alleviating depression proved difficult to identify. The breakthrough was the discovery that fluoxetine hydrochloride can block reuptake of the neurotransmitter serotonin. This compound, the first major specific serotonin reuptake inhibitor (SSRI), was marketed in 1987 as Prozac. It works because serotonin controls neural pathways affecting mood. Some depressed individuals have too little serotonin to enable fully effective communication to occur between neural cells. SSRIs prevent serotonin removal, thus enabling serotonin levels to rise and reestablish cellular communication without affecting other neurotransmission pathways. Over a period of weeks, Prozac raises serotonin to normal levels and has proved highly successful in relieving anxiety and depression.

Behavioral regulation with psychotropic drugs

Many of the tens of millions of current SSRI users do not fall into clinical definitions of severe depression but take the drug to relieve what may be mild and transient unhappiness, a situation that has given rise to ethical debate. More controversial still is the widespread prescription, particularly in the United States, of psychotropic stimulant drugs such as methylphenidate and its relatives, compounds related to amphetamines. These psychostimulants, the best known of which is Ritalin, are prescribed for the treatment of attention deficit disorders (ADD), usually in male children and adolescents.

D. E. ARNOT

SEE ALSO:
Antidepressant Drugs • Classification of Drugs • Controlled Substances • Hallucinogens • Narcotic Drugs • SSRIs

Reserpine

Reserpine is derived from a plant used to treat high blood pressure. It works by reducing neurotransmitters such as dopamine and norepinephrine in nerve cells, which makes it an interesting drug for studying the natural causes of depression.

Reserpine is obtained from the dried roots of the snakeroot plant *(Rauwolfia serpentina)*, a small evergreen climbing shrub native to the Indian subcontinent. Known in India as *sarpaganda*, the plant has been used for centuries as an antidote for snakebites, treatment of high blood pressure, fever, insomnia, and wounds. However, it was not until 1952 that an active chemical, reserpine, responsible for the effects of the plant, was isolated from *Rauwolfia*. Reserpine occurs as an odorless, white or pale yellow-colored crystalline powder that is sensitive to light and is insoluble in water.

The main clinical use of reserpine is to treat mild to moderate hypertension (high blood pressure). It acts by depleting the stores of signal-carrying transmitters such as catecholamines (dopamine and norepinephrine) and serotonin in many organs, including the heart and the brain. Catecholamines in general have a stimulatory effect on the heart and act to constrict blood vessels. By depleting catecholamine stores, reserpine prevents blood pressure from rising. The usual adult daily dose for hypertension treatment is up to 0.5 milligrams by mouth.

The effect of reserpine on transmitters in the brain causes central nervous system depression. Early use of reserpine exploited this to produce a tranquilizing effect and was used for the management of conditions such as schizophrenia and psychoses. Although reserpine is no longer used to treat these conditions, since newer and better antipsychotic drugs have been developed, it has often been called the original tranquilizer. Reserpine is often used as a tranquilizer in veterinary practices, especially to sedate show horses.

The side effects of reserpine are generally mild and infrequent. The commonly observed problems include drowsiness, dizziness, lethargy, increased dreaming, nightmares, abdominal cramps, and diarrhea. Reserpine is an unusual drug as it may take days to several weeks to reach its full effect and continues to have some sedative effects for weeks after treatment is discontinued. Its major side effect,

> ## KEY FACTS
>
> **Classification**
> Not scheduled in US, Canada, UK, or INCB.
> Antihypertensive.
>
> **Short-term effects**
> Reduced blood pressure, diarrhea, dryness of mouth, loss of appetite, nausea, stuffy nose
>
> **Long-term effects**
> Some effects persist several weeks to months after drug withdrawal and might include mental depression severe enough to cause suicide, sedation, decreased sexual interest, and slow heartbeat.

however, is mental depression, which can lead to suicide. The fact that the drug is known to reduce concentrations of many of the brain's mood-enhancing chemicals makes it a useful tool for research into the causes of naturally occurring depression, which can be a trigger for drug abuse.

Although there are no documented reports of reserpine being abused as a psychedelic (producing visual hallucinations), the plant has traditionally been used by holy men in India to achieve detachment while meditating. The use of reserpine has dropped dramatically over the years because of the introduction of newer drugs. However, it is still the cheapest antihypertensive agent available. In the wake of mounting costs of treating hypertension, many have suggested that inexpensive older drugs such as reserpine should be given a second chance.

A. KAPUR, J. DERRY

SEE ALSO:
Dopamine • Norepinephrine • Serotonin

Ritalin

Many children diagnosed with attention deficit disorder are prescribed Ritalin to improve their concentration. However, Ritalin is a member of the amphetamine family, and therefore has potential for drug abuse.

Ritalin is the trade name for the drug methylphenidate used by the pharmaceutical manufacturer Novartis, and it has also become the common name for the drug. Methylphenidate is available from a number of other drug manufacturers as well, under a variety of names. Methylphenidate is a psychostimulant drug and, as such, belongs to the same pharmacological class as cocaine and amphetamine. Ritalin is most well-known as the treatment for attention deficit disorders (ADD), though it has also long been used in the treatment of narcolepsy and is sometimes used in the treatment of stroke.

Methylphenidate was first synthesized in 1944 and went on the market as a prescription drug in the mid-1950s. At the time it was recommended for the treatment of lethargy, narcolepsy, and depression. Since the mid-1960s, Ritalin has been the primary pharmacological treatment for ADD. In ADD, which is found most often in boys, though it is seen in girls and adults as well, patients are unable to concentrate, usually on schoolwork, and may become loud and disruptive in search of stimulation. Ritalin has been found to increase the ability of ADD patients to focus attention and to reduce the impulsivity and behavioral disruptions the disorder can produce. The exact mechanism by which Ritalin acts remains poorly understood. Like cocaine and amphetamine, Ritalin acts at the transporter proteins for the neurotransmitters dopamine and norepinephrine. There is some evidence that at therapeutic doses Ritalin principally effects norepinephrine, rather than dopamine. Dopamine is more strongly correlated with abuse potential, which may explain why methylphenidate is not as widely abused as cocaine or amphetamine. Therapeutically it is less likely to produce tolerance and toxic side effects than its relatives, and it is thus preferred for clinical uses.

Ritalin is not entirely benign, however. Concerns about its potential for abuse have been voiced since the early 1960s. The oral form used in prescriptions is not the preferred form for abusers; more often abusers will grind the pills into a powder and then either inject or snort it. All three routes have been reported clinically in abusers, and the latter two have been associated with a number of deaths. Ritalin is sometimes injected mixed with Talwin (pentazocine) or heroin as a speedball. Reports of abuse and toxicity have become more common as diagnosis of ADD has increased and the drug has become more available. During the period from 1985 to 1995, methylphenidate production in the United States increased nearly eightfold to more than 10 tons a year.

R. G. HUNTER

SEE ALSO:
Amphetamines • Dopamine • Norepinephrine

KEY FACTS

Classification
Schedule II (USA), Schedule III (Canada), Class B (UK), Schedule II (INCB). Stimulant.

Street names
R, Rit, Ts and Rits (with Talwin), Vitamin R, West Coast

Short-term effects
Like other psychostimulants, Ritalin can produce reduced appetite, agitation, increased activity, constricted pupils and verbosity. Anxiety and paranoia are common negative states associated with Ritalin abuse. In ADD patients, Ritalin has a paradoxical calming effect at therapeutic doses.

Long-term effects
Ritalin may increase the chances of seizures and cardiovascular events in predisposed individuals or in overdose situations. Withdrawal from Ritalin may produce major depressive episodes.

Rohypnol

Rohypnol is a brand name for flunitrazepam, a benzodiazepine drug similar to Valium. It is one of the so-called date-rape drugs, because some criminals use it to render their victims vulnerable to sexual assault or robbery.

Rohypnol (flunitrazepam) is a benzodiazepine, a class of drugs that also includes Valium (diazepam), Restoril (temazepam), and Xanax (alprazolam). These drugs reduce anxiety and can cause sedation by enhancing the action of GABA (gamma-aminobutyric acid), a neurotransmitter that calms brain activity. Sedative benzodiazepines also block memory formation during their period of action, which makes them useful for surgery.

Differences in potency, speed of onset, and duration of effect between individual benzodiazepines make them suitable for diverse applications. When Roche launched Rohypnol in 1975, its intended uses included insomnia treatment and the induction of anesthesia, since the drug takes effect within 30 minutes and has up to 10 times the sedative potency of diazepam. The effects of a dose of Rohypnol usually wear off within 10 hours.

Recreational use

Rohypnol soon became a street drug through the diversion of prescription supplies. In common with other benzodiazepines, it amplifies the effects of other central nervous system (CNS) depressants, such as alcohol and opiates. The high potency of Rohypnol increases the danger of death by accidental overdose for people who are accustomed to taking less potent benzodiazepines, such as temazepam. The combination of Rohypnol with alcohol can in some cases unleash violent and cold-blooded behavior by suppressing inhibitions and conscience.

Rohypnol counteracts the effects of CNS stimulants such as cocaine and amphetamines. Hence, some stimulant users take Rohypnol to reduce symptoms of anxiety produced by the stimulant or to bring the stimulant effect to an end and allow them to catch up on sleep.

Whether taken alone or with other drugs, the regular use of Rohypnol or any other benzodiazepine rapidly leads to increased tolerance and physiological dependence. Withdrawal symptoms are diverse and include irritability, restlessness, headaches, delirium,

In itself, the blister packaging of Rohypnol pills is no guarantee of legitimate manufacture or purity. The importation of Rohypnol to the United States has been banned since 1996, and supplies are of clandestine origin. Street names for Rohypnol pills include roofies, rope, ruffies, and Mexican Valium.

and hallucinations. Sudden withdrawal can cause seizures and heart failure several days after taking the last dose, and people who have become dependent on Rohypnol should reduce their intake gradually, with medical guidance and supervision.

Drugged assaults

Rohypnol is odorless, neutral tasting, and colorless, and it dissolves easily in water. Hence, a person who intends to rape or rob can easily slip a sedative dose into the drink of an intended victim without detection. The drug also eliminates all memory of the crime, thereby protecting the criminal.

Roche has introduced a blue dye and sediment-forming material into Rohypnol pills in Europe, but illicitly manufactured doses have no such additives to assist detection. Partygoers should be vigilant of their drinks at all times and contact a responsible friend or staff member if sudden unexpected drunkenness indicates that a drink might have been contaminated.

M. CLOWES

SEE ALSO:
Benzodiazepines • Chloral Hydrate • GHB • Valium

Secobarbital

Secobarbital is a barbiturate, one of a family of sedative drugs that can induce sleep and reduce anxiety. Although rarely used clinically, secobarbital is still used by addicts to reduce the excitatory effects of stimulants.

Secobarbital, also known by its trade name Seconal, is a sedative drug abused for its effects in reducing anxiety and producing relaxation and euphoria. Polydrug abusers use it as a "downer" to reduce the unpleasant side effects of repeated stimulant use. Conversely, secobarbital abusers will use stimulants to remain alert. Secobarbital is sometimes used for sleep induction prior to surgical anesthesia, as the antianxiety effect is very helpful in this setting. It is occasionally used by psychiatrists for its disinhibitory effect to help patients recover repressed memories after psychological damage.

Pharmacological effects

A typical adult oral dose of secobarbital for sleep induction is 100 to 200 milligrams, though abusers may take increasing amounts as tolerance develops. Secobarbital passes relatively quickly through the blood-brain barrier, though not as rapidly as pentobarbital. The drug is metabolized in the liver by the cytochrome P450 enzyme system and prolonged use induces the liver to synthesize more of these enzymes, leading to faster breakdown and contributing to tolerance. The half-life for elimination of the drug is 19 to 34 hours.

Barbiturates such as secobarbital work by enhancing the action of the inhibitory neurotransmitter gamma-aminobutyric acid (GABA) at its receptor on brain neurons. Secobarbital acts as a central nervous system depressant, slowing reflexes and reaction times, dulling the senses, and causing incoordination and slurring of speech before inducing sleep. Sedation occurs within 15 to 30 minutes after oral ingestion, more quickly for other methods of administration, and lasts 6 to 8 hours.

As with other barbiturates, breathing becomes depressed, hence, the risk of a dangerous overdose increases with prolonged use. Street addicts will sometimes dissolve the contents of the capsule in water and inject secobarbital intravenously, a particularly dangerous practice since an overdose can kill within minutes. Secobarbital is often taken

KEY FACTS

Classification
Schedule II (USA), Schedule IV (Canada), Class B (UK), Schedule III (INCB). Sedative.

Street names
Barbs, F-40s, Mexican reds, pink ladies, red birds, red devils, secco, seggy

Short-term effects
Relaxation, euphoria, decreased inhibitions, coordination problems, sleepiness progressing to coma if taken with other depressants

Long-term effects
Insomnia, tremulousness, agitation, erratic behavior, paranoia, social isolation. Risk of fatal overdose.

Signs of abuse
Confused or drunken behavior, sleepiness, shallow breathing, unresponsiveness

together with other depressant drugs including the opiates and alcohol, a dangerous practice that can lead to coma and death. Barbiturate intoxication also impairs the memory, so users may forget that they have taken it and take additional doses. Tolerance develops quickly and contributes to the addictive potential. Dependence on the drug manifests initially as insomnia but can result in a severe withdrawal syndrome consisting of tremulousness, anxiety, delirium, hallucinations, and seizures.

L. J. GREENFIELD, JR.

SEE ALSO:

Amobarbital • Barbiturates • Gamma-aminobutyric Acid • Pentobarbital • Sedatives and Hypnotics

Sedatives and Hypnotics

Sedatives decrease excitement and produce a calming effect. Hypnotics induce sleep. Both effects are part of the same continuum that can lead to unconsciousness, anesthesia, and fatal depression of the respiratory system.

Probably the oldest sedative known is ethanol. Its effects are dose dependent and, as the dose is increased, the subject progresses through all of the stages identified above. Similar effects can be produced by bromide salts, which were introduced specifically as sedatives in the middle of the nineteenth century. Unfortunately, bromide salts produce significant liver and kidney toxicity. Subsequently, chloral hydrate, paraldehyde, urethane, and sulfonal were used for the same purpose before they were superseded by the barbiturates. Barbital appeared in 1903 and phenobarbital in 1912. The barbiturates were used widely for many years as both sedatives and hypnotics, despite the fact that many suffered fatal overdoses from their use. Indeed, one of the most difficult issues with the sedative drugs is their ability to augment the effects of other sedatives. Taking a barbiturate before bedtime would certainly facilitate a rapid induction of sleep, but taking a barbiturate with alcohol may mean that one does not wake up in the morning—the sad fate of both Marilyn Monroe and Jimi Hendrix.

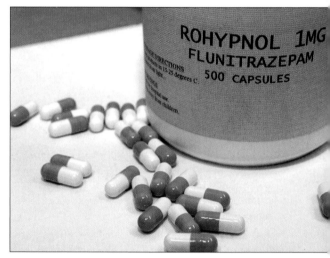

Benzodiazepines such as Rohypnol are much safer than barbiturates but can be used as date-rape drugs.

Safer sedatives

It was not until the introduction of the benzodiazepines in 1960 that efficacious and essentially safe sedative-hypnotic drugs became available to the clinician. As sedatives they proved to be extremely effective in the treatment of anxiety disorders. One such compound is diazepam, which is still widely prescribed today. The hypnotic effects of the benzodiazepines make them particularly suitable for the treatment of insomnia. Three commonly prescribed sleeping pills are zolpidem, zolpiclone, and zaleplon, which produce their sedative properties by binding to the same receptor sites in the brain. The effects of all of these drugs are exacerbated when taken with alcohol. However, the benzodiazepines have a singular advantage: when taken alone they display only part of the spectrum of activity of the older sedative agents. These drugs, even when taken

at extremely high doses, rarely produce respiratory and cardiovascular depression. Despite their widespread use, there remain few, if any, documented fatalities from uncomplicated benzodiazepine overdose. The reason for the limited effects of the benzodiazepines is probably quite simple: that is, they have a particularly specific mechanism of action.

The benzodiazepines produce their overt effects by interaction with accessory recognition sites on a single family of receptors in the brain, the $GABA_A$ receptors. These are the receptors for gamma-aminobutyric acid (GABA), a simple amino acid that is responsible for essentially all of the inhibitory transmission within the brain. GABA interacts with two classes of receptors in the brain; the first one to be studied in any detail was the $GABA_A$ receptor, and the second, now commonly referred to as the $GABA_B$ receptor, plays no part in the action of the sedative-hypnotics. The clinically used benzodiazepines produce their effects by reducing the amount of GABA that is required to activate the $GABA_A$ receptor. The result is an increase in neuronal inhibition, leading to sedation and hypnosis. Many of the older sedatives appear to interact in a similar, though mechanistically distinct, manner with the GABA$_A$ receptor, but they are rather "dirty" drugs in the sense that they interact with several other proteins in the brain, which leads to the side effects that compromise their routine clinical use.

When the benzodiazepines were introduced into clinical medicine their advantages were immediately apparent: they were sedative and hypnotic but failed to cause fatalities in overdose. Clearly this was an enormous advantage; they quickly replaced the barbiturates and became the most widely prescribed medications in general practice. In 1983 some 28 million prescriptions for benzodiazepines were issued to a population of 54.8 million in the United Kingdom. They rapidly gained something close to notoriety in the popular press, and in 1985 an attempt was made to restrict what was seen as an overprescription of these agents. A limited list of benzodiazepines was made available for funding by the National Health Service. This approach proved effective and, although the worldwide sales of the benzodiazepine anxiolytics rose by 13 percent between 1981 and 1989, the figures in the United Kingdom fell by 58 percent. During this time, they were most often used to treat clinically debilitating anxiety disorders, allowing sufferers to once again lead productive lives. They remain the most effective pharmacological intervention for generalized anxiety disorder, which is thought to have a prevalence rate of around 10 percent of the population.

In the treatment of anxiety, there is essentially no evidence to suggest that people become tolerant to the benzodiazepines. There is also no evidence of dose escalation, which is a common indication of the development of tolerance. Everyone suffers from occasional anxiety; at times this can be beneficial because it provides motivation to achieve things such as a good grade in an examination or an improved sports performance. Most of us learn to live with a little anxiety. However, there is inevitably a proportion of the population who become dependent on prescribed drugs. Personality type certainly plays a part in defining individuals who become hooked on the benzodiazepines. Only about 20 percent of patients who have been taking benzodiazepines for a significant period of time will exhibit withdrawal symptoms upon cessation of treatment. These symptoms vary from mild, such as difficulty in sleeping for a few days, to more severe, in which the patient feels anxious and jittery once the drug has been withdrawn. Rarely, except after very high doses for prolonged periods, will the patient experience convulsions during withdrawal. Many of these withdrawal symptoms can be alleviated by slowly tapering the drug dose prior to stopping its use.

Drawbacks of sedatives

Since the 1960s, the benzodiazepines have been the drugs of choice for the treatment of the majority of the anxiety and sleep disorders. They are not without their problems but, for the vast majority of patients, they are a means of getting through a difficult time and returning them to a productive and effective way of life. However, the benzodiazepines have also been used as drugs of abuse. In the past, temazepam (Restoril) has been widely abused because it could be removed from gelatin capsules in a form that could be injected. Although changes in drug formulations have significantly reduced this problem, some drug abusers still use oral preparations of temazepam that have been acquired either through prescription or from illicit sources. There has also been an increasing use of some of these agents as so-called date-rape drugs. Rohypnol (flunitrazepam) has proved particularly troublesome in this regard, especially when combined with alcohol. Here an additional property of the benzodiazepines is being exploited: these drugs have pre-amnesic effects, meaning that the recipient is unable to recall what occurred immediately prior to the ingestion. This effect can be clinically useful, for example, when a benzodiazepine such as the short-acting midazolam is used as a pre-anesthetic.

Sedatives and hypnotics are valuable in therapeutic intervention. They improve the quality of life for many people who suffer from anxiety or sleep disorders. Like all drugs, they have their disadvantages. With appropriate medical advice, it is the responsibility of the individual to decide whether the putative gains outweigh any risks that may be involved.

I. L. MARTIN, S. M. J. DUNN

SEE ALSO:
Barbiturates • Benzodiazepines • Chloral Hydrate • Paraldehyde • Rohypnol

Serotonin

Serotonin is one of the principal neurotransmitters implicated in the actions of psychoactive drugs. In its normal function it regulates sleep, mood, and body temperature through its action at various receptor sites in the body and brain.

Serotonin produces the psychoactive effects of psychedelic drugs such as LSD, as well as of entactogenic-empathogenic drugs such as Ecstasy. Serotonin also contributes to the unpleasant and sometimes life-threatening side effects of such drugs.

Insufficient serotonin activity is believed to be a cause of anxiety, depression, eating disorders, sleep problems, vulnerability to stress, and obsessive-compulsive behavior such as repeated unnecessary hand washing. Excessive serotonin activity causes serotonin syndrome—a variety of psychiatric and physiological disorders that can sometimes kill.

Formation and function
Serotonin forms from tryptophan—an amino acid derived from food—via 5-hydroxytryptophan (5-HTP). Both tryptophan and 5-HTP can cross the blood-brain barrier, whereas serotonin cannot. Hence, all serotonin in the brain forms there and cannot escape. Serotonin also forms in the gut, where it governs secretion into the gut and peristalsis, the wavelike contractions that propel material through the intestines. Serotonin also has roles in causing vomiting and the aggregation of blood platelets.

Serotonin in the brain accumulates in vesicles, or small vessels, near the transmitting ends of serotonergic neurons. When a nerve impulse arrives at the end of such a neuron, vesicles disgorge serotonin into the synapse, or junction, between the transmitting neuron and the receiving neuron.

The serotonin molecules can either stimulate or inhibit activity in the postsynaptic (receiving) neuron by attaching to receptor sites on its surface. Presynaptic receptors on the transmitting neuron restrict serotonin release when stimulated, and this helps prevent excessive serotonin release.

The attachment of serotonin to receptors is temporary, and dispersal of serotonin from the synapse prepares the receptors between bouts of neurotransmission. Transporter proteins in the

Two sets of serotonergic neurons emerge in opposite directions from the dorsal raphe. Those that descend toward the spinal column through the brain stem mediate pain signals. Those that ascend into the brain affect aspects of consciousness such as depression, aggression, compulsive behavior, and hallucinations.

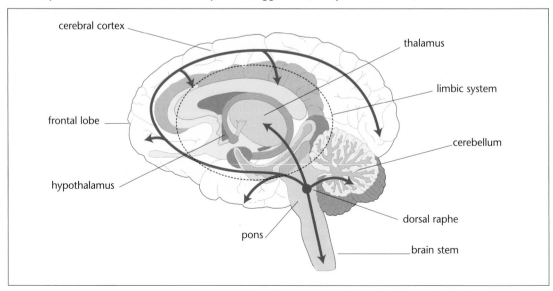

SEROTONIN SYNDROME

The normal Ecstasy trip typifies a mild case of serotonin syndrome. Its physical symptoms include overheating, sweating, shivering, jaw clenching, nausea and diarrhea, and increased heart rate and blood pressure. Psychiatric symptoms include confusion, euphoria, and hallucinations.

In more severe serotonin syndrome, extreme overheating can cause rhabdomyolysis—a breakdown of muscle tissues that releases toxic substances into the bloodstream. Those substances can cause kidney failure and other potentially fatal conditions. Serotonin syndrome also includes the formation of blood clots throughout the body, resulting in strokes and other circulatory problems.

Factors that increase serotonin levels include various types of antidepressants; stimulants such as amphetamine, cocaine, and Ecstasy; tryptophan-based food supplements; and electroconvulsive therapy. Any of these factors can be the sole cause of mild to moderate serotonin syndrome.

The risk of severe serotonin syndrome increases greatly by the combination of two factors that boost synaptic serotonin levels by different means. An example would be the combination of Ecstasy with a monoamine oxidase inhibitor (MAOI) antidepressant: Ecstasy triggers release of serotonin into synapses, while the MAOI impedes one of the means of removing serotonin from synapses.

A further risk arises from the length of action of MAOIs and many SSRIs, such as fluoxetine (Prozac). Users of amphetamines, cocaine, or Ecstasy can have severe serotonin reactions many weeks after finishing MAOI treatment because their MAO enzymes are still inhibited.

presynaptic neuron provide a reuptake mechanism that pumps serotonin back into the neuron, where some of it returns to vesicles for reuse. Some is destroyed by monoamine oxidase, an enzyme.

There are seven distinct types of serotonin receptors, and these are 5-HT_1 to 5-HT_7. (The abbreviation 5-HT refers to 5-hydroxytryptamine, an alternative name for serotonin.) These types include receptor subtypes identified by additional letters, such as 5-HT_{1D} and 5-HT_{5B}. Some of these receptors are on other neurons that transmit using serotonin; others are on dopaminergic neurons, where serotonin receptors regulate dopamine release.

Recreational drugs

Hallucinogenic tryptamines such as DMT have similar chemical structures to serotonin, so it is unsurprising that they produce their effects by interacting with serotonin receptors. Early studies suggested the hallucinogenic effect was due to drugs binding to 5-HT_{1A} receptors and impairing the filtering of sensory input by serotonergic neurons. In this model, disturbed perception occurs because the raw visual and auditory data overwhelms the brain. Subsequent studies have revealed that hallucinations

are at least in part due to stimulation of 5-HT_2 receptors, but it is as yet uncertain whether 5-HT_{2A} or 5-HT_{2C} receptors are the main targets.

The hallucinations caused by LSD and some tryptamines and phenethylamines appear to occur by the same mechanism, despite significant differences in molecular structures. Evidence for a shared mechanism comes from reports of cross-tolerance—reduced sensitivity to a group of drugs through exposure to a single drug of that group.

The use of $5\text{-HT}_{2A/C}$ antagonist ketanserin diminishes the visual disturbances experienced with Ecstasy, which suggests they have a common origin to that of LSD trips. Ketanserin fails to reduce the stimulant and mood-lifting effects of Ecstasy, which suggests these effects occur through the action of Ecstasy at other receptors. These may be the same receptors as those stimulated by serotonin-boosting antidepressants, such as the selective serotonin reuptake inhibitors (SSRIs).

M. CLOWES

SEE ALSO:

Amphetamine Sulfate • Dopamine • Ephedrine • Epinephrine • Norepinephrine • Phenethylamines

SSRIs

Selective serotonin reuptake inhibitors (SSRIs) are first-choice drugs for the treatment of depression, social phobia, obsessive-compulsive behavior, and eating problems. They produce fewer side effects than older antidepressants.

Depression is an alarmingly common condition that blights the lives of its sufferers by dulling their capacity for hope and pleasure in life. A study of data from 2006 and 2008 by the U.S. Centers for Disease Control (CDC) indicated that around 9 percent of the population was currently suffering from some sort of depression.

SSRIs are now the drugs in most frequent use for the treatment of depression, and they can help 60 to 80 percent of patients feel better within two to six weeks. Several SSRIs have come into use since the 1987 launch of fluoxetine (Prozac). The top sellers in 2010 were generic sertraline, accounting for around 20 percent of antidepressant prescriptions; escitalopram (Lexapro; 15 percent); and generic fluoxetine (14 percent).

Accumulated experience with SSRIs has revealed their usefulness in the treatment of bulimia, general anxiety disorder (GAD), and obsessive-compulsive disorder (OCD), as well as major depressive disorder (MDD), the original target for the drugs. Growing confidence in the safety of SSRIs led to their being prescribed "off label," that is, for conditions and age groups beyond the original scope of the drugs. That trend has reversed, however, and regulatory bodies such as the U.S. Food and Drug Administration (FDA) are requiring or recommending more restricted use of SSRIs, particularly for adolescents.

Before Prozac

Since the 1950s, antidepressant medications have targeted neurotransmission by norepinephrine and serotonin, since these systems are usually underactive in the brains of depressed people. Two older classes of antidepressants use different means to increase the persistence of these neurotransmitters in synapses (the junctions between neurons) so as to reinforce neurotransmission. The tricyclic antidepressants (TCAs) inhibit the reuptake mechanisms that return neurotransmitters to the neurons that secrete them; monoamine oxidase inhibitors (MAOIs) block the enzymes that render neurotransmitters inactive.

Both TCAs and MAOIs are effective treatments for depression, giving improvements in around two in three patients, compared with one in three patients treated with inactive placebo tablets. A major problem with these types of drugs is that they can be fatal in overdose. They also have side effects that can discourage patients from taking the drug.

Many of the side effects of TCAs and MAOIs stem from the fact that they produce overactivity of other neurotransmitters apart from those implicated in depression. In particular, they cause undue increases in the activities of acetylcholine, histamine, and epinephrine; the resulting side effects include dry mouth, blurred vision, altered heart function, constipation, and urinary retention.

Benefits of selectivity

SSRIs resemble TCAs in that they inhibit neurotransmitter reuptake and have similar success rates in lifting depression. The important difference is that SSRIs act only on serotonin reuptake, so there is less scope for adverse effects due to over-activity of other neurotransmitters. The selectivity for serotonin also vastly reduces the risk of death by overdose.

SNRIs (serotonin-norepinephrine reuptake inhibitors) such as venlafaxine (Effexor) and duloxetine (Cymblata) selectively inhibit reuptake of two neurotransmitters as does bupropion (Wellbutrin), an NDRI (norepinephrine-dopamine reuptake inhibitor). They can be helpful for patients who fail to respond to SSRIs, especially if lethargy is a symptom.

Adverse effects and withdrawal

Some side effects are caused by serotonin itself. They are usually mild, and they include excessive sweating, nausea, and headaches. Disruption of male sexual function can occur and is more problematic, since it makes patients more likely to abandon treatment.

Greater problems are likely to occur if SSRI treatment overlaps with MAOI treatment, since the combined actions of these drugs can cause high levels

"EVERGREENING" SSRIs

By the time a new drug comes to the market it may have fewer than 10 years of patent remaining. After the patent period expires, any manufacturer can produce a generic version. With increased competition the price of the drug falls and hence the profit for its developer.

"Evergreening" is a process by which a drug developer improves return on investment by acquiring a new patent with minimal effort. The new patent can result from proving the effectiveness of a drug in a new application or by making a slight change to the drug that makes it a new product in terms of patent law.

In 1997 the manufacturer of Celexa (citalopram) produced a successor by separating two mirror-image components, R- and S-citalopram. The S form has the therapeutic effect while the R form counteracts this effect to some extent, and citalopram contains the two forms in equal amounts. By 2002, pure S-citalopram (Lexipro) was approved and patented in its own right, two years before the Celexa patent expired.

Fluoxetine (Prozac) was the first SSRI to enter widespread use for the treatment of depression and other disorders, but it is now outsold by more effective SSRIs.

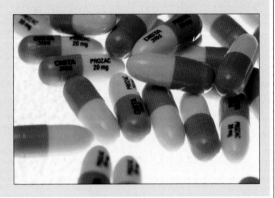

of serotonin. The result is serotonin syndrome—a collection of unpleasant symptoms that can be fatal. For this reason, courses of MAOIs and SSRIs must be separated by at least two weeks for the drug to clear from the system and, in the case of MAOIs, for monoamine oxidase activity to return to normal.

Discontinuation of SSRIs can be problematic, as the brain has to adapt to falling levels of serotonin. Slow dose reduction over a period of weeks or months can keep to a minimum symptoms such as dizziness, disturbing dreams, and fatigue. There is also less likelihood of falling back into depression if the drug is withdrawn gradually.

Abuse potential

The fact that sudden SSRI discontinuation can cause adverse reactions does not equate to SSRIs being addictive in the sense of a recreational drug. There is no evidence for SSRIs provoking drug-seeking behavior in humans or animals, and a drug user seeking a high from SSRIs is likely to be disappointed when the physical side effects of SSRIs set in without there being a noticeable high. Combinations of Ecstasy with SSRIs are also ineffective, since SSRIs block the mechanism by which Ecstasy and its analogs produce their euphoric effects. There have been some cases where SSRIs have caused flashbacks in individuals who had taken LSD in the past, but the mechanism of this effect is unknown.

Caution for young people

There have been cases where patients have become agitated and attempted suicide within a few days of starting on SSRIs. In the main, these patients have been adolescents suffering from depression, and there has been much debate about whether the depression or the drug is to blame. In 2007 an FDA study revealed an increased risk of suicide linked to SSRIs in depressed people under 25 years of age. This finding was later confirmed by a World Health Organization study that also suggested a reduced risk of suicide in older patients.

M. CLOWES

SEE ALSO:

Antidepressant Drugs • MAOs and MAOIs

Tobacco

Tobacco, the main source of the addictive chemical nicotine, is a major crop in many parts of the world. It is estimated that one-sixth of the global population smokes tobacco, which is a significant factor in the health of millions of people.

The National Survey on Drug Use and Health, published by the U.S. Department of Health and Human Services, reports that in 2009, 69.7 million Americans aged 12 or older used a tobacco product in the past month, nearly 30 percent of the population. Of these, 58.7 million were cigarette smokers, 13.3 million smoked cigars, 8.6 million used smokeless tobacco, and 2.1 million smoked tobacco in pipes.

For a drug whose use causes such a wide range of potentially fatal diseases, tobacco has an innocuous pedigree. The tobacco plant *Nicotiana tabacum* is a member of the Solanaceae family, the same group as the potato, tomato, chili pepper, and deadly nightshade, and is native to North and South America. European civilization first encountered the plant in November 1492, when the explorer Christopher Columbus was given dried tobacco leaves by Native Americans.

History

The tobacco plant has a long and complex history of use. Native Americans appear to have used the tobacco plant some 1,500 years ago, smoking it in pipes for medicinal and ceremonial purposes. The Mayans of South America wrapped the dried leaves in corn husks or palm leaves to form crude cigarettes, and the Aztecs are known to have both smoked

When tobacco leaves have been harvested, they are hung onto racks for drying. The racks are then placed in barns away from sunlight, where they cure in the air or with the assistance of heat. Curing produces the familiar yellow and brown colors and brings out the aromas of the tobacco.

tobacco and used it as snuff. Tobacco was also chewed, eaten, rubbed onto the body, and drunk as an infusion during this period.

However, details of the plant's history during this period are unclear. Some authors claim that tribes were smoking tobacco as long ago as 6000 BCE, and there have been various arguments about whether it was used purely for ceremonial purposes or on a casual basis, as well as which tribes did or did not smoke.

Tobacco's spread across the Atlantic began with Spanish sailors who became avid cigar smokers. The Portuguese were instrumental in spreading tobacco use to the rest of Europe, being the first to cultivate the plant outside the Americas. By 1558, snuff (dried and ground tobacco) was on sale in Lisbon's markets.

It was the French who gave the plant its botanical name, *Nicotiana,* after the French ambassador to Portugal, Jean Nicot de Villemain, sent specimens of the plant back to Paris in 1559. By 1620, snuff had become highly fashionable in the French court.

Tobacco traveled to Italy again through Portugal, after the Papal Nuncio at Lisbon sent specimens to Pope Pius IV. The plant then spread to the rest of Italy and into Germany, Hungary, and (aided considerably by the traveling soldiers of the Thirty Years' War, 1618–1648) into northern and central Europe.

Historians have concluded that tobacco probably came to England in 1565 directly from the New World. Records show that John Rolfe began cultivating tobacco commercially in Virginia as early as 1612, subsequently shipping it to England. The early English settlements were in Virginia, where the Native Americans smoked pipes. The English preference was for pipe smoking, whereas Portuguese-influenced tobacco users tended to take it as snuff. Walter Raleigh claimed to have been the first to have brought tobacco to England, along with its cousin, the potato. The English spread tobacco to Holland and those parts of Europe not reached by the Portuguese and Italians.

By the end of the sixteenth century, tobacco had reached Turkey, probably brought by the Portuguese. The Turks planted tobacco in Macedonia and spread its use east to Persia and central Asia. The well-

HOW CIGARETTES AND CIGARS ARE MADE

Manufacturing cigarettes is a fast and highly automated process. Cigarette-making machines produce between 8,000 and 12,000 cigarettes a minute. Spools of cigarette paper up to 6,000 yards long are rolled out and a mixture of shredded tobacco and processed tobacco pulp is released from a hopper onto the center of the unrolled paper. The wrapper is then closed over the tobacco, making one long cigarette known as a rod.

Machines slice the rod into shorter lengths, insert filters, and then cut the shorter lengths into single, filter-tipped cigarettes. Next, the cigarettes are sorted into groups according to the size of pack they are intended for, wrapped in foil to preserve their aroma, and placed into cartons.

A premium or super-premium cigar is handmade and is built up from three parts—filler, binder, and wrapper. The filler is the interior of the cigar. "Long filler" means the cigar's interior consists of full tobacco leaves, which require skillful rolling to ensure that the cigar burns evenly. "Short filler" consists of loose clippings of tobacco leaves left from long filler cigar production. The binder consists of several layers of leaves that the cigar maker will wrap around the filler, forming it into a cylindrical shape. The final component, the wrapper—a smooth, high-quality tobacco leaf—is then rolled around the outside of the binder.

Machine-made cigars use homogenized tobacco leaf (HTL) as a binder. This is made from tobacco stems and fiber, mixed with water and cellulose, forming a paste that is spread on a drying belt and emerges in rolls, similar to cigarette paper. The cigars are then made in a process very similar to that used for cigarettes. A few premium machine-made cigars use tobacco leaves rather than HTL as a binder.

traveled Portuguese were again instrumental in bringing tobacco to India, and it was in fact from India that the cigar was introduced to England.

The Portuguese also took tobacco to Japan, in the 1570s, from where it spread to Korea, where it is still the country's main agricultural export. China had various routes of entry: from Korea and from Portuguese Macao and Spanish settlements in the Philippines. Tobacco spread from India and China to the remainder of Eurasia. Western Africa was introduced to tobacco as early as 1607 by the Portuguese, with the Dutch taking the habit, and the plant's cultivation, to the south of the continent in 1652.

Tobacco types and uses
There are a number of different types of tobaccos and methods of curing the plant; choices depend on its intended use. The three main types grown in the United States are Virginia, burley, and oriental tobaccos. Virginia tobacco is widely grown for its mild and sweet flavor and is most popular for pipe and flake tobacco mixtures. Burleys have little natural sugar and are dryer and more aromatic than Virginia tobaccos. They are usually air cured and burn more slowly at a cooler temperature. Oriental tobaccos come from Turkey and the Balkan regions. These tend to be dry and have a sour aroma and are popular in the cigarettes smoked in Arabic countries. Curing, by which moisture is removed from the leaves, is either a natural process, where leaves are left to hang in open barns or spread out in the sun, or is heat assisted. Of these, flue- or fire-cured tobaccos are used for snuff and chewing tobacco. Dark air-cured tobaccos are used for chewing tobacco, and flue-cured Virginia tobaccos are used for cigarette and smoking mixtures. Air-cured cigar tobaccos are used for cigar wrappers and fillers. Air-cured burley tobacco is used for cigarette, pipe, and chewing tobacco. Most oriental tobaccos are sun cured.

Manufactured cigarettes are the main form of tobacco used around the world. They are made from shredded tobacco leaves, processed with hundreds of different chemicals and encased in a paper cylinder. In 1939 Brown & Williamson introduced the tobacco industry's first cork-tipped filter cigarette. Filter-tipped cigarettes jumped from under 1 percent of the market in 1950 to 87 percent by 1975.

Lower tar and nicotine cigarettes were introduced from the mid-1970s to the early 1980s, with manufacturers producing a variety of "light" and "ultra-light" cigarettes. Smokeless tobacco contains nicotine, which is absorbed into the blood through the oral mucosa and the gastrointestinal tract and has been shown to have similar health effects to normal tobacco.

Reynolds Tobacco began producing two purportedly safer cigarettes, the Premier in 1988 and the Eclipse in 1996. Both of these produce smoke by heating rather than burning tobacco, thus reducing the effects of tar and nicotine. Flavorings, mainly menthol, are also added to cigarettes to increase their appeal.

Tobacco products exist in many other guises: the next most popular form after cigarettes, the cigar, comes in various shapes and sizes and consists of air-cured, fermented tobacco in a tobacco-leaf wrapper. Varieties include the cigarette-sized cigarillo, coronas, and cheroots. Pipe smoking involves placing a small amount of tobacco in a pipe bowl and inhaling through the stem. A variant of this, the water pipe, or hookah, in which tobacco is burned in a bowl and then passed through a container of water before inhalation, is popular in western Asia, North Africa, the Mediterranean, and parts of Asia.

Bidis, popular throughout Southeast Asia, are small, cigarette-like smokes made from a tiny amount of tobacco, wrapped by hand in a temburni leaf and tied with string. *Kretek*s, widely smoked in Indonesia, are clove-flavored cigarettes that contain a range of flavorings and eugenol, an anesthetic, which allows the smoke to be inhaled more deeply. Sticks of sun-cured tobacco known as *brus* are wrapped in cigarette paper and smoked.

Chewing tobacco, known as plug, loose leaf, or quid, is most popular in Southeast Asia. In this region pan masala, or betel quid, consists of tobacco, areca nuts, and slaked lime wrapped in a betel leaf. This type of tobacco product can also contain a variety of flavorings and sweetening agents.

Moist snuff is often packaged in small paper or cloth packets, or is wadded and placed in the mouth between cheek and gum. Dry snuff is inhaled, usually through the nose but also orally.

Production and consumption

The manufacture of tobacco started modestly enough. Records show that in 1616, Virginia sent just 2,300 pounds (1,050 kg) to London. Two years later, Virginia was sending more than 20,000 pounds (9,100 kg), and by 1620, 40,000 pounds (18,200 kg) were being exported.

Cigarette smoking enjoyed a similar exponential increase. In 1865, less than 20 million cigarettes were produced in the United States. By 1880, this figure had risen to 500 million; five years later, 1 billion cigarettes were being made. Another five years later, the number had doubled to 2 billion. By 1895, 4 billion cigarettes were being produced annually.

In some countries, consumption is leveling off or decreasing, but worldwide the number of smokers (about one billion) continues to rise. More than 80 percent of the world's smokers live in low and moderate income countries.

Tobacco is now grown in more than 125 countries, over a wide variety of soils and climates on nearly 10 million acres (over 4 million hectares) of land, a third of this in China alone. More than 1 percent of all agricultural land around the world is devoted to tobacco growing. The global tobacco crop is a small fraction of the total profits from selling tobacco-related products. Brazil, China, Turkey, India, and the United States produce most of the world's tobacco. Growing the crop alone has caused serious environmental problems with 45 percent of the deforestation in the Republic of Korea attributed to tobacco plantations.

Health effects

For much of its history, it was believed that tobacco gave, rather than took, health. Native Americans believed it could be used to cure toothache, frostbite, burns, venereal ulcers, and tumors. European and Chinese doctors believed it healed wounds, sores, and broken bones and cured bubonic plague, breast cancer, goiter, and malaria.

Medical research since the mid-1950s has proved something very different. Smokers have a considerably greater risk of dying from many different cancers, notably lung cancer. Cigarette smoking accounts for 90 percent of lung cancer cases in the United States. The list of other directly linked illnesses is long: emphysema, heart disease and strokes, macular degeneration and cataracts, peripheral vascular disease, stomach and duodenal ulcers, infertility and impotence, osteoporosis, early menopause, and diabetes. About 38,000 deaths per year in the United States can be attributed to secondhand smoke. In addition, chewing tobacco has been shown to cause cancer of the tongue, lip, and mouth.

Research in the United Kingdom has shown that about 20 percent of deaths from coronary heart disease (CHD) in men and 17 percent of deaths from CHD in women are due to smoking. Smoking has also been linked to low birth weight in babies. There is also an increased risk of spontaneous miscarriage, premature or stillborn births, birth defects, and possible long-term physical and mental side effects. If a pregnant woman smokes, she also increases the number of nicotine receptors in the fetal brain, making the child more likely to eventually start smoking.

Regulation of tobacco

Although smoking even in moderation and the effects of secondhand smoke have been recognized as harmful for many years, efforts at national and local prohibitions against smoking in public did not gain momentum until the early 21st century. Despite increasing awareness of the dangers of tobacco, there are few restrictions around the world on the purchase of tobacco by adults.

Partly, this is an accident of history. The addictive nature of nicotine ensured tobacco's spread around the world following its introduction to Europe in the fifteenth century. Until firm medical proof of harm began to surface, tobacco smoking was seen as promoting steady nerves (cartons were given to soldiers during wars) and, through movies, as a glamorous pastime.

A picture has slowly emerged since the mid-1930s of the true nature of tobacco and the harm that smoking causes, beginning with an early U.S. study in the 1930s linking smoking to lung cancer and a Reader's Digest article, *Cancer by the Carton*, in the 1950s. However, it was not until 1995 that the U.S. Food and Drug Administration (FDA) declared nicotine a drug. This opened the door for federal

The highest-quality cigars are made individually by skilled workers in factories in Cuba. Cigar rolling is considered an art that takes many years to perfect. The skill lies in wrapping loose tobacco in a binding leaf so that it does not fall out. The fastest workers can produce around 400 cigars in a day.

legislation regulating the sale and marketing of tobacco products. A law had already passed in the United States in 1985 prohibiting the sale of tobacco to minors. In 1993 Vermont's Clean Indoor Air Law became the first statewide statute to completely ban smoking.

Statistics show that tobacco kills half of all lifetime users. At the same time, it is the leading preventable cause of disease, disability, and death in the United States, claiming more than 400,000 lives each year. One of the most significant factors is the young age of first-time smokers. World Health Organization statistics show that more than 30 percent of smokers sample their first cigarette before the age of 10; evidence suggests that tobacco is attractive to minors due to shrewd marketing (smoking is depicted as "cool") and peer pressure. The younger a person is when he or she begins to smoke, the more likely it is that he or she will contract smoking-related diseases.

The tobacco industry has acknowledged that it targets young people. In 1987 U.S. tobacco product manufacturer Liggett Group issued a statement saying: "We at Liggett know and acknowledge that, as the Surgeon General and respected medical researchers have found, cigarette smoking causes health problems, including lung cancer, heart and vascular disease, and emphysema. Liggett acknowledges that the tobacco industry markets to 'youth,' which means those under 18 years of age, and not just those 18 to 24 years of age."

Why not just ban smoking? Attempts have been made. In 1901, there were only two U.S. states—Louisiana and Wyoming—that had not passed laws restricting the sale and public smoking of cigarettes. Some states prohibited both, but the antismoking lobby was unable to obtain a federal prohibition, so the suppression did not last. While the number of cigarettes produced fell to 2 billion in 1901, it was back up to nearly 8 billion by 1910. By 1928 the number of cigarettes produced annually in the United States had reached 100 billion.

The reason that no modern government has simply banned tobacco purchase or consumption is largely due to the tax benefits from the sale of tobacco, along with the sheer difficulty of enforcing a wholesale ban and opposition from the influential tobacco lobby. Nonetheless, in 2009 the United States Congress passed the Family Smoking Prevention and Tobacco Control Act, giving the Federal Food and Drug Administration the ability to regulate tobacco products, including especially the way such products are advertised and marketed to young people.

L. STEDMAN

SEE ALSO:
Nicotine • Plant-Based Drugs

Tryptamines

The tryptamines are a group of compounds that includes hallucinogens as well as the neurotransmitter serotonin and the hormone melatonin. Many tryptamines occur naturally in plants and animals; others are synthetic substances.

The tryptamine structure is present in a number of known psychoactive substances, such as DMT, LSD, and the psychoactive constituents of various "magic" mushrooms and other fungi, plants, and animals. As a group, the tryptamines have much in common with another class of compounds that includes some hallucinogens, namely the phenethylamines.

Availability to the brain

The first similarity between the tryptamines and the phenethylamines is that neither parent compound has detectable psychoactive effects if swallowed or otherwise absorbed into the bloodstream. Both tryptamine and phenethylamine have unmodified amino ($-NH_2$) groups that are good targets for monoamine oxidases. Hence, these enzymes rapidly convert unmodified tryptamine into inactive compounds as the start of its elimination from the body. Furthermore, the same amino groups are

These "magic" Psilocybe mushrooms contain psilocin and psilocybin—both tryptamines that cause hallucinations and emotional disturbances as well as muscle relaxation and pupil dilation. The toxic and psychoactive components in mushrooms are extremely variable, and the effects from their use can be unpredictable.

significantly polar, and this property prevents tryptamine from passing through the nonpolar membrane material of the blood-brain barrier.

Psychedelic tryptamine derivatives tend to have alkyl groups such as methyl ($-CH_3$) or ethyl ($-C_2H_5$) in place of one or both hydrogen atoms of the amino group. Such groups hinder the action of monoamine oxidase, so the compounds persist in the body for longer. Alkylation also reduces the polarity of the amino group and makes it easier for such compounds to cross the blood-brain barrier, a prerequisite for any kind of psychoactivity.

Nature uses polarity to keep serotonin inside the brain. Serotonin (5-hydroxytryptamine, or 5-HT) is more polar than tryptamine because of its hydroxy ($-OH$) group. Hence, serotonin that forms in the brain is unable to escape through the blood-brain barrier. Conversely, this effect explains why it would be futile to attempt to boost serotonin in the brain by taking serotonin food supplements or injections.

Psychoactivity and receptors

Once a tryptamine gets inside the brain, its profile of psychoactive effects depends on how it interacts with receptors there. Most of the psychoactive effects of tryptamines stem mainly from interactions with serotonin receptors. In a few cases, interaction with norepinephrine receptors causes stimulation.

The implication of serotonin receptors in the effects of tryptamines is no surprise, since serotonin itself is a tryptamine. Other members of this group of compounds have more or less similar shapes and charge distributions to those of serotonin. These are the key factors in determining how well a molecule fits a receptor and whether the molecule activates it.

The interaction with serotonin receptors can be agonistic, in which case the tryptamine binds to the receptor and activates it in the same way as serotonin does. Alternatively, antagonistic tryptamines bind to serotonin receptors but fail to activate them and also prevent serotonin from activating them as long as the tryptamine occupies the receptor site.

CHEMICAL ANALOGY TO PHENETHYLAMINE

A brief look at the tryptamine molecule reveals its similarity to phenethylamine. Knowledge of the structure also helps explain names of tryptamines.

The first point of similarity is that both tryptamine and phenethylamine consist of an amino group ($-NH_2$) linked by a two-carbon chain to a ring structure. The twin-ringed indole structure in tryptamine also resembles the phenyl ring by its aromatic bonding. Such bonding makes the rings flat and puts diffuse clouds of negative charge on either side of the plane of the rings.

As is the case for phenethylamine, there are various sites where nature and laboratory processes can introduce chemical groups to substitute for hydrogen atoms in tryptamine. The principal sites are labeled at right. Alkyl (hydrocarbon) groups such as methyl ($-CH_3$) can also replace one or two hydrogen atoms on the nitrogen at the end of the

ethylamine chain. Hence, N,α–dimethyltryptamine has one methyl group attached to the ethylamine nitrogen and a second on the α carbon. Similarly, 5-hydroxytryptamine (serotonin) has –OH at the 5 position of the indole structure.

The nature of the psychoactivity of any given tryptamine depends on its balance of agonistic or antagonistic effects at different subtypes of serotonin receptors. Some tryptamines can therefore cause hallucinations, while other drugs that alter the serotonin system are not hallucinogens, such as various types of antidepressant drugs.

Studies of LSD (lysergic acid diethylamide) suggest that this and other psychoactive tryptamines might produce their hallucinogenic effects by interactions with $5\text{-}HT_2$ receptors—most likely by activation of $5\text{-}HT_{2A}$ and $5\text{-}HT_{2C}$ subtypes. Stimulation of $5\text{-}HT_2$ receptors has also been linked to anxiety and might provide the mechanism that can cause nightmarish bad trips on certain occasions.

Hallucinations can occur in various sensory modes, notably those of sight, sound, and touch. These hallucinations are often distortions of what is actually seen or heard, although visual hallucinations can sometimes be increased by closing the eyes to shut out visual input. The curious effect of synesthesia occurs when one form of sensory input creates a hallucination in a different sense. For example, visual hallucinations may occur when

listening to music. The intensity of hallucinations depends on the type of tryptamine, the dose, and the individual.

DMT and related compounds

As previously explained, alkyl groups on the amino group of tryptamine produce compounds that are less easily destroyed by monoamine oxidase (MAO) and that pass into the brain more readily than is the case for tryptamine itself. The simplest of these compounds is N,N-dimethyltryptamine, or DMT.

DMT occurs in numerous plant sources and is present in *cohoba*, a traditional Amazonian snuff. The two methyl groups fail to give full protection against MAOs, and it is usually smoked to ensure fast delivery to the brain so the psychoactive effect can take place. Hallucinations can be strong when DMT is taken this way, but the experience is brief. MAOs destroy DMT at a sufficient rate to terminate the trip within 30 minutes to one hour, although the DMT user often feels the trip has lasted much longer.

An alternative means of taking DMT is in ayahuasca, a traditional brew used in South American shamanic rituals. In this case, DMT-bearing plants are mixed with others that contain natural MAO inhibitors, or MAOIs. The combined infusions produce longer-lasting hallucinations, as the MAOI protects the DMT from destruction. The same principal applies to pharmahuasca, a mixture of synthetic DMT and a pharmaceutical MAOI.

Bufotenine is simply DMT with a hydroxy (–OH) group at the 5 position of the tryptamine system. It is present in various frog venoms, but the polar hydroxy group limits its psychoactivity by hindering its entry to the brain. Test subjects injected with bufotenine often reported hot flashes, which are consistent with stimulation of serotonin receptors around the body. This is no surprise, since bufotenine is a dimethylated version of serotonin.

Bufo alvarius frogs produce 5-methoxy-DMT in their venom, which can be milked from the frog and dried before smoking. The methoxy (–OCH$_3$) group is much less polar than hydroxy, so this compound gets into the brain more easily than bufotenine and is a much more potent hallucinogen.

Psilocin and psilocybin are the main hallucinogens in species of "magic" mushrooms, such as *Psilocybe cubensis*. Psilocin is 4-hydroxy-DMT, and psilocybin is the phosphate ester of the same compound. Human experiments with the pure compounds

reveal them to be equally potent, which suggests that the human body might convert psilocybin into psilocin. These compounds seem less prone to destruction by MAOs, since they are effective even when eaten and their effects typically last for 3 to 6 hours—much longer than DMT, for example. It is probably their greater persistence in the body that allows them to be psychoactive despite their polarity.

Other tryptamines

Chemical synthesis allows scientists to produce a multitude of tryptamines that have never been found in nature, in addition to many that have. One chemist who has explored the possibilities of producing new psychoactive tryptamines is Alexander Shulgin. He reported the results in *Tihkal (Tryptamines I Have Known and Loved): The Continuation,* the sequel to *Pihkal,* a similar book about the synthesis and testing of phenethylamines.

Two synthetic tryptamines that have come to the attention of drug enforcement agencies in recent years are Foxy Methoxy and AMT. The chemical name of Foxy Methoxy is 5-methoxy-*N,N*-diisopropyltryptamine. The position of the methoxy group makes it a relative of the hallucinogen in *Bufo alvarius* venom, but the replacement of methyl groups with isopropyl (–CH(CH$_3$)$_2$) provides more protection against MAOs, so the hallucinogenic effects are stronger and last for longer than for 5-methoxy-DMT.

AMT is alpha-methyltryptamine, the tryptamine analog of amphetamine (alpha-methylphenethylamine). As with amphetamine, the methyl group at the alpha position makes this compound an analog of norepinephrine, and this gives AMT a stimulant effect in addition to its hallucinogenic effect, a combination similar to that of Ecstasy.

More distant relatives of tryptamine include lysergic acid derivatives and harmines. The former group includes the potently hallucinogenic LSD, and the latter are natural MAOIs that are often used to potentiate tryptamines and phenethylamines.

M. CLOWES

Lysergic acid diethylamine (LSD) has the amino group of tryptamine bound up in a complex four-ringed molecular structure.

SEE ALSO:
Bufotenine • DMT • Harmine and Harmaline • LSD • MAOs and MAOIs • Phenethylamines • Psilocybin and Psilocin • Serotonin

Valium

Valium is a tranquilizing drug often used by stimulant abusers to overcome the excitatory effects of amphetamines and cocaine. Valium itself has dependence potential and can produce unpleasant withdrawal symptoms.

Valium is the trade name for diazepam. It is the most widely prescribed and thus the most well-known member of a family of drugs called benzodiazepines. At the height of its clinical use (mid-1960s through to the mid-1980s), Valium was a household word, but the name is less well recognized today because the patent is long expired and Valium has been largely replaced with generic versions of diazepam.

Diazepam is used clinically to reduce the symptoms associated with a range of anxiety disorders without producing overt sedation. Typical doses of diazepam are 6 to 30 milligrams daily in divided doses taken by mouth. With increasing dosage, sedation and sleep induction become apparent, hence its use to treat insomnia. Diazepam is also used to treat the convulsions associated with alcohol withdrawal in dependent subjects.

The sedative and hypnotic effects of diazepam and other benzodiazepines have led to their illicit use to "come down" from abuse of central nervous system stimulants, such as amphetamines and cocaine. The availability of benzodiazepines in liquid form (including syrups and capsules) has been restricted to minimize illicit intravenous use.

Although all benzodiazepines produce similar effects, they differ in their duration of action. Diazepam is classified as long acting, which means that its effects will be apparent for at least eight hours after a normal single oral dose. Common adverse effects of diazepam are slowing of reaction time, impairment of concentration, and reduced performance in carrying out skilled tasks. Subjects taking diazepam are routinely advised against driving motor vehicles or operating machinery, because the drug's adverse effects may result in hazards to themselves or others. The occasional use of diazepam to promote sleep will also result in impaired function the following day. Diazepam can also depress respiration, which may become significant in those with breathing disorders, such as bronchitis or asthma.

The most important drug interaction of diazepam is its additive effect with other drugs that suppress

activity of the central nervous system. The interaction with alcohol is particularly important. Small amounts of alcohol in combination with diazepam produce sedative effects that are greater than the sum of the individual effects and can be fatal.

Tolerance and dependence have long been recognized as a problem when benzodiazepines are taken in large doses for long periods of time. Diazepam, with its long half-life and moderate potency, has a moderate dependence potential. Drug withdrawal in dependent individuals results in a distinct withdrawal syndrome, the symptoms of which are clearly distinct from preexisting medical conditions. Withdrawal symptoms may take up to two weeks to develop and may persist for up to six months.

R. W. HORTON

KEY FACTS

Classification
Schedule IV (USA), Schedule IV (Canada), Class C (UK), Schedule IV (INCB). Sedative and anxiolytic.

Street names
Downers, tranks, V

Short-term effects
Relaxation, intoxication, mild drowsiness, slurred speech, confusion, lack of coordination

Long-term effects
Physical and psychological dependence, confusion in elderly patients. Withdrawal symptoms include tremor, cramps, vomiting, insomnia, and sweating.

SEE ALSO:

Benzodiazepines • Librium • Rohypnol • Sedatives and Hypnotics

Vicodin

Vicodin is a pain reliever used as an analgesic and cough suppressant. Vicodin tablets are composed of hydrocodone, an opioid analgesic, and acetaminophen, a nonopioid analgesic commonly marketed as Tylenol.

Vicodin, a combination of hydrocodone and acetaminophen, is an effective painkiller because these drugs have different mechanisms of action in the body. Hydrocodone is a synthetic narcotic analgesic that is structurally related to morphine, a natural component of the poppy plant, *Papaver somniferum*. The pharmacological effects of hydrocodone include analgesia, respiratory depression, constricted pupils, reduced gastrointestinal motility, and euphoria. Chronic use or abuse of this class of drugs leads to tolerance (decreased responsiveness to the same dose of a drug over time) and physical dependence (the need to continue to take the drug in order to prevent the development of withdrawal symptoms). Withdrawal from this drug may include some or all of the following symptoms: mydriasis (dilation of the pupils), irritability, insomnia, vomiting, weight loss, dehydration, diarrhea, increased heart rate, and abdominal pain. Morphine and morphinelike drugs can cross the placenta; therefore, abuse of these drugs during pregnancy can produce neonatal dependence. Drugs from this class exert their effects through interaction with different classes of opioid receptors in the spinal cord and brain. The effects of hydrocodone last 4 to 6 hours, and overdose can be treated by intravenous infusion of the antagonist naloxone. Hydrocodone should not be given to alcoholics or patients suffering from respiratory depression.

Acetaminophen is a common household analgesic that is taken to relieve mild pain and fever. Its effects are similar to aspirin and ibuprofen. This drug is safe provided that the recommended dosage is not exceeded. In overdose, acetaminophen is dangerous, as it can cause severe liver and kidney damage. The initial sign of overdose is abdominal pain, though this may not occur until 24 to 48 hours after ingestion and tends to worsen within 72 to 96 hours. Gastric lavage (neutralizing the overdose with charcoal) may be necessary. Liver damage may be exacerbated by consumption of alcohol.

Of the 4 million Americans who admitted that they abused drugs in 2001, 65 percent reported misuse of prescription pain relievers. Of these, Vicodin is one of the most commonly abused combination analgesics. In 2010, 8 percent of twelfth grade students in the United States reported using Vicodin for illicit purposes. Vicodin has gained notoriety in recent years. It has become a common drug of abuse among celebrities, as it produces the same effects as drugs such as heroin but does not yet have the same social stigma. Vicodin should not be taken in combination with alcohol, antihistamines, barbiturates, benzodiazepines, or general anesthetics, all of which cause drowsiness and may impair respiration. Vicodin has been reported to cause anxiety or fear in patients and to precipitate panic attacks in predisposed patients.

J. G. NEWELL, S. M. J. DUNN

KEY FACTS

Classification
Schedule II (USA), Schedule I (Canada), Class A (UK), Schedule I (INCB). Opioid.

Street names
Vike, Watson-387 (name on generic tablet). Trade names: Hycodan, Lorcet, Lortab, Tylox.

Short-term effects
Euphoria, nausea, vomiting, drowsiness, confusion, and constipation

Long-term effects
Respiratory depression, liver damage, dependence

SEE ALSO:
Morphine • Narcotic Drugs • Opiates and Opioids • Prescription Drugs

Resources for Further Study

BIBLIOGRAPHY

American Psychiatric Association (APA). 2000. *Diagnostic and Statistical Manual of Mental Disorders.* 4th ed. Washington, D.C.: APA.

Brick, John, and Carlton K. Erickson. 1998. *Drugs, the Brain, and Behavior: The Pharmacology of Abuse and Dependence.* New York: Haworth Medical Press.

Brick, John, ed. 2004. *Handbook of the Medical Consequences of Alcohol and Drug Abuse.* New York: Haworth Press.

DuPont, Robert L. 2000. *The Selfish Brain: Learning from Addiction.* Center City, Minn.: Hazelden.

Frances, Richard J., Sheldon I. Miller, and Avram H. Mack. 2005. *Clinical Textbook of Addictive Disorders.* 3rd ed. New York: Guilford Press.

Karch, Steven B. 2009. *Karch's Pathology of Drug Abuse.* 4th ed. Boca Raton, Fla.: CRC Press.

Liska, Ken. 2009. *Drugs and the Human Body.* 8th ed. Upper Saddle River, N.J.: Pearson Prentice Hall.

McKim, William A. 2003. *Drugs and Behavior: An Introduction to Behavioral Pharmacology.* 5th ed. Upper Saddle River, N.J.: Prentice Hall.

Spence, Richard T., et al. 2001. *Neurobiology of Addictions: Implications for Clinical Practice.* New York: Haworth Social Work Practice Press.

WEB RESOURCES

The following World Wide Web sources feature information useful for students, teachers, and health care professionals. By necessity, this list is only a representative sampling; many government bodies, charities, and professional organizations not listed have websites that are also worth investigating. Other Internet resources, such as newsgroups, also exist and can be explored for further research. Please note that all URLs have a tendency to change; addresses were functional and accurate as of February 2011.

Al-Anon / Alateen
www.al-anon.org
Al-Anon, which includes Alateen for younger members, helps the families and friends of alcoholics. It focuses on the importance of recovery and explains how to cope with the effects of problem drinking. The website operates in English, Spanish, and French.

Alcoholics Anonymous
www.alcoholics-anonymous.org
A fellowship of men and women who share experiences to help solve their common problems. The aim is to help other alcoholics achieve sobriety. The website operates in English, Spanish, and French.

American Society of Addiction Medicine
www.asam.org
An association of physicians dedicated to promoting research, educating health care workers, and improving the treatment of individuals suffering from alcoholism and other addictions.

Canadian Centre on Substance Abuse
www.ccsa.ca
CCSA is Canada's national addictions agency. It provides information and advice to help reduce the harm associated with substance abuse and addictions. There is a list of recommended reading to download on the topic of young people and drugs at *www.ccsa.ca/index.asp?ID=10*

Canadian Society of Addiction Medicine
csam.org
Policy Statements are available under Non-Member Services.

Center for Education and Drug Abuse Research
cedar.pharmacy.pitt.edu
Based at the University of Pittsburgh School of Pharmacy, Cedar's mission is to carry out long-term research into substance abuse. The research encompasses both genetic and environmental factors in abuse.

Center for Treatment Research on Adolescent Drug Abuse
www.miami.edu/ctrada/
CTRADA was established to conduct research on the treatment of adolescent drug abuse. It evaluates different treatments to develop a greater understanding of successful treatment factors.

Drug Enforcement Administration
www.usdoj.gov/dea
News bulletins, briefings, and background reports on a wide range of issues about illegal drugs. Part of the United States Department of Justice.

Food and Drug Administration
www.fda.gov
The FDA approves drugs for legal use in the United States. Information on over-the-counter, prescription, and generic drugs as well as the illegal use and trafficking of controlled drugs is available on this website.

Hazelden
www.hazelden.org
A not-for-profit organization, Hazelden helps those addicted to alcohol and other drugs. It provides treatment and care services, education, research, and publishing products.

Mothers Against Drunk Driving
www.madd.org
MADD's mission is to stop drunk driving, support victims of this crime, and prevent underage drinking. This website has the latest statistics on the impact of drunk driving, plus information on the laws, underage drinking research, and other issues related to MADD's mission.

National Center on Addiction and Substance Abuse
www.casacolumbia.org
CASA is based at Columbia University. It is the only national organization that brings together the professional disciplines needed to study and combat abuse of alcohol, nicotine, and illegal, prescription, and performance-enhancing drugs.

National Council on Alcoholism and Drug Dependence
www.ncadd.org
The NCADD provides education, information, and help to the public. This website has statistics, interviews with experts, and recommendations about drinking from leading health authorities. A nationwide network of affiliates can be accessed through the site.

National Inhalant Prevention Coalition
www.inhalants.org
NIPC promotes awareness and recognition of the problem of inhalant use. It campaigns on the issue, promotes the latest research, and can advise on individual local programs. The website operates in English and Spanish.

National Institute on Alcohol Abuse and Alcoholism
www.niaaa.nih.gov
NIAAA conducts and publishes research on alcohol abuse and alcoholism. Click on "Resources" for textual and graphical information.

National Institute on Drug Abuse
www.nida.nih.gov
This site provides information on particular drugs as well as statistics on drug use, treatment advice, and research.

The Partnership at Drugfree.org
www.drugfree.org
Successor to the Partnership for A Drug-Free America, the organization helps parents prevent, intervene in, and find treatment for children's drug and alcohol abuse.

Substance Abuse and Mental Health Services Administration
www.samhsa.gov
SAMHSA's website is an important resource for data, briefings, and reports. SAMHSA's Office of Applied Studies (*oas.samhsa.gov*) provides national data on drug-abuse issues.

Substance Abuse Treatment Facility Locator
findtreatment.samhsa.gov
This searchable directory, run by the U.S. Department of Health and Human Services, shows the location of treatment facilities around the country that treat alcohol and drug abuse problems.

Tobacco Free Kids
www.tobaccofreekids.org
This site offers news, research, and facts to discourage children from smoking. It presents the latest federal and state initatives and provides facts and figures on young smokers in each state.

United Nations Office on Drugs and Crime
www.unodc.org
The UNODC is a global leader in the fight against illicit drugs and international crime. The organization's website provides information on the fight against illegal drugs, including legislation passed by the United Nations.

University of Michigan Documents Center
www.lib.umich.edu/govdocs
A central reference point for government information: local, state, federal, and international. Includes news and statistics.

World Health Organization
www.who.int
The World Health Organization offers support to countries to prevent and reduce drug abuse. It presents recommendations to the United Nations about which psychoactive substances should be regulated. Information about substance abuse, including WHO projects, activities, and publications, is available at www.who.int/substance_abuse, including profiles of substance abuse by country.

Glossary

acetylcholine Neurotransmitter that occurs throughout the brain and at the junction between motor neurons and muscle fibers, causing the fibers to contract. Cholinergic neurons are those that release acetylcholine at the synapse when stimulated.

action potential A rapid change in the electrical potential between the inside and outside of a neuron, resulting in the cell "firing" and a nerve impulse traveling along the axon.

addiction Problematic dependence on, and craving for, a drug or activity. Addictions can cause physiological changes (as in alcoholism) or have a solely psychological basis (as in gambling).

adrenergic Neurons that release epinephrine when stimulated. Adrenergic pathways are made up of adrenergic neurons.

adrenoceptor An adrenergic receptor; that is, a receptor that uses epinephrine or norepinephrine as the neurotransmitter.

adverse reaction (ADR) Negative side effects of drugs (prescribed or otherwise).

affect Used by psychologists to mean emotion, feeling, or mood. Adjective: affective.

agonist A drug that has a stimulating effect on physiological activity, increasing the effect of a natural hormone or neurotransmitter, or of another drug.

AIDS Acquired immune deficiency syndrome. The condition caused by the human immunodeficiency virus (HIV).

alcoholism Addiction to alcohol, taking the form of the habitual consumption of excessive amounts of alcoholic drinks.

alkaloid A group of organic (carbon-based) compounds containing nitrogen and produced by various flowering plants. Many alkaloids, including caffeine, nicotine, and quinine, have physiological effects.

allele One form of a specific gene. Many genes occur in a variety of different forms depending on the precise DNA sequence. People inherit two copies of most genes and can therefore have similar or different alleles of any gene.

allostasis Maintaining stability through change, as when the body adapts to a challenging or stressful situation. While this adaptation is helpful in the short term, allostatic loading occurs if the stress response continues, with potentially damaging effects on the brain, immune system, and cardiovascular system.

amphetamine A class of drugs that act as stimulants. Amphetamines suppress appetite and increase pulse rate and blood pressure, in addition to causing psychological effects.

anabolic steroid A steroid drug chemically related to male sex hormones, used to enhance the build-up of muscle tissue.

analgesic A substance that has a painkilling or pain-relieving effect. In contrast to anesthesia, the sense of touch is maintained during analgesia.

analog A substance that has a similar chemical structure to another substance, and which therefore has a similar chemical action or physiological effect.

anesthetic A substance that produces a lessening or complete loss of sensation, usually temporarily. General anesthetics cause the temporary loss of conscious awareness, while the effect of local anesthetics is limited to a particular body area.

anion A negatively charged ion, chemical group, or molecule. Adjective: anionic.

antagonist A drug that has an opposing effect, decreasing the effect of another drug or blocking the action of a natural hormone or neurotransmitter.

antidepressant drug A prescribed drug that alleviates the symptoms of depression. Classes of antidepressant drugs include MAOIs, tricyclics (such as imipramine), and SSRIs (such as fluoxetine, marketed as Prozac).

aphrodisiac drug A drug intended or with the actual effect of increasing sexual desire or enhancing sexual performance, for example, by facilitating erection.

arrhythmia An abnormal heart rhythm.

autoreceptor A receptor on a presynaptic neuron that acts as a feedback control to prevent excessive release of its corresponding neurotransmitter.

aversion A dislike or fear of something. Aversion therapy is a behavior modification technique that aims to treat those affected by pairing the addictive substance or habit with an unpleasant experience, thus building up an aversion to the addictive substance or habit.

dendrite

cell body

axon

◄ **axon** The elongated fiberlike protrusion that extends from the body of a neuron (nerve cell) and along which the nerve impulse travels. Axons connect with other neurons through the dendrites, which are shorter protrusions of the cell's body that receive the incoming signal.

synaptic button or terminal

barbiturate A large class of drugs with a sedative effect, formerly prescribed as sleeping pills and still used in anesthesia. Barbiturate drugs are highly addictive.

benzodiazepine A group of tranquilizer drugs (for example, diazepam, marketed as Valium) used in the treatment of anxiety and stress and to help sleeping. These drugs were, in the past, prescribed liberally but are far less used today because of problems associated with discontinuing their use.

bioconversion See biotransformation

biopsychosocial Refers to a combination of biological, psychological, and social factors that may influence drug abuse and efforts to treat it.

biotransformation The chemical changes undergone by a substance within the the body as the substance is metabolized.

blood-brain barrier The means by which many toxic substances circulating in the bloodstream are inhibited from entering brain tissues. The walls of the capillaries in the brain are less permeable to some substances than capillaries elsewhere in the body.

cannabinoid Any chemical (including tetrahydrocannabinol, THC, the active ingredient of marijuana) that activates the body's cannabinoid receptors. Herbal cannabinoids occur in the cannabis plant; endogenous cannabinoids are those produced naturally in the body; synthetic cannabinoids are produced in the laboratory.

cannabis The plant known formally as *Cannabis sativa,* or hemp. Also, any of the psychoactive preparations (such as marijuana or hashish) or chemicals (THC) that are derived from the plant.

catalyst Anything that triggers, speeds up, or slows down a chemical reaction without itself being altered by that reaction. Enzymes are biological catalysts within the human body.

cation A positively charged ion, chemical group, or molecule. Adjective: cationic.

central nervous system (CNS) The brain and the spinal cord. Only vertebrate animals have a central nervous system, which is responsible for higher functions such as thinking and reasoning, and for integrating incoming sensory information and producing appropriate responses. The spinal cord is a bundle of nerves that conducts nerve impulses from brain to body and vice versa; it is protected by vertebrae (units of bone that make up the spine).

brain

spinal cord

cerebral cortex The surface layer of the brain, also known as gray matter, where the brain's higher functions (such as language, thinking, and reasoning) take place and perceptual information is processed.

characteristic A specific inherited feature of an individual. A characteristic is a particular value or version of a trait: for example, the characteristic of having blue eyes is one version of the eye color trait.

cholinergic Relating to the neurotransmitter acetylcholine. Cholinergic neurons are those that release acetylcholine; acetylcholine is the neurotransmitter within cholinergic neural pathways

club drug Any drug commonly used recreationally at nightclubs or other similar social events.

CNS *See* central nervous system

cognition Thinking; including mental functions such as memory, problem solving, language use, deliberation, reflection, and so on, which are often described as cognitive processes. Cognitive psychology focuses on how information is processed within the mind, constructing theoretical models to describe mental processing, including unconscious processes such as perception.

comorbidity Refers to diseases or disorders occurring together, such as alcoholism with depression. Adjective: comorbid.

conditioning Learned associations (in animals and humans) induced, deliberately or otherwise, by repetition of paired events. Classical or Pavlovian conditioning involves the pairing of an "unconditional" stimulus that has an obvious beneficial or harmful value (such as food or an electric shock) with a neutral stimulus (such as a ringing bell). In time, the neutral stimulus comes to be associated with the unconditioned stimulus and to elicit the same behavior or physiological effects (such as salivation). Instrumental (or operant) conditioning results when specific behaviors are reinforced or inhibited by being paired with reward or punishment.

conjugation Modification of a (natural or synthetic) chemical by enzymes, usually to make it more soluble in water and thus more easily excreted.

contractility A measure of the ability to contract, for example, like muscle fibers. Adjective: contractile.

counterculture movement Any social (often also political and artistic) movement that questions society's established conventions. A highly influential movement developed in the United States and Europe during the late 1960s.

cross-sensitization The process by which a sensitivity to one drug can produce an accelerated response to another drug.

cross-tolerance The transfer of tolerance from one drug to another drug within the same family. For example, prolonged use of heroin produces tolerance to all other opiate drugs, as well as to heroin itself.

delirium Mental confusion that can result from a variety of causes, including intoxication. Symptoms of delirium include disorientation, hallucinations, drowsiness, and fear of imaginary disasters.

dementia Loss of mental capacity, usually progressive, to the extent that normal social and intellectual functions (memory, reasoning, and so on) can no longer be carried out. Dementia has many causes, including severe alcoholism, strokes, and Alzheimer's disease.

dependence State in which an individual has a compelling desire to take a drug, drink alcohol, or indulge in a particular behavior despite the harm it is causing to the individual and the people around the individual.

depolarization The reduction of the electrical potential across the membrane of a neuron, such as occurs during a nerve impulse. When a neuron "fires," a wave of depolarization travels along the axon. Verb: depolarize.

depressant An agent that reduces a bodily functional activity or an instinctive desire (like appetite). A drug that has a depressant, rather than stimulating, effect, generally causes relaxation. The most commonly used depressant is alcohol. Adjective: depressant.

depression A common mood disorder in which the affected person typically feels sad and pessimistic and is unable to be normally active and interested in what is usually pleasurable. Bipolar depression is a clinically separate disorder from the more common unipolar depression. As well as depressive phases, bipolar depression includes phases of abnormally high activity and excitement, called mania.

designer drug A chemically modified version of an illegal recreational drug, designed to have similar effects but to avoid the problems of illegality through its distinct chemical identity.

detoxification The process of treatment for the physiological damage caused by drug abuse, involving medication, rest, and other procedures.

Diagnostic and Statistical Manual of Mental Disorders Standard reference work used by clinicians to classify, diagnose, and treat psychiatric and other mental disorders. First published in 1952, the manual is updated frequently to reflect changing medical and social opinion. Editions are signified by the use of Roman numerals after the book's acronym; for example, DSM IV refers to the current, fourth edition.

diathesis Medical term for a predisposition (usually inherited) to specific disorders.

dilation of pupils The enlargement of the pupil. Dilation of pupils occurs under the influence of certain drugs.

dopamine A neurotransmitter that plays an important role in movement. Dopamine deficiency produces the tremors and movement difficulties of Parkinson's disease, and there is evidence that some symptoms of schizophrenia are caused by excessive dopamine.

drug courts Courts established for the purpose of dealing with offenses that stem from drug use. Rather than punishment, drug courts emphasize treatment for drug addiction and monitoring to guard against further drug use, with the goal of rehabilitating the defendant.

DSM or **DSM IV** *See* Diagnostic and Statistical Manual of Mental Disorders

dysfunction Impairment in normal functioning of any kind, whether social, psychological, or physiological.

dysphoria The opposite of euphoria. Dysphoria is an inappropriately negative mood or feeling, often associated with anxiety or depression.

dysregulation The changes that occur in the central nervous system and body generally in response to the long-term use of drugs. Normally, systems of the body are regulated to stay at an optimal value. Prolonged drug use causes disturbances in this balance, and regulatory systems respond by producing compensation effects.

endocytosis The process by which material, including fluids and particles, is taken into a cell. Certain specific molecules can gain entry to the cell by initiating endocytosis when they attach to receptors on the cell's surface.

enzyme A specific molecule that has a particular function in cells or in the body generally, from digestion to DNA synthesis. Enzymes are proteins, and their structure enables them to attach with great specificity to other molecules and act as biological catalysts by bringing the reactant molecules together.

epidemiology The study of the incidence and spread of diseases within a population. Epidemiologists use statistical methods to identify possible causes for diseases by examining a great deal of data obtained over time. For example, epidemiology was used to identify smoking as a major cause of lung cancer.

euphoria A sense of extreme elation and optimism. In addition to such positive feelings, euphoria can sometimes be accompanied by delusional states of mind.

excitation, neuronal ▶ The state of a neuron resulting from its stimulation. Neuronal excitation occurs when incoming signals from neighboring neurons build up, resulting in a nerve impulse traveling along the axon. Incoming signals can be excitatory or inhibitory, so the degree of neural excitation depends on the balance of these opposing effects.

exocytosis The expulsion of substances from inside a cell.

extinction In behavioral conditioning, the elimination of a behavior by withholding the stimulus or event that maintains the behavior. In Pavlov's classical conditioning experiment, presenting the bell without the food would result in extinction of the association. Learned responses can similarly be extinguished through withdrawal of the reward.

fetal alcohol syndrome (FAS) Physical and mental abnormalities in a baby resulting from the mother's alcohol intake during pregnancy.

EXCITATION AND DEPOLARIZATION OF A NEURON

An "unexcited" neuron during the resting stage. The neuron has a slight negative charge on the inside of the cell and a positive charge on the outside.

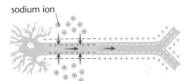

sodium ion

Excitatory signals build up (sodium ions flood into the cell), reversing the local polarity (charge). This is depolarization.

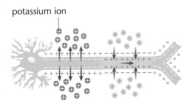

potassium ion

A nerve impulse travels along the axon as a wave of depolarization. Meanwhile, potassium ions flood out of the cell, repolarizing the interior of the cell and making it negative again.

functional group Chemical groups such as methyls, ethyls, and amides that determine the classification of organic (carbon-based) molecules. For example, hydrocarbon chain molecules with one or more hydroxyl (OH) group are classed as alcohols. Organic molecules often have more than one functional group.

GABA An amino acid (full name: gamma-aminobutyric acid) that acts as an inhibitory neurotransmitter in the central nervous system. GABA imbalances are thought to play a role in anxiety disorders.

gateway drug A controversial designation for drugs believed to open the way to the use of other, more damaging drugs. For example, according to this theory, use of marijuana is likely to lead to the use of "hard" drugs such as cocaine and heroin.

gene A unit of hereditary information comprising a segment of DNA. A single gene contains the information for producing a single substance used in the cell, usually a polypeptide (protein). Many genes take a variety of forms, called alleles.

genetics The study of heredity in living organisms based originally on abstract concepts such as genes, dominance, and inheritance. Many of these concepts are still used in modern genetics, which is based on an understanding of genes at the molecular, or DNA, level.

glutamate An amino acid that functions as a neurotransmitter; also known as glutamic acid.

habituation A reduction in a person's response to a stimulus due to repeated exposure to it. In terms of drug use, repeated use causes habituation in the form of desensitization and, eventually, dependence.

hallucinogen Any substance that induces hallucinations, which are sensory experiences (typically visual or auditory)

that appear real but which are not produced by external reality. Some drugs are mildly hallucinogenic, while others (such as LSD) are strongly hallucinogenic.

heritability Also known as the "heritability ratio," the proportion of the variation of a particular trait in a population that can be traced to inherited factors. The term is a technical one and is not equivalent to the degree to which variation in a trait has a genetic, as opposed to environmental, origin.

hippocampus A structure within the limbic system of the brain that has a key role to play in many brain functions, including long-term memory, learning, and emotion.

HIV Human immunodeficiency virus; the virus that causes AIDS. HIV is a retrovirus: its genetic information is copied and incorporated into that of the host cell (the cell it infects).

homeostasis The regulation and maintenance of stability in biological systems, such as a stable internal environment in the body maintained by regulation of temperature and concentration of glucose, water, and oxygen.

hormone A protein that acts as a messenger substance within the human body. Hormones are secreted into the bloodstream and may act on several organs. Examples of hormones include epinephrine, insulin, testosterone, and estrogen.

hyperpolarization An increase in the electrical potential across the membrane of a neuron, inhibiting a nerve impulse. Verb: hyperpolarize.

hypnotic drug Drugs that depress the central nervous system, either acting as sedatives or inducing sleep, depending on the drug and its dose.

hypothalamus A structure situated at the base of the brain that plays an important role in controlling many aspects of body regulation and behavior, including thirst, hunger, sleep, growth, and sexual behavior.

immunoassay Method for determining the amount of a specific antigen (substance that generates an immune response). Immunoassays are used for clinical testing; for example, in pregnancy tests.

INCB International Narcotics Control Board, an organization within the United Nations that oversees the implementation of international treaties limiting the availability of controlled drugs.

incentive salience The extent to which an incentive is noticed and desired by an individual; in other words, its value as an incentive. Salience is a matter of the individual's response and therefore varies over time and between individuals.

inhalant Any substance that is used as a mind-altering drug by being inhaled. Inhalants are vapor-producing substances such as solvents, and the abuse of these substances can cause serious harm.

inhibition, neuronal Reduction in the likelihood of a nerve cell firing. Neuronal inhibition occurs when an inhibitory neurotransmitter (such as GABA) reaches the postsynaptic (message-receiving) membranes of a neuron, causing an increase in the electrical potential across the membrane. In contrast, excitatory neurotransmitters (such as acetylcholine or glutamate) cause a decrease in electrical potential and increase the likelihood of a nerve impulse being transmitted.

intercellular Occurring between cells. For example, intercellular fluid is the fluid that surrounds body cells.

intervention Any treatment or procedure for a specific purpose. For example, antidepressant medication and cognitive therapy are both possible interventions in the treatment of depression.

intoxication The effect of an intoxicating substance, usually alcohol but also caffeine, amphetamines, and other drugs. Literally, intoxication means having been poisoned. Adjective: intoxicated.

intracellular Occurring within a cell. For example, the nucleus and mitochondria are intracellular structures.

ionotropic receptor ▶ A receptor site that is triggered by molecules of neurotransmitter binding to its surface, which changes the shape of the receptor and opens the channel, allowing ions to pass through and trigger an action potential. Ionotropic receptors are the direct, faster-acting of the two main classes of receptor (compare with metabotropic receptors).

ligand-gated channel ▶ Channel associated with an ionotropic receptor within a cell membrane that opens in response to a ligand (a chemical group that donates electrons), in contrast to voltage-gated channels. The neurotransmitters serotonin, acetylcholine, and GABA operate by activating ligand-gated channels in the neuronal membrane.

maladaption A behavior pattern that is unlikely to be beneficial to the person displaying it. Describing behavior as maladaptive avoids the issue of whether psychiatric conditions are physiological illnesses. Adjective: maladaptive.

MAO Monoamine oxidase; an enzyme that breaks down substances called amines, some of which (such as dopamine, epinephrine, and serotonin) act as neurotransmitters.

MAOI Monoamine oxidase inhibitor; a group of substances that work by

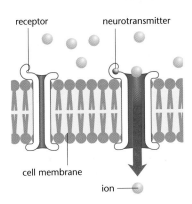

receptor · neurotransmitter · cell membrane · ion

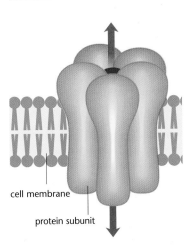

cell membrane · protein subunit

Ligand-gated receptors are composed of five structurally similar protein subunits that assemble to form a central channel through which ions can pass.

inhibiting the action of the enzyme monoamine oxidase. Because this enzyme breaks down amines, the effects of MAOIs are to increase the amounts of amine neurotransmitters, including dopamine, epinephrine, and serotonin. See encyclopedia entry "MAOs and MAOIs."

MDMA 3,4 methylenedioxy-methamphetamine, better known as Ecstasy, a commonly used illegal recreational drug. Ecstasy generates feelings of euphoria but can have dangerous side effects, including loss of control of body temperature and increased heart rate.

mesocorticolimbic dopaminergic system *See* mesolimbic dopaminergic system.

mesolimbic dopaminergic system An important dopamine-secreting system within the brain, extending from the pons through the limbic system to the cortex.

metabolism The various vital processes by which substances are chemically converted in the body, including both the building up and breaking down of complex molecules such as proteins, and the use and production of energy. A metabolite is any substance involved in a metabolic process.

metabotropic receptor A receptor that influences the activity of a cell indirectly by first initiating a metabolic change in the cell. This metabolic change may ultimately affect the opening or closing of an ion channel or may alter some other activity of the cell, such as protein transcription. Metabotropic receptors are the slower acting of the two main classes of receptor, with longer-term effects (compare with ionotropic receptors).

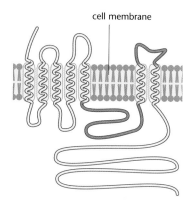

cell membrane

Metabotropic receptors are long proteins that pass in and out of the cell membrane seven times. Binding of a neurotransmitter causes a change in shape that allows the receptor to interact with a protein.

monoamine An amine with a single amino (NH_2) group. Monoamines include some hormones, proteins, and neurotransmitters.

Motivational Enhancement Therapy (MET) A form of one-on-one psychotherapy that aims to help people to reduce or eliminate their harmful use of a particular drug. Motivational Enhancement Therapy seeks to evoke a person's own motivation for change as a personal decision and to support that decision, using a technique called motivational interviewing.

narcotic drug Any drug that has both sedative and analgesic effects. Strictly, the term should be used to refer only to opioid drugs such as morphine and heroin, but sometimes it is also used for other psychoactive drugs, such as cocaine and marijuana.

neuron A nerve cell. The nervous system is made up of billions of neurons, each comprising a cell body, a long fiber called an axon, and several shorter projections, or dendrites. There are three main

types of neurons: sensory neurons transmit information from sense receptors toward the brain; motor neurons transmit signals toward muscles and glands; and interneurons transmit signals within the central nervous system. Adjective: neuronal.

neuroplasticity The ability of groups of neurons to adapt their function. Neuroplasticity allows an infant's brain to learn and develop and also allows recovery after neural damage caused by strokes. Adjective: neuroplastic.

neurotoxin A substance that is toxic (poisonous) to nerve tissue, including the central nervous system.

neurotransmission ▶ The sending of signals within the nervous system. Transmission takes place between neurons using chemical messengers emitted by nerve cells that trigger an impulse in neighboring cells, thus transmitting the signal.

norepinephrine A neurotransmitter that occurs in the central nervous system and sympathetic nervous system. Alternative name: noradrenaline.

opiate, opioid Drugs such as the natural opiates opium, morphine, and codeine; or synthetic versions (heroin, fentanyl) that have a similar effect. Opioid drugs have both sedative and analgesic effects.

oxidase Enzymes that have the function of producing chemical oxidation—that is, the removal of hydrogen atoms—in the substances on which they act.

paranoia A psychiatric disorder characterized by jealousy, suspicion, and delusions of persecution. People with paranoia usually function well

NEUROTRANSMISSION

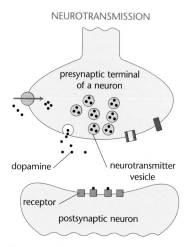

presynaptic terminal of a neuron

dopamine

neurotransmitter vesicle

receptor

postsynaptic neuron

A neuron releases neurotransmitters such as dopamine to trigger a response in a neighboring neuron.

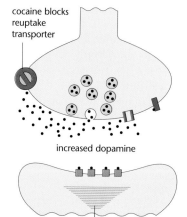

cocaine blocks reuptake transporter

increased dopamine

greater response to dopamine

Cocaine blocks a presynaptic control point (the reuptake transporter) that removes excess dopamine (above). Prolonged cocaine use causes tolerance (below).

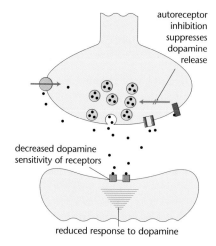

autoreceptor inhibition suppresses dopamine release

decreased dopamine sensitivity of receptors

reduced response to dopamine

intellectually, so their beliefs may be internally coherent although delusional.

parasympathetic nervous system Part of the autonomic nervous system, which controls involuntary actions, particularly digestion and excretion. Nerves of the parasympathetic nervous system release the neurotransmitter acetylcholine, while those of the sympathetic nervous system release epinephrine.

peripheral nervous system (PNS) The part of the nervous system that extends from the central nervous system to the rest of the body, within the head and trunk and along the limbs to skin, muscles, and internal organs.

pharmacokinetics The study of the chemical mechanisms by which drugs act within the body, including the bodily absorption, distribution, metabolism, and excretion of drugs.

pharmacology The scientific study of drugs and their actions.

pharmacophores The physiologically active parts of the molecules of a drug substance that produce the drug's effect.

pharmacy drug An over-the counter drug bought without a prescription. Common pain-killers such as paracetamol and aspirin, as well as some mild sedative drugs, are available in this way.

phenethylamines Chemicals derived from phenylethylamine, $C_8H_9NH_2$. Phenethylamines occur widely in nature, in plants as well as in the body. Dopamine, epinephrine, and norepinephrine are phenethylamines, as are some drugs, including Ecstasy and the amphetamines.

polar compound A chemical compound in which the molecules have a distinct electrical charge at one end in relation to the other. Water (H_2O) is a polar compound, since electrons are drawn to the oxygen atom, which thus has a negative charge with respect to the hydrogen atoms. Many organic (carbon-based) compounds in the body are nonpolar and have a relatively even charge distribution.

polysubstance dependence Term used by psychiatrists to describe multiple addictions involving three or more substances as a group, not including caffeine or nicotine, over a 12-month period.

postsynaptic After the synapse (the junction between one neuron's axon and the next neuron's dendrite). Nerve impulses are passed from a presynaptic neuron to a postsynaptic neuron.

post-traumatic stress disorder Disorder resulting from a traumatic event that causes the sufferer to experience a variety of psychologically distressing phenomena, such as recurrent and distressing dreams in which the traumatic event is re-experienced.

presynaptic Before the synapse (the junction between one neuron's terminal button and the next neuron). Nerve impulses are passed from a presynaptic neuron to a postsynaptic neuron.

prohibition The legal prohibition of the sale, manufacture, or use of a drug.

proteomics The study of proteins. Proteins are large, carbon-based molecules that are extremely important in cells

and the body as a whole, both structurally and functionally.

psychoactive The ability of a substance to produce a psychological effect, particularly on mood, consciousness, experience, and so on. Although common painkillers and other mild drugs could be said to affect consciousness in a limited sense, the term is generally used to indicate a more marked effect.

psychopharmacology The scientific study of the action of drugs on the mind and brain. Psychopharmacology includes both the endeavor to design drugs with desired psychological effects (such as antidepressants) and to understand why particular substances have their observed effects.

psychosis Any psychiatric disorder in which the person affected has beliefs that are grossly inappropriate and disconnected with external reality, involving delusions or hallucinations. Psychotic disorders include schizophrenia and bipolar depression

psychotropic drug Any mind-altering psychoactive drug, including hallucinogens, tranquilizers, and antipsychotic drugs.

receptor Any nerve cell that responds to sensory stimuli by producing a nerve impulse, for example, light-sensitive cells in the retina. The term also refers to receptor sites; that is, regions on the surface of a cell that bind specifically to particular molecules such as neurotransmitters and hormones, triggering characteristic changes in the cell.

reinforcement ▶ Any stimulus or event that rewards a particular action and thus makes that action more likely to happen again. In instrumental conditioning, for example, presentation of a food reward acts as a reinforcement for a rat's lever press.

reinstatement Restoration to a previous, often satisfactory, state. In the biological context, reinstatement can refer to a return to normal physiological or psychological functioning—for example, reinstatement of normal brain function after withdrawal from drug abuse.

relapse A worsening of any medical condition after previous improvement. In the addiction context, a relapse occurs if an addicted person returns to drug abuse after a period of reducing or eliminating the abusive behavior.

retrovirus A type of virus with RNA as the genetic material and that uses an enzyme (reverse transcriptase) to produce DNA from the RNA, with the viral DNA then being incorporated into the host cell's DNA. HIV is an example of a retrovirus.

reuptake The reabsorption of a neurotransmitter by the neuron after the neurotransmitter has been released into the synaptic gap (or cleft).

reward A pleasurable event or object obtained after a specified task or action has been carried out.

scheduled drug A drug that has its use and distribution tightly controlled because of its abuse risk. Controlled drugs are placed in schedules in the order of their abuse risk; drugs with the highest abuse risk are placed in Schedule I, and those with the lowest in Schedule V.

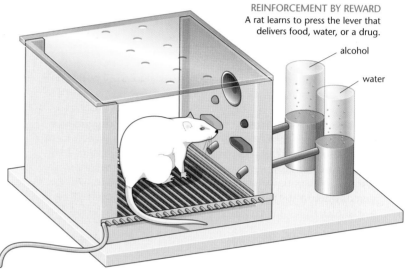

REINFORCEMENT BY REWARD
A rat learns to press the lever that delivers food, water, or a drug.

alcohol
water

schizophrenia
A group of psychiatric disorders in which thinking, emotions, and behavior are disrupted and often delusional. One characteristic of schizophrenia is hallucinations, often auditory ("hearing voices") rather than visual. Paranoid schizophrenia involves delusions of persecution.

sedative A drug that produces sedation—that is, drowsiness and a reduction in anxiety or aggression. Sedatives are most commonly used as sleeping pills.

self-medication The self-treatment of health problems by individuals without medical supervision. Medicines for self-medication are available without a doctor's prescription through pharmacies.

sensitization The effect by which repeated intake of the same drug and dosage produces a progressive increase in particular drug effects, such that eventually a lower dose will produce the same effect as the original dose.

serotonin A neurotransmitter found in the central nervous system; also known as 5-HT.

signal transduction The transformation of a signal from one form to another. For example, a signal meeting a sensory receptor (such as light meeting a light-sensitive retinal cell) is transduced (transformed) into a nerve impulse.

SNRI Serotonin norepinephrine reuptake inhibitor. This class of drugs is thought to act by limiting the reabsorption of serotonin and norepinephrine by neurons in the brain.

sobriety The state of being sober—that is, not under the effect of any drug, particularly alcohol.

speedball A combination of heroin with cocaine, amphetamine, or other stimulating drug injected directly into the bloodstream.

SSRI Selective serotonin reuptake inhibitor. SSRIs are a relatively new class of antidepressant drugs, of which one of the best known is fluoxetine (Prozac). These drugs increase the amount of the neurotransmitter serotonin by inhibiting its reuptake.

standard drink The amount of an alcoholic drink that contains the alcoholic equivalent of 14.7 ml of pure ethanol.

step program A strategy for overcoming dependence, involving graduated aims and the approach of taking "one step at a time." The original twelve-step program was developed by the organization Alcoholics Anonymous to help people overcome alcoholism.

stimulant A drug that produces a stimulating effect by activity in the central nervous system. Amphetamines, which increase alertness and raise levels of norepinephrine, are stimulants.

synapse The junction between two neighboring neurons, formed where the terminal button on the axon of one neuron meets a neighboring neuron. There is no direct physical contact between neurons at the synapse, and signals pass by means of chemical neurotransmitters.

synaptic cleft The gap between two adjacent neurons at the synapse, which is bridged by the release of neurotransmitters.

syndrome A collection of symptoms that tend to occur together, indicating a specific disorder.

synthesize To produce a particular substance by building it up from smaller components. For example, proteins are synthesized in the body from amino acids.

tachycardia An abnormally fast heartbeat; that is, a pulse rate of more than 100 beats per minute in a resting adult.

telescoping A phenomenon in which something develops at a faster rate than usual, such as the faster progression from alcohol use to alcohol abuse that some studies have found in women compared with men.

tetrahydrocannabinol (THC) The main psychologically active ingredient in marijuana.

thalamus A pair of structures in the center of the brain that function as a relay station between sensory information and the cortex, where the information is processed, resulting in the perception of sensations.

tolerance A reduced response to a drug due to repeated exposure to it, and a corresponding need to take larger and larger doses to achieve the previous effect.
toxicity The potency of a substance such as a toxin (poison). Adjective: toxic.

trait In genetics, a genetically determined variable. For example, height is a trait (in contrast, a particular person being tall or short is a characteristic).

transduction *See* signal transduction

tryptamine An organic (carbon-based) chemical, formula $C_{10}H_{12}N_2$. Tryptamine is formed in plant and animal tissues from the amino acid tryptophan and is an intermediate in various metabolic processes. Tryptamine derivatives include the neurotransmitter serotonin and the hallucinogenic drug DMT(dimethyltryptamine).

urinalysis Tests on a sample of urine to detect drugs.

ventral tegmental area (VTA) Region of the brain containing dopamine-secreting neurons; thought to be important in arousal.

voltage-gated channel Channel within a cell membrane that is opened by a change in electrical potential, rather than by the presence of a particular chemical. Compare with ligand-gated channels.

withdrawal The process of discontinuing the use of a drug or substance by a person who is dependent on it. Unpleasant physical and mental symptoms often accompany withdrawal.

Drug Table

COMMON NAME OR TRADE NAME	CHEMICAL, GENERIC, OR BOTANICAL NAME	STREET NAMES AND OTHER NAMES	TYPE OF DRUG
2C-T-7		Blue mystic, 7-up, beautiful, tripstasy	Phenethylamine
Acetorphine and etorphine		Elephant juice, M99	Opioid
Amyl nitrate		Aimies, boppers, pearls, poppers	Inhalant
Amytal	Amobarbital	Blues, blue heavens	Barbiturate
Ativan	Lorazepam		Benzodiazepine
Atropine			Belladonna alkaloid
Benzedrine	Amphetamine sulfate	Speed, bennies, amp	Amphetamine
Bufotenine	5-HO-DMT (5-hydroxy-dimethyltryptamine)		Tryptamine
Caffeine			Stimulant
Chloroform			Sedative/Inhalant
Cocaine	Cocaine hydrochloride	Coke, snow, blow, Bolivian marching powder, Charlie, big C, nose candy	Stimulant
Coca leaf	Erythroxylon coca	Coca	Stimulant
Codeine	methyl morphine		Opiate
Crack cocaine		Smack, rock	Stimulant
Demerol	Meperidine, pethidine		Opioid
DET	Diethyltryptamine		Tryptamine
Dexedrine	Dextroamphetamine (amphetamine sulfate)	Dexies	Amphetamine
Dilaudid	Hydromorphone	Hospital heroin	Opioid
DMT	Dimethyltryptamine	Businessman's LSD, Fantasia, 45-minute psychosis	Tryptamine
DOB	Brolamphetamine		Amphetamine
Doriden	Glutethimide		Sedative
Ecstasy	MDMA (3,4 methylene-dioxymethamphetamine)	XTC, love drug, Adam	Amphetamine
Ephedrine			Amphetamine
Equanil, Miltown	Meprobamate		Sedative
Erythropoietin		EPO	Hormone
Ethanol	Ethyl alcohol		Alcohol
Ether			Anesthetic/Inhalant
Ethyltryptamine	3-(2-aminobutyl)indole	ET, alpha-ET, love pearls, love pills	Tryptamine
Eticyclidine	PCE		PCP analog
Fentanyl		Jackpot, China white, TNT, friend, goodfellas	Opioid
GBL	Gamma-butyrolactone	Lactone, firewater, revivarant	Depressant/see GHB
GHB	Gamma-hydroxybutyrate	GBH, Georgia Home Boy, jib, liquid E (or X), organic quaalude, sleep	Depressant
Halcion	Triazolam		Benzodiazepine
Harmine and harmaline	Banisteriopsis caapi	Ayahuasca	Hallucinogen
Hashish	Marijuana	Gram, hash, soles, pollen	Hallucinogen
Heroin	Diacetylmorphine/diamorphine	Antifreeze, brown sugar, China white, gold, H, horse, shit, stuff	Opioid
HGH	Human growth hormone		Hormone
Ibogaine	Tabernanthe iboga		Hallucinogen
Isobutyl nitrate		Aroma of men, bullet, locker room, snappers	Inhalant
Jimsonweed	Datura stramonium		Belladonna alkaloid
Ketamine		Special K, cat Valium, jet, kit-kat, vitamin K	Dissociative
Khat	Cathine/cathinone	Somali tea, African salad	Stimulant

COMMON NAME OR TRADE NAME	CHEMICAL, GENERIC, OR BOTANICAL NAME	STREET NAMES AND OTHER NAMES	TYPE OF DRUG
Klonopin	Clonazepam		Benzodiazepine
Laudanum			Opioid
Levorphanol	(-)-3-hydroxy-N-methylmorphinan		Opioid
Librium	Chlordiazepoxide		Benzodiazepine
LSD	Lysergic acid diethylamide	Acid	Hallucinogen
Magic mushrooms	Psilocybin and psilocin	Musk, mushrooms, shrooms, Simple Simon	Tryptamine
Marijuana	Cannabis sativa	Pot, weed, grass, hashish	Hallucinogen
MDA	3,4 methylenedioxy amphetamine	Eve	Amphetamine/Ecstasy analog
Mecloqualone	3-(o-chlorophenyl)-2-methyl-4(3H)-quinazolinone		Sedative/see Methaqualone
Mescaline	3,4,5-trimethoxy-phenethylamine	Buttons, cactus, mescal, peyote	Phenethylamine
Methaqualone	2-methyl-3-o-tolyl-4(3H)-quinazolinone	Quaaludes, ludes, 714s, sporos	Sedative
Methanol	Methyl alcohol	Meths	Alcohol
Methamphetamine		Crank, crystal, ice, meth, redneck cocaine, ya-ba	Amphetamine
Methcathinone	2-(methylamino)-1-phenylpropan-1-one	Cat, Jeff, ephedrone, bathtub speed	Stimulant
Morphine		God's drug, Miss Emma, morf, unkie	Opiate
4-MTA	4-methylthioamphetamine	Flatliner, golden eagle	Amphetamine
Nembutal	Pentobarbital	Yellow jackets	Barbiturate
Nexus	2-CB, BDMPEA	Bromo, spectrum, toonies, Venus	Phenethylamine
Nicotine			Stimulant
Nitrous oxide	NO	Laughing gas, buzz bomb, whippets	Inhalant
Noctec	Chloral hydrate	Mickey Finn, knockout drops	Sedative
Opium	Papaver somniferum	Poppy, Auntie, big O, Chinese tobacco, God's medicine, midnight oil, zero	Opioid
OxyContin	Oxycodone (14-hydroxy-dihydrocodeinone)	Oxy 40s/80s, hillbilly heroin, kicker, oxycotton	Opioid
Parahexyl			Depressant
Paraldehyde			Depressant
PCP	Phencyclidine	Angel dust, crazy coke, mad dog, ozone, rocket fuel	Dissociative
Prozac	Fluoxetine		SSRI
Restoril	Temazepam		Benzodiazepine
Ritalin	Methylphenidate	MPH, vitamin R, west coast	Stimulant
Robitussin	DXM (dextromethorphan)	Robo, Velvet, DXM	Dissociative/opioid
Rohypnol	Flunitrazepam	Forget-me drug, pingus, roofies, roaches, rope	Benzodiazepine
Rolicyclidine	PHP, PCPy		Dissociative/PCP analog
Scopolamine			Belladonna alkaloid
Serax	Oxazepam		Benzodiazepine
Talwin	Pentazocine		Opioid
Toluene		Tolly	Inhalant
TCP	Tenocyclidine		Dissociative/PCP analog
Thorazine	Chlorpromazine		Sedative
Valium	Diazepam		Benzodiazepine
Versed	Midazolam		Benzodiazepine
Vicodin	Hydrocodone		Opioid
Xanax	Alprazolam		Benzodiazepine

Index